British Politics

British Politics

An Analytical Approach

Peter John

Head of the School of Politics and Economics and Professor of Public Policy,
King's College London

OXFORD
UNIVERSITY PRESS

Great Clarendon Street, Oxford, OX2 6DP,
United Kingdom

Oxford University Press is a department of the University of Oxford. It furthers the University's objective of excellence in research, scholarship, and education by publishing worldwide. Oxford is a registered trade mark of Oxford University Press in the UK and in certain other countries

First Edition published in 2022

Impression: 1

Published in the United States of America by Oxford University Press
198 Madison Avenue, New York, NY 10016, United States of America

British Library Cataloguing in Publication Data

Data available

Library of Congress Control Number: 2021941329

ISBN 978–0–19–884062–6

Printed in Great Britain by
Bell & Bain Ltd., Glasgow

To Mike

Preface and Acknowledgements

I have always been fascinated by British politics, right from when I was a teenager growing up in the turbulent 1970s. Then big questions about the economy, Europe, and the constitution were regularly debated just as they are now. I remember playing chess with my dad by candlelight because there was no electricity available owing to industrial action that, in the end, crippled the government led by Prime Minister Ted Heath. Later, I recall being drawn to a cartoon in *The Times* on the occasion of Harold Wilson's resignation as prime minister in 1976, which showed a pilot leaving a sinking ship. When my sister Ros accidently caused a fire in our home in December 1978, it was the Green Goddesses (emergency replacement vehicles) and soldiers who arrived rather than the regular fire engines and firefighters because of the famous dispute with trade unions, the Winter of Discontent, that preceded the fall of the Callaghan government the following year. Then, as an undergraduate and research student, I had full exposure to the period when Margaret Thatcher was prime minister. Voting in the 1983 general election, I was shocked to observe that the police officer on duty at the polling station had placed his copy of *The Sun* with its front-page headline, 'VOTE MAGGIE', right next to the ballot box for everyone to see.

My first academic job, from 1992 to 1995 at the University of Keele, was teaching British politics, which I enjoyed immensely, being the 'British politics person' in the department for a short while. My research has almost solely been on British politics and public policy in some way, such as on English local government (for example, John 2014), and in particular my work on agenda-setting, which addresses the classic literature on British politics (John et al. 2013), as well as experiments on voting and participation (John et al. 2019).

My recent passion goes back to a series of real-world events that started with the Scottish referendum campaign leading up to the vote in September 2014. I spent what was the start of many 'all-nighters' watching television waiting for results to come in, with the Scottish referendum being joined by the 2015 general election, the 2016 United Kingdom European Union membership or Brexit referendum, and the 2017 and 2019 general elections, all momentous and nail-biting events that had me on the edge of my sofa in increasing amazement as the hours slipped by until dawn. It did not get much better when the Covid-19 crisis unfolded on television every day. I have spent the last six years in a state of obsession with British politics, following daily events with a sense of incredulity. As a result, I am addicted to all kinds of news and commentary. In this period, I discovered the joys of podcasts that can feed my anxiety at any time of day or night: *The New Statesman Podcast*, *The Spectator Podcast* (including the excellent daily *Coffee House Shots*), BBC Radio 5 Live's *Brexitcast*, *The Financial Times UK Politics Podcast* (now *Payne's Politics*), and *Talking Politics* (University of Cambridge and *London Review of Books*). Then endless Twitter posts keep me engaged when torn away from the broadcast media. To friends and significant other, I was able to say that I was *working* while consuming all these media, which in a way is true (academics do have an unusual profession). I often say, 'what is wrong with a professor of politics being so obsessed with politics?'

The thought I had at the time of these big events is that I ought to have been able to draw on a secure body of knowledge and research which would offer me some explanation of what was happening, so that I could draw implications for future governance, the party system, and electoral politics. With good theory, backed by different kinds of research, whether qualitative or quantitative, I should have been able to do better than the journalists and podcasters I had been listening to, or at least offer a different perspective. But I was not sure I could. I found it a particular challenge when travelling outside the United Kingdom, where hosts always asked the 'Brexit question' and wanted authoritative ideas and answers. Partly for this reason, I re-read a lot of the classics on British politics as well as recent research published in academic journals, both with my hat on as a general political scientist as well as engaging in my new hobby of British politics obsessive.

Before moving to King's College London in January 2018, Adrian Blau, head of teaching in the Department of Political Economy at that time, kindly asked me what I wanted to teach in my new job. Top of my list was British politics. Rather than being told that others were teaching this subject already and suggesting that it would be much better for King's if I stuck to public policy or nudge theory, he said there was a 'bog-standard' ten-week optional course for second-year undergraduate students called 'British Politics' with no one assigned to it. I jumped at the chance: not only would I have an excuse to obsess about British politics to those who had to listen to me, I also had to explain it in ways that students could understand and benefit from—a true pleasure for me and a great opportunity to express my ideas and make them more concrete. I found it helpful in a therapeutic way, so I could get back to my personal equilibrium about politics: after all, I have a job researching politics that benefits like any other from detachment, balance, and ultimately being able to switch off. I am not sure the students realised I had this personal motive! Writing this book has been just the same kind of therapy, so I am grateful to Oxford University Press, and to my editor Katie Staal for her work on the book, allowing me to shape it in ways that worked for both the students and me. I also thank the OUP reviewers who provided incredibly insightful and helpful comments that improved the book for its second draft.

I thank my students in three successive classes of teaching the course of the book as I tested out different ideas with them. I also thank Mitya Pearson, who was a research student in the department, who co-taught the course with me and very much helped me think about its rationale, logic, and organization as well as suggesting many readings and quiz questions. The same encomium applies to his successor, Stuart Smedley. One thing that struck me when teaching was that when things are changing fast in British politics there is even more of a premium on knowing the basics about the political system—the mechanics of how an election is called or a government is formed—which even the most experienced students, even those who have done A-level politics, find tricky at times, and which can be important foundational knowledge when discussing more advanced readings. I found I could remind these students of the basic institutional facts as a way of preparing them for the more advanced readings to come later on in the lecture at the same time as introducing the political system to other students, some of whom were newly arrived in the UK and needed that information for the first time.

I would like to thank some of my original teachers of politics who made the subject so interesting for me at the University of Bath: Roger Eatwell for his exciting first-year lectures on British politics, and the late Elizabeth Meehan for my first seminars on British politics. By some timetabling quirk, I was the only student in one of her classes, so we spent the hours talking about politics and occasionally taking breaks by smoking cigarettes out of the window (probably not permitted on campus even then!). Nuffield College, Oxford, where I was a research student, is a centre for the study of British politics, with many events to go to and with politicians dropping by. I particularly loved hearing Bernard Donoghue give a series of impromptu talks based on his diary of the 1974–9 Labour government (Donoughue 2006, 2008). I also had my first ever experience of teaching at that time, which was on British politics. I thank Niamh Hardiman for giving me that opportunity.

I also thank colleagues with whom I have worked on British politics, especially Tony Bertelli for suggesting I re-read the classics on British politics when we researched policy investment (Bertelli and John 2013). As an experimentalist, I have worked directly on political projects along with party workers and citizens, whether doing Get Out the Vote in Wythenshawe and Sale East (John and Brannan 2008) or a campaigning experiment in North East Somerset (Foos and John 2018). Special thanks also go to Helen Margetts with whom I worked on a separate project that led to our book *Political Turbulence* (Margetts et al. 2015), which provides a particular take on current politics and influenced my thinking in this book.

I benefited from the help of colleagues and friends who patiently read the rather patchy first draft and who suggested some tremendous improvements. Jonathan Bradbury, Rosie Campbell, and Mitya Pearson commented on the whole manuscript; others contributed their expert knowledge on individual chapters: Oli James (Chapter 8); Martin Moore and Helen Margetts (Chapter 6); Roger Mortimore (Chapter 4); and Brian Salter, Keith Smith, and Stuart Smedley (Chapter 10). Gerry Stoker provided encouragement, agreeing with my insight that political leaders had messed up British politics more than anybody else. I had help from several talented students on my course, who edited and fact-checked many of the chapters. My appreciation goes to Christina Fernandes, George Byham, Rhys Pearson-Shaul, Luca Siepmann, and Angeles Ribeiro Perez. I am also very grateful to another King's student, Francisco (Paco) Tomas-Valiente Jorda, for his assiduous work on the figures and source data.

Outline Contents

Detailed Contents

Guided Tour of the Learning Features

British Politics provides a range of carefully selected learning tools to help you navigate the text and contextualize your understanding, supporting development of the essential knowledge and skills you need to underpin your British and UK politics studies.

Helpful **Key terms** boxes throughout the text briefly summarize key concepts and reinforce your understanding of new terminology.

Key term 1.1 Britain or United Kingdom?

It might sound surprising, but there are several names in use for the British political system(s). In this book, the term Britain or British is used to describe the political system in general terms, hence 'British politics'. United Kingdom or UK is referred to as the formal name of the nation state, for example as used in international law. The UK is also used to describe Westminster political institutions when compared to those in other parts of the country, for example to distinguish between the UK Parliament and the Scottish Parliament or Senedd Cymru (Welsh Parliament). At various points, it becomes important to refer sep-

Engaging and relevant **Case Study** boxes in every chapter illustrate how ideas, concepts, and issues are manifested in the real world.

Case Study 1.1 The *Ministerial Code*

Recently, many of these conventions have been written down in documents, such as the *Ministerial Code* and *The Cabinet Manual*, which emerged from an initiative under Gordon Brown when he was prime minister. By writing them down, something has happened akin to a written constitution as they can be referred to in disputes and where

manuals can change or be updated to tice. They are not enforceable and it observe governments behaving diffe conventions outlined in the manuals. the manuals refer to the convention dentiality of the cabinet, but under T government this was regularly brea

Zoom-In boxes provide extra information on particular topics and help to explain key ideas in more detail.

Zoom-In 1.1 Parliamentary sovereignty

Parliamentary sovereignty is a key principle of the UK constitution, which affects how Parliament, courts, and the executive operate. It was asserted during the seventeenth century and set out in the Bill of Rights 1689 and other documents.

It is defined as legal supremacy of Parliament, which can undo any law it makes: 'the right to make

- Difference between legal (de jure) and practical (de facto) sovereignt
- Whether EU membership limited s by ceding power to a higher court, an Court of Justice (ECJ).
- Whether parliamentary sovereignty means legality, and is not about Par

Useful **Essay and examination questions** at the end of each chapter help to encourage critical reflection on what you've learnt, highlight the 'classic' questions on the subject, and provide useful prompts for exam preparation.

Essay and examination questions

One general question could be about the Westminster model and take the form 'How convincing is the Westminster model in understanding British politics today?'. What is needed in the answer is a clear statement about what the model is or could be, then an assessment of the basic criticisms of the model. To help structure the answer see Dunleavy

picked up in the question 'How d politics?'. It is possible to have a tion on the constitution that c 'Does Britain have a written con possible to pose a question on along the lines of 'Is Britain uniq disasters?'. There is much more

Each chapter's **Further reading** section explores the key academic literature in the field, helping you to develop your interest in particular topics in British and UK politics.

Further reading

There are many sources on British politics which introduce the political system and review debates about British democracy. For someone new to British politics needing a user-friendly introduction, the short book by Anthony King, *Who Governs Britain?* (2015), is helpful. For an introduction to the constitution, see Martin Loughlin's *The British Constitution* (2013).

Westminster model by Patrick D Rod Rhodes (2005). Another cri model, with more of a focus on pu topics later in this book, is Jordan a

It is important to incorporate feminism (Lovenduski 1996) an race in British politics (Gilroy 201

Guided Tour of the Online Resources

This textbook is accompanied by many helpful additional resources for both students and lecturers, providing opportunities to take your learning further:

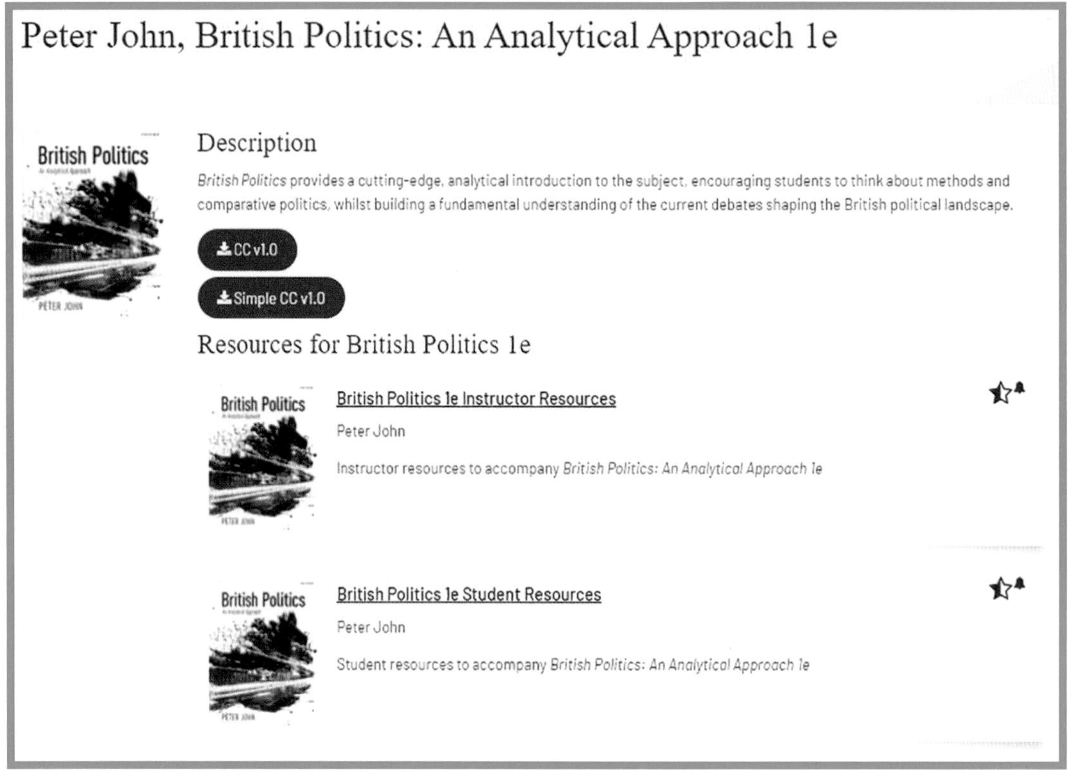

www.oup.com/he/John1e

Student resources

- **Multiple-choice questions**—a popular interactive feature that provides instant feedback, helping you test your knowledge of key points in each chapter and also at revision time.
- **Web links** to datasets and multimedia sources deepen your understanding of key topics and explore your research interests.
- **Biannual online updates** from the author keep you up to date with the latest developments in British politics.

Lecturer resources

These resources are password-protected, but access is available to anyone using the book in their teaching. Please contact your local sales representative.

- Customizable **PowerPoint® slides**, arranged by chapter, for use in lecture or as hand-outs to support efficient, effective teaching preparation.
- All **figures and tables from the book** available to download, allowing clear presentation of key data to support students' data analysis.

About the Author

Peter John is Head of the School of Politics and Economics and Professor of Public Policy at King's College London. He was previously Professor of Political Science and Public Policy, University College London. He is known for his work on agenda-setting, local politics, behavioural interventions, and randomized controlled trials.

He is the author of *Analyzing Public Policy* (2012), which reviews the main theories of public policy and the policy process. He has carried out empirical work on agenda-setting to find out why governments focus on particular policies, which is represented in *Policy Agendas in British Politics* (Palgrave, 2013).

He is interested in how best to involve citizens in public policy and management, often deploying behavioural interventions. He tests many of these interventions with randomized controlled trials. Some of these trials appeared in *Nudge, Nudge, Think, Think: Experimenting with Ways to Change Civic Behaviour* (Bloomsbury, 2011, 2nd edition with Manchester University Press in 2019). Practical issues with the design of experiments are covered in *Field Experiments in Political Science and Public Policy* (Routledge, 2017). Experiments are also used to examine the impact of social media and politics in *Political Turbulence: How Social Media Shape Collective Action* (Princeton University Press, 2015).

A more general approach to the use of the tools of government to achieve policy change is contained in his *Making Policy Work* (Routledge, 2011). In 2018, he published a critical review of the use of behavioural public policies called *How Far to Nudge: Assessing Behavioural Public Policy* (Edward Elgar).

Peter John has had a long interest in local politics and public management, focusing on citizen choices. Such work culminated in *Exits, Voices and Social Investment: Citizens' Reaction to Public Services* (Cambridge University Press, 2012). He is currently researching the effectiveness of deliberative behavioural public policies, a programme of work called 'nudge plus'.

Part A

Constitutional and Institutional Foundations

This book is divided into three parts, which are designed to help make sense of the different elements or 'moving parts' of the British political system. The idea is to convey what aspect of politics is being studied and show how it all fits together. This first part is called Constitutional and Institutional Foundations, which is about political institutions—the formal set-up of politics—embedded in laws and procedures, and also customs and informal rules, evolving over many centuries and still changing rapidly today. These formal and informal rules create the familiar and distinctive features of a political system, making it recognizable to everyone, even if part of a family of types of political institutions across the world that may be compared with the UK. These rules tell individuals in politics like politicians how they can operate so they may advance their careers and follow their interests. It is important to understand these institutions. Getting through the first three chapters helps provide a basic understanding of the political system as a whole and provides springboards into other parts of the book. These chapters allow the reader to become familiar with what is going on in day-to-day politics and enables them to understand more theoretical treatments and empirical studies.

It is important to stress that the three chapters in Part A need to be seen in relation to the other parts of the book. The intention is to avoid giving a 'top-down' perspective on British politics, whereby the whole political system is seen as an expression of UK national institutions operating only in relation to the centre. Moreover, these institutions are internally complex and divided. In particular, as devolution gets more defined, with stronger parliaments in Wales and Scotland and arrangements for democratic government in Northern Ireland, many of the topics need to take account of government and politics right across the UK.

It is in part a matter of perspective about which way to look at the political system. In Part B, Political Behaviour and Citizenship, the table is turned and politics is examined from the viewpoint of the everyday citizen. Then there are parties that seek power and influence, represented within the very institutions set out in Part A. Elites and citizens are also connected through the public agenda and mass media, as set out in Chapter 6. With a bottom-up perspective, it is possible to observe the diversity and variation of Britain's cultures, ethnicities, and identities, as they feature today.

Part C, Policy-Making and Delegation, shows how UK power and authority are dispersed in different ways, either through delegating to agencies and subcentral authorities, or sharing powers with international bodies, each of which is pursuing their own interests and goals different to that of the UK government. The elements described in Parts A, B, and C interact with each other in ways that help produce the drama, complexity, and even chaos of contemporary British politics.

Across the three parts are threaded the five themes of the book, which each chapter addresses in different ways. These culminate in a digest of the book, which appears in the final concluding Chapter 11, summarized in Table 11.1. The *first* theme is the summary of the nature of the political system as it has changed rapidly in recent decades. This is the essence of what is described in each chapter, as the early part of the 2020s is reached. The *second* theme is the extent to which party government is in operation. This term is explained in section 1.3.12, but it is the way in which a single political party or a coalition is able to dominate decision-making so as to get re-elected and to implement policies that reflect its worldview and ideology. The *third* theme is core to this book: the extent to which the political system has become more turbulent and unpredictable in recent years with electoral shocks, media storms, and erratic decision-making from politicians and policy-makers. The task is to find out why this has happened: how institutions affect political incentives in Part A, the role of political behaviour in Part B; then, in Part C, how the practice of delegation and its complexity may enhance this instability.

The *fourth* theme is the degree to which policy disasters and blunders characterize British politics, perhaps more so than other countries, emanating from Britain's institutions, and perhaps exacerbated in recent years as British institutions change and become more complex. The *fifth* and final theme relates to British democracy, which is the extent to which the electorate can obtain responsiveness and accountability from its political system—what is called agency. This is the idea that it is hard for those with power and authority—that is, the electorate in a modern political system, who are supposed to be the principals in any political relationship—to get what they want from those charged with delivering their wishes. With these five themes addressed, the book becomes an assessment of the state of British democracy.

Chapter 1

The Starting Point

Understanding the Political System

1.1 What is going to be in this chapter?

This chapter is about what makes British politics distinctive and recognizable: its parliamentary democracy, uncodified constitution, and pattern of party government. It describes the political system in the 'basic facts' section (section 1.3) (a common feature of each chapter in this book), in particular the institutional rules that govern how politics takes place. There will also be a summary of the British constitution. The chapter also places the UK in a comparative context, to be studied alongside other nation states. It sets out the information and concepts that help in understanding the nature of and limits to British democracy. But before all this, the chapter starts with some recent events that have made British or UK (see Key term 1.1) politics so fascinating and controversial.

Key term 1.1 Britain or United Kingdom?

It might sound surprising, but there are several names in use for the British political system(s). In this book, the term Britain or British is used to describe the political system in general terms, hence 'British politics'. United Kingdom or UK is referred to as the formal name of the nation state, for example as used in international law. The UK is also used to describe Westminster political institutions when compared to those in other parts of the country, for example to distinguish between the UK Parliament and the Scottish Parliament or Senedd Cymru (Welsh Parliament). At various points, it becomes important to refer separately to the nations/territories of the UK: England, Northern Ireland, Scotland, and Wales.

The terms Great Britain and British Isles are old-fashioned (Team GB excepted), so are not used much in this book; but may appear in some of the readings.

1.2 Introducing British politics

1.2.1 Getting started with a thought experiment

Think about contemporary British politics for a minute. Try to sum up what images and impressions come to mind. Are they about unpredictable recent events? Perhaps unexpected election results, close-fought referendums, dramatic parliamentary battles, hastily convened press conferences chaired by the prime minister, or last-minute negotiations in Brussels come to mind? Do these images convey a sense of turbulence and disruption to politics? If the answer is 'yes', you will not be alone in thinking in this way: many experienced observers of British politics also report a sense of not knowing what is going to come next and of politics not being normal in recent times. For example, on 13 November 2018, the BBC correspondent Chris Mason said on BBC *Breakfast* TV: 'So, where are we in this Brexit process? You know what? People like me are paid to have insight and foresight and hindsight about these things, and to be able to project where we're going to go. To be quite honest, looking at things right now, I haven't got the foggiest idea what is going to happen in the coming weeks' (*Washington Post*, 14 November 2018).

1.2.2 Recent events in British politics

There are some big events that might suggest that something bizarre has happened to British politics recently. First, the Scottish independence referendum

Photo 1.1 The British Union Jack flag flying in front of Elizabeth Tower (Big Ben) and the Houses of Parliament at Westminster Palace, London.

Key term 1.2 Brexit

The vote to leave the European Union (EU) which triggered the lengthy, controversial, and complex process that came to be known as Brexit: Britain exiting the EU (see sections 4.7.2, 4.8.1, and 10.4.8).

of 18 September 2014 asked whether Scotland could become independent as a nation separate from the United Kingdom. There was a dramatic campaign and a real sense of momentum for independence (see section 9.7.3). Though the final result was a clear vote to remain in the United Kingdom (55:45), it was much closer than many expected and some experts thought that Scotland was not far off voting for independence (see Curtice 2015a).

Second, the general election of 7 May 2015 saw the Liberal Democrat Party lose all but eight of its fifty-seven seats in the UK Parliament and the defeat of all but one Labour candidate in Scotland to the Scottish National Party (Cowley and Kavanagh 2016). This was striking because Labour has had a significant electoral presence in Scotland since the founding of the party in the early years of the twentieth century (see section 5.3.2).

Soon after the 2015 election, the third surprising event occurred. With the position of Labour leader being vacant following the resignation of Ed Miliband, the party went through the procedures needed to elect a new leader. Rather than one of the established front-line Labour politicians coming through, the post went to a complete outsider: the left-wing rebel, Jeremy Corbyn. He only got the necessary thirty-five nominations by Members of Parliament (MPs) because some of them wanted a diversity of candidates, but did not necessarily intend him to win (Quinn 2016, 763). Yet he was elected leader on 12 September 2015 by a clear majority of Labour Party members (59.5 per cent of first preferences), a result repeated a year later when he was challenged again (he won with a 61 per cent vote share).

The fourth event was the referendum of 23 June 2016 to decide whether the UK should leave the European Union. This referendum was agreed by most members of the political establishment, with a massive majority of MPs voting in support of the legislation required to make the referendum possible (544 to 53). Rather than there being a comfortable win for Remain as many had expected, Leave won by about four percentage points (52:48), a result that massively surprised commentators and experts alike. After the result had come through in the early hours of the morning of 24 June, the prime minister, David Cameron, decided to resign.

But the turbulence did not stop there. Within a year of the Conservative Party selecting Theresa May as prime minister, someone thought to be a cautious politician, and therefore the safe pair of hands needed to get the country through Brexit (Seldon and Newell

'I'm studying politics. The course covers the period from 8am on Thursday to lunchtime on Friday'

Photo 1.1a Politics moves fast in turbulent times.

2019, 35–36), she boldly decided to call an election for 8 June 2017 to secure a larger majority in Parliament so as to have her own mandate, and to be able to deal more securely with Brexit (Shipman 2017). Rather than the election increasing her majority, however, it was close to a disaster for the Conservative Party: she nearly lost, ceding seats to Labour, with the Conservative Party continuing to govern only with the support of the Democratic Unionist Party (DUP). The Labour Party came within a few percentage points of votes of being elected with a majority of seats and forming a government with Jeremy Corbyn as prime minister, something that no one would have predicted given prevailing expectations of what kind of leader attracts electoral support in British politics.

There followed two years of indecisiveness where Theresa May tried to govern without a majority, desperate to get a Brexit Withdrawal Agreement with the EU through Parliament, but each of the three attempts was voted down in the House of Commons, not just by the opposition but also by members of her own political party. Eventually resigning on 24 May 2019, with leader-in-waiting Boris Johnson becoming prime minister on 24 July 2019, there followed an even more extraordinary period of infighting within the Conservative Party. These deadlocks and manoeuvres seemed to go on forever. But then the Liberal Democrats and Labour allowed for a general election to be called on 12 December 2019. Thought to be a close-run contest, seats that had been Labour for generations swung to the Conservative Party, thus delivering a decisive eighty-seat majority, appearing to lance the Brexit boil, and causing the resignation of Jeremy Corbyn as leader of the Labour Party.

Just when the crises in British politics appeared to have receded, with the election of the more moderate and mainstream Sir Keir Starmer as leader of the Labour Party, a Withdrawal Agreement from the EU finally passed through Parliament, and the Conservative Party planning for its next electoral contest with the 'levelling-up' agenda to divert resources to its newly won northern England seats, in March 2020 the Covid-19 crisis struck. The speedy spread of a deadly virus with no cure knocked governments sideways across the world. But it seemed that the British government struggled more than most, with massive U-turns and huge policy failures over procurement and testing. It failed to respond with lockdowns in good time, errors that possibly reflected an over-centralization of public policy-making (Gaskell and Stoker 2020) (see section 11.3.4). As well as the aftermath of Covid-19, there is the renewed demand for a second Scottish independence referendum, not to mention uncertainty about the future of Northern Ireland, making future years likely to be just as unstable as those since 2014.

Overall, British politics in recent years has experienced many profound shocks, such as unexpected election and referendum results. These have often come from decisions made by political leaders, which in retrospect look like risky and rash actions. Such events convey a sense of unpredictability and turbulence about British politics.

Key term 1.3 Mandate

An endorsement of a policy or programme as sanctioned in a manifesto and voted on in an election. A mandate gives a political party the legitimacy to act, and may be used in political debate to underpin a programme and to encourage the bureaucracy to act decisively.

1.2.3 The traditional account of British politics as stable

Such an account of turbulence would have puzzled scholars writing on British politics a generation ago, say in the 1950s and 1960s, who thought Britain was an example of a stable political system that produced predictable electoral and policy outcomes mediated by a moderate governing culture. Britain does not have a codified constitution (see Key term 1.4), but observers believed it had adapted its flexible arrangements so that it can be governed effectively at the same time as incorporating democratic representation. Consider a book published in the 1960s, *Representative and Responsible Government* (Birch 1964), which described the accommodation between effective representation and responsible government. The argument put forward by Birch is that the political system can deliver on both these aims by being representative in ensuring that people's views and goals are respected with responsive political decisions, while at the same time having an effective government that makes sensible and effective public policies.

It was believed that citizens supported the system of government and were content to vote into office parties that made minor changes to public policy, which kept Britain on a path of gradual adaption to socio-economic changes and acceptance of a reduced international role.

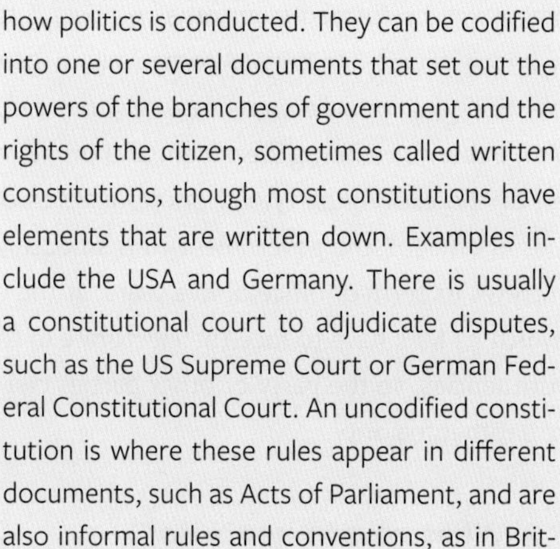

Key term 1.4 Codified constitution

A constitution comprises the rules that guide how politics is conducted. They can be codified into one or several documents that set out the powers of the branches of government and the rights of the citizen, sometimes called written constitutions, though most constitutions have elements that are written down. Examples include the USA and Germany. There is usually a constitutional court to adjudicate disputes, such as the US Supreme Court or German Federal Constitutional Court. An uncodified constitution is where these rules appear in different documents, such as Acts of Parliament, and are also informal rules and conventions, as in Britain. See discussion about constitutional conventions in sections 1.3.10 and 1.3.11.

1.2.4 Or is instability baked into British politics?

If the conventional picture outlined above were true, how did this country apparently go from one extreme of stability to one of apparent reckless policy-making and volatile citizen choices? Is there something that has happened to British politics that explains these recent events? Is this experience systematically different from politics in other political systems in Europe, which might appear to be more placid and slow-moving?

Or it may be the case that the political system always possessed some special general qualities that lead to poor decision-making and rapid changes in executive priorities (Finer 1975), in particular a lack of effective scrutiny (Dunleavy 1995b). Is there something about the process of competition between parties seeking high office, working with the incentives of a First-Past-the-Post (FPTP) electoral system (see Key term 1.5) to get a majority of seats (discussed in sections 5.3.3 and 5.4), which causes political leaders to act so rashly? Perhaps Britain is so centralized that its leaders make bad choices? The chapters in this book aim to find out answers to these questions. First there is a need to learn some basic facts about the political system.

Key term 1.5 First-Past-the-Post (FPTP)

A voting or electoral system where the winner needs to get a plurality of the votes cast; they only need more votes cast over any rival candidate to win.

1.3 Basic facts: British politics

1.3.1 The task of description

How does British politics work? It is important to have a clear grasp of the basic institutions and their rules, and in particular to understand how a government is formed. A bit of historical context is also necessary. There is also a need to understand the British constitution. These elements are kept short on a 'need-to-know' basis: the minimum amount of information to be able to comprehend how British politics operates. That is the aim.

1.3.2 The historical context

Although Britain is now a parliamentary democracy, with legal and political power concentrated in the legislature, executive power in the past was in the hands of the sovereign or monarch who appointed ministers to carry out the business of government and to rule the country. The king or queen's power was constrained by Parliament as laws and taxes required the agreement of the House of Commons (see section 1.3.5) and House of Lords (see section 1.3.6), as well as the sovereign. The unlimited legal power of Parliament became described as a doctrine of parliamentary sovereignty (see Zoom-In 1.1). The term means that any law passed by Parliament takes precedence over any other and Parliament cannot be bound by any convention or rule or even its own prior decisions (see sections 1.3.11 and 1.3.12 on the constitution). Parliament, composed of the House of Commons, House of Lords, and the Crown, is the supreme legal authority in the UK.

Over time, the House of Commons gained ascendency and became the focus for electoral politics. Rather than the monarch, the prime minister appoints MPs and Lords as ministers and members of the government.

1.3.3 How governments are formed

The key decision point in British politics occurs when a person is appointed or continues as prime minister. This person is usually the leader of a party with the majority of seats or MPs, or the leader of the largest party, who can secure a majority in the House of Commons. General elections are 'counting exercises' for which a party or parties need to have a majority of MPs (out of the current 650), so the monarch can be advised which party leader (or other representative) may be appointed as prime minister.

The government stays in power so long as it has a working majority of MPs (326 or more). It needs its MPs to adhere to the programme of the party or parties, at least for most of the time and over crucial votes. Governments can fall if they lose their majority from irreconcilable internal divisions within their parties or when coalition partners and/or other allies abandon them, making the business of government impossible. Even though governments can stagger on for many months without a majority, seeking to win each vote of confidence, eventually a new government will be formed from other parties, if they can find a secure majority. Alternatively, a general election may be called so a new majority can be found, either for a new government and prime minister, or the existing party and prime minister continues in office. If the government runs smoothly, it completes its term of office of five years, at the end of which its MPs have to face the electorate in their constituencies, so the party or other parties can secure another majority.

1.3.4 What governments do

Once a government is secure in office, with a working majority of MPs it can rely on, it can then ask

Parliament to pass its programme or manifesto into legislation. Ministers are in charge of government departments, directing a permanent cadre of public officials or civil servants tasked with implementing government policies. The most senior ministers, about twenty in number (though more may attend), are formed into a cabinet, chaired by the prime minister, which discusses and approves the key business of government. The prime minister can also exercise the monarch's powers, called prerogative powers (see Zoom-In 1.2), to conduct foreign policy as well as engage in treaties and military actions (though now heavily constrained by Parliament); the government can also bring a budget to the House of Commons for approval and use the power of the finance ministry, under the charge of the Chancellor of the Exchequer, to levy taxes and approve public spending. In this way, the key feature of the British political system is how members of the House of Commons form, sustain, and topple a government.

1.3.5 The House of Commons

As section 1.3.3 indicates, the House of Commons is central to British politics as it is where governments are formed and fall or are renewed, and to which governments are accountable. It is composed of 650 MPs, elected in single constituencies across the UK. Its members may be part of the government. As the first chamber of the legislature, laws must pass through the Commons, usually initiated there. Government dominates law-making and parliamentary business and most legislation is usually controlled by the government party through the loyalty of its MPs and the work of the whips (see Key term 1.6) in getting MPs through the voting lobbies (see also section 3.3.1).

Photo 1.2 The interior of the House of Commons, at the State Opening, December 2019.

1

Key term 1.6 Whip

Parties have what are called whips, who are MPs or members of the House of Lords who hold formal government (ministerial) or opposition posts, and whose job is to convey the party's line and ensure that MPs vote accordingly.

1.3.6 The House of Lords

The second chamber of the legislature, through which legislation must also pass, is the House of Lords (see Photo 1.3). Members are not elected by the voters, but its operation follows the same pattern as the House of Commons: appointed ministers sit in the Lords and seek to promote the government's legislative programme. However, the chamber does not always have a majority of seats controlled by political parties who are in the government and there are many independent members. Though the House of Lords has significant input in legislation and public policy (Russell 2013), it cannot delay things for long if there is a decisive Commons majority, and it may not oppose the government's budget or amend money bills (see section 3.5.5).

1.3.7 The party system

The two necessary features of the British political system are Parliament, whose members make laws and authorize taxes and expenditures, and a government with executive powers, which forms when the monarch appoints a prime minister who can command a majority

Photo 1.3 A House of Lords vote during debate on the European Union Withdrawal Bill (2019).
Source: Copyright House of Lords 2021/Photography by Roger Harris

of votes in the House of Commons. The political system could operate with just these features in place, but in practice political parties, which are embedded in the formal institutions, shape much of how British politics takes place. In particular, parties determine how the government and the opposition are organized. Parties and the party system as a whole operate in very different ways at different points in time, such as in the 1950s, when there were (just about) only two parties represented, or with today's more fragmented array of parties at different levels of government. Nonetheless, parties in Parliament still need to work within the basic constitutional features of parliamentary democracy and government, as outlined in section 1.3.3.

For historical reasons, from the power of the establishment, based on the influence of the Crown and the Church of England, and the presence of a more liberal alternative, there were two coalitions, then becoming two parties: the Tories and the Liberals, respectively. The Tories became known as the Conservative and Unionist Party—or just the Conservatives—which survives to this day. In the early decades of the twentieth century, the Liberal Party was replaced by the working-class- and trade-union-organized Labour Party, as the main progressive or left-wing force in British politics. Yet this transfer retained two political parties as the main parliamentary alternatives for voters. As a result of elections, one can be a party in government, holding ministerial offices as mentioned above; the other becomes the opposition, with a 'shadow' cabinet/ministers ready to replace the government should the government fail to govern or lose its majority at a general election. Smaller parties, such as the Liberal Democrats and the Scottish National Party (SNP), can also be opposition parties with formal roles too, but they are less significant in the House of Commons than the official opposition. That two parties have dominated at various times in British history does not mean that other parties do not attract votes and seats, especially at other levels of government, such as the Scottish Parliament or the Greater London Authority, both of which have proportional electoral systems; nor does it mean that other parties do not gain significant numbers of seats in the House of Commons, even under FPTP, such as the Liberal Democrats before 2015 and the SNP since then; nor does it mean the current set-up will last for decades. It is simply that, for significant periods of recent British history, the vast majority of MPs who can form a government come from two main parties. For example, at the 2019 general election 567 out of 650 MPs were from the Labour and Conservative Parties: 87 per cent of the total number of MPs. Later in the book, we will discuss whether this system of two-party dominance is weakening and changing out of recognition (see section 5.6).

1.3.8 General elections

General elections have to happen at least every five years, when each MP has to contest their seat in a competitive race under FPTP. In the past, prime ministers had the power to call an election when they wanted, which was the power of the monarch to dissolve Parliament (one of the prerogative powers). From 2011, the prime minister has been constrained by the Fixed-Term Parliaments Act (which may be repealed before 2024), which sets out the rules by which an election may be called: a two-thirds majority of MPs or a loss of a vote of confidence in the government. In practice, the system remains similar to before 2011 with much power in the hands of the prime minister as leader of the majority party, who is secure in office provided MPs in their parties support them and their majority is assured. The prime minister may call an election by ensuring the party's MPs vote for it, and the opposition's MPs are usually expected to want an election so that they have a chance of becoming the next government. It is hard for opposition parties to hold out against an early election, or 'snap' election, for long, such as the general election of 12 December 2019, caused by a motion proposed by the Liberal Democrats and SNP on 28 October 2019.

1.3.9 **The role of opposition parties**

The parties in opposition have an official role, especially as some opposition posts have salaries paid for by the state. The opposition is there to challenge the government, symbolized by the structure of the House of Commons with its government benches on one side and opposition parties on the other: ministers/opposition spokespersons sit at the front and their party supporters behind them. The main opposition party presents itself as a plausible government in waiting. It does so by criticizing the government, even if it may be important on occasion to offer support, as was seen at times during the Covid-19 pandemic. It needs a political crisis to form a new government, such as the governing party losing the support of its MPs, revealed in a confidence motion. Otherwise, an election is needed for a new intake of MPs so it can form the new government with its leader as prime minister. Then the roles of government and opposition reverse.

1.3.10 **Britain has a written constitution (in places)**

To understand how a political system operates, it is important to know about a country's constitution, which is a set of rules and conventions that guide how politics takes place; in particular, it sets out the powers of those who make political decisions, elaborates the basic rules of decision-making, specifies the relationships between different institutions of the political system, and protects the rights of the citizens. Every country has some kind of constitution. Britain's is based on the doctrine of parliamentary sovereignty (see Zoom-In 1.1) and executive (prerogative) powers (see Zoom-In 1.2), exercised by whom the monarch appoints. Some parts of the constitution are written down in statutes, such as the Parliament Act of 1911 (revised in 1949) that limits the powers of the House of Lords. Much of the constitution is not written, or only recently has been (Blick 2016), and what texts there are do not have the legitimacy and longevity of a document like the US constitution with its statement of the powers of the different branches of government and enforcement by the US Supreme Court. Even key doctrines are not defined in one authoritative document. For example, to define parliamentary sovereignty, courts have to look to various sources and documents, as the Supreme Court had to do in the famous *Miller* case of 2017 to decide whether Parliament had to vote to authorize leaving the European Union (see section 3.7).

Britain is best described as having an uncodified (see Key term 1.4) rather than unwritten constitution because some of it is contained in written documents, such as Acts of Parliament, though they are not brought together in one place. When writers refer to the unwritten constitution they should be taken to mean that the constitution has many flexible features and no one defining document that can be interpreted by a constitutional court. However, it is also possible to overemphasize the difference between codified and uncodified constitutions, as all countries have living constitutions that adapt according to interpretation of the courts and from changing practices, as social and political changes create new circumstances that the founders might never have thought possible.

1.3.11 **Constitutional conventions**

Many features of British politics are based on unwritten rules called constitutional conventions (see Zoom-In 1.3), which are about how the government is formed and how ministers report to Parliament (Marshall 1987). These conventions require understanding from political participants who need to choose to follow them in some way; but they are not strictly enforced, such as by the courts. Conventions can work well when they are about the exercise of executive political power, such as the rules of the cabinet; but they tend to be weakly observed when they are about democratic review, such as ministerial accountability

Zoom-In 1.1 Parliamentary sovereignty

Parliamentary sovereignty is a key principle of the UK constitution, which affects how Parliament, courts, and the executive operate. It was asserted during the seventeenth century and set out in the Bill of Rights 1689 and other documents.

It is defined as legal supremacy of Parliament, which can undo any law it makes: 'the right to make or unmake any law whatever; and further, that no person or body is recognized by the law of England as having a right to override or set aside the legislation of Parliament' (Dicey 1889, 38).

Debate:

- Difference between legal (de jure) sovereignty and practical (de facto) sovereignty.
- Whether EU membership limited sovereignty by ceding power to a higher court, the European Court of Justice (ECJ).
- Whether parliamentary sovereignty in effect means legality, and is not about Parliament per se (Lakin 2008).
- Whether the founding of the United Kingdom as a union of nations shows the lack of coherence of the doctrine (McLean 2010).

to Parliament, being prepared to resign because of wrongdoing, or a failure of policy.

Why are there conventions? In the view of the famous jurist Dicey (1889), these conventions were thought to soften the potential harshness of parliamentary sovereignty or unlimited legal power in the hands of the government, and to ensure that accountability is fostered and more moderate government conducted. These conventions can be very flexible and change according to convenience and purpose. For defenders of the British constitution, they lead to a pragmatic form of governance (Dicey 1889). Critics, however, regard conventions as weak and malleable, subject to the demands of the

Zoom-In 1.2 Prerogative powers

These are powers of the Crown or sovereign that are executive in nature, though they might be subject to a vote in the House of Commons (see 5, 6, 7 below). They have been handed over to the prime minister to exercise or delegate to others. They cannot be created, but can be changed by statute (e.g. 2, 6, 7).

Examples:

1. Appointment and dismissal of ministers
2. Dissolution of Parliament (to call a general election), amended by the Fixed-Term Parliaments Act in 2011
3. Royal assent to bills
4. Conduct of foreign policy
5. War and military action
6. Agree treaties (role for Parliament since Constitutional Reform and Governance Act 2010)
7. Organization of the government departments
8. Grant honours

executive that can easily override them. The constitutional lawyer Ivor Jennings, writing over seventy years ago, saw conventions as subject to the power relations at play in British politics (Jennings 1948). This weakness has caused people to worry that there are no principles behind the constitution, which means British government tends to stumble from crisis to crisis, adopting pragmatic solutions that work for the moment but where the constitutional framework offers no coherence to the system as a whole. The conventions permit the unlimited power of the executive because of the absence of powerful constraints that, it is claimed, leads to an over-mighty and over-centralized form of government, lurches in policies, and inefficient decisions (Finer 1975). There is a long line of critics of the lack of a codified constitution, coming from all parts of the political spectrum. They have sought to put in place a written document that would replace the existing collection of laws and conventions. A written constitution, in their view, would modernize the British state, entrench citizen rights, and limit the power of the executive (e.g. Hirst 1989). This campaign carries on through advocacy, such as in the work of openDemocracy (https://www.opendemocracy.net) and in the writing of academics (King 2019).

In spite of the lack of enforcement and politicization of the conventions, they can suddenly spring to life, such as when the former Home Secretary, Amber Rudd, resigned on 29 April 2018 because of not remembering the advice she received from her officials over the Windrush scandal about how the Home Office gave targets over illegal migrants, which long-term residents from the Caribbean had been caught up in. The scandal resurfaced in 2017, highlighting how the Home Office had wrongly detained, denied legal rights to, and deported Commonwealth citizens who had migrated to the UK in the late 1940s up to the 1970s (Wardle and Obermuller 2019).

1.3.12 **Summarizing the political system**

British politics has always been recognizable because of the clear route to power through voting

Zoom-In 1.3 Constitutional conventions

These are informal non-enforceable rules that guide the practice of government and seek to ensure accountability of the government to Parliament.

Examples:

1. Individual ministerial accountability to Parliament (reporting to Parliament and resigning for personal errors in policy, misconduct, or for the actions of public officials).
2. Collective ministerial responsibility. Agreement of members of the government to follow and publicly agree to government policy. If they do not, they are obliged to resign. Applies to the cabinet in particular, where there is a right to debate and disagreement behind the cover of secrecy.
3. The House of Lords does not oppose items in the government's manifesto (Salisbury convention).
4. The sovereign must assent to any bill passed by the two houses of Parliament.
5. Parliament does not legislate on devolved matters without first seeking the consent of the devolved body (the Sewel convention).
6. Ministers are members of the House of Commons or the House of Lords.

Case Study 1.1 *The Ministerial Code*

Recently, many of these conventions have been written down in documents, such as *The Ministerial Code*, and *The Cabinet Manual*, which emerged from an initiative under Gordon Brown when he was prime minister. By writing them down, something has happened akin to a written constitution as they can be referred to in disputes and where there is a conflict of interest (Blick 2016). The manuals can change or be updated to reflect practice. They are not enforceable and it is possible to observe governments behaving differently to the conventions outlined in the manuals. For example, the manuals refer to the convention of the confidentiality of the cabinet, but under Theresa May's government this was regularly breached with no consequence.

blocks of MPs, and for procedures to be in place for a government to be formed. It is true that politics can at times seem to be chaotic and uncoordinated, such as when one party does not have a majority of MPs; for example, from 1976 to 1979 when Labour lost its tiny majority from by-election defeats, and from 2017 to 2019, after Theresa May called her fateful general election, or when there is a small majority and frequent rebellions, as when John Major was Conservative prime minister from 1990 to 1997. But there is usually a means for getting government back on track. A fresh election can, if the conditions are right, yield a majority of MPs for a single political party which has the capability of gaining control of the system. This happened in 1979, when the Conservative Party led by Margaret Thatcher achieved successive majorities in the 1980s and changed British politics fundamentally; similarly, in 1997 Tony Blair's 'New Labour' Party reformed British politics through decisive election victories, repeated in 2001 and 2005, that generated secure majorities from which to govern. Then, in 2019, the Conservative Party led by Boris Johnson secured a majority of eighty seats, seeming to put to an end the parliamentary uncertainties of the May years, for example by voting through the final Brexit deal—the UK's free trade agreement with the EU—in one day on 30 December 2020. Whether this marks a return to traditional party government is not clear, as the likelihood of secure majorities may now be reduced in future elections; nor has Boris Johnson fully succeeded in returning to old patterns of government dominance of parliamentary business. More is said about this topic in Chapters 3 (on Parliament) and 5 (winning elections).

This description has been boiled down to its essence for the purpose of explaining it in simple terms. It is possible to conclude that Britain has a potentially straightforward political system, at least at first glance. It is about how parties seek to gain majorities that allow them to exercise power. Once in power, a government, either controlled by a single political party or a coalition of parties, has freedom to act; but it can be swiftly replaced and then the party or parties can spend many years out of office with not much power at all. It is an executive-dominant system designed to sustain what is called party government (see Key term 1.7), where political parties have the right to govern and to drive public policy (Rose 1974).

British national politics is a high-stakes game in that it benefits those in power and excludes those who are not. At the same time, it also generates the conditions for a fall from power. It has the means

Key term 1.7 Party government

Control of policy and decision-making by a single party that has a majority in the legislature and can implement its policies by law-making and the bureaucracy. Government aims to get re-elected at the end of its term of office and to impose policies that reflect its worldview and ideology.

for replacement of the government, which can happen because of the outcome of regular elections or at any time from the simple failure of government when it cannot govern anymore. The system is designed to ensure the monarch is never forced to make an executive decision: it should be very clear whom to appoint as a new prime minister. If there is uncertainty about who should be prime minister, the incumbent stays in office until another person can be found. But the very simplicity of the political system and exercise of power by the government might put too much power in the hands of a small group of party leaders.

1.3.13 **A centralized polity?**

Both formal and informal rules create a potentially centralized polity as once a party has access to the levers of power in government, it can potentially do what it wants (subject to the rule of law and international legal obligations), through its control over the business of the House of Commons, commands by ministers, and exercising powers over finance, sanctioned by its majority in the House of Commons, and ability in due course to override the House of Lords.

But running such a system in a centralized way is not practicable, neither politically in terms of keeping good relations within parties, which are electoral coalitions under the façade of unity, nor practically in that it is not possible to concentrate power in the hands of the prime minister and run a complex policy-making machine efficiently without government overload. Hence there are extensive delegations of power to agencies, subcentral governments (including law-making to the Scottish Parliament, Northern Ireland Assembly, and Welsh Senedd), interest groups, and international organizations, which are considered in Part C of this book. It was always a complex, varied, and decentralized system, but since the devolution of power to parliaments across the UK from 1999, this asymmetry has intensified and deepened. Now the central state, described in sections 1.3.1–1.3.13, has had to adapt and operate in a cooperative way across the territories of the UK. This decentralization and fragmentation of the central state came to the fore during the Covid-19 crisis, with different policies across the UK and the need for the Johnson government to seek agreement with other UK governments over which it has no real power (see Case Study 1.2).

One of the paradoxes of parliamentary sovereignty is that it is compatible with both centraliza-

Key term 1.8 Separation of powers

A doctrine that states the executive, legislature, and judiciary should be independent of each other, and is seen as a limit on arbitrary power. It is usually backed up by a codified constitution, as in the US. With its fusion between the executive and the legislature, the UK does not have separation of powers in the full sense, though there are ways for the legislature to hold the executive to account (see section 3.4) and the courts have independence (see section 3.7).

Case Study 1.2 The Covid-19 pandemic and the nations of the UK

During the Covid-19 crisis the complexity of the governance of the UK was revealed in a very public way. England, Scotland, Wales, and Northern Ireland each have responsibilities for public health and the NHS, so they were able to make decisions based on advice from their own scientists and public health professionals, such as the timing and extent of lockdown, social distancing, testing, track and trace, foreign travel, providing personal protective equipment, and who is vaccinated. The UK government in Westminster was not often successful in coordinating policies, while at the same time having to manage a complex array of agencies to deliver England's response, whether test and trace, local lockdown, providing and building new hospitals, and developing and rolling out a vaccine (see section 11.3.4).

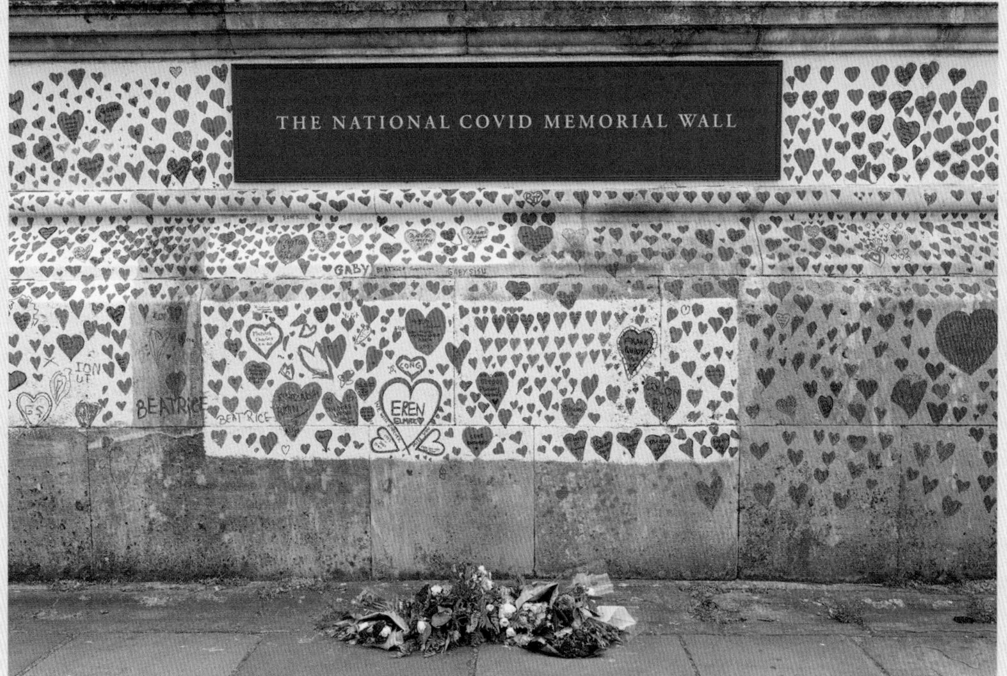

Photo 1.4 The national Covid-19 Memorial Wall, Westminster, London, in April 2021.

tion *and* decentralization, as each can be enacted by an Act of Parliament. The UK can delegate what powers it likes to the Scottish Parliament and even enact Scottish independence in a way that is much more straightforward than other countries with codified constitutions and formal separation of powers (see Key term 1.8). For example, in Spain the integrity of the state is protected by the constitution, making it very hard for a region like Catalonia to secede, whereas the UK Parliament could make Scotland independent with one Act of Parliament, if it wished.

1.4 The political system in comparative context

1.4.1 British politics as a political system

Now the basics have been set out, essential for the first-time student of British politics, but hopefully also useful for those who already have a strong grasp of the political system and its institutions, it is important now to stand back and ask what is being conveyed with these institutions and personnel. What is the character of the political system (Key term 1.9), the British political system, or the system or systems that pertain to the United Kingdom?

In comparative terms, Britain is a parliamentary democracy rather than a presidential or separation-of-powers system; power is concentrated in the legislature. In a world of institutional hybrids, Britain is a pure example of a parliamentary system with no president. It also combines a parliamentary system with a majoritarian one whereby a winning party or parties in a general election can gain control over the levers of power. A simple majority of legislative seats is needed for a government to be in power.

1.4.2 Majoritarian and consensus democracies

The comparative scholar Lijphart (1999) proposed two types of democracy: consensus or majoritarian, determined mainly by their respective electoral systems. They can be represented as a set of features (see Figure 1.1). Lijphart says that majoritarian systems lead to a single party in power, while consensus democracies encourage coalitions between political parties, which can represent a wider range of citizens than a single party might be able to do. For example, Germany has a proportional representation system, a multi-party system, coalition governments, a balance of power between the executive and Parliament; it has a decentralized system in a federal division of powers, where there are two strong chambers of the Bundestag (the Parliament) and the Bundesrat (representation of states); and it has a codified constitution with an independent constitutional court.

As a majoritarian and parliamentary system without a codified constitution, Britain appears as a pure example of a majoritarian democracy, whereby the political system appears to be less geared to produce consensus and not suited to producing effective policies based on negotiation between political parties. It is often noted as not having veto players (see Key term 1.10), which exist in separation-of-powers systems (Tsebelis 2011), and are able to prevent radical and non-consensual policies from happening.

Lijphart's scheme is a simplification of a complicated array of democratic systems, even Britain's. In spite of the many changes in recent years that have moved Britain closer to other European political systems in terms of multi-party politics, proportional electoral systems, and more decentralization of power, as with the Scottish Parliament (Dunleavy 2005), political parties still seek to be and often are majority governments at Westminster with access to (in theory) unlimited power.

Key term 1.9 A political system

Describes how the different participants in politics—leaders, representatives, bureaucrats, citizens, and interest group members—work together and/or exercise power to make choices, represent others, and shape public policies. It works in different ways depending on the institutions and cultures of the country.

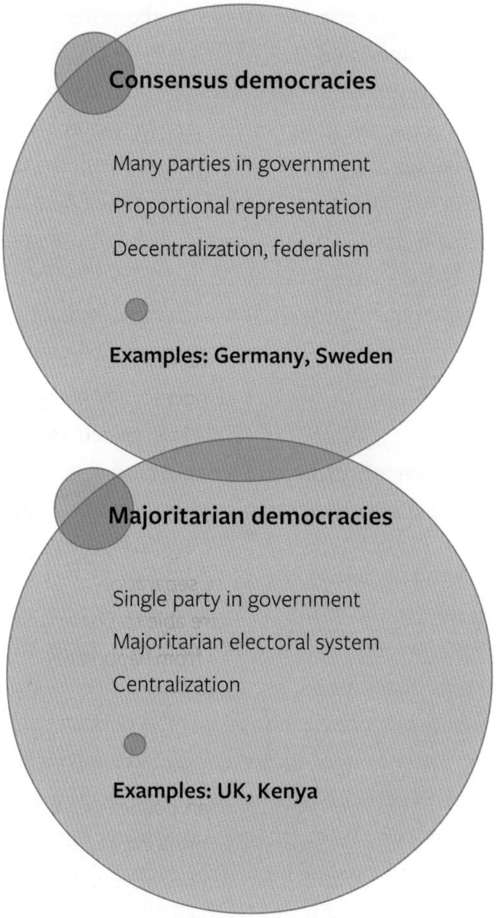

Figure 1.1 Consensus and majoritarian democracies.

Key term 1.10 Veto player

A political actor who has the formal power to block a measure or policy. For example, a constitutional court in a separation-of-powers system can stop a law or policy.

1.4.3 **The 'Westminster model'**

Having located Britain in comparative context, it is important to assess how the system can be thought to embody a version of democracy, even if one thought to be less desirable in Lijphart's scheme. Britain's democracy is often assessed by reference to what is called the 'Westminster model' (Lijphart 1999, chapter 2), which is about the concentration of power in a government accountable to the Westminster Parliament and therefore to the electorate as a whole, thus giving a democratic justification for the institutions set out descriptively in section 1.3. This model emerged from how executive power, which was in the hands of the monarch, had become moderated by democratic politics (Bagehot 1873). In practice, there is no authoritative statement of the British version of democracy. Nobody designed the system: it is made up of different elements that have evolved over time. It is not clear what are its necessary (have to be there) and sufficient (important to have) features. It is also important to note that its familiar features do not always operate predictably, especially when there is a political change or crisis, such as when a war is going badly as in May 1940 when a coalition of government and opposition had to be formed.

To oversimplify, for the purposes of exposition, the key features of the Westminster model include: centralized strong government at the centre with control over laws and policy; close scrutiny of the executive responsible to Parliament; clear choices between government and credible opposition political parties at election times; and the possibility of decisive electoral punishment by voters, who can use their choices to deliver either support or electoral defeat for the incumbent government, which is decisive and leads to a secure majority for the next government that gets a chance to test out its ideas. The idea is that the institutions produce a coherent government at the centre, giving a democratically elected party access to the levers of power over policy, laws, and finance to move a government forward. The government can get on with the business of governing and is responsible to the House of Commons for its

Key term 1.11 Clarity of responsibility

The idea that a single institution vested with power and regular elections can be held to account, partly because it cannot shift blame onto other actors.

performance and ultimately to the electorate, who vote its MPs in or out of office at general elections. The government has power, but it can be reviewed and judged. Errors can be costly, as there is no other branch of government to transfer blame to. Clarity of responsibility (Key term 1.11) reveals to the electorate who is responsible for decisions so they can make an evaluation about the government accordingly. Then, the government becomes responsive and accountable to the electorate.

Parliament is considered to be crucial in providing scrutiny and debate, with the role of the opposition in holding the government to account. Given the weakness of many parliamentary procedures, at least until recently, this only made sense when combined with an electoral threat, so that Parliament can be used to increase the credibility of opposition parties, so they may launch an effective attack on the government when the time comes.

The Westminster model relies on voters being able to deliver decisive government in an electoral contest. If parties are in a position to be a government, this incentive may affect their behaviour and the extent to which they fashion their policies to please the electorate. They are incentivized to be responsible, either as the government party for fear of being kicked out of office, or as an opposition waiting to get their chance to govern.

1.4.4 British politics in terms of principals and agents

It is useful to have an intellectual framework that can help analyse the relationships between key actors in the Westminster model (see Zoom-In 1.4). In the principal–agent model, some actors are called principals while others are known as agents. Principals command a service from agents. For example, a principal might be a politician wanting to carry out a policy, with the agent being the bureaucrats in an agency who are charged with carrying it out (see section 8.4.1). Or the principal could be voters wanting an agent, the political party, to carry out its wishes. The important issue is that control is limited by an information

Zoom-In 1.4 The principal–agent model

The model originates in work by economists (Coase 1937) on how organizations internalize transaction costs to reduce the need for costly contracts with outside bodies.

It is a model of control where two parties have different roles: one is the principal that commissions a service; the other is an agent who delivers it.

The expertise of the agent in delivering the service creates an information asymmetry between the two, which means the principal finds it difficult to monitor the agent without costly acquisition of information. This agency problem creates an incentive for the agent to slack (also called moral hazard).

Key sources: Moe (1984); Strøm, Müller, and Bergman (2003)

imbalance between the principal and agent: the latter has expertise and discretion about how to carry out instructions. The agents can withhold information from the principal or ensure it would be very costly for the principal to find out about something. For example, a political party might not tell the voters about all the choices available to it or voters might find it very hard to monitor whether the government had carried out their wishes after the election.

1.4.5 The single chain of command

Using the lens of the principal–agent model, British politics potentially has a single chain of command from voters to MPs to government (Saalfeld 2003): voters are the principals with respect to their MPs, who are their agents; then MPs are the principals with respect to the government, who is the agent. The voters task their MPs to put in place a government that reflects their wishes. The government's job is to implement these wishes, knowing that it cannot blame-shift or deflect responsibility for a failed policy. The principal can punish or reward the government by voting in a general election against or for the government based on its past performance. There is a clear mechanism through which the principal can monitor and punish the agent. Figure 1.2 sets out this representation of the political system, with the roles of voters, MPs, and the government. Note that unified political parties make the task of the agents, the voters, much easier, so they vote in an MP in the knowledge that that person will put in place a government that has promised policies and programmes to the voters.

The single chain of command makes the political system apparently simpler than other kinds, which may have multiple principals and agents; for example, in the US, executive agencies report to Congress and the president, which are both principals. But this simplicity in the UK was always more apparent than real, and more complex chains of relationships emerged in the late part of the twentieth century, such as to devolved administrations, interest groups, international organizations, and agencies and regulators (Richards and Smith 2016). The government can in fact shift blame onto these other organizations, avoiding electoral accountability (see Part C of this book). It also requires voters to have a large amount of information about the performance of the incumbent, the current office-holder, to overcome the information asymmetry, so as to be able to monitor and, if need be, punish the incumbent government correctly by voting. The other issue is whether principals, the voters, are able to punish agents at all as this depends on a clear connection between vote choices and seat outcomes that deliver the result of the choice, which does not really occur, especially in recent years, partly through the vagaries of the electoral system (see section 5.8.4). And even with incentives in place, the single chain of command still needs democratic elites, leaders in the political parties, to believe they should respond to voters and adhere to norms of democracy, at least between elections.

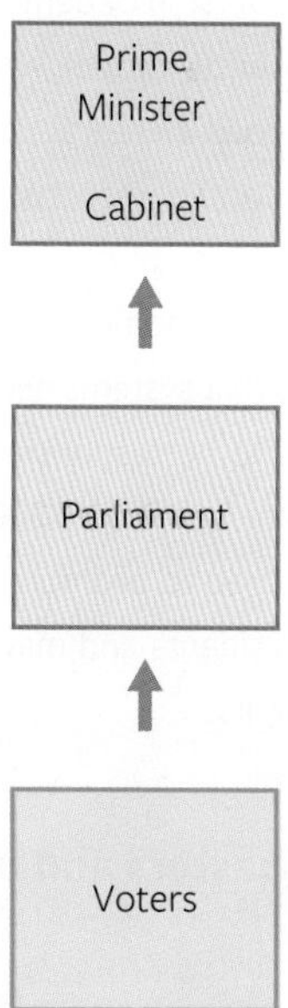

Figure 1.2 The basic principal–agent framework of British politics. *Note: Arrows indicate from principal to agent*

1.4.6 **Clarity of responsibility and responsible party government**

The British democratic model is based on a single party forming the government. It has the freedom to get on with the job of governing, but in due course faces the judgment of the voters on the basis of its performance. This goes back to the responsible party government model of the 1950s (Ranney 1954), which questioned the benefits of diffusion of power and shared responsibilities implied by separation-of-powers constitutions. It was a time when outside observers saw much to admire in the British party system.

If power is concentrated and actors cannot shift blame onto others, this creates a government that Parliament and the electorate can hold to account. If there is clarity of responsibility, voters can judge the past actions of the government and, if they are not happy with the incumbent government, can vote in an alternative in its place. The last feature is very important, because voters need a viable alternative if they are to express their discontent.

This is a distinct version of democracy. It contrasts with Lijphart's consensus model, which prioritizes the importance of a broad electoral coalition to achieve citizen satisfaction and a responsiveness of policies to opinion. Clarity of responsibility is an alternative model proposed by economists (Persson and Tabellini 2005) that says that systems need incentives to be efficient as well as to be responsive to voters (for a review of this debate, see Powell 2000). Political institutions that are alleged to promote efficiency include directly elected presidents and mayors as well as single-party governments.

1.4.7 **Policy disasters and the decay of British politics?**

A common view today is that the British system may have worked effectively in the past, but has now broken down irretrievably. The late Anthony King (2007) believed the essential features of the British political system had decayed because politicians stopped believing in the basic principles of governing and placed short-term advantage above serving the interests of the people. The system now lacks coherence and tends to stumble from one crisis to another. Writing with Ivor Crewe (King and Crewe 2014), King argues that the British system of government increasingly produces what are called 'blunders of government'. These are policy disasters, thought to have come about because the British political system centralizes decision-making and limits deliberation and debate, which derive from the way the very constitutional arrangements described in sections 1.3.10 and 1.3.11 affect the business of government (Dunleavy 1995b). This sense of decay of British politics is a familiar theme in recent decades, influencing accounts of the poor decision-making process and miscalculations by the governing elite. The theme is picked up in work by Michael Moran, who saw increasing disorder and confusion in British politics and policy-making (Moran 2007). In his final book, *The End of British Politics?* (2017), he takes the criticisms one step further to discuss the possible breakdown of British politics as a model of government. If the normal operation of government has broken down, it makes performance or retrospective voting largely meaningless, as each government will blunder and voters cannot ensure an improvement in performance by voting out the incumbent. They get policy failures no matter which government is in power. Rather than showing the virtues of the Westminster model of accountability and responsiveness to the electorate, with responsible government, the British system now shows what many democratic scholars call backsliding (Runciman 2018) (Key term 1.12), whereby the democratic practices that guided political systems in the past have been eroded. If the political system is also becoming more turbulent and characterized by shocks and surprises, as outlined in section 1.2.2, then voters are also unlikely to get the

Key term 1.12 Backsliding

How political systems lose the essential features of democracy, such as the rule of law. Unlike direct challenges to democracies, such as military coups, the process is a step-by-step erosion of freedoms and fair procedures, and evasion by governments of democratic scrutiny. It is about the acquisition of power by a narrow elite not interested in democratic accountability.

electoral outcomes they were expecting, undermining the punish–reward model that needs citizens to be able to give governments a clear, predictable signal (see section 11.3.4).

1.4.8 Should the Westminster model be scrapped?

Partly for the reasons stated in section 1.4.7, scholars tear their hair out over the use of the term 'Westminster model' to describe British politics (for example, Rhodes 2005; Dunleavy 2006). They believe it is particularly not applicable now. Then there is the litany of mistakes and policy errors (see section 1.2) showing that the sheer risks taken by today's political leaders would seem to point against the use of the term responsible to describe party government. Scholars find the Westminster model too simplistic an account of British politics, not taking full account of the range of policy-making and large numbers of decision-makers in play in the UK (Jordan and Cairney 2013), and neglecting the complex structure of the central state (Richards and Smith 2016). The title of Russell and Serban's (2020b) recent blog summarizes this as: 'An ageing and distinctly cloudy term: why it is time for the "Westminster model" to be retired'. They review the academic literature, observing the inconsistent use of the term, and the lack of attempt at definition of key terms in most studies and reviews (Russell and Serban 2020a).

1

1.4.9 Alternatives to the Westminster model

Discontent with the fundamental principles of British politics appears in radical and/or alternative critiques of the British model of accountability and electoral responsiveness. These approaches criticize the nature of the political institutions, which democratically elected parties need to work within, focusing on their non-democratic origins and claiming that they serve to perpetuate a degree of continuity with established interests. Ideas of responsible government and accommodation are thought to be really about the tempering of democratic preferences in line with established and elite opinion. Even though the British system of democracy may appear responsive and deliver accountable government, in this view it is very narrowly conceived and operates within a strict range of choices that are in effect sanctioned by the establishment and maintained by its institutional rules. It is a democracy, but of a limited sort. Such ideas strongly influenced left-critiques of British politics right from the start of the twentieth century when Labour became more electorally successful. They regard British institutions, like the civil service (Kellner and Crowther-Hunt 1980), as part of the establishment, which has a consensus about how decisions are taken. In particular, the nature of the parliamentary system affects political parties, which needed to moderate their stances to be credible as parties of government, rather than fulfil their radical mandate (Miliband 1972, 1961). The criticism by Labour politician Tony Benn, when writing in the 1970s (Benn and Mullin 1979), was that the Crown has an indirect influence on the operation and culture of government, which deadened change. This approach to British politics influenced the constitutional reform movement, Charter 88, based on the idea that the modernization of the institutional framework and greater transparency would also be associated with a broader agenda for democracy in Britain (Hirst 1989). Currently, the Democratic Audit's review of British democracy makes this case (Dunleavy, Park, and Taylor 2018). The negative evaluation of institutions is extended in feminist critiques of British politics as perpetuating male domination, a bias that is codified into institutional routines that circumscribe the political agenda (Lovenduski 2012). The lack of representation of many ethnic minorities in political institutions is also part of this underlying culture and institutional pattern that contrasts with the diversity of the British population. Britain's prosperity was linked to its dominance of people in other parts of the world through its history as a colonial power, and citizens from these countries came to live in the United Kingdom, experiencing discrimination (Gilroy 2013; Byrne et al. 2020). Much work on the constitution and party politics is blind to this diverse past. Often these histories are hidden in the operation of these central institutions so they do not appear very much, if at all, in writing about them. It is at the subnational level, where policy is made on the ground, where it is possible to see and read about how class and race influence British politics in more direct ways (see section 9.6). In Part C of this book, these issues of private power, race, and class emerge more strongly.

1.4.10 **The heuristic (learning) value of the Westminster model**

While not denying the importance of the radical critique and alternatives, the contention in this book is that it is still useful to know something about the framework of the Westminster model, since so much is written about it and against it. It is something that is quite easy to knock down or at least to criticize, such as from the radical approaches outlined above. The basic elements may still be in place, even if working in an odd, dysfunctional way. Some writers, such as David Judge (1993), who work in the new institutionalist tradition (see Zoom-In 1.5), believe that the logics and routines of public organizations matter very much in how everyday politics takes place and that includes Westminster institutions. Other writers, working within the interpretivist approach (Rhodes 2011), stress that ideas and beliefs matter. Key actors in the process, politicians and civil servants, still believe in the fundamental tenets of the Westminster model and so bring these ideas into their everyday work. Institutions have 'lives of their own' and are very persistent, carrying on even when the fundamentals upon which they are based have eroded in the era of political turbulence. Then odd terms pop up in politics and the law, such as 'parliamentary sovereignty' and 'collective responsibility', that are not comprehensible without a link being made between democracy and the constitution. This becomes crucial when constitutional law cases come before the courts, as with the *Cherry* case (Case Study 1.3).

To understand where British politics has got to now, it is important to delve back into the foundations of the system and know how it developed over time. Doing so shows the use of the Westminster model in helping understand British politics, even if it does not offer a complete explanation of how power and decision-making operate in Britain today. Finally, it is important to be wary of thinking that a concept has no use just because it is not easily defined, which is the essence of the complaint by Russell and Serban (2020a). The philosopher Ludwig Wittgenstein wrote in *Philosophical Investigations* (1958, section 31) that many concepts are unclear, but people are still able to understand them when they come across examples. For example, many people might find it hard to define a game played between two people, such as a game of chess; but when they see it being played or play it themselves, they understand it more easily. So it is with the

1

Case Study 1.3 The *Cherry* case

In 2019, the *Cherry* case came up in front the UK Supreme Court ((*on the application of Miller*) *v The Prime Minister; Cherry and Others v Advocate General for Scotland (2019) UKSC 41 (24 September 2019)*). A litigant took Boris Johnson's government to court over its decision to have a long suspension (prorogation) of Parliament on 12 September to end the start of the new parliamentary year on 14 October. Normally, prorogation lasts a few days between sessions; this suspension of Parliament was seen as an attempt by the government to avoid scrutiny. It could be seen as an attempt at democratic backsliding (see Key term 1.12) whereby the executive seeks to avoid democratic accountability. The government lost the case because the power to suspend Parliament by the monarch under the advice of ministers was, in this case, an abuse of power. To make its decision, the court relied on the constitutional conventions of parliamentary sovereignty and democratic accountability. Without a model of democracy, it is hard to understand what is happening in this case. The courts in this and other cases (see *Miller* case, Case Study 3.3) have upheld a parliamentary version of accountability.

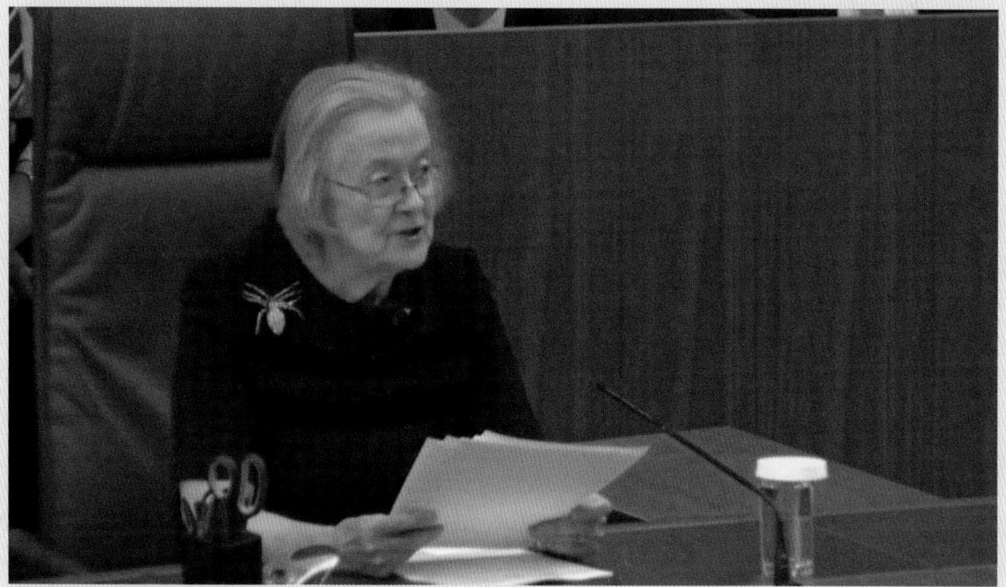

Photo 1.5 The head of the Supreme Court of the UK, Lady Brenda Hale, announces the ruling that the British Prime Minister Boris Johnson's decision to prorogue Parliament was unlawful.

Westminster model: it needs to be seen in operation, just like with the *Cherry* case.

So, it is just not possible to scrap the Westminster model, much as there might be applause at doing so! In any case, it is only ever regarded as one among many lenses through which to examine British democracy (Gamble 1990). The Westminster model should be treated cautiously, like any conceptual approach, and can be compared with the others on offer (see Zoom-In 1.5).

Zoom-In 1.5 Theories of British politics

A theory is a conceptual scheme that highlights key causal relationships at work in politics, and is usually a simplification of complex realities, stressing one or two core features that dominate others.

1. *Traditional institutionalism* (Westminster model): constitutional features as drivers of politics and policy, and role of party government. Key authors: Norton, Birch, Rose (see section 1.3.3).
2. *New institutionalism*: stresses formal and informal rules of the parliamentary state. Key authors: Judge, Kelso (see section 3.2.1).
3. *Feminist institutionalism*: stresses the way institutions embed patriarchal (male-dominated) relationships. Key authors: Lovenduski, Campbell, Childs (see sections 3.2.1, 3.6.2).
4. *Political economy*: importance of the economy, especially globally, in structuring relationships. Key authors: Gamble, Hay, Thompson (see section 7.2.4).
5. *Rational choice institutionalism*: importance of choice structures to generate outcomes and the difficulty of achieving collective action. Key authors: Dunleavy, Dowding, Dewan (see sections 2.4.7, 5.6.7).
6. *Neo-pluralism*: fracturing of decision-making and lack of coordination, complexity, extensive decentralization, complex governance. Key authors: Marsh, Smith, Cairney, Flinders, Moran, Stoker (see sections 2.6.8, 7.2.2, 7.4.5).
7. *Sociological determinism*: impact of social change, role of identity, social movements, globalization, and geographic inequality. Key authors: Ford and Sobolewska, Goodwin (see sections 4.4.7, 10.4.8).
8. *Interpretivism*: importance of ideas and narratives, such as the British political tradition. Key authors: Rhodes and Bevir (see sections 5.6.5, 8.4.2).
9. *Chaotic pluralism*: unstable agenda-setting, dominance of social media, political turbulence, voter volatility, and breakdown of traditional routines. Key authors: Margetts, John, Fieldhouse (see sections 5.8.1, 6.6.2).

1.5 Conclusion

The material presented in this introductory chapter provides the information and set of arguments to prepare the reader for the consideration of more detailed accounts of British politics that follow. The chapter started out with the current turbulence of British politics and whether this represents something systemic about radical decision-making and greater electoral volatility. But it is not clear whether these are recent trends or whether such turbulence is woven into the fabric of British politics and its institutions.

A brief summary of the central institutions of the political system was offered, either to remind the more experienced reader and to bring out its essential features, or to sum it up for those coming to British politics for the first time. Then an account of how the system might embody a version of democracy as well as some trenchant criticisms of why it might not, and alternative perspectives, were explored. Big questions of the strength of democratic mechanisms, the quality of representation, and the efficiency of public policy were discussed. They still need further attention, which they will get in the following chapters and in Chapter 11, the conclusion to the book.

Further reading

There are many sources on British politics which introduce the political system and review debates about British democracy. For someone new to British politics needing a user-friendly introduction, the short book by Anthony King, *Who Governs Britain?* (2015), is helpful. For an introduction to the constitution, see Martin Loughlin's *The British Constitution* (2013).

It is important to get a grip on or be aware of the basic readings on British politics. The classic paper by Andrew Gamble (1990) on theories of British politics is worth reading closely. There are strong critiques of the Westminster model by Patrick Dunleavy (2006) and Rod Rhodes (2005). Another critical account of the model, with more of a focus on public policy, useful for topics later in this book, is Jordan and Cairney (2013).

It is important to incorporate perspectives from feminism (Lovenduski 1996) and the experience of race in British politics (Gilroy 2013). The latter has a great title: *There Ain't No Black in the Union Jack*. The recent edited volume, *Ethnicity, Race and Inequality in the UK* (Byrne et al. 2020), reviews the inequality in representation and public policy.

Essay and examination questions

One general question could be about the Westminster model and take the form 'How convincing is the Westminster model in understanding British politics today?'. What is needed in the answer is a clear statement about what the model is or could be, then an assessment of the basic criticisms of the model. To help structure the answer see Dunleavy (2006) and Jordan and Cairney (2013; see also Russell and Serban 2020b, 2020a). A similar but broader question is 'Does Britain deliver representative and responsible government?'; this can cover much of the same ground but might reference the wider debate about representation and policy stability as articulated by Birch (1964). Similar themes can be picked up in the question 'How democratic is British politics?'. It is possible to have a more specific question on the constitution that could take the form, 'Does Britain have a written constitution?'. It is also possible to pose a question on the policy disasters along the lines of 'Is Britain uniquely prone to policy disasters?'. There is much more discussion and further readings on policy disasters in section 11.3.4, especially on government responses to Covid-19. Finally, the principal–agent model can be used as a framework to understand British politics, as in the following question: 'To what extent does the principal–agent model offer insights into the operation of British democracy?'.

Access the online resources for this chapter, including biannual updates, web links, and multiple-choice questions: www.oup.com/he/John1e

Chapter 2

2

Leadership from the Top

2.1 What is going to be in this chapter?

This chapter is about the apex of the British political system, where the drama of high politics takes place, and what drives the headlines and news stories. It is about the general issue of leadership and the stresses and strains of this task, examining the role of the prime minister, the readiness of its occupants for the demands of high office, and the impact of being in frontline politics on their capacity to do the job. It is also about the particular system of government in the UK, based around the prime minister, and the power and influence of this person to shape policy and politics, the extent of that influence, and whether it is a factor behind political turbulence. The chapter also gives more basic information about how British politics works and some background information about recent premiers, as well as covering leadership at other territorial levels.

2.2 The role of leaders

2.2.1 What are leaders for?

Political systems vest power and authority in one person or a small group of people who make or shape the key decisions in a country. This does not mean that this person or group of people have complete power and can rule as dictators; but they do have considerable power, to initiate policies and to sign them off, as well as being able to guide the rest of the political system. As politics is about collective choices and making authoritative decisions, as well as the contentious process of getting to those choices, leaders are placed at a crucial point, even though many people are involved down the chain and up to the international sphere. In the British system, prime ministers also need to lead their political parties, especially in the House of Commons, as well as offer more general leadership for the country in the context of the nations of the UK. One task of leadership is to persuade others to do things (Neustadt 1960), which may be not in their immediate interests but are in the collective interest, and where the prime minister does not have complete hold over them. The prime minister also needs to lead internally by managing the official realm of the bureaucracy and agencies and generally overseeing the policy process, which includes tiers of colleagues as ministers and many other actors, such as leaders of interest groups, much of which goes on behind closed doors. Much of the job is symbolic in seeking to provide identity and meaning to members of a national state and being capable of responding effectively in times of national crisis.

2.2.2 Power of the prime minister

One question that needs to be addressed in this chapter is the extent of the power of the prime minister. This is the ability of the office-holder to get things done when faced with decisions made by other actors in the policy process. This leads to one of the classic questions of British politics, about the power of the prime minister and the role of the cabinet. Everyone needs to know about this, partly to be able to look at other ways of examining leadership in British politics, to show the extent to which leadership at the top is moderated by collegial discussion, or whether it is driven by the prime minister with little input from anyone else.

Once the prime ministerial power debate is discussed, there are more general approaches to central coordination work as offering good descriptions of policy-making that typically involve senior officials and politicians. As part of this discussion, it is important to acknowledge the role of political leadership at other territorial levels, such as the devolved territories, and also within local government, although most of that discussion can be found in Chapter 9. The penultimate section of this chapter looks at recent work on the UK prime minister using the framework of what is called rational choice, which will be introduced in this chapter as a set of tools to help understand power play at the centre (see Key term 2.1). While much of this chapter is about the limitations of central executive power in Britain and difficulties prime ministers have

Key term 2.1 Rational choice theory

An approach in the social sciences that stresses individual choices based on ranking objectives based on their perceived utility. Individuals act on the basis of these choices, when the benefits exceed the costs. An important element is game theory (see Zoom-In 2.4).

in overcoming the limits of their personalities and the sheer difficulty of the task in the current political environment, rational choice theory suggests that behind much of the day-to-day struggle to survive, longer-term strategic interests are being gamed. This also highlights the influence and latent power at the centre of government, which may be exerted behind the scenes and not overtly.

2.3 Basic facts: leadership from the top

2.3.1 Back to the constitution

The role and power of the prime minister flows from the general discussion about the nature of British politics and its model of democracy covered in section 1.3.3. The role of the prime minister is crucial in understanding the nature of British government and its elections, party politics, and parliamentary procedures. To recap briefly: the monarch appoints the prime minister on the basis that this person can lead a majority of MPs who will back the government, typically a single party after a general election, but it could be a leader with a minority of MPs who can put together a coalition with another party and its leader, or has an arrangement with a party, sometimes called 'confidence and supply', which was the arrangement the Conservative Party had with the Democratic Unionist Party between 2017 and 2019 (see section 1.3.3). Once appointed, the prime minister has the powers of the Crown to use, and at their command is the machinery of government and the civil service. Moreover, as head of the government, with the consent of cabinet, they can seek to put in place a legislative programme through the House of Commons and the House of Lords, using the allocated time for government business.

2.3.2 Leader of a party and prime minister

The prime minister remains a party politician as head of their party. Very rarely is the head of the party a different person; this happened when Winston Churchill became prime minister in May 1940, with the former prime minister Neville Chamberlain remaining as leader of the party. Usually, if the prime minister is not leader of their party, they have to stand down from office. This is what happened when Theresa May was forced to resign on 24 May 2019. She had to remain in office until 24 July when the Conservative leadership election had taken place and her successor was ready to meet the sovereign. Then she could resign, leaving 10 Downing Street just before Boris Johnson arrived.

2.3.3 Challenges to prime ministers

Prime ministers are sometimes challenged directly in office, as with Theresa May, but it is rare. It is a big thing for MPs to mount such a bid and they need to be convinced that the party is going down to electoral defeat or that the leader is leading the party in what some MPs think is fundamentally the wrong direction. It is easier when the prime minister leaves office, facing a party that has been defeated at the polls, as with Edward Heath who was successfully challenged in 1975 after losing the elections of 1974. Under current Conservative Party rules, the consent of only 15 per cent of the parliamentary party is required for this to happen. In 2018, this amounted to forty-eight letters that had to be sent to the chair of the 1922 Backbench Committee of Conservative MPs; now it is fifty-five. The Labour Party also needs 20 per cent of its MPs

Photo 2.1 Tony Blair. In 2007, Blair resigned as prime minister and Labour leader, and Gordon Brown was elected unopposed to replace him.

2

to mount a challenge to its leader, which Jeremy Corbyn faced in 2016; but the party has never challenged a sitting prime minister in recent decades. More likely the prime minister will face an internal rival, which Tony Blair (Photo 2.1) did with Gordon Brown, his Chancellor of the Exchequer, who planned to take his place and succeeded in 2007, helped by Blair's increasing unpopularity over his decision to go to war in Iraq in 2003 (Rawnsley 2010).

Even if no election campaign takes place, the effect is the same in that the prime minister holds office but can face a challenger at any time, likely to be a senior party colleague. Taken with the problem that given certain conditions a government can fall if it loses

2

its majority, there is much insecurity in the post, even with a comfortable majority of MPs. If the government cannot get its programme through, then this starts to drain the prime minister's authority. This cannot happen in a different system where the term of office is fixed, such as a US president who has a four-year term and where impeachment proceedings need to be brought to remove a leader from office, and in France, where the president has a five-year term. It is a feature of the British system which needs to be remembered when assessing the role of the prime minister, and how this insecurity might be an explanation for rash decisions and over-defensive behaviour. At any time, the prime minister can fall from office.

2.3.4 The advantages of the office of prime minister

Although being leader of the party has its risks for the prime minister, it also has a lot of advantages because the party leader chairs key internal committees and is responsible for discipline (subject to internal procedures and lawfulness). The prime minister can decide the content of the next manifesto, on which MPs and candidates will need to fight their local campaigns. It is this manifesto that then becomes the programme of the government, which ministers and the party's MPs have to follow in office. This ability to shape the party's agenda can increase over time. A prime minister who enters office mid-term will inherit the manifesto of the previous leader and party; however, over time, once a new mandate has been bestowed by a fresh election, the prime minister as party leader can become more potent. Overall, it is important to judge prime ministers over time: they can start out as appearing to be weak and then end up strong as they gain control over the levers of power; or they start confidently, but then lose control over and confidence of their parties. In fact, it could be said the clock is running on all the leaders as they can only make mistakes and alienate their supporters and voters. Most British prime ministers know that the time will come when they are either pushed out by their colleagues (Edward Heath, Margaret Thatcher, Theresa May), get a drubbing at the polls (James Callaghan, John Major, Gordon Brown), simply feel they do not have the level of support to carry on and resign mid-term (Tony Blair), or make such a mistake that they feel they have to go (David Cameron). Very few go at a time fully of their choosing (the exception is Harold Wilson, but this may have been caused by his impending illness). To help compare and contrast prime ministers, Zoom-In 2.1 is a summary of the occupants since 1970, with some key facts that relate to the extent to which they exercised power during their time in office.

Zoom-In 2.1 List of British prime ministers since 1970 with key facts

Edward Heath, 1970–4: Conservative; secure majority; early activist phase of privatization, reform of structure of government and joining the European Economic Community; famous U-turn in economic policy; then inflation and industrial relations conflict; later period of loss of authority; thought to have poor communication skills within party; used power to call early election in February 1974, but was not successful in renewing mandate.

Harold Wilson, 1974–6: Labour; small majority; long experience from being prime minister 1964–70, but declining energy at this time; reputed as clever at keeping party united in face of radical left, the economic downturn, and splits over Europe; resigned from office of his own choice.

James Callaghan, 1976–9: Labour; took over from Wilson at a time of economic challenge; lost majority; found it hard to control trade unions; in survival mode; made decision to run to end of term of office, but caught out by industrial action of Winter of Discontent, 1978; lost 1979 election.

Margaret Thatcher, 1979–90: Conservative; right-wing reformer; started cautiously in 1979–83

Photo 2.2 Boris Johnson, UK prime minister from 2019 to the present, delivers a speech outside 10 Downing Street.

without many supporters in cabinet; lucky in facing divided opposition, successful Falklands War of 1982, and economic upturn before 1983; increasing radicalism of policies after third election victory in 1987; placed supporters in cabinet and exerted command over the machinery of government; caught out by unpopular tax proposal, the poll tax, and economic downturn; cabinet members told her she had to leave office.

John Major, 1990–7: Conservative; early successes in first Gulf war, EU treaty negotiations, and securing re-election in 1992; loss of reputation for economic competence after Black Wednesday currency devaluation; suffered from divisions of his party over Europe; large loss in 1997 general election, affected by long Conservative incumbency.

Tony Blair, 1997–2007: Labour; large majorities; initially transformative and skilful at repositioning of Labour; over-confidence from 2001; unpopular war over Iraq in 2003 was mainly his decision; rivalry with Gordon Brown as Chancellor limited effectiveness of government; reputation damaged by time of resignation in 2007 in spite of winning three successive elections for his party.

Gordon Brown, 2007–10: Labour; secure majority; dealt with financial crisis and was an effective international leader; appeared to lack the common touch and did not exert clear approach in government; suffered from end of long Labour incumbency.

David Cameron, 2010–16: Conservative; no majority, but coalition with Liberal Democrats that acted like a majority government and a coalition agreement; won a small majority at the 2015 general election; caught up in Conservative controversy over EU membership; rash decisions on referendums; loss of EU referendum prompted resignation.

Theresa May, 2016–19: Conservative; inherited small majority; compromise candidate elected without opposition to deal with Brexit; reputation for toughness behind closed doors; put Brexit supporters into cabinet to create unity; called the 2017 election, then weak with no majority; used power of civil service machine to agree Brexit with EU, but found it impossible to win over enough MPs to support the deal.

Boris Johnson, 2019– (Photo 2.2): Conservative; inherited no overall majority from May and the difficulty of achieving Brexit; reputation as a chancer and humourist; popularity among party members; secured a large majority in 2019; got Brexit deals agreed; early activist phase, then preoccupied by the Covid-19 crisis.

2.3.5 **Executive power away from the UK government**

The prime minister is not the only executive authority in Britain. At the subnational level, there are executive bodies and political leaders. In Scotland, there is the first minister, who is voted into place by the Scottish Parliament, and has similar powers to the UK prime minister in appointment and dismissal. Similarly, the first minister of Wales is nominated by the Senedd Cymru and has executive powers. In Northern Ireland there is a dual leadership structure of the first minister of Northern Ireland and the deputy first minister, who must both be in place, nominated by the different political groups in the assembly. Then there are executive authorities in local government right across Britain, such as executive mayors, or leaders and cabinets. There is more on these arrangements in Chapter 9.

2.4 The powers of the prime minister

2.4.1 Powers and resources

The political realities of being prime minister need to be balanced against the considerable powers and resources of the office, which can be used to control the very party members that can create the problem of insecurity, and also can help keep a government on track with its programme and policies, with MPs following the party line, as led by the prime minister, in Parliament (see Zoom-In 2.2). It is important to be careful about these powers and roles, as many are held by convention, so are not strictly powers of office in the way the president of the United States has powers, for example; but unless convention changes, they are in effect powers that are legal in character or cannot be challenged except by Act of Parliament. Other kinds of resource are not powers in the strict sense of the term, but may be seen as roles, such as chairing the cabinet, which in the end become de facto powers or resources because the prime minister is expected to carry out a function. Exercising such a role in the political system can increase the power of the prime minister because information and reporting need to pass through them or their office and may be used strategically.

2.4.2 Appointment and dismissal

The first of these *powers* is appointment and dismissal. A government is typically composed of about 120 ministerial posts, which range from senior cabinet offices, such as the Chancellor of the Exchequer, the Foreign Secretary, and the Home Secretary, to junior (even unpaid) posts (see Zoom-In 2.3). A key aspect of the power is that it is solely in the prime minister's hands. It is not subject to approval by anyone else, so the leader can use the power strategically, and it is important that the politicians that the prime minister wants to control realize that. It is not just a power to appoint, but to sack as well or to move ministers

Zoom-In 2.2 Powers and roles of the British prime minister

A. **Powers**

1. Appoints and dismisses ministers and other public posts
2. Awards honours and peerages (subject to nomination)
3. Oversees the operation of the civil service and its structure
4. Conducts foreign policy, negotiates treaties, and authorizes military action (subject to parliamentary approval)
5. Calls elections (subject to Fixed-Term Parliaments Act 2011)

B. **Roles**

6. Chairs cabinet
7. Leader of political party
8. Leader of political party in the House of Commons
9. International leader (role on G7, UN, etc.)
10. Head of security services
11. Authorizes official information provision

Zoom-In 2.3 Main ministerial offices and their rank in UK government

Prime Minister—also called the First Lord of the Treasury (has the ancient office of Lord High Treasurer); also Minister for the Civil Service

Chancellor of the Exchequer—chief finance minister

Secretary of State—this is the senior cabinet post with powers to run a department

Minister of State—next rung down from Secretary of State; has a more specialist role in the department

Parliamentary Undersecretary of State—the most junior paid post

Parliamentary Private Secretary (PPS)—unpaid, the most junior post, seen as a stepping stone to higher office or a return to backbenches if performance is not satisfactory

between posts. King and Allen (2010, 251) note that other political systems, such as Italy and the Netherlands, do not have such unfettered power and this is a unique feature of the British system, which should bolster the power of the office-holder. In King's (1991, 43) view, 'the British prime minister is probably able to be more powerful inside his or her own government than any other head of government anywhere else in the democratic world'.

In general, ministerial posts go to MPs, though House of Lords government posts need to be filled as well, so that reduces the number available to about ninety MPs (the House of Commons Disqualification Act 1975 says that no more than ninety-five ministers may sit and vote in the House of Commons at any one time). For a politician, these posts are very important as they form part of a career, perhaps the pinnacle of it, or a step to that pinnacle. They may have been following this career since they decided to go into politics. As a backbench MP for a few years, they may have realized that (until relatively recently) there is not very much to do, unless they want to become a specialist and sit on a select committee, or devote their time as a policy or special interest advocate. A ministerial post is important for a politician and a post they do not want to lose. It also comes with a salary and prestige. In Anthony King's (1991) view, the importance of the power of appointment has become more salient because most MPs are career politicians; that is, their whole working life is spent in politics with no other source of employment, so they value political office above all else. However, there has been little change in the average age of MPs since 1979, suggesting the era of mainly professional politicians is not as immanent as King thought (Lamprinakou et al. 2017, 21).

2.4.3 Is control over appointments such a source of power as is commonly thought?

Does the appointment of MPs as ministers buy loyalty? It is likely that many MPs are to a degree loyal to begin with, as they are elected on a party ticket. As a government member, the MP or Member of the Lords is expected to follow the government line and to defend it. They are part of the state, have the support of the civil service, and are very much part of a government machine with the prime minister at the top who is effectively their boss. The prime minister can fire ministers too, which is always a possibility, or there arises situations where a minister has to resign and then return to the backbenches without access to the power they may have craved their whole career.

But it is not possible to extend the government payroll to the rest of the government party, which will be several hundred MPs, so it is easy to overstate the power of appointment over backbench MPs. It is possible to appeal to a wider group of MPs wanting to be ministers, creating an incentive to behave so they might be appointed; but many MPs may not want such a role, or may have been a minister already and are effectively out of the government or happy to take a role in chairing a select committee—this has become a more important role in recent years as these committees have become more prominent (see section 3.5.3). In any case, MPs since the 1970s have become increasingly disloyal and increasingly likely to vote against the government, as will be discussed in section 3.5.1. Prime ministers who are trying to lead their party in the House of Commons may find it difficult to win votes if they rely on the appointees alone. The realities of parliamentary politics weaken this crucial power of the prime minister, and it is perhaps the case that it is now not as important as Anthony King once thought.

2.4.4 **Appointments and public policy**

The power of appointment is not just important politically; it is important for the direction of policy in government. The prime minister appoints ministers to run departments with the secretary of state as the senior minister having a team below them who are responsible for directing policy, which gives them a degree of autonomy to get things done. The prime minister needs to appoint politicians who get on with the job and solve problems as well as taking forward the party's policy, such as elements of the party manifesto the party was elected on. The prime minister may develop ideas when in office so as to follow a personal agenda, or deal with new problems that may involve working closely with ministers with particular portfolios. The prime minister will need to keep an eye on what ministers are up to in their departments as new issues come up and they get ideas for policies they wish to follow. Being the person who appoints ministers, the prime minister will assume there is a degree of trust from the office-holder and that the likelihood of being fired might be a deterrent for not behaving badly. If things do go wrong, the minister can be fired or put in a situation where they either have to resign or accept being moved to another post with less prestige.

2.4.5 **Firing ministers and resignations**

Overall, the firing of a minister is rare, but resignations of ministers in the expectation that if they do not resign, they will be fired are much more common. The calculation the prime minister needs to make concerns when it makes sense to back the minister concerned, and when to withdraw support. This is not just an issue of managing the government and reducing the conflicts in it, but also sustaining the outward face of the government in the political system and its reputation. Too many losses of ministers may negatively affect a government's image of competence, but keeping on poorly performing ministers too long will also damage the reputation of the government, and make the prime minister look indecisive.

In the end, prime ministers may be tempted to lose ministers over time. This course of action has the advantage of increasing the popularity of the government. Looking at the incidence of resignations, Torun Dewan and Keith Dowding (2005) found that a resignation increased the popularity of the government, giving the prime minister a weapon if the timing is right. The government gets a public opinion boost of 15 per cent resulting from losing an unpopular minister who is causing bad headlines, with the government being able to blame the minister rather than itself. Often resignations are in effect the loss of the prime minister's confidence, so can be seen to be similar to a dismissal where the timing can be calculated. Often it is hard to work out whether the minister resigned out of choice or encouragement. Some resignations are a matter of conscience, such as Jo Johnson, the

Key term 2.2 Reshuffle

A reshuffle occurs when there is a change in the ministerial posts, especially at cabinet level, with some ministers leaving government, others joining, and many moving to posts that others have been vacated from. Can also occur with opposition spokespersons and in devolved cabinets.

brother of the current prime minister, who was Minister of State for Universities, Science, Research and Innovation and resigned on 5 September 2020, stating that he was 'torn between family and national interest'. Amber Rudd MP was Secretary of State for Work and Pensions, but resigned over Boris Johnson's top-down control of the Conservative Party and lack of a deal with the EU. Alun Cairns was Secretary of State for Wales and resigned on 6 November 2019, following claims he had known about his former aide's role in suspending a rape trial.

2.4.6 **Reshuffles**

Appointment is tricky to get right and needs a lot of preparation to ensure it does not backfire and create more problems down the line. The prime minister may be forced to put people in certain positions, which can constrain the choices available in the other positions; or someone might be in a position already and doing a good job so cannot be moved; or another person, less able, has to be kept in government for fear of them returning to the backbenches and causing trouble there. It is important that different wings of the party are represented in ministerial ranks, not just the prime minister's supporters or faction or a particular ideological group, as this would create divisions in the party, and might affect the course and survival of the government more generally. It is important to get a range of gender and ethnic representation in the cabinet because of commitments to diversity and to avoid negative commentary in the media. In the past, the cabinet has had very few women and ethnic minority members; though representation has improved. Figure 2.1 shows there has been a rise in the number of women cabinet members, from one or two up to 1991, increasing to between four and eight, which is still not half the cabinet. Ethnic minority representation has improved from none before 2002 (Paul Boateng was the first as Chief Secretary to the Treasury in 2002) to seven in 2021: Priti Patel as Home Secretary; Alok Sharma as President for COP 26; Rishi Sunak as Chancellor; and Kwasi Kwarteng as Minister for Business, Energy and Industrial Strategy, Sajid Javid as Secretary of State for Health and Social Care, Nadhim Zahawi as Secretary of State for Education, Suella Braverman as Attorney General—23 per cent of the full cabinet compared to 14 per cent in the population. This consideration gives the prime minister opportunities in being able to promote talented women and ethnic minorities, but also makes the whole process of filling ministerial posts very complicated.

The diversity of personnel who need to be in place also makes the business of running the cabinet and getting agreement very hard, as there are many strong personalities and people who want to be independent figures. This is revealed when government is reshuffled (see Key term 2.2), which can be easily botched and reveals how limited the prime minister's choices sometimes actually are. A reshuffle can happen when the prime minister wants to refresh the government, bring on new talent, dispose of unpopular or difficult colleagues, and give a new direction to public policy, which might be helpful mid-term. Others might be caused by resignation and firing and it may not be possible to promote someone directly into the cabinet, so each post moves round. For example, on 13 February 2020, Johnson undertook his first main reshuffle, partly because the Chancellor of the Exchequer, Sajid Javid, resigned his post over a dispute about government advisors (Javid subsequently came back into cabinet, taking the health and social care portfolio when Matt Hancock had to resign over a personal scandal). Then five cabinet ministers were sacked, including the Northern

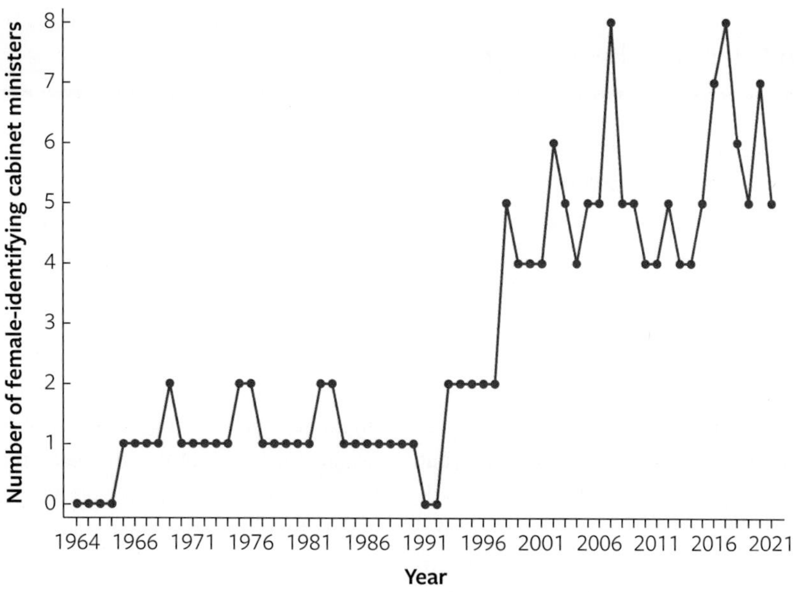

Figure 2.1 Number of female-identifying cabinet ministers by year.
Source: Mortimore and Blick (2018, 101–2); Colebrook and Priddy (2021)
Note: as of 1 January each year

Ireland Secretary Julian Smith. On 15 September 2021, Johnson sacked Gavin Williamson, Robert Buckland, and Robert Jenrick, and moved other cabinet members, to make room for new talent and to focus on delivery of policy.

Reshuffles are a bit like musical chairs and can get very complicated, with civil servants using a large whiteboard to plan the changes. An Institute for Government report found that between 1970 and 2016 there had been eighty-two reshuffles, an average of just under two per year. Most of these were held to accommodate minor changes, usually after resignations. However, nineteen were unforced (that is, not prompted by resignations, sackings, or a general election) (Sasse et al. 2020). Reshuffles can go wrong. Ministers can refuse to be moved, for example Jeremy Hunt in January 2018 as Secretary of State for Health, so Theresa May kept him in post. This means that the prime minister is often constrained in the choices available, yet the need for reshuffles means that ministers have a short tenure in office, which may be one factor behind policy errors in British government as ministers do not get the chance to learn on the job before they have to move on. But tenure is not just a problem for Britain: 'in some countries, including the US and France, the average tenure of a secretary of state (or their equivalent) is even shorter, suggesting this problem is not restricted to the UK. In others, such as Germany, Sweden and Spain, it is considerably longer' (Sasse et al. 2020, 7).

2.4.7 Insights from game theory

It is possible to use what is called game theory to understand the nature of the choices the prime minister faces, as this technique can model one choice as based on the expected actions of others (see Zoom-In 2.4). The prime minister needs to pick a minister from a limited talent pool, but has to balance all other choices and anticipate how other actors are going to react. Such ideas influenced the work of Torun Dewan and David Myatt (2008, 2010), who have examined the choices of the prime minister when appointing ministers from a limited talent pool of politicians. The problem resembles that of a team coach, as the prime minister has to pick the players from a limited pool. So why not pick the

Zoom-In 2.4 Game theory and political science

A rational actor model of human action says that individuals rank options according to the extent they maximize their utility and then choose the best one. As a form of rational choice (see Key term 2.1), game theory sees these choices in interaction with each player by the institutional rules. Second-guessing other choices can lead to suboptimal outcomes for both players, as in the famous prisoner's dilemma where each participant chooses a safe option, fearing freeriding by the other, but they are both worse off than had they cooperated.

The prisoner dilemma example is derived from a hypothetical situation where two prisoners are accused of the same crime. They are arrested, put into separate cells, and interrogated. The police and criminal prosecution service present the prisoners with the following options: if both stay silent, they each receive a mild punishment; if one confesses and the other does not, the former gets off and the latter receives a severe punishment; and if they both confess, they receive a heavy punishment. The game predicts they both confess because they fear that the other one will admit the crime first and will receive a worse punishment as a result. They are not capable of choosing the outcome that benefits them both because they do not trust each other. The game produces the powerful insight that people do not cooperate to pursue their best interests because they fear others will freeride on their gullibility. There is a wide application across political science to all forms of collective action.

For an introduction, see Hargreaves-Heap et al., *The Theory of Choice: A Critical Guide* (1992).

best players? The problem in politics is that ministers need to do other things, such as be loyal to the prime minister. The number of talented politicians is also limited, so the talent of the cabinet goes down over time, which might explain why governments often start off so well but then get mired in problems as the years pass—another reason for policy fiascos or disasters.

2.4.8 Other appointments

It is also important that the prime minister appoints many other public posts, or at least is the person who signs off on these appointments. These powers formally come from the Crown, such as the power to appoint the head of the established church, the Church of England, given that the monarch is the 'supreme governor'. In the past, the prime minister exercised this power by giving advice to the monarch; now the Crown Nominations Commission draws up a list of candidates and the prime minister picks one from two, so as to advise the monarch. Many such appointments are now made in this way, with another body drawing up a list or coming up with a nomination and the prime minister acceding. But it is still a non-trivial power to have people in place who correspond with the prime minister's preferences, which might increase the ability for the prime minister to shape policy, particularly if the prime minister is in office for several terms, as Thatcher and Blair were.

2.4.9 Honours and privileges

The second power is to award honours and grant peerages. Principal among these are appointments to the House of Lords, which can be a way of rewarding party followers and of seeking to influence the agenda of the second chamber. But this power is double-edged because appointees may become more independent once they are settled into the Lords (see section 3.5.5). As a result, this form of appointment cannot stem the tendency for the Lords to act independently from government (see section 3.5.5). Lords appointments are circumscribed by the House of Lords Appointments Commission, which is another way in which the prime minister and their party's powers have been constrained, delegated by the prime minister to another body in 2000. The Commission makes the recommendations, which the prime minister approves. Party nominations seek to achieve political balance, reflecting the composition of the House of Commons; but it can take many years to achieve given the limited number of Lords that can be appointed each year. Constitutionally, the prime minister can accept these recommendations. In fact, the prime minister could ask the monarch to appoint anyone, such as many hundreds of peers, who could be put in place to get government business through the second chamber. But in practice it is hard to imagine how a prime minister could overturn the Commission except in unusual circumstances.

This has important implications for the balance between the executive and legislature, which again constrains prime ministerial power (see section 3.2.4). The prime minister is limited in using other honours, such as knighthoods. It may be possible for the prime minister to reward supporters after their service (which can be done by a departing prime minister via the convention of resignation honours). For example, John Redwood, a Conservative Brexiteer, was given a knighthood in 2019, which was part of a wave of honours given to rebels to try to get a Brexit deal through. But, as this example shows, this does not buy loyalty, as politicians can take the honour but carry on regardless with their rebellious behaviour. Even though honours are mainly decided by the Honours Committee at the Cabinet Office, with the prime minister not having a role in many cases, it is often perceived that rewards are for doing favours such as raising money for the government party. The resulting scandals, such as 'Cash for Peerages' in 2006, show this power of the prime minister can come with a cost if not handled correctly.

2.4.10 **Head of the civil service**

The third power of the prime minister comes as head of the civil service: Minister for the Civil Service, which is a separate ministerial role held at the same time (see Zoom-In 2.2). Because of this, the prime minister is effectively in charge of the operation of government. The senior civil servant, the cabinet secretary, reports to the prime minister. Holding the sovereign's power (codified in the Ministers of the Crown Act 1975), the prime minister can reorganize the structure of government departments, which can then be tasked to reflect policy preferences. For example, in July 2016 Theresa May, when she started as prime minister, created a new Department of Exiting the European Union, which was thought to be needed to deal with Brexit. Another example is in 2020, with the folding of the Department for International Development (DFID) into the Foreign and Commonwealth Office (FCO). The role of the prime minister over the civil service also means that civil servants have a higher duty than to their ministers as they serve the government of the day with the prime minister at its head. This has the effect of officials looking to the cabinet secretary, and by implication the prime minister, for leadership. It creates a network of civil servants who report upwards to the centre. This consequently increases the reputation of the prime minister and makes it hard to oppose what they do within government. It helps power over, but is also about capacity—the power to do things as a government. It is limited by the independence of the civil servants in that the prime minister cannot directly appoint civil servants, which is done by the Civil Service Commission, an independent body. Even though there are ways in which the prime minister can influence the appointments to the civil service (see section 8.4.9), this is a subtle process and the takeaway is that the prime minister has the power of authority and direction, subject to the rule of law, legislation, and the civil service code that limits that power. This is quite different to other political systems like the United States where the president appoints top-level officials, who may be party politicians. The comparison to the US in the UK is the special advisors who serve as short-term appointees in government, working alongside civil servants and also appointed by the prime minister (see section 8.4.2). In France, there are ministerial cabinets to advise the minister, which are composed of politicians and civil servants without a clear dividing line between the two.

2.4.11 Prerogative powers

The fourth power comes from the prerogative powers discussed in Chapter 1 (Zoom-In 1.2). These are principally in the field of foreign policy: to have relations with foreign states, to engage in treaties and military action and in general direct the armed forces. These powers have been constrained, for example by treaties which need parliamentary approval, so power has shifted more to Parliament, which then depends more on the prime minister as a party politician to command a majority. With war, the situation is more ambiguous and the prime minister can authorize military action without needing approval. However, it might depend on the scale of the action and a calculation of practical politics. For example, David Cameron put the intervention in Syria to the vote on 29 August 2013, which he lost; but Theresa May (Photo 2.3) did not ask approval for the bombing of Syria in April 2018. Much negotiation with the EU happened through powers delegated to ministers, even though Parliament then had to approve the legislation after the main decisions

Photo 2.3 Theresa May. In 2018 Prime Minister May refused to grant a parliamentary vote to launch air strikes against the Syrian government.

had been taken, as it did in December 2020 after the UK and EU agreed the EU-UK Trade and Cooperation Agreement.

2.4.12 Call elections (before and after 2011)

The fifth power before 2011 was to call elections. Here there was an unlimited prerogative power up to the five-year term (see Zoom-In 1.2), which is now limited by legislation. Since the Fixed-Term Parliaments Act 2011, it is not so easy for the prime minister to call an election as it has to be done through Parliament (see section 1.3.8); but it is possible, as the act allows the vote of two-thirds of MPs to approve. The assumption is that MPs of the government party would support this motion from a sitting leader and the opposition needs to always be ready to go to the polls, which is what happened for Theresa May's 2017 election and for the December 2019 election (see section 1.3.8). The Conservative government elected in 2019 is committed to the repeal of this Act.

There is an argument for claiming that the power to call elections might increase the power overall of the prime minister, because it might be a way to keep the government on its toes and keep the opposition guessing, and if successful can lead to election victories which can increase the prime minister's power. An example was Margaret Thatcher in the 1980s. She called elections early, at about four years into her term, rather than the statutory five-year maximum. The government was able to stoke up the economy before the 1983 and 1987 elections by its control of interest rates, which it lowered, boosting its popularity from the resulting economic booms (Sanders 1991).

2.4.13 The impact of election timing

It is hard to produce evidence of different election timing choices, or to know whether the government would have done better at calling them at other points in time. For example, Edward Heath called an early election for February 1974 to test out his power in relation to the trade unions, but the Conservative Party lost seats and Labour formed the minority government instead even though Edward Heath had a year left in office. But would it have been even more risky in 1975? In contrast, Labour arguably hung on too long until 1979, when it could have called an election in 1978 while industrial unrest had eased. Then there was Theresa May's election in 2017, which hamstrung her in the Brexit negotiations and weakened her power and authority considerably, which shows the limits to this power. These examples demonstrate how this is a double-edged power at best.

A technical account of election timing is set out by Alistair Smith (2004), who examined whether these choices helped prime ministers to win elections. Smith argues that the power is useful because prime ministers might have access to information about external conditions, such as the economy, that voters do not have access to, so this should be a significant power. The data show that elections that were called early led to worse conditions than comparable elections that run to term, suggesting the prime ministers know something the voters do not, and they need to run early. When conditions are fair, they run to term as, other things being equal, they prefer to stay in office. As Smith (2003, 418) writes, 'The more confident leaders are of their ability to perform in the future, the weaker their incentive to announce early elections.' As with other powers, it is possible to overstate the power of the prime minister to call elections on government survival, even before the recent change in the law; but the power may have other consequences, which is keeping the party on their toes as no government MP wants the challenge of a surprise election, and opposition parties can be caught on the hop too.

2.5 The roles of the prime minister

2.5.1 **The difference between powers and roles**

The next set of factors are the roles and positions of the prime minister, which are naturally assumed once the person enters office. They resemble powers, but are more informally based. They occur because the prime minister is in a role through which decisions or information flow to whom others defer. This gives the prime minister what can be called a network form of power in that information flows through the office, and the ability to structure the information, which is a tool of government, called 'nodality' in Christopher Hood's (1983) typology (see Key term 2.3). In addition, by being in a prominent position prime ministers are able to structure their reputation for being powerful and influential, partly by being successful in the first place which then continues over time, and from their visibility in the role. This reputational effect can work in the opposite direction: the very visibility of the prime minister may make other actors more aware of their failings and ability to lose battles, so as to encourage challenges. As ever, power is double-edged.

Key term 2.3 Tools of government and nodality

Tools of government are resources, such as laws and finance that get the job of government done. Hood (1983) devised the NATO scheme of **N**odality, **A**uthority (laws), **T**reasure (finance), and **O**rganization (bureaucracy). Nodality is the power to coordinate a network of actors from being in a central position.

2.5.2 **Chair of the cabinet**

The first of the prime minister's *roles* is as chair of the cabinet (Photo 2.4). The prime minister chairs the meetings and decides the agenda. Officials who support the cabinet are responsible to the prime minister for its organization and they take minutes of these meetings, which are government decisions. The key business of government passes through the cabinet and is approved by it. The prime minister calls the cabinet meetings when needed and is in a position to ask it to approve all government papers.

2.5.3 **Cabinet committees**

The other important feature of the chair of the cabinet is that the prime minister controls the structure and membership of its committees, which is where the business of cabinet is done (see Zoom-In 2.5). Some of these committees are permanent features of government, such as the Parliamentary Business and Legislation Committee, which oversees the legislation presented to Parliament; others may reflect more temporary concerns. It is up to the prime minister to organize remit, number, and membership of these committees, according to the policies they wish to pursue, reflecting their style as a premier, and this can be used tactically to isolate factions in the cabinet and to manage the business of government. The prime minister can ensure that the membership of committees produces preferred outcomes, which are then presented to cabinet.

The distribution of ministers across these committees affects their power as it gives them a voice in decision-making. Dunleavy (1995a) proposed using weights reflecting the status of the committees to create a power index for each member of cabinet (see Zoom-In 2.6). The prime minister can determine

Photo 2.4 The Cabinet Office, Whitehall, Westminster, London. This is the UK government department responsible for supporting the prime minister and senior ministers.

the relative power of each minister by shuffling them around. There are some weaknesses with these power indices, which have to do with the arbitrary way in which committee reputation is allocated, and there may be differences between these committees not picked up by this measure. But it is useful for measuring change over time if the same measure is used and shows how prime ministers strategize.

Allen and Siklodi (2020) compared prime ministers' scores using the Dunleavy index and revealed how prime ministers differ (see Table 2.1). Theresa May increased her control by chairing a small number of large subcommittees, with smaller subcommittees underneath; David Cameron, who was more relaxed in power and faced a less fractious and divided cabinet, stood back. These indices reveal the powerplay at work, in particular the extent to which the prime minister needs to exercise direct or indirect control over the proceedings.

2.5.4 Collective responsibility

The final aspect of being chair of the cabinet is the use of the convention of collective responsibility, which means that a minister must hold to the line that has been agreed and defend it (Zoom-In 1.3). This means that once the agenda has been set, it is hard for a minister to go against the prime minister, which ensures the decision-making process moves on, and an opposing minister has to campaign against a policy in secret. The erosion of the convention probably started in the 1960s (Brady 1999), but emerged more strongly in John Major's period of office when he was faced with rebellions in the party that spilled over into the cabinet. The prime minister thus can find it hard to assert power based on the secrecy of government. Sometimes collective responsibility is suspended and ministers can speak freely, such as for the European referendums of 1975 and 2016. More often it reflects the breakdown

Zoom-In 2.5 List of cabinet committees and subcommittees in 2020

National Security Council

National Security Council Sub-Committee: Nuclear Deterrence and Security

Covid-19 Strategy

EU Exit Strategy

Domestic and Economic Strategy

Climate Action Strategy

Crime and Justice Task Force

Covid-19 Operations

EU Exit Operations

Economic Operations Committee

Domestic and Economy Implementation

Union Policy Implementation

Parliamentary Business and Legislation

National Space Council

Climate Action Implementation Committee

Source: gov.uk list of cabinet committees: www.gov.uk/government/publications/the-cabinet-committees-system-and-list-of-cabinet-committees

Zoom-In 2.6 Power index of ministers in cabinet

An index based on the number of positions ministers have on subcommittees weighted by the reputation of the committee (Dunleavy 1995a, 306–7).

Step 1: calculate the committee weighting

$$\text{Committee weighting} = 100 * S * (C/N)$$

S = the status of the committee: full ministerial committee = 1, subcommittee = .5

C = number of cabinet members who sit on the committee

N = total number of ministers who are members

Step 2: calculate the total score for each committee

$$(100 * S * (C/N))/(N+1)$$

A double share is assigned to the chair (one for membership and one for chairing).

Then the scores are assigned to each member, then summed for each role they have to reveal the score per member (or percentage of total power). For example, in Table 2.1 the figure for the Chancellor in Boris Johnson's cabinet comes to 218.83 out of a total of 1271.39 for all cabinet members, which makes for 17.2 per cent power and first ranking.

of prime ministerial authority, such as during Theresa May's second period in office after the 2017 election when secret meetings, such as those at the prime minister's residence at Chequers, were reported in the newspapers with accounts of who said what, even with photographs. With Johnson in power, the convention has resumed once again, as the prime minister is more secure in office with a comfortable majority and a cabinet of his own choosing. As Theresa May found, these things can change rapidly (see Case Study 2.1). In 2021 Boris Johnson has faced his own leaks, such as regarding decisions over Covid-19 lockdowns.

Table 2.1 Key ministers' share of positional power, 2005–20

Source: Allen and Siklodi (2016); 2020 calculations from gov.uk list of cabinet committees: www.gov.uk/government/publications/the-cabinet-committees-system-and-list-of-cabinet-committees

Government	Prime minister (ranking)	Chancellor (ranking)	Chief secretary (ranking)	Cabinet Office minister (ranking)
Tony Blair	8.5%	5.7%	4.5%	4.9%
September 2005	(1st)	(3rd)	(7th)	(4th)
Gordon Brown	5.3	8.1	5.2%	6.8%
July 2007	(4th)	(1st)	(5th)	(2nd)
David Cameron	4.7	10.4%	9.3%	3.9%
September 2010	(8th)	(1st)	(2nd)	(9th)
Theresa May	10.6%	7.1%	2.8%	3.0%
October 2016	(1st)	(3rd)	(18th)	(13th)
Boris Johnson	15.0%	17.2%	1.3%	14.8%
December 2020	(2nd)	(1st)	(17th)	(3rd)

2.5.5 Leader of the party

The seventh resource or role is as leader of their party, which is usually the case for the prime minister. Although the party is not a branch of government, parties are involved with government to help make policy and get re-elected. The leadership comes with powers over the party as provided by its internal governance, so the Labour Party leader chairs the main decision-making body of the party, the National Executive Committee (NEC), which makes the basic rules. The leader cannot impose their views, but as chair of the NEC and with key allies on the committee, they can get their way. When in government the prime minister is more distant from the party, but still has access to these resources, which can help command loyalty, such as of MPs as party members. Party loyalists serve as whips. When a MP rebels, they act against their party and leader of the party—not that this always stops them, but it is a big step especially as MPs need to report back to their constituency parties. MPs can 'lose the whip' if they rebel too often, which means they would not be selected as an official parliamentary candidate in the subsequent election. Boris Johnson withdrew the whip from twenty-one Conservative MPs in November 2019. Ten got it back, but the others did not and they had to stand down from politics or run as independents in the 2019 general election. They lost their seats.

Party leadership does not bestow massive power, but it is symbolically important. And it can be very important, as Johnson's actions show. But strong exercises of party leadership can also backfire as leaders can become unpopular in their parties. They need to manage the factions, who can limit the power of the prime minister. Their representatives often need to be placed into the cabinet, so limiting the room for manoeuvre of the prime minister; but when out of the cabinet they can coordinate backbench rebellions and put in place a plan to challenge the leadership.

2.5.6 Leader of the party in Parliament

The eighth factor is the position of the leader of the party in Parliament, taking a prominent position in the House of Commons, leading key debates, and answering the weekly Prime Minister's Questions. Here the leader is responsible for mobilizing their party's MPs, helping party unity, and wielding symbolic power in relation to the opposition. The prime minister exercises power in the House of Commons, as the government is usually in control of the business and timetable of the House (though the Leader of the House of Commons has this formal role: see Key term 2.4). Overall, this is an important role and leaders can use their skills as public speakers to mobilize their parties and try to embarrass the opposition.

2.5.7 Head of the security services

The ninth role is as head of the security services in Britain, such as MI5, which is part of the central state and where the prime minister chairs the cabinet committee. There is a national security service which is set up as a network of committees around the prime minister, where ministers play a role. It is hard to see how this power helps the prime minister in normal times when the country is not at war, but it adds a further positional resource and could make the prime minister very powerful in a national emergency.

Key term 2.4 Leader of the House of Commons

The Leader of the House of Commons is a ministerial role in cabinet, where the MP is responsible for the business of the House of Commons in terms of introducing government bills. The different post of Speaker of the Commons is an elected position from MPs who is responsible for chairing the proceedings and for ruling on procedure.

2.5.8 International role

The tenth role as international leader sees the prime minister take centre-stage in international forums such as the United Nations and the G7, taking part in these decisions which in the end have consequences for domestic politics and policies, and where these agreements can bolster or undermine the power of the prime minister (see section 10.3.2). Again, it is double-edged as it can preoccupy the prime minister and therefore reduce their capacity to do other things closer to home. For example, when Margaret Thatcher was challenged as leader in December 1990 she had to attend an international meeting in Paris, using valuable time she could have spent lobbying her fellow MPs to vote for her in the contest (even though she had a campaign group to do this). Tony Blair became preoccupied with his international role in seeking to build a strong alliance with the US, possibly alienating his own party and supporters. Boris Johnson has sought to increase his stature as an international politician and environmental champion as chair of the G7 at the COP26 summit in November 2021.

2.5.9 Control of official information

The final position is control of the provision of official information, which means the prime minister can influence the coverage of the government in the media. This involves preventing leaks to the media and helps keep control over their colleagues in cabinet. With extensive leaking now common practice, this role is more limited, but the prime minister still has at their command a large information-producing machine, such as the prime minister's press secretary and official spokesperson. During the Covid-19 crisis in the first half of 2020, daily press briefings were broadcast from the No. 10 press room, with Johnson taking centre-stage, flanked by scientific advisors. It is not a direct power, but can bestow status and authority upon the prime minister.

2.6 Prime ministerial power assessed

2.6.1 Summarizing the limits to prime ministerial power

So, how powerful is the British prime minister? One way of answering this question is to list the powers and roles of the prime minister (see sections 2.4 and 2.5) and to assess these resources in an even-handed fashion. The powers look very extensive and decisive in many senses, and greater than equivalent positions in other countries (section 2.4.2). But it is possible to see limitations and downsides to these powers, which can backfire if not used correctly, as for example with appointments, and where there are practical constraints on the use of the power. Then there are limits to these powers, often self-imposed, to give Parliament a say, often needed for legitimacy and party management, which can constrain the prime minister's freedom to manoeuvre. There is also the way in which visibility and reputation have double edges, so the positional power of the prime minister increases when things are going well, but then can undermine power when errors happen and where the prime minister loses autonomy and reputation. Then there are limits to the office, which is not set up as a chief executive or president. It has weak capacity, which derives from its origins as a delegate of the monarch, its role in Parliament, and the small size of the central staff (see section 2.6.1). Much power is held by convention rather than having a formal and legally sanctioned ability to command. There are no lines of control throughout Whitehall as departments are empires in their own right and pursue policies over a long time period, whereas prime ministerial interest may wax and wane. Recall in section 1.4.5 the setting out of the basic tenets of the principal–agent model, where the asymmetry of information is the cause of the lack of the ability of the principal to realize their interests. This insight applies to the relationship between the prime minister and the rest of the policy-making system, where information and expertise are in the departments, whereas the centre lacks personnel and time to monitor them effectively.

2.6.2 The role of Chancellor of the Exchequer

The relationship between the prime minister and the chief finance minister, the Chancellor of the Exchequer (Photo 2.5), who has extensive power across Whitehall, is important for understanding the power of the prime minister. If the two offices are working in harmony, the prime minister has extensive power as the Chancellor is their appointee so should do their bidding. Budget approvals have to be run past the prime minister. The prime minister is First Lord of the Treasury so has a direct role in financial and tax policy, at least in theory, with the Chancellor of the Exchequer being the Second Lord. But the two office-holders sometimes fall out. For political reasons the prime minister sometimes cannot fire the Chancellor of the Exchequer if the person is too powerful to place on the backbenches. Gordon Brown was Chancellor

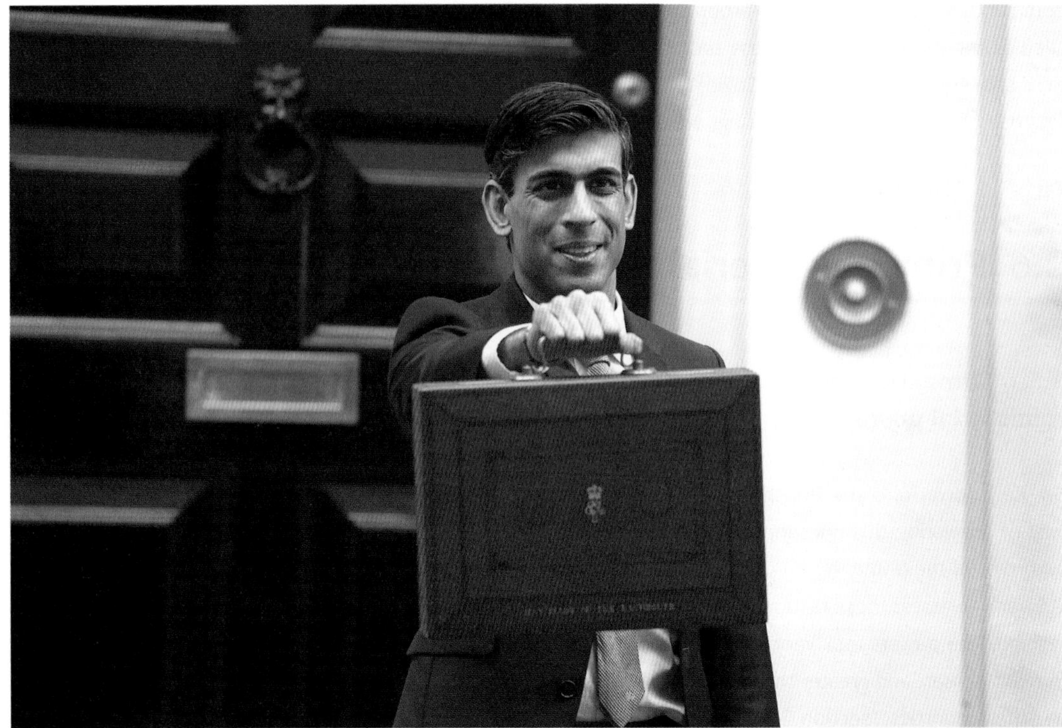

Photo 2.5 Rishi Sunak, Chancellor of the Exchequer from February 2020 to the present, leaves No. 11 Downing Street to present his budget at the House of Commons.

from 1997 to 2007, but he was a rival to Tony Blair (Rawnsley 2001). Blair never sacked Brown or even got close to doing so, which shows the limits to the power of appointment, or it might show, as Seldon (2008) argues, that Blair was able to dominate the domestic policy process even with a powerful rival in the cabinet. The continued rivalry limited Tony Blair's power as prime minister in the latter part of his premiership and contributed to his decision to resign from office in 2007.

2.6.3 **Cabinet government**

The other factor that limits the power of the prime minister is the cabinet itself, whose members need to agree government policies, and where the prime minister chairs but does not direct. Here it is important to introduce some more constitutional theory. The cabinet is supposed to be the centre of power where debate about the course of government policy should take place. This is the forum of collective decision-making, which was thought to be a central part of the British approach to government. It is not government by the prime minister, but rather by a committee with the prime minister as chair, with the implication that important decisions are preceded by cabinet debate in its weekly or special meetings. In Bagehot's famous account of the British constitution, it was not the prime minister who is the 'join' between the executive and legislature, but the cabinet, what he also called the 'buckle' (Bagehot 1873). This was Bagehot's 'efficient secret' at the heart of the British political system which really made it work amid the pomp of the monarchy and Parliament, achieving 'the near complete

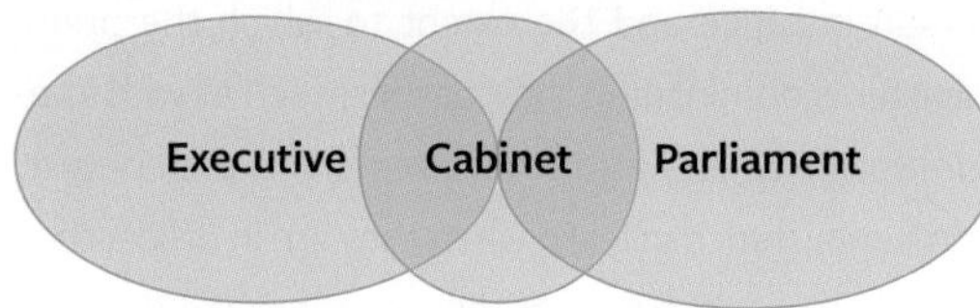

Figure 2.2 The cabinet as the 'buckle' or 'join' between the executive and legislature. *Note: inspired by Bagehot (1873, 12)*

fusion of executive and legislative powers' (1873, 12). This hinge or buckle idea is represented in Figure 2.2: the executive is separated from Parliament, but members of the cabinet (and the rest of the government) are part of the legislature and answerable to it.

If the cabinet is the key constitutional unit of analysis, it implies a degree of collective decision-making at the heart of the system. This is the idea that policy could be tempered and fashioned through debate within the cabinet, perhaps moderating and improving policies, creating more pluralism (Key term 2.5) at the top of government than there otherwise would be with just one person in charge, and allowing different forms of representation to become part of argument and debate. The prime minister then is what is called *primus inter pares* (first among equals), which denotes a collective form of governance at the top of the British state. But how powerful the prime minister is in this system became subject to extensive debate.

The origins of this academic debate go back to the 1960s in the thesis of Richard Crossman, a former senior Labour politician and cabinet minister. In his introduction to a new edition of *The English Constitution* (Bagehot and Crossman 1963), he argued that the power of the office had increased from internationalization, the centralization of the party machine, and the growth in the size of the state and its centralized bureaucracy, making cabinet government less important. This debate continued, partly stimulated by the increasing leaks from the centre of government, not least Crossman's own diaries as a cabinet minister (Crossman 1979), with the complaint that the decisions were being made by a 'kitchen cabinet' of a small group of advisors and trusted ministers. Margaret Thatcher was thought to decide controversial policies away from cabinet in subcommittees and other working groups, like the poll tax, even though cabinet and its committees approved the measure (Butler, Adonis, and Travers 1994). Tony Blair was believed to be keen on 'sofa government', taking decisions in small informal groups away from cabinet. He was perceived to have kept the cabinet not fully informed of the decision to go to war in Iraq in 2003, though formal processes, including decisions by cabinet and its committees, were followed very carefully (Chilcot 2016).

Michael Foley (2001) talked of the arrival of the 'British presidency' summing up this prominent international role and more assertive control over policy-making. The prime minister appeared to have acquired a slicker media machine and loyal cadre of staff members to back them up, much like a directly elected president. Yet, as many academics, such as Dowding (2013b), point out, the use of the term 'presidency' does not make sense in the British context where there is no separation of powers and the constitution does not give powers to the prime minister, which are exercised on behalf of the monarch. Reality then is somewhere in between the stylized ideal of cabinet government, which cannot sustain a 'first among equals' when that first person appoints the other

Key term 2.5 Pluralism

The claim that power and authority are dispersed, with no one key actor dominant, where policy emerges from negotiation and the balance of interests. More generally, it refers to a type of political system, a polyarchy, in which all groups and ideas can access the decision-making process, with many entry points, producing policies that are responsive to public opinion.

ministers, and a more dictatorial account of the role. Just because the prime minister meets small groups of other politicians to talk about policy does not necessarily undermine cabinet government, which is there to discuss and approve decisions that emerge from within government, wherever they come from. The prime minister is limited by a variety of practical and political constraints that reduce direct control over the administrative machine and ensure dependence on senior colleagues in cabinet (Jones 1964).

2.6.4 **Variation over time**

Many commentators argue that prime ministerial power is itself variable (Heffernan 2005). As Jones (1990, 2) writes, 'as a convention the office is like an elastic band. It can be stretched to accommodate an assertive prime minister and contracted for a prime minister with a more relaxed style'. It tends to vary over time, partly because of the personality of the person in office and the extent to which the prime minister is dominant in their parties, such as with a secure majority, and also from events and the context. Prime ministers can learn when they are in office; they are able to get the people they want around the cabinet table; they can also lose a sense of direction and sound judgment.

2.6.5 **Pluralism?**

Many argue that cabinet government is not dead. G. W. Jones was prominent in advocating this position in a series of articles (Jones 1964, 1990). Jones pointed to evidence that decisions are made in cabinet where different points of view are articulated. Jones focuses on the importance of intra-party politics in limiting prime ministerial power with the famous quote, 'a prime minister who can carry his colleagues with him can be in a very powerful position, but he is only as strong as they let him be' (Jones 1964, 185).

Case Study 2.1 Comparing Theresa May and Boris Johnson

Theresa May became prime minister in July 2016 after the Brexit referendum, facing a divided party. Showing the importance of the cabinet, she placed key Brexit supporters in the key roles of Foreign Secretary (Boris Johnson), Brexit Secretary (David Davis), and International Trade Secretary (Liam Fox). The government was divided but still functioned and she was able to use her control of the agenda in cabinet and the civil service to fashion policies, such as a negotiating position on Brexit. She used her two advisors, Fiona Hill and Nick Timothy, to great effect in dominating government business and managing the cabinet. Once Theresa May lost her majority in 2017, this balance and equilibrium fell apart with open divisions in cabinet. The party split on the Brexit deal, and then cabinet resignations followed. The episode shows the crucial role of the unity of the party in government to ensure both prime minister and cabinet function effectively. It is possible to contrast this with the Johnson government from 2019, which has a Commons majority and cabinet unity. The Covid-19 crisis shows both the importance of cabinet and the prime minister. The prime minister is crucial in authorizing government policies. But when Johnson was in hospital with Covid-19 in April 2020, the government still functioned with cabinet minister, Dominic Raab, Foreign Secretary, acting as deputy. But in practice, the machine needed the prime minister to direct it, so no major decisions were made during his absence.

During Theresa May's incumbency, debates about key issues such as Brexit took place within cabinet, even with the prime minister, backed up by civil servants and other loyal ministers, as the agenda setter, such as for the Chequers meeting of July 2018, when a new model of cooperation with the EU was pushed through (see Case Study 2.1). Cabinet government is a process: it ensures that key actors are an important part of the government machine and are needed to sign off policies. Cabinet can occasionally assert its power, as shown by the fall of Margaret Thatcher, as she could not proceed with a leadership re-election without their support. The cabinet becomes more powerful when the Commons majority is slim, as in John Major and Theresa May's periods in office.

2.6.6 The concept of power

Part of the problem surrounding the debate about the prime minister and cabinet is that power is a hard concept to understand and to measure. It is composed of power *over* when the power-holder wants to win against opponents, but more commonly it is blended into power *to*, which involves shaping the agenda and gradually crafting a response for collective benefit as well as the power-holder's reputation (see Key term 2.6). Power *to* involves creating capacity, where the sum of human actions generates more than their parts because everyone is working together (Dowding 2013a). Just winning might be a poor measure of the prime minister's performance, and they get a reputation just as a fixer (like Harold Wilson allegedly was) or someone just hanging on for survival (like Theresa May). Getting things done collectively is much harder. Moreover, it is hard to draw conclusions from what is happening in cabinet: just because there is conflict does not prove there is pluralism, as the prime minister still sets the agenda and authorizes the minutes and decisions. The constant leaks from within government to the media give an impression of chaos, but once the public records are available (there is a thirty-year rule on their access), the extent of control over the process can be more evident. It is a complex set of relationships where the term 'power' of the prime minister and cabinet may not always make much sense, particularly because the two elements of prime minister and cabinet are so bound up with each other in a mutually dependent relationship. Nor does the cabinet being involved guarantee a diversity of views around the table, leading to better or more informed decision-making. If the government feels under threat, it may push cabinet members closer together, creating blind-spots that some people call 'groupthink' (Janis 1972), which has been applied to foreign policy decisions (Allison 1971), mainly in the US but also UK foreign policy (for example, Walker and Watson 1989) (see Key term 2.7). Just because the cabinet is in play does not guarantee pluralism exists. Both prime minister and cabinet are often locked into a common project.

2.6.7 The core executive

Many academics became frustrated with the prime ministerial power debate (e.g. Judge 2005, 145), seeking to replace it with a more sophisticated understanding of the power balance across the executive. A key idea of critics of the prime ministerial power debate or prime minister and cabinet debate is that a broader unit of core executive politics needs to be considered (Dunleavy and Rhodes 1995; Burch 1996;

Key term 2.6 Power *to* and power *over*

Power *over* occurs when someone forces an opponent to act against their interest.

Power *to* is about generating collective capacity; getting things done for the benefit of all.

Key term 2.7 Groupthink

The idea that small groups of decision-makers tend to develop a common approach, helped by close relationships and the desire for harmony in the group, which can be enhanced in a crisis with a sense of us and them, and when facing criticism in the media. It encourages conformation bias whereby facts are interpreted as in support of an initial hypothesis when that need not be the only interpretation. It becomes hard for alternative points of view to emerge.

Smith 1999). This captures the larger unit of the executive beyond the prime minister, which goes to the departments of states and the policy networks within which many decisions are taken. The message is of complexity and complex relationships of power beyond the cabinet and prime minister but highly connected into it. It is important to include the Treasury, the role of cabinet committees, and the top level in government departments, which are formed into a close web of relationships (see Figure 2.3).

The concept is useful in explaining how decisions are made, for example in Burch and Holliday's (1995) account of cabinet government and its complex structures, uncovered by a painstaking mapping of the structures and decision-making within British government. It links to the idea that many decisions are delegated to communities of decision-makers, either territorially, functionally, or in complicated networks rather than within the Westminster system of government (Jordan and Cairney 2013). An understanding of executive power needs to incorporate this underlying complexity to decision-making. While offering additional understanding of a complex system, the core executive model is not a theory and does not on its own say how and when power is exercised.

2.6.8 The prime minister as agenda setter

Another way of examining power is to take more of an agenda-setting approach to prime ministerial

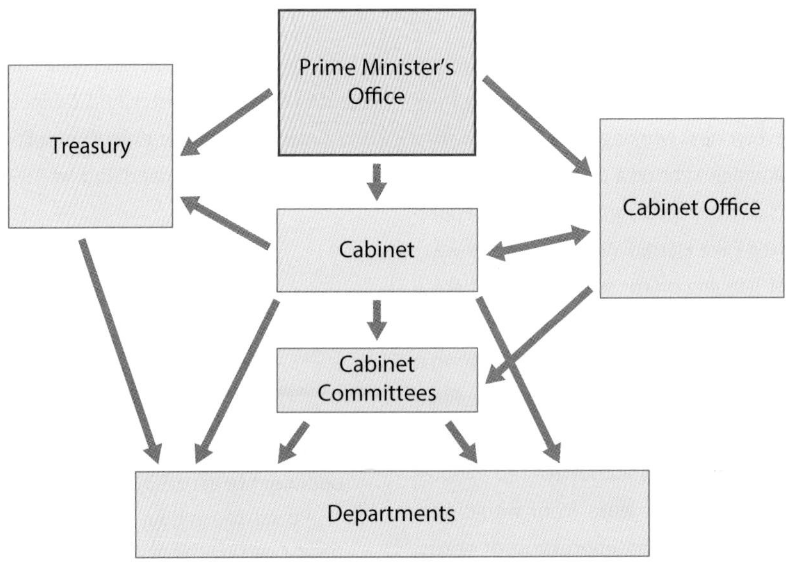

Figure 2.3 The core executive. *Source*: Adapted from Smith (1999)

Key term 2.8 Core executive

A term to describe the institutions and power relationships at the heart of government, extending beyond the prime minister and cabinet to include personnel in key institutions proximate to the prime minister/cabinet. Decision-making is characterized by complex interdependence, rather than a battle between prime minister and cabinet.

decision-making (see section 6.2 for a definition), which acknowledges the limits to prime ministerial power and the considerable delegation that goes on, but recognizes the prime minister's need to control the agenda and use resources to shape it, which include allowing a lot of debate and discussion to get there. Cabinet discussion is important as the prime minister needs to manage the cabinet like any politician would any committee or decision point, where interests need to be accommodated and a winning strategy embarked on or retreats made gracefully. The British system does give a lot of direct power to the prime minister, but this is not likely to be unconditional. The power is highly contingent on the general political context, such as the security of the government. Detailed case studies are required to understand it (Dowding 2013b). The issue of cabinet versus prime ministerial government is just not resolvable. A lot depends on the cunning and instincts of the person in high office in structuring the agenda.

2.6.9 **The prime minister as strategist and heresthetician**

When reviewing decision-making, there are a lot of opportunities for the prime minister to shape the agenda of politics and decision-making, which may be seized by prime ministers who vary in their capacity to think strategically. Iain McLean (2001) applies rational choice theory (see Key term 2.1) to British prime ministers, taking a historical perspective. The key idea comes from heresthetics (see Key term 2.9), which is the study of how actors can manipulate the structure of decision-making so as to be more likely to win. The theory is drawn from the work of political scientist, William Riker (1986). It requires cleverness, which allows a person to calculate each actor's moves quite a way ahead so as to anticipate reactions, lay traps, and take opportunities. Central to this concept is that there are issue dimensions in politics that people vote and act on, and that these might not be stable, so giving the leader an opportunity to manipulate the choices of other actors. It is more than rhetoric; it is persuading everybody that the world is the way you say it is. In McLean's view, Thatcher was good at this: 'the best rhetorician of our period is neither Peel nor Gladstone nor Disraeli nor Lloyd George, but Margaret Thatcher. During her time in office as prime minister, she evolved a novel economic policy that marked a radical break with the Keynesianism that had dominated British policy-making since 1945. She did not only say that the previous policies had failed. She said that there is no alternative to the policies she put in their place, and dumbfounded the critics within and without' (McLean 2001, 12). But she was lucky as the opposition was divided and the economy bounced back. It was later that her luck and judgment ran out.

Key term 2.9 Heresthetician

A term used by Riker to describe a decision-maker who gains advantage by thinking through the moves in a game, as described in game theory. Rhetoric and skill at presentation also play a role.

McLean applies this method to study British prime ministers, like the early twentieth-century Liberal prime minister, David Lloyd George (McLean 2001). But it is relevant to more recent prime ministers too. McLean's study ends with Blair, but he fares badly in McLean's scheme. Blair might be more of a candidate for this kind of politician, as he had the skills to overcome obstacles early in his career and even his policy error of the Iraq war still did not prevent him from winning the general election of 2005. Blair was very skilful at presentation and made tactical choices in the early part of his career which grew his reputation, surprising his opponents, such as the successful campaign in 1995 to rewrite clause 4 of the Labour Party constitution that had committed the party to public ownership. Instead of alienating Labour followers, he inspired them, up until the decision to go to war in Iraq in 2003.

John Major was very talented in negotiating opt-outs to the Maastricht Treaty, for example, but could not face down the Eurosceptic rebels in his party who were opposed to the treaty. It is an open question as to whether successive premiers have these qualities or not, as McLean's book only goes up to early Blair. Cameron made many errors of judgment (see section 2.7.1). The same can be said of Theresa May and her decision to call an election in 2017. Then, Boris delayed decisions to deal with Covid-19 (see section 11.3.4). It may be the case that Britain in the 2010s and 2020s is not such a fertile ground for the heresthetician when compared to the leaders in the early twentieth century studied by McLean. These considerations about tactics bring the argument about power to the character of the prime minister and their capacity to do the job. That is the topic of the next section.

2.7 The capacity of the prime minister to do the job

2.7.1 Is political leadership harder in Britain than elsewhere?

Leadership is not an easy job in any political system, but is it harder in Britain? The challenge comes because of some of the special features of Britain's institutions. The prime minister is simultaneously leader of a party, head of a party in Parliament, chief executive with control over the government machine, and a figure playing an international role, as the UK has a legacy of a world power with formal participation in many international institutions, including NATO and the United Nations, and has a seat at the table of international organizations, such as the G7 and G20 (see sections 2.5.7 and 10.3.2). It may be the case that the evolution of the post of prime minister, effectively from the chair of a cabinet and leader of the party in the House of Commons, creates a legacy of lack of capacity when compared to other countries, such as the US or France, and even across Whitehall (the civil service) compared to the Treasury (Thomas 2021). In other countries, a president, such as Emmanuel Macron in France, can rely on the prime minister to get on with the job of running the government while he can focus on the big crises and the international role. In the UK, there is a head of state, the monarch, who has official duties, but in practice the prime minister has to have the important meetings with heads of state or other prime ministers, and meanwhile needs to keep backbenchers happy by inviting them to Downing Street and visiting the House of Commons. A prime minister who does not do the latter will lose the confidence of the parliamentary party and that can be very damaging in keeping the government on track and can even

Key term 2.10 Backbencher

A Member of Parliament (MP) who is not a government minister or official opposition spokesperson. This refers to the ordinary MPs who are elected on a party ticket and need to be whipped through the voting lobbies in the House of Commons in support of the party line. They play a key role in election of the party leader.

cost the premier's job. In fact, the job might be or have become impossible in many ways because of the pressures involved. Prime ministers might overcompensate for their lack of capacity by making decisions that are too quick and rash. The UK government's response to the Covid-19 crisis illustrates these points (see section 11.3.4).

It may be the case that the prime minister does not have enough backup from staff, access to intelligence, and strength over the levers in the centre to manage the machine of government (King and Crewe 2014, 314–15). The prime minister has responsibility and power, but perhaps does not have enough heft in terms of the capacity of the machine around the office-holder and the tools needed to get the job done, which might lead to costly blunders (King and Crewe 2014, 306–14). Recently, the number of personnel working for the prime minister as advisors has increased; twice as many as that in 2010 with forty-four in 2019 and over a third of all special advisors working at No. 10 (Durrant, Blacklaws, and Zodgekar 2020, 17).

2.7.2 Are prime ministers a source of political turbulence and policy disasters?

The structural features of the job might be one of the factors that contribute to political turbulence in British politics, as the prime minister might be tempted into making poor decisions or rash ones, which are partly encouraged by the system with its incentives to perform strongly and to do quick turnarounds. In particular, prime ministers can be unseated by members of their own party while in office, which they need to anticipate and have strategies in place to prevent, and this in turn may feed into a series of defensive strategies that might work in the short term in fending off rivals, but could lead to poor decisions in the long term.

In section 1.2, there was a short history of recent key recent events in British politics, such as the Scottish referendum, Brexit, the 2017 and 2019 general elections, and the management of the Covid-19 crisis. These owed much to the personal decisions of prime ministers, such as David Cameron, Theresa May, and Boris Johnson. For example, before 2014, then prime minister David Cameron decided that it was not advisable to delay the Scottish referendum. In what is perhaps the most striking example of all, he announced in January 2013 that he needed to offer the voters a referendum on membership of the European Union. Tim Shipman, a political journalist, has pieced together the debate at the top of the Conservative Party shortly before the referendum decision. His account suggests that Cameron was strongly opposed by George Osborne, the chief finance minister in his capacity as Chancellor of the Exchequer and his key political ally (Shipman 2016). The message that comes from Shipman's account is that David Cameron did not need to offer the referendum (even if he sensed it was coming anyway and wanted to get it out of the way) and that his close allies realized the risks both of losing it and of the British leaving the European Union. But he proceeded with it as a Conservative promise regardless. By the time the Conservative Party became the government after the 2015 general election, the 'in-out referendum' was in the manifesto so he had to do it. Rather than take the time needed to negotiate a new settlement with the EU to present to voters, he rushed to get a deal from Europe so as to get the referendum out of the way in the second year of the new parliament, so that he could then spend the rest of his term consolidating his reputation. Using his power as leader of his party, he chose to promise the referendum that in the end led to Brexit.

The penultimate case in this series of what turned out in hindsight to be poor decision-making is Theresa May, who inherited Cameron's majority of fifteen gained in May 2015. She could have easily stayed on in office, but she used her power as leader of her party to call an early election for 8 June 2017, getting the measure through the House of Commons easily in spite of the Fixed-Term Parliaments Act seeming to favour five-year terms of office for governments. She was probably right that given the divisions in the Conservative Party, the small majority might not have been enough to get the Brexit legislation through the House of Commons, and opinion polls were riding high in her favour; but with hindsight she would have been better off sitting tight and not calling an election. And Boris Johnson has also had his share of self-inflicted disasters, in particular over the Covid-19 crisis (see section 11.3.4).

Prime ministers have very different personalities, and may even have opposing mind-sets; but all are capable of rash and ill-thought-out decisions, suggesting that the system is at fault as much as particular personalities. The question is whether politicians of different temperaments, perhaps some who were initially quite balanced personalities, and who may have had considerable success as a party leader or minister before entering the highest office, become destabilized by the nature of the job. To get their way and to be successful, they need the right skill-set and good negotiating qualities which they should have by virtue of succeeding in politics and getting to the top. But often the arrival at No. 10 can be quite rapid, such as a surprise leadership election or a snap selection. Once in the role, they have to work out how to do this challenging job which nothing has prepared them for. Politicians are not perfect: they are human beings just like everyone else, with the same defects and blind-spots, as recent studies comparing the biases of citizens and politicians show (Linde and Vis 2017; Sheffer et al. 2018). They make mistakes and get into situations they cannot get out of. They are trying to reconcile difficult tasks of governing at the same time as keeping their political parties unified. From the strains of office, they make decisions in ways that are not predictable or fully rational, tending to make policies that may be taken too quickly. The centralization of power and the isolation of the office-holder give leaders false signals of the extent of their power and sagacity, like a medieval court, where factions seek to curry favour with the leader. They may be subject to various kinds of bias that affect the judgment of human beings like politicians. For example, confirmation bias is where decision-makers take on board evidence that supports their basic hunches; and availability bias is where certain views are seen as more representative than they actually are (Hallsworth 2018). The lack of critical culture may also lead to too much self-confidence and overreach. Then the changes to British politics that have increased rebellions within political parties and re-discovered the power of Parliament may have constrained the prime minister in ways that an earlier occupant would have found it hard to comprehend and manage. Politicians who hold the highest rank, like Boris Johnson, Theresa May, and David Cameron, should be able to use the powers of office to sustain them in power, and be experts in securing their re-election and in pursuing their preferred outcomes selected from their personal views and ideology. That such experienced people should sometimes make decisions that, on the face of it, go so badly wrong should cause some pause for thought.

2.8 Conclusion

This chapter has taken a look at the centre of UK government to understand how a core feature of British politics works. It follows from the description of the constitution and its model of democracy, offered in Chapter 1 (see sections 1.3 and 1.3.3), which is based on the fusion of executive powers with the institutions of parliamentary democracy and party organizations. The prime minister is at the centre of this potentially centralized system of party government, so the office and its occupant are crucial in understanding how politics and decision-making work day-to-day. As well as being leader of the largest party in the House of Commons, able to command a majority, and potentially able to get government business through Parliament and into law, the prime minister has executive powers, which helps keep this focus. These powers include the appointment and dismissal of ministers, and other powers and roles that mutually reinforce each other. On the back of these functional needs of the system, the prime minister can follow their own objectives and craft policies to win against their opponents as well as promote the collective interest.

Despite the power of the position and its importance in the British system of government, there are fundamental weaknesses in the role that come from the instabilities of party politics, in particular the threat of an internal coup against the leader, the need to include rivals in the cabinet, and the challenges of gripping a highly complex political-administrative machine. Much gets decided within a wider core executive rather than the prime minister acting alone. Prime ministers have limited capacity in terms of time and suffer from the pressures of the job. The endless and constant exposure to the media and public scrutiny takes its toll. Overall, the picture of prime ministerial and core executive power and capacity is a mixed one that is changeable over time. Much depends on conjunctions of events and personalities: in one period the prime minister can appear weak and out of control; but in another a course of events can mean the same person is assertive and victorious. In recent years, over Brexit and the Covid-19 pandemic, the prime minister's fate can change dramatically, even week-by-week. It is one of the characteristics of British politics that it can move very quickly, in ways that can destabilize one prime minister but then give opportunities to another. This protean or changeable character of British politics will be picked up in Chapters 4 and 5 as the issue of turbulence is discussed in more detail.

Further reading

There are some classic readings on this topic, such as by Anthony King (1991), George Jones (1964), and Rod Rhodes (2017). Very useful are the reviews of the debate by Keith Dowding (2013a) and Richard Heffernan (2005). A recent volume by Garnett (2021) stresses the limitation of the office and the difficulty of being prime minister, taking account of the difficulties of Theresa May's premiership. Biographies are a good source of information about premiers and the character of their governments, such as Margaret Thatcher (Moore 2014, 2015, 2019). Journalists also write well on these topics, for example Polly Toynbee and David Walker (2015) on the Cameron government.

Essay and exam questions

The classic question is 'How powerful is the British prime minister?'. The other side to the question is cabinet government, such as 'Is Cabinet government dead?'. The party dimension to the prime minister's power can be emphasized, such as a discussion of the phrase 'Prime ministers are only as powerful as their party allows'. Alternatively, a question could be asked about the nature of the job and the pressures on it, such as 'Is it impossible to succeed at the job of prime minister?' or 'Have prime ministers contributed to the turbulence of British politics?'.

Access the online resources for this chapter, including biannual updates, web links, and multiple-choice questions: www.oup.com/he/John1e

Chapter 3

Debating Politics and Making Laws

3

3.1 What is going to be in this chapter?

This chapter is about representation, looking mainly at the institution of the UK Parliament, where parliamentarians have a chance to debate issues of the day and to make laws. Classic arguments about the power of Parliament in relation to the executive are discussed and reviewed. The debate about the role of the House of Lords is also considered alongside that of the House of Commons. Then we will look at the evidence about what MPs and other representatives do in office, and how their behaviour links to other features of the political process, such as public opinion and constituency interests. Other legislatures, such as the Scottish Parliament, are also discussed and compared with the UK Parliament.

3.2 Introduction

Political systems need ways of making authoritative rules and ensuring they are seen to be legitimate by all involved with politics. The power to make decisions could emanate from one person or be in a small group, but citizens in advanced societies and democracies usually want more than just elite and executive-led decisions. There is a demand and expectation in most societies, especially in large democracies, for a wide range of opinion and forms of representation to come to bear on public decisions, and done in a way that is transparent to all. So, how does this happen?

In most democracies, decisions about laws and rules are usually made by groups of representatives in designated institutions that have their own rules of election and formal procedures. These institutions are called legislatures, usually operating at the national level as with the UK Parliament, but also existing at other levels, such as the Scottish Parliament, Senedd Cymru, and Northern Ireland Assembly. Even local councils make regulations that are authorized by locally elected politicians. Legislatures are often thought of as physical spaces, such as the House of Commons or House of Lords, which generally have a debating chamber into which all the representatives are regularly gathered. They take part in debates on the issues of the day and vote on laws and regulations, even though there are many other parts to these buildings where smaller groups of legislators meet, like committee rooms. Increasingly, much can be done online, such as online select committee hearings and, for a while during the Covid-19 pandemic, even votes in the House of Commons were cast remotely.

3.2.1 The UK Parliament as an institution

Like the executive, a legislature is a political institution, with its own rules, and forms part of the constitution. The UK Parliament has a long history and tradition, going back many centuries, but is constantly adapting. These rules, traditions, and habits of understanding, as well as the formal rules and legislation, determine what happens in the contemporary House of Commons and House of Lords. They also shape the practice of representation (see Key term 3.1). Although the electoral connection between voters and representatives is a key means by which representation happens, the process is mediated by these very rules and procedures. Even the design of the space where these institutions are located can contain in-built assumptions about how people are to be represented (Puwar 2004; Judge and Leston-Bandeira 2018). There are many conventions and rules, such as the televised Prime Minister's Questions (PMQs), when the prime minister is asked questions in a noisy chamber, for which theatrical performances on all sides matter.

Zoom-In 3.1 Why are there opposing benches in the House of Commons?

It seems natural to assume that the design of the House of Commons, with its benches on either side of a wide aisle, reflects the pattern of two-party politics, with government and opposition arranged against each other; but this design was an accident resulting from the decision by Edward VI in 1547 to allow the Commons to use St Stephen's Chapel after the dissolution of St Stephen's College. Parliamentarians simply took places on benches either side of the nave. See the UK Parliament website for more details.

Key term 3.1 Representation

How citizens' voices, opinions, identities, and perspectives are incorporated into politics and public decision-making. Those who hold public offices speak, advocate, and act on behalf of others in the political process. Can be descriptive (where representatives are from the same group as those who are represented), substantive (leading to policies), and symbolic (about identities).

These rituals, many of which are informal, govern how the institution works and affect what issues are addressed (Lovenduski 2012). Some of these conventions are relatively recent, with PMQs only being instituted as a twice-weekly occasion in 1953 (confirmed in 1961), with the modern format of the weekly event on Wednesdays decided as recently as 1997 when Tony Blair became prime minister. Being aware that institutions change all the time can be an impetus to reform and modernization.

3.2.2 Political parties

Political parties seek common representation across the country or territory/nation (see section 5.3.2). Elected representatives in Parliament are almost always members of and have loyalty to a political party. For example, there are no current MPs who ran as independent candidates in the 2019 general election despite former Conservative Party rebels standing for office. Party leaders and senior party officials approve who runs as a candidate and can suspend someone who does not follow the party line (though it can take a long time to get to that stage). Parties have values and ideologies that can turn into programmes for office. Legislatures are made up of representatives of these parties in different numbers across the legislature, whether left, right, green, or nationalist. At the level of the individual MP, representation is a blend of these factors: party membership/ideology, the makeup and values of the constituency, and the legislator's own values and identities.

3.2.3 Executive–legislative relations

In understanding the legislature, it is important to consider the link between it and the executive. As discussed in Chapter 2, in a parliamentary system of government like in the UK, one party or parties may become the government with the prime minister at its head, who has control of executive power. In addition to exercising executive powers, the government seeks to govern through the legislature: it has a programme of legislation set out at the start of each parliamentary session in the Speech from the Throne (Queen or King's Speech) (Key term 3.2) or it may bring other legislation forward for approval as it sees fit. It needs to get a budget passed for each financial year; and overall it wants to structure the agenda and public debate in these chambers. Such party-based representation is linked to electoral responsiveness, but is also about the influence of an ideology on public policy.

With one party or several parties in government, it becomes the task of parties that are not in power, the opposition, to hold the government to account, to keep it on its toes, to try to amend legislation, and to prepare for the next electoral contest, using the procedures of Parliament, and hoping that the government suffers a loss in popularity while being held to account. It is parliamentarians who lead this activity, whether party leaders defending the government or spokespersons from the opposition parties attacking and scrutinizing it. Backbenchers can also independently perform these activities, but the extent to which they can is limited given the importance of party organization and the dominance of the government and opposition over the business and agenda of these chambers. The legislature is where the opposition can

Key term 3.2 Speech from the Throne (Queen or King's Speech)

A formal speech given by the monarch to open the Houses of Parliament at the start of the parliamentary session (Photo 3.1). Although a highly ceremonial occasion, the speech is written by the government and signed off by prime minister and cabinet. It is a summary of the government's legislative programme, usually for a year.

Photo 3.1 Queen Elizabeth delivers the Queen's Speech alongside Prince Charles at the State Opening of Parliament at the Palace of Westminster in London, December 2019.

challenge the government and prepare the ground for the occasion, such as after a general election, whereby they can replace the government.

3.2.4 Methodology of studying Parliament

In answering questions about power and representation, it is important to be aware of the methodological difficulty of studying Parliament, mainly because in a parliamentary democracy the executive and legislature are fused in the sense that the government seeks to rule through Parliament in terms of exercising control over law-making. There are many actors involved, such as factions within parties and backbenchers (see the typology set out by King 1976). It is hard to know how powerful each actor is compared to the other and whether it is a party faction that is powerful rather than the legislature as a whole. It is no surprise, then, that scholars disagree about the importance of Parliament and the different elements within it (Butt 1967; Adonis 1990; Russell and Cowley 2016), and whether it does an effective job at representing the people.

3.3 Basic facts: debating politics and making laws

The UK Parliament is made up of two chambers of the House of Commons and House of Lords. It is a law-making body first and foremost, with bills usually starting in the first chamber, then passing through the second, which then need to be approved by the monarch: see section 3.3.1 and Figure 3.1. Though technically royal assent may be refused, no monarch has done this since the start of the eighteenth century.

3.3.1 Procedures and powers of the House of Commons and House of Lords

The House of Commons is the elected chamber made up currently of 650 Members of Parliament (MPs) who each represent one constituency. They usually run for office on a party label, which means they need to be selected by their local party association whose decision is then approved by the national party. The House of Lords is made up of about 800 unelected members. There are hereditary peers (members of the aristocracy), whose number was reduced to ninety-two in a reform that took place in 1999. There is an elaborate election procedure when these Lords need to be replaced: hereditary peers who are office-holders, deputy speakers or committee chairs who are elected by the whole house, and the remainder who are elected by the other hereditary peers in their respective party/cross-bench groups. There are other members who are there by virtue of their office, such as religious leaders. The rest are nominated, usually by the political parties, with the final decision made by the House of Lords Appointments Commission.

3.3.2 Role of political parties

Parties dominate the business of the House of Commons in terms of votes for legislation and motions that are put through. They are also important in the Lords where the government needs to get its business through that opposition parties scrutinize and review. But the government is not guaranteed a majority in the Lords, partly because there are many members who are not formally aligned to any party who are called crossbenchers (see Key term 3.3). Section 3.5.5 on the House of Lords contains more material on these issues, in particular the relationship between the two chambers.

The role of political parties is essential in understanding the business of the House of Commons and much of what goes on in the House of Lords. During the nineteenth century, political parties gained greater internal organization and central control by their leaders. Needing to form a government with credible promises to the electorate, there was an incentive for parties to be unified, with members of the parliamentary party voting according to an agreed

Key term 3.3 Crossbencher

A member of the House of Lords who is not directly affiliated to a political party, so votes with their conscience or on the basis of expertise.

line made by leaders, enforced by whips (see Key term 1.6). The term comes from hunting: a 'whipper in' was someone who was charged with keeping the headstrong hounds within the pack (Searing and Game 1977, 361). According to legend, whips were rumoured to keep MPs' secrets (in a so-called 'black book'), which they would threaten to divulge if the MP voted against the party line. How much cajoling by whips actually happens is up for debate. In general, the task of getting the votes through the lobby is of persuasion, especially as MPs are increasingly likely to rebel against the party line in recent years (see sections 3.5.1 and 3.5.5), making it a much harder job. It is a complex role; feeding information up to the party hierarchy about what is happening in the party and what MPs are unhappy about is as important as exercising control.

3.3.3 Committees

It is important to know about the role of committees in both chambers to understand the influence of the legislature. In Parliament, committees scrutinize and debate legislation as a bill passes through the legislature; others are designed to offer extra scrutiny on matters of public policy and hold the government and others to account. The former is whipped and is part of the law-making process. Law-making works as in Figure 3.1: in what is called a first reading, a bill is introduced (usually by a minister), either in the Commons or Lords, though usually the former. It then gets a second reading where the chamber gets a chance to debate the measure. When the chamber (either House of Commons or Lords) votes on the bill, it moves to what is called the committee stage, where its clauses are examined one by one by a group of MPs. Then it returns to the whole chamber to consider the amendments done in committee. This is followed by the third reading where amendments may be considered. After the bill is approved, it is sent to the House of Lords or House of Commons where it goes through much the same process, and if approved by both houses it gets royal assent. Section 3.5.5 will cover what happens when the two chambers do not agree, but in essence this is the basic procedure.

Other kinds of committees consider aspects of government business and specialist activities. These are often called select committees and the current system was introduced in the House of Commons in 1979, though the influential Public Accounts Committee, which runs the National Audit Office and scrutinizes public expenditure decisions, was created in 1861. Select committee members are elected within parties and allocated according to party representation in the Commons, and their chairs (also proportional to party balance) are elected by the whole chamber. Commons committees are organized to reflect the names and structure of government departments, and their agendas are usually concerned with government business. They are supported by clerks of the house and follow an agenda of investigations, having the power to request witnesses and documents. Although the government is not obliged to follow their recommendations, it will consider them and respond in writing. Committees in the Lords follow specialist topics, such as the Science and Technology Committee that carries out inquiries into specialist science and technology matters.

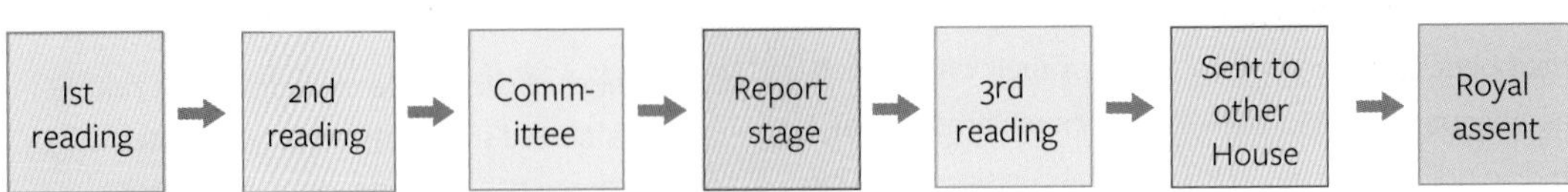

Figure 3.1 UK law-making procedure.

3.4 The debate about the power of the UK Parliament

One key debate that needs to be resolved is about the power of the UK Parliament. It is important to assess the influence the institution has over making laws and creating policy in relation to the power of the executive, and more generally to appraise the influence of elected representatives exercising their right to debate and scrutiny. It is an important debate about the relationship between the executive and legislature, even bearing in mind the complex relationships within parties and among elected representatives. In most constitutions, the legislature checks the executive and its tendency to exercise overmighty power; that is, to make decisions in an overcentralized way, without taking account of a wide range of views, ignoring public opinion, and/or without using evidence effectively, or even abusing power by making decisions that are to a party's advantage, but not in the national interest (variously defined). In terms of constitutional thinking in the UK, it is the job of the legislature to hold the executive to account and influence the direction of the government and its policies. In some political systems, the legislature co-determines laws and policies with the executive, which does not happen in Britain. But recent developments may point to a stronger role for the legislature.

3.4.1 Historical perspective

In Britain, the debate about the power of Parliament goes back to the seventeenth century when the executive was headed by the monarch, and Parliament was acquiring powers to review the decisions of the executive, which emerged in a series of foundational events in British politics, such as the Glorious Revolution of 1688–9 (Miller 2014). In many political systems, the balance is sustained by the doctrine of the separation of powers (see Key term 1.8), which can be understood narrowly as the guarantee of independent political institutions carrying out different functions (Vile 1967), but more broadly occurs when independent political institutions share in the making of policy, which is more common in countries with codified constitutions, such as the US, and with a constitutional court to adjudicate disputes (see Key term 1.8). Because political parties have dominated the business of the House of Commons since the mid-nineteenth century, this separation is harder to achieve. All executives have some powers in the legislature in any system (for example, the role of the vice president in the US in deciding tied votes), but the extent of executive control is (or has been) much stronger in Britain. In particular, government controls much of the business and the timetable of the House of Commons, with very little time devoted to laws and business that are not the government's own. The opposition has twenty days per session for debate; backbenchers can ask questions and participate in debates as well as propose a small number of laws in private members' legislation (ten bills allocated by ballot once a year), but this is different to the ability to get a programme for the government through the legislature.

3.4.2 A weak Parliament?

When there are disciplined political parties and governments have secure majorities, rebellions over votes on government bills will be rare, which means that the government business determined in the executive almost always succeeds. Indeed, there were decades in British politics where very few rebellions occurred, such as the 1950s and 1960s (see Figure 3.2). For example, from 1955 to 1959 only 2 per cent of all divisions had any dissenters (Norton 1987, 144). It is easy to see how Parliament was thought to be redundant and dominated by the executive. This became standard commentary, such as Ronald Butt's *The Power of Parliament* (1967), written in the 1960s but looking back over previous decades, even though he realized the informal power of parliamentarians behind the scenes. It reflects the common view of Britain as an executive-dominant political system, which was discussed in the last two chapters. In comparative studies, the Westminster Parliament is often described as passive (Polsby 1975), in contrast with systems where the legislative has much more power, such as the US. It fits into a wider narrative about British politics as centralized and dominated by the elite in one party when in office: the so-called 'elective dictatorship' (Key term 3.4).

3.4.3 **Alternative account: informal power**

The complete dominance of the executive is a powerful argument to make, but it is also possible to come up with a different, more nuanced account. A lot happens behind the scenes in the everyday work of Parliament in terms of informal influence and work on the committees, so that what might appear to be executive influence actually is shaped by the everyday work of parliamentarians who participate in the law-making process but whose contribution is not always seen. The work of the academic lawyer John Griffith, based on detailed case studies carried out in the 1970s, seeks to show this influence (Griffith 1974). Such findings can be found in later studies, for example in Russell and Gover's (2017) study of twelve pieces of legislation using the same case study method as Griffith.

Institutions such as Parliament are not monolithic, but composed of factions that need to be placated and reconciled, which is the task of leadership within the Commons. Political parties are not unitary, as we will see in Chapter 4, and the institution may work in ways where factional influence is important. Moreover, it is important to rule by consent which involves trading off objectives and making concessions even if it appears that the government programme remains in place. In this view, decision-making is shared, and the policy process comprises multiple influences, which is a feature of pluralism (Key term 2.5). This view is articulated in an article by Russell and Cowley (2016), who sum up much evidence of the influence of Parliament, looking at the impact of parliamentary rebellions, the role of the House of Lords, and the influence of select committees. They argue that 'parliament is powerful at the decision-making stage, but that much of that power is exercised through anticipated reactions, in terms of ministers facilitating last-minute negotiations to avert rebellions and defeats' (Russell and Cowley 2016, 133).

> **Key term 3.4** Elective dictatorship
>
> Coined by the Conservative politician and former minister Lord Hailsham (Marylebone 1976) to sum up the idea that British governments are elected but have few constraints on their power between elections. Hailsham was not deterred from serving as a cabinet minister in 1959–64, 1970–4, and 1979–87.

3.4.4 **Institutional presence**

Another related argument is that Parliament remains at the centre of debate. It is where ministers have to appear, and it is reported to by government, which structures the accountability of departments, and most official business has to pass through it (see Adonis 1990). This power of the institution in its informal sense of determining the routines and standard operating procedures in politics has been put strongly by David Judge (1993), conveyed by the term 'the parliamentary state'. It also illustrates the difficulty of dissecting the power of Parliament, which is harder to ascertain than the power of the prime minister. Parliament is quite a large institution, made up of many parts. There is also the existence of power *to* and power *over*, both of which are hard to measure and evaluate, as was found in section 2.6.7. It is hard to uncover the counterfactual (Key term 3.5) of no parliamentary influence because the institution is a necessary part of the political system so has some role in any decision by default. Because the executive and Parliament, and also parties, are so fused in the British system, it is hard to work out their relative impact of each as they are constituted of each other as well as containing overlapping factions.

Key term 3.5 Counterfactual

A fair comparison of the state of affairs of an intervention, process, institution, or policy, which allows the observer to claim its influence or causal impact (see Zoom-In 6.1).

3

3.5 Changing behaviour in Parliament

A key part of the argument about the power of Parliament is based on changes in MPs' and Lords' behaviours, which reflect wider changes in the political system that point to less hierarchical parties, loss of deference within parties, reflecting social changes, and also changes in Parliament itself that have improved the prospects of MPs so they can have an alternative career other than just as a minister or opposition spokesperson. These changes have taken time to work through, but may have increased the power of Parliament through the greater independence of backbenchers (see Key term 2.9).

3.5.1 **MP rebellions**

MPs rebel if they do not follow the party whip on a government bill or an opposition line, either by voting in the opposite way to the whip, respectively for the opposition or government, or abstaining. After a period when MPs followed the party line in the 1950s and 1960s, there were increasing rebellions. As political parties have at various times sought to define their agenda more strongly, with leaders keen to push a new programme, they have encountered resistance. The other argument is that as rebels form a habit of rebelling, so they become more inclined to join rebellions at a later date (Cowley 2004). There is thus a baseline so that times of rebelling do not fully dampen down, so that the next period of activism will ratchet up the effect. The other factor is that voters prefer MPs who rebel (Vivyan and Wagner 2012; Campbell et al. 2019).

This change in behaviour started to occur in the 1970s, partly stimulated by the insensitive leadership of Prime Minister Edward Heath, 1970–4 (Norton 1978), when the proportion rose to one in five of all divisions as having rebels. The change in behaviour was observed in successive papers and books by Philip Norton (Norton 1975, 1980, 1978). The tendency for increased rebellions was then picked up in the work of Phil Cowley who looked into later rebellions, first under John Major's government, 1992–7 (Cowley and Norton 1999), when the prime minister had a slender majority, then under Labour from 1997 to 2010, where rebellions became the norm in spite of governments having large majorities (Cowley 2005; Cowley and Stuart 2014). One example happened in 2003 when the government looked for MPs' support for its decision to invade Iraq in that year, when 139 Labour MPs voted against. In this period, Blair found it hard to control former ministers whose careers were over and believed they had nothing to lose, as well as those who were more ideologically opposed (Benedetto and Hix 2007). Then 143 MPs voted against the party leadership under the prime ministership of Gordon Brown (Cowley and Stuart 2014). There were rebellions during the Conservative and Liberal Democrat coalition government of 2010–15. This fell during 2015–17, perhaps reflecting the slim Conservative majority. Figure 3.2 gives an indication of the change over time. They then continued after Brexit (Case Study 3.1), though the number of rebellions needs to be considered against the extent to which governments put votes to the Commons, which they might not do if they believe they are going to lose, so reducing the number of defeats.

Such change in behaviour exemplifies the observation that MPs are less likely to follow the party line and to obey the whip. If MPs do not follow the government line and defect to the opposition, particularly in sufficient numbers, it follows that the government will find it hard to get its measures through because it cannot rely on the loyalty of its MPs, depending on the size of the majority. It also follows that the government needs to make concessions before the rebellions occur to avoid losing and being humiliated. In this way, the power of backbench MPs amounts to more than counting the number of rebellions in votes in the House of Commons, but extends to the whole business of government in ways that are not easily observable.

Work on rebellions has been carried forward by Slapin and colleagues who looked at the 1992–2016 period (Slapin and Kirkland 2019; Slapin et al. 2018). They show there were more rebellions on the government side, with between 2 per cent for the opposition and 7.4 per cent for the governing party experiencing ten or more MPs rebelling in the period from 1992 to 2016 (Slapin and Kirkland 2019). This could also reflect the need for the opposition to be unified in order to be credible. Defeats might suggest that backbenchers are getting concessions by rebelling more, though it might indicate that governments have to make more difficult decisions based on wide consultation and cannot follow party factions in the way an opposition can. Rebels are often 'grandstanding' to signal to voters and other groups (Slapin et al. 2018). Rebellions may be more 'position taking' rather than a sign of real

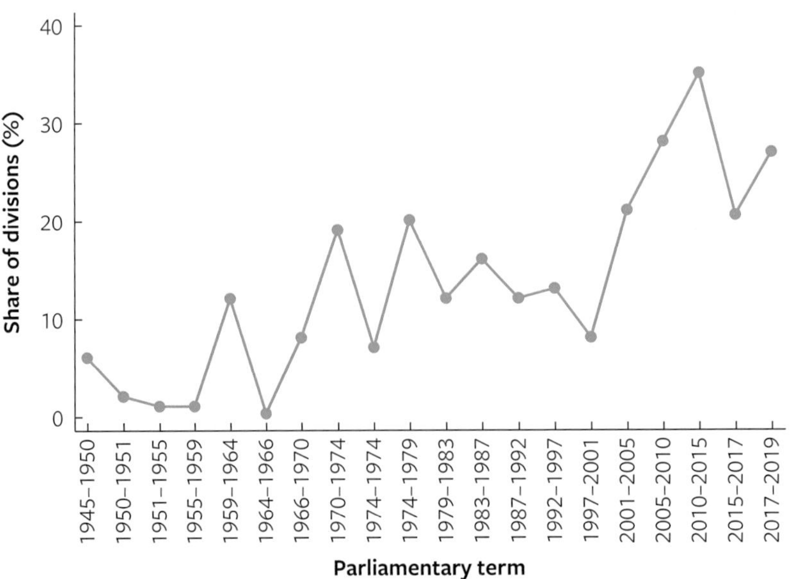

Figure 3.2 MP rebellions, 1945–2019.
Source: Cowley and Norton (1999); Mortimore and Blick (2018, 324); further calculations made using Hansard

Case Study 3.1 The UK Parliament and Brexit 2017–19

Rebellions by MPs became the norm after the Conservative Party lost seats in the 2017 general election, and had to govern with the support of the Democratic Unionist Party (DUP). MPs from two wings of the Conservative Party regularly rebelled either to keep the plan for Brexit on track or to try to stop or modify it. When all the votes of allies were counted, the government had an effective majority of thirteen. Attempts to get the government Withdrawal Agreement through the Commons, which was needed to implement Brexit, failed because of the opposition of the DUP and the twenty-eight Conservative opponents. The Withdrawal Agreement was rejected by 432 votes to 202 in January 2019, then by 391 votes to 242 in early March.

The UK Parliament of 2017–19 illustrated the power of the legislature over the executive to block policy. But it is hard to see this Parliament as an example of making effective policy decisions. Parliament was not able to come up with a constructive alternative to the government's method of dealing with Brexit and get it through. Given that factions in Parliament had very different goals, none got its way, and each blocked each other. Having power is partly about the ability to coordinate and to achieve common goals. This relates back to the difference between power *to* and power *over* (see section 2.6.7): Parliament excelled in the former, but failed in the latter.

influence. They could even indicate a lack of power if the measure gets through, despite their rebellion, or if nothing is done.

Just when commentators were getting used to disloyal MPs and even cabinet ministers abstaining on government legislation without punishment (Russell 2020), the wheel of British politics turned once again. With the election of Boris Johnson as Conservative Party leader in July 2019, replacing Theresa May, there emerged a real push to enforce party loyalty. On 17 November, shortly before the 2019 election, each Conservative MP was required to sign a declaration to honour the Withdrawal Agreement negotiated with the EU. Then the large majority of eighty as a result of the 12 December 2019 snap general election meant that the government could get most of its measures through, making rebellion pointless or just grandstanding. For those newly elected Conservative MPs enjoying the taste of victory, it did not make sense to rebel at first either because of the Conservative government's commitment to the levelling-up agenda. The volatile nature of British politics means it changed again, all too quickly, and before long Boris Johnson faced his own rebellions over new Covid-19 restrictions, with fifty-five Conservative MPs voting against his proposed plan of action on 1 December 2020, though not defeating the government. There were also several government U-turns because of protests by MPs, as well as the media storm over Marcus Rashford's free school meals campaign on 16 June 2020, which occurred again on 8 November 2020. Table 3.1 gives some examples of some bills or motions that have had rebellions since 2019.

3.5.2 Power behind the scenes

The discussion of MP rebellions draws attention to the key problem of interpreting data about the power of different actors. Just because there are rebellions does not prove who is powerful or not, as rebellions might be merely symbolic, and sometimes a

Table 3.1 Examples of House of Commons rebellions or adverted rebellions since 2019

Date	Measure	Rebellion	Outcome
8 January 2019	Amendment to the finance bill limiting the government's powers in a no deal Brexit scenario	Passed 484–76 (20 Conservatives voted against)	The amendment was approved
25 March 2019	Amendment allowing Parliament to take control of the order paper	329–302	Led to a series of indicative votes on Brexit, but no decision overall
3 April 2019	Amendment to European Union Withdrawal Bill to ensure government did not have to accept an extension if offered by the European Council	304–313 (15 votes against)	Government forced to accept an extension to membership of EU
13 November 2019	A humble address to force government to publish legal advice on the Brexit Withdrawal Agreement	Passed without division (govt ordered Tory MPs to abstain after it became clear they would lose because DUP decided to back the motion Labour presented)	Legal advice published
1 December 2020	A new tougher tier system of Covid-19 restrictions for England	Passed 291 to 78, but 53 Conservative MPs voted against (18 abstained)	Government's Covid-19 policy proceeds, but Johnson's first test of loyalty from his party
25 March 2021	6-month extension of the Covid-19 legislation	Passed 484–76	Government's Covid-19 policy proceeds, but another test for Johnson

government concedes a battle, but does not give up on its strategy down the line. All it shows is that parliamentary politics has changed. Also, vast amounts of government business still go through without opposition. The figures on rebellions appear high because they concentrate on the number of divisions that have rebels (of a certain number), but that does not give much of a sense of whether the government was under threat or not.

A subtler argument is put forward by Russell and Cowley (2016, 128) over amendments to legislation, which are done less in the public glare, and instead in the committee stage of a bill. This gives more of a sense of the influence of parliamentarians, and thereby of Parliament itself. In the past, academics noticed that the vast bulk of government bills went through unamended (Mezey 1979), but Russell and Cowley calculate that 60 per cent of amendments in their sample were due to backbench parliamentarians. They note that governments when threatened by a potential defeat withdraw bills first, to prevent appearing weak. A similar argument is made by Thompson, who explains that there are important cases of backbench influence, that these bill committees have experts on them, and that the debates have a deliberative quality (Thompson 2015). However, as Dunleavy et al. (2018, 165) say, the data show 'an exceptionally modest role, and one that falls well below the rationale of careful deliberative debate and consideration that other legislatures in Europe can claim'. The key problem in this debate is the difficulty of ascertaining the strength of Parliament as strong or weak because the same data can support both propositions. It is a bit like saying whether a glass of water is half-full or half-empty: the former indicates plenty; the latter dearth. It is possible to find in Thompson's study that evidence of government power: 0.6 per cent of amendments proposed by backbench and opposition MPs succeed in bill committees whereas 99.9 per cent of amendments proposed by the government to its own bills succeed (see Berry 2015).

The other issue is whether government accepts right from the start that amendments are going to happen and are even desirable, often then improving a piece of legislation, rather like Microsoft introduces early or beta versions of its computer operating system, in the full knowledge that an army of coders are going to suggest improvements, effectively doing the company's work. The government is in a similar position, which means that successful amendments are not examples of power *over*, from Parliament to the executive, but power *to* (Key term 2.5), which is about collective capacity in a joint project of producing legislation.

3.5.3 **Select committees**

Another dimension to the power of Parliament is the rise of influence of select committees in the House of Commons (see Zoom-In 3.2). These have developed over time and are now a normal part of the business of government. Select committees have become established and have gained experience of scrutinizing government policy, in spite of changing membership. Their role has been enhanced following the 'Wright reforms' of 2009–10 which introduced election of the chairs by the whole chamber. Furthermore, select committees have received increasing attention in the media, rising from 100 mentions per year in 2008 in the newspaper database LexisNexis to 350 in 2013 (Dunleavy and Muir 2013), though this might be a low baseline and does not indicate the extent of the interest in select committees by the media. Some select committee chairs have become public figures who step forward to comment directly to the media, such as Meg Hellier, the current chair of the influential Public Accounts Committee in 2021. In 2020, several former secretaries of state put themselves up for election as select committee chairs, demonstrating the appeal of the post. For example, Jeremy Hunt, former Secretary of State for Health and Social Care, became chair of the Health and Social Care Select Committee and took a prominent role in the Covid-19 crisis. Stephen Crabb, former Secretary of State for Work and Pensions, became chair of the Welsh Affairs Select Committee. Other chairs have been frontbench spokespersons, such as Hilary Benn for Labour, who was chair of the Committee on the Future Relationship with the European Union.

Given the large amount of MPs' time these committees take up, the large number of reports they produce, and the resources they consume, the key question is whether they successfully challenge the executive and other powerful actors so that scrutiny and accountability take place. There are a large number of hearings and reports—several hundred over the life of a government. For example, seven committees produced 695 reports over a thirteen-year period (Benton and Russell 2013, 778). It may be the case that this is just a necessary checking process and that not many changes are needed as a result of committee

3

Zoom-In 3.2 Select committees

A select committee is a small group (minimum of eleven) of MPs or Lords, drawn from across the political parties, who are authorized to investigate and make reports within a specialist field. In the Commons, they scrutinize government departments. For example, the Defence Committee shadows the Ministry of Defence. There are other Commons committees on more general matters, such as the Public Accounts Committee, and committees set up for special purposes which are time limited. The committees in the Lords are more generalist, such as the Science and Technology Committee. Their composition and membership are determined by the political parties within each chamber. They receive administrative support from the clerks (civil servants who support Parliament and parliamentarians) and may appoint special advisors. They have powers to request 'persons and papers', so as to call witnesses and receive documentation to support their inquiries and reports. The government must respond to committee reports within three months. House of Commons chairs have been elected by all MPs since June 2010.

scrutiny, and that it is reasonable not to expect much government policy to change from select committee investigations, especially as it is overseen by professional civil servants and those working for public bodies. But things do go wrong, some decisions are badly made, short-term electoral advantage is seized, and governments try to cover up their mistakes. It is the job of scrutiny and accountability to expose this, so it is fair to ask whether select committees actually make a difference, and to focus on whether they can effect change.

3.5.4 **Select committee influence**

How can the question about the influence of select committees be answered? There has been a lot of research and commentary on select committees as they have developed. Some studies are descriptive, examining how they work in a particular time period (Drewry and Study of Parliament Group 1985; Jogerst 1993). There are also accounts of the roles of particular kinds of committee, such as the Intelligence and Security Committee (ISC) (Bochel, Defty, and Kirkpatrick 2015). These accounts are useful as they show how the system has become institutionalized and has bedded down over a period of time. Select committees are more settled in their work as an established part of the policy-making process. Committees have sought to use what powers they have to better effect (Mellows-Facer, Challender, and Evans 2019).

Many studies do not, nor do they claim to, address the issue of influence (for example, Drewry and Study of Parliament Group 1985). But some do, bearing in mind the limitations of research methods in trying to answer questions about power (see section 3.2.4). Hindmoor et al. (2009) followed up on the recommendations of the then Education and Skills Committee. They compared the proposals of the committee with the actual legislation that was enacted later. This research strategy does not entirely get around the counterfactual of what would have happened without the committee's action (see Key term 3.5), but it is a good way to track the influence on parties and the media. A second study takes the same approach (Benton and Russell 2013), which uses a mixture of quantitative (statistical) and qualitative (more intensive research with a small number of subjects) methods to find evidence, claiming about a 50 per cent success rate of select committee proposals. A third study is by the Institute for Government (White 2015) based on case studies. As Benton and Russell (2013, 793) say, a case study may 'overestimate committee influence if, for example, many of the recommendations that succeeded had also been pressed on the government by outside groups'. Bates et al. (2017, 780) note that it is hard to come to definitive conclusions when the case study evidence is drawn from those most closely involved in the process and that claims of the increased role of the committees need to be approached with some caution. They seek to find out whether the committees increased in influence following the Wright reforms in 2009–10. Taking quantitative measures, such as data on attendance and turnover, they find no change over that period, including when the reforms took place. The lack of proved influence does not mean such committees are not useful or interesting to study. Some studies of committees seek to go beyond the tricky question of proving a causal inference, such as Geddes' (2019) study, seeking to understand the ideas, beliefs, practices, and traditions, and in particular that the beliefs of the actors involved matter.

Any assessment of the power and role of select committees needs to be sensitive to the basic problem that they can only influence the political and policy agenda and need to persuade government to change course. They have to rely on the goodwill of governments to listen to these reforms when governments also have other objectives such as getting re-elected, ensuring a good reputation, and avoiding too much criticism. There is also a massive information asymmetry between the committee, with its limited resources of clerks and special advisors, and the large bureaucracies they monitor, as well as a fast-moving agenda where reports need writing quickly and the personnel of the committees changes at each parliamentary session. At best, they can set the agenda of reform.

3.5.5 The House of Lords

The final leg of Russell and Cowley's argument—that Parliament is more powerful than is commonly supposed—is an examination of the greater independence of the House of Lords. This is based on the idea that a second chamber of Parliament can contribute to the content of legislation and the general scrutiny of the executive, because legislation has been considered, amended, and maybe even introduced there, and there is a framework of committees and reporting that feeds into government policy. Traditionally, the House of Lords was seen as passive, particularly because it lacks a legitimate role in a democratic political system, and also because the Parliament Act limits the extent to which it may resist government legislation. Legislation can be introduced in the Commons and is then considered in the Lords (see Figure 3.1). If the Lords make amendments to the legislation, these are then considered by the Commons, which can accept the amendments, so the bill goes for royal assent, or they can send the legislation back to the Lords for further consideration. This is called 'ping pong', which can go on for a long time, but is limited by the Parliament Act (see Zoom-In 3.3). Also, by the terms of the Salisbury convention, the Lords do not vote down items that are in the government party's manifesto (see section 1.3.11).

Compared to other second chambers, such as the Senate in the US or the Bundesrat in Germany, the House of Lords is relatively weak in terms of its formal powers. But a number of authors (Russell 2013; Dixon 2021) have noted that it plays an important role in shaping legislation and policy. The idea is that it allows a 'second thought' to take place for legislative measures. This means that effective revisions can be introduced, preventing ill-thought-out legislation being rushed through Parliament and causing potential problems implementing it down the line. Given the composition of the House of Lords, with many former civil servants and scientists, experts can become

Zoom-In 3.3 Parliament Acts of 1911 and 1949

Emerged from a historical dispute between the Liberal government and the House of Lords over the 1909 budget. The Parliament Act, passed in 1911 and amended in 1949, limited the power of the House of Lords to amend or reject legislation proposed by the Commons. After a year of 'ping pong'—that is where legislation passes back and forth between the Commons and Lords without agreement—the Act requires the version passed by the Commons to be sent to the monarch for assent without the input of the Lords. 'Money bills', matters of taxation and public spending, must be approved within a month of being passed by the Commons. Only seven bills have been invoked by this procedure, though it influences other bills where the Lords climb down beforehand. The Act does not apply to what is called secondary legislation, statutory instruments, though it is believed that there is a constitutional convention that the Lords do not oppose them (see Case Study 3.3).

involved with amending legislation so that the policy process improves as a result. It can improve policies by greater deliberation (Parkinson 2007), with the second chamber paying less attention to partisan party politics and point scoring. The lack of direct election and consideration of policy by experts and those not dependent on party preferment might have some advantages in being able to use delaying tactics yet not challenging the democratic legitimacy of the Commons. Dixon's (2021, 7) study of government bills in the 2016–17 session shows that most were substantially amended, 'on average 31 percent of the lines of text were altered during the parliamentary process, up to a maximum of almost 80 percent'. The process of influence is quite subtle with the government accepting most amendments.

The argument about power goes further than influence, claiming that the House of Lords exerts actual power over the Commons and over the government, and sometimes flexes its muscles. In part, this depends on the costs of delay to a government programme so that the government cannot afford slippage in a packed programme of legislation, so it makes sense to concede first or come to a compromise rather than resist. The other factor is that it is not possible to separate out what happens in the Lords and Commons. If the government has a large majority and a unified approach, it does not make sense for factions in the Lords to oppose government policy; but when government is divided and there are factions of MPs ready to rebel, there can be alliances between groups in both chambers to try to outwit the government, so rebels in each chamber are stronger when working together.

With the 1999 Act that reformed the House of Lords, most of the hereditary peers were removed (see section 3.3.1). Thereafter, the Lords lost its inbuilt majority for the Conservatives, making divisions more likely. Whereas in an earlier period there were few Lords voting against the wishes of the House of Commons (Shell 1992), behaviour has changed since 1999. Figure 3.3 shows this rise in 2000/2001, though this was under the Labour government. Also, the number of rebellions then went down, except during the Brexit Parliament. The rebelliousness of the Lords is cyclical, reflecting the current politics.

Looking to the evidence more broadly, Russell and Cowley (2016, 127) report that 'detailed tracking of the 406 unique legislative defeats over the period 1999–2012 found that 44 per cent resulted in a Lords policy "win," or at least a draw'. This is impressive evidence, but as with backbench rebellions, it is worth

Case Study 3.2 Lords exerting power

Following the government's defeat on the Tax Credits (Income Thresholds and Determination of Rates) (Amendment) Regulations 2015, it appeared the House of Lords was using its power to evade the Parliament Act and challenge a 'money bill' in the government's welfare and tax reforms.

On 26 October 2015, the House of Lords voted to delay changes in tax credits until certain reservations were made. Its power came from voting on a statutory instrument so the Lords were able to defeat the measure until the government changed tack.

considering the counterfactual, and whether the government may have other ways of changing policy long term after a Lords defeat (for example, by placing measures in the finance bill). Overall, it may be the case that the Lords tend to choose the fights they wish to have and avoid a showdown with the Commons (Dixon 2021, 31). As Norton (2003, 172) points out, members of the Lords come from a variety of back-

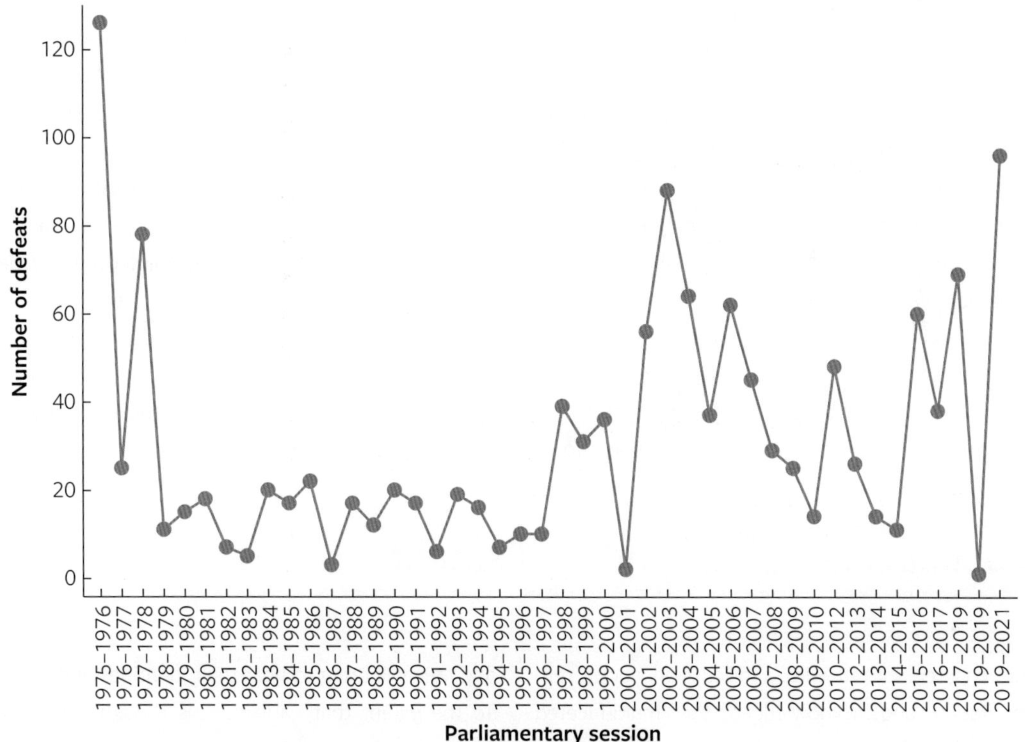

Figure 3.3 Number of government defeats in the House of Lords, 1975–2021.
Source: Parliament House of Lords FAQs, Lords Government Defeats: www.parliament.uk/about/faqs/house-of-lords-faqs/lords-govtdefeats*Note: exclusion of one case in 2012–13 where coalition was split; 2010–12, 2017–19, and 2019–21 parliamentary sessions spanned over two years; the 2019 session lasted for only two months*

grounds and not all them wish to get involved with party fights. Overall, the Lords needs to be thought of as seeking to be a legitimate policy-making body in a democracy, which means playing within the constraints of the agenda being set by the democratically elected first chamber. This self-denying ordinance limits the Lords' power to brief periods of rebellions and a less observable drip-drip of incremental adjustments through amending legislation. The tendency for British politics to produce unified government for some periods of time (if less so than in the past) creates the conditions for Lords' deference, in spite of occasional rebellions and victories, especially when there are small majorities.

3.5.6 Concluding on the power of Parliament debate

This part of the chapter has reviewed the debate about the power of the UK Parliament. It has acknowledged that it is a hard question to answer because of the problem of identifying key actors, who may be associated with the power of Parliament, and of attributing influence. Claims about the end of parliamentary influence and absence of scrutiny of the executive are overblown, but it is important to realize that most of the cards in terms of influence are still in the hands of the government, which has control of information and expertise, as shown by the principal–agent model, as well as over the rules of the game. Parliamentarians usually work within this system and know how to get the best from it, given these imbalances. When the system looked like it was falling apart over the Brexit legislation from 2017 to 2019, Parliament was unable to operate as an alternative executive and revealed its weakness. If Parliament is to be an effective policy-maker, there needs to be a more fundamental rethink of the constitutional set-up that gives it a role-sharing power with the executive. It may be the case that Parliament needs more control over its own business and timetable so it can learn to be an effective partner with the executive (Russell and Gover 2021). In Senedd Cymru or the Welsh Parliament there is a 3:2 split between government and Senedd time.

A lot depends on judgment when looking at the evidence. Examine this statement by Russell and Cowley (2016, 132): 'British parliament has significant influence, at all stages of the policy process'. Much turns on the word 'influence' and the relative input of Parliament and its different elements (for example, a group of party rebels) compared to others. When looking at the figures on rebellions (see Figures 3.2 and 3.3), is this another case of deciding whether something is half-full or half-empty? It is possible to use the same data to argue both rebellious influence or conformity to the executive's wishes.

3.6 Representation and Parliament

This chapter started with a discussion about representation and acknowledged the multi-faceted nature of this concept (see Pitkin 1967) (see Key term 3.1). It has been implied in many of the discussions in this chapter, in that the exercise of power from groups both within the executive and without will involve representation of different interests and groups, and MPs will bring to bear their identities and values. To the extent that Parliament is thought to matter determines how much representation occurs. But it is important to drill down into the different elements of representation. Even governments, when they are elected, are representing the people, so how does this kind of partisan and government representation mesh with the other kinds based on gender, ethnicity, social class, and territory?

3.6.1 **Descriptive representation**

Descriptive representation is the idea that who someone is matters to those who are represented (see Key term 3.1). People often wish to see people like them as elected representatives and ministers. It also affects their engagement with politics and their sense of influence (called 'efficacy'). Comparative studies show that perceiving someone as similar to oneself in office is very important for people from different ethnic backgrounds, and affects their attitudes and behaviour (Tate 2003). As there are people from many different backgrounds in the UK as a whole, descriptive representation is the extent of their presence in politics. Given that in the past and still to an extent up to the present day, MPs have often been drawn from a similar background of white, privileged, and male, the common conclusion is that the Houses of Commons and Lords are not adequately representative of the population.

3.6.2 **Gender**

One key area is gender, with the UK often observed to be below the average of all countries (House of Commons 2016, 3). But there have been improvements. The House of Commons has, after the 2019 election, 33.8 per cent female-identifying MPs, which has risen from 17.9 per cent in 2001 and from 3.0 per cent in 1979: see Figure 3.4a. Now the UK is higher than any regional average for most parts of the world, except the Nordic countries (Inter-Parliamentary Union 2021). There are variations across the political parties with Labour having higher representation, helped by having all-women shortlists (AWS), especially effective before the 1997 election, giving them a higher baseline from which to project the current growth in numbers (see Figure 3.4b).

There have been trends across the world to increase the representation of women. Factors influencing representation include the electoral system as well as political-cultural factors and institutional barriers in political parties (see Lovenduski and Norris 1989) as well as in Parliament itself, which have been widely recognized as an environment that is not receptive to female and non-binary people (Childs 2004; Catalano 2009), in spite of improvements. For example, the Commons sits for longer and has a less predictable timetable than many other chambers, making it incompatible with a private and family life (UK Parliament 2018, 11–12). The key is the supply of candidates, as local constituency associations are still reluctant to nominate candidates in the absence of AWS (Wäckerle 2021). As well as Labour, the Conservative Party, under the leadership of David Cameron, promoted women in A-list candidates, as did the Liberal Democrats since 2017, initiated by former leader Tim Farron (Morris 2017). AWS have helped drive up the numbers over time.

The Lords is not often discussed in terms of descriptive representation, but unsurprisingly it is not representative. In May 2020, there were 216 female-identifying Lords out of 785 total members, 27.5 per cent, which is behind the House of Commons (https://members.parliament.uk/parties/lords/by-gender). Like the Commons, this figure has risen in recent years, from 7 per cent in 1995.

3.6.3 **Ethnic minority representation**

Ethnic minorities—sometimes called BAME (Black, Asian, and Minority Ethnic)—make up 14 per cent of the population according to the 2011 UK census (Office for National Statistics 2018). In 2017, there were fifty-two ethnic minority MPs, rising to sixty-five in 2019 with twenty-two Conservative and forty-one Labour (see Anstis 2020). There have been some improvements in diversity in recent years (Figure 3.5a), at about 10 per cent of MPs, so they

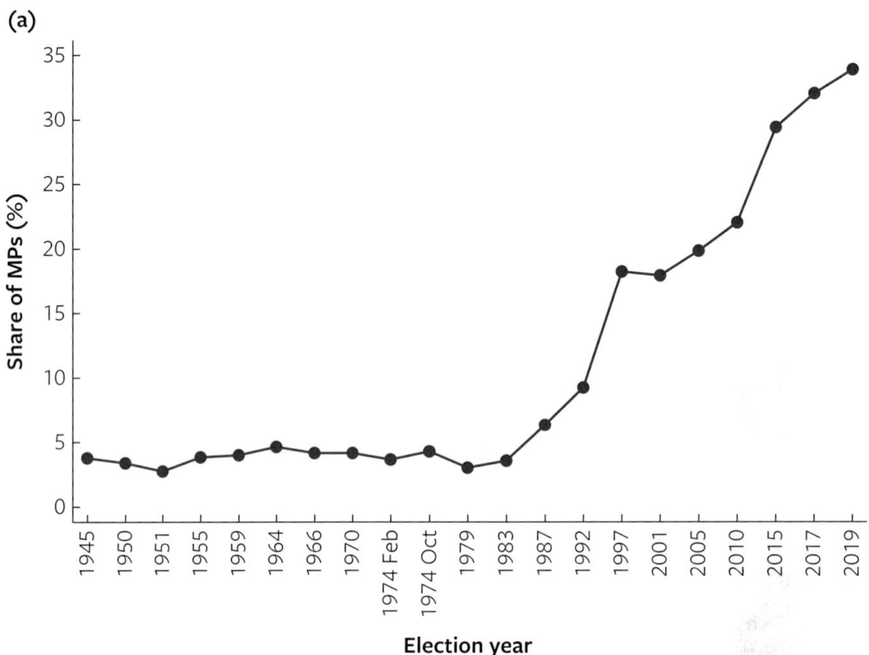

Figure 3.4a Share of female-identifying MPs in Parliament, 1945–2019.
Source: Audickas et al. (2020, 28)

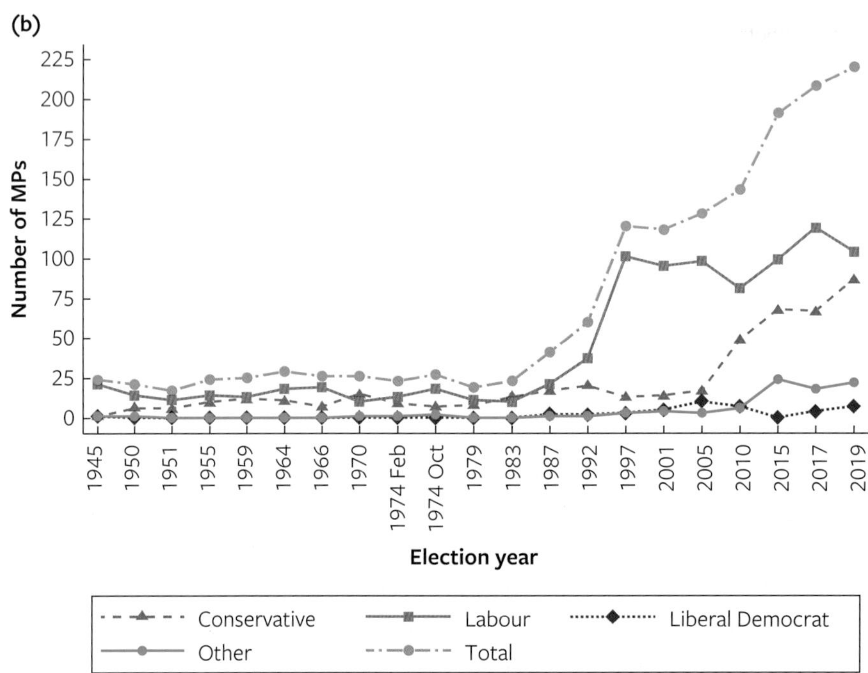

Figure 3.4b Numbers of female-identifying MPs in Parliament, 1945–2019, by party.
Source: Audickas et al. (2020, 28)

Photo 3.2 Diane Abbott was the first Black woman elected to Parliament, and is the longest-serving Black MP in the House of Commons.

are underrepresented by four percentage points when compared to the general population. It is important to recognize that these communities are very different from each other in terms of the makeup of the UK population (which is one of the reasons BAME terminology is sometimes hard to use).

The political parties have paid attention to ethnic minority recruitment (see Figure 3.5b). Labour has been successful in urban ethnically diverse areas in recent years, such as Dawn Butler, MP for Brent South and Brent Central, and Kim Johnson, MP for Liverpool Riverside. The Conservative Party has had some recent success, often in constituencies with largely white populations, such as Darren Henry, MP for Broxtowe. Quotas are not lawful in this area, limiting what political parties can mandate in terms of representation.

3.6.4 Social class

Another dimension to representation is social class. Researchers used to pay a great deal of attention to the class background of MPs (Mellors 1978), a concern that has recently re-emerged (Allen 2018). Class is usually taken to be the social divisions identified by the early twentieth-century sociologist Max Weber, who defined social class as the agglomeration of wealth, status, and power (Weber 1978, 302–10), which systematically varies across society. Class divisions in the past were linked to the support and membership of political parties, with Labour representing the working class (unskilled, skilled, and semi-skilled occupations, and other deprived groups), and the Conservatives representing the upper and middle

3

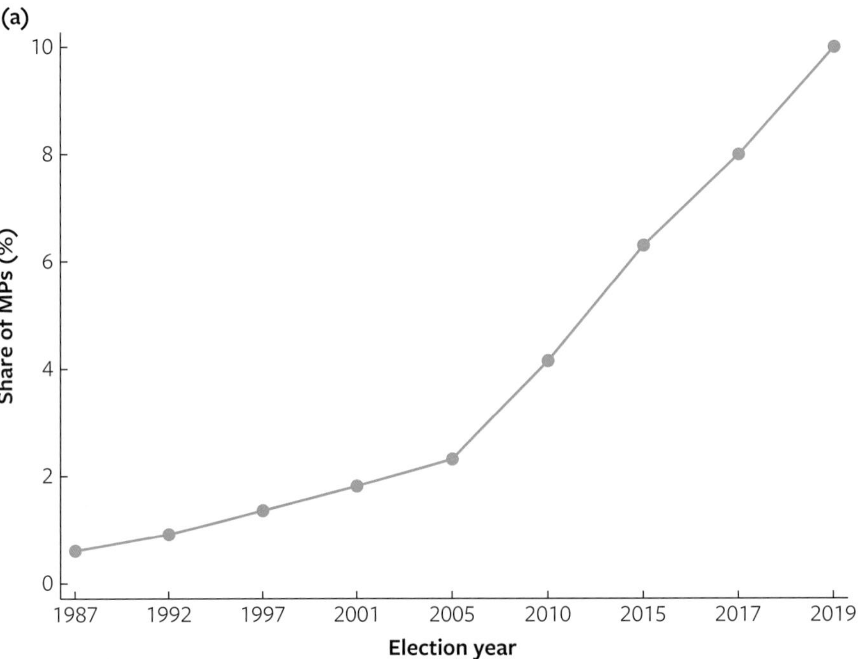

Figure 3.5a Share of ethnic minority MPs, 1987–2019.
Source: Audickas et al. (2020, 28)

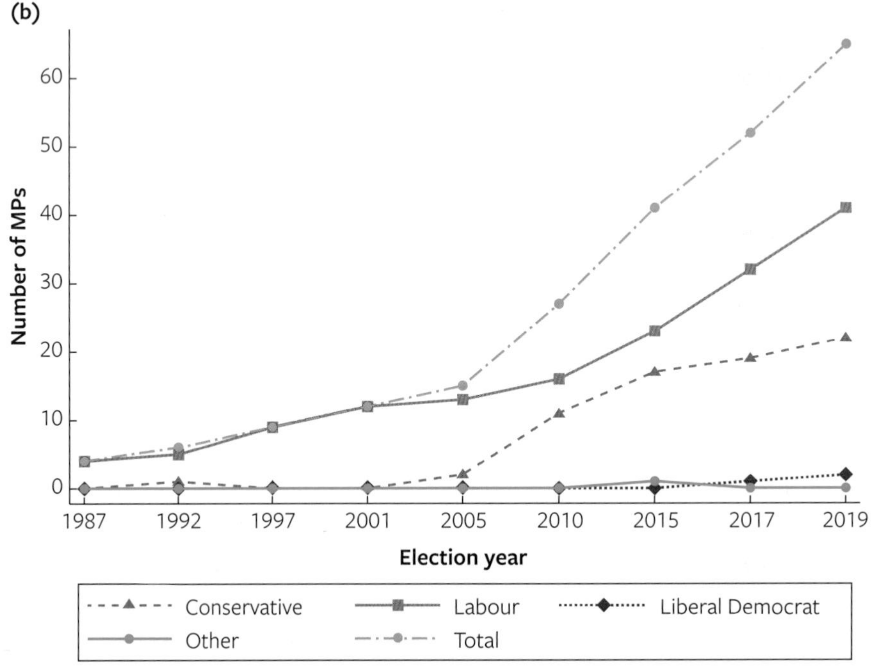

Figure 3.5b Numbers of ethnic minority MPs, 1987–2019, by party.
Source: Audickas et al. (2020, 28)

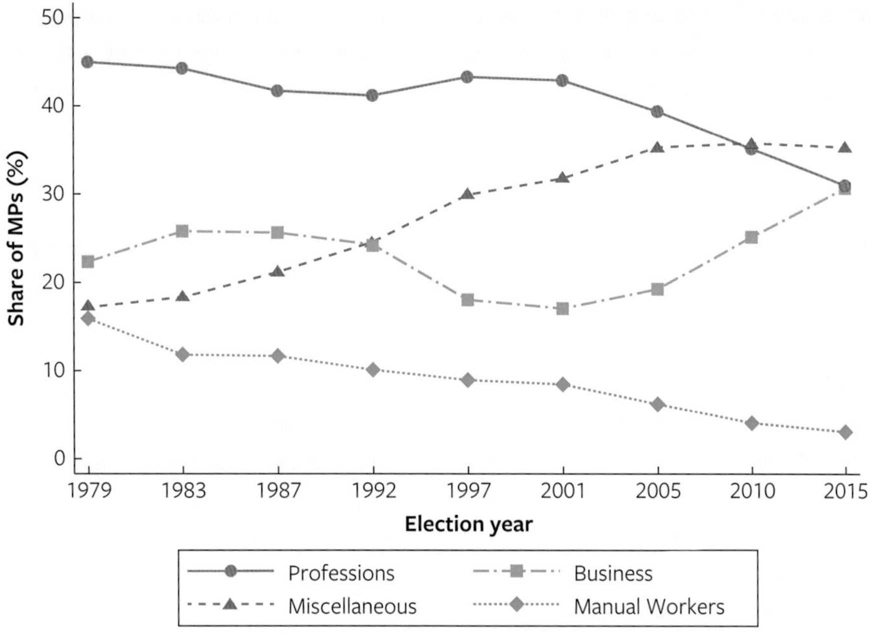

Figure 3.6 MP occupations, 1979–2015.

Source: Audickas et al. (2020, 28)

Note: *data up to 2015 include only Labour, Conservative, and Liberal MPs, while data from 2015 include these three parties plus Scottish Nationalists*

classes, but needing to forge a cross-class coalition to get elected (see sections 4.7 and 5.3.2). In the past, Labour helped bring into politics working-class MPs, often through sponsorship. But such representation has declined. In 1951, 37 per cent of Labour MPs came from working-class occupations; by 2015 that number had decreased to 7 per cent (Heath 2016, 306). Figure 3.6 maps recent trends. They reflect a reduction in the size of the working class, declining trade union membership, and a more general trend for MPs to enter politics in order to have a professional career, perhaps having been exposed to party politics at university, rather than having a career in an occupation and then coming into politics (King 1981). The middle classes have tended to become more important in local Labour parties, first identified by the political sociologist Barry Hindess (1971) in Liverpool in the 1960s. Bale (2017) shows 77 per cent of Labour members fall into the ABC1 (middle-class) category.

3.6.5 Analysis of descriptive representation of candidates and MPs

Representation reflects social factors and the experience of discrimination, which is reinforced in the media and family roles, and sustained by other institutions in society, such as workplaces, schools, and government institutions. As more progressive ideas and tolerance diffuse across society, and government policies are implemented to address forms of inequality, these biases should reduce. By this argument, Parliament's representation should in the long term reflect these more general trends in society.

But there are special features of a political career that need to be considered, relating to the costs and risk of being in politics; moreover, groups with fewer resources may find it difficult getting started in a political career (Lawless 2012). Recruitment is also dependent on decisions to select candidates by political parties, which tend to be quite autonomous, and local party members may wish to apply a range of personal criteria to candidate selection. Political party central organizations have tried a range of measures, such as AWS, to improve representation, which usually improve gender representation to some extent (Ashe et al. 2010). The other factor affecting representation in the House of Commons and English local government is the electoral system, which may encourage constituency selection committees to focus on one candidate who they believe reaches across many social groups. Indeed, there are a larger number of female-identifying candidates in electoral contests outside the House of Commons, such as the Scottish Parliament and Senedd Cymru; but it is not clear whether it is the different electoral systems that affect this, or whether more candidates come forward, or are promoted by political parties at these levels, or a combination of these factors (Evans and Harrison 2012). For example, Wales saw twenty-five female-identifying members elected in 2016—41.7 per cent. Table 3.2 shows the figures from Scottish Parliament and Welsh Assembly elections since 1999. The decline in Wales is because political parties stopped using positive action, such as AWS, which had been used to select candidates in the early elections (Brooks and Gareth 2016, 6). This points to commitments within the political parties as the crucial factor in encouraging female-identifying candidates to stand for election. The international evidence also supports this conclusion (Hughes and Paxton 2016).

3.6.6 The impact of descriptive representation

A lack of descriptive representation affects how the House of Commons works, such as the subjects that are debated and who gets to speak. It may create a culture that can shape the agenda of Parliament and, by implication, the policies that come out of government. In this way, descriptive representation affects other forms of representation, both substantive and symbolic.

For female and non-binary MPs, there is some evidence that they concentrate on different issues to cisgender male MPs, traditionally termed 'female issues', such as violence against women and access to childcare (Campbell and Childs 2015). There is a danger of 'female issues' bias, as female and non-binary MPs may get encouraged to talk more about 'women's issues' and then not input into other issues (Catalano 2009). As a result, female and non-binary people may

Table 3.2 Female-identifying MSPs (Members of the Scottish Parliament) in the Scottish Parliament and MSs (Members of the Welsh Senedd) in the Welsh assembly/Senedd Cymru, 1999–2021
Sources: Breitenbach (2020, 22); Brooks and Gareth (2016, 15); BBC News Scotland: www.bbc.com/news/uk-scotland-scotland-politics-57,047,370

Wales Online: www.walesonline.co.uk/news/politics/full-list-wales-60-members-20,532,580

Year of election	**1999**	**2003**	**2007**	**2011**	**2016**	**2021**
No. of female-identifying MSPs	48	51	43	45	45	58
Proportion of female-identifying MSPs	37%	40%	33%	35%	35%	45%
No. of female-identifying MSs	24	30	31	25	25	26
Proportion of female-identifying MSs	40%	50%	52%	42%	42%	43%

get side-lined into what are considered to be 'less important' portfolios, such as ministerial posts that are associated with 'women's issues', for example welfare (Krook and O'Brien 2012).

Other evidence that female-identifying and non-binary politicians advance more slowly in their careers because of the 'glass ceiling' effect is less clear. The term 'glass ceiling' is used to represent the invisible barrier to success that women, non-binary people, and those of ethnic minority backgrounds face in the workplace. However, one study shows that once women enter the Commons, they proceed up their careers at the same rate as men (Vannoni and John 2018). Another study finds that the presence of female-identifying ministers stimulated other women parliamentarians to participate in debates, speaking about 20 per cent more often, which is indicative of a gradual change in culture (Blumenau 2019). It may be the case that long-term change takes decades to unfold. Over time, shifts in perception have occurred, so that previously siloed 'female issues' have entered the mainstream, with all legislators addressing 'women's issues' more often, reflecting the international pattern (for example, Switzerland; Höhmann 2020). Other studies of the impact of increasing women's representation show resistance and sometimes backlash, as in in the US and New Zealand, as well as progress (O'Brien and Piscopo 2019). It continues to be an open question as to whether increases in the proportion of female-identifying MPs, especially if they move up towards 50 per cent of members, will cause significant cultural and institutional changes. Many of the traditional practices that put women off participating in politics have not receded (for a review, see Campbell, Childs, and Hunt 2018). Internationally, there is evidence that a critical mass of female-identifying MPs can make a difference (Childs and Mona 2008), such as in Scandinavian countries (Dahlerup 1988), though one study shows there is not necessarily a relationship between representation and changes in institutions and policies (Studlar and McAllister 2002). It may be more important that women and non-binary people are in place in key positions of power in legislatures, as critical actors, rather than simply making up a raw number of legislators (Childs and Krook 2009). That there are also more UK cabinet members who are female-identifying (see Figure 2.2) could also be an important factor.

3.6.7 **Ethnic minority representation**

Evidence of the impact of ethnic-minority citizens in the UK Parliament is not conclusive internationally. Moreover, the numbers of ethnic minority MPs in the UK are too small to make strong generalizations. It appears that Black MPs have been successful in keeping minority issues on the parliamentary agenda (Nixon 1998; Saalfeld and Kyriakopoulou 2010). For example, from looking at 16,000 parliamentary questions, Saalfeld (2011) finds that immigrant-background MPs tend to ask about more ethnic diversity and equality issues. Overall, they contribute to the more deliberative side of parliamentary business, but at the same time some of these MPs wish to perceive themselves as part of the general task of being a representative, rather than purely defined by their background, and still believe they need to represent all groups in their constituencies (Saalfeld and Kyriakopoulou 2010). Linked to this point, Black MPs are more likely to ask about the problems and rights of minorities and about immigration if they represent communities that have those constituents, which could be based on electoral factors.

3.6.8 **Working-class alienation**

Lack of representation has been argued to have alienated sections of working-class people, which may have led to lower voter turnout (Heath 2016). Heath tests for a variety of explanations of declining turnout in working-class constituencies, though these conclusions are drawn from analysis of surveys of attitudes and party positions, rather than inferring a direct change between MPs' representativeness and differences in behaviour. Working-class voters tend to give more positive evaluations to working-class representatives, as has been shown in experiments (Key term 3.6) using surveys (Vivyan et al. 2020). The change in representation may have contributed to the loss of working-class support for Labour since 1997, which has been observed in studies by Evans and Tilley (2017), and which will be discussed further in section 4.7.1.

The other impact is on the behaviour of MPs, which might have electoral consequences. Whereas earlier research showed no difference in the attitudes of MPs according to social class (Norris and Lovenduski 1995), more recent studies demonstrate differences in observed behaviour. A study by O'Grady (2019) highlights that the decline of working-class representation in Parliament is associated with MPs not supporting policies that favour the interests of the working classes. O'Grady looks at speeches by MPs about welfare policies, then examines the change over time for the impact on representation.

Overall, descriptive representation matters, showing the importance of making Parliament more representative of the population as a whole. But it is important to take account of other elements of this debate, which come out in the discussion of ethnic minority MPs. We can also examine how MPs with minority-ethnic backgrounds reach out to other constituents, and how non-minority MPs respond to different kinds of constituents. In the US, there is considerable evidence from doing experiments sending 'fake' emails to state legislators that they were more likely to respond to co-ethnic constituents, therefore reinforcing inequalities (Butler 2014). In an experiment carried out by writing to House of Commons MPs, Habel and Birch (2019) find MPs do not exhibit such strong differential responses, with MPs less likely to respond to a person who is both working class and a specific ethnicity rather than these two categories on their own.

Key term 3.6 Experiment

In the social sciences, an experiment refers to where random assignment or its equivalent determines the allocation of an intervention, so as to establish a counterfactual (see Key term 3.5). It can be a randomized controlled trial, where the allocation is carried out by the researcher, or a natural experiment where randomness occurs in the world. Experiments can establish causation (see Key term 6.4).

Overall, the pattern seems weaker than the US, and there is a more equal responsiveness to constituents in the UK illustrated by this study.

3.6.9 **Home-style politicians?**

The UK was thought to differ from other political systems, such as the US, where representatives have much more freedom to act and more power, and where voting patterns create an incentive to benefit constituents in their home constituency (Cain, Ferejohn, and Fiorina 1984). In the US members of Congress have a personal vote, relying on a reputation as a 'home-style' politician (for the use of this term, see Fenno 1978). In fact, there has been a personal dimension to what UK MPs do in order to build a good reputation, which was acknowledged in the classic studies (Searing 1994). The personal vote in the UK has increased since the 1980s (Wood and Norton 1992), with local campaigning also having an effect (Pattie, Johnston, and Fieldhouse 1995; Pattie, Hartman, and Johnston 2017). Following on from Cain et al.'s (1984) comparison with the US, Wood and Norton (1992) carried out a study of UK representation which found that constituency links had increased as MPs have become more career orientated. It matters for them to build up a personal following. The public notice when MPs rebel and get an electoral benefit (Campbell et al. 2019). Citizens also appreciate the work politicians do for their constituents in terms of mentioning the constituency in Parliament, and those who know their MP's name typically trust them more (McKay 2020). MPs behave differently when their electoral margins are close, for fear of not getting re-elected. They tend to ask more parliamentary questions, with MPs from vulnerable seats asking 15 per cent more questions in the 1997–2010 period (Kellermann 2016). They also make greater use of early day motions (see Key term 3.7) (Kellermann 2013). MPs who are given the opportunity to present a private members' bill in the House of Commons get an electoral boost (Bowler 2010). In this way, MPs can ensure there is bias in favour of incumbency, but by comparative standards this advantage has been quite modest for Labour and Conservative MPs: about 1 to 2 percentage points in the 1983–2010 period (Smith 2013).

3.6.10 **Territorial representation**

The local connection alerts us to the territorial dimension to representation. MPs represent local areas, and will seek to ask questions about their constituency, such as in parliamentary questions (though in practice PMQs are dominated by national issues and what is important in public opinion (Bevan and John 2016)). The local focus can be enhanced if the candidate is from the local area, and there is some evidence that voters prefer candidates with local origins (see Childs and Cowley 2011). Survey experiments (Campbell and Cowley 2014) show that voters exhibit stronger preferences for occupation and place of residence than for sex, age, religion, and education. By analysing a two-wave survey, Evans et al. (2017) find that distance from the voter and the candidate in terms of miles from local area matters for the personal vote.

Key term 3.7 Early day motions (EDMs)

A procedure available to MPs in the Commons. They are a written proposal designed to highlight an issue, event, or campaign. Other MPs may add their signature to the EDM to show their support. For example, Layla Moran tabled 'Humanitarian crisis in Yemen and UK arms sales to Saudi Arabia' on 13 April 2021, which received twenty-four signatures.

MPs also represent larger spaces, such as English regions and nations, and MPs will seek to represent a large city and its regions. MPs will have connections in local government, and some of them may have served as local leaders or councillors. As devolution has progressed (see Chapter 9), MPs have adjusted to national representation by working with devolved institutions, though they will forward constituency matters of the devolved institution to relevant politicians, such as the Members of the Scottish Parliament (MSPs), for example (Russell and Bradbury 2007). The greater number of MPs from the Scottish National Party (SNP) and Plaid Cymru in the House of Commons means that there is coordination between what the party wants in the devolved territory and in the UK Parliament. Like the UK state as a whole (Bradbury 2021b, 274–75), the House of Commons has not been very good at dealing with territorial concerns at the higher levels than the constituency, especially in England, though there was Scottish legislation and committees, and now a means of coordinating business between the Parliaments. There are select committees for Scotland, Wales, and Northern Ireland and grand committees for Scotland and Wales. There was a brief experiment during the Gordon Brown government of having committees for each of the regions of England, which was later abandoned by David Cameron. In the 2010–15 Parliament measures were set out to deal with England-only business to manage

Key term 3.8 West Lothian question

A term associated with the former MP for West Lothian, Tam Dalyell. Argument that there is a constitutional inconsistency between Scottish (and other devolved nations) MPs voting on English-only legislation while England MPs do not vote on devolved matters. Does not occur if the same powers are devolved to regions across the whole of the UK.

what has been called the 'West Lothian' question (see Key term 3.8), so that Scottish MPs could not vote at the committee stage on English legislation.

3.6.11 **Law-making and debating politics in the rest of the UK**

The territorial dimension to the work of MPs is an important reminder of the extensive delegation of law-making functions to the devolved territories/nations of Scotland, Wales, and Northern Ireland, which will be explored fully in Chapter 9, but can be considered here as these Parliaments increase in scope, and also where there is conflict between representation by different kinds of representatives, such as MSPs (Shephard and Carman 2007; Lundberg 2014). Many of the same arguments appear about the extent of executive dominance in devolved legislatures, such as the role of MSPs over amendments in the period of devolution up to 2015, showing the dominance of ministers (Shephard and Cairney 2005). In the Scottish Parliament, there was much hope of a 'new politics', which involves a more constructive and cooperative relationship between executive and Parliament, and within Parliament itself, with a stronger role for committees (Arter 2004). There has been scepticism as to whether this new politics has actually come about (Mitchell 2000; McMillan 2020), while Shephard and Cairney's research offers some support for a more cooperative executive–legislative relationship. The constituency role of representatives in Scotland and Wales has been developing given different roles bestowed by the electoral system (Russell and Bradbury 2007). The issue of divergent views between voters and representatives has also been researched, such as for members of the Senedd Cymru (Trumm 2018).

Across the whole of the UK, there are local authorities, which have their own chambers for discussing policies, budgets, and the local equivalent of laws and regulations, given to locally elected councillors, though here the executive (often the local authority cabinet) has much more control than at other levels of government, with little role for elected representatives who are not cabinet members (Gains, John, and Stoker 2005).

3.6.12 **Qualitative studies**

The stereotype of passive backbench MPs, who are thought not to have an incentive to voice and act independently, does not apply in British politics, and probably never did. As well as voting or threatening to vote against the party line (see section 3.5.1), there are opportunities to participate in Parliament by speaking in debates, asking parliamentary or prime ministerial parliamentary questions, working on select committees, or introducing a private members' bill if they win a ballot. The whole point of having a single constituency is for an MP to have a direct relationship to constituents, but there are other interests to balance too. The complexity of this role is shown by a study of representation in *Westminster World* by Donald Searing (1994), which illustrates MPs' roles as policy advocates, ministerial aspirants, parliamentary animals, and constituency representatives.

Searing takes the qualitative route to understanding MPs by interviewing them—work he repeated some thirty years later, interviewing surviving MPs to find that their values have not changed much (Searing, Jacoby, and Tyner 2019). Other studies use the vast amount of data that has appeared in recent years, such as the corpus of Hansard, to understand how MPs use speech to represent themselves for groups of constituents, examined in section 3.6.13.

3.6.13 **Roll call studies**

More common are quantitative studies. In the US, scholars have sought to classify the votes of each member of Congress from what are called 'roll-calls', according to a scale from left to right ideologically, with each member placed somewhere along it. A roll call is a US term for votes by legislators on bills, counting which way they voted. Statistical work (called ideal point estimation) shows whether representatives have become more polarized and more distant to the average North American voter (McCarty, Poole, and Rosenthal 2016). Because UK MPs vote on party lines, it has been very hard trying to map the House of Commons in this way as the method needs some variation between MPs. Early attempts were unsuccessful (Spirling and McLean 2006). Some authors have tried to use other activities carried out by MPs to generate estimates, such as early day motions (Key term 3.7) (Kellermann 2012), but it is hard to generalize to the whole of MP behaviour in this way. It has been possible to use these data to see if MPs behave close to the views of their constituents, which is a crucial question going back to Miller and Stokes (1963), who argued that representatives are responsive to their local voters. By linking public opinion in each constituency, and testing with early day motions and 'free' votes, research by Chris Hanretty and colleagues shows MPs moderately responding to changes in public opinion in a constituency (Hanretty, Lauderdale, and Vivyan 2017). It is possible to tie different data sources together to examine this question, for example by finding out from an MP's personal website whether they have a personal approach to representation, rather than just conveying the party's approach (Pedersen and vanHeerde-Hudson 2019).

Scholars have used large datasets to identify the voting blocs in the House of Commons (Spirling and Quinn 2010). Other work on speeches deploying advanced methods (Goet 2019) examines large ranges of debates to track patterns of change over time, understand procedure changes, and uncover the extent of polarization (Goet, Fleming, and Zubek 2020). These papers yield a simple conclusion: the more positive tone of debates in recent years in terms of language used is predicted by the positive state of the national economy on average (Rheault et al. 2016).

3.7 Law-making and judges

So far, this chapter has covered law-making by parliamentarians, which is a key aspect of British politics; but law-making and debate do not stop there. Law-making, and by implication policy-making, happens when the legislation or the actions of government are tested in the courts. When a law is passed, a litigant may wish to challenge the government or other organization, and the courts are an institution designed to resolve these disputes. There is a formal process of appeal and the representation of sides to the legal case, making arguments to try to ensure their side wins in the adjudication. The case is heard by judges who are appointed and who can make a ruling (if there is no jury, as is usually the case with

3

Photo 3.3 The exterior of the Supreme Court building on Parliament Square, Westminster. The Supreme Court is the highest court in the United Kingdom legal system.

political or policy decisions). Cases may also emerge through the system of administrative and constitutional law run by county courts or tribunals and other bodies, but they can raise matters of law which can be appealed, and these cases can appear in the High Court. They can then be appealed to the Court of Appeal, and then on to the Supreme Court (Photo 3.3), composed of twelve judges who then rule on a case, which is the final decision in the UK (see Figure 3.7). It is fundamental to the doctrine of the rule of law that courts are independent from the executive and that governments accept the rulings.

In the British system, the doctrine of parliamentary sovereignty means that the courts are supposed to interpret the will of Parliament (not the government) in the language of the statute and other relevant supporting documents. If the government has a majority in the House of Commons, it can then seek to change the law if does not like a ruling, but would need to get its change through the whole parliamentary process, in particular the House of Lords. Given that there is no codified constitution, the role of the courts is to interpret the meaning of the statute. Overall, this set-up in the past led to the courts being believed to be relatively passive in the face of executive power, focusing on the letter of the law to ensure powers had been drafted correctly and consistently, and ensuring that fair procedures had been followed (Marshall 1971).

An alternative view is that the courts are more active. As a result, they have been targets of left-wing criticism (Griffith 1997). More mainstream accounts of judicial decision-making also demonstrate that judges are forced to make political choices as they need to choose sides on a case (Bell 1985). The argument is that there is usually discretion over the interpretation of the statute, which means that a judge can choose

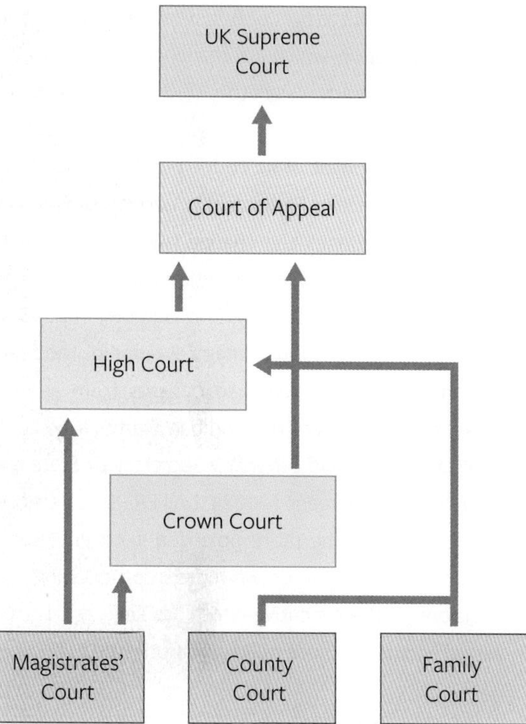

Figure 3.7 Structure of the court system (relating to England).
Source: Adapted from judiciary.uk: www.judiciary.uk/wp-content/uploads/2020/08/courts-structure-0715.pdf

an interpretation that favours a prior viewpoint. In any case, judges will hear learned arguments by advocates, so when the decision reaches the highest court it is likely to be finely balanced and also legally defensible. Because of the role of precedent, future cases use past cases as a guide to their decisions, then these decisions become judge-made law which then guides the actions of public authorities and the rights of citizens, until the law is changed again by Parliament or another court case. As well as interpreting statutes, judges can apply what is called the common law, which is legal doctrines that have been handed down by courts over generations, such as the doctrine of reasonableness that decisions need to be based on matters that are relevant or natural justice that relevant groups have been consulted. These common law principles can be interpreted in different ways so offer an opportunity to increase the range of decisions that are reviewed by the courts.

Judges have been more inclined to use common law principles and interpret statutes more broadly, as part of a more assertive approach to decision-making happening since the 1960s. This is called judicial activism, which is an international phenomenon (Sweet 2000),

Case Study 3.3 *R (Miller) v Secretary of State for Exiting the EU* (2017)

The courts questioned the government's decision to trigger article 50 of the Treaty of the European Union that permits a country to exit the union. The decision in the Supreme Court case *R (Miller) v Secretary of State for Exiting the European Union* (2017) UKSC 5 required the government to put a vote to the UK Parliament to leave the European Union. In a judgment that referred to the classic jurists from the seventeenth century, such as Edward Coker, the case involved a detailed consideration of the legislation and principle involved.

The right-wing press saw it as the imposition of judge-made law. The *Daily Mail* ran the headline, 'Enemies of the People', with pictures of the judges on the front page, which caused a lot of controversy (Rosenberg 2020). But it could be said that the courts were simply applying a basic principle of parliamentary sovereignty that a fundamental change in UK law would need to be authorized by Parliament. It did not stop Theresa May's government putting article 50 to Parliament and winning the vote on 7 March 2017.

associated with the growth of rights-based arguments in public life. A further argument is that creation of the Supreme Court in the UK in 2009 (which replaced what appeared to be an anachronism in that the highest court of appeal was a committee of the legislature, the House of Lords, which seemed to breach the key idea in the separation of powers) may have given the judges a great sense of independence, even though the formal powers and fundamental role of the court were unchanged. The legislation that set up the court formalized the appointment process of Supreme Court judges and also ensured the Lord Chancellor (a cabinet minister) was not the formal head of the judiciary.

A more important development for understanding judicial activism is the incorporation of human rights law into British law from 1998, which meant that judges could directly interpret European Court of Human Rights judgments as part of British law, which may give more basis upon which to challenge the executive. The UK was already a signatory to the European Convention on Human Rights, so was already obliged to follow the judgment of its court, but this took a long time to take place as Parliament needed to change the law. Now the judges can change law made in Parliament by referring to the convention and judgments of the European court directly. For example, in 2003, a court decision questioned the provisions of the then Nationality Act that removed benefits from asylum seekers as a breach of their human rights (*R (on the application of Q and others) v Secretary of State for the Home Department* (2003) 2 All ER 90.). Because politics has become more polarized in recent years, the courts have been drawn more into reviewing the decisions of the executive which are seen as controversial and hence more politically motivated.

Photo 3.4 Judicial activism is the philosophy that justices should use their position to promote desirable social outcomes from their rulings.

As illustrated by these examples, it is often thought that there is now more judge-made law in the UK, and that judicial discretion reflects the underlying political preferences of the judges (Ewing 2009), but it is hard to prove the latter point without looking into the minds of judges as the legal text alone cannot alone settle the point. There is some indication from looking at quantitative judicial decisions using ideal point estimation (see section 3.6.13) that judges are arrayed on a continuum of policy preferences (Hanretty 2013). Another quantitative study shows that litigants are not favoured systematically, with the government side tending to win cases overall (Hanretty 2014). The conclusion to draw is that judges tend to be cautious in getting involved in UK politics, given the constitutional primacy of Parliament and its relationship to elected government, and the absence of a constitutional document that defines a legitimate role for the courts in making controversial policy-related decisions, so judges have tried to avoid being seen to be political and opposed to government (Dickson 2015). Often judicial activism is followed by more passive periods of bedding down judgments. The ability of Parliament to change the law, except about matters relating to the European Convention on Human Rights and international treaty obligations, means that the executive retains the ability to correct any imbalance, which also reduces the incentive to challenge government too often. The courts do play a political role, but limit themselves from getting involved too much.

3.8 Conclusion

This ends the introduction to how laws are debated and made, and more generally how elected representatives affect the agenda and outcomes of politics. The account is still influenced by the Westminster system of government, whereby the executive in the form of the government is sustained in power by having a majority in the House of Commons. It then seeks to govern through the UK Parliament by using its majority to get laws passed and to ensure the reputation of the government is intact and survives scrutiny. This fusion of executive and legislative power inevitability squeezes out some of the autonomy of the legislature to act through control over the parliamentary timetable and the need to get government business through in good time. But it is wrong to see the UK Parliament as passive, partly because it retains primacy in legitimate policy-making, so it is always the reference point for decision-making; it needs to be reported to; and the government structures its activities around parliamentary authorization. This is the argument behind what Judge (1993) calls the parliamentary state. Given the diversity of politics and the difficulty of exercising control from the prime minister, diverse factions within Parliament will have their say even if it is behind the scenes, though today it is increasingly in the open. Revisionists, such as Norton, then Cowley and Russell, question the standard view, and stress the importance of the power of Parliament and the recent changes of more rebellions, the greater role for select committees, and an enhanced influence of the Lords. These changes may be thought to derive from wider changes in British politics, pointing to less stability in party control, which makes it harder to exercise executive control. However, just because there are massive changes does not mean the system has fundamentally changed out of recognition. Governments still govern; they seek majorities which they more often than not get; they have policy programmes; and they get most of their business through Parliament. To a certain extent, MPs and Lords exercise influence within this system of executive dominance that gives structure to politics, partly because there is no overt constitutional set-up to generate an alternative form of influence. When the system appeared to fall apart in the period when Theresa May's government did not have a majority, policy-making hardly worked at all and British politics became directionless rather than showing a resurgent legislature. As soon as Boris Johnson got a majority for the Conservative Party after the general election in December 2019, political routines appeared to return to the standard pattern, at least for a while.

The question of parliamentary power and influence is a subtle one to grasp, though there are some clear conclusions. It is also the same with representation, partly because of the complexity of the concept. Parliament can be critiqued for a lack of descriptive representation, though there have been improvements in recent years in favour of women, non-binary people, and ethnic minority communities. Representatives embody other forms of representation, and there are subtleties in how these roles emerge, and now there are more opportunities for parliamentarians to represent diverse interests.

Further reading

A good place to start is one of the many books written by Philip Norton (for example, Norton 2013) and a review by Alex Kelso (2009). There is also a lot of relevant material in a recent Oxford University Press volume, *Exploring Parliament* (Leston-Bandeira and Thompson 2018).

In terms of getting into the power of Parliament debate, the Russell–Cowley piece (and the papers that feed into it) can be read directly as it reviews the debate, summarizes the facts and evidence, and conveys their point of view (Russell and Cowley 2016; Russell, Gover, and Wollter 2016). From these papers, further more detailed materials can be read, such as on select committees (Mellows-Facer, Challender, and Evans 2019; Geddes 2019), and the House of Lords, including Meg Russell's (2013) book. There is a growing amount of work on subcentral Parliaments in articles by James Mitchell, Paul Cairney, Jonathan Bradbury, and Mark Shephard (for example, Shephard and Cairney 2005; Russell and Bradbury 2007; Bradbury and Mitchell 2007).

For representation, one title is Judge and Leston-Bandeira (2018). A more general volume on women and representation is Lovenduski's *Feminizing Politics* (2005); also see Paxton and Barnes (2020). There are a number of papers on women. There is literature on women (Childs 2008; Campbell, Childs, and Hunt 2018), ethnic minorities (Saalfeld and Kyriakopoulou 2010), and social class (O'Grady 2019). There are more technical pieces on MP responsiveness (e.g. Hanretty, Lauderdale, and Vivyan 2017).

Essay and examination questions

One question might be about the power of Parliament which can cover the debate in this chapter, with an answer that reviews different positions, taking Russell and Cowley (2016) as the starting point. The article has some quotable sentences that can be used to frame the question such as 'Westminster is more influential than is widely believed' (Russell and Cowley 2016, 121). Other questions may be asked more directly about the influence of select committees and the House of Lords, or about the impact of backbench rebellions. Or it may be possible to frame a question comparing representation across the Parliaments of the UK.

Representation can be explored with 'How effective is the UK Parliament at representation?'. The essay might be targeted to MPs more specifically, such as 'Discuss the role MPs play in representing constituents'. Taking all the themes of the chapter, it might be possible to ask a more general question, such as 'Is Parliament fit for purpose?', where an answer could review scrutiny of the executive, the role of the House of Lords, and the quality of representation.

Access the online resources for this chapter, including biannual updates, web links, and multiple-choice questions: www.oup.com/he/John1e

Part B

Political Behaviour and Citizenship

The next part of the book, unfolding over the next three chapters, is primarily about political behaviour, which concerns how individuals and groups take action (or inaction) in a political system. Behaviour includes citizens acting on their own, for example complaining to a public official, and also how they organize themselves collectively to influence politics, as in political parties and interest groups, voting in elections, or petitioning the government or another public authority. As well as describing and measuring political behaviour, scholars seek to explain what influences these political actions (or non-actions) in terms of citizen demographics (e.g. gender, age), attitudes/values (e.g. left–right), and incentives (e.g. chance of influencing an outcome), which can help us understand the underlying drivers of British politics.

Political behaviour is very much about what occurs outside the formal institutions of the central state (even if what people do is guided and constrained by state rules and conventions), so is designed to contrast with what was covered in Chapters 1 to 3. But it is also important to frame the topics of institutions, the constitution, and formal politics alongside that of the behaviour and attitudes of citizens, as both operate in close relation to each other. There are powerful influences of citizen beliefs and actions on the operation of political institutions, and of decision-making and the practice of politics more generally; then institutions and constitutions, and conduct of formal politics, have an impact on citizen attitudes and behaviours. There is thus an interactive relationship between those in office and citizens who experience politics but also influence it. In understanding how behaviour intersects with political institutions, a continuing theme in this book is addressed: how political institutions and actors holding formal roles interact, and even may stimulate, changes in political behaviour, as well as how citizen behaviour can deliver shocks to the political system (such as surprise election and referendum results). In this way, the following three chapters can help explain some of the political turbulence Britain has experienced since 2014.

In part, this task is about understanding causal relationships, as with an eco-system whereby one element of the system influences another. But such relationships are also about democracy: the responsiveness of government and governors to citizens as well as guidance and leadership from government so that citizens can respond to decisions made on their behalf (Powell 2000). Then politicians may seek to influence citizen views and behaviours for their own benefit, such as getting re-elected and/or successfully shifting blame for mistakes. This returns the discussion to the core question about representation, as discussed in Chapter 3, and relates to the quality of British democracy overall.

The first chapter (Chapter 4) in this part of the book is about the attitudes and core behaviours in British politics, covering what people think about politics, what influences their views, how much people get involved, and what causes changes over time. It ranges from basic attitudes, to beliefs on getting involved with politics, to voting and protest. Chapter 5 is about the relationship between participation and the party system, as affected by electoral systems, and factors that drive election victories and successes. Chapter 6 examines the role of the media, and how the agenda of politics and public policy is shaped, which can influence both citizens' attitudes and behaviour, and also the wider agenda of politicians and policy-makers at the same time.

Chapter 4

What People Think and Do about Politics

4

4.1 What is going to be in this chapter?

This chapter is designed to introduce citizen attitudes, values, cultures, and behaviours, which underpin the political system. Particularly important is voting for elected representatives (as discussed in section 3.6.9), whether MPs, Members of the Scottish Parliament (MSPs), Members of the Senedd (MSs), Members of the Northern Ireland Assembly (MLAs), directly elected mayors, police and crime commissioners (PCCs), local councillors, or even parish councillors. Then there are extensive forms of participation from citizens and groups, ranging from complaining to public authorities to protesting. Both voting and participation are linked to wider attitudes and beliefs about politics. This chapter is also a guide to understanding the different forms of turbulence that have emerged in recent years, in particular since 2014, with the arrival of populist movements, and the more frequent use of referendums. After reading this chapter, it is possible to understand recent changes in citizen attitudes and behaviours and how these have affected British politics.

4.2 Introduction

In an economically prosperous country, without recent experience of war or revolution, many UK citizens believe they are not primarily interested in formal or party politics. Crises happen, such as the big financial and economic crash of 2008 or the Covid-19 pandemic of 2020 and 2021, which increase people's worries about their futures, thereby drawing their attention to matters of politics, and to the words and deeds of politicians. But these periods often pass or become the 'new normal'. Most of the time, the overwhelming majority of people think they want to get on with what they see as the important things in their lives, which might include being part of a family, progressing in a career and/or getting gainful employment, pursuing leisure interests, such as sport, or travel, or music, or following their spiritual inclinations, which initially do not appear to be political. Formal politics is something most people would often consider to be distant from everyday life. Of course, there is a subset of people for whom conventional politics is the most important or one of the most important things in their lives, and members of political parties mix their personal lives with politics (see section 5.8.5 and Whiteley and Seyd 2002). This, however, is not the norm for most people.

Furthermore, people sometimes find party politics and media reporting of politics to be alienating, disliking the games played between the political parties, such as the cheers and jeers at Prime Minister's Questions (PMQs), which they do not see as relevant to their own lives (for a review of attitudes to politics, see Stoker 2016). As will be shown in section 4.4.10, this tendency to be antagonistic to conventional politics appears to have grown in recent years in a phenomenon called 'anti-politics', which is hostility to the practice of representative and party politics as a whole (see Stoker and Hay 2017). Anti-politics has big consequences for the business of politics and operation of government more generally. It is, however, wrong to say that people are completely turned off from politics. We can extend the definition of politics beyond matters of party politics to embrace collective issues, which includes many important matters in people's personal lives, such as climate change, pollution, access to good employment, equality in the family, and so on. The very things that appear to be private, such as family life and employment, are actually intrinsically political as they are the result of collective choices. People are more interested in what may be called 'small-p' politics, general issues that affect them, but are disengaged from formal party and electoral politics, at least most of the time (for young people, see Marsh, O'Toole, and Jones 2007). People are able sometimes to make links between what might seem to be 'local-level' worries, such as discrimination, car pollution in the streets, and the quality of treatment in the NHS to the very issues which are being hotly debated in the House of Commons. How people make these connections is at the core of understanding how democracy in Britain works (or, perhaps, does not work).

4.3 Basic facts: citizen attitudes and behaviours

As with other chapters, this section details the basic facts that everyone needs to know. It differs from previous chapters, where it was important to grasp the rules of how institutions work, which requires paying some attention to the minutiae and vagaries of the British constitution. Here are basic facts about citizen attitudes and behaviours, and some key concepts that come from political science and sociology that help build an understanding of public opinion and election data.

4.3.1 **Attitudes/values and political behaviour**

A foundational idea is that there is a difference between attitudes, values, and knowledge on the one hand, and actual political behaviour (like voting) on the other. Attitudes fall into various categories of politics. They may be citizen assessments of the quality of the political system, and of its representatives and political parties; they could be self-assessments of the capability citizens think they have to influence government, called efficacy (see Key term 4.1). There can also be basic values regarding the kinds of political and social outcomes which citizens see as desirable, such as left- or right-wing ideas, or pro-environmental and/or pro-rights issues. Values are more-deep seated, linked to morals and principles, whereas attitudes can change in response to what is happening in the outside world, such as a scandal in government, for example.

Key term 4.1 Efficacy

Influence citizens think they have over the political system, conventionally divided into *individual* efficacy, about their sense of personal influence, and *collective* efficacy, which is about the influence citizens think they have in general over the political system and its outputs.

4.3.2 **Political participation**

Behaviour is about acting in politics, like voting or being a member of an interest group. There are different kinds of participation, often divided up into what are thought to be conventional acts, like voting, and the

4

Photo 4.1 A polling station sign and the Union Jack flag.

more unconventional, such as protest (Barnes and Kaase 1979). The other way to understand participation is between high- and low-cost activities—ones that involve a lot of time and effort for individuals, and others that do not (de Rooij 2012)—with the implication being that high-cost acts might restrict the range of participation possible (see discussion about equality in section 4.5.1). In recent years, the range of participation acts has increased, such as participating in local public services like citizen forums or public consultations (John 2009). Some academics argue that new individualized forms of participation, such as boycotts of certain commercial products, have grown in importance since the 1970s (Pattie, Seyd, and Whiteley 2004). It is also possible to think of participation quite broadly, and include what one might think of as social activities, such as volunteering (be it in one's local community or internationally), which is political in the broad sense of the term because people are getting involved with activities that affect others collectively. The other aspect of participation to consider is that nearly all of it now takes place online (except voting), whether by e-mail, on websites, on apps, or through social media, which not only makes participation easier and more convenient, but also changes its nature to being more networked and focused on person-to-person communications happening in real time (see section 6.6). It is important to understand the full range of political acts, summarized in Table 4.1, classified broadly according to conventional or non-conventional forms of participation in the first two columns, and high and low cost in the last two columns.

4.3.3 The legal framework

People have rights to carry out certain activities, though there are limits to how they exercise them, for example if people break the law or behave in a way that damages national security when acting politically. There is a legal framework in place which governs political behaviour, so voting rights are set out in law, where it is determined who may vote. Furthermore, the conduct of elections is governed by a set of laws which are regulated by the Electoral Commission: the Boundary Commission for England, and equivalents for Northern Ireland, Scotland, and Wales, determine the size and borders of UK parliamentary constituencies. There are equivalent bodies for local government and associated elections. There is also a legislative framework for governing other political activities, such as donating money to political parties.

4.3.4 How attitudes/values link to behaviours

There is a link between attitudes/values and political acts, because people often need motivation to carry out the act, such as a sense of civic duty causing people to turn out to vote. If people do not trust politicians and believe the political system is unresponsive, they might be less likely to turn out to vote in elections (though sometimes discontent has the opposite effect of increasing voter turnout because people are angry and want to hold politicians to account). Sometimes the relationship is the reverse, and political behaviour causes attitudes (Quintelier and Deth 2014). For example, if someone turns out to vote because they have been mobilized in a Get Out the Vote (GOTV) campaign, they might be more likely to turn out to vote in subsequent elections because they have developed a habit of voting (Gerber, Green, and Shachar 2003; Cutts, Fieldhouse, and John 2009). Usually, the causal arrow points from attitudes to behaviour. Figure 4.1 shows this causal relationship, and also shows the influence of social background on both.

4.3.5 Sources of data

The other basic fact that is useful to know concerns citizen attitudes and behaviours. Systematically collected data are useful to be able to generalize across many types of people, either to the population of the United Kingdom as a whole, or to subgroups within it, such as people in a geographic area (for example, Scotland) or

Table 4.1 Types of political participation in Britain
Sources: Pattie et al. (2004); de Rooij (2012); John (2009)

	Conventional	Unconventional	High cost	Low cost
Vote in elections (parish, local, devolved, national)	X			X
Vote in referendums	X			X
Display campaign materials, e.g. sticker	X			X
Become a member of a political party	X		X	
Donate money to political/community cause (e.g. by SMS, #donate)	X			X
Become a member/supporter of an interest/interest pressure group	X		X	
Volunteer in the community		X	X	
Participate in public service consultation or deliberation		X	X	
Attend political meeting or webinar	X			X
Contact official	X		X	
Contact politician	X		X	
Sign e-petition		X		X
Interact with online information, e.g. subscribing, following, retweeting		X		X
Post/organize material online (e.g. Twitter, Snapchat)		X		X
Take part in a lawful demonstration		X	X	
Boycott or buy a product for ethical reasons		X		X

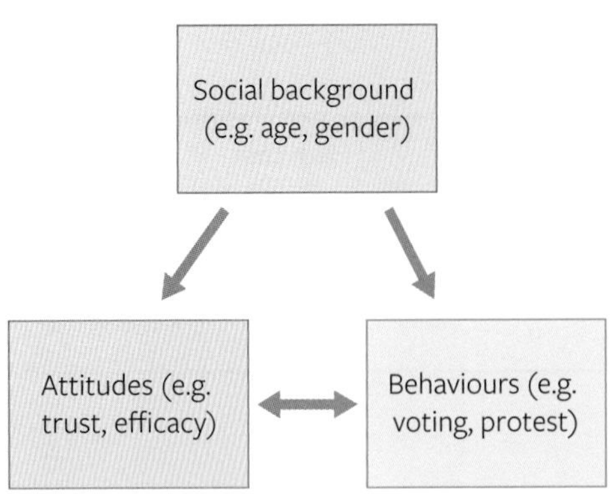

Figure 4.1 The relationships between social background, attitudes, and behaviours.

4

a particular ethnic group (e.g. Black Caribbean). Mass surveys are important, whereby a specialist company selects a sample that is representative of a population (such as all adults living in Britain), then asks respondents a set of questions that are either binary in response, or where the participant places their answer on a scale, such as the degree to which they support a political party or extent to which they consider themselves to be left or right wing. With sufficient sample size (say of about 2,000 people), the analysis of a survey allows for the presentation of figures that can be generalized from the sample to the population, such as the proportion who support a political party. Then it is possible to look for relationships within a survey, such as the proportion of working-class voters who vote for the Labour Party (see discussion of class voting in section 4.7.1). Many of the questions, such as about a person's identification with a political party (see section 4.4.7), have become standard, and so have been repeated many times in successive surveys which can then be compared, such as the regular British Election Study (BES) surveys (www.britishelectionstudy.com) and with the British Social Attitudes survey (www.bsa.natcen.ac.uk). This method becomes crucial in understanding whether public attitudes change over time, shedding light on potential recent changes in British politics. It is possible to access these data to create tables and figures, such as Figure 4.2, which is stored at the UK Data Service (https://ukdataservice.ac.uk). The Nesstar Catalogue (www.nesstar.ukdataservice.ac.uk) allows the presentation of tables from the survey directly and easily from the website. Survey companies, such as Ipsos-MORI (www.ipsos.com/ipsos-mori/en-uk), also carry out many surveys and report findings on their websites.

4.3.6 Methodological issues

When reading about attitudes and behaviour it is important to be aware that the data are collected using research methods, such as surveys and interviews, and it is important to be aware that these methods have both strengths and weaknesses. Surveys (and qualitative research) are important for recording political behaviour as it can be hard to find out from other data what people are doing, such as how many consumer boycotts there are. Real-world data such as votes for parties (aggregated) and voter turnout are important too, and some other data sources exist, such as members of political parties. These can be compared with figures produced in sample surveys, though they do not always give the same results. For example, people often overstate in surveys how much they vote in local elections, which is called 'social desirability bias', a common problem in survey research whereby respondents answer in the way they think they ought to rather than what they really think (Grimm 2010). Observed data should be treated carefully too as they may have gaps and be subject to different recording conventions. For example, how members of political parties are counted may depend on the definition of the party member, and also local party associations keeping effective records. Analysing aggregate data provides challenges as much of it is not tied to the individual, such as at district or constituency level. Finally, many researchers on political behaviour have been using new methods to find out about what influences behaviour, such as field experiments that randomize whether one group gets a treatment and the other not, and then assess the impact of the treatment by comparing the average outcome (e.g. voter turnout) in two groups (Key term 3.6). Field experiments can find out how campaigns can raise voter turnout (John 2017b), which have been carried out in the US (Green and Gerber 2019), and are also used in the UK to understand the mobilization of voter turnout, either from a non-partisan source (John and Brannan 2008, building on the pioneering work of Bochel and Denver 1971) or by political parties (Foos and John 2018). Then there are survey experiments, which have become ever more popular since Covid-19 made face-to-face research much harder to do. Here participants are recruited to carry out an online survey, often by a company such as Prolific (www.prolific.co), then randomized to get different pieces of information to test for impact on attitudes and intended behaviour (see egap.org, https://egap.org/resource/10-things-to-know-about-survey-experiments), which can be generalized to the population (Mutz 2011).

4.4 Attitudes and political values

4.4.1 **Political socialization**

In sizeable, wealthy countries like Britain, there are long-developed attitudes that citizens have acquired about formal politics, which are passed down the generations. These partly reflect historical events and transitions, but also the transfer of ideas about democracy, the impact of past struggles, such as for workers', women's, and migrants' rights, common experiences, such as war, and the survival of older attitudes, such as deference to elites and support for traditional social institutions. In the views of post-colonial thinkers, British politics has a particular set of social attitudes that come from a sense of self-importance based on prior history of empire (Rich 1990), which also negatively affects attitudes to new citizens (Sobolewska and Ford 2020, 85–118). Beliefs can survive to the present day, sustained by formal and informal institutions. Ideas about politics are transmitted through families, friendship networks, neighbours, workplaces, and schools, as people come into contact with others and exchange ideas, thereby influencing each other.

4.4.2 **The role of elites in transmitting values**

Attitudes and values can also come from elites, with classic works in political science (Zaller 1992) paying particular attention to these elite-driven attitudes. People's attitudes to politics are believed to be malleable, subject to influence and change, particularly because the political world is distant to most people, and citizens do not have a great deal of knowledge about it. Ideas and facts about politics cannot be corrected easily from everyday experience. Given favourable circumstances, such as external events highlighted in the media, elites may be able to convert underlying attitudes into more active forms of politics, such as protest and voting choices. For example, underlying attitudes to race can be stimulated by reports of migration, which can be stoked up by political leaders, such as the right-wing politician Enoch Powell in the late 1960s and early 1970s, then latterly in the 2010s

Key term 4.2 Political socialization

How people acquire values and ideas, usually from the immediate social background of family, school, friends, and workplaces, as well as wider influences. Generally thought to be a slow process, ensuring continuity particularly as people get older they keep their attitudes and behaviours.

by Nigel Farage as part of the campaign to leave the EU (see sections 4.8.1 and 10.4.8).

On the other hand, it is important not to move too quickly to adopt an elitist point of view that public opinion is easily manipulated, and that there are no stable preferences that last over time. There is a long line of work in the study of political behaviour that suggests that values and attitudes are reinforced by family, friends, neighbours, and colleagues (for example, Lazarsfeld and Merton 1948). Even if these preferences change, such as towards left and right, academics claim they can be relied on as stable measures of citizen attitudes (Evans, Heath, and Lalljee 1996). These preferences get aggregated at points in time, particularly at elections. Voters translate their preferences into votes for a party, but also make judgements about politicians, such as punishing or rewarding them for their performance as constituency representatives or as part of the governing party. Of course, these preferences and behaviour can be shaped by campaigning and framing, and influenced by the media, which is explored further in section 6.7.

4.4.3 **Rational ignorance?**

Do voters in democracies, such as in the UK, have sufficient knowledge to make political judgements and choices? How can people who are pressured for time make sophisticated evaluations of a record in government? In classic political science literature, voters use cues which are thought to approximate to a full evaluation (Downs 1957), economizing on the amount of information they need for a particular task, what is called 'rational ignorance' (Key term 4.3). Of course, it is possible for citizens to make mistakes and for manipulation to occur, something that will be examined further in Chapter 6 on the media (see section 6.4). As in many democracies, knowledge about politics is usually quite low (Carpini 1997), especially in English-speaking countries like Britain (Grönlund and Milner 2006, 397). These low scores are often derived from responses to standard survey questions, which can pose questions in an odd way, such as asking about the number of MPs in the House of Commons. In 2017, only 9.5 per cent of the BES survey respondents answered that question correctly. It might be better to find out whether citizens have the capacity to judge whether the government has exercised its power correctly, such as making effective decisions during the Covid-19 crisis, which requires some knowledge, such as an awareness of who is responsible for decisions. It might be possible not to know that the House of Commons has 650 members, but at the same time be able to assess the qualities of Dominic Raab as Secretary of State for Justice, for example (see the discussion in Boudreau and Lupia 2011). Here the media can provide relevant information to citizens and interrogate political actors on citizens' behalf.

There is also a debate about the extent of citizen competence needed in a democracy (Druckman 2001). There is a common assumption that a lack of education is a limit to making political judgements (Milner 2002). This debate about the extent of knowledge needed is important to bear in mind when looking at voting behaviour and also when citizens vote in referendums. It also affects how well British democracy is doing, if voters rationally update their preferences based on an evaluation of governments and politicians or if they do not pay much attention and make 'incorrect' judgements. Also, in terms of the

Key term 4.3 Rational ignorance

An idea from rational choice theory (see Key term 2.1) that explains low knowledge of citizens as the result of a calculation not to expend effort collecting information about politics when a series of shortcuts, such as voting for a party that usually represents a person's interests, work with less effort.

principal–agent model (see Zoom-In 1.4), if the principal (the voters) does not have much information, they cannot monitor the agents (the politicians), who might present what they are doing favourably based on selective reading of official information they cannot challenge, though those in the media can question politicians based on information they have gathered on the citizens' behalf (see section 6.3 on the media), as do opposition politicians.

4.4.4 Do opinion surveys reveal a golden age of British democracy?

In thinking about British democracy, it is important to consider whether there was some 'golden age' of strong participation, from which the current period of alienation and turbulence is a great falling off. Almond and Verba (1963), in one of the classics of political science, the civic culture surveys carried out in the 1950s, found that people felt willing to participate in politics and believed that their actions had an effect (efficacy) and were accepting of the system as a whole and the decisions that come out of it.

Ideas of a so-called 'golden age', however, are not borne out in the findings of these surveys. Even in the 1959 civic culture survey, only 23 per cent of people reported talking about public affairs and politics, consistent with the lack of interest in politics as discussed at the start of this chapter (see section 4.2). Only 16.6 per cent had a belief in their own ability to change a law, though 42 per cent felt that they had a say in government.

Clarke, Stoker, Jennings, and Moss (2016) have investigated this issue systematically, using focus groups and survey data. BIPO/Gallup collected survey data on approval and satisfaction during the 1940s and 1950s. It found that on average just over 40 per cent of citizens disapproved of the record of the government during this period. The period between 1945 and 2015 showed an increase in negative feeling, with a trend rise by 20 per cent to 60 per cent of respondents expressing disapproval of the government. In 1944, 35 per cent of respondents felt that politicians were 'out merely for themselves'; 48 per cent of respondents gave the same answer in 2014.

The portrait of Britain illustrated in civic culture surveys from the 1960s reveals relative homogeneity—a very different society when social class was the main divider, there were fewer ethnic minorities, and there was much less differentiation according to age, place, and religious affiliation. This pattern differed from other European countries in the twentieth century where religion and ethnicity were important factors and sources of division (Lipset and Rokkan 1967). That said, there are some variations in the data according to education, age, and nation/region even in the early 1960s (John, Fieldhouse, and Liu 2005), which become more marked as the decades proceeded and were to become more important drivers of attitudes in the era of Brexit. In particular, there were important differences in political attitudes and behaviour linked to religion and/or ethnicity, depending on where people lived, such as Protestants and Catholics in Northern Ireland, Scotland, and parts of England (like Liverpool), who tend not to get discussed in general narratives on British politics (for an exception, see Rose 1968, 140–41).

4.4.5 The British Election Study and party identification

Another important starting point for understanding political attitudes is the first British Election Study, which led to the famous book, *Political Change in Britain* (Butler and Stokes 1969). As with the civic culture survey, the intellectual framework is important. This is the Michigan model, the set of ideas that influenced the US study of elections, which in turn influenced British scholars. The Michigan model entails people developing their attitudes about politics through loyalty to a political party. This attachment persists over time, reinforced within the family, employment, and local community. It is also transferred down the generations, sustained by social cleavages based on class—broad classifications of occupations, such as unskilled workers, semi-skilled, and so on—which are also inherited given limited population mobility. This strength of attachment then dominates attitudes to politics in general, hence party identification (Key term 4.4).

What this model suggests is a relative dominance of party loyalty in terms of general attitudes to politics, such as a strong level of party identification. The Michigan model also suggests that this dominance generates stability, as it assumes that these orientations remain fairly constant; and this might be thought to provide a bedrock for UK politics, a core or stable element of party supporters that can offer general support to the party system. There were some powerful statistics from the BES surveys. In 1964 respondents were asked, 'Generally speaking, do you usually think of yourself as . . . or what'; they answered Conservative (39 per cent), Labour (42 per cent), and Liberal (12 per cent), with 'none' at 5 per cent and 'don't know' at 2 per cent (Butler and Stokes 1969).

Key term 4.4 Party identification

The attachment a person feels with a political party. This long-term support for a party is formed in the early years, from family influences, and stays with a person over their lives, causing them to vote for the party in successive elections. It is measured by asking survey respondents whether their identification is very strong, fairly strong, or not very strong.

Photo 4.2 The three main political parties in the UK: Conservatives, Labour, and Liberal Democrats.

4.4.6 **Left and right**

The disputes of the nineteenth and twentieth centuries produced powerful ideologies that still influence politics today. These belief systems range from defence of the existing order, such as traditional institutions and private property, with a limited role for the state, to views that challenge or want to modify society and the economy through state intervention. There is a continuum of support, ranging from right to left, bestriding the moderate centre ground (see Figure 5.6). These differences influence the policies of the political parties, such as Conservative (right) and Labour (left). Left–right is a foundational idea in political science, and survey evidence in the UK shows that it continues to dominate over other kinds of debates and continua (Evans, Heath, and Lalljee 1996), though it has come under challenge in recent years as other dimensions of attitudes, such as authoritarian to liberal, have come to prominence, particularly after the Brexit referendum (Fieldhouse et al. 2019) (see Figure 4.5).

4.4.7 **Attitudes to parties and politics today**

Moving to the present day, how best to summarize how people think about politics? The twenty-first century is commonly thought to be one when people lost faith in politics and became disengaged from the offerings of the two parties. As was pointed out not long after Butler and Stokes' book came out in 1969 (Crewe 1974), citizens had already been loosening themselves from their attachments to parties. In recent years, the decline has become marked: using data from the BES surveys, in 1964, 45 per cent of respondents felt very strong party identification, but by 2017 the number of respondents who felt this way had dropped to around 15 per cent. There are changes at the extremes of party identification: a large decline from 45 per cent to 10 per cent of those who have very strong party identification, and a rise from below 5 per cent in the 1960s to around 15 per cent in the 2010s, though with less change in the totals for the middle categories. It would be wrong to say that party identification is not an important aspect of public opinion today, but this kind of attachment has weakened markedly overall.

But there has also been relative stability since the late 1980s. Figure 4.2 shows the trend of party identification over time since 1987 using the British Social Attitudes (BSA) surveys (for a more regular source of data than BES). After a fall in the early part of this series, slight increases have occurred in recent years, such as the survey responses in the 'very' category. The no identification category continues to rise, if slowly in this figure. When looking at recent explanations of political turbulence in British politics (see Key term 4.5), it is not possible to identify changes in party identification as the immediate cause, though it could be argued that the dramatic fall in party identification in the decades before 1987 was a necessary precursor to more electoral instability upon which populist movements and challenger parties could build (Key term 4.6). It is important to be very careful about a measure like party identification, which has attracted a lot of criticism over the years, in particular whether party identification is a long-term sense of association, or more of a running record of how citizens update their views regarding political parties (Fiorina 1981).

Key term 4.5 Political turbulence

Increased volatility and lack of predictability across the whole political system, affecting voting behaviour, public opinion, the media, the policy agenda, and implementation of public policies.

Key term 4.6 Challenger parties

New political parties that seek to challenge the mainstream political consensus and do not usually enter government.

4.4.8 **Anti-politics and stealth democracy**

In a book called *Why We Hate Politics* (2013), Colin Hay describes the discontent people have with the practice of contemporary democratic politics. In 2009, members of the public found out that many Members of Parliament had not made honest claims in their expenses, which escalated into what was called the expenses scandal. Electors then had the experience of political parties breaking promises, such as the Liberal Democrats in coalition with the Conservatives, which participated in a decision to raise student fees in 2010, after promising in their election manifesto not to increase them. The financial crisis of 2008–9 saw large parts of the financial sector over-extended and close to collapse, with the government bailing these organizations out at many billions of pounds, whilst the Liberal–Conservative government implemented an austerity programme. In this context, it does not seem surprising that trust in government fell. There has been a similar pattern across democracies (Dalton 2004).

It is quite common for commentators in any era to find problems and crises, but the claims seem stronger in the twenty-first century. In the views of some writers (Hay 2013; Stoker 2006), this is an era of 'anti-politics', when people have not just turned

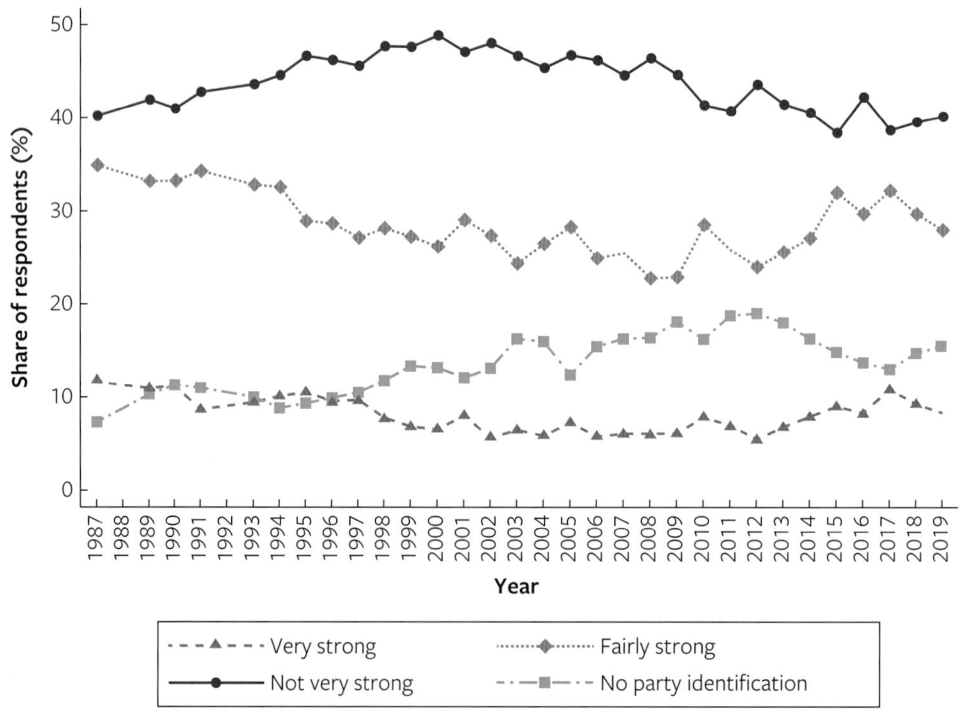

Figure 4.2 Party identification in Britain, 1987–2019.
Source: British Social Attitudes: https://bsa.natcen.ac.uk/downloads; Nesstar.uk: http://nesstar.ukdataservice.ac.uk/webview

Key term 4.7 Anti-politics

Hostility to conventional electoral and party politics, based on a suspicion that politicians are acting in their own interest, not that of voters. Associated with discontent, such as outrage with scandals. Linked to stealth democracy (see Zoom-In 4.1).

off the policies of a particular government or party, but lost faith in party and electoral politics (see Key term 4.7). It is an important change in attitudes, which may underlie other changes in political behaviour, such as support for challenger parties, and may even lead to political turbulence as people are more willing to change support for political parties (see section 5.8.1).

It is important to realize that many measures of attitudes towards politics show relatively little change. For example, interest in politics does not change much over time, as shown in Figure 4.3, with about 30 per cent of people usually saying that they are interested in politics a great deal or quite a lot, with the same proportions saying respectively that they have some interest or not very much/not at all. This makes for two-thirds of the population having some interest in politics. The period since 2016 did see a jump in interest in politics following the 2016 referendum, which dampened down again in 2018.

The relative lack of feeling and engagement with politics on the part of voters supports the suggestion that people are only partially engaged with British democracy, but they feel a need to intervene from time to time. This partial engagement can be described as 'stealth democracy' (Hibbing and Theiss-Morse 2002) (see Zoom-In 4.1).

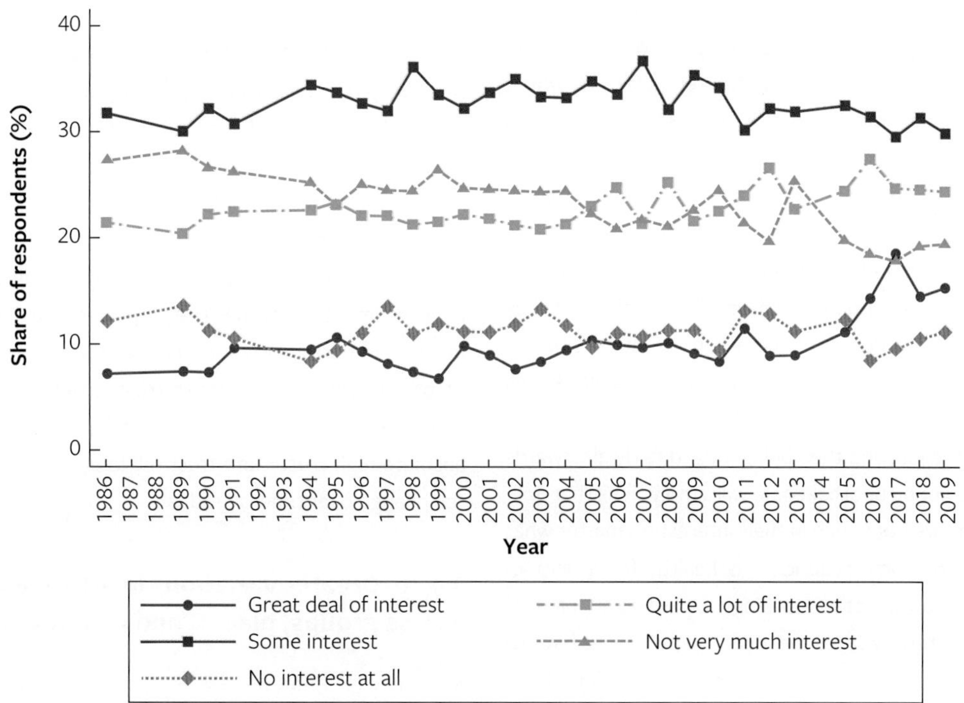

Figure 4.3 Interest in politics, 1986–2019.
Source: British Social Attitudes, UK Data Service

Zoom-In 4.1 Stealth democracy

Developed by Hibbing and Theiss-Morse (2002) to describe the limited engagement of citizens with contemporary democracies. Stoker and Hay (2017, 5) identify the prevalence of stealth politics in this way: 'Stealth populists think that in a democracy, the political system should deliver what the people want without them having to pay continual attention to it. From such a perspective, the perceived failings of the current political system are a simple product of too much politicking. Politicians talk rather than act, make too many compromises to special interests and do not have sufficient cognisance of expertise to come to sensible decisions'. Stealth politics is arguably not a new state of affairs, as Moss et al.'s (2016) account of the mass observation surveys done just after the Second World War identified the same kind of attitudes some seventy-five years ago. There are many continuities from then to now.

4.4.9 **Trust**

One big change, backed up by extensive data, is that citizens have less trust in politicians (Bowler and Karp 2004). Trust is a general feature of human life, for example social trust is the idea that people trust others in general, such as strangers who could help them if they got lost in a different place to where they lived. Political trust is another kind, which is important because it implies that politicians cannot be relied upon to carry out their promises, which is crucial in the Westminster model, and to make judgements in the national interest without citizens assuming that politicians have other motives, or they just will not deliver. If there is no trust by citizens, then a representative democracy cannot work well because it relies on citizens letting politicians get on with the job, and then being judged fairly afterwards at the voting booth. People will simply think that politicians are not acting in their interest no matter what they do (some scepticism is healthy for a democracy), so will vote accordingly or not at all. Lack of trust in turn reduces the incentive politicians have to listen to citizen concerns and to craft a medium-term strategy, as they might think that citizens are going to punish them whatever they do.

There are different kinds of political trust, such as for different politicians and also for bureaucrats and other authority figures. Political trust has gone down since the 1990s (Jennings et al. 2017). These findings are from a set of surveys that draw similar conclusions; for example, the British Social Attitudes survey shows that in 2012 one in five (18 per cent) trusted governments to put the nation's needs above those of a political party, down from 38 per cent in 1986 (Alice Park et al. 2012, xvi). This trend is not just confined to Britain, but affects most advanced democracies, such as the US (Dalton 2004). Figure 4.4 presents the change in trust in government over time. The graph shows a decline in trust, in particular an increase in the percentage of people who almost never trust government. It should also be noted that the starting point is not absolute high trust (and trust fell long before) and the change over time is gradual.

4.4.10 **Greater variations in attitudes across groups, places, and generations**

As society becomes more complex and multicultural, it is becoming increasingly difficult to speak of a single entity called UK public opinion, even though it was

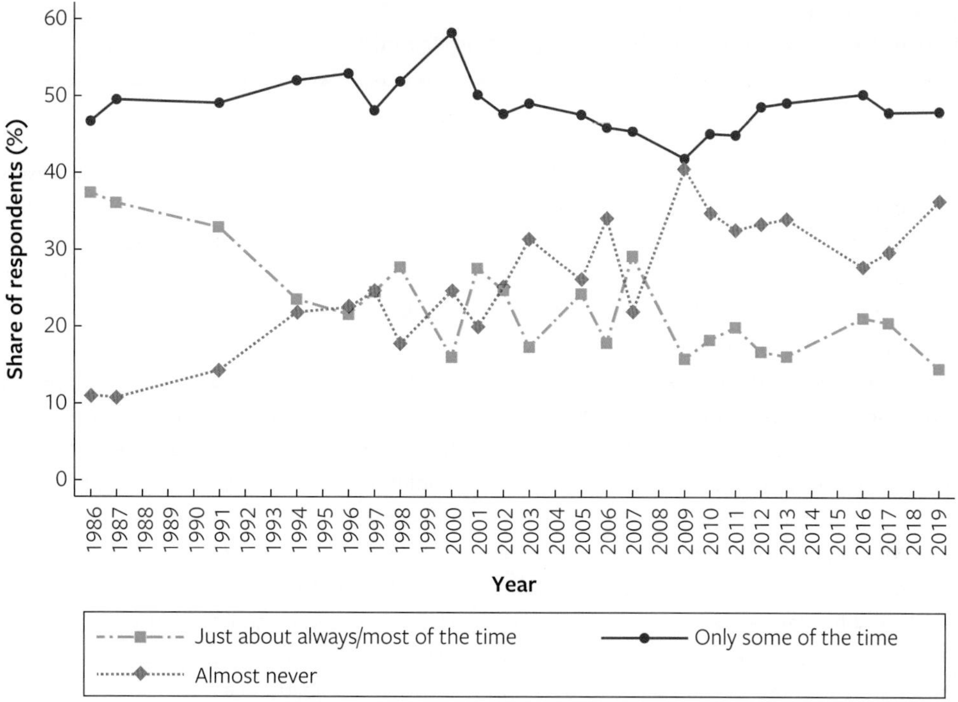

Figure 4.4 Trust in government, 1986–2019.
Source: British Social Attitudes (BSA), UK Data Service

always differentiated to a degree (see section 4.4.4). There are different views according to subgroup and place, findings that were there in the original foundational studies, such as the civic culture survey, but have become stronger over time.

Social class remains an important dividing line even if there is much sharing of political attitudes (see Zoom-In 4.4). In higher social classes there is much more interest in politics (Hansard Society 2019, 31). There is also much greater knowledge of politics, with more people in higher classes reporting that getting involved is effective than in the other groups.

There are differences according to whether someone is part of an ethnic-minority group, though there are very different kinds of groups within this. Ethnic-minority citizens broadly support a policy agenda around anti-discrimination and welfare policy issues, and their party affiliation leans towards Labour (Sobolewska 2005).

There are different political attitudes among those who identify as female, which research has concluded are less interested in politics than men (49:57 per cent), and have less knowledge about politics (43:59), partly explained because women are more willing to respond with a 'don't know', whereas men are likely to guess (see for the US, Mondak and Anderson 2004; Lizotte and Sidman 2009). Furthermore, women are less satisfied with the performance of politics and government, and less likely to think that getting involved is effective (Hansard Society 2019, 31–32). These differences correlate to the power and status disparity between men and women, which create different gendered role models, and also because women tend to have more sense of communion with others, as shown in a detailed study by Campbell and Winters (2008). These gaps reverse when respondents are more aware of female role models. In a study that compared responses cross-nationally: 'Women of all ages are more

Zoom-In 4.2 A quick guide to measuring social class

Social class refers to divisions within society between groups with different levels of power and wealth (see section 3.6.4). In general, it is measured according to similar kinds of occupations that vary according to pay, status, degree of autonomy, and power.

For many years and even now, polling companies and many researchers used a six-point class scale of A—upper middle class as higher managerial, administrative, or professional; B—middle class as intermediate managerial, administrative, or professional grades; C1—lower middle class as supervisory or clerical and junior managerial, administrative, or professional; C2—skilled working class as skilled manual workers; D—working class as semi-skilled and unskilled manual workers; and E—non-working as state pensioners, casual and lowest-grade workers, unemployed with state benefits. For simplicity, it is possible to divide the classes into non-manual (A, B, and C1) and manual (C2, D, and E) so as to see the basic link between class and voting (it is also possible to use the four-point scale of AB, C1, C1, and DE as in Figure 4.7). Sociologists have been discontented with these scales as they do not reflect power relationships in the workplace, such as within a factory. Goldthorpe and others proposed a seven-point scale (Goldthorpe, Llewellyn, and Payne 1987), which influenced the BES studies and the debate about social class (see section 4.7.1).

Also important is the subjective sense of social class—how the person feels in terms of class—which means that people who are middle class in terms of occupation can self-identify as working class, say because of their family background.

likely to discuss politics, and younger women become more politically active, when there are more women in parliament' (Wolbrecht and Campbell 2007, 936). In the US, even allowing for statistical controls, the gender gap in political knowledge disappears when the share of women in the state legislature exceeds 20 per cent (Wolak and McDevitt 2011, 519).

There are also differences in political attitudes according to age, which partly reflect what happens as people get older (Danigelis, Hardy, and Cutler 2007), for example increasing interest in politics (Glenn and Grimes 1968), and then what are called cohort effects that are about socialization during periods of time, and increases in levels of education for all, which are also associated with attitudes to politics. There is less knowledge about Parliament in the 65+ age group, with most age groups having higher levels of knowledge, but this is lower for the under-39 age group. There are less strong relationships for interest in politics.

4.4.11 Rightward or liberal (progressive) shifts in public opinion?

Has the British electorate become more polarized? Some parts of the electorate have become more liberal and tolerant over time as Britain has become a more multicultural and accepting society (Ford 2008). A recent study of attitudes in successive waves of the European Social Survey shows that young people are becoming more tolerant of immigration (McLaren, Neundorf, and Paterson 2020), which suggests as younger generations replace older cohorts, the UK population in general will become more tolerant.

At the same time that parts of the electorate have become more liberal or progressive, other parts retain more right-wing views, particularly in regard to immigration, but also a sense of culture divide and resentment at what appears to be the unfair division of wealth and resources and public spending across England in particular (Sobolewska and Ford 2020, 85–113). There is a debate as to the extent to which parts of British public opinion have moved to the right, partly influenced by the policies and stance of right-wing governments that were in power from 1979 to 1997, which arguably influenced the policies of Labour when it returned to power with Tony Blair in 1997. This is the idea that people might support markets and stronger policies to control welfare rights, and have strong views about preventing migration. Researchers have sought to find out whether individuals have become more individually orientated, such as support for private ownership of council houses, for example if they bought them or became share owners, but the analysis of the BES scotched this claim (Heath, Jowell, and Curtice 1985). The consensus from survey results was that the electorate had not at that time become 'Thatcherite'—that is, become more supportive of markets and traditional values associated with the former prime minister (Crewe 1988). But more recently, the analysis looking at the British Attitudes Survey shows younger generations believing more in economic liberalism and an authoritarian state (Grasso et al. 2019a).

4.4.12 **Populism**

Linked to these changing attitudes, there has emerged support for populist movements in the twenty-first century. Populism goes back to the late nineteenth century (see Zoom-In 4.3), but emerged more strongly in the aftermath of the financial crisis of 2008–9.

The presence of populism and populist ideas links to other important changes in how people think about politics, such as anti-politics, so can be seen as a set of more general anti-system attitudes. Furthermore, there are links between the survival of authoritarian/non-liberal attitudes, growth in anti-politics, and increasing spatial and income/wealth inequality, especially in regard to housing wealth (Ansell 2014), and the disengagement of the working class with the rise in support for extreme-right parties in the 2000s (John and Margetts 2009). This discontent was one of the key factors that caused some citizens to vote to leave the European Union in 2016. It is also possible to have a left version of populism, which uses some of the same ideas (Custodi 2020), such as criticism of Westminster elites in the interests of the common people, which emerged in the Momentum movement when Jeremy Corbyn was leader of the Labour Party (Watts and Bale 2019).

4

4.4.13 **Variation in attitudes**

Overall, political attitudes are increasingly varied across the UK, showing greater polarization, trends that began during the Thatcher decade of the 1980s (Fieldhouse 1995). People who live in small towns, away from London and the South East of England, have since the 1990s come to feel marginalized and believe that establishment politicians do not take account of their views (Jennings and Stoker 2018)—a populist or anti-politics view. This highlights how different dimensions to attitudes now exist rather than just ranging on the left–right continuum. There is also a liberal–authoritarian axis that intersects with the left–right one.

Figure 4.5 is a schematic representation of how attitudes can vary across two dimensions, so it is possible to think of some left-wing people as more authoritarian (say, wanting stronger policing or immigration control), while others are more liberal (say, interested in EU citizenship and mobility). On the right are free marketeers and libertarians (say, opposed to Covid-19 regulations) ranged against more traditional conservatives interested in law and order (say, wishing to clamp down on demonstrations). It is also possible to think of alliances across left and right, such as between left- and right-wing authoritarians, for example.

Zoom-In 4.3 Populism

Populism is a comparative phenomenon (Mudde and Kaltwasser 2012), defined by Cas Mudde (2004, 543) as 'an ideology that considers society to be ultimately separated into two homogeneous and antagonistic groups, "the pure people" versus "the corrupt elite", and which argues that politics should be an expression of the *volonté générale* (general will) of the people'. It has long roots, going back to rural discontent in the US in the late nineteenth century expressed through the People or Populist Party, and the Poujadists in France in the 1950s, which was an anti-establishment movement, representing small businesses and artisans. Populism is linked to anti-politics (see Key term 4.7), but tends to be more extreme and linked to support for outsider or challenger political parties (Key term 4.5).

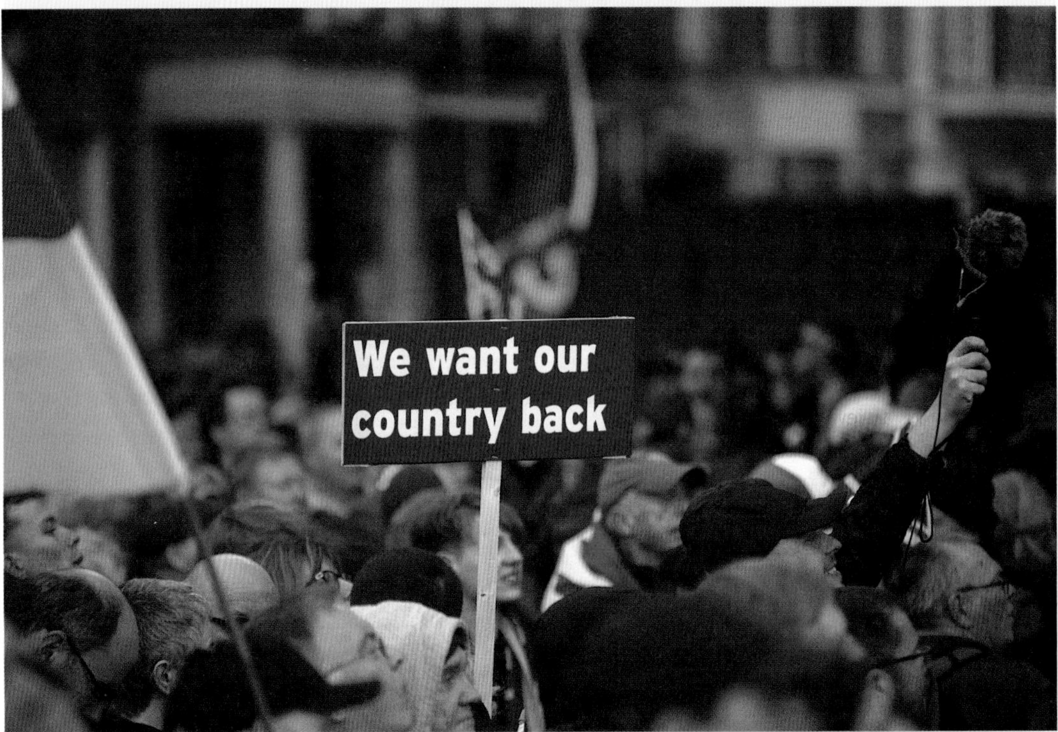

Photo 4.3 A 2018 UK Independence Party (UKIP) rally. UKIP are a right-wing populist political party in the UK.

4

4.5 Political participation

Linked to attitudes towards politics are the range of participation acts that citizens can undertake to get involved with politics, either directly in terms of contacting or mobilizing, or more indirectly in the form of group memberships that might have political objectives but encompass more general features, for

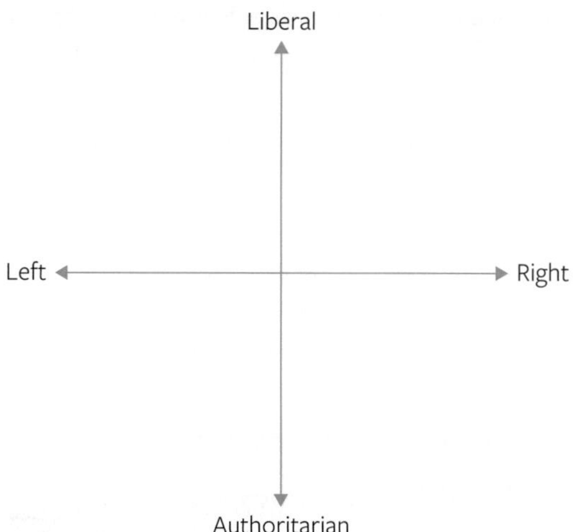

Figure 4.5 A representation of attitudes: left v. right, authoritarian v. liberal.

example membership of the National Trust, or volunteering, which is called civic engagement (see Key term 4.8) (Ekman and Amnå 2012; John et al. 2019; see also Table 4.1).

An active citizenry, who carry out political acts between elections, is often seen as an essential feature of a democracy, a view that is ascribed to classical Greek writers, such as Pericles, and which extends to Rousseau, J. S. Mill, de Tocqueville, and more recently to the US scholar Robert Putnam. In a modern representative democracy, covering the size of the UK and its 66 million population, participation is a way for citizens to signal their interests and concerns between elections. These signals allow political elites to be responsive at other times than elections, with citizens acting as 'fire alarms'. Citizens who are active are easier to communicate with than citizens who are passive, so it makes it easier for government to achieve collective policy objectives, such as getting citizen cooperation during the Covid-19 pandemic in 2020 and 2021. Although the benefits of participation, when described in this way, can be seen to be paternalist—that is, government knowing what is best for citizens—it is possible to imagine a two-way relationship made possible by a wider range of participation choices, with governments listening to citizens and vice versa. Naturally, participation does not mean that governments necessarily or even often listen or take notice, and some non-participation can be a rational assessment by citizens, as their voice does not usually count (meaning there is no point being involved). The possibility of achieving collective action—that is, citizens working together—is often thought to be limited because it is in no one person's interest to cooperate (see Key term 4.9 and Zoom-In 2.4).

Since the 1990s, there has been much commentary about a sharp drop in levels of participation

Key term 4.8 Civic engagement

The degree to which citizens are engaged with a wide range of participation acts and have a positive attitude to public authority in a democracy. It is more than conventional forms of political participation, such as voting and membership of political parties, and embraces civic acts such as volunteering, helping neighbours, and co-producing public services alongside other citizens, as well as responding to government consultations. It often has a local or neighbourhood focus.

Key term 4.9 Collective action

Achieving cooperation when it is not in the interests of any individual to cooperate, for fear of others free-riding. Arises out of the prisoner's dilemma and other problems in game theory (see Zoom-In 2.4).

Key term 4.10 Social capital

A stock of social bonds and ties in society that can contribute to collective action, individual welfare, and government performance. Defined as trust, networks, and voluntary action.

across Western democracies, mainly focusing on voter turnout (Flickinger and Studlar 1992) and membership of political parties (Whiteley 2011). In addition, there is a wealth of discourse on what is called social capital (Coleman 1988; Putnam, Leonardi, and Nanetti 1994) (see Key term 4.10), which suggests that there is a more general decline in civic engagement, such as membership of voluntary groups as well as social trust, mainly in the US, where there have been large declines in participation as measured in terms of membership of associations and groups (Putnam 2000).

It is hard to assess the overall health of participation as there is no agreed standpoint about what the standard might be. At one extreme, a lack of participation might signal that the public are content: if people are happy with the outputs of a political system, then non-participation might be rational, rather like the people who are members of political parties but who never go to meetings, e.g. giving donations to compensate, the so-called 'check-book' participation (Maloney 1999). This claim links to the debate on rational ignorance (see section 4.4.3). At the other extreme, it is thought that only when there is a massive amount of participation can democracy be fully realized, and where the limited range seems not to be sufficient today (Barber 1984).

Figures on participation can be seen to be high or low depending on perspective. For example, the 2019 Audit of Political Engagement found a range of participation in answer to the question, 'In the last 12 months have you done any of the following to influence decisions, laws or policies?', ranging from 22 per cent signing an e-petition, to 3 per cent attending a political meeting, as shown in Figure 4.6. That 39 per cent report doing nothing implies that about 60 per cent of the population are involved in some kind of political participation.

4.5.1 Equality, education, and participation

One of the key features of participation to explore is whether some groups get more involved in politics than others. This difference in levels of participation may affect the quality of the democracy in favour of those who participate and therefore influence the output of democracies, such as public policies. If some people do not participate, then they do not get the chance to guide policies, even if indirectly, as politicians are incentivized to respond to those who vote and lobby. Participation increases in certain segments of the population can exacerbate divisions and reinforce inequalities (Dalton 2017). The main source of bias stems from those who have more resources, partly from greater wealth and levels of education, which increases their knowledge about politics and in turn creates the security and confidence to deal with it, as well as having more time to be able to do politics (which applies to those who have retired from full-time work, hence linking participation with age). People with more resources are more likely to engage in political participation in its different forms. This inequality is an internationally consistent finding (Verba, Nie, and Kim 1987), from countries as different as France and Peru (Marien, Hooghe, and Quintelier 2010). The UK is not different in terms of the basic drivers (Pattie, Seyd, and Whiteley 2004).

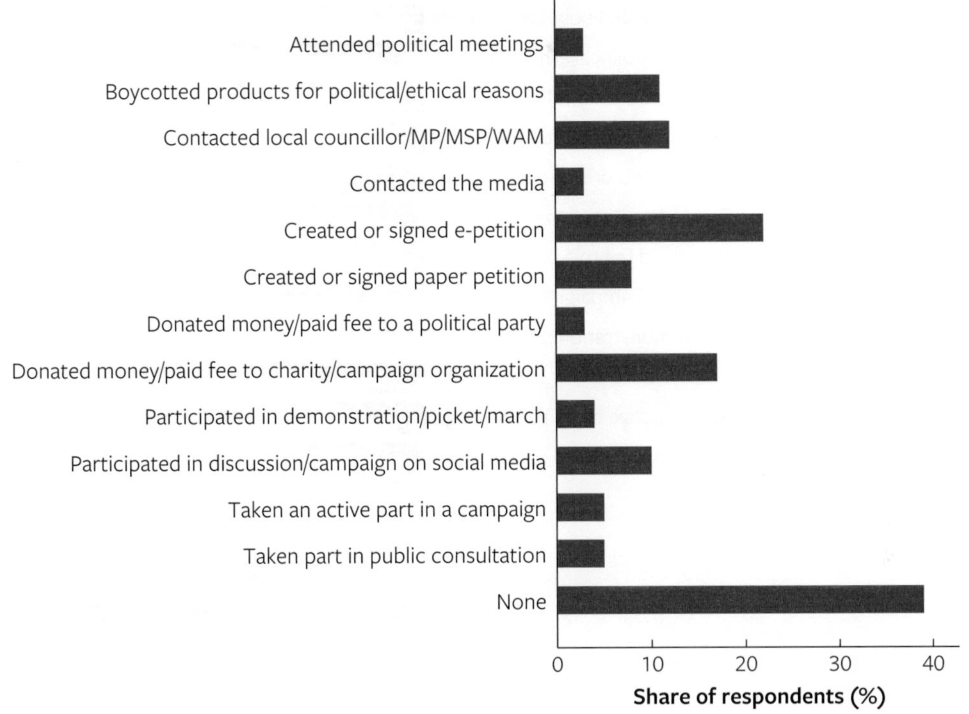

Figure 4.6 Political participation in Britain in 2018.
Source: Hansard Society (2019, 38)

4.5.2 How social background affects participation

Social class is often thought to be an important element of inequality. Figure 4.7 reports the same items of participation that were summarized above, but shows the percentages within each class category (using the C1 and C2 measures: see Zoom-In 4.2). For virtually every category, the AB class groups participate much more than other groups, with the C2 group as close to if lower than AB, while other groups do much less.

Differences exist for ethnic-minority citizens as they do for political attitudes, which is shown in Figure 4.8. The main difference is in contacting an MP, but most categories see ethnic minorities participating less than white citizens.

Gender plays a role too, especially with respect to social capital. Female-identifying people tend to do more 'gendered' roles, such as family-based volunteering, which have persisted over time (Lowndes 2004). Figure 4.9 reports the same activities by male and female respondents. There are not many differences here, though there are some slight variations according to the type of activity, such as women signing more e-petitions, and men being more likely to boycott certain products.

Another key feature is age, as different generations experience politics at different times, for example from experiencing how communities work together and the state take a more interventionist role in wartime (notably during the Second World War), and also the feelings of affluence in the post-1945 economic boom, as well as more confidence and trust in the political system which means that generations of older people participate strongly because they acquired the habit of participating when

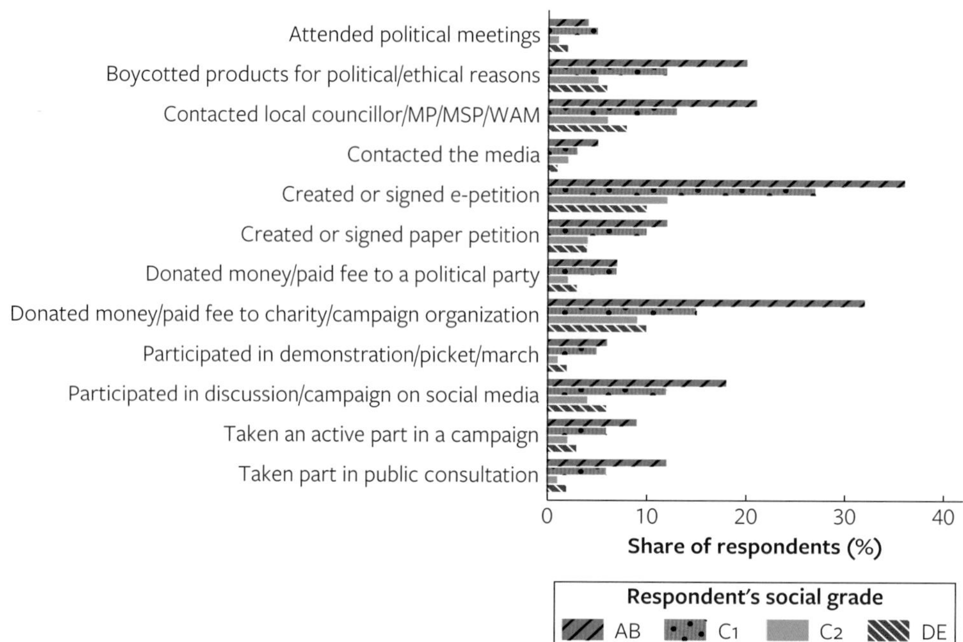

4

Figure 4.7 Political participation in Britain by social class.
Source: Hansard Society (2019, 31–32 and tables in annex); data are for 2018

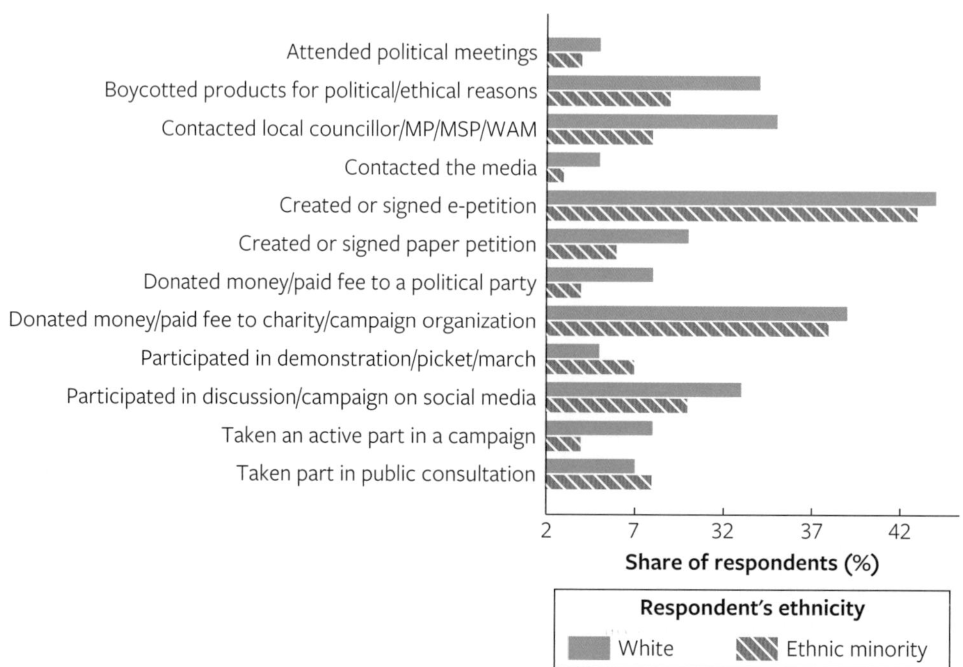

Figure 4.8 Political participation in Britain by ethnic-minority background.
Source: Hansard Society (2019, 31–32); data are for 2018

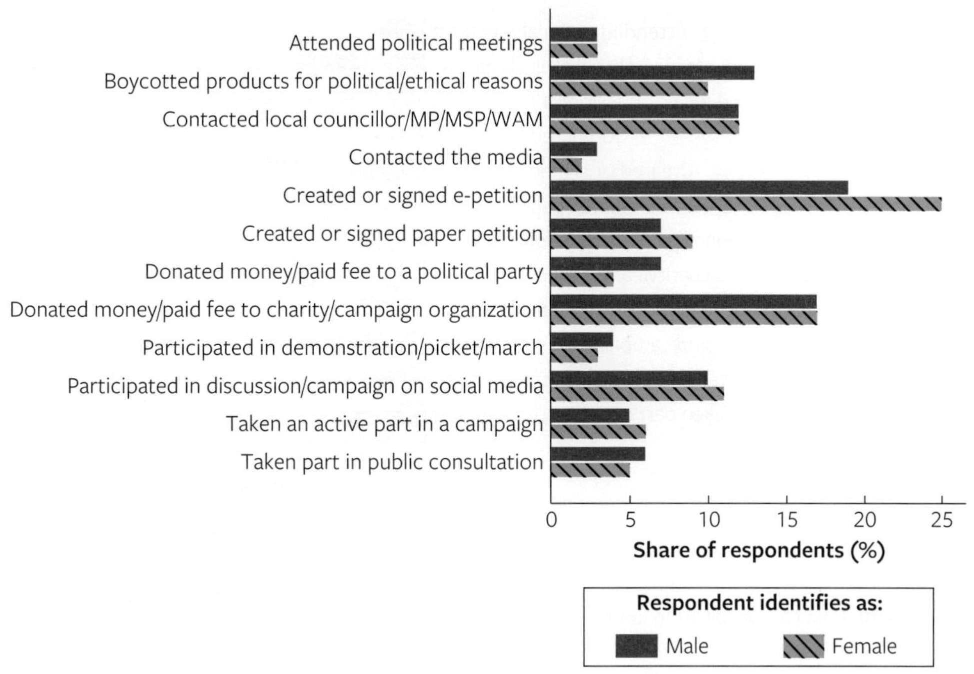

Figure 4.9 Political participation in Britain by gender.
Source: Hansard Society (2019); data are for 2018

they were younger (Grasso et al. 2019b). Norms of civic duty, such as voting at each election, were important in earlier decades, whereas younger generations have lived through the period of anti-politics and greater cynicism. Figure 4.10 maps these patterns, highlighting that younger groups report lower participation across most categories. On the other hand, Russ Dalton (2015), writing about US politics, suggests that the portrait of decline in participation among young people is misleading and that young people are transferring to new forms of political participation, often via social media. In the UK, there are some signs that this is the case, with younger groups with similar levels of participation for other activities, such as demonstrations and donating money. Note that the differences in taking part in a demonstration are not statistically significant as the numbers are very small in this part of the survey.

4.5.3 A decline in political participation?

Levels of participation can change over time. In the view of Putnam and others (Putnam 2000; Pharr and Putnam 2000), there has been a crisis in political participation and social life, but figures for the UK show relative stability in participation over time, with fluctuations that are correlated to other factors in politics such as discontent with governments, and the state of the economy. There does not appear to be a reduction in social capital in the UK, such as volunteering activities, making the UK similar to other countries, and the US is rather singular in this respect (Hall 1999). If anything, there has been a small increase in non-electoral participation, as observed by Curtice and Seyd (2003), though partly explained by the rise in the numbers of 'super-activists' who drive up the figures, as well as a long-term increase from rising levels of education which are correlated with participation.

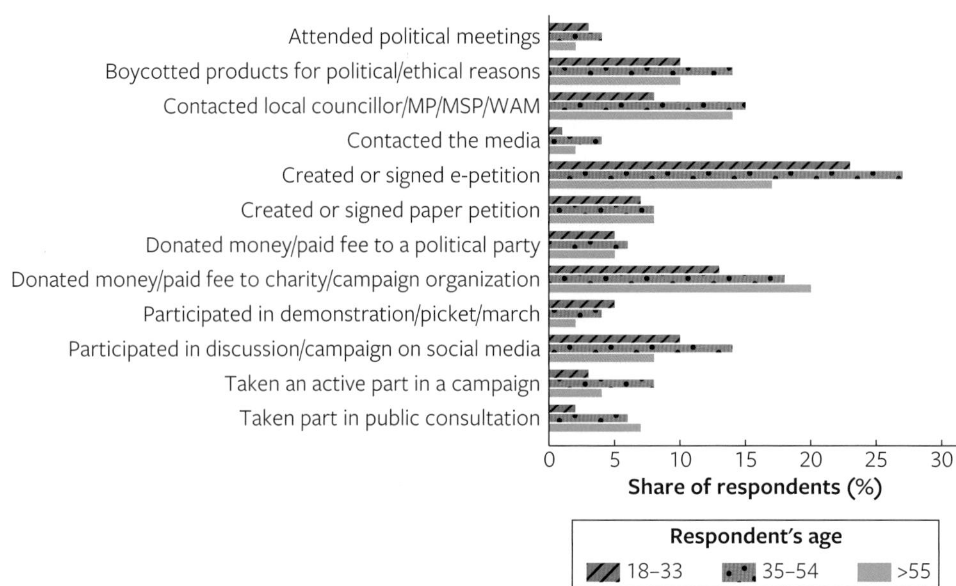

4

Figure 4.10 Political participation in Britain by age group.
Source: Hansard Society (2019) and its data tables
Note: Represents participation activities the respondents said they had completed in the previous 2–3 years. Data are for 2018

Overall, the picture of changing participation is mixed, with some indication that participation, broadly defined, has increased. For example, the British Social Attitudes surveys show an increase in levels of participation from its repeated question, 'And have you ever done any of the things on this card about a government action which you thought was unjust and harmful?', with 29 per cent saying they signed a petition in 1983 with 37 per cent in 2011, 10 per cent contacting an MP in 1983 compared to 16 per cent in 2011, and small rises or no change for other kinds of participation (Lee and Young 2013, 68).

It is very hard to find recent data that can be compared over time. The most recent series is the Audit of Political Engagement surveys, commissioned by the Hansard Society, which have been carried out on samples of respondents in England, Scotland, and Wales since 2003. These studies, however, suffer from a change in question wording in 2012 (and other changes in the categories of activities to respondents), so they need to be read with great caution when comparing across the years. Figure 4.10 shows stability in key participation items of contacting politicians and engaging in protest, but the percentage who donate money seems to have reduced after the financial crisis of 2008, and also shows that people moved from paper petitions to e-petitions in this period.

4.5.4 **Non-conventional participation: protests and riots**

If most people are drawn to a familiar menu of activities, such as petitioning or writing to their MP, some do more unconventional forms of participation, such as protest and taking to the streets, though these figures are much smaller, running at about 5 per cent in most surveys. This is a high-cost activity, and involves appearing in a public place, perhaps holding a placard, and being monitored or arrested by the police, even when the internet makes them easier to organize

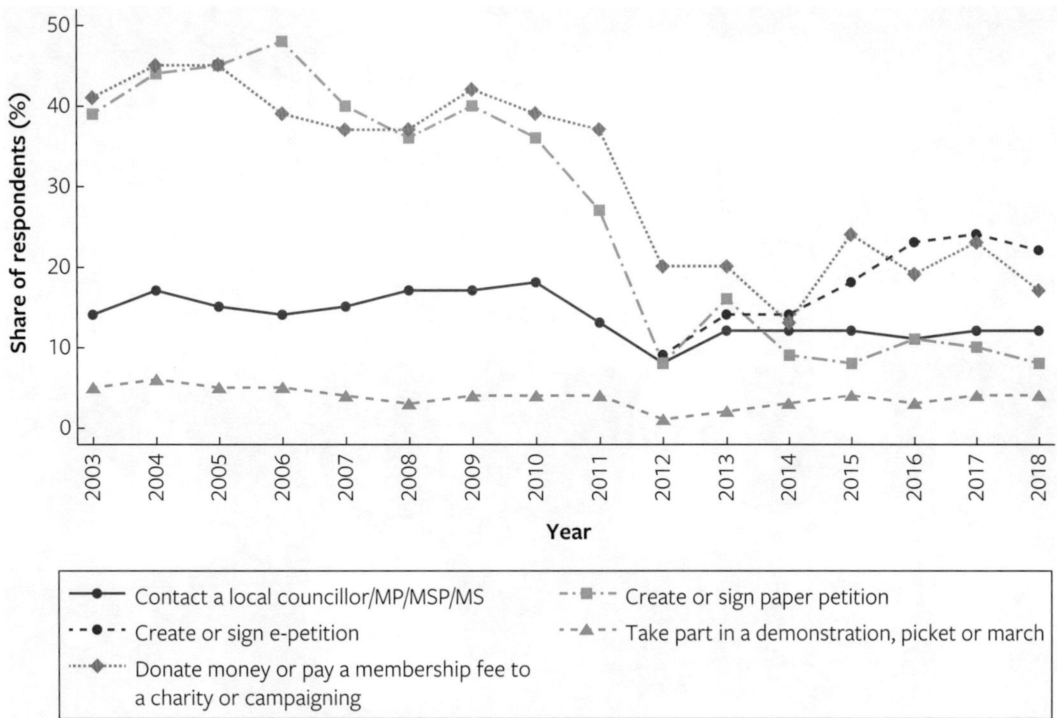

Figure 4.11 Political participation, 2003–18.
Source: Audit of Political Engagement series
Note: dates refer to the survey, not the publication of report

(Ghonim 2012). It is linked to other activities, such as e-petitioning and contacting MPs, which are often done at the same time, but can at times involve violent conflict with the police, even at peaceful protests. There is a long tradition of protest in Britain linked to progressive social changes, such as voting reform and gender equality. People often protest against government policies, such as the Extinction Rebellion UK (XR) (Gavin 2010). The Black Lives Matter and Stand Up to Racism protests from May to June 2020 (Photo 4.4) were peaceful protests taking place across cities in the UK, which also involved more assertive acts, such as tearing down a statue of slaver Edward Colston on 7 June 2020 in Bristol. The protests were in response to the murder of George Floyd in the US, an African-American man who was killed during an arrest. There was also aggression and arrests from the police towards mourning protesters at a vigil for the murder of Sarah Everard on 15 March 2021, organized by the direct-action group Sisters Uncut. In this case, the arrests were made for breaching the Coronavirus Act 2020, which granted the government emergency powers to handle the Covid-19 pandemic. These examples demonstrate how protest can be peaceful, but conflict with the police can still occur. In early 2021, controversial legislation (the Police, Crime, Sentencing and Courts Bill) was proposed by the UK government to gain more power to further control protests. Human rights charities and groups critiqued the legislation for being detrimental to civil liberties.

Whereas protest is often planned and has organizations, such as pressure groups, behind it, there are some kinds of action that are more spontaneous. Riots can occur in public places, and are often triggered by mass discontent or linked to protests, and the police response to control people on the street. They have

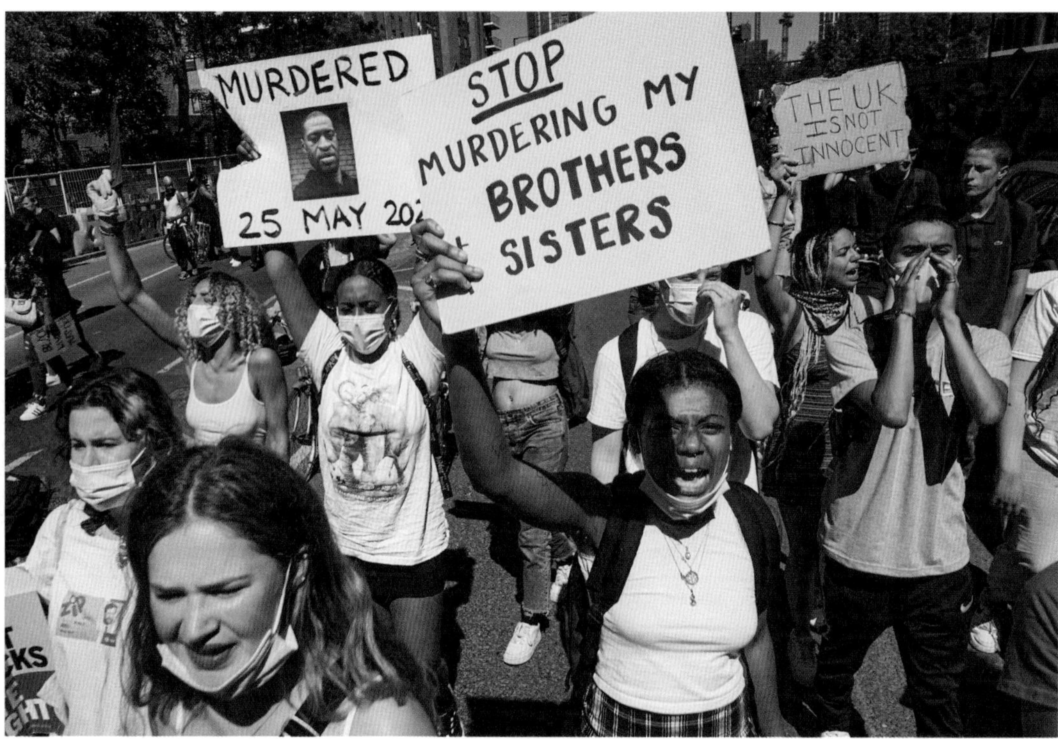

Photo 4.4 Black Lives Matter protesters in London, 31 May 2020.

a long history going back to the eighteenth century (Thompson 1971), if not before to medieval times (Clement 2016). However, riots have emerged as people have expressed anger and frustration, for example at injustices against ethnic-minority citizens. In 2011 there were riots in London and across England that emerged in response to the shooting by the police of an unarmed Black suspect, Mark Duggan. These events can be associated with criminal acts, such as setting properties and cars on fire, and looting. For some, these acts are not seen as political—rioting 'for fun and profit', as described by US sociologist Edward Banfield (1970). But given that they reflect collective grievances, such as against the police, they represent a non-conventional form of political participation. Even though politicians often condemn riots, they often lead to important policy changes such as more funding for cities and reform of the criminal law and policing (John 2006).

4.6 Voter turnout

An act of participation that has received a great amount of attention is voter turnout, which is the extent to which people and subgroups turn out to vote in elections. In many democracies, turning out to vote is a right that citizens may take up: they do not have to vote, unlike countries with compulsory voting, such as Australia. Turnout is determined by the percentage of eligible voters for a particular election. Voters need to

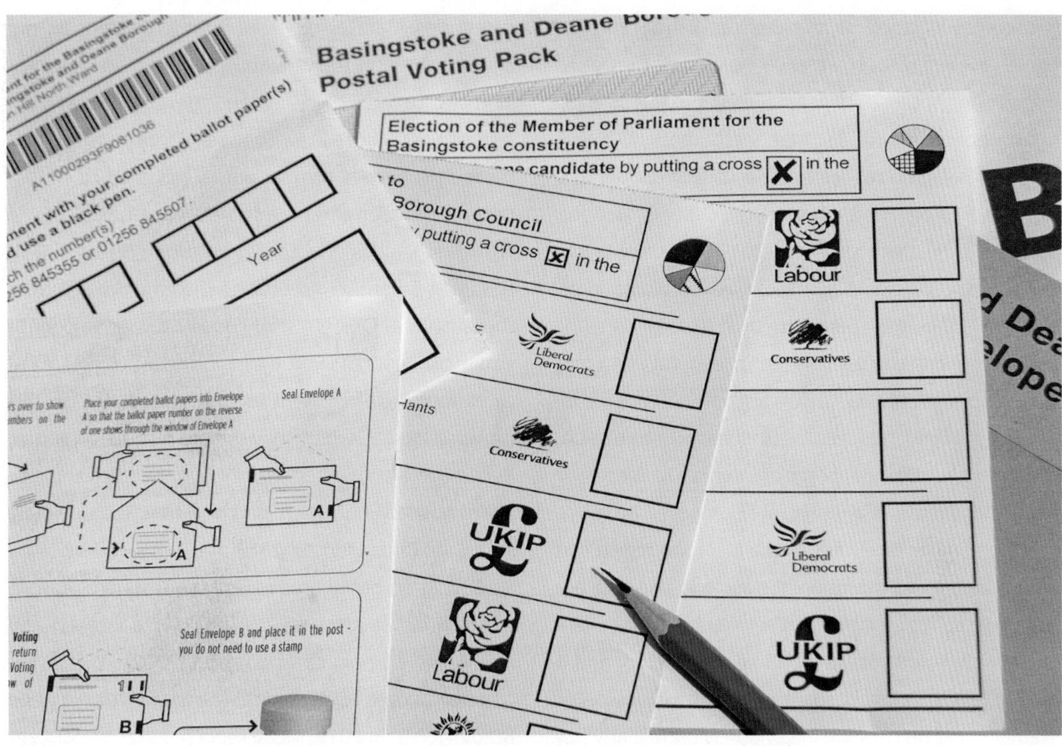

Photo 4.5 Ballot forms for postal voting in the local and general elections for May 2015.

register to vote, which is compulsory, but not strictly enforced. Commentators are interested in voter turnout as a measure of participation because the level of voter turnout can link to the outcomes of an electoral contest (Handsford and Gomez 2010). If people do not vote, they cannot influence the outcome of the election, and they might not get the party and government they want. If this is just a random draw of non-voters, then it might not matter as the outcome would be the same as if all people voted (other than from the possible increased legitimacy and citizen sanction of the system as a whole from everyone voting). But if those who do not vote are different from those who do, then the latter will have more influence over politics and public policy. If governments are just relying on the votes of a small number of people, they will follow their interests and not the others. This is concerning, as it is the case that (as with other kinds of political participation) the more affluent vote may have precedence, which might mean a government is not elected on the basis of equal participation, and some groups who may already have more power in the economy and society replicate that power in the political system as a whole.

4.6.1 **Voter registration**

Very close to voter turnout is voter registration, which is the legal requirement to enter details and make a declaration to enter the ballot. Low registration rates, especially for some groups who are marginalized by the political process, such as ethnic minorities, young people, and those who move around a lot (such as private sector renters), mean that these people are in effect excluded from the political process (Bite The Ballot et al. 2016). Because not everybody who should be registered to vote has taken the steps to have themselves included on the register, official turnout figures overestimate the real proportion of the voting population. At the 2019 general election, just over 32 million people voted. As there were about 47.6 million names on the register, that is usually quoted as a turnout of 67 per cent. However, the Office of National Statistics estimates that in mid-2019 the voting population of the UK was 52.7 million, which would imply a turnout of only 61 per cent (or a bit over as some people are not eligible to vote in general elections, such as foreign nationals). This also affects voting constituency boundaries as the Boundary Commission, who revise boundaries at regular intervals to keep their populations reasonably equal, are compelled by law to use the number of entries in the electoral register as their measure of population. If people in one area are less likely to register than those in another, its share of the population total will be underestimated, and it will get less than its fair share of MPs. It is known, for example, that registration in London is particularly low (see ONS report: www.ons.gov.uk/peoplepopulationandcommunity/elections/electoralregistration/datasets/electoralstatisticsforuk). That means that when the constituency boundaries are next redrawn, metro areas such as London will have several MPs fewer than they would if everyone registered or was required to do so, thus reinforcing spatial, ethnic, and party inequality. The issue of registration is closely linked to inequalities in participation in general.

In practice, those who do not vote are similar in characteristics to those who are not registered, so even if more people are registered to vote, it is not clear theywill go out and vote (for US evidence, see Nickerson 2014).

4.6.2 **How social background affects turnout**

Social class has an association with turnout, with those in more highly paid and professional jobs having participated more than those in less well-paid skilled occupations. In 2019, 63 per cent of those in categories A and B reported voting, whereas 53 per cent of those in the D and E group did so. A similar kind of category is housing tenure, with those who are homeowners more likely to vote—70 per cent of fully owned properties turning out—compared to 51 per cent of private renters. International studies show a link to difficulties of voter registration (Brians 1997), though it is hard to disentangle the effect of age from these figures. One UK study does show an impact of voting procedures (Pattie and Johnston 1998). In the UK, a factor is the extent to which people frequently move residence, which may reduce turnout as people become less connected to their communities and lose their knowledge of where and how to vote (Dowding, John, and Rubenson 2012).

Education has an impact for the resource reasons discussed in section 4.5.1 in that more interest and knowledge of politics (Denny and Doyle 2008) encourage people to take part (Verba, Schlozman, and Brady 1995). In 2019, MORI reported that 59 per cent of those without qualifications turned out to vote, whereas 69 per cent of those with a degree turned out. Once the relative influences, such as age, have been allowed for, the relationship between education and voter turnout in UK is less strong than in other countries, such as the US, with some studies suggesting there is no relationship at all in the UK (Milligan, Moretti, and Oreopoulos 2004). From the reported 2019 figures, it is possible to observe that the differences between those with high and low education are less than for ranges of the age category, for example.

Ethnic-minority voters are less likely to vote, with 52 per cent reporting voting in 2019 compared to 63 per cent of white voters, though there are large differences according to type of ethnic group (Heath et al. 2011), which reflects a combination of factors, such as social class, less contact with the political parties, including campaigning (Sobolewska, Fieldhouse, and Cutts 2013), and less mobilization from other organizations (Heath et al. 2011). Ethnic-minority men and women vote at similar rates, with ethnic-minority men voting by 2 percentage points more than women in 2019, according to MORI and YouGov's surveys. This convergence is a relatively recent development, as pre-1964 research highlighted that ethnic-minority women voted less (see LSE blog post: https://blogs.lse.ac.uk/politicsandpolicy/gender-and-voting-behaviour-in-ge2017) (Electoral Commission (Great Britain) 2004).

Women in all groups turned out less than men because of less exposure to public life and family obligations (Electoral Commission (Great Britain) 2004, 11–12). In the past women tended to have less knowledge and interest in politics. As women have gained independent employment and more equal rights, their participation has risen to be close to that of men. So, in the 2019 Audit of Political Engagement, intentions to vote were 62 per cent for men and 60 per cent for women.

Age is a powerful factor, with older people more likely to vote, as verified by cross-national studies (Smets 2012). In the 2019 general election, MORI's survey showed that 47 per cent of eighteen- to twenty-four-year-olds reported voting compared with 74 per cent of over sixty-five-year-olds, with a gradually increasing level of voting for each group in between (see Ipsos-MORI: www.ipsos.com/ipsos-mori/en-uk/how-britain-voted-2019-election). Age has become a more important feature of politics in recent years with many age-friendly policies being introduced, such as free public transport, whereas younger people often find it harder to access a good pension scheme, need to pay student fees if going to university, and face barriers in the housing market. The question to ask, which is hard to prove, is whether differential turnout according to age makes older voters more important in the calculations of political parties, hence possibly skewing policies in favour of older voters. There appear to be some recent changes to reverse this age gradient, such as the so-called 'youth-quake' of 2017, a perceived rise in young people's turnout, which helped the Labour Party get a good vote share in that election, but detailed analysis by the BES team shows that there were not many genuine new young voters with the upsurge actually being existing voters re-registering to vote (Prosser et al. 2020; for a different view see Sturgis and Jennings 2020). Overall, the evidence still says that turnout is strongly related to age.

More collective factors are the influences of neighbourhood and place on voter turnout, whereby people are influenced by those who live near them. There are concentrations of people who share the same cultures and voting histories (Johnston and Pattie 2006). For example, ethnic-minority voters tend to live in certain locations, affecting voter registration and turnout, for example (Fieldhouse and Cutts 2008). There are differences in voter turnout at general elections across the UK: high in Scotland in 2019 at 68.1 per cent, and higher in the South West of England at 72.0 per cent and the South East at 70.2 per cent, with Northern Ireland with the lowest turnout at 61.8 per cent. These differences reflect a combination of factors, such as socio-demographic differences across the UK, historical patterns of voting, different levels and kinds of campaigning, and then the accumulation of these factors that persist over time.

These regional or local factors alert us to the importance of context to the determinants of voter turnout in Britain, which includes political factors, but also how the political contest feeds into the voter choices. Turnout is related to the sense of influencing the outcome, so if the contest is regarded as 'safe', then it does not make sense to turn out to vote. In the classic theory of voter turnout, the decision is based on weighting costs and benefits, adjusted by level of civic duty, so that if the probability of an individual vote affecting the outcome reduces, then the decision to vote reduces accordingly. This can work at the aggregate level as certain contests are regarded as competitive, which will be discussed in section 5.8.4, with respect to changes over time, but they also vary by constituency. Under FPTP (see Key term 1.6 and section 5.3.3), MPs can pile up large majorities that are sustained for one party for long periods of time, so that once the contest comes, the voter thinks their individual vote will not make any difference, if the majority is, say, 20,000 (Vowles, Katz, and Stevens 2017). The other factor behind this phenomenon is the extent to which parties seek to mobilize voters in these constituencies in the hope of winning an election, which increases turnout and may even affect the vote outcome (Pattie, Johnston, and Fieldhouse 1995). However, in recent elections the relationship between marginality and turnout has reduced, not appearing in 2019 (Commons Library: https://commonslibrary.parliament.uk/insights/general-election-2019-turnout). It may be the case that voters in safe seats, who were mobilized to vote in the 2016 Brexit referendum (when the margin was very slim), continued to vote in other elections despite low marginality. Voters had been targeted to vote in greater numbers. This draws attention to the large impact that political parties and other organizations, including the media, have in raising turnout (Heath et al. 2013).

4

Finally, there are a range of other factors that influence voter turnout. Poor weather on the day can put off some voters, and more elderly voters who find it more difficult to get to the polls (for the Brexit referendum, see Leslie and Arı 2018). There are a range of personal factors, such as cognitive ability and political interest (Denny and Doyle 2008), which increase turnout. The level of political information may have an impact on turnout, but this may be affected by the consumption from the media, which is yet another influence on voter turnout (Larcinese 2007).

Then there is the level of electoral contest, with citizens at local elections voting much less than general elections. In the 2018 local elections, voter turnout was 35 per cent, for example, compared to 67.3 per cent in the general election the following year. Some contests have very low levels of turnout, such as elections for police and crime commissioners; 27.3 per cent in 2016. Turnout is better for the devolved legislatures with 55.9 per cent voting in the 2016 elections for the Scottish

Key term 4.11 First- and second-order elections

The claim that voters attribute importance to the national-level context, which appears to be more high stakes than local or regional or supranational elections, so they are more likely to vote and less likely to defect from established parties.

Parliament, 45.6 per cent for the 2016 elections to the Welsh Assembly, and a turnout of 64.5 per cent for the Northern Ireland Assembly election of 2017. The reasons for these variations in turnout have to do with the relative importance of these levels of government, with national governments having more responsibilities and more significance in cultural terms. These are called first- and second-order elections (see Key term 4.11). There is also the impact of electoral systems to consider, as there are a variety of these in British politics. This is covered in more detail in sections 5.3.3 and 5.8.4.

4.6.3 Turnout decline

In terms of understanding British politics, it is crucial to examine changes in turnout over time. Here, the arguments are similar to those for political participation more generally, in that it is hard to know without a prior normative standpoint what counts as high and low turnout, so as to judge the change and its magnitude. So, it is important to ask: if turnout changes, what is the impact on democracy, and are there any tipping points when it should matter or not? Also, given that turnout varies according to age, education, place, and so on, reducing turnout may increase inequalities, if the rate of decrease varies across these categories. The extent to which the evidence suggests that these inequalities affect representation overall will also affect concern about levels of turnout. How Britain compares to other countries may play a role in coming to a judgment, for example that the 68.8 per cent turnout at the 2019 elections was twelfth from the top in terms of European countries, or seventeenth from the bottom in the same ranking, or just above the average of 66.5 per cent (for the ranks, see Uberoi 2017, 7).

The key focus is on general elections, as voter turnout used to be much higher. In 2019, voter turnout was 67.3 per cent, which is down 1.5 percentage points from 2017. Back in 2001 it was as low as 59.4 per cent, its lowest level since people over the age of eighteen got the right to vote, whereas in the general elections of 1950 and 1951, turnout was 80 per cent. Figure 4.12 shows the turnout for the UK general elections since 1945, which demonstrates the decline in turnout since the 1950s. The sharp turnout fall of 12 percentage points in the general election of 2001 caused commentators to believe there was a democratic crisis (Clarke et al. 2003), though you can see a marked decline since 1992; but turnout did go back up again, if not to the 'golden age' of the 1950s, at least into the late sixties, as with the general elections of 2017 and 2019. The main difference across the countries of the UK is the lower turnout and different trends in Northern Ireland.

Growing levels of education, such as more people going to university, should raise turnout (see section 4.6.3); if this is taken account of, the fall is even greater. Also, as the class composition of the electorate changes, a greater proportion of middle-class citizens with more resources should raise average turnout (Heath 2007, 499). It should be noted that turnout has been falling in elections across Europe (Uberoi 2017, 9), and that turnout in local elections has declined too, but from a low starting point (see Rallings and Thrasher 2013). There have been relatively static levels of turnout for the devolved administrations, with a large increase in 2021 for the Scottish Parliament elections.

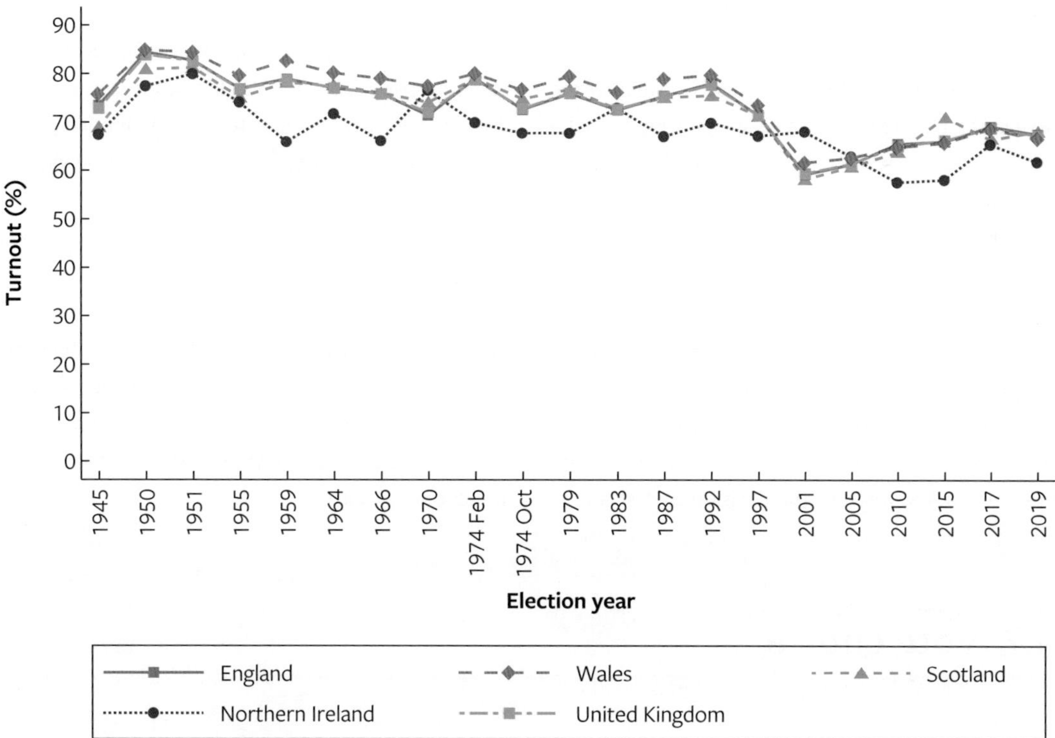

Figure 4.12 Voter turnout in UK general elections, 1945–2019.
Source: Audickas et al. (2020, 25)

4.6.4 Why does turnout change over time?

Turnout change may be related to many factors, some of which may reverse or partially reverse a turnout decline or increase, such as voter perceptions of the closeness of the race, anger at the political system, and new forms of engagement that spill over into electoral participation. In the literature (Heath 2018, 494), it is assumed that the factors that determine the general level of participation, education, and class size changes as discussed in section 4.6.2 do not explain turnout decline as these demographics change very slowly, and much slower than the change in turnout. Even other changes, such as generational change, are moving too slowly to be a key factor. It would be rash to neglect these demographic factors entirely, as it may be the case that certain groups react to general political factors more than others, as was shown in section 3.6.8 with the decline in turnout among working-class voters reacting to the absence of working-class politicians representing them (Heath 2018). It is more accurate to focus on the particular context, such as whether the political parties are offering a meaningful choice to the voters: if there is no perceived difference between the main parties capable of forming a government, then the voters might think it is better to stay home, as has been thought to be the case in the 2000s when Labour moved to the centre ground in British politics, and there was no effective challenger (Clarke et al. 2006).

Turnout decline may also be linked to the general trends in attitudes to politics in recent years, such as decreasing trust and the rise of anti-politics discussed in section 4.4.8, whereby the decision to cast a vote might be seen as pointless, or assenting to a form of politics that voters do not approve of. However, many of these same factors may also cause rises in turnout, if people feel angry about politics and then vote for challenger parties. There is a need to disentangle the factors at work. Oliver Heath (2007) examines change over time using data from the BES surveys from 1964, finding declining party identification as the main factor, though naturally this relates to other factors too (though precedes the large declines in trust and loss of confidence in government). Consistent with the rise in turnout, Heath identifies the contextual factors that cause turnout to change from election to election, such as the perceived difference between the parties and the closeness of the electoral contest.

4.6.5 Summing up on participation and voter turnout

This section shows all the ways in which people become involved with politics. It gives a sense of the diversity and varying character of contemporary British politics, and how different groups engage with it, based on their attitudes and resources. Whether it indicates British democracy is in rude health or perilous decline is hard to say; reality is probably in between these extremes, with lots of evidence of civic engagement and participation, from a variety of groups, as well as non-participation, and less conventional participation, such as protest and riots. Naturally, the big element to democracy is voting, which is considered in sections 4.7 and 4.8.

4.7 Vote choice

Once a voter turns out, they are faced with a choice of candidates, who for most contests in the UK run under a party label, often for what are thought to be the main parties capable of forming a government (see section 5.3), and traditionally arrayed from the left to right and/or other dimensions, such as pro- or

Key term 4.12 Partisanship

Partisanship is the strong support for a political party expressed by an individual, a similar term to party identification (see Key term 4.4), but more overt and all-encompassing. Partisans often see the political process in competitive terms and cast other partisans in a negative light. They may even interpret facts in ways that are favourable to their political party; what is called partisan-motivated reasoning or partisan information processing. Members of political parties are often called partisans. Partisan or partisanship can also refer to the conduct of politicians—whether they are independent and listen to argument, or behave only according to the interests of their party.

anti-environmental, or nationalist/unionist. In studies of British politics, such as those based on the BES surveys (Butler and Stokes 1969; Särlvik and Crewe 1983; Heath, Jowell, and Curtice 1985; Heath 2016; Clarke 2004; Clarke et al. 2009; Fieldhouse et al. 2019) (see section 4.4.5), considerable attention is paid to explaining why people vote the way they do, particularly over a number of elections, which links to the general discussion about participation and voter turnout in section 4.6, but is related more to partisanship (see Key term 4.12).

Moreover, given that there are party members who are important in sustaining parties in office as campaigners in elections, and who provide candidates, there is a complex relationship between candidates, party members, different kinds of supporters, and those who might vote for a party (see Bale 2019 and discussion in section 5.8.5).

A considerable amount of intellectual effort is used to seek to explain electoral choice in the UK and elsewhere to examine sources of party support. In the UK in particular, there is a great focus on the role of social class, which is still a large influence on politics and social life in general, and where a degree of class conflict and compromise is part of an ongoing history and forms a backdrop to contests on public policy, such as over levels of taxation and the distribution of public resources (see Savage 2015). Much centres on the growth of the power of the working class, which expanded in numbers in the nineteenth century from industrialization. In time, advocates argued for a working-class electoral organization, which led to the formation of a separate party in 1906, the Labour Party (see section 5.3.2).

Given this history and the places where Labour got its electoral support, from the industrial heartlands where working-class support was concentrated, it is not surprising to see working-class support as crucial to Labour's electoral project, and this was based on consistent support across elections sustained by strong party identification. Casting a vote for Labour was historically associated with class position. In 1964, 64 per cent of Labour voters were from manual classes (Denver 1998, 67).

The conclusion that has been drawn is that class was key to understanding party politics. There is a famous quote by Peter Pulzer (1967, 98) that has been a stalwart of examination questions: 'Class is the basis of British party politics; all else is embellishment and detail'. Yet this statement should not be taken to mean that all voting falls into expected class categories. Both main parties did not draw support overwhelmingly from single social classes. There is a long tradition of working-class support for the Conservative Party going back to the franchise extension of 1867. Leader and prime minister Benjamin Disraeli sought support for the Conservatives by appealing to patriotism, class deference, and pride in empire. The Conservatives realized that they could not win elections based on the middle-class vote alone. It was a simple matter of calculating the relative size of the classes at that time as the working class was a lot larger then: if most of

Zoom-In 4.4 How to measure class voting

There are various ways to measure class voting, which is the extent to which members of a social class support a political party in elections. The easiest is absolute class voting: the proportion of the working class voting for a party, plus the proportion of the middle class voting for the other party or parties. But this means that as classes change in size, so does the measure, so this does not measure the extent to which members of a class vote for other parties. It is also possible to create various indices of relative class voting, such as the Alford index. This is calculated by subtracting the party's vote share of the working class from the non-working class (Alford 1967). For example, if a party gets 50 per cent of the vote share of manual workers and 30 per cent of non-manual workers, the index is 0.2. But this measure also depends on the size of classes, which change over time. The measure of odds ratio, which is a statistical measure of the likelihood of one class voting for a party divided by the odds for another class, gets round this problem of the size of classes (Heath, Jowell, and Curtice 1985).

the working class voted for another party, the Tories were sunk in electoral terms. The party built up a network of local associations to sustain working-class support, whose buildings can still be seen in many a British town centre. There is also a link between working-class support and belief in the union of the UK, partly based on commitment to a Protestant state. Unionism was important in Scotland (Seawright and Curtice 2008), and some parts of England, like Liverpool (Jeffery 2017). It is often forgotten that the full title of the Conservatives is 'The Conservative and Unionist Party'.

Roughly about a third of working-class voters continued voting Conservative during the twentieth century and were the subject of a classic sociological study called *Angels in Marble*. This found that working-class Tory supporters were better paid and had more supervisory roles within the working class, seeing themselves as a 'cut above others' (McKenzie and Silver 1968). Labour was a working-class party, but it also drew on middle-class support from the caring professions, such as teachers, and intellectuals, a trend that has grown over time. Class support for political parties is thus a complicated set of relationships, especially as classes themselves are internally differentiated, with party support varying within classes as well as between them. This means that the quotation by Peter Pulzer needs to be treated cautiously, even at the highpoint of class politics.

4.7.1 Has class voting declined?

In the 1980s, there was an academic debate about whether class voting had declined. The claim is based on the weakened association between class and vote for Labour (Franklin 1985). Survey data indicated that voters had become de-aligned or detached from parties they had previously identified with (Särlvik and Crewe 1983). The dispute about whether social class voting had declined was partly over measurement, with the BES studies proclaiming the survival of class politics when using a better definition of working class and deploying the odds ratio statistic (Heath, Jowell, and Curtice 1985) (see Zoom-In 4.4). The debate got technical and heated (for example, Dunleavy 1987).

In the end, no one could dispute that the detachment of the working class, however defined, from the Labour Party became very marked in the years of New

Labour from 1997 to 2010, for some of the reasons discussed in sections 3.6.8 and 4.4.8. In the research of Geoff Evans and colleagues, traditional Labour voters not only did not turn out for their party, but increasingly voted for other parties, such as the United Kingdom Independence Party (UKIP) (Mellon and Evans 2016) (see section 5.3.2). Working-class Labour voters reacted against the preference of the Labour leadership to occupy the centre ground and to articulate a classless style of politics (Evans and Tilley 2017). They were sympathetic to messages based on strong immigration controls and law and order. Even though Blair and senior Labour colleagues understood these concerns, they were stressed more clearly by far-right parties, such as the extreme British National Party (BNP) and UKIP (John and Margetts 2009; Ford and Goodwin 2014). Working-class support from Labour voters was crucial in support for Brexit in the referendum of 2016. In time, many of these voters forgot their hostility to the Conservative Party, and turned out to vote against Labour in the 2019 general election (Evans and Mellon 2020) and the 2021 local elections.

For graphical representation the easiest technique is to divide classes into managerial and professional occupations (Figure 4.13a), and semi-routine and routine occupations (Figure 4.13b). This shows the changing relationships between party and the vote over time that precedes the 2019 result, with the working-class base of Labour support, and the reversal of the normal pattern of class voting. The

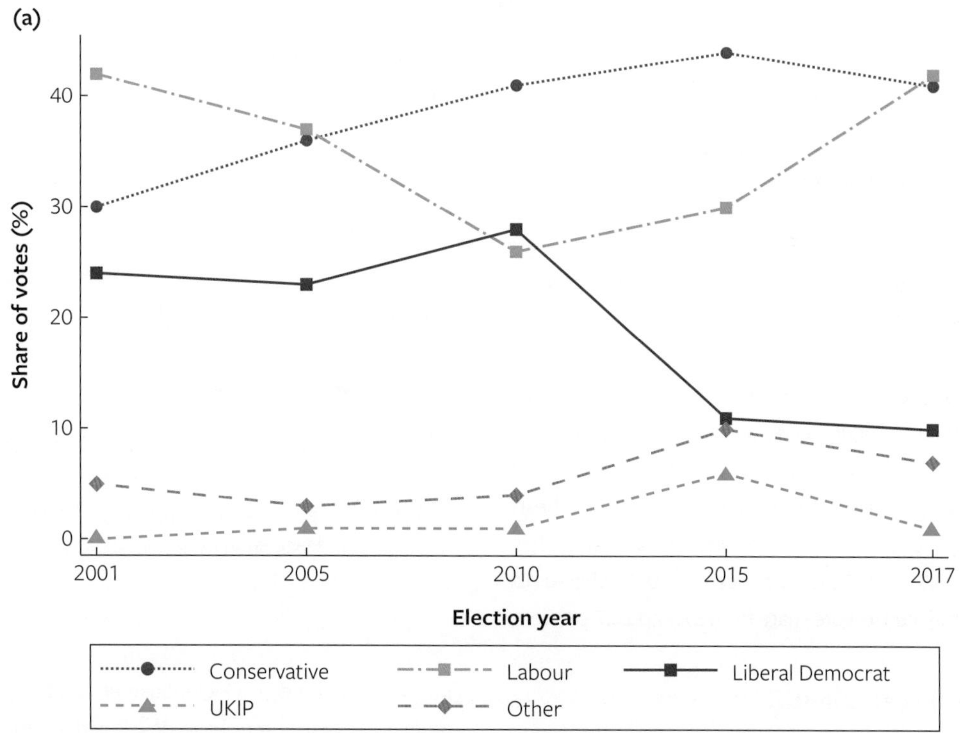

Figure 4.13a Party vote shares, 2001–17: professionals and managers.
Source: Phillips et al. (2017, 25)
Note: In this figure, social class was measured using the National Statistics Socio-economic Classification (NS-SEC): 'managerial and professional'; 'intermediate', composed of self-employed, lower supervisory, or employer in a small organization; and 'routine', composed of those with routine or semi-routine occupations

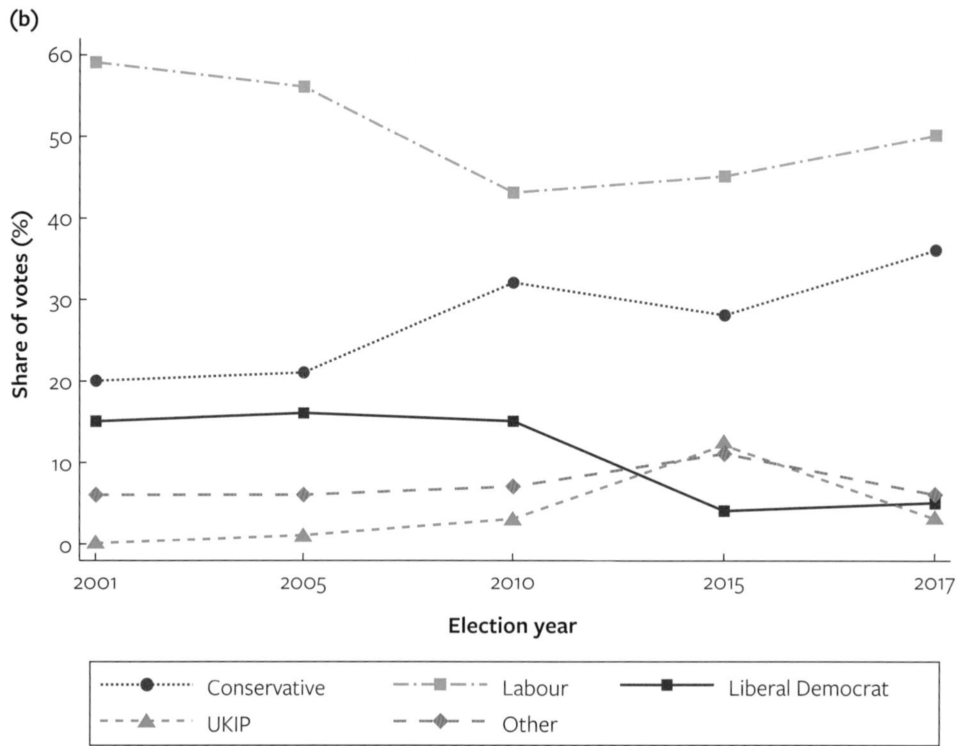

Figure 4.13b Party vote shares, 2001–17: routine occupations.
Source: Phillips et al. (2017, 25)

4

Conservative Party increased its lead of 9 percentage points among working-class voters in 2017 to 21 points in 2019. Results from the 2021 local elections suggest the Conservative Party has increased its appeal among working-class voters, such as in the 2021 Hartlepool by-election, located in the 'northern wall' of new Conservative seats in Labour's former heartlands. The Conservative Party increased its vote share from 28.9 in 2019 to 51.9 per cent in 2021, whereas Labour reduced its vote share from 37.7 to 28.7 per cent.

Key term 4.13 Affective polarization

Affective polarization is the tendency for partisans to show strong animosity to the opposing partisans, such as seeing opponents as less intelligent and less open minded.

4.7.2 **Brexit identification**

The argument of many academics is that voters have started to adopt what is called a 'Brexit identity' (see section 4.8.1), which replaces a class-based identity. It is a new dimension to politics based on anti-elite (populist) sentiments (Fieldhouse et al. 2019). The argument is that voters have developed an affective polarization (Druckman and Levendusky 2019) (see Key term 4.13), whereby partisans show strong animosity towards their opponents, identifying negative traits. Studies show that this phenomenon is emerging in British politics, linked to the Brexit Remain/Leave vote divide (Hobolt, Leeper, and Tilley 2020; Duffy et al. 2019).

It is important to note that Brexit was just one of the factors behind these attitudes, and they had been building up over many decades. Brexit stimulated but did not directly cause affective polarization. It does not mean that beliefs in left and right do not also continue to affect voting behaviour, but that other dimensions are now more important (Hobolt and Rodon 2020). In the BES survey of 2017, 26 per cent of respondents said they had a Conservative identity and 30 per cent a Labour one; whereas 43 per cent said they identified as a leaver and 44 per cent as a remain supporter (Hobolt, Leeper, and Tilley 2020, 13). Brexit identity, including that of many working-class supporters, drove working-class support for the Conservative Party. The long-term question is whether Brexit, having been achieved on 31 January 2020, by a government elected by many of these voters, will be superseded by concerns about the Covid-19 crisis and the economic fallout in its wake (which might harm working-class areas in cities and cause these voters to turn against the Conservatives), or whether these Brexit attitudes will shape the responses to Covid-19 itself. The findings so far indicate a link between Brexit identity and Covid-19 responses, but it is not strong (Sturgis, Jackson, and Kuha 2020), with some studies indicating not much of a connection (Dennison and Duffy 2021). US evidence is suggestive, as the polarized electorate has different assessments of the federal government's Covid-19 response (Druckman et al. 2020a, 2020b), but Britain is not as polarized as the US (Duffy 2020).

Beneath the decline in the relationship between class and vote are long-term social factors, in particular linked to the decline of party identification discussed in section 4.4.5, which reduced the number of voters who were prepared to maintain allegiance to Labour through thick and thin, such as during the electoral disaster of 1983 when the Labour vote reduced to 28 per cent of the electorate. While Labour's performance in 2019 was better, they gained votes from outside the working class. However, they lost seats in areas that had been loyal in previous generations. The other factor is the growing importance of what can cause new cleavages that cross class, based on new identities and interests, such as by age group, region, and Brexit identity. It is important to stress that this does not mean that class is not important, as class issues intersect with other new dimensions in politics, with some working-class Brexit supporters articulating class animosity to bankers and middle-class metropolitan types.

4.7.3 The multi-factor approach to vote choice

In studies of vote choice, there are many factors at play, without the necessary dominance of one factor, even class, which reflects the diverse and varied social geography of Britain today. Age becomes increasingly linked to vote choice, with younger voters more attracted to Labour who also happened to be middle-class voters, but facing more pressures in the labour and housing market than their parents' generations. Thus, in the 2019 election as reported by MORI, 62 per cent of eighteen- to twenty-four-year-olds voted Labour whereas 64 per cent of the over sixty-fives voted Conservative, which contrasts with the social class figures, showing the importance of this cleavage in British politics, which has been growing rapidly since the 1990s. There is a debate as to whether the changes are generational or based on particular influences on a cohort, with the evidence pointing to the latter (Tilley and Evans 2014).

4.7.4 Gender, education, LGBT+, and ethnic-minority voters

Gender tends to moderate these differences according to age, with the MORI 2019 survey reporting that women are more likely to vote Labour, with a 3 per cent lead among women, whereas women were less likely to support Conservative by the same margin. Young women were more likely to vote Labour than young men and vice versa for older voters. Research for many years has highlighted the independent role of gender as a determinant of partisan choices, with a 'gender gap' in evidence independent of other factors (Campbell 2006). The gender gap initially involved women leaning towards voting for the Conservative Party for historical and deeply gendered reasons relating to family values and religiosity, but this reduced from 1992, and then switched in favour of Labour from 2015 (see Figure 4.12, which reports the difference between the Conservative and Labour lead for women and for men).

Education plays a role, though it is closely linked to social class, so voters with qualifications were more likely to vote Conservative, whereas there was more balance among Labour voters. This relationship has weakened in recent years, with less educated and older voters supporting the Conservative Party, as Labour has lost support with its old working-class base. In 2019, more of the less educated voters voted Conservative, reflecting also the switch in social class as well as age.

Ethnic minorities continue to vote for Labour, which is a long-term phenomenon to do with social disadvantage, and negative perceptions about the race policies of the Conservatives (Heath et al. 2011; Sanders et al. 2014). These studies show there is differentiation of values within the ethnic-minority groups, with religious observance, traditional values, and private sector business ownership pointing to a weakening of the relationship to Labour. The Conservative Party has not benefited in spite of efforts at improving recruitment of candidates. Sobolewska (2005, 210) uses regression analysis to show that traditionalist values are driven by African, Caribbean, Indian, and Pakistani respondents.

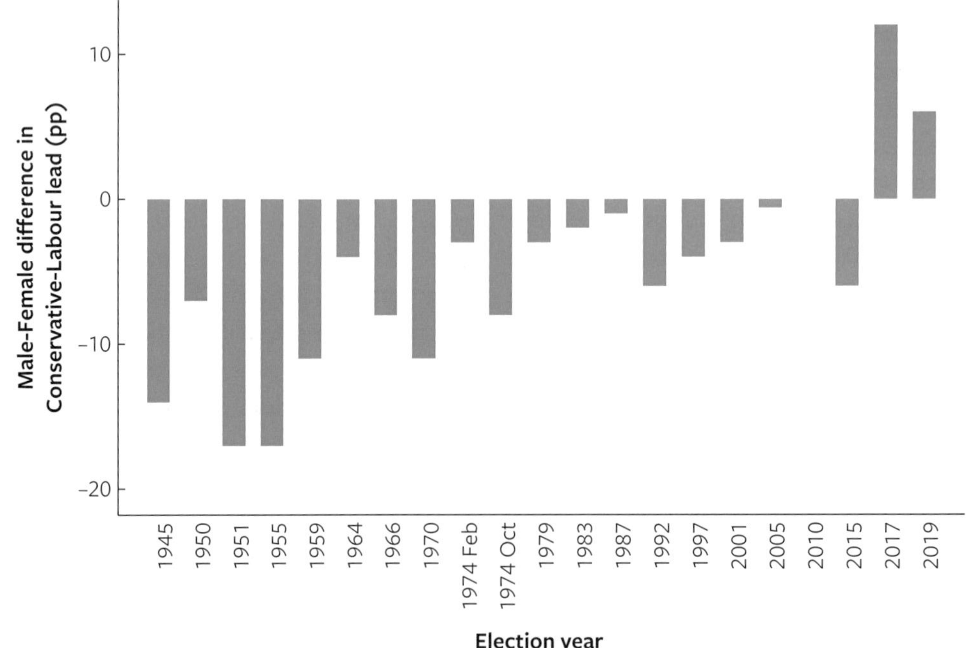

Figure 4.14 Gender gaps at British elections, 1945–2019.
Source: Campbell (2019); (Skinner, Mortimore, and Spielman 2019)
Note: These data are based on cisgender people, and do not account for non-binary voters

There has not been very much research on LGBT+ voters as these identities are not often recorded in surveys and the numbers tend to be small for statistical analysis. But Stuart Turnbull-Dugarte (2020) managed to locate same-sex couples in the European Social Survey, finding that lesbian and gay respondents identify with the left, support leftist policy objectives, and vote for left-of-centre political parties. In Britain, he uses the *UK's Understanding Society* dataset to show that Labour benefits, especially from younger voters (Turnbull-Dugarte 2020).

4.7.5 **Place-based vote choices**

Linked to age and identity is the growing importance of place, such as the politics of voters in large metropolitan areas tending to be more liberal, left-wing, and Green or Liberal Democrat voting, with more rural and small towns having more Conservative voters (Sobolewska and Ford 2020, 48–54, 303). Researchers have been aware of the spatial aspect of voting behaviour for some time now (Johnston and Pattie 2006), whereby variations across space because of different geographies are accentuated over time because people tend to imitate the behaviour of those living close to them.

Overall, there is more differentiation in voting in the British electorate, with less clear class voting, and with other demographic and social factors impacting on vote choice, as age cohort, gender, and Brexit identity are now increasingly important. In fact, these elements interact considerably and reinforce each other (Johnston, Jones, and Manley 2018), and need statistical models using many variables, as the causal order (for example, whether class is more important than age) is not easily ascertained.

4.7.6 **Second-order elections**

It is important to add the factors that explain voting in a subnational context, which have some similarities to the UK national level because voters are asked to support many of the same parties and because voters often use these elections to give a signal to the UK government, or perhaps correlate with the national vote if held on the same day. Because these are what are called second-order elections, voters may be more inclined to vote for other parties, such as the Liberal Democrats or UKIP, because the stakes are lower as it is not a vote for or against an incumbent government (Heath et al. 1999). Second-order elections, with the exception of English local government, are not FPTP contests so there is a better chance of small parties winning. There are other parties, such as the Northern Ireland parties, that have their own social basis for support as well as class voting (Evans and Tonge 2009), as do the nationalist parties in Scotland (for example, Johns and Mitchell 2016) and Wales (Scully and Jones 2012). As the UK becomes more differentiated and separated, it may be the case that rather than second-order elections, there are separate nationally based systems, each with their own determinants of vote choice, as in Wales (McAllister and Awan-Scully 2021) and Scotland (Mitchell and Henderson 2020).

4.8 Voting in referendums

So far, this chapter has covered general participation in politics, in particular voting in elections. Before the 1970s that would have ended the review of political action in British politics, but since 1973 there have been exercises in what is called direct democracy (Key term 4.14). One form of direct democracy is a referendum where citizens, by Act of Parliament, are given the chance to vote on a proposition and to determine the outcome in subsequent policy (see Zoom-In 4.4). In the UK, these referendums are non-binding, though it would be hard for a government to ignore the result having accepted the principle, and they would need to have a second referendum to reverse the first. Although the first UK referendum was in 1973, over the border in Ireland, the first national referendum arose from the divisions within the Labour Party over Europe, specifically European Economic Community (EEC, the precursor to the EU) membership, which the prime minister, Harold Wilson, decided to settle by allowing the referendum in 1975. This referendum saw the suspension of cabinet collective responsibility, with members campaigning on both sides (see Butler and Kitzinger 1976). Apart from two devolution referendums in 1979, they were not used again until the Labour government of 1997 deployed them to legitimate a series of constitutional reforms which included: directly electing mayors, a new authority and mayor for London, a new Parliament with law-making powers for Scotland, an assembly for Wales, and then an attempt to introduce regional assemblies, with the failed plan of getting sanction for an assembly for the North East of England. Then there was a second referendum on Scottish independence in 2014. The latest referendum was in 2016 on whether Britain should leave the European Union (the Brexit referendum).

Key term 4.14 Direct democracy

Instead of representative democracy, where citizens elect someone to represent them, in direct democracy citizens participate directly, either where everyone participates in an assembly or makes choices in referendums or online polls (see Zoom-In 4.1).

In some accounts (for example, Weale 2018), referendums are not thought to fit well within a representative democracy, as political authority should rest with the elected representative, and this provides democracy with both intelligence and responsiveness. Referendums appear to work for politicians who believe (maybe erroneously) that they solve problems and conflict within their parties, or if they wish to seek extra consent for their policies. However, referendums can unleash the less tolerant and more emotional side to politics, often through populism (see Zoom-In 4.3). Partisan politics, however, is not far from the surface in many referendums, such as in 2011 on the alternative vote, which was informally opposed by the Conservative Party, and also Labour, which helped ensure its defeat (Curtice 2011). Referendums give people a chance to vote against party positions; they can encourage citizens to use these contests to punish elites, and to use them to express long-held resentment against the established party politicians. In the referendum of North East England in 2004 to introduce a regional assembly, citizens punished the government for promising more politicians and another layer of government (Tickell, John, and Musson 2005). In elections, parties can dominate campaigns and frame them as government issues, whereas in referendums, it is possible for campaigns to highlight issues that the parties do not wish to discuss. If there is an undercurrent of dissatisfaction with established politics, it is possible that referendums can be a vehicle for populist movements that use the campaign to influence voters (Topaloff 2017). There is some evidence that opinion change in a referendum can be stronger than for election campaigns (Leduc 2002). Whereas in elections, many nuanced issues can be discussed, the referendum reduces the issue to just two sides, therefore encouraging the oversimplification of arguments, and polarization as a consequence.

The opposing argument is that there is nothing to stop the UK Parliament from engaging in populist and

Zoom-In 4.5 Referendums in British politics

Definition: a poll of citizens, resident in a jurisdiction, to decide a proposition, usually by simple majority.

Practice in Britain: needs to be authorized by an Act of Parliament; government is not required to implement the decision, but has done so.

Examples:

8 March 1973: Northern Ireland—Northern Ireland sovereignty referendum on whether Northern Ireland should remain part of the United Kingdom or join the Republic of Ireland (yes to remaining part of the UK).

5 June 1975: UK—Membership of the European Community referendum on whether the UK should stay in the European Community (yes).

1 March 1979: Scotland—Scottish devolution referendum on whether there should be a Scottish Assembly (40 per cent of the electorate had to vote yes in the referendum; although a small majority voted yes, this was short of the 40 per cent threshold required to enact devolution).

1 March 1979: Wales—Welsh devolution referendum on whether there should be a Welsh Assembly (no).

11 September 1997: Scotland—Scottish devolution referendums on whether there should be a Scottish Parliament and whether the Scottish Parliament should have tax-varying powers (both referendums received a yes vote).

18 September 1997: Wales—Welsh devolution referendum on whether there should be a National Assembly for Wales (yes).

7 May 1998: London—Greater London Authority referendum on whether there should be a Mayor of London and Greater London Authority (yes).

22 May 1998: Northern Ireland—Northern Ireland Belfast Agreement referendum on the Good Friday Agreement (yes).

3 March 2011: Wales—Welsh devolution referendum on whether the National Assembly for Wales should gain the power to legislate on a wider range of matters (yes).

5 May 2011: UK—referendum on whether to change the voting system for electing MPs to the House of Commons from first past the post to the alternative vote (no; FPTP will continue to be used to elect MPs to the House of Commons).

18 September 2014: Scotland—referendum on whether Scotland should become an independent country (no; the electorate voted 55 per cent to 45 per cent in favour of Scotland remaining within the UK).

23 June 2016: UK's membership of the European Union—whether to leave or remain in the EU (52 per cent voted in favour of leaving the EU).

Note: since 2001 there have also been referendums on whether to have local mayors.

Further information is on the Parliament UK website: www.parliament.uk/get-involved/vote-in-general-elections/referendums-held-in-the-uk.

emotional policies without referendums, especially on the back of decisive election results, whereas some referendums can reflect a more reasoned choice and the build-up of consensus, such as for new electoral bodies in London, Wales, and Scotland. A middle course in this argument is to say that *some* referendums do allow more extreme arguments to come into play. But referendums can work well when there is a lot of preparation and public debate beforehand (University College et al. 2018). Some countries, such as the US and Switzerland, have integrated referendums into their decision-making process over many years, showing that representative and direct forms of democracy can work alongside each other (Mendelsohn and Parkin 2001). Campaigns in referendums can gain momentum. But many referendums are more sober exercises, where they suffer from lower turnout and acceptance of the official line, such as the one for the London mayor, and to set up the Welsh Assembly (see Figure 4.13). Partly because referendums are unusual in British politics, they vary a lot. This is shown by the levels of turnout that occur, as illustrated by Figure 4.12, where some get over 80 per cent of the vote, whereas others barely get over 30 per cent (note the 1973 poll was boycotted by the nationalists who wanted unification of Ireland). In spite of the variation, few contests are as dramatic as the Brexit referendum, reported in full in section 10.4.8 but discussed briefly in section 4.8.1.

4.8.1 **Brexit and vote choice**

A significant example of a referendum in UK politics is the choice to leave the EU in 2016 (see more extended discussion in section 10.4.8), which had been caused by Prime Minister David Cameron's promise to his Eurosceptic backbenchers in the belief that the public opinion would back both the main parties and experts. But deep divisions caused by anti-politics and Euroscepticism, stoked by parts of the media and social media, dominated the campaign. The 2016 poll also highlights that referendums typically give one vote to each citizen, which means that voters in safe Westminster seats can find that their vote makes a difference, thus increasing turnout from those voters (Abreu and Öner 2020, 1437), though it is hard to disentangle this

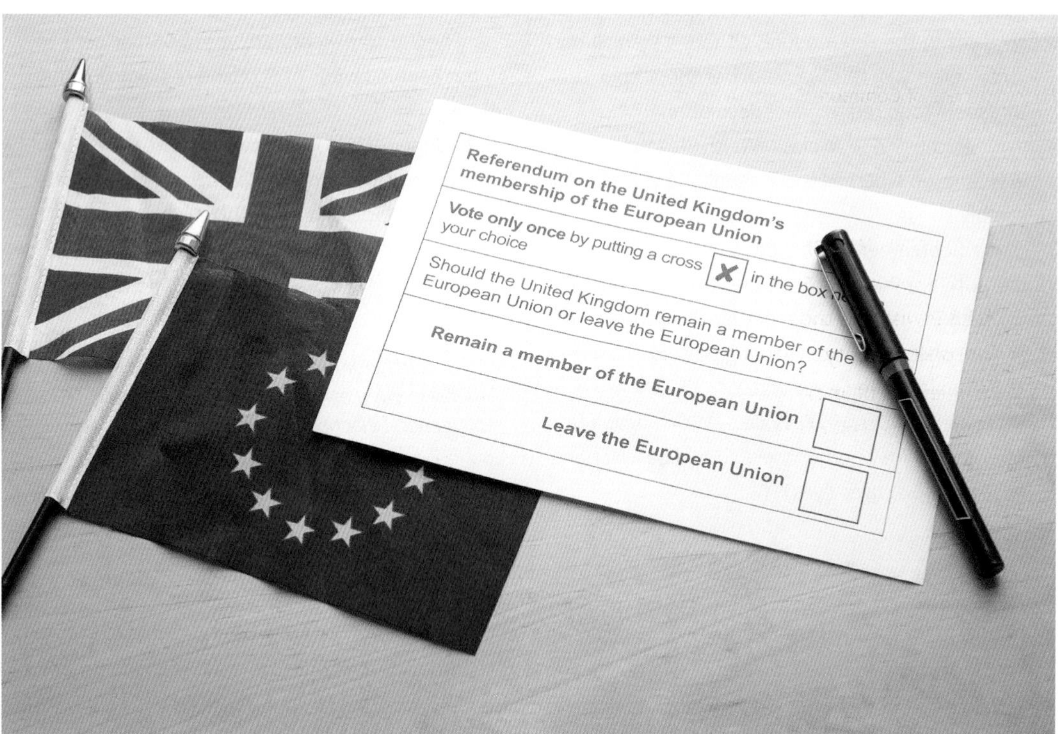

Photo 4.6 Voting ballot for the referendum on the United Kingdom's membership of the European Union.

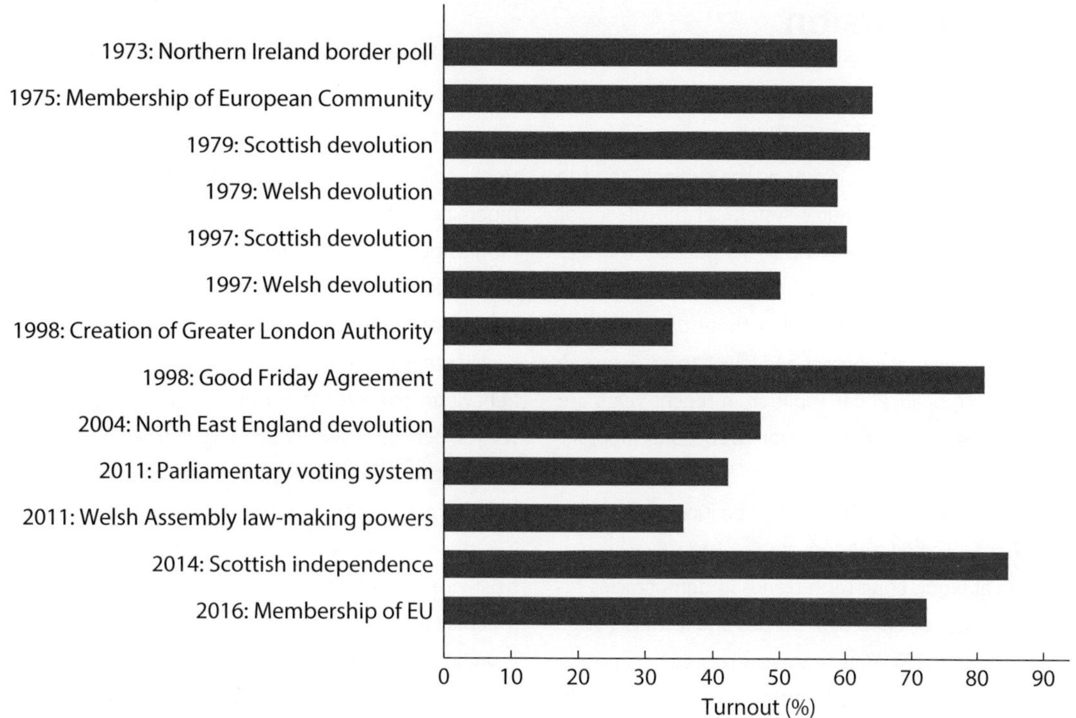

Figure 4.15 Voter turnout in UK referendums, 1973–2016.
Source: House of Commons Research Briefing: https://researchbriefings.files.parliament.uk/documents/CBP-7692/CBP-7692.pdf

effect from other determinants of turnout and vote choice, such as education and age. We discussed in section 4.7.2 whether the 2016 referendum helped foster a Brexit identity, which can in part replace traditional left–right party identification of voters, and shows the power of referendums to shift the agenda of politics.

We can observe that the occasion to use some referendums in British politics can be a source of political turbulence. Although many UK referendums were called to solve problems that political parties or governments faced, they actually unleashed stronger views on these issues that either split the parties, as with the EU referendum, or benefited one party over its competitor, as with the SNP over Labour in Scotland. David Cameron was keen on calling referendums (2011, 2014, and 2016), but he was only successful in the first of them in dampening the political agenda. For example, the 2014 referendum strengthened the SNP and support for a second Scottish independence referendum; the 2016 Brexit referendum prompted cultural divisions, affecting the 2017 and 2019 elections. With Brexit 'done', it remains to be seen whether these forces will weaken and if more routine or 'bread and butter' issues, such as the state of the economy or quality of public services, will return to the core of the agenda of British politics. If the pre-Brexit changes that have been documented in this chapter are projected into the future (also see Sobolewska and Ford 2020), then the answer is probably 'no'.

4.9 Conclusion

In this chapter, the perspective of the book has been reversed: it takes the citizens as the subject, and the formal part of the political system as the object of attention. This is about citizens as political thinkers and actors, who have views about politics. They still support democratic politics, but these days display a higher degree of discontent and lower trust. Even the increases in political participation in recent years are linked to greater dissatisfaction with contemporary politics.

4

The changes show how British politics has become more complicated and less stable. There are several factors at work. Long-term trends in democracies favour outsider or challenger parties and leaders (Vries and Hobolt 2020). Voters are less rooted in supporting conventional political parties, which is a trend in Britain going back to the 1970s (Särlvik and Crewe 1983), bolstered by some new tendencies towards political turbulence more generally. British citizens are divided, often not sharing the same cultural views about politics and life in general (Duffy et al. 2019). The difference is especially marked across different age groups, with younger people voting and thinking differently to older generations. Anti-politics (Clarke et al. 2018), which entails greater distrust of conventional politics and politicians, has emerged across democracies, which makes voter turbulence more common as people become less likely to put their faith in conventional political parties and to follow the recommendations of those in office.

Whether democracies need a set of attitudes and behaviours to ensure they function effectively is a matter for debate. There is certainly a baseline needed, but whether different levels of trust and confidence in politics make a difference is hard to ascertain. While it is the case that a degree of scepticism and lack of trust are important for democracy, the stealth democracy model that many citizens hold is not a great foundation for democratic politics. When citizens and voters are not fully engaged, they are likely to behave in dramatic ways. It is harder for political leaders and parties to adapt, perhaps causing them to make rash decisions. Add to that the fact that many stable features of political orientation have weakened in recent years, such as falls in party identification, and greater differentiation in the drivers of attitudes and participation. It is a complex environment for both politicians and citizens to make sense of.

Further reading

The best source, even if from a few years ago, is the book of the Citizenship Audit, which was based on a national survey (Pattie, Seyd, and Whiteley 2004). Also, the book *Why Democracy Matters* (2006) by Gerry Stoker is a concise introduction to the field. The topic of anti-politics is best conveyed by the work of Clarke, Jennings, Moss, and Stoker (2018). There are more specific publications on trust and discontent (Jennings et al. 2017). Sobolewska and Ford's *Brexitland* (2020) is a mine of information on changing attitudes in British politics.

The social determinants of voting are best conveyed by publications emerging for the regular BES surveys, written up into regular books to cover key elections (the most recent is Fieldhouse et al. 2019), supplemented by other edited volumes (for 2019,

Tonge, Wilks-Heeg, and Thompson 2020), also useful for the next chapter. There are materials looking at the drivers of voting, especially class (Evans and Mellon 2020), sex/gender (Campbell 2006), ethnic minorities (Heath et al. 2011), and age (Tilley and Evans 2014). Many of these references require a bit of technical knowledge to understand (or patience to read around the statistical discussions). To help the reader *Elections and Voters in Britain* (Denver, Carman, and Johns 2012) is a very clear introduction to the field.

There is a lot of material on referendums (e.g. Qvortrup 2017; University College et al. 2018). There is a growing amount of work on voting and participation across the nations, such as Wales (McAllister and Awan-Scully 2021), Scotland (Mitchell and Henderson 2020), and Northern Ireland (Tonge, Wilks-Heeg, and Thompson 2020). For attitudes in Scotland there is survey work carried out by the Scottish NatCen (https://whatscotlandthinks.org).

Essay and examination questions

In terms of attitudes, one question could point backward and ask, 'Is there a civic culture in Britain?'. The current period can also be captured by the question, 'What is anti-politics? What are its consequences for democracy in Britain?' or 'To what extent has the electorate turned away from politics?'. This could link to a more general question about populism, such as 'What is the influence of populism in British politics?', though this would also need materials from the following chapters, which cover party systems and media/campaigns.

One question could focus on equality and participation, such as 'What are the factors that affect political participation in Britain today?'. Another question could address recent changes, such as 'Is there a crisis of political participation in Britain?'. In terms of voter turnout, the question could be 'Why does voter turnout in elections vary between groups, places and over time?'. Referendums could be linked to wider concerns about political change in British politics as in 'Are referendums a vehicle for populism?'.

Then there are questions about voter choice, especially about the various influences, such as class and party, and whether it has declined. The question about Brexit data could be posed in a reformat of the Peter Pulzer quotation: 'Brexit is the basis of British party politics; all else is embellishment and detail'. Discuss'.

Access the online resources for this chapter, including biannual updates, web links, and multiple-choice questions: www.oup.com/he/John1e

Chapter 5

Winning and Losing Elections

5

5.1 What is going to be in this chapter?

This chapter explores what politicians and members of political parties really care about: getting into office on the back of a successful election campaign. Rather than the general determinants of voting outlined in Chapter 4, this one is about the choices voters and parties face within a particular system, so they can organize themselves to win. For that they need to play by the rules of the game, which includes developing strategies within electoral systems. In this chapter, there is discussion of the impact of electoral systems on that calculus, and how the number of parties is affected by the electoral system in place. The chapter then looks at the factors that assist the winning of elections, and the extent to which the choices of parties and voters are affected by growing instability in the system. Overall, this chapter provides an overview of British political parties and party systems.

5.2 Introduction

The key feature of democratic life is elections, which can happen at different territorial levels, such as national, regional, and local governments, or for specific offices, such as an elected mayor, or a police commissioner. From these events, winners and losers emerge; then, as a consequence of winning, certain groups of people or a person may exercise power and decide policy for a period of time, until the next contest decides whether they may continue or not. Losers are denied this access to power, so they have to bide their time; instead of governing, they seek to influence public and elite opinion about the competence of the incumbents, and convey their own credibility as potential replacements (or at least as effective critics). Electoral contests are fundamental to democracy, so it is important to understand them, and find out what determines who wins or loses. They matter in terms of the outcomes that everyone gets, both for winners and losers, and for a sense of fairness of the system and its legitimacy.

Even though understanding electoral contests is the topic of this chapter, it is important to introduce a set of organizations that affect how these elections take place. In the UK, it is rare for people to run for office on their own as independents (as Ken Livingstone once did for the election of the mayor of London, 2000); they are usually candidates who have a political party as a label, such as the Labour Party, Scottish National Party, and so on. Parties are political organizations that seek to hold public office and win power, and approve candidates who represent the party and adhere to the party line. Political parties are distinct from pressure groups that lobby on a range of issues, which might be quite similar to parties in having ideologies, and policy positions, and members, but they do not seek office. Parties usually have a set of ideas of how to change the country or to maintain it in its current state, which they simplify as promises made to the electorate at elections, via manifestos and party-political broadcasts. Given changes in public policies that result from elections, it really matters which party wins.

In democracies, parties also compete with each other for votes: they operate in relationship to each other in what is called a party system. In this set-up, they need to adjust their policy positions to be able to succeed. If parties are in government or in office, they need to ensure the outputs of government meet the approval of voters and their leaders appear competent and worthy of re-election. When planning for elections, parties need to take account of the various voting systems in play to forge a strategy that can win against their rivals. Then they need to campaign for support in election campaigns, which involves social media, broadcast media like TV, and the old-fashioned door-to-door Get Out the Vote (GOTV) exercises (see section 6.7).

Politics takes shape as a result of these processes, which again informs how a democracy in Britain works, as parties can provide a bridge between the experiences of citizens discussed in Chapter 4, and the world of leaders and Parliament covered in Part A. Parties can perform this linkage function in terms of bringing coherence to policies and issues, providing a perspective on politics, representing interests, and even mobilizing the general population to take part in politics (for a review of these functions in comparative perspective, see Dalton, Farrell, and McAllister 2011). Furthermore, if parties have an important role, then how does the possible decline of parties, in terms of party identification in the electorate (see section 4.4.5) and reductions in the numbers of party members, affect the political system as a whole?

5.3 Basic facts: political parties

5.3.1 Defining terms

The first basic fact is about what distinguishes a political party from an interest group. There are some ambiguities in this distinction, as some parties tend to be focused on single issues (sometimes called 'niche parties'), such as the Green Party with its mission for the environment, or what are called 'challenger parties' (Vries and Hobolt 2020), such as the United Kingdom Independence Party (UKIP) and the Brexit Party, with their (achieved) goal of Britain leaving the European Union (see Key term 4.5). These parties may have little initial hope of winning a large number of seats in national elections, but their main objective is to shape the political agenda, often quite successfully, as in the case of UKIP. Some political parties, such as the Labour Party, have a very close relationship to trade unions, and have them as part of their governance. Trade unions, as well as representing their members in particular occupations, have wider policy objectives and sponsor MPs. But in practice there is a big difference between the trade unions and the Labour Party, with the latter being an electoral campaign organization and either a party of government or opposition. Similarly, niche or focused parties often feel compelled to produce a policy programme across many areas not connected to the party's original mission to campaign effectively and they need to answer questions from journalists, such as a policy for the NHS, for example. The distinction between parties and interest groups still makes sense: parties seek elected office; interest groups do not.

5.3.2 Names of and facts about political parties

Another set of basic facts includes information about the family of political parties in the UK today and an understanding of their history (for a summary, see Table 5.1). There is a lot of information available on party histories and organization (Driver 2011; Awan-Scully 2018), but it is useful at least to know the very basic outlines. It is important to begin by looking at the historic parties, which have tended to dominate Parliament, and then move on to discuss newer parties. The Conservative and Unionist Party, commonly referred to as the Conservative Party, was founded in 1834. Its roots go back much earlier to the Tory Party (Conservatives are referred to today colloquially as 'Tories'), which was a more informal organization closely allied to the monarch and established interests, formed in the 1770s. The Conservatives are what might be called a centre-right party—that is, on the right of the political spectrum, but often tacking to the centre. As represented in the views of its foundational political thinkers, such as Edmund Burke (1790), Conservatives are interested in preserving the current order, and are thought to be pragmatic and electorally focused above all. However, ideology and lack of pragmatic politics are often evident in Conservative Party politics, such as in the 1990s and 2010s when the Party was tearing itself apart over membership of the European Union. This kind of internecine split had happened before over free trade at the start of the twentieth century (Green 1996), though the Party overcame its divisions by 1914. Even with these tendencies towards self-destruction, the Party has been very successful electorally throughout its history. Since 1945, the Conservatives have been in power (singly or in a coalition) during 1951–64, 1970–4, 1979–97, and 2010 to the present. In 2021, it is led by Boris Johnson.

The other major party is the Labour Party (Photo 5.1), which was formed in 1900 as the Labour Representation Committee, changing its name to the Labour Party in 1906. At root it is a working-class party seeking to represent workers from unskilled and skilled trades. It traditionally gained support in areas

Table 5.1 List of the main parties in the United Kingdom

Name	Date formed	Basic description
Conservative and Unionist Party	1834	Right of centre, pragmatic instincts (usually)
The Labour Party	1906	Social democratic, strong trade union links
Liberal Democrats	1988	Defender of liberal values, e.g. freedom and individual rights
The Scottish National Party (SNP)	1934	Campaign for Scotland's independence from the UK
Plaid Cymru	1925	Campaign for Wales' independence from the UK, champion of the Welsh language
Green Party	1990	Radical environment transformation
Sinn Féin	1905	Unified Ireland
Social Democratic and Labour Party (SDLP)	1970	Unified Ireland, social and civic rights
Ulster Unionist Party (UUP)	1905	Defend the union and its values
Democratic Unionist Party (DUP)	1971	More radical unionist
Alliance Party	1970	Moderate non-sectarian party
United Kingdom Independence Party (UKIP)	1993	Independence of UK from EU
Brexit Party	2019	Independence of UK from EU

with heavy industry, such as in the north of England and central Scotland. But middle-class and intellectual input has been important right from the start, and like many parties, it is a coalition of interests. Ideas play a prominent role through the debates about the meaning of socialism (Key term 5.1) and its commitment to progressive social change as represented in the term 'social democracy' (Key term 5.2). As with the Conservative Party, it has a national electoral organization and is capable of tacking its programme and policies to the centre to attract votes, winning elections for significant periods in the twentieth and twenty-first centuries (1945–51, 1964–70, 1974–9, and 1997–2010), producing six prime ministers since its founding: in reverse order, Gordon Brown, Tony Blair, James Callaghan, Harold Wilson, Clement Attlee, and Ramsay MacDonald. In 2021, it is led by Sir Keir Starmer.

The other historic party is the Liberal Democrats, though only formed in 1988. The Party, originally called the Whigs, goes back to the same period as the

Key term 5.1 Socialism

A critique of private ownership and the power of capital as a cause of social problems, such as economic and political inequality. Advocates the rights of working-class and poor citizens. Common cause either advanced at the ballot box or by direct action, including revolution. When a socialist party gains power there is radical economic and social change, including extensive public ownership.

Photo 5.1 The Labour Party logo.

Key term 5.2 Social democracy

Linked to socialism, but a more moderate philosophy that seeks gradual progressive social changes by building coalitions between the working class and other groups for electoral victory.

Tories as a grouping less connected to the establishment. It was in favour of the power of Parliament, and was an espouser of ideas of limited government. The nineteenth-century version of the Party was called the Liberal Party, which emerged as a coalition of Whigs, Radicals, Peelites (breakaway Tories), and the Independent Irish Party, which gradually formed into a modern political party in the 1870s. It was initially a competitor to the Conservative Party, forming governments in the nineteenth and first two decades of the twentieth century, but was overtaken by Labour. It languished in the years since 1945, yet survived, emerging in some places as a challenger to the two main parties since the 1960s. Its electoral success tends to go in phases: challenging Labour along with the breakaway Social Democratic Party (SDP) in the 1980s; presenting an alternative to Labour over the Iraq war in the 2000s; entering coalition government with the Conservatives from 2010 to 2015, then a slow rebuild after a disastrous election defeat in 2015. In 2021, it is led by Sir Ed Davey.

The Green Party is another national-based party. Set up in 1972 as the PEOPLE Party by a small group in Coventry, it changed its name to the Ecology Party in 1975 and the Green Party in 1985. In 1990 it separated into three separate but allied parties: Northern Ireland, Scotland, and England and Wales. Its main ideological influences and divisions are a deep green ecological focus and a red-green approach, which joins environmentalism with socialism. In 2021, its co-leaders are Carla Denyer and Adrian Ramsay.

Other parties have a territorial focus but are no less important. The main one is the Scottish National Party (SNP), formed in 1934 from a union of the National Party of Scotland (founded in 1928) and the Scottish Party (1932). It has the aim of independence from the United Kingdom. It has sought to challenge the UK or unionist parties in Scotland. As with the Liberal Party, its support and popularity run in cycles, such as the revivals of the 1960s and then the 1970s, but it has been increasingly dominant in Scottish politics since devolution in 1999. In 2021, it is led by Nicola Sturgeon.

Plaid Cymru in Wales was formed in 1925 after Welsh nationalists had begun to organize themselves. Its principal focus is on gaining Welsh independence and promoting Welsh interests, including championing the Welsh language. It is generally seen as centre left. Its current leader is Adam Price.

Northern Irish parties are distinctive and compete between themselves. There are the nationalist and leftist parties: Sinn Féin and the Social Democratic and Labour (SDLP) Parties, with the former an all-Ireland party, with links in the past to the armed struggle against British rule, overtaking the SDLP in recent elections. Sinn Féin is led by Mary Lou McDonald (as president) and Michelle O'Neill (currently deputy first minister). The SDLP is led by Colum Eastwood. Then there are the unionist, protestant parties, such as the Ulster Unionist Party, which was the long-standing party that was in power in the devolved government up to 1972. It is led by Doug Beattie. Then the more radical party is the Democratic Unionist Party (DUP), which gained votes in the period since the Good Friday Agreement set up the current democratic arrangements in Northern Ireland (see section 9.3.4). Its leader in 2021 is Sir Jeffrey Donaldson. Aiming to occupy the centre ground is the Alliance Party. There are also a large number of other smaller parties in Northern Ireland.

There are more minor parties that stand for office in the rest of the UK, sometimes acquiring large shares of the popular vote. In recent years, UKIP leapt to prominence with its single issue of independence from the EU. Created as a Eurosceptic party in 1993 by the academic Alan Sked, its main focus was opposition to Britain's membership of the EU (with its main objective of Brexit successfully achieved in 2020); but it has also traditionally been an economically libertarian party and has campaigned to reduce immigration. As with the Green Party, these parties find it hard to get national representation, but they may come to dominate the political agenda. In the midst of the Brexit negotiations, its leader, Nigel Farage, broke away and formed the Brexit Party, which had considerable success in the 2019 European Parliament elections, topping the popular vote at 30.8 per cent, though its support has rapidly fallen away since then (now it is known as Reform UK).

There are other parties, but they tend to be based on special issues and poll low numbers of votes. In some accounts, it is estimated that there are around 400 political parties (Driver 2011, 5). Almost all of these parties are very small and do not really count for much when seeking to understand the British political system.

5.3.3 **Electoral systems**

The third set of facts concerns the rules of votes and elections, which affect how parties compete and campaign, and have a big effect on how well parties perform in electoral campaigns and results. Electoral systems convert votes into seats for a candidate or group of candidates and there is considerable variety in the UK (see a summary in Table 5.2). In the UK, the key unit is the single parliamentary constituency, in which a candidate needs to get a plurality over the other candidates in a constituency in order to win the seat. The winner does not need to get a majority of votes cast, just more than any other front-runner. This is called the First-Past-the-Post (FPTP) electoral system and is used to elect Members of Parliament to the House of Commons,

Table 5.2 Electoral systems in the United Kingdom
Source: Adapted from Parliament UK: www.parliament.uk/about/how/elections-and-voting/voting-systems

Name of system	Brief description	Where in operation
First-past-the-post (FPTP)	Winning candidate needs to poll the highest number of votes in single seat	House of Commons, English local authorities
Supplementary Vote (SV)	As with FPTP, where voter gets an additional vote. If a candidate fails to get 50 per cent of the vote, the second preferences of the first two ranked candidates are added to the first preferences to find out who gets more combined first and second preferences	Mayor of London, other English mayors, and police and crime commissioners
Alternative Vote (AV)	Voters rank each candidate. If the 50 per cent threshold is not reached, the candidate with the fewest first preference votes is eliminated, with the second preferences of these candidates reallocated to the others. This process continues until the candidate with the highest number of votes wins	Chairs of most committees in the House of Commons and the Lord Speaker, and by-elections for hereditary peers
Additional Member System (AMS)	Voters get one vote for a constituency representative, another for a party list. Members for each constituency are counted first, using FPTP. Then the additional members are selected from the votes for the party lists, according to the proportion of votes available	Scottish Parliament, Senedd Cymru, and the London Assembly
Single Transferable Vote (STV)	Multi-member constituencies, where voters rank the candidates. Each candidate needs to reach a quota which can be done on the first preferences for the first-ranked candidates. Once these votes are used up, the remainder second preferences go to the other candidates. Once the quota is used up, excess votes are redistributed. This process continues until all the seats in the constituency are taken	Northern Ireland Assembly elections and local elections in Scotland and Northern Ireland. It is also used for election of deputy speakers in the House of Commons

commonly called a majoritarian system. FPTP is also referred to by some academics as a single-member plurality system (Curtice 2018) (Key term 1.5). It is how a party can get into power at the national (UK) level. It also is used to elect local councillors in England, who run for an individual seat (even in multi-member wards).

FPTP is only one kind of electoral system, and other electoral systems are more common across the world, and have been increasing in prevalence in UK politics. These alternatives are often called proportional representation systems because they ensure that there is a close relationship between electoral preferences in the form of votes cast for political parties and the number of seats they get. These systems also vary amongst themselves and to the extent of proportionality they offer. Usually, they improve the proportionality achieved when compared to FPTP, rather than offer a fully proportional outcome between votes and seats. They also vary in the degree to which a voter can cast a ballot for more than one candidate or a party in a seat (see Renwick and Pilet 2016). Most countries in Europe have some version of proportional representation.

One system that is similar to FPTP is the Supplementary Vote (SV) as it is also based on single constituencies; but the voter gets an additional vote, often presented in a second column on the ballot paper, which are second preferences. If a candidate fails to get 50 per cent of the vote, the second preferences of the first two ranked candidates are added to the first preferences to see who gets more combined first and second preferences. It is used to elect the mayor of London, other mayors in England, and police and crime commissioners. Note that there is some similarity to the Alternative Vote (AV) system where voters rank each candidate as 1, 2, 3, etc., and then if the 50 per cent threshold is not reached, the candidate with the fewest first preference votes is eliminated, with the second preferences of these candidates reallocated to the other candidates. This process continues until the candidate with the highest number of votes wins. It has not been used in the UK, but has been proposed as a replacement for FPTP and was subject to a national referendum in 2011, which was decisively lost (see Chapter 11). The system is used to elect chairs of most committees in the House of Commons and the Lord Speaker, and by-elections for hereditary peers. It is used in some Australian elections (its federal House of Representatives and in Parliaments of Australian states) and in Papua New Guinea. The president of Ireland is elected by AV.

One of the most common forms of proportional representation is the Single Transferable Vote (STV), which involves constituencies with several representatives. Voters rank the candidates as 1, 2, 3, etc., as many ranks as they like, up to the total number of candidates. Each candidate needs to reach a quota, which can be done on the first preferences if these candidates are popular. Once these votes are used up, the remaining second preferences go to the other candidates and as a result they may reach the quota and their excess votes are redistributed. This process continues until all the seats in the constituency are taken. This system is used for Northern Ireland Assembly elections and local elections in Scotland and Northern Ireland. It is also used for electing deputy speakers in the House of Commons. A closed regional list, allocated by the D'Hondt system (the first seat goes to the party that has the most votes, then a formula is applied to a party's original total vote each time it wins a seat: number of votes/number of seats won + 1), was used to elect members of the European Parliament from 1979 to 2019, except in Northern Ireland which had STV. It is used in the Republic of Ireland and Malta.

Another system that is commonly used is the Additional Member System (AMS), which is used for the Scottish Parliament, the Senedd Cymru, and the London Assembly. Under AMS, voters get two votes, one for a constituency representative, the other for a party list (the parties draw up a list of candidates who are selected in order). This is organized by region in Scotland and Wales, and for the whole of London. Members for each constituency are counted first, using FPTP; then the additional members are selected from the votes for the party lists, according to the proportion of votes available for each seat. To be more precise, taking the difference between mixed-member proportional (MMP) and mixed-member majoritarian (MMM) types of AMS, the Scottish and Welsh systems are examples of the MMP type, with different proportions of regional list seats from the classic MMP model in Germany. It is used for elections to the New Zealand House of Representatives.

5.3.4 **Party systems**

Another set of basic facts concerns how political scientists discuss how parties operate together within a jurisdiction and/or level of government, using the term party system (see Key term 5.3). Party systems concern the number of parties typically in place in a democracy, usually in operation for long periods of time (see Mair 1990). They can be one-party dominant, whereby one party stays in power, maybe even for decades; there are two-party systems, where two parties take a large share of the votes and seats, alternating at regular intervals; or there are multi-party systems, with many parties where governments or coalitions are formed out of many partners, which tend to share the same ideological approach or are closer to each other than to other parties (though odd combinations are possible). A party system is often thought to be on an array, with parties placed on a continuum according to ideology or values, such as from left to right. One core idea is that these parties are in competition with each other, so a party system can yield different outcomes in terms of who wins depending on voter preferences and party strategies. One party might think that it can dominate electoral politics and stay in government for successive elections, or even longer, especially at the subnational level where there can be clusters of party identifiers, such as former workers in old industrial towns, who support a local party for decades. But parties also know that their dominance can be challenged and opposing parties can gain in popularity, win an election, and throw the incumbent out of power. After election, parties start to work out their chances of winning next time, deciding how to get ahead in choosing the issues to stress or policies to adopt, which might become a strategy for an electoral campaign. For these calculations, the nature of the party system matters, as well as which parties to compete with, such as minor parties in attracting votes away from a larger party that is not able to satisfy an intense minority of its supporters (for example, UKIP taking votes from the Conservative Party in the 2010s).

Key term 5.3 Party system

The number of parties typically in place at a territorial level in a democracy, such as two-party systems or one-party systems or many parties as in a multi-party system.

A party system can benefit one political party and disadvantage another; it can mean that a party can see it has a route to holding power by exclusively winning a majority of seats over others; or it can suggest which parties need to see others as coalition partners, so as to be able to share power when it comes. We will discuss later which party systems are prevalent in Britain today.

5.4 **Electoral systems and party systems**

Now some basic facts have been outlined, it is possible to assess the character and operation of the party systems across the whole of the UK. Here are ideas that come from foundational claims in political science concerning how electoral systems and party systems relate together. The basic claim is that majoritarian systems tend to reward established parties and penalize smaller ones. This is because of the electoral effort at winning a particular seat. When one or two parties are very dominant in those seats, say getting 70 per cent of the vote between them or where one party say gets 60 per cent overall but the vote is split be-

Key term 5.4 Wasted votes

Votes cast by electors that do not contribute to the winning of a candidate in a constituency or district. For example, if candidate A for a Westminster seat gets 55 per cent of the vote and becomes the MP, but candidate B gets 45 per cent, those votes for candidate B are 'wasted'. A feature of FPTP, though occurs to a lesser extent in proportional systems, such as AMS through the use of thresholds.

tween other parties, smaller parties do not get much of a chance of winning a seat, even though they may get a sizeable vote share, like 30 per cent. When votes are aggregated across many constituencies, people are voting for parties who do not get seats—what are called 'wasted votes' (Duverger 1963, 226) (Key term 5.4). Wasted voting affects voting behaviour, because the main parties are usually those that are viable potential winners, either in the seat or at the national level. If people want to influence the election outcome, they need to vote for one of the contenders for entry into government. This means that votes for the two main parties are higher than they would otherwise be in electoral systems that are more proportional.

5.4.1 Duverger and the two-party system

It is commonly believed that there is a tendency for majoritarian systems to create party systems with two parties, which is called Duverger's 'law' (Duverger 1963). The idea is that majoritarian systems privilege the larger parties and penalize the smaller ones, so encouraging votes to pile up for those parties and to be reduced for the smaller ones. At the level of the constituency, it only makes sense to vote for a party that is likely to win, which means one of the top two in the last contest, encouraging voters for other parties to cast their ballots for one of these two to avoid wasting their votes. Once this system is in place it is likely to continue over time as voters are often making choices based on past election results in each constituency, so each election replicates the pattern of choices of the last one and so on, though massive electoral shocks do occur and can even be encouraged by FPTP. There is more on this point later in the chapter in section 5.8.

The electoral system is not the only reason for the number of parties normally in operation in a political system. The structure of social cleavages, such as class and/or ethnicity, and how these differences map on to parties is a major factor, or even just how some parties become 'catch-all' (a term coined by Kirchheimer 1966) (see Key term 5.5) or electoral machines keen to move ahead of rivals. History is important in explaining why parties are in existence and last for long periods of time, often because of past disputes that are long forgotten. If people want to vote for one of the two parties, there is nothing to stop them, whatever electoral system is in place. Similarly, many parties can appear in FPTP electoral systems, especially where there is a regional concentration of the vote of the challenger party that can push out the two main parties, as with the nationalist parties (the SNP in Scotland and Plaid Cymru in North and West Wales). The Liberal Democrats as a national party, and the 'third' party, have often focused on local targeting to get ahead, such as in the South West of England, and in the past in Scotland, trimming their campaigns to local issues and concerns (see Russell and Fieldhouse 2005).

It is difficult to directly observe the relationship between an electoral system and a party system as both do not change very much, especially within a political system. Even looking at correlations over time, for example in a comparative systems design (where countries are compared systematically along a number of dimensions), does not prove the relationship, as it may be the case that shifts in the party system may be causing changes to the operation of the electoral system rather than the other way around, even

Key term 5.5 Catch-all party

A political party that designs its policy platform so as to appeal to wide groups of voters, often moving away from ideological principles that may have influenced its founding and less reliant on a traditional base of support.

promoting change in that system itself (for discussion and comparative research, see Renwick 2010). The likely party system can influence the choice of electoral system, as with the Greater London Authority (GLA) and the Welsh and Scottish systems, as their single-member components came out of the debates and decisions to set up the new authorities. The plans of electoral system designers can go wrong and party systems emerge in ways reformers do not expect, as with the dominance of the Scottish nationalists in a system Labour was central to designing.

It is rare to find an example within a country of a new electoral system emerging within the same jurisdiction to see what happens to the party system when one system is replaced with another. New electoral systems have usually been introduced for new institutions, such as the devolved Parliaments, or the GLA, so it is not known what party systems would have been existence in an earlier period to make the comparison. For example, for the GLA, the previous Greater London Council (GLC), an elected authority on the same boundaries, was abolished in 1986, and there was no London elected government between 1986 and 2000, the period when it would have been useful to look at the party system prior to the introduction of the mayor and assembly (see Case Study 5.2).

Duverger, then, did not produce a law, and political scientists are very cautious about assuming a close and necessary relationship between the number of parties and the electoral system, though few would go as far as Dunleavy to say the law is a 'dead parrot' (Dunleavy 2012). Some countries have both FPTP and many parties, such as India and Canada, and now they are partly joined by the UK.

5.5 Seats and votes

As the party and electoral systems debate illustrates, it is important to understand how votes turn into seats. To understand this relationship, political scientists use a measure of disproportionality, which is called the deviation from proportionality or DV score (see Dunleavy, Park, and Taylor 2018, 50, for more explanation). The idea is that in the most proportional system (say, electing under STV the whole country in one constituency) there will be a close correlation between votes cast for a party and the seats it gets in the chamber; but most electoral systems do not achieve this, so there is a need for a measure that captures the extent of the lack of relationship. One common score, the Gallagher measure, is created by adding up the squared differences between votes and seats for any one party then dividing by two (to avoid double counting). For example, if the vote for party A was 10 per cent and the proportion of seats it got was 5 per cent, then the difference is 10 minus 5 = 5; when squared, this equals 25. If the vote for party B was 20 per cent and the proportion of seats it got was 30 per cent, then the difference is 20 minus 20 = 10; when squared, this equals 100. Adding the squared differences together yields 125; dividing by two gets

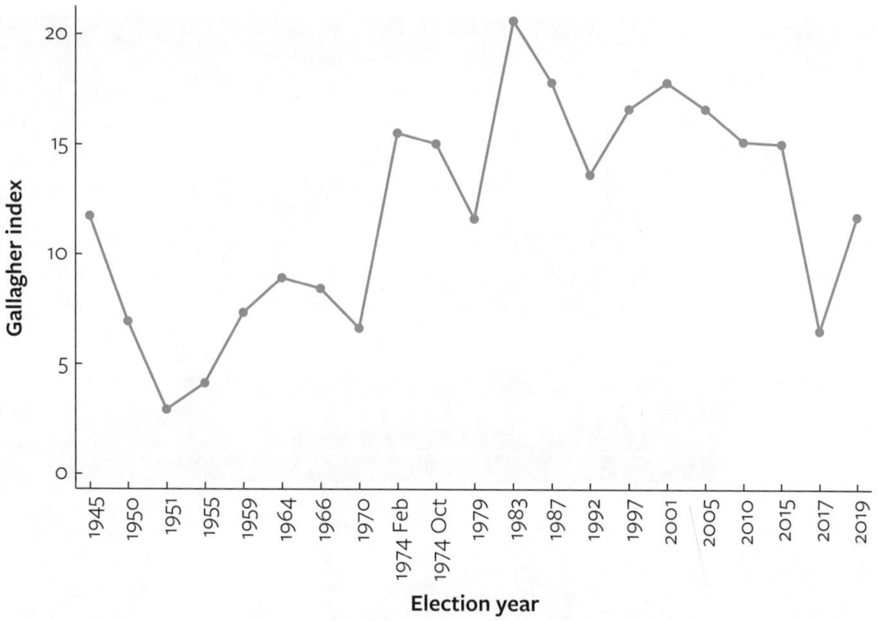

Figure 5.1 Index of disproportionality for UK national elections, 1945–2019.
Source: http://www.tcd.ie/Political_Science/people/michael_gallagher/ElSystems/index.php

to 62.5, the Gallagher index value. There are other indexes to use, but this is the most commonly reported.

In general, British national elections are disproportionate according to this and other measures, though it is important to be aware that many voters correct their party choice to take account of wasting their vote, making it hard to establish a counterfactual (see Key term 3.6) of what a more proportional system would be like. Figure 5.1 shows the change over time for the Gallagher score since 1945. It was quite low in the 1950s, which shows that under special conditions, with just two parties that are equally matched, FPTP can yield proportional outcomes. But this changed after this unique period in British politics, especially from the 1974 elections with the emergence of stronger third parties, such as the Liberals, which did not get many seats under FPTP. There was another leap upwards in the early 1980s when the Liberal/Social Democratic Party (SDP) alliance (the SDP was a breakaway party from Labour, created in 1981) emerged as an electoral force. Since that time, the index has dropped back again, and remains stable at about 15, which is still quite disproportionate.

5.6 A two-party system?

Traditionally, the UK is seen as a two-party system. This means that two parties are thought to dominate the shares of the UK-wide votes and seats, and this predominance structures the political system in general, as in a duopoly when two companies supply the market with their products. There are two parts to

Photo 5.2 Labour and the Conservatives are the two major parties in the UK.

5

this claim: one is about vote and seat shares that persist over time; the other is about how this dominance affects how the political system operates in general.

5.6.1 Vote shares

Consider vote and seat shares. Figure 5.2 shows the shares of the popular vote taken up by the two main parties since 1945.

Figure 5.2 shows that the two parties received nearly 100 per cent of the votes cast in some elections in the 1950s, but this has been reducing since 1970 to just over 80 per cent, then dropping to just over 60 per cent in the 2000s. The two parties are much less dominant than before, but they still mop up most of the votes. It is a matter of judgment as to whether the data support a two-party system or not, as it could show surprising resilience of the two parties or loss of support. In the view of critics (Awan-Scully 2018; Dunleavy 2005), the two-party system is about to fall apart, but the voting trends at the UK level may be seen to have a more gradual trend pointing to decline rather than a replacement of two-party dominance with a fully operational multi-party system.

5.6.2 Seat shares

Looking at the seat shares in the House of Commons, the two parties increase their dominance from votes. Figure 5.3 shows the percentage of seats for each party (the maximum number of seats differs over the decades, ranging from 625 to 650), but the figure shows the basic pattern with a vast proportion of seats going to the two main parties, with a gradual

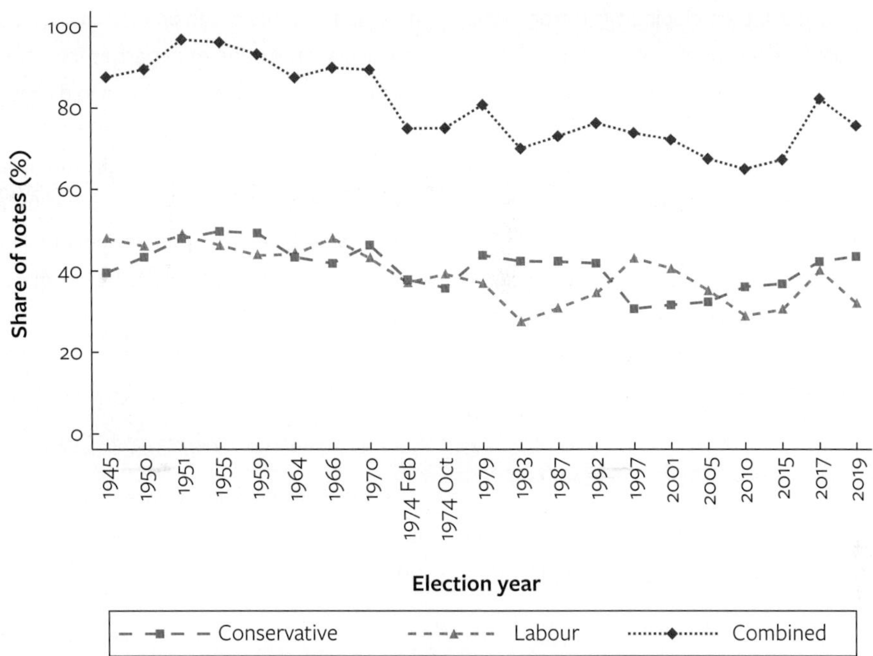

Figure 5.2 Shares of the popular vote in British general elections for the two main parties, Conservatives and Labour, 1945–2019.
Source: Audickas et al. (2020, 13)

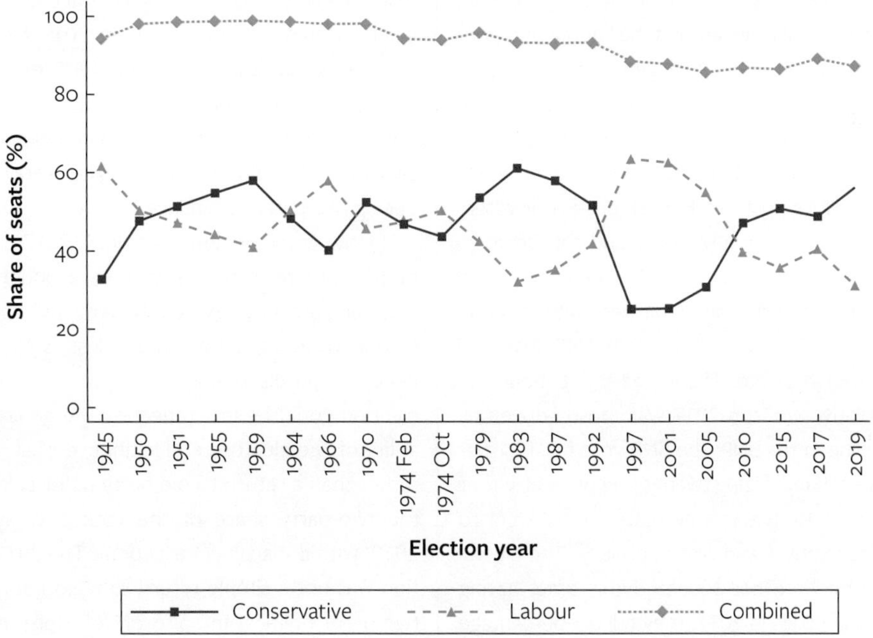

Figure 5.3 Shares of House of Commons seats held by the two main parties, Conservatives and Labour, 1945–2019.
Source: Audickas et al. (2020, 28)

reduction from 1970, then dipping again from 1992, settling at about 85 per cent of seats.

As discussed in section 5.4.1, the electoral system is a factor behind this seat representation, which conveys greater dominance than vote shares would indicate, and enhances the extent to which the UK political system at the national level may be considered still two-party dominant, especially if only England is looked at. The general elections of 2017 and 2019 are useful case studies of the resilience but also the frailty of two-party politics (see Case Study 5.1).

5.6.3 The effective number of parties

Another way of looking at the party system is to count the effective number of parties. Rather than make judgements based on vote shares, it is possible to calculate the number of parties from their relative strength in the electorate. This avoids counting very small parties. The idea was introduced by Laakso and Taagepera (1979). It is calculated by adding the proportion of the squared vote shares for all parties with at least one vote, then dividing this number by one. For example, if there are three parties which get vote shares respectively of 60 per cent, 30 per cent, and 10 per cent, then the effective number of parties is:

$$1/\left((.6*.6)+(.3*.3)+(.1*.1)\right)=2.17$$

Examining vote shares since 1945, it is possible to calculate the effective number of parties at the UK national level, reported in Figure 5.4.

Case Study 5.1 The 2017 and 2019 general elections

A surprising uptick in the percentages of the vote for the two parties occurred at the 2017 election, when voters polarized around the Labour and Conservative Parties. This poll generated shares of seats at respectively 88 and 87 per cent; and 82.4 and 75.7 per cent of the vote. This poll was not a return to two-party politics, but reflected the travails of politics post-Brexit when pro-Brexit voters went to the Conservative Party and anti-Brexit to Labour. The two parties in 2017 benefited from vote switches from minor parties, with a fall in votes from 2015 to 2017 for UKIP: UKIP lost 10.8 per cent of the vote. The increase in Labour and Conservative votes in 2017 was mostly driven by the decline in the SNP: the SNP vote fell 13.1 per cent in Scotland, losing twenty-one of its fifty-four seats (of these twenty-one seats, twelve went to the Conservatives and six to Labour). The Liberal Democrats were not squeezed this time, having suffered in 2015. In 2017, they fell 0.5 percentage points compared to 15.1 in 2015. In 2019 they increased by 4.2 percentage points over the 2015 result, rising to the highest level since 2010, with Liberal Democrats benefiting in 2019 from the not-so-clear position of Corbyn over Brexit, rather than getting squeezed out by Labour. In 2019, Labour was squeezed by the Conservatives in certain seats, with the Labour vote dropping overall, so reducing two-party dominance.

In the view of John Curtice (2017), many of the long-term trends that have undermined two-party politics have continued, with age predicting voting and class much less, which connects to the discussion in Chapter 4. The 2017 election could be just reflecting the greater volatility of the electorate (Fieldhouse et al. 2019) rather than a return to old party politics. Indeed, the two-party share of the vote decreased in 2019, with a sharp fall for Labour. The 2019 election was not a simple return to majoritarian and two-party politics, in spite of Johnson's eighty-seat majority (Curtice 2020b).

Photo 5.3 Dejected Labour Party supporters after the Vale of Glamorgan general election vote count at Barry Leisure Centre, Wales, 13 December 2019.

The figure illustrates the gradual change over time since 1970, but no massive shift in the effective number of parties: about two parties up to 1970 for seats, between two and two and a half in votes; then rising to between two and two and a half in seats, and ranging from three to four in votes. Even with this measure that limits counting smaller parties, Britain is now not a two-party system, neither in terms of votes nor seat shares. This would comport with other commentators, who say that the UK has become a two-party-plus system (Heffernan 2003) or a two-and-a-half party system (Siaroff 2003).

Flip to other jurisdictions and these vote shares for the two parties do not seem to be so dominant. For example, in the devolved nations, there are more parties reflecting the presence of nationalist sentiments and electoral systems that do not punish minor parties, such as the Liberal Democrats. Figure 5.5 displays the calculations for Scotland and Wales in the same format as Figure 5.4.

There are more parties at the devolved level. There is also a slight decline in Scotland over time, which may reflect the dominance of the Scottish National Party. There is the continuing dominance of Labour in Wales, then a slight rise in the number of effective parties. Overall, the trend over time shows how these are not two-party systems, but three-party at least.

5.6.4 The two-party system as narrative

A two-party system is more than just about electoral dominance, although this is the essential driver. It also reflects the dominance of Labour and the Conservatives in the UK political system more generally, which is over the business of the House of Commons in debates (see section 3.2.4), and the institutionalization

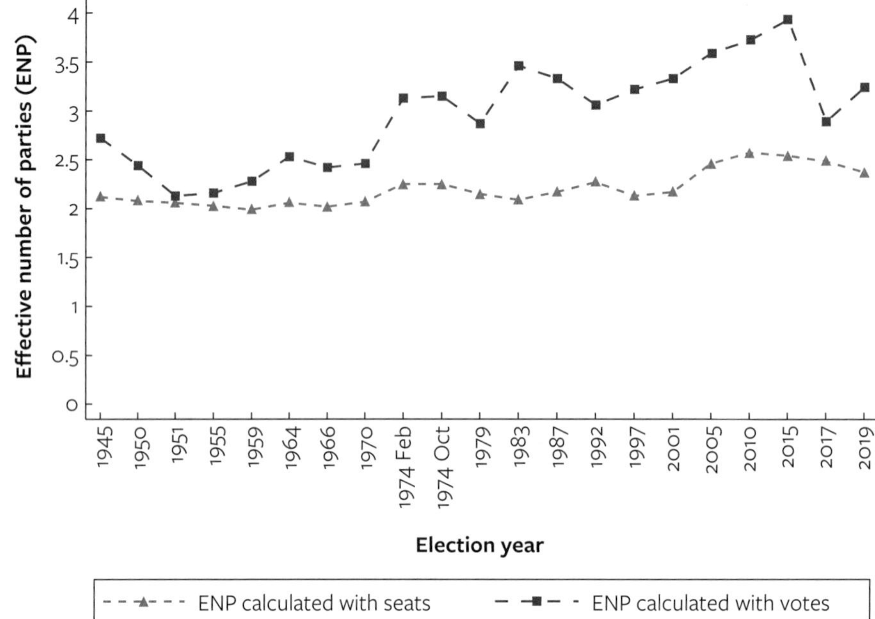

Figure 5.4 The effective number of parties in the House of Commons, votes and seats, 1945–2019.
Source: www.tcd.ie/Political_Science/people/michael_gallagher/ElSystems/index.php. 2019 figure is calculated separately from source data

of government and opposition. It is also about the dominance of the two main parties in national debate, as reported in the media. This is in essence a new institutionalist argument (for a review of institutionalisms, see Peters 2011), which is about the persistence of institutions over time, and how procedures and rules of the game reinforce each other, creating an equilibrium that is hard to break out of. It is about understanding what the political system is in terms of its core ideas, which was discussed in Chapter 1, in the frameworks used to understand British politics—particular narratives that shape how actors think and behave (Bevir and Rhodes 2006). It also relates to incentives, as parties benefit from the institutional arrangements, such as the electoral system. Although the relationship between seats and votes is complicated, it is still the case that a new party breaking in on the political scene, without much of a local or regional powerbase, say in local government, can get high levels of percentage support at a national poll but very few seats. In 1983, the SDP/Liberal alliance got 25.4 per cent of the vote, but only twenty-three seats. Even though the social democratic movement was a strong opponent to the main parties, especially Labour in the early 1980s, it eventually lost steam and extinguished, demoralized by the lack of electoral success (Crewe and King 1995). It also gave time to the Labour Party to recover from its loss of seats while in opposition rather than being destroyed as an electoral force, trying out Neil Kinnock and then John Smith as leaders, before landing on the reformist Tony Blair who led the party to overwhelming victory in 1997. The same might be said of the Conservative Party after its defeat in 1997, taking time to get back into government in 2010 and with a majority in 2015 and 2019. Both parties needed their base of MPs to make the case that as the single opposition party it was able to replace the government when it was ready. Although political parties do not get funding from the government, they get various financial advantages, such as funding for

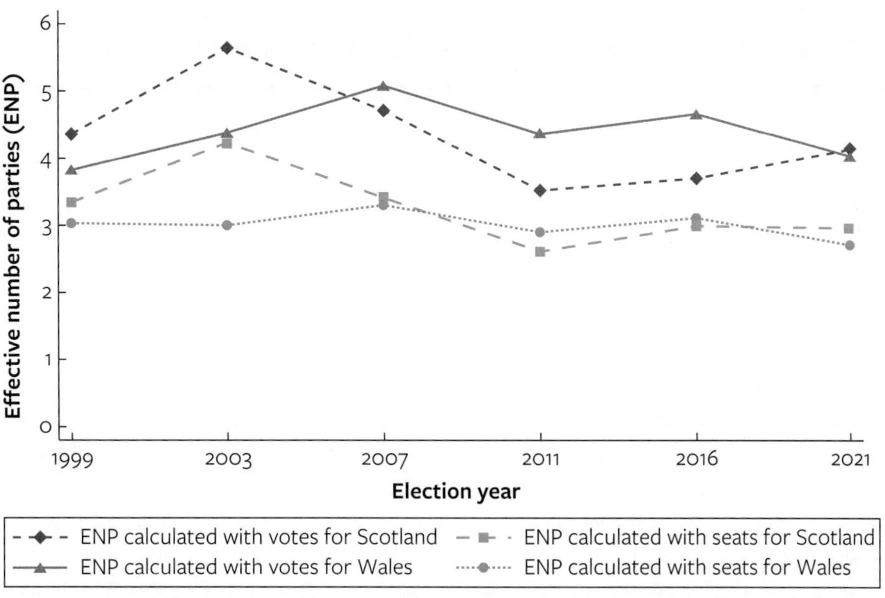

Figure 5.5 Effective number of parties in Scottish Parliament and Welsh Assembly/Senedd elections, 1999–2021.
Source: Election indices dataset at www.tcd.ie/Political_Science/people/michael_gallagher/ElSystems/index.php. 2021 data from BBC Welsh Parliament results: www.bbc.com/news/topics/cqwn14k92zwt/welsh-parliament-election-2021 and BBC Scottish Parliament results: www.bbc.com/news/topics/c37d28xdn99t/scottish-parliament-election-2021
Note: based on list (regional) votes and total seats

parliamentary groups, that keep them in business as well as the electoral system, which make it hard for challengers to get started or to continue contesting elections for long periods.

5.6.5 An alternating predominant party system?

A critical argument about two-party dominance is about the experience of one of the two parties holding national office. This has been the pattern since 1945 as one of the two parties either achieved a majority (Labour: 1945–51, 1964–6, 1966–70, 1997–2010; Conservative: 1951–64, 1970–4, 1979–97, 2015–17, 2019–), or were the main party in a minority or coalition government (Labour: 1974–9: Conservative: 2010–15, 2017–19), or were the main opposition party in terms of seats and votes. In a two-party system, there should be a reasonable chance at any time for the opposition to gain office. In UK politics there were times when this did not happen, such as between 1918 and 1945 when coalition governments occurred as a matter of course rather than two-party competition (Butler 1978); then there were other periods when one party was thought to dominate elections, which meant it was hard for the opposition to win power. This is what Quinn (cited in Nadeau, Bélanger, and Atikcan 2019) calls an 'alternating predominant party system' (see Key term 5.6). The Conservative Party was in power between 1951 and 1964, but then Labour managed to gain office between 1964 and 1970, and then from 1974 to 1979. Similarly, the

Case Study 5.2 London as an example of different electoral systems

The Greater London Authority (GLA) is another example of multi-party politics appearing with a proportional representation system. In 2016 a large number of parties stood for office, with many getting good proportions of the popular vote: Labour, Conservative, Green, UKIP, Liberal Democrats, Women's Equality, Respect, Britain First, Christian People's Alliance, Animal Welfare, BNP, The House Party, Socialist (GB), Take Back the City, and the Communist League (https://data.london.gov.uk/dataset/london-elections-results-2016-wards-boroughs-constituency). But the main parties still get the vast proportion of the popular vote, with Labour getting 45.5 per cent of the constituency vote and 40.3 per cent of the regional vote, with the smaller parties getting very small percentages, e.g. Respect getting 1.3 per cent. In terms of seats from both constituency and regional methods, the main parties dominate, with Labour getting twelve Assembly Members and the Conservatives eight. Other parties gained a small number of seats in the assembly: the Greens gained two, UKIP two, and the Liberal Democrats one, with other small parties getting nothing. This is a better result than these parties often get at the national level, but it reveals that there are a set of contingent factors at work between the electoral system and party system. There is not a great difference between the GLA and what happens in the FPTP London borough elections: in the 2018 local elections in London, Labour got 1,123 seats, Conservatives 511, Liberal Democrats 154, Greens 11, and independents 34. In terms of the percentage of the seats, the Liberal Democrats do better at the borough level in London with FPTP at 8 per cent, with 4 per cent of GLA seats with AMS. What this case shows is that there are usually many reasons other than the electoral system for the extent of party representation at any level of government. It is important to state that the elections were two years apart in 2016 and 2018, and that the Liberal Democrats did better with FPTP in 2018 which may be unrelated to the electoral system and arise because of growing support for the party.

Conservative Party was in power between 1979 and 1997, but then Labour managed a long spell from 1997 to 2010. In these periods of one-party dominance, the opposition parties were often divided, which is part of the explanation for one-party dominance, but often a consequence of it. For example, Labour in the early 1980s drifted leftwards and became unpopular. In the 1990s and 2000s, the Conservatives were divided over Europe, and challenged by right-wing parties, such as UKIP, and had a succession of ineffective leaders. The ideological space occupied by the parties has become more polarized and manifestos more distinct from each other (Downs 1957).

It is important to note that even with polarization between the parties, the electorate still consents to the winner, with the UK conforming to the general pattern of 'loser's consent' (Key term 5.7) of other European democracies (Anderson and Tverdova 2001). The main exception to this is over the 2016 Brexit referendum result (Nadeau, Bélanger, and Atikcan 2019), which spilled over into the views of voters for parties in elections. But overall, the electorate are happy to accept switches in power as legitimate, and this acts as a stabilizer for the system and limits the power of challenger parties.

In some periods, commentators believed that the UK could have become a one-party system (e.g. *The Guardian*, 18 April 2020). But it has never happened so far. In the late 1980s, after losing successive general

Key term 5.6 Alternating predominant party system

Where one party dominates electoral politics and occupies government for successive elections; then the dominant party loses office and the pattern reverses with an opposition party taking the reins for another set of electoral periods until the next reversal of roles.

elections since 1979, Labour moved to the centre, and the Conservatives did much the same thing in 2005 when electing David Cameron as leader. He adopted more moderate policies as a reaction to the losses of elections in 1997, 2001, and 2005. The Cameron case is not straightforward as he could not shake off the challenge from the right-leaning wing of the party, and the Liberal Democrats had benefited from some shrewd policy choices in opposing the unpopular war in Iraq, a long-run campaign to target seats based on local government successes in parts of the country overcoming the electoral system, and they also benefited from the growth of anti-system politics and anti-politics in the 2000s (see section 4.4.8). The Conservatives could not return to office with a classic majority like Labour and had to share power with the Liberal Democrats following the 2010 election. Yet the two parties then appeared once again in 2015 when the voters were angered at the Liberal Democrats and punished them heavily at the polls. Even though the Tories lost their majority in 2017, it was still a largely Labour-Conservative contest, so they were able to get it back again decisively in 2019 under Boris Johnson, again in mainly a two-party race. After Labour was defeated, the new leader Sir Keir Starmer used the institutionalization of two-party politics in the House of Commons to challenge the government over its management of the Covid-19 pandemic, so trying to become the effective government in waiting, seeking to build up credibility with voters. There is something more like two-party politics at Westminster once again, at least for a while, even when there are several credible opposition parties alongside Labour, such as the SNP.

Key term 5.7 Loser's consent

An important feature of democratic politics whereby the losers in elections consent to the winning party, believing it to be a legitimate occupant of government. If consent ebbs, then losing parties and their supports do not accept the legitimacy of incumbent government, believing the outcomes of the election to be unfairly won, and do not accept the policies. Although opposition parties cannot do much out of office, loss of loser's consent may mean they take office wanting to reverse the policies of the previous administration. It can undermine support for democratic politics as a whole, leading to backsliding (Key term 1.12).

5.6.6 Spatial models of two-party competition

The debate about party competition prompts a discussion of the spatial model or the Hotelling-Downs model, which is an important tool that political scientists use to understand how parties compete with each other and respond to the electorate. It appeared in Downs' famous book, *An Economic Model of Democracy* (Downs 1957). It is a good example of an application of rational choice theory (Key term 2.1).

The model represents two parties who select policy proposals on a left–right continuum upon which the electorate is arrayed. The electorate's preferences take the form of a 'single peak' from left to right with more extreme positions getting less support than the larger numbers in the central portion (see Figure 5.2).

Even though parties, such as party A on the left and party B on the right in this example, have preferences for particular packages of policies, they ultimately wish to maximize their votes. They know that they can increase their votes by changing the composition of their policy programmes, so they move closer to the centre ground, where the voters are. So, in Figure 5.6, they both move in the direction of the arrow to the centre, the median voter, and towards each other. In theory, party positions do not converge completely because it makes sense to have a distinctive platform to distinguish them from their opponents. Nor do they leapfrog each other because they need to retain a coherent ideology to keep their reputation to please an information-economizing electorate that prefers clear ideological differences from which to vote. There is an equilibrium point that stays in place until the electorate moves again. In this way the electorate retains its choice of parties, but it does not cause parties to offer extreme policy positions; it can base its choice on which leaders are likely to do best and which party is closest to its preferences.

Key term 5.8 Single-peaked preferences

A term in rational choice theory that describes when a person's or people's preferences are arranged in a way so it is possible to find a single equilibrium point when welfare is maximized. In Figure 5.6 preferences are arrayed on the scale from left to right, taking the form of a single peak. It is possible for a party to move towards the centre ground and increase overall welfare at a single point in the middle. If preferences had several peaks, there would be two humps in the figure, where the party would not know from which point on the left–right scale to choose its policies.

There are some problems with this model, which have largely to do with the assumptions about single-peaked preferences (Key term 5.8). For example, if preferences have two extreme peaks when the electorate is polarized, there is no single equilibrium point. If there is more than one party, electoral competition can take voters away from one or both main parties, which again undermines the extent to which they will move to the centre, as they may wish to compete with another party instead. There may be other ways in which parties may move towards the median voter rather than only in a two-party model, as parties may see themselves as part of a coalition so all parties move in line with the median voter, in what is called the median mandate view of democracy (McDonald and Budge 2005). They may be incentivized to be catch-all parties (see Key term 5.5), which can appear in any political system (Wolinetz 1991). Nonetheless, the model provides an imperfect route whereby citizen preferences may be turned into public policy by parties competing for the median voter. In section 5.6.7, we will discuss whether this model of two-party competition actually works in the UK.

5.6.7 Does two-party competition actually work?

Despite the problems with the simple spatial model, it can provide a useful explanation about why UK parties sometimes change their programmes to appeal to the middle or median voter, and hence try to win elections. When the Labour Party lost successive elections to the Conservative Party in the years since 1979, it realized it needed to drop some radical policies and adopt centrist policies to win, which they eventually did in 1997. After 1997, when the Conservative Party had spent successive elections in the wilderness with radical policies on the right, David Cameron when elected leader in 2005 presided over moderation of his party's policies to make a more attractive offer that might have helped him become prime minister in 2010 (Kavanagh and Cowley 2010). In both these examples, a lot more is going on to

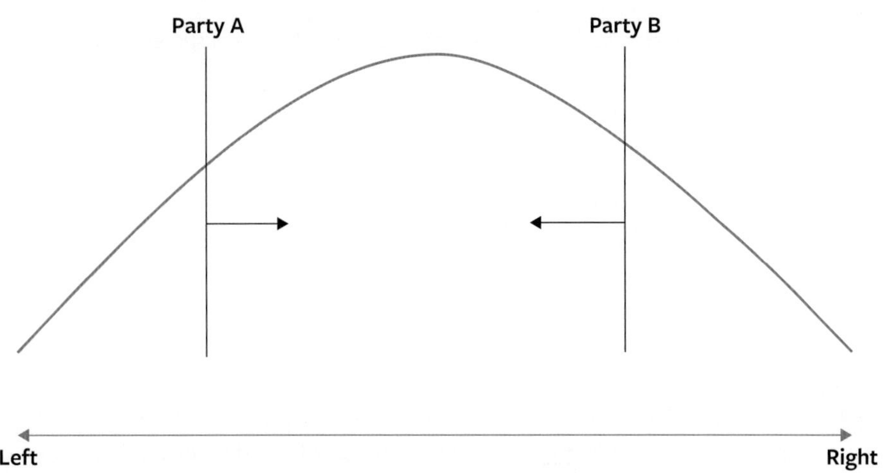

Figure 5.6 Hotelling-Downs model of party competition.

explain both the party positions and electoral outcomes than electoral competition for the median voter, not least the presence of other challenger parties, divisions within one of the two main parties, and clever rhetorical strategies by new party leaders to exert control (see Hindmoor 2004 for an account of this strategy with New Labour in the 1990s). A study of party positions at elections shows that even though conditions for the convergence to the median voter have been in place, they have not been met in the UK, such as at the 1992 election (Schofield 2004). There is scant evidence from surveys and aggregate analysis that voters even notice whether party programmes are moving left or right (Adams, Ezrow, and Somer-Topcu 2011). Nor have party programmes fully converged in public policies, as claimed in the consensus model of British politics that was thought to operate between 1945 and 1979 (Jones and Kandiah 1996), with parties having fundamental differences, for example over economic policy (Kelly 2002).

But the model provides *some* indication of the electoral incentives of the British system that force a major party to expand its programme and move to the centre ground. When Jeremy Corbyn was Labour leader from 2015 to 2020, it appeared to make sense for the Party to appeal to core voters and a new group of radicalized younger voters. In the Party there was a frustration about the moderate politics of the New Labour years and a desire to strike out with a new radical set of policies. In practice, the leadership in the person of John McDonnell, shadow chancellor, made strenuous efforts, such as talking to City representatives, to moderate Labour's image so as to capture moderate voters that might tip it over the final line of getting a majority of seats at a future general election. It appeared to succeed in this double aim in the 2017 general election, increasing its share of the popular vote from 30.3 to 40.0 per cent, but a degree of hubris and overconfidence, as well as defensiveness from the leadership and the inner circle, undermined this strategy in 2019 (see the accounts in Pogrund and Maguire 2020; Jones 2020). Sir Keir Starmer presented his campaign to be leader as showing elements of continuity with the radical approach of Corbyn; in fact, it is more of a move to the centre, especially in terms of the image of the Party and its reputation, even if the actual policies might not be so different to Corbyn's.

The spatial model of party competition has limitations, so the challenger parties may start to sap at parties on their more extreme ends, moving them away from the centre to head them off (as Cameron did with UKIP). Add to this the fact that the left–right dimension is not the only dimension that parties compete on, as parties articulate on other issues, such as cultural matters or environmental policies, as well as liberal versus more authoritarian values (Wheatley 2015) (see Figure 4.5). This means it is not possible to compile sets of policies that appeal to all centre-ground voters. Parties also compete on other factors as well as policy position, such as the competence in government and as credible challengers. Party members who have ideological objectives may shape the party's line as they provide support for leadership and are still essential in campaigns, so need to be kept on board. In Quinn's (2013) view, polarization can occur because the median voter is in a different position in different constituencies where there are separate party races. But there is a shred of truth to the Downsian model, as it provides an explanation of what parties and voters are seeking to do in much of England at least. It also ensures the dominance of the two-party monopoly when much of its social support has eroded.

It is important to realize that there are powerful factors behind the survival of a version of two-party politics in Britain, even if it is not as strong as it was before. It is also the case that these factors are themselves changing in the way they operate, so weakening the existing system, which might point to future changes.

5.7 The costs of incumbency and economic voting: support for two-party alternation

5.7.1 Economic voting and the political economic business cycle

The political system can be biased in favour of parties that are in government, as they control the levers of power so therefore can decide popular policies to help them get re-elected. If these policies meet with public approval and voters, opposition parties may be excluded from power for long periods of time; then it might reverse, creating a sustained pattern—what may be called incumbent advantage (see Key term 5.9). To understand how this works, concepts from political economy are helpful. One is the idea of economic voting (see Key term 5.10), which is where the votes for the incumbent will be based on objective (and some subjective in the form of perceptions) economic indicators, with voters rewarding a government that has achieved rises in core economic indicators, such as aggregate growth and employment. Punishment and reward in electoral politics arises from retrospective voting, and is conveyed by former US President Clinton's much-quoted phrase, 'it's the economy, stupid'. The economy can go up and down for all sort of reasons that may have nothing to do with the decisions of incumbents, but the economic voting hypothesis implies just that incumbents benefit whether they managed the economy well or not (Powell and Whitten 1993). For electoral punishment to occur, it helps if there is a unified government as countries with one-party in control government have more economic voting (Norpoth 2001). Where power is shared between the legislature and the executive, or between federal and state government, as in Germany, voters find it harder to attribute blame.

The other question is whether a party in government can control the economic aggregates enough to ensure re-election, which engineer what is called a political business cycle, another concept in political economy (Key term 5.11). In the period before 1997, the Treasury could reduce interest or borrowing rates, thereby stimulating the economy. There was a debate whether governments got re-elected on the back of lower interest rates, with the evidence pointing from interest rates to economic expectations and to the vote (Sanders 1991). Even with interest rates now set by the Monetary Policy Committee, political leaders can still get a boost from a well-performing economy, which they can affect in their tax and spending decisions. David Cameron secured re-election in 2015 with a better-performing economy and after fiscal austerity had been achieved. He got an incumbent advantage while his coalition partners the Liberal Democrats did not. Boris Johnson (and other UK leaders, such as Nicola Sturgeon, Photo 5.4) may have got an incumbent advantage in the May 2021 elections for getting their countries through the Covid-19 crisis without observable damage to the economy.

Governments have levers other than the economy. They can direct public resources and make promises of resources shortly before election time. Ward and John (1999) show that governments targeted public funds to areas with marginal or swing seats

Key term 5.9 Incumbency advantage and loss

The incumbent is the current office-holder with access to the levers of power. This incurs advantages because the levers of power can be used to secure re-election, e.g. through control of the political business cycle. Incumbents can claim credit for policies for which they have control or accidental factors that help their performance; or get punished if outcomes are not favourable. Then there is the opposite phenomenon of incumbency loss, because governments are blamed for the state of the economy or poor public policies. There is also a cost of governing (see Key term 5.16): as administrations go on, they lose support month on month.

Photo 5.4 Nicola Sturgeon, first minister of Scotland (2014–present).

Key term 5.10 Economic voting

Voters cast their choices in the light of real or perceived economic conditions. For example, increasing unemployment can lead to electoral punishment of the incumbent, or a pre-election boom can help the incumbent to return to office as in the political economic business cycle (Key term 5.11).

Key term 5.12 Swing or marginal seats

Some majorities for Westminster seats are quite narrow, which indicate that these need to be defended by the incumbent party and be the subject of an opposition campaign at subsequent general elections. A lead of 10 percentage points or fewer is often considered to be marginal, but other ranges can be used. Marginals feature in single constituencies and the FPTP electoral system. They are less in evidence in other electoral systems (see section 5.3.3).

(Key term 5.12) to help the UK incumbent and also benefit local authorities under Conservative control (see also Fouirnaies and Mutlu-Eren 2015). Using comparative evidence from Britain, Denmark, Finland, France, and Germany, Wenzelburger et al. (2020) show that governments time welfare reforms to be close to elections, with expansions just after and just before.

5.7.2 **Economic voting in the age of globalization**

In the age of globalization, the independence of the Bank of England, and constraints over boosting the economy mean the room for manoeuvre for governments may be more limited over economic policy than it was in earlier years. Moreover, academics question the extent to which economic voting actually occurs, which can be context bound and endogenous, and vary in impact considerably across different social groups (Dorussen and Taylor 2003; Linn, Nagler, and Morales 2010). In terms of re-election, voter perceptions are bundled into a number of what are called valence factors by which voters evaluate incumbents, which include the economy but also a range of other issues, such as foreign policy (Clarke 2004) (see Zoom-In 5.1). British governments find it hard to shift the blame for mistakes and policy errors onto other actors because of the unified nature of its government, even though they try this tactic; in the end they face what is called the cost of governing, which tends to reduce their electoral support each year. Governments find it hard to avoid losing popularity as time goes by. Winning elections can depend on the government's own competence, but it may get blown off track by making mistakes, acting in the short term, or being the victim of events happening beyond its control, and for which the voters may attribute blame.

Key term 5.11 The political business cycle

How political leaders are able to use the tools of government, especially control over economic policy, to ensure that levels of economic activity improve and reach a peak in the period immediately before an election, so that voters reward the incumbent. Often, the economy has to be dampened down immediately afterwards, hence the cycle of economic activity linked to election periods.

Zoom-In 5.1 Valence

Valence captures the idea that voters reward government for its performance over generic issues, such as the economy and running public services. This contrasts with topics that are thought to be owned by political parties (Issue ownership, Key term 5.13); valence issues are more general and might be important to voters. Valence is designed to be a critique of spatial models where it is assumed there is one dimension to politics, such as left–right. Associated with the work of Donald Stokes (1963) in the US and with several British Election Study volumes (Clarke 2004; Clarke et al. 2009).

Key term 5.13 Issue ownership

Idea that parties have an advantage in the public's mind in discussing or handling certain topics, associated with left or right issues, or with events in the past, e.g. Labour with the NHS.

Key term 5.14 Cost of governing

When the incumbent government faces a loss of popularity and electoral support that increases the longer it is in office and occurs inevitably in the absence of concerted policies to improve popularity (e.g. by manipulating the political business cycle) (see Key term 5.11).

5.7.3 Incumbency loss and the cost of governing/ruling

Electors also react against the policy positions of the incumbent, so if a left government is in power, they tend to move rightwards and vice versa. Stimson and colleagues pooled a large amount of survey data over time and found this is the case for the US (Stimson, MacKuen, and Erikson 1995), results that have been replicated in the UK (Bartle, Dellepiane-Avellaneda, and Stimson 2011). There are links to more general costs of governing (see Key term 5.14) or ruling that governments experience from voters, who are increasingly inclined to punish governments because of their mistakes and wish to try an alternative, so wishing to 'chuck out the rascals' and put in a new government ready to test its mettle. This claim has been tested for the support of US parties in the mid-term if they occupy the party of the presidency (Erikson 1988), and why, across Europe, incumbent parties lose votes when seeking re-election (Paldam 1986). Voters attribute responsibility to the government and the media can highlight these faults. Green and Jennings' (2012) statistical analysis of party competence across many issues in Britain finds a cost of governing across these issues, with the driver being the voters' sense of party competence. Parties can be in danger of losing their reputation for competence over certain issues for which they had a premium. For incumbents, statistical analysis of the 1979–97 period shows that a process of punishment and reward explains voter intentions and electoral outcomes for incumbents (Green and Jennings 2012). This affects the incumbent rather than the opposition, partly because voters have more information about what governments are doing (such as during the Covid-19 pandemic when citizens had to rely on daily press briefings from No. 10 to find out what was going on). This is particularly the case with information about the economy, examined by Butt (2006), who compared the economic evaluations of voters, when a party is in or out of power, using survey evidence.

Government survival depends on campaigns, the presentation of policies, and controlling the agenda, which is the topic of Chapter 6, but it is hard to change opinions once they set in, such as the Conservative Party's handling of the exit from the Exchange Rate Mechanism in 1992. This was an attempt by the UK government to enter into a fixed currency scheme, which did not work out, where the government spent billions of pounds trying to prop up the pound only to have to withdraw in a national humiliation, damaging the Conservative Party's reputation for economic competence (Thompson 1996; Heath, Jowell, and Curtice 2001; Green and Jennings 2012). Even Labour's relatively successful handling of the financial crisis of 2008–9 cost the Party in the elections of 2010 and 2015 (Cowley and Kavanagh 2016, 72). Other tactics to get re-elected such as cabinet reshuffles (see section 2.4.6) may prove to be short-lived exercises. As has been shown in section 5.7.1, governments can try other things rather than seeking to influence the economy, such as targeting swing voters with more public spending (Ward and John 1999), but these kinds of tactic are unlikely to decide the fate of all elections. The argument then points again away from one-party dominance. Provided the main opposition party remains unified and competent, it can reap the advantages of incumbent loss of popularity in due course. As is often pointed out, governments usually lose elections, rather than opposition parties winning them.

5.8 Electoral and institutional instability, not two-party politics?

Section 5.7.3 seems to point to continuities behind the British political system: there are incentives for the government to stay in place, but opportunities exist for opposition party challenge. The opposition wishes to become a party of government in waiting, with shadow ministerial posts, and trimming policies to the centre ground of politics, waiting for government scandals and failures that cause the voters to lose their trust in the incumbent. Yet there are recent changes in the political system that undermine this picture of government and opposition competition and switches. The next sections set them out.

5.8.1 Electoral shocks

In Section 4.4.7 we saw how the dominance of the two parties is weakening, in particular the relationships between class, party identification, and voting choices. This set of relationships was always complicated with a lot of cross-class party voting, even in the 1950s. Nonetheless, party leaders and those co-ordinating election campaigns could rely on a bedrock of support, especially in particular parts of the country where votes were certain. Even in unpropitious elections, parties could rely on electing a phalanx of MPs, located in safe seats protected by FPTP. The electoral system made it very hard for parties to overthrow large majorities in many constituencies. Even bad election results could then be the baseline for an opposition party's revival, allowing for the regrouping of the party before the next election. Since the 1970s, voters have become detached from their parties and attracted to challenger parties (Key term 4.5). Any party can face losing nearly all its seats and even its safe seats. This happened to Labour in Scotland and the Liberal Democrats in England in 2015; then Labour again lost many of its northern England seats in 2019.

The 2017 and 2019 elections back up this argument. Even though the two parties still seemed like monopolies in the campaign, and in 2019 there was a traditional victory of one of the two parties with a sizeable majority of seats, it was based on more insecure footing than before (see Case Study 5.1). Electoral swings are now normal, so wins can be easily gained and lost. This is the phenomenon of political turbulence, which is about the greater likelihood of unpredicted changes across the whole policy and political agenda (see Key term 4.5). A key part of this turbulence is the greater chance of electoral shocks. The argument is that voters, now detached from their moorings and traditional identities, can be swayed by appeals from new parties or even by new strategies by the existing parties. Volatility has always been a dimension of political behaviour, where de-aligned voters have been increasingly likely to switch votes since the 1970s (Denver 1998, 85–92). The argument is that political turbulence has increased and is more likely to produce surprising electoral outcomes, such as the surprise result for the Conservatives in 2015, the good performance of Labour in 2017, then the return to form of the Conservatives in 2019, none of which was fully expected by pundits and forecasters.

5.8.2 **Measuring volatility**

What is the best way to measure volatility over time? A common measure is the Pedersen index (Pedersen 1979). It shows net change within the electoral party system resulting from vote transfers: the index is equal to the net percentage of voters who changed their votes (not considering negative signs) divided by 2. For example, in 2019, Labour's vote changed from 40.0 to 32.1 = 7.9, Conservative from 42.5 to 43.6 = 1.1, Liberal Democrats from 7.4 to 11.6 = 4.2, and SNP from 3.0 to 3.9 = 0.9. Percentage changes for Greens = 0.0, DUP = 2.0, Sinn Féin = 0.0, Plaid Cymru = 0.0, SDLP = 2.0, and Alliance = 1.0. Adding up the percentage point changes for all the parties equals 17.3, then dividing by 2 gives 8.6, the Pedersen score. The higher the score, the higher the volatility. The tally since 1945 is shown in Figure 5.7. Surprisingly, it has not increased very much. As Fieldhouse et al. (2019, 11) point out, there was greater voter volatility in the more distant past, such as in 1918 and 1931. In their latest analysis, the BES team find that net volatility actually decreased in 2019, back to levels last seen in 1997 and 2001 (The British Election Study Team 2021).

To examine vote shifts, it is important to analyse data from individuals rather than in aggregate, which can understate the amount of movement of voter choices. These kinds of data can only come from surveys. Ed Fieldhouse and the BES team (Fieldhouse et al. 2019) map this out using their unique data source of the regular surveys of elections since 1964. They find that 3 per cent of voters switched between the 1964 and 1966 elections whereas 43 per cent of voters switched between the 2010 and 2015 elections, and 33 per cent of voters switched between the 2015 and 2017 elections. The biggest period of vote switches often occurs when there is a change in the governing parties, such as in 1997 or 2015, and once a government settles in for a number of successive election victories based on relatively stable vote shares, the number of switches goes down, so party switches alone are not a measure of turbulence, as it could be the case of an unpopular government being kicked out by voters.

Although Fieldhouse et al.'s thesis is of greater electoral shocks, these measures show more gradual changes and a cyclical pattern, as Figure 5.7 shows. The record of change in UK politics is subtler than the grand narrative of electoral shocks suggests. It is the case that these trends have been unfolding gradually over several decades rather than 2014 representing a particular turning point. Nonetheless, it is still plausible

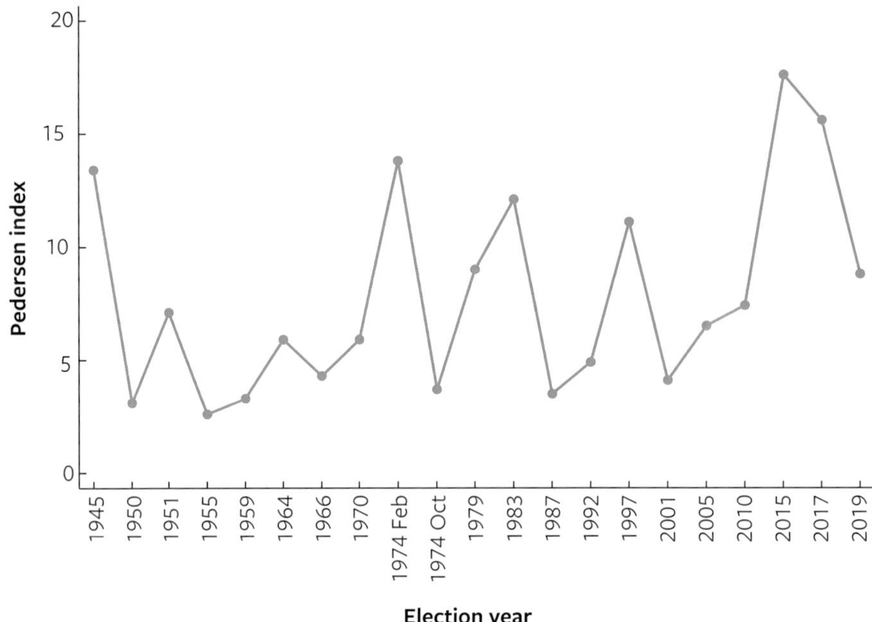

5

Figure 5.7 Volatility of British elections, 1945–2019.
Source: Adapted from Audickas (2020)

to argue that the context of voter behaviour and level of attachment makes it less secure territory for the two political parties, as the example of Labour's loss of heartland voters shows.

5.8.3 Institutional change

Another element of the argument against the longevity of the two-party system is that the very institutional foundations behind the system are becoming less firm. Dunleavy (2005) argues that the scale of the reforms of the system show a degree of institutional change, with new proportional representation systems at different levels of government and the emergence of multi-party politics in terms of voter and party strategies. The FPTP system looks increasingly isolated and out of date. The direction of travel is towards modernization and a more European style of party politics, with many parties and regular coalition governments. The key element of the change is the dispersion of votes across more parties, whereby voters take increasing account of the multi-level nature of politics. Increasing partisan dealignment across the UK is accelerating the transformation of both voter and party strategies: 'the institutional framework is slowly tilting towards more use of PR [proportional representation] and multi-preference elections' (Dunleavy 2005, 525).

As with the argument for the longevity of the two-party system itself, this line of thinking is also a form of new institutionalism (see Zoom-In 1.5), which is about how the routines of politics are changing and adapting—a more sophisticated institutionalist argument than the one about stability. But it is a hard claim to resolve with evidence as it relies on assessment of the extent of embeddedness of electoral institutions that is hard to measure. One key part of the claim that times are changing was the multi-party politics of the European Parliament elections (which no longer run in the UK post-Brexit), which might have tilted the balance away from the old system. The nations of the UK are developing separate forms of competition and party systems, usually based on very different cleavages. Even though some of the same parties operate in Westminster, they compete in different ways and in different dimensions to government and opposition politics in Westminster (Awan-Scully 2018).

Newer parties, such as the Greens (Photo 5.5), have become permanent parts of the electoral landscape; despite their defeat in 2015, and only partial revival since, the Liberal Democrats continue as a powerfully organized party seeking electoral contexts across the nations of the UK at different levels of government. Institutions are changing, such as the TV election debates, which are no longer just between the two main party leaders, such as in 2010 when they included the Liberal Democrats. In 2019, on 29 November, the BBC hosted a live debate with seven major political parties: the leaders of the Liberal Democrats, the SNP, and Plaid Cymru were present. The Conservatives, Labour, Greens, and the Brexit Party fielded senior politicians rather than the party leader. There still remain events just for the two main parties: on 6 December on the BBC there was a live head-to-head debate just between Boris Johnson (the Conservative leader) and Jeremy Corbyn (the then Labour leader).

5.8.4 Perversity and electoral choices

One key aspect of the British system, as was classically argued (Pulzer 1967), was that it produced strong and stable government. In part this was because of

Photo 5.5 The UK Green Party is a political party based on the principles of green politics including social justice and environmentalism.

the two main alternatives for the voters and a clear route to power for both parties and the electorate to work towards. Not only did the electoral system reinforce the dominance of the two parties against challengers, it increased the chance that if a party was ahead in the polls, it could rely on multiplying its majority in seats on election day. This was because as a party's lead increased, more marginal or swing seats came into play, flipping over to the challenger, creating what are called landslide elections. This is because there was uniform swing of the vote in most constituencies ensuring that a large vote swing reached across the country (Key term 5.15). This phenomenon, sometimes called the cube law, was popularized by one of the founders of British psephology (the study of elections), David Butler, as set out in a famous article in *The Economist* on 7 January 1950 (Crick 2018). From looking at a large number of election results in the early part of the twentieth century, Butler found that the proportion of seats gained or lost in an electoral contest was far greater than the swing in the share of the vote. The numbers of seats increase more rapidly as the swing increases, which is the result of many constituencies which have been marginal tipping over to the other side and the numbers of these vulnerable seats increasing rapidly as the swing gets larger (Taagepera 1986). This relationship was thought to have the function of a cube: cube the percentage swing in the vote to find out the swing of seats the winning party or losing party had or were likely to achieve (Key term 5.16). A swing of 2 per cent in the vote leads to an 8 per cent shift in seats, a swing of 3 per cent generates a 27 per cent shift in seats, and so on. An unpopular government can lose decisively and then give the reins of power to a new group of politicians who can be similarly judged four or five years later. The cube law shows how decisive election victories were possible (Tufte 1973). It provides a useful addition to the Westminster model that electoral correction is severe and outcomes decisive, or so people used to think.

Key term 5.15 Uniform swing

The idea that the percentage change in vote share received by winning candidates in constituencies across the UK is constant. For example, a percentage change of the vote in Islington South and Finsbury, say an increase of 5 percentage points, would be the same as in North East Somerset, as well as in other constituencies.

Key term 5.16 The cube law

An expected relationship between the swing of votes between the two leading parties and the number of Westminster seats they get at a general election, where the vote swing is cubed to turn into the seat swing (for example, 2:8, 3:27).

The cube law may have only operated (if at all) for a relatively short period of time in British politics, weakening in the 1980s (Curtice and Steed 1986). It depends critically on the number of marginal and swing seats in play, which are in decline (Blau 2004). Now it fails to work at all. The psephologist John Curtice (2010) produces convincing data to show that it is much harder for a political party to get a majority in Britain under FPTP. Curtice shows that the system does not discourage people from voting for third parties. It does not give a consistent bonus of seats to whoever comes first in votes, nor does it award any bonus in an even manner.

Figure 5.8 shows the relationship between the percentage swing in votes and seats for elections since 1945. For much of the period, there is such a relationship, but not cubed; instead, there was something resembling a 'two and a half law' (Laakso 1979). By 2015, however, this relationship had broken down. Instead of the smooth production of secure majorities, FPTP now delivers perverse and unpredictable outcomes, partly from the complex nature of party politics, with different combinations of three or more parties in constituencies in England, and other combinations of parties in races in Wales and Scotland, and a reduction of the number of marginal seats (Curtice 2010, 2018). Vote swings are less likely to lead to a majority at all, as in 2010 and 2017. Even the 2019 election did not resurrect the cube law, and many aspects of the new politics continue, such as the decline of the number of marginal seats and third-party wins (Curtice 2020b).

5.8.5 Decline in political parties?

The final part of the argument about the decline of two-party politics is that parties themselves are in decline, in particular the two main parties: Labour and Conservative. As documented in Chapter 4, parties have become less popular and trusted, alongside party politicians. They have lost their natural bases of support from distinctive class groups and party identifiers have become a smaller group. There are many more distractions for people these days, including single-issue groups to get involved with. Family and work life are pressing in the UK today, where household members are often working long hours and looking after family members: there is no time for meetings and door-to-door canvassing (though perhaps increased usage of online meetings will improve matters). Central organizations of political parties are themselves less interested in all local constituencies, preferring to focus their efforts on the small and reducing numbers of marginal seats. As the main parties tend to

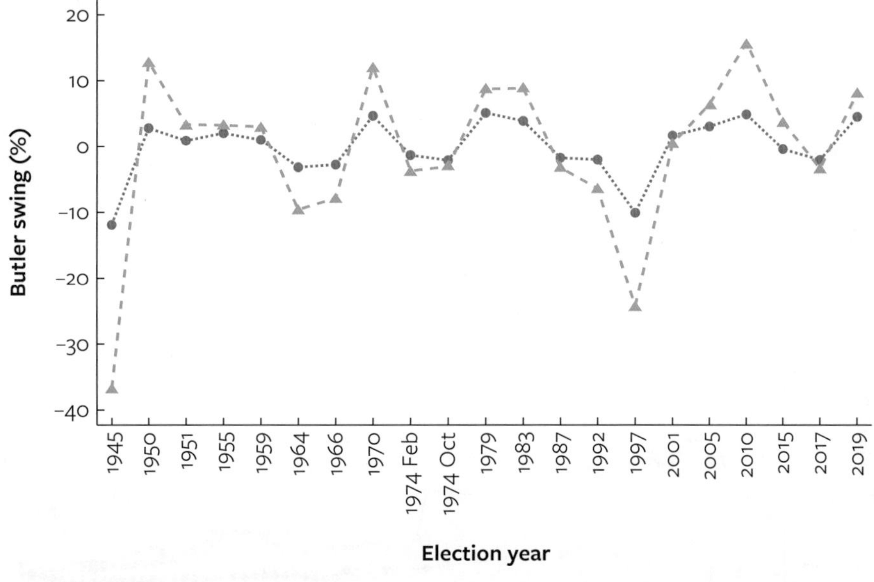

Figure 5.8 Comparisons of percentage swings in votes and House of Commons seats, 1945–2019.

Sources: Adapted from Audickas et al. (2020), Mortimore and Blick (2018), and internet sources (www.bbc.co.uk/news)

Note: Butler swing is per cent change in votes and seats of two largest parties added together and divided by 2

converge their policies on the median voter, many voters have migrated to other parties (Spoon and Klüver 2019).

However, these data are a bit more complex than this story would suggest. Figure 5.9a shows the change in party membership for political parties in Britain since 1945, with Figure 5.9b zooming in on the changes since 2002, including the SNP, the Greens, and UKIP, giving a more vibrant picture, such as the increase for Labour.

Alongside the decline in the major parties has been the rise of new parties with mass memberships, such as the SNP and the Green Party. Even the old parties can revive as membership increased massively in the Labour Party with Corbyn's leadership and the movement, Momentum, which is a left-populist organization within the Labour Party that became popular in the 2010s. Whether these surges can arrest long-term decline remains to be seen.

The other dimension to party politics is factionalism, and increasing conflict within parties preventing them from presenting a united front to the electorate. This is hard to measure, as parties are by definition composed of different elements, and intra-party politics has always been important in understanding how parties operate (Mule 2001). But it is possible to see the growth of party disunity in rebellions of MPs, for example (section 3.5.1), then the impact of Brexit on party unity, especially the Conservative Party, which had a group of MPs called the European Research Group (ERG) bent on securing a hard or pure form of Brexit and breaking most ties with the European Union. There still remain powerful incentives for parties to stay unified as the electorate punishes disunified parties (Greene 2014; Greene and Haber 2015), but the temptations of rebellions and grandstanding can prove too much for politicians wishing to appeal to their constituents and get a good billing in the media.

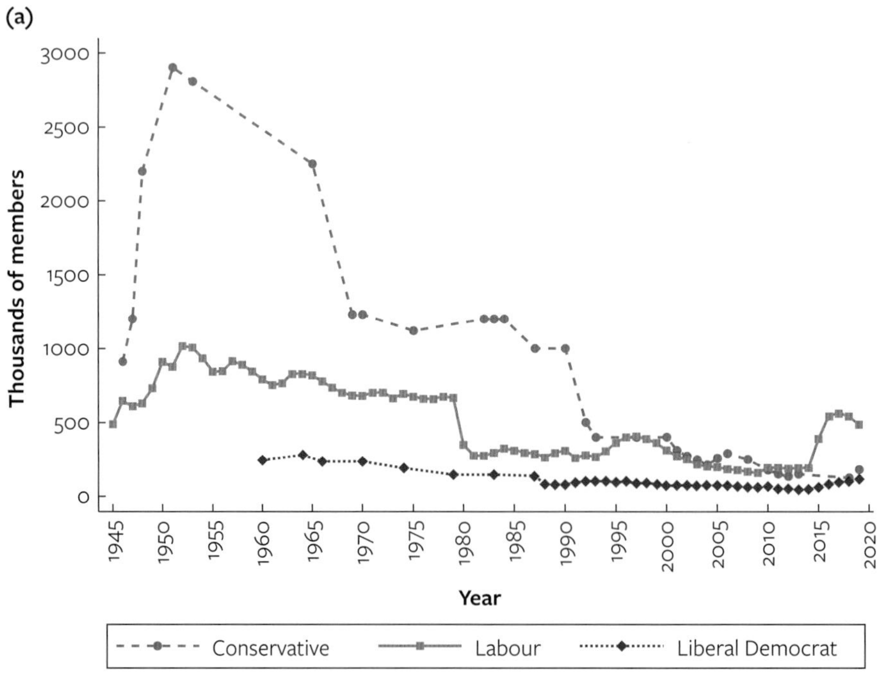

Figure 5.9a Membership of political parties (thousands), 1945–2019.
Source: Adapted from Audickas (2019, 7)

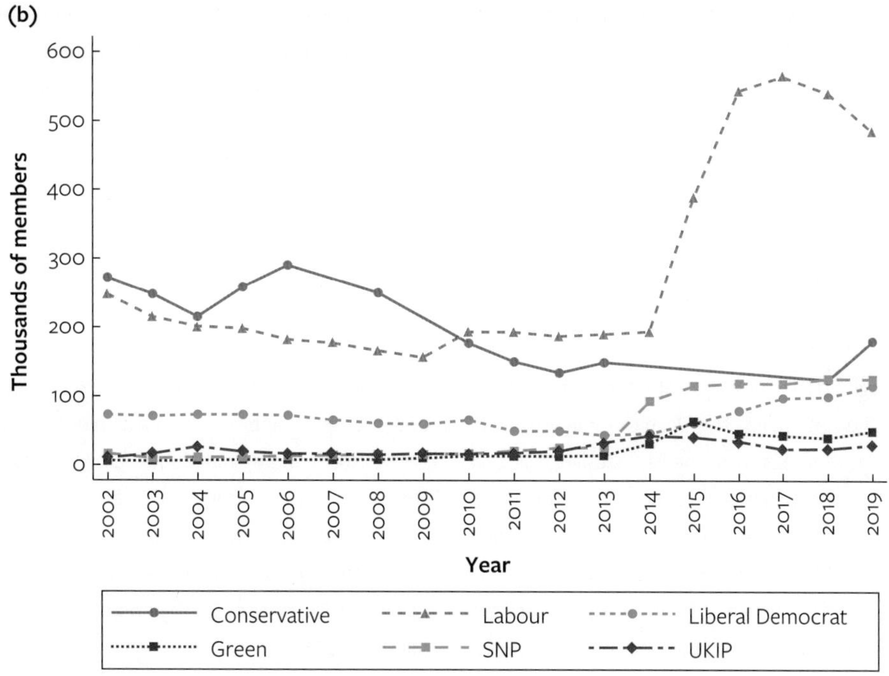

Figure 5.9b Membership of political parties (thousands), 2002–19.
Source: Adapted from Audickas (2019, 7)

5

5.9 Conclusion

This chapter has reviewed the process of competing for elections through the operation of the party system. It has painted a picture of a polity that was dominated by two main political parties that competed to win elections, and stressed how that process structured the nature of the British political system. This argument joins with the one made in Chapter 4 about stable voting blocs. There is also a link through the changes in the party system which reflect big social changes in British politics towards less support for the established parties, and diverse voting patterns and preferences. The two parties have challengers, such as the Green Party, or the powerful parties in the devolved governments, especially the SNP; periodically, they then face competition with the Liberal Democrats, who even entered a coalition government in 2010. Some elements of two-party dominance remain in place, in terms of seats in the House of Commons and incentives to vote for those parties to have a chance to enter government, which keeps the system in place at the UK level. There is an impact of the FPTP in keeping challengers from entering the House of Commons in greater numbers; but the same system delivers perverse results and can at times not yield a majority for either Labour or Conservative, and deliver significant numbers of seats for smaller parties that have regionally concentrated votes, such as the SNP, Plaid Cymru, and the Liberal Democrats. At other levels of government, parties operate with different electoral systems and participate in regular coalitions, though the two major parties are still dominant in London and most English localities. At times the old incentives can return when there is a clear choice for the electorate, such as in 2017 and 2019, on the final Brexit outcome. Such returns to two-party politics can, however, be illusory and the underlying volatility of the system means such gains can vanish as quickly as they appear.

Further reading

The Nuffield election studies (for example, Cowley and Kavanagh 2018) are very useful for each election, especially the appendix, 'The Results Analysed'. Also useful are the volumes from the BES studies that test models of voting behaviour based on performance politics and party competition (for example, Fieldhouse et al. 2019). For the operation of the electoral system, read John Curtice (2015b, 2018). There are many books on parties, such as the introduction by Driver (2011), and a recent book based on surveys of party members (Bale 2019). There is not a massive amount on party systems in the devolved nations, but discussion appears in recent pieces on elections (McAllister and Awan-Scully 2021; Mitchell and Henderson 2020; Tonge 2020; also see Awan-Scully 2018). There is work on individual parties in the devolved territories, such as on the Democratic Unionist Party (Tonge et al. 2014) and the SNP (Johns and Mitchell 2016).

Essay and examination questions

The classic question that gets posed is the extent to which Britain is a two-party system. There are various approaches to answering this question, such as using Dunleavy's (2005) critique. The article by Quinn (2013) is about the kind of party system at work at the UK level (also see Raymond 2016). It is wise to include a discussion of recent elections and what they mean for the party system, such as 2017 (Curtice 2017; Prosser 2018) and 2019 (Curtice 2020a; Cutts et al. 2020). Other questions could be directed to the appearance of electoral turbulence and the Fieldhouse et al. (2019) arguments, so aspects of party and partisan change can be reviewed in a question like, 'Has electoral politics become more volatile/turbulent in recent years?'.

The other set of questions are about the electoral systems of the UK and their impact, such as 'What is the impact of the electoral systems in the UK?', which allow for the exploration of different electoral systems. To answer these questions, especially over the operation of FPTP, pieces by Dunleavy (for example, Dunleavy 2005; Dunleavy, Park, and Taylor 2018) and Curtice (Curtice and Steed 1986; Curtice 2010, 2015b, 2018) are particularly useful.

Access the online resources for this chapter, including biannual updates, web links, and multiple-choice questions: www.oup.com/he/John1e

Chapter 6

The Media and Agenda-Setting

Political Turbulence

6.1 What is going to be in this chapter?

This chapter is about media in politics, including newspapers, television, the internet, and social media. It seeks to answer the question of how influential the media is over politics, such as voting behaviour. This discussion gives a broad overview of politics and the media, about the agenda of politics and its framing, and what shapes it. It then covers the classic question of the influence of the media in British politics. The importance of social media, and how it is now part of all media today, is covered, especially in relation to elections and referendums. The chapter also covers media and social media campaigning in elections. The chapter introduces the concept of chaotic pluralism as a way of characterizing today's social media-dominated and fluid political environment.

6.2 Introduction

This chapter in Part B of the book on behaviours and attitudes outside the traditional institutions of British government is about the agenda of politics, exploring the ways in which issues and ideas take hold and become important over time, or diminish in importance. This is key to debates in politics, and for understanding the diffusion of information more generally in the political system. This chapter is aimed at understanding this more intangible aspect of politics, what is called the policy agenda (Kingdon 1984, 3) (see Key term 6.1), and whether it has changed radically in recent years under the influence of social media as well as from more traditional outlets. Even though ideas and information exist in their own right, they need a means of communication provided by the institutions of the media and social media, which are political organizations, like broadcasters, even if heavily regulated (for the argument that the media is a political institution, see Cook 2005). Private companies, such as those that own Twitter or Facebook, have their own agendas and potential for bias. Moreover, the changes wrought by social media have become part of the way to understand whether and how the UK has experienced political turbulence in recent years under the influence of ever-increasing information and swings in the policy and public agenda. With a 24/7 media presence, and fast-moving stories, such as campaigns on social media, which draw the attention of politicians and other policy-makers, it could be claimed that the media and the public agenda create an environment of short-termism and endless U-turns. Such an environment undermines the long-term thinking and deliberation needed for policy-making, increasing the turmoil of politics, especially as politicians experience much of politics through the media and discuss media content among themselves (Schudson 1989, on the US).

Key term 6.1 The policy agenda

The range of salient issues that the government and other key decision-makers, such as ministers, civil servants, journalists, and parliamentarians, concentrate on at any one point in time.

6.2.1 Framing and bias

The media is crucial in processing the agenda of politics, so it is important to understand how it is organized to help explain the outputs and outcomes of British politics. In democratic theory the media can be a source for debate and scrutiny in politics (Keane 1991), providing a critical source of information and ideas for policy-makers and citizens, as well as scrutinizing politicians and other leaders, and helping to hold them to account alongside opposition and campaign groups. But media coverage of stories and scandals can allow those who are in positions of power to influence ideas and behaviour more generally, in line with their political preferences. The media can also frame issues in a certain way, and positive or negative word choices can impact on neutrality (no selection can be entirely neutral). For example, the same story of a family receiving state benefits could be framed as a story of dependence on the state or of brave survival in parlous circumstances.

6.2.2 The influence of the media on politics

A lot depends on the extent of the influence of the media, which is part of what is called agenda-setting (McCombs and Shaw 1972) (see Key term 6.2,

Photo 6.1 A cameraman films Westminster Palace, London. The city is a location for the largest broadcaster in the world, the BBC, and many other national and international media companies.

6

definition (1)). Accounts vary considerably from authors who think the media has a strong influence on politics (Zaller 1992), to those who think that it reinforces existing beliefs. Classic studies of the media show that individuals can resist new information that does not conform to their prior beliefs, processing information through their social networks of friends and family members (Klapper 1960). In an age of polarization, it is often thought that people are reading views that they agree with in the first place, and are screening out information that does not confirm them, interpreting information in a favourable light from their partisan lens, a process called partisan information processing (see Key term 4.12). On the other hand, with easy access to information from a variety of sources on social media, people might be subject to influences on topics on which they do not have prior information to be able to decide for themselves, and sources might be disguised with the direct objective of influencing them in a certain direc-

Key term 6.2 Agenda-setting

Referred to in three linked ways:

(1) How the media affects the content and tone of communication and hence politics as a whole.

(2) The general process of how policy-makers, the public, experts, and the media shape the content of debate and thence public policy. Agenda-setting often refers to the process before a final decision is made and authorized.

(3) The extent to which one actor or set of actors can set the agenda, for example the prime minister (see section 2.6.9).

tion. Even though much information appears neutral, space can be bought by campaign groups, particularly on social media. In the classic works on the democratic citizen (Downs 1957), reviewed in section 4.4.2, low knowledge and interest in politics is thought to be common, which means that people might be easily manipulated (or they may stick to established cues from the political parties they may trust as in section 4.4.3). The media can act on behalf of citizens to overcome the information asymmetry implied in the principal–agent model (see Zoom-In 1.4). Part of this chapter will be about the extent of the media's influence in UK politics, thereby helping us to understand the agenda-setting process and the character of the policy agenda.

6.3 Basic facts: forms of media

In this section, there are some basic facts about the different aspects of the media, in particular the different organizations involved. It should be remembered that all media are connected today and operate through the internet and in particular social media, and each media outlet seeks to influence its reach and impact on social media. In many ways, we are looking at how the media is part of a wider system of media dominated by big companies, such as Facebook, Snapchat, and Twitter.

Photo 6.2 The British newspaper *The Daily Telegraph* in print and digital editions.

6.3.1 The 'print' media

The main set of basic facts that will be covered here are the main media organizations in the UK. Key is print media, even though print media can also be published online; some are online-only, like the *i* newspaper, or have a dual presence. But the past is very much associated with the printed page, a folded document that is produced each morning (there are some evening or afternoon newspapers, such as the *Evening Standard*, London's daily newspaper). Although they lost their monopoly of news coverage, they still retain a massive hold on the population, and are part of people's daily reading habits, whether read online or in print.

There is a key distinction between what is called the tabloid press, printed on a small page, sometimes called the 'red tops' because of their front-page red banner, and the quality press, the 'black tops', which are larger-sized broadsheets papers like *The Daily Telegraph* or *The Financial Times*. There is less of a distinction between the two these days, but the quality press in the past typically included longer stories, with more of an intellectual tone and content, whereas the red tops are more popularly orientated, with a focus on sport and gossipy stories, shorter stories, and eye-catching headlines. In practice, the press has become more homogenous in tone and content, with *The Times*, *The Guardian*, and *The Independent* moving to tabloid-size editions in the 2000s. The big change was the move to online publication or joint print/online publications, which means it is possible to count both in circulation figures. The daily totals of traditional news media are reported in Figure 6.1a, with the total reach including the internet in Figure 6.1b. Then there is the concentration of ownership of these media organizations, as shown in Figure 6.2.

The print media ownership is narrowly concentrated (see Figure 6.2).

6

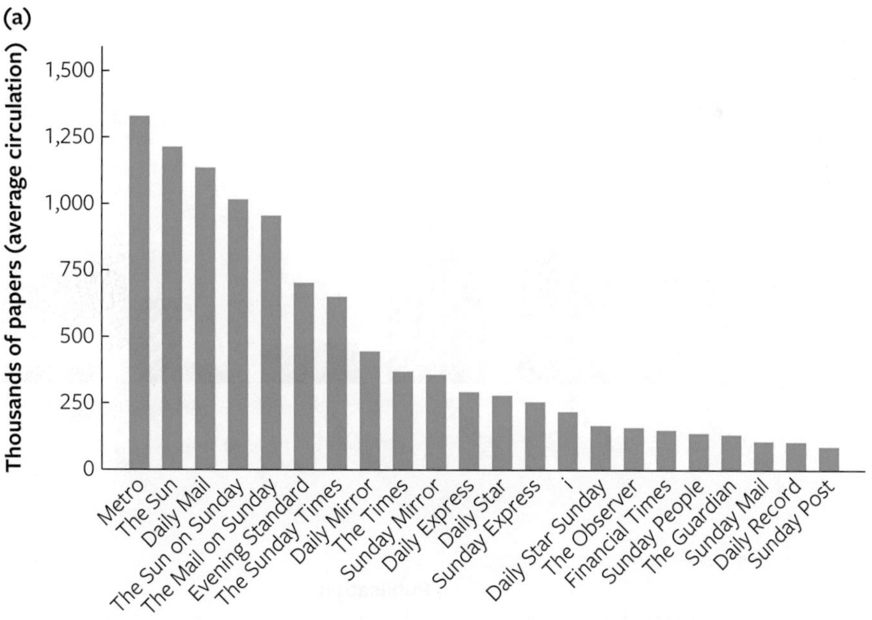

Figure 6.1a Newspaper average circulation, 2–22 March 2020.
Source: ABC: www.abc.org.uk/data/national-newspapers

(b)

Total brand reach (millions)
0 2 4 6 8 10
The Sun
Daily Mail
Daily Mirror
Guardian
Metro
Daily Express
The Times
Evening Standard
Daily Telegraph
Daily Star
i
Publication

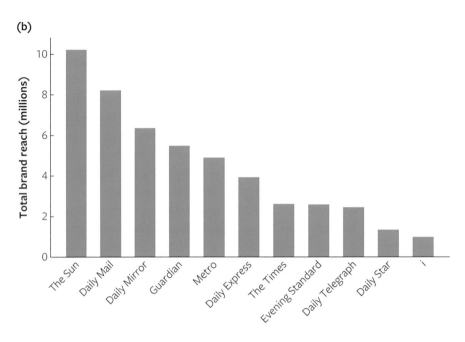

Figure 6.1b Total brand reach.

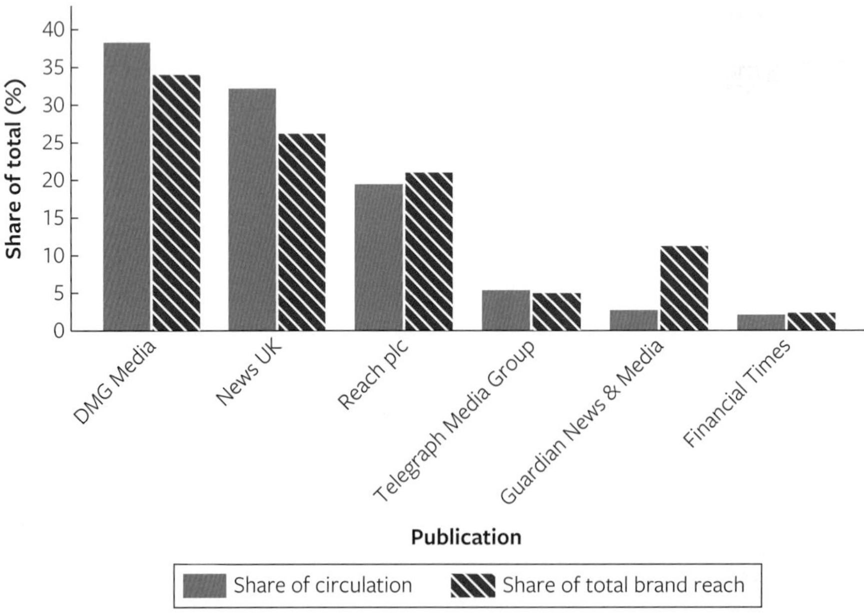

Figure 6.2 Media ownership in 2020.
Source: Chivers, Who Owns the UK, 2021: www.mediareform.org.uk/wp-content/uploads/2021/03/Who-Owns-the-UK-Media_final2.pdf

6.3.2 Broadcast media

Broadcast media can be received on a radio or television, or online through a website or app. Traditionally these programmes were listened to or watched live, but increasingly are downloaded pre-recorded to play later on phones, laptops, and tablets, though news usually needs to be consumed immediately. Television and radio have been key means of communicating political information in the UK during the twentieth century, and are still important today. The BBC (British Broadcasting Corporation) is a key player for both radio and television; then there are private stations, such as ITV and Channel 4, which have legal obligations as public service broadcasters (with the latter having a statutory remit to make high-quality, innovative, and alternative content, which challenges established conventions), and private radio providers. Even with many other sources of information being available, these media outlets still have very large audiences. In 2019, 89 per cent of UK adults listened to at least 5 minutes of live radio each week (Ofcom 2019, 8); people watched on average 3 hours 12 minutes of broadcast television in 2018, but this was 49 minutes less than in 2012 (Ofcom 2019). TV remains the most used platform for news (75 per cent). The average adult watched 95 hours of TV news in 2019, with the over-sixty-fives watching 204 hours and sixteen- to twenty-four-year-olds watching 16 hours. Podcasts are becoming more popular, with one in twenty receiving their news in this way (Ofcom 2019).

6.3.3 Internet and social media

The web and social media have become ubiquitous and all-embracing, especially for young people, with 90 per cent getting their news this way (compared to 12 per

Photo 6.3 The BBC or British Broadcasting Corporation headquarters building in Portland Place in London.

Photo 6.4 The majority of young people receive their news via social media.

cent print) (Newman 2020). Also, news organizations have different ways of reporting the news, such as the BBC's live updated website, or a newspaper, like *The Financial Times*, having a Twitter feed. There are some online-only news organizations, often based in the US, with UK editions, such as *The Huffington Post*. Even search engines have news feeds, such as Google, which uses an algorithm to select its content, and technology companies, like Apple, provide stories and curate news. Figure 6.3 demonstrates the variety of sources available for news and Figure 6.4 shows how concentrated is the reach of social media companies.

6.3.4 **Subcentral media**

There is a considerable media presence at the subnational level (Franklin 2006), with newspapers based in cities, like *The Manchester Evening News*, as well as small towns having print and/or online news outlets (though many of these are dying out). The impact of the media revolution has been very painfully felt at a local level with the decline in local newspapers and thus sources of investigative reporting, which can hold local politicians to account (Ramsay and Moore 2016, 35). There has been a concentration of ownership, with 83 per cent of all local titles owned by six publishers, with the three largest publishers—Newsquest, Reach, and JPI Media—owning a fifth each (Media Reform Coalition 2021, 8).

There is a more vibrant media economy in the devolved territories, with Scotland having very distinctive newspapers, such as *The Scotsman*, or special editions of UK national newspapers, like *The Sun*, though with the same fears of decline in the face of the internet (Dekavalla 2015). Scotland, Wales, and Northern Ireland also benefit from the regional organizations of the media, such as the BBC, that broadcast from these places and other regional locations in England.

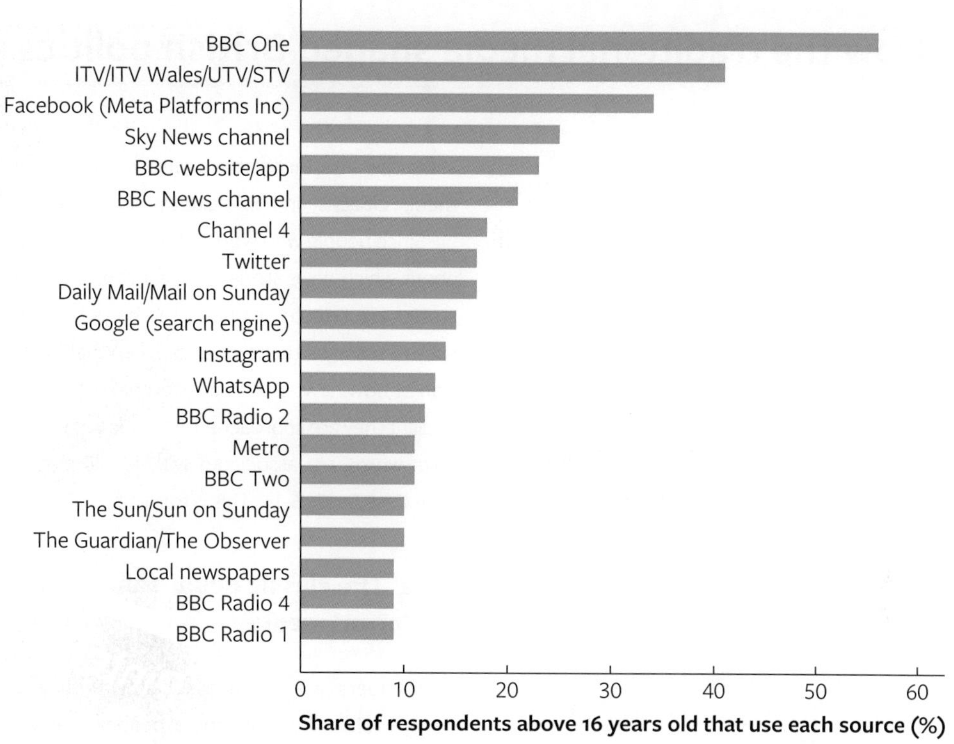

Figure 6.3 Top twenty news sources 2020.
Source: Ofcom 2020: www.ofcom.org.uk/__data/assets/pdf_file/0013/201316/news-consumption-2020-report.pdf

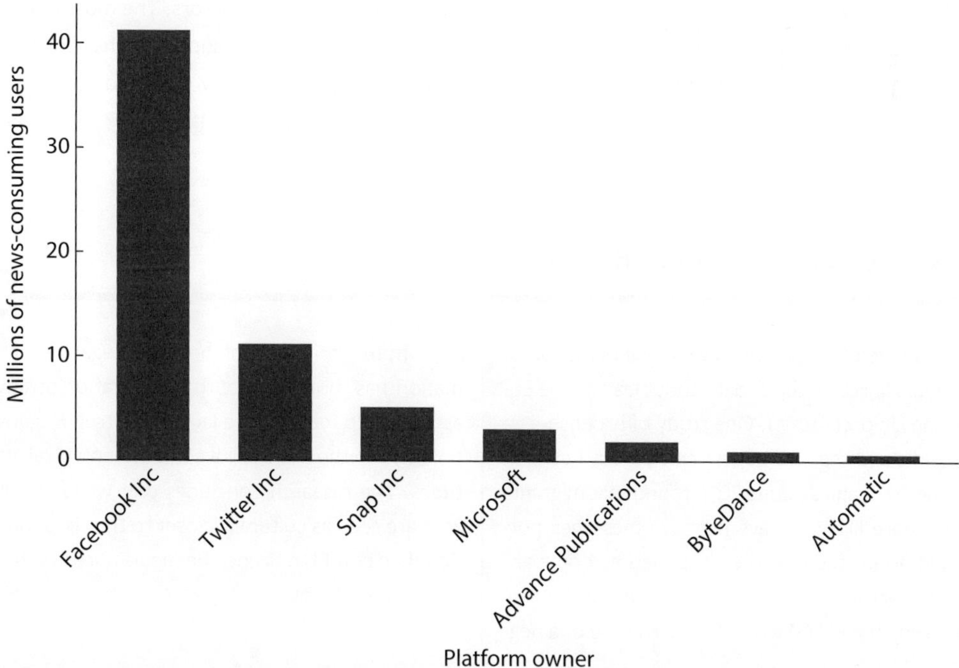

Figure 6.4 Social media reach.
Source: Chivers, Who Owns the UK, 2021: www.mediareform.org.uk/wp-content/uploads/2021/03/Who-Owns-the-UK-Media_final2.pdf

6.4 How the traditional media shaped British politics

6.4.1 Methodological issues

The key question about the media is how it shapes politics, in particular its influence on the opinions and behaviours of citizens as voters, as measured by public opinion and other citizen data. The media can also influence the actions of politicians and other key actors in politics who are also directly influenced by consuming news and other content. Politicians and other policy-makers also need to react indirectly to citizens who are influenced by the media. Figure 6.5 represents this set of interactive relationships between the media, citizens, and politicians/policy-makers.

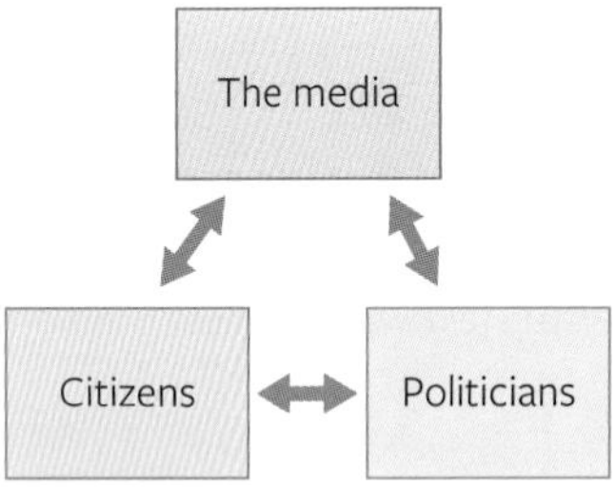

Figure 6.5 How the media, citizens, and politicians/policy-makers influence each other.

Since people who work in the media make decisions about which news stories to prioritize, certain kinds of stories are selected to be in the news or highlighted, such as being on the front page. Then there is the question of how news stories are described, and what tone or slant they are approached with, such as whether negative words are associated with ideological positions (see Case Study 6.1). This is framing.

6.4.2 The classic debate about the 'print' media

Newspapers are often associated with a political slant, such as support for a political party, as well as left- or right-wing views. The private ownership (which includes print media hosted online) means that a paper reflects the political views of its owner, subject to commercial factors. The most read newspaper, *The Sun*, often supports the Conservative Party (though it famously switched to the Labour Party led by Tony Blair in March 1997, shortly before

Case Study 6.1 Migration in the EU

An example of bias in the news is the depiction of migrants linked to the debate about leaving the European Union (Brexit). One study of broadsheets, tabloids, and regional papers carried out between 1 June 2015 and 23 June 2016 found that migrants were more likely to have negative messages portrayed about them, to be described as criminals, and to feature in stories linked to the desirability of leaving the EU (Walter 2019). The use of a negative frame is important because negative information has more impact than neutral or positive as it leads to feelings of a lack of control. Negative portrayal in the news is linked to stereotypical attitudes. The research concludes that while EU citizens are seen as culturally closer to the UK population than non-EU citizens, the media portrays them as a greater threat.

the general election), with only a few other papers tending to support Labour, such as *The Daily Mirror* and *The Guardian*. With the concentration of ownership favouring right-wing newspapers and their large readerships, the suspicion has been that the bias in headlines would affect the outcomes of elections as well as moving the agenda of politics rightwards and affecting the extent to which non-Conservative parties can pursue a radical agenda, especially when they are in power.

Whether political influence can be attributed to *The Sun* and other papers is, however, a hard claim to prove. Studies tend to use survey evidence from one time period (for example, Curtice and Semetko 1994). A key issue is that people in these studies have already self-selected into reading particular papers. Finding out that a *Sun*-reading working-class person votes Conservative is not a guide to the influence of the paper, as these people chose to read the paper. Even Labour voters might be inclined to buy the paper rather than *The Mirror* because they may be Conservative-inclined and know *The Sun* supports the party they might vote for. Newspapers also target certain kinds of readers because they have done their market research, so their readers may be more likely to swing with the newspaper's preferred party. Even switches during a campaign, say with *Sun*-reading Labour voters switching more than *Mirror*-reading Labour voters, could occur because they might be latently more sympathetic to a right-wing party in the first place, hence more likely to be activated to vote Conservative in a campaign—not a direct influence of the newspaper. This latency would need to be controlled for in statistical analysis, but is a hard attitude to measure in surveys. There is a need for a research method that can detect a causal influence where there are unobserved differences between groups (see Zoom-In 6.1). To try to get around some of the methodological problems, Newton and Brynin (2001) decided to look at data from the long-running British Household Panel Survey (BHPS) to find out whether long-term exposure to print newspapers affects political preferences. The BHPS is a panel survey, which interviews the same respondents at successive time points. They find that those who have a Labour Party identification but read a Conservative newspaper are more likely to vote Conservative.

6.4.3 Experimental methods detecting media influence

Reeves et al. (2015) offer a stronger test than Newton and Brynin. They leverage an opportunity offered by *The Sun*'s switch in allegiance from Conservative to Labour just before the 1997 election, and also the paper's switch back to the Conservative Party before the 2010 poll. This creates what they claim is a quasi-experiment (see Key term 6.3), whereby it is possible to compare what happens to the same voters before and after the papers switch, to measure whether the paper had influence in swinging those voters. It is a good test of the influence of the media, even if just for a short period, and if it is assumed that *The Sun*'s switch was independent of any likely movement in voter preferences. To show this, Reeves et al. (2015) use the same data source, the BHPS, as well as the British Social Attitudes Survey; but they look at the impact of switches on voter preferences. They find that 'the swing in support for Labour among consistent readers of *The Sun* was 6.62 percentage points larger than all other persons in the sample' (Reeves et al. 2015, 7). When *The Sun* switched back to support David Cameron in 2010, they similarly concluded that, 'any increase among *Sun* readers in support for the Conservative Party over and above the background trend occurred in the period after *The Sun* campaigned to get David Cameron elected' (Reeves et al. 2015, 9). This change happened more after the campaign had started than at the immediate point of the switch. The authors concluded that these switches affected the voting behaviour, and were important in influencing the result in 2010.

Key term 6.3 Quasi-experiment

In an experiment, people or places are assigned randomly, so it is possible to compare treated and non-treated areas and to attribute causal impact. In a quasi-experiment the assignment is non-random, but it is reasonable to make comparisons.

Ladd and Lenz (2009), again using the BHPS, show similar results, using the data in a slightly more sophisticated way.

The use of panel data does not get around the challenge of attributing causation (see Zoom-In 6.1). Experimental methods can address this issue, shown in the research of Foos and Bischof (2019). They are interested in the role of the press in encouraging negative attitudes to the European Union, which had been fostered by stories of regulations that appeared to undermine British laws and customs, such as over the size of fishnets, the content of sausages, or the curvature of bananas. *The Sun* once again took the lead (along with *The Telegraph*, whose stories were often written by their former Brussels correspondent, Boris Johnson), with a campaign against the former president of the EU Commission, Jacques Delors, with the characteristic rhyming headline, 'Up Yours Delors'. When it came to the campaign to leave or remain in the European Union in 2016, *The Sun* was very prominent (see Figure 6.6).

So, it is not implausible to think the newspaper had an influence on attitudes to the European Union. How do the researchers tackle this issue? Foos and Bischof (2019) take advantage of the fact that *The Sun* was boycotted in the Liverpool area after its coverage of the Hillsborough disaster of 1989. These residents did not get a chance to read the paper at this time while those in the surrounding areas did, creating a natural experiment in terms of people in the study who are very similar in outlooks and preferences, only differing by being exposed to *The Sun*. Looking at data from the British Social Attitudes (BSA) survey, which covered respondents in both areas, they find a 10-percentage-point shift in attitudes in support of the EU, as measured by responses to the question, 'Britain should continue its EC/EU membership'.

Analysis from Gavin and Sanders (2003) finds a modest effect of print media influence, this time on economic attitudes. In a statistical model, they link change in press coverage of the economy, personal

Zoom-In 6.1 Causation

Causation is about the attribution of a relationship, say between A and B, where the observer can be confident that A influences B, and there is no other variable, say C, that explains the relationship. So, if a newspaper says to vote Conservative (A) and the reader (B) votes Conservative, that is a relationship that might be observed, but need not be causal. It is possible that the reason B buys A is that they are voting Conservative anyway and expect to read this. The newspaper might offer pro-Conservative stories because its readers are expecting them, so the causal arrow runs from B to A. It is very hard to prove a causal relationship in the social sciences, because it is hard to rule out a confounding variable like C and many other variables might be unobserved. Experiments can overcome this problem (see Key term 3.7).

THE Sun

Tuesday, June 14, 2016 BRITAIN'S BEST-SELLING PAPER 50p thesun.co.uk

Oh Roo behave

WAYNE'S PLEA TO ENGLAND FANS

SEE SUNSPORT

INSIDE 8-PAGE ROYAL ASCOT GUIDE

BeLEAVE in Britain

THE Sun SAYS

WE are about to make the biggest political decision of our lives. The Sun today urges everyone to vote LEAVE.

We must set ourselves free from dictatorial Brussels.

Throughout our 43-year membership of the European Union it has proved increasingly greedy, wasteful, bullying and breathtakingly incompetent in a crisis.

Next Thursday, at the ballot box, we can correct this huge and historic mistake.

It is our last chance. Because, be in no doubt, our future looks far bleaker if we stay in.

Outside the EU we can become richer, safer and free at long last to forge our own destiny – as America, Canada, Australia, New Zealand and many other great democracies already do. And as we were the first to do centuries ago.

If we stay, Britain will be engulfed in a few short years by this relentlessly expanding German-dominated federal state. For all David Cameron's witless assurances, our powers and values **WILL** be further eroded. Staying in will be worse for immigration, worse for jobs, worse for wages and worse for our way of life.

Greece is bankrupt. Italy is in danger of going the same way, with even more disastrous consequences. In Spain, 45 per cent of those under 25 are out of work. And numerous even poorer and worse-governed countries are now joining the EU.

'Remain' is bigger risk in every way

To remain means being powerless to cut mass immigration which keeps wages low and puts catastrophic pressure on our schools, hospitals, roads and housing stock.

In every way, it is a bigger risk.

The Remain campaign, made up of the corporate establishment, arrogant europhiles and foreign banks, have set out to terrify us all about life outside the EU. Their "Project Fear" strategy predicts mass unemployment, soaring interest rates and inflation, plummeting house prices, even world war.

The Treasury, Bank of England, the IMF and world leaders have all been wheeled out by Downing Street to add their grim warnings.

Nonsense! Years ago the same politicians and economists issued apocalyptic predictions about our fate if we didn't join the euro.

Thank God we stopped that. The single currency's stranglehold has since ruined the EU's poorer nations and cast millions on the dole.

We are told we cannot be in the single market without accepting all the rules, free movement of people included. If so, let's leave it and, using our enormous clout as the world's fifth biggest economy, strike great trade deals with the other 85 per cent of the world. And pick and choose the best migrants from the whole world. If we stay in the EU, as Cameron wants, we will finally give up any chance of controlling our population. Cameron admits it.

Vote Leave, and we will reassert our sovereignty – embracing a future as a self-governing, powerful nation envied by all.

We will re-establish the basic principle that we are governed by politicians we elect or eject every five years, not foreign bureaucrats.

Our country has glorious history

The Sun has campaigned relentlessly against the ever-expanding superstate. But the EU cannot reform.

Remain has conducted a deceitful campaign. It has been nasty, cynical, personally abusive and beneath the dignity of Britain.

Our country has a glorious history. This is our chance to make Britain even greater, to recapture our democracy, to preserve the values and culture we are rightly proud of.

A VOTE FOR LEAVE IS A VOTE FOR A BETTER BRITAIN.

VOTE TO QUIT EU ON JUNE 23

Figure 6.6 *The Sun*, 14 June 2016.

economic expectations (how well people think they are going to be doing economically), economic management competence, and party support. They find that the content of the 'black-top' press influences middle-class respondents' positive economic expectations, which then go on to influence vote choices, increasing Labour support, but with no impact for the popular red-top press.

Taking these studies together, there is good evidence that the print media (now mainly hosted online), especially *The Sun*, influenced political attitudes and behaviour in the UK in a rightward direction on the political spectrum. Whether such influence remains in an era of declining print sales, with the internet as the key source of political information, remains to be seen.

6.5 Broadcast media

6.5.1 Bias on TV

There is less evidence about the impact of the broadcast media, such as TV, because there are rules on impartiality which make it harder to determine a relationship between news content and political attitudes/behaviour. The case must be made more subtly, focusing on the influence of elites in the media and the hidden routines that create bias even if not consciously articulated. While some research sees the broadcast media as biased to the right (Group 1976), a more balanced approach appears with Neil Gavin (2007), who argues that journalists do try to find the right story and seek political balance, both in TV and press news, though he notices there has been a decline in attention to 'serious' economic news over time. Miller (1991, 210) also finds no evidence of right-wing bias from the BBC. Even with these balanced findings, the role of visual media in conveying frames and common understandings should not be neglected.

6.5.2 TV and vote choices

Whether TV does influence voters is questionable, with the classic studies indicating that voters process this information rather than being directly influenced by it (Trenaman and McQuail 1961), though this research is limited to campaign broadcasts, rather than assessing the influence of television more generally. A lot of the evidence from studies of campaigning show that voters tend to use campaign broadcasts as sources of information, as well as television and press having a modest effect on perceptions and attitudes (Miller 1991).

Probably the best study carried out in Britain is by Norris et al. (1999), which tested for the impact of the election campaign using experiments with video clips, some of which had pro-party messages in them. They recruited people to participate in a laboratory experiment, who were surveyed after seeing the clips. The research showed a modest impact on voter preferences.

6.6 Internet and social media

A revolution in the media saw most communications happen electronically through the internet, starting first with static websites and e-mail, then from 2005 moving to dynamic interactions involving feedback through social media with real-time responses. Today, there is mass engagement with the internet and social media. In early 2020, 96 per cent of households in Great Britain had access to the internet, up from 93 per cent in 2019, and 57 per cent in 2006 (ONS 2020), drawn from the Opinions and Lifestyle Survey (OPN). There were fears that the internet would cause a digital divide between those with or without access, which might reinforce existing inequalities related to income and social class (Norris 2001). Now most people in the Western world have access to the internet. Not only are there more households using the internet, there has also been a massive increase in frequency of usage. Figure 6.7 shows the increase in recent years, up to some 40 million people, with 47 per cent of the population using it daily.

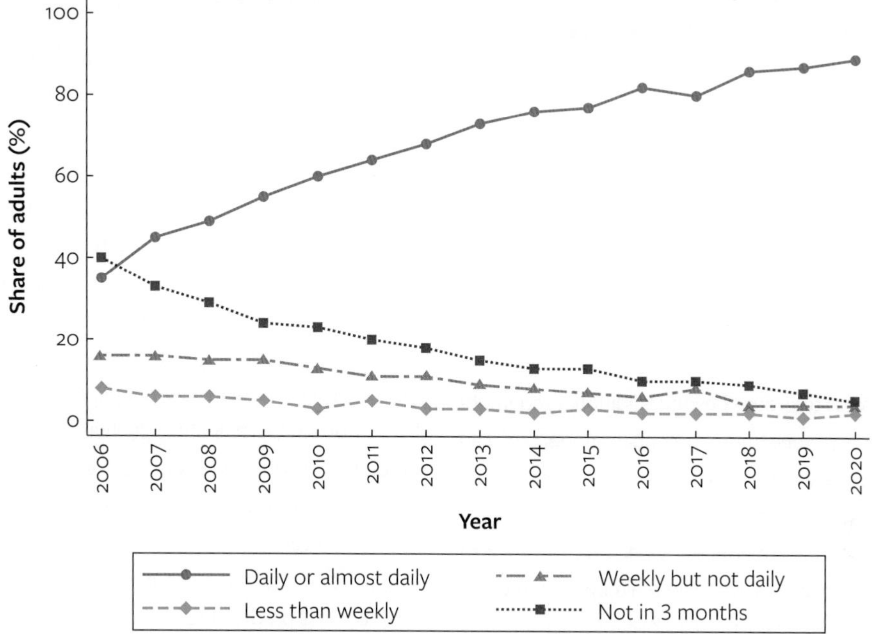

Figure 6.7 Internet use, 2006–20.
Source: ONS: www.ons.gov.uk/peoplepopulationandcommunity/householdcharacteristics/homeinternetandsocialmediausage/datasets/internetaccesshouseholdsandindividualsreferencetables

6.6.1 More or less participation from the internet?

Most if not all engagement with politics is now done online. This was evident during the Covid-19 pandemic, when rules around social distancing prevented people from meeting and gathering. So, what impact does this have on participation? Some researchers regard the internet and social media as substitutes for older forms of political participation (Ward, Gibson, and Lusoli 2003). Whereas previous generations went canvassing door to door, had face-to-face meetings, and posted mailshots, now the same things can be done online, which could suggest that the basic levels and patterns of behaviour in politics pre-internet, including inequalities, extend into the future. But this research came from an early period when there were much fewer people online, and those who were already active in politics had shifted their existing behaviour from off- to online. Over time, as use of the internet and social media has become ubiquitous, researchers have begun to understand their impact. A combination of factors is at work, in particular that the internet is lower in cost to use, which means more people can get involved from particular groups that have fewer resources, as they do not need to travel to meetings, for example. There is some evidence internationally that social media attract people to politics who were previously not interested (Borge and Cardenal 2011). A comparative study of the UK, Australia, and the US (Xenos, Vromen, and Loader 2014) shows the internet to be the 'great equalizer'; that is, being used right across the social spectrum rather than confined to a small minority, and revealing a positive relationship between social media use and interest in politics. There is some evidence of this in the UK too with the survey showing that young people are more inclined to engage in online politics (Gibson, Lusoli, and Ward 2016), with different results for women (increase overall, but less interest in campaigning). A study from the 2010 general election showed that people who are drawn into online participation also do other kinds of activities, such as e-petitions; what is called spill-over (Cunill, Cutts, and Gibson 2016).

With access to groups beyond traditional geographic boundaries, many more potential supporters can be reached, allowing political movements to scale up considerably. With many more people involved, money can be raised more effectively because citizens can make 'micro-donations' that can scale up to many millions very quickly. This makes collective action (Key term 4.9) easier. On the other hand, some sites do not have regularly disseminated political content, reducing engagement with politics and political behaviour as a result. A study of increased broadband use in the UK by Gavazza and colleagues (2019) found that citizens consumed less news as a result, and so turned out less in local elections. The internet might depend on its users being curious and willing to search out new content, rather than it being delivered for passive consumption, like in a news bulletin.

The impact of the media on consumption links to the argument that the internet is associated with greater polarization in politics, which is being experienced in the US, and in part in the UK (Duffy et al. 2019). The mechanism is isolation in 'echo chambers' and 'filter bubbles' (Sunstein 2017), which is about how internet users tend to select content that is close to their own opinions and interact with like-minded people. The international evidence, from the US in particular, however, is not conclusive, and does not support the claim that citizens have become more isolated from each other in chambers or bubbles (Jungherr, Rivero, and Gayo-Avello 2020, 85–92).

6.6.2 Chaotic pluralism

Another dimension to the internet and to social media in particular is that horizontal communication makes it easier to connect with people online who share interests. By following and messaging them, political influence can occur. Such reciprocated mass engagement can lead to cascades of interest in a particular topic, where everyone focuses on one issue because of a 'feeding frenzy'. An internet-induced bandwagon can take off, with large upswings in political participation. Social media allow people to know the numbers of others participating, such as when 1 million e-petitions are reached (Margetts et al. 2011). Once these kinds of thresholds are reached, they also draw in further interest, and even more upswings in interest. With these kinds of factors at work, the internet might lead to a less predictable kind of politics and increased turbulence, which reflects the dramatic swings in politics that have characterized UK politics in the past few decades (Margetts et al. 2015). There is also a link between movements on social media and how they may be picked up by the political system itself, with more traditional media outlets paying attention to campaigns on social media, which, in turn, through the process of agenda-setting, causes issues, such as immigration, to rise up and down the agenda in rapid succession, which in turn affects the conduct of political campaigns and the outcomes of elections. This destabilizing nature of contemporary politics where it is hard to predict issues and with the effect of the social media has been called chaotic pluralism (Margetts et al. 2015). As a result, social media encourages support for some political candidates, such as the former leader of the Labour Party, Jeremy Corbyn (#Grime4Corbyn), with one interview with him being viewed on Facebook by 2.5 million people (Margetts 2017).

6.6.3 Bias and manipulation

Finally, as with traditional media, bias and manipulation can be conveyed with social media. This argument is

Photo 6.5 The prevalence of fake news, post-truth politics, and confirmation bias has increased with the rise of social media, especially the Facebook news feed.

more difficult to make than for news organizations where there is one or several bodies and groups of people tasked with presenting information to the public. Because there is such a diversity of views on social media and many sources of information, people are exposed to many sources, where they can compare views, or select social media sources that confirm their pre-existing views. More opportunities for discussion moderate the possibility of manipulation. But certain kinds of stories may emerge on social media that give a voice to more extreme groups, such as the far-right, who would usually be shut out of mainstream debates, and where more moderate and liberal voices might find it harder to be heard (Jungherr, Rivero, and Gayo-Avello 2020, 189). Furthermore, money plays a role in social media such as the purchase of advertising. The users of some social media sites, such as Facebook, are less knowledgeable about politics than other users, such as Twitter (Mellon and Prosser 2017), and may be susceptible to social media campaigns via algorithm-filtered content. It may also be the case that because people are referred to by friends and people they trust, they may be more susceptible to influence on the internet.

The environment of the internet might be a means to disseminate lies or questionable facts, much more common in the era of 'post-truth' or 'alternative facts', giving power to less conventional groups. It is often thought that referendum campaigns, such as Brexit in 2016, are susceptible to this kind of influence from discussion on social media (Hall, Tinati, and Jennings 2018) (see Case Study 6.3 on Cambridge Analytica).

6.7 Media and political campaigning

As explored in Chapter 5, campaigning is an important feature of elections, usually lasting a matter of three or four weeks (though this can be longer, as was the case in 2017, when it was seven weeks), whereby parties seek to get ahead. Parties throw money at their campaigns, seeking to highlight issues that they think are useful to them, and to highlight the failings of the opposition over those issues. Parties focus on certain issues because they are closer to them on the left–right scale (see section 4.4.6), or because of historical factors meaning that an issue has been associated with or 'owned' by a political party (see Key term 5.13) (Budge and Farlie 1983). In the UK, the issue of publicly funded healthcare in the form of the National Health Service (NHS), and its sustainability over time, is associated with the Labour Party. The secret of the campaign is to ensure that the debates and discussions happen on the party's owned issues where the party can win arguments and the respect of voters, but if the main parties are both seeking to do this, then it can be hard if there is similar campaign effort. Occasionally it can make sense to move on the opponent's ground and show that you are better than them, which was Tony Blair's strategy in seeking to show the credibility of New Labour. Recently, Boris Johnson's Conservative government has been adopting policies, such as more public borrowing, control over public utilities, and increasing taxes on businesses, which are more reminiscent of Labour's policies. Parties hope for an event, such as a scandal over NHS treatment, which highlights their owned issue, and for which they can adjust their campaigning to take advantage.

There are a variety of techniques that parties can use to campaign effectively, which range from door-to-door canvassing to delivery of leaflets, which are carried out by local party organizations. Then central party organization can use phone calls and targeted advertising, either on broadcast or digital media, the latter of which can be targeted using postal codes from e-mail addresses. These campaigns aim to do two things: one is to raise the turnout of existing supporters at the upcoming election—that is, to get them to the polls; the other is to sway the vote if turnout is assured; or target both turnout and vote choice at the same time. It is hard to change people's minds on the doorstep, especially from one party to another. US evidence shows that campaigns find it hard to change the views of voters (Kalla and Broockman 2018); but it is easier to persuade people to turn out to vote or not, especially if they support a party but are a bit reluctant to vote or think the election is not important. There is also some experimental evidence from the UK which shows how party campaigns using leaflets or door-knocking can improve voter turnout (Foos et al. 2020), and can benefit the turnout of partisans and even depress those of opponents (Foos and John 2018).

Campaigning involves the spending of considerable amounts of money, regulated by the Electoral Commission. For example, the Conservative Party spent £16 million on the 2019 election. This can be a local campaign, either from money raised locally or from the national party, which often gets targeted to marginal seats for national campaigns. There is a huge amount of expenditure on social media which can be targeted to very precise postcode districts, with no limits on advocacy organizations spending money (though spending by political parties is controlled).

There is a wealth of research which seeks to explain this distribution and to see whether greater expenditure does increase voter turnout (see section 3.6.10 on MPs and voting) (Pattie, Hartman, and Johnston 2017). However, it is very hard to know for certain whether this expenditure influences voter choices because campaigners may be targeting areas that they think are going to swing their way in any case.

Case Study 6.3 Brexit and Cambridge Analytica

Social media campaigning where resources are targeted to citizens has been an important topic of debate in UK politics, particularly since it has been alleged that the 'Leave' Brexit campaign appeared to be more skilful in using resources on the internet and social media than 'Remain'. Vote Leave acquired a large list of potential supporters, allowing it to send half a million text messages in the final twenty-four hours of the campaign (Shipman 2016, 406). It built a database of users by creating a football competition and collecting the names and contact details of people who had entered it (Jungherr, Rivero, and Gayo-Avello 2020, 202). The campaign was alleged to have been connected to the company Cambridge Analytica (now not in business), which claimed to be able to identify the personalities of its users, gained from a research project, so as to target them (Jungherr, Rivero, and Gayo-Avello 2020, 125). Vote Leave did not use Cambridge Analytica directly. It did, however, use the services of Aggregate IQ, spending about 40 per cent of its total budget on a firm that appears to have had ties to Robert Mercer (former principal investor in Cambridge Analytica), and via Mercer to Cambridge Analytica. The other campaign, Leave.EU, paid Cambridge Analytica, but Leave.EU claimed that the firm did nothing of substance for them (*The Guardian*, 20 July 2019). The Leave campaign may have benefited more generally from the way in which information and 'alternative facts', often ranged against the more established sources of knowledge, can circulate over the internet, perpetuating rumour (Dobreva, Grinnell, and Innes 2020).

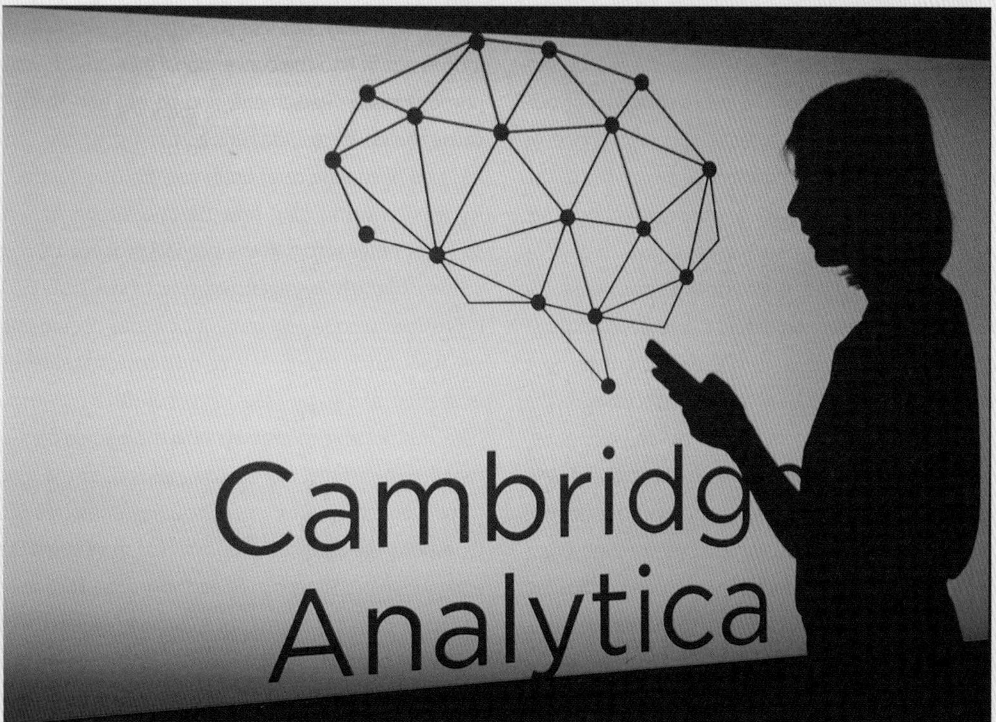

Photo 6.6 The British Parliament's Fake News Inquiry indicated that Cambridge Analytica did work for the UK's Leave.EU Brexit campaign during the 2016 EU referendum (which they denied).

6

Some researchers question whether campaigning makes any difference (Pattie, Johnston, and Fieldhouse 1995), and whether parties cancel out each other's efforts by pulling the voters in both ways. The determinants of election results are often set in place before the campaign, such as the economy, which affect the performance of the incumbent as conveyed to voters' minds before the election (see section 5.7.1). Nevertheless, campaigns can have momentum, and the party or government or leader gets revealed to voters, or weaknesses in their campaigns are exposed, and opposition leaders and their followers can get mobilized during the campaign. Many studies of elections show that voters do move support between parties during the campaigns, making media influence a likely impact (Norris et al. 1999, 173–79). Norris (2006) shows that the consumption of media, in particular party election broadcasts, affects vote choices and increases turnout. In these studies, as in many others (see Zoom-In 6.1 and section 6.4.2), it is impossible to control for self-selection into consuming media. Nevertheless, the media can become very important in conveying information and in providing stories that shape the narrative of a campaign. Given that the impact of campaigns depends on their contexts (Farrell and Schmitt-Beck 2002), the impact of the media is also conditional on the particular circumstances of each contest.

6.8 The agenda of politics and policy

In this section, the pattern of the policy agenda in Britain is outlined more generally, including the influence of the different forms of media, and where these influences connect to public opinion, and the concerns of politicians and other public figures. Ultimately, concerns expressed by the public or in the media connect to the decision-making process, such as the organizations that implement public policies, such as local government or public agencies, changing their priorities as a result, for example spending more on defence or the NHS following a rise in issue salience. In turn, the decisions of those government agencies influence what is discussed in the media, as decisions or implemented public policies become unpopular, and may need to be changed. These government organizations may also seek to influence the media agenda themselves, such as through press releases, from ministers appearing on TV and radio, and more recently the activities of organizations to influence the public agenda through social media, such as in official Twitter accounts (Jeffares 2014).

This pattern of multiple influences across different arenas is called the policy agenda (John et al. 2013), and has been studied extensively in the US (Baumgartner and Jones 1993), but less so in the UK, partly because it does not fit into the conventional divisions of cabinet, prime minister, Parliament, and so on, and partly because the policy agenda runs across institutions. There has also been little data, until recently, on how the policy agenda works, and how the media connects to a range of other actors in the political process. Using the scheme of the policy agendas project (see Table 6.1), it is possible to code government or media documents to see how much attention is paid to topics like defence, education, and so on (see John et al. 2013). With such data, it is possible to examine how the agenda connects together over time, from public opinion, to the media, to parliamentary questions—including Prime Minister's Questions—and executive priorities as mentioned in the annual Queen's Speech or Speech from the Throne (see Key term 3.3). It is thus possible to find out whether the agenda of the Queen's Speech follows changes in public opinion, so if public concern on the economy goes up, so does the number of economic items in the speech (Jennings and John 2009). It is also the case that the topics mentioned in Prime Minister's Questions follow public opinion, allowing backbenchers to draw attention to issues that concern them (Bevan and John 2016).

It is possible to plot these levels of attention in a graph. For illustration, Figure 6.8 shows how attention to three selected topics of the economy, health, and defence changes over time. This figure is for statutory instruments, which is a form of legislation, that often back up Acts of Parliament. It is possible to see how attention to certain topics, like health, goes up in the years before the financial crash, reflecting international trends (Mortensen et al. 2009).

These data sources help us understand the nature of the agenda in British politics. They can account for the extent of instability in British politics through the tendency for the agenda to move to extreme points after long periods of stability—what are called policy punctuations (Key term 6.4), which have been shown to exist in British public budgets (John and Margetts 2003), Queen's Speeches (Jennings and John 2010), and Acts of Parliament (John and Bevan 2012). This tendency for the agenda to change can be seized by a government seeking to anticipate changes in the policy agenda. Overall, these data demonstrate how unstable UK politics is, which is consistent with the turbulence hypothesis outlined in section 4.4.7. However, it should be noted that there is not a massive difference in the number of punctuations over time (John and Bevan 2012) and the patterns of change are broadly comparable with other countries, such as Denmark (Mortensen et al. 2009).

6.8.1 The left–right agenda

It is important to recognize that policy agendas are not the only dimension of agenda-setting in UK politics. Another way to look at this is through the left–right spectrum (see section 4.4.6) rather than according to issues, or to blend the change in issues with changes in tone and ideological focus being the

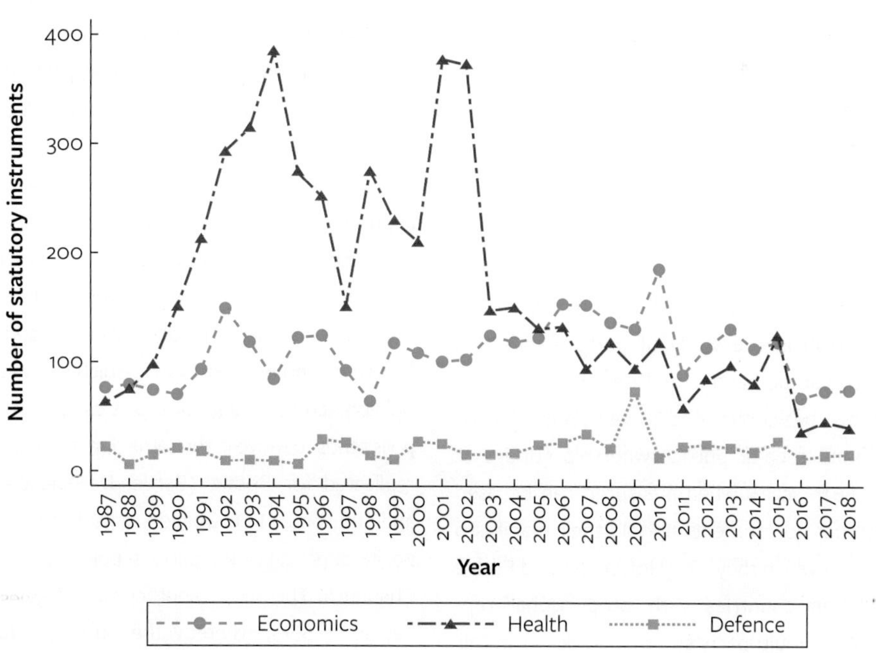

Figure 6.8 Attention to selected policy agendas topics (statutory instruments), 1987–2018.
Source: Bevan (2015); data supplied by Shaun Bevan

Table 6.1 The policy agendas coding scheme (major topics)
Source: Comparative Agendas: www.comparativeagendas.net/datasets_codebooks

0. Non-policy content
1. Macroeconomics
2. Civil rights, minority issues, immigration, and civil liberties
3. Health
4. Agriculture
5. Labour and employment
6. Education and culture
7. Environment
8. Energy
9. Transportation
10. Law, crime, and family issues
11. Social welfare
12. Community development, planning, and housing issues
13. Banking, finance, and domestic commerce
14. Defence
15. Space, science, technology, and communications
16. Foreign trade
17. International affairs and foreign aid
18. Government operations
19. Public lands, water management, colonial and territorial issues

Key term 6.4 Policy punctuation

A surge in the attention to a public policy after a long period of stability.

main drivers of agenda-setting. This kind of approach was first shown in the study of party manifestos, whose items can be hand-coded on a scale by picking out items that correspond to well-known left or right positions, such as public ownership (Budge et al. 2001). Such scales when measured can be used to see whether governments uphold their manifesto commitments, which they did (Hofferbert and Budge 1992), though countries with proportional representation and multi-party systems do better in this respect (McDonald and Budge 2005). The conclusion to draw is that the positioning of agenda items as left–right still matters for the inputs and outputs of government, part of the common pattern in Britain and elsewhere (Adams, Bernardi, and Wlezien 2019).

Keeping with left and right as important aspects of the agenda of politics are studies of long-run changes in public opinion. It is possible to gather together many opinion polls and to see how opinion moves from left to right by looking at the correlations across these polls. This uses a technique introduced by Stimson (Stimson, MacKuen, and Erikson 1995), which shows that public opinion across a range of topics as captured by these polls tends to move in the same direction. This has been replicated for Britain (Bartle, Dellepiane-Avellaneda, and Stimson 2011). Opinion tends to move in the opposite direction of the party in power, as was found in Chapter 5. This shows another cost of governing (see Key term 5.9), whereby the public gradually turns against the ideas of the party in power, becoming more right-thinking when the left is in power and vice versa.

6.9 Conclusion

The role of the media and agenda-setting in British politics is very important, for all political actors, and for the citizens who observe and participate in politics. The policy agenda and media are the essential transmission lines in politics, providing essential information so different parts of the political system can connect together. But is the media biased and does that bias have influence? In this chapter, there are enough studies that show this, for example on the influence of *The Sun* newspaper on Euroscepticism (Foos and Bischof 2019), and by implication influencing Brexit.

Most of all, the agenda of politics is not stable, with frequent changes in priorities, which cannot simply be seen as a consequence of objective conditions, such as the state of the economy, or changes in party control. The agenda has a momentum of its own, with the ability of issues to rise and fall off the agenda, and where other actors need to respond quickly. Amid this instability in the processing of ideas, some political organizations can keep ahead, and political parties can respond. For example, the Covid-19 pandemic precipitated a massive change in the public agenda, after the dominance of Brexit since 2016. Covid-19 shows how a significant event can shift the priorities of government so quickly that no other news story predominates, but other public problems do not go away.

6

Further reading

The general topic of agenda-setting and the media is dealt with in *Policy Agendas in British Politics* (John et al. 2013), with chapter 8 on the media. The issue of the media is covered in Gavin's (2007) book focusing on economic news. A general introduction to the internet is Graham and Dutton (2019), which includes an essay on political turbulence by Margetts et al. A review of internet campaigns and digital politics is *Retooling Politics* (Jungherr, Rivero, and Gayo-Avello 2020).

Essay and examination questions

The classic question is about the influence of the media, such as 'How influential are media in British politics?'. The internet specifically can be covered by the question, 'What is the influence of social media on politics and/or elections in Britain?'. Or there can be a question about campaigning in general, such as 'Do political campaigns influence election outcomes, and what is the role of the media in those campaigns?'. For the role of the media and democracy, the question could be 'Is the media (still) the watchdog of democracy?', which can tap into the debates about media independence, the decline of print media and investigative journalism, and the quality of the debate on social media.

Access the online resources for this chapter, including biannual updates, web links, and multiple-choice questions: www.oup.com/he/John1e

Part C

Policy-Making and Delegation

The third segment of this book explores decision-making beyond the central state. Not everything can be run from Whitehall—neither practically nor politically—even though, under the doctrine of parliamentary sovereignty, it could be done legally. It just is not possible to take every policy decision in central London and to deliver all public services from there, even if London is itself decentralizing its functions and activities to other parts of the UK. The task of decision-making would be too complex, and blockages would occur at the central level, which would be immensely frustrating for all. Government would become overloaded with having to make too many detailed decisions. In any case, the public would probably not put up with such a degree of centralization as they expect a degree of local organization for public services, which has been a tradition since the medieval period, and more recently through local elected councils and devolved governments. There may be some functional advantages in task specialization of particular bodies and learning from local and specialist client groups and residents which may not be possible simply through centrally run units. Furthermore, it suits central government to hand over powers and functions as it can avoid taking the blame for many decisions or outcomes (Hood 2002). There may even be a reflex within the central establishment that it makes sense to offload functions: so that the centre can concentrate on the key decisions of the overall state regarding the economy and foreign policy, leaving what appear to be more detailed and minor matters to the purview of delegated bodies (Bulpitt 1983).

Many of these factors cause modern states to delegate public activities, necessarily requiring central government to accept that delegated bodies will enjoy a degree of independence and separate organization, but still arranging matters so that the wishes of those at the centre are reflected, often indirectly, in the decisions that are produced on the ground. This goes back to the principal–agent problem, introduced in Chapter 1 (see Zoom-In 1.4), whereby the principal loses the expertise and capacity to be able to supervise the agent and the agent can behave in ways that suit itself and cannot be effectively monitored. The principal–agent model or framework does not mean that the state loses power completely, and writers on principal–agent theory stress that the principal–agent problem can be overcome, often by building allies that monitor the agent (Moe 1984). But it does mean that the polity becomes much more complex—much more than a simple version of the Westminster model would imply. It is also more complicated because there are chains of delegation (Bergman, Müller, and Strøm 2000), whereby local authorities and other public bodies delegate to others, such as regional and national governments delegating to other local authorities, who delegate to private contractors, voluntary organizations, and so on.

Part C of this book is an exploration of the difficulties of exercising control over a complex delegated system. Agency problems partly caused by decentralization may act as fuel for political turbulence because of the centre's diminished formal oversight which can, in turn, lead to negative feedback into the Westminster system itself. Chapter 7 begins with delegation, in terms of interest groups and advocacy, because much of the energy and resources of these groups come from the grassroots, being largely self-organized without the involvement of the central state. In fact, as shown in Chapter 7 (see section 7.2.3), most groups often have close relationships with the central state (as well as other public bodies at different territorial levels), from which they may even receive funding, and are frequently involved with delivering and implementing government policies, for instance those concerning agriculture rules or how hospitals should be run. Interest groups then become a way for the state and other bodies to deliver their policies, without which not much government action can happen. But they still need to deal with the dynamism and independence of an increasingly large and diverse range of groups, which can be hard to control.

Other forms of delegation are covered in subsequent chapters: in Chapter 8, the delegation of the powers of ministers to civil servants and other public officials is covered, both in government departments and in a range of public agencies—what has been called 'delegated governance' (Flinders 2008); then Chapter 9 concerns decentralization, covering local, regional, and other national governments, as in Scotland, Northern Ireland, and Wales. Delegation can occur upwards too, whereby activities normally performed and regulated by the central state are transferred to international bodies, such as the European Court of Human Rights (ECtHR), which enforces the European Convention on Human Rights (ECHR), or the World Trade Organization (WTO). In all three of these contexts, the same issues of control and agency from the central state arise. Therefore, the task of these chapters is to make sense of these complex patterns of governance, to understand whether British politics can work coherently with such a framework and whether the central state can still fulfil its objectives when so much is delegated. It is important to understand how the delegated agencies and bodies express their preferences, especially from their own democratic mandates and sources of legitimacy, which they seek to realize.

Key term C.1 Delegated governance

Idea that government transfers responsibilities for decision-making to a range of bodies with unclear lines of accountability to Parliament and where decision-making and internal procedures are often obscured from view. It reflects an attempt at depoliticization or shielding from public debate.

Chapter 7

Interest Groups, Advocacy, and Policy-Making

7.1 What is going to be in this chapter?

This chapter is about interest, pressure, or advocacy groups, which organize separately from political parties, seeking to influence public opinion and public policy. The chapter discusses the nature of these groups and what they do, before reviewing the debate on the power of interest groups, in particular whether business has a privileged position.

7.2 Introduction

Interest groups, sometimes called pressure groups or advocacy groups, are an essential part of the political process, operating alongside the contributions of parties and voters. These groups arise out of a sense of common interest that some citizens (or other bodies) feel they have with each other, such as in employment, and/or by having a sense of common identity over certain issues, concerns, and beliefs. Section 5.3.1 was about how interest groups and political parties can be alike in many respects, as some interest groups are invested in wide varieties of topics, while some political parties, such as the Green Party, are mainly focused on one issue. The fundamental difference is that interest groups do not usually seek to run candidates directly for public office, even though they may support political parties that do.

7.2.1 The contribution of interest groups

Interest groups do not substitute for political parties, but they can offer a different perspective on public problems for which they can deploy their expertise, and thereby seek to influence the decision-making process. They provide information about policy issues upon which they are expert by directly lobbying policy-makers and seeking to influence public opinion at the same time, as in campaigning, via leafleting, advertising on the media, Tweeting (and other uses of social media), and sometimes organizing direct action and protest, which aims to get attention from the media. This freedom of association is often seen as fundamental to democracy. It is the right citizens have to associate and to represent their interests, which often appear in codified constitutions, such as in the First Amendment of the constitution of the USA. In terms of the political system as a whole, there are possible benefits to this kind of representation; groups can bring issues and problems to attention along with potential solutions for which they have drawn on the expertise of their professional memberships, or the input of activists and experts who are supporters. The range of representation enabled by interest groups may compensate for the aggregation of issues by political parties preparing policies for elections, where issues that are far from the concerns of the median voter may be neglected in political debate. In the view of the empirical political theorist Robert Dahl, interest groups can convey 'intense preferences' so that small groups have a presence in debate, balancing out less intense preferences held by larger-sized groups and interests (Dahl 1956). Dahl is the academic most associated with the claim of pluralism that there is diversity of representation, with each group having equal access to the political process (see Key term 2.4).

7.2.2 Negative aspects of group politics

Interest groups do have negative aspects, conveyed by the term 'fear of faction' (Hamilton and Madison 2015, 10), as some groups (because of unequal distribution of property in society) can dominate politics and neglect the public interest as a result. The balance of resources, in terms of education, networks, and wealth between groups, is massively unequal in most societies. If this imbalance is systematic, and links with other power imbalances in society, there may be an effect on policy outcomes that reflects this inequality, where more powerful groups get more access and resources allocated in their favour, thereby biasing democracy in favour of some outcomes, but not of those who are less powerful. As Schattschneider

Key term 7.1 Neo-pluralism

Describes systematic inequalities of power and resources between groups that generate unfair outcomes. It is also about how informal routines and anticipated reactions favour business and other systematically powerful groups.

famously wrote, 'the heavenly chorus (still) sings with a strong upper-class accent' (1960, 35), identifying who is normally powerful in a political system as those with more resources to deploy. This is a classic debate which allows an understanding of the role of groups in British democracy: whether a pluralist conception, which involves fair competition between groups and a level playing field for access (see Key term 2.4), or a modification to pluralism of neo-pluralism (see Key term 7.1), where some groups such as businesses have more power (Lindblom 1977), or whether there is a structural imbalance in political power in the system as expressed in institutions, cultures, and media as well as through the exercise of covert political power (Lukes 1977).

7.2.3 **Interest groups and public policy**

There is a close link between interest groups and public policy. Public policy is the set of concrete decisions leading to outcomes and concrete outputs. This concerns such decisions as how hospitals should be run that should lead to better health or subsidies for employers to cope with Covid-19. Public policy has already been mentioned in this book as this is the output of the executive, and what Parliament accordingly scrutinizes, yet it comes into much more focus in this chapter and in those that

Key term 7.2 Policy implementation

A defined stage of decision-making about turning intentions into programmes and policy outcomes on the ground.

follow. Chapters 7–10 are concerned with the details of getting policies into place and ensuring they work, known as policy implementation (Pressman and Wildavsky 1984) (see Key term 7.2), which is seen as distinct from but very strongly connected to policy formulation (which the executive and also Parliament primarily do). Public policy formulation is usually carried out prior to policy implementation, as decision-makers seek to anticipate policy outputs and outcomes when they design the policy. Politicians will monitor the process, such as from Number 10 or the Treasury. Likewise, those who deal with policy implementation in agencies and local governments usually have ideas about policy formation that they feed in to the central decision-makers if they can, and they are usually consulted. Still, it is fair to say that closer to the front line, more detailed implementation issues appear as important factors to resolve. This is where interest and advocacy groups become important in providing feedback, while also jointly participating in the implementation of those policies. This collaboration can be useful to policy-makers in improving public policies; interest groups can be used as an additional way to overcome the principal–agent problem, by providing information to the centre about how agencies are doing, being 'fire alarms' for the politicians or principals at the centre (McCubbins and Schwartz 1984). Governments can delegate the running of the policy to the interest group, such as training hospital doctors (see section 7.3.1).

In the study of British politics and policy-making, it was fashionable once to say that policy outputs were not much affected by which party was in control (Rose 1980), with governments making incremental and gradual decisions, such as over budgets. This was due to group politics operating within and without the central state, bargaining for resources (Rose 1990; Rose and Davies 1994). This view of slow, incremental decision-making has largely been rejected, as there are frequent changes in public policies. The large changes in budgets question the 'parties do not make a difference' hypothesis (John and Margetts 2003). There are still many decisions that can be laid at the doors of parties and their ministers as well as consulting in policy networks of agencies, experts, and interest groups. This discussion of the literature on interest groups highlights the impact of partisan leadership from the centre on structuring the influence and behaviour of these groups. The debate about British politics almost turns full circle: moving away from belief in party government towards a recognition of the insignificance of parties and power exercised in policy networks, then returning to partisan politicians seeking to control the complex and unstable system (for a recent example of the party government argument, see Maggetti and Trein 2021).

7.2.4 Public policy and political economy

It is important to take a broad perspective when studying public policy to understand how public decisions are intertwined into the power and networks of the global economy of which Britain is a part. Political and policy decisions reflect the constraints of these relationships, conditioning the approach of political parties when making policy choices. A number of writers since the 1960s have used variants of this framework, notably Gamble (1974, 1994), and it appears in studies of British economic policy-making (Thompson 1996). This field of work extends into more ideas-centred approaches to British politics (Hay 2002), as there are interpretations of how governments and politicians should respond to economic pressures, such as globalization (Hay and Rosamond 2002). This line of work focuses on the constraints of policy-makers and their need to work within a framework of ideas that are acceptable to a wide elite audience and work well as a narrative.

7.3 Basic facts: interest groups

7.3.1 Numbers and range of groups

It is important to take account of the scale and scope of interest groups in Britain. Back in 2005, it was estimated that there were 22,402 interest groups in the UK, which had grown from 12,491 as recorded in 1975 (see Jordan et al. 2012), which comes from editions of the *Directory of British Associations: And Associations in Ireland*, though no longer in print. It is also important to take account of the different kinds of interest groups. These can be sorted according to the policy agendas codebook of topics (this scheme was explained in section 6.8 and Figure 6.7). Figure 7.1 shows the breakdown and presents the vast diversity of these groups showing the large numbers of business and science groups. It is also possible in this figure to get a sense of the expansion of interest groups, which is an international phenomenon going back many decades (Bischoff 2003), though growth has fallen for some

Agriculture
Art
Business
Civil Rights
Defence
Economy
Education
Energy
Environment
Family
Government
Health
History
Hobby
Housing
Ideological
International
International Trade
Labour
Lands
Law
Local Government
Other
Religion
Science
Social Welfare
Sports
Transport

0 500 1,000 1,500 2,000 2,500 3,000

Number of interest groups

Year

1970 2006

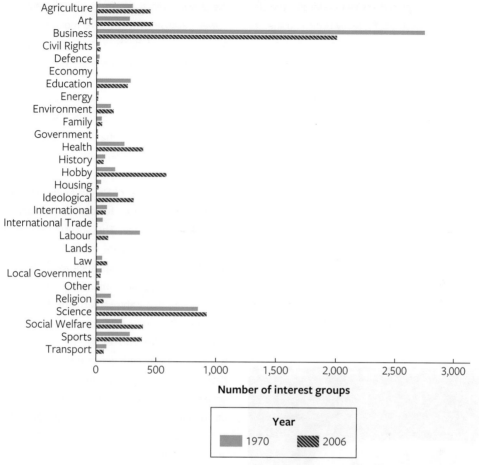

Figure 7.1 Numbers of UK interest groups.
Source: Jordan et al. (2012, 151)

sectors, such as defence. In an earlier period, Jordan and Maloney (2007, 3) found that 48 per cent of groups had start-up dates post-1968.

7.3.2 **How lobbying works**

Many interest groups focus on the Westminster government and Parliament with offices in London, employing specialist consultancy firms to represent them to the executive and/or Parliament (see section 3.4.5). The lobbying scandal in 2021 involving Greensill Capital, with former Prime Minister David Cameron making representations directly to ministers, illustrates the importance of this kind of politics and the close access that lobbyists have. Interest groups can cross jurisdictional boundaries by representing themselves at different levels of government, playing one side off against another. When Britain was a member of the European Union (EU), many interest groups had a presence, such as an office in Brussels to seek to influence the policies made there as these would be implemented in the UK (Coen and Richardson 2009). Now the UK has left the EU, there is less direct interest for lobbies in a direct presence in Brussels, yet lobbying by British trade associations and trade unions continues as many regulations in Brussels affect Britain through successive revisions to the UK–EU trade deal (UKICE 2021). Many British businesses are part of long supply chains right across Europe, for example over vaccine production that became so controversial in response to the Covid-19 pandemic; and they operate within complex patterns of ownership of enterprises across Europe, which are affected by European regulations. There are also local-level interest groups, focused on one local authority area, but also seeking to influence central government at the same time in partnership with other interest groups and professional bodies.

7.3.3 Examples of interest groups

As well as the aggregate figures and accounts of different levels of government, it is useful to provide some examples of different kinds of interest groups. One of the classic interest groups, which allegedly has great power because of its relative monopoly over membership, medical doctors, and great expertise and resources, is the British Medical Association (BMA) (Photo 7.1).

Photo 7.1 A junior doctor wearing an armband with the BMA logo.

The BMA, founded in 1832, has been subject to a number of studies (Eckstein 1960; Marmor and Thomas 1972), showing its strong influence on public policy. Famously, the Labour government elected in 1945, which set up the NHS under the guidance of Minister of Health Aneurin Bevan, managed to get a contract for doctors in place, despite the BMA's resistance. The government still had to agree reluctantly to many of the BMA's demands on behalf of its membership, such as private pay-beds within NHS hospitals, which allowed some patients to receive favourable treatment from the public purse. Because of its size—about 159,000 fully qualified doctors and 19,000 medical students—it is the main body with which the government negotiates on working conditions for doctors. The association does not approve doctors' qualifications, but is heavily involved with training members. It has a dedicated parliamentary unit and an income of about £139m per year.

A very different kind of interest or pressure group is Stonewall (www.stonewall.org.uk), a campaign group formed from supporters for the cause of lesbian, gay, bisexual, and transgender (LGBT) rights. The group was formed in 1989 as part of a campaign against the homophobic climate fostered by the then-Conservative government. The name Stonewall comes from the Stonewall Inn (Photo 7.2), the location of the 1969 Stonewall riots in Greenwich Village, New York City. Its founders include the actor Ian McKellen, campaigner Lisa Power, and politician and former actor Michael Cashman. It is mainly a campaign group focusing a great deal on parliamentary activity, such as on transgender rights. It raises its funds from members and campaigns. In 2019 it had an income of just over £8.3m per year.

Photo 7.2 The Stonewall Inn, site of the 1969 riots in New York.

Another example, showing a more diffusely organized social movement, is Black Lives Matter (BLM: https://blacklivesmatter.com; Photo 7.3), which is organized internationally and has a presence in the UK. Its foundation was a reaction to occurrences of racial injustice that have shaken the world over the last decade, particularly involving deaths of Black citizens at police hands, such as George Floyd. BLM does not resemble a formal interest group, with a public budget and fee-paying members, but it does raise resources and seeks to build a contact base of supporters rather than members. In Britain, in September 2020, it was registered as a charity, with the name Black Liberation Movement. Although a group like Stonewall can

Photo 7.3 BLM is not a formal interest group, but a political group and registered charity, protesting against incidences of police brutality and racially-motivated violence.

engage in some direct action, it is more of a formal lobbying organization, seeking to influence policy, such as to change the clauses of a bill going through Parliament. Conversely, BLM is more interested in securing change through direct action and protests against deaths in police custody.

There are many other examples to find out about, be it via an organization's web page, information provided elsewhere online, or news reports. Published financial accounts also yield a lot of information. As well as reading about those groups above, why not choose to research other groups according to interest or even membership? This can make some of the drier academic reports more interesting when applied to a familiar group. Doing so would illuminate the variety of organizations that range from professional bodies to grassroots campaign groups.

Key term 7.3 Social movement

A loose alliance of people who share a common cause and may contribute to direct action and protest, but who are not defined by a formal organization, as in an interest group. Sometimes these can be called protest movements to signal the wider purpose. In practice, the difference is more about interpretation as interest groups may resemble a social movement, as with Momentum.

7.4 The study of interest groups: in search of a typology

7.4.1 Producer and consumer groups

7

Scholars have been preoccupied with classifying interest groups into different types as a way of understanding the nature of the system. One crucial classification, which has proved very helpful, was originally made by Sam Beer (1965, chapter 12) in his account of the 'new group politics', which focused on the differences between producer and consumer groups. The former is associated with key industries or public activities, where the participants often work in these sectors of activity, whether as employers or workers (in trade unions or professional associations). Consumer groups come from more diffuse sets of people whose well-being is affected by government decisions. As a result, these people become active and then organize accordingly, seeking to draw others in from the general population.

7.4.2 The state and group politics

Beer was charting a form of group politics closely linked to the development of the state in the post-1945 period, when more government provision and regulation emerged, creating a form of group politics closely connected to the outputs of government. This links to a separate literature derived from public choice theory (see Key term 7.4) concerning the size of government and the numbers of groups, claiming that—as a result of the large number of groups—policy-making has become overloaded. These groups use their monopolies to get benefits from the state to the public's detriment in increasing the size of the state (Mueller and Murrell 1986). In turn, this expansion of government and the number and influence of interest groups contributed, in the 1970s, to the conclusion that government had

Key term 7.4 Public choice theory

A theory originating in economics based on individuals maximizing their utility, and theorizing about the nature of the state, politics, and society as a result. Similar to rational choice theory (see Key term 2.1), public choice theory prioritizes individual freedom, consumer choice, and limiting the purview of the state.

lost its capacity to govern, as it was too dependent on powerful producer groups, which explained its lack of power in the face of trade unions and the lack of coherent economic policy at the time. As a result of these pressures from interest groups and awareness of the loss of direction in policy-making, the 'overload' thesis was applied to British government for a time (King 1975). Governments were thought to have been paralysed by interest group pressures and the sheer scale of problems they faced.

Many of these arguments were pre-figured in Beer's book, but the main use of the distinction between producer and consumer groups is to explain the factors that contribute to the power of interest groups, and the relationship to the policy process. Producer groups are more integrated into the state because it needs them to implement policies, and prefers to have expert advice to formulate public policy too. With the BMA example, it is very hard for government to work without the support of doctors, as their active cooperation is essential for policy implementation; they could passively resist or even actively resist through industrial action. Government needs the advice of doctors and to engage them in actual policies, such as training. To get its way, government still has resources or tools to deploy in the form of laws, money, and executive power (see Key term 2.2), but it needs to proceed with caution, often having to retreat from a course of action as often as proceeding with new policies and directions. It is not as negative as the overload thesis surmised, as there is give and take on both sides; and from the government perspective it is better to have producer groups inside government consulted first and involved throughout, which gives them power, but both sides need to compromise too.

Consumer groups need to leverage different resources, having more diffuse sources of support. However, this can change, and it is possible to find consumer groups deeply involved in the policy process for many of the same reasons as the producer groups with their sources of expertise and legitimacy, combined with their ability to communicate with supporters and the wider public. Beer's distinction does remain helpful, however, in alerting us to the power and roles of different kinds of groups, and to the compact between the state and certain powerful groups.

7.4.3 The corporatist debate

Beer's and other academic work generated a lot of theorizing on the nature of producer group politics, which led to the claim that the UK and national politics in other European countries had become corporatist because of the integration of trade unions and employers into the policy process, in a tripartite relationship between the state and the other two groups (Grant 1985).

Corporatism had its origins in the 1920s and 1930s, when fascist states tried to set up formal arrangements between the state and industry groups (Schmitter 1974). The modern form is not seen as ideological, being more about how policy is closed off to outsiders, and there are formal and informal processes whereby businesses and unions make policy jointly with state organization. This arrangement benefits certain kinds of employees and businesses, usually in large enterprises. The term 'corporatist' describes the long-term relationship between businesses, trade unions, and the state in northern European countries, such as Sweden, Austria, and Germany (Schmitter and Lehmbruch 1979). In Britain, the influence of market thinking and the tendency towards executive dominance was always thought to make corporatism unstable (Panitch 1977, 82).

Key term 7.5 Corporatism

Describes a close and structured relationship between the state, businesses, and trade unions, who jointly make key policies, often in times of economic crisis.

7.4.4 **Insiders and outsiders**

7

A distinction has been made between insider and outsider groups (Grant 1978). The assumption is that some groups get the credibility to be insiders—that is, they are regularly consulted in the policy process—whereas others are outsiders and are not invited in, or, if they are invited, they only participate in a formal way, such as part of a formal consultation process. This argument draws on empirical research showing that some groups were found to be helpful to policy-makers while others were not (Dearlove 2011). Overall, insider/outsider is a helpful distinction, although a somewhat oversimplification of what in reality are complex relationships (Grant 2004). It is also hard to find groups that are genuine outsiders, as Page's (1999) survey of 381 groups reveals: relatively few groups could be classed as pure outsiders, while a much larger number have the features of the insider. Page's article opens with the line: 'As they used to say about the Ritz, the process of consultation between groups and government is "open to everyone".' In other words, you are free to book a table at a very expensive restaurant, but if you don't have the money to pay for it, you are not really free to go there for a meal. Similarly, lobbying access may only be available to those with connections and money.

The insider and outside typology appears again in a study of the interest group Amnesty International (Christiansen and Dowding 1994), which lobbied different government departments. To the then-Foreign and Commonwealth Office (now Foreign, Commonwealth, and Development Office), it was the insider group because it helped put pressure on foreign governments over poor human rights records; perhaps unsurprisingly, however, when Amnesty International raised human rights concerns to the Home Office, they were treated as an outsider group. This example suggests insider status does not equate to political power without central government recognition. Insider and outsider status depend on the prior policy goals of a government department.

Despite the example of Amnesty International seeming to discredit the importance of distinguishing between different groups, Binderkrantz and Pedersen (2019) recently produced a study of lobbying in Denmark and the UK, based on survey data collected on Danish and British interest groups in 2011–14, contrasting citizens and economics groups. They show that different types of lobbyists engage in distinct strategies, with economic groups deploying insider strategies and citizen groups using outsider strategies, showing that the distinction still has some use in empirical research.

7.4.5 **Policy styles and institutions**

The next set of literature is also linked to policy-making, which is about policy styles. The claim is that the routines of government and of decision-making, standard operating procedures, create a certain kind of interest group behaviour, the policy style (see Key term 7.6), and to a certain extent cause the pattern of insiders and outsiders. Richardson and Jordan (1979) set out this case in the classic work on British politics, *Governing Under Pressure: The Policy Process in a Post-Parliamentary Democracy*, which found evidence of the lack of interest group presence at the parliamentary stage. This was down to the lack of a role for Parliament in the policy-making process, particularly at the time that the research for the book was conducted. As a result, interest groups focused on government departments and sought to influence civil servants and ministers, getting drawn into a consensual pattern of decision-making, and standard operating procedures for making decisions. By conforming to the standard practices of this arguably secretive aspect of British government, interest groups could work behind the scenes to exercise influence even before bills were drawn up before Parliament. Richardson and Jordan's argument does not fully account for the massive changes in parliamentary behaviour happening already in the 1970s (see section 3.5.1), which meant it became much more worthwhile for groups to lobby Parliament. The change since the 1970s in interest group behaviour in terms of an increasing readiness to approach the media and to engage in direct action did break down this consensus to some degree. Nevertheless, the approach of Richardson and Jordan has been very influential and has helped coin the term 'policy styles' to capture a particular approach to policy-making in Britain and elsewhere. It is an institutionalist or new institutionalist approach for understanding the behaviour and pattern of interest group mobilization. It also made observers aware that there are networks and communities of groups around Whitehall and other agencies (Marsh and Rhodes 1992).

Key term 7.6 Policy style

Idea that a nation state or other territorial unit has a particular approach to working with interest groups and processing decision-making, which comes from its constitutional arrangement and informal ways of conducting business.

7

7.5 The power of interest groups

A key question about interest groups revolves around the power they hold. The examples reviewed in section 7.3.1 give some indication as to the scale of the power of groups, such as in discussion about producer groups, corporatism, and insiders and outsiders. The case studies, such as of the BMA, do indicate power and influence, even if mediated by government and executive power, but these studies do not offer strong backing for a causal claim about the power of pressure or interest groups. This is because it is very difficult to establish a counterfactual (see Key term 3.6) of what would have happened if the group had not been present or had not lobbied. It is hard, though not impossible, to randomly assign an interest group to a policy venue to find out about the influence of that group independent of any other factor. There is one example of a randomized controlled trial of lobbying in the UK, which is Richardson and John (2012), discussed in section 7.6. Notwithstanding this particular study, it is hard to ascertain the influence of individual lobbies and to research the anticipated reactions of policy-makers, especially when the policy agenda is set in place before the lobbying starts and decisions are made informally behind closed doors.

7.5.1 Bernhagen's study

Bernhagen (2012) carried out newspaper analysis from British and Scottish newspapers with a dataset of 163 policy proposals advanced by UK governments, between 2001 and 2007, to record the reported policy position of organized interests, such as their view about a new proposal. The study was specifically designed to test the idea that business is a powerful interest group, with its unique role in generating wealth, which should be greater in recent years because of a global market. The policy proposals were found through 'an archival search of seven major UK broadsheet newspapers (*The Daily Telegraph*, the *Financial Times*, *The Herald*, *The Guardian*, *The Independent*, *The Scotsman* and *The Times*)' (p. 563), looking for clear statements of intent by government of a policy change (this included the Scottish government). The final agreed policy positions were then coded along with the final policy outcomes to see whether they had changed. The idea is that these changes can be associated with the presence of business as an indication of its power.

Bernhagen found that support from interest groups is positively related to a proposal becoming policy. But the positions of business groups are no better reflected in policy outcomes than those of non-business groups, which is a similar finding to US studies (Baumgartner et al. 2009). In sum, insider status is no guarantee of success. Neither, Bernhagen found, are donations to political parties related to the extent to which policy outcomes are in line with a firm's policy positions, which appears to undermine the argument that resources are the key factors in the degree of success of lobbying or pressure action. This study does not prove a causal relationship between lobbying and policy outcomes; it only reports an association between the two, and factors other than business presence could have caused the policy outcome. As Dowding (1996) points out, getting the outcomes one prefers is not necessarily a signifier of power; some groups can simply get lucky in getting favourable outcomes, being in the right place at the right time. Still, multiple interest groups may achieve success in some way, which is an outcome to be expected under the pluralist thesis. It can also mean that issues that subside before the decision-making stage, called 'non-decisions' (Bachrach and Baratz 1962), are dealt with before the policy issue can come out into the open.

Vannoni (2015) later replicated Bernhagen's study. He argued that it failed to consider the 'second agenda-setting face of power', a concept put forward by Bachrach and Baratz (1962). He introduced an alternative method of approaching the concept of influence, which allows the researcher to identify the 'second face of power': what is determined prior to the formal decision-making process. He breaks up Bernhagen's variable into different elements, finding varying results: 'both issue salience and the stage of the policy cycle are associated with the correspondence between business policy position and the policy proposal' (p. 5). He finds preliminary evidence that the policy cycle stage and issue salience matter when policies are formulated, especially when the media and public opinion are not paying attention to the lobbying issue.

Bernhagen and Bräuninger's (2005) next study was qualitative and comparative, concerning the regulation of small business banking in England and Wales. Despite an informationally and structurally privileged position, 'business sometimes has little choice but to back down and bear the costs of policy for the sake of preserving its good reputation as an advisor to political actors' (p. 57). Bernhagen (2013) then applies this model to the UK dataset to classify different kinds of lobbies where these costs are incurred.

Case Study 7.1 Brexit and the City of London

James and Quaglia's (2018) study of the City of London (see Photo 7.4) and the Brexit process showed that even though the City of London has structural power, and there was the possible threat of exit (though often exaggerated), it was constrained by the political statecraft of Brexit, leading the government to downgrade the concerns of the financial industry, which undermined the City's voice within government. The City was also hemmed in by constraints on its organization and an inability to organize collectively. There were too many lobbying proposals that were not wielded into one coherent policy, leading to conflicts within the lobby group. Through research based on interviews and testimonies of officials and lobbyists, James and Quaglia showed that the UK government's neglect of financial services was a consequence of it choosing to prioritize ending freedom of movement once Britain had left the EU. Still, given how politicized a period this has been in British politics, when the Conservative Party was preoccupied with delivering the Brexit deal, it may not be a generalizable case study. The City may have been influential in other time periods, such as under New Labour from 1997, and under the Coalition government in power from 2010 to 2015. Its influence might return as Britain tries to forge a global economy, where selling financial services is an important strategy.

Photo 7.4 Tower Bridge in the City of London.

7.6 Lobbying

Key term 7.7 Lobbying

The active process by which interest groups seek to influence public policy. Involves providing information to policy-makers and actively seeking to persuade them to support their cause.

Much of the discussion surrounding the influence of lobbying is limited to an assessment of whether an interest group is present in the decision-making or consultation process. But other less observable factors may be at work, such as the threat of exit, the use of expertise, and deployment of resources, which may indirectly influence government policy. There are also more active attempts to influence policy, such as by direct persuasion or carefully presented information. Studies of lobbying bring up the tricky question of the influence of groups, but are more concerned with evaluating active strategies while also keeping the strategic costs and benefits of lobbying in mind, in that if one group puts an argument forward, another group can put across the counter-argument, potentially negating the lobby (see Austen-Smith and Wright 1994). Additionally, many policy-makers have already made up their minds before they are lobbied, which again points to the more informal techniques of providing information, and the use of agenda-setting rather than a full-frontal persuasive campaign. In fact, rather than being manipulative, it is in the interests of the group to get a reputation for providing good information so that policy-makers—who are supposed to act in the public interest—respect these arguments and the quality of the evidence, which then can underpin future influence.

In another of Bernhagen's (2013) analyses of UK lobbying, he placed predictions of lobby success against data on the policy positions and lobbying activities of firms and other organized groups in the context of twenty-eight policy proposals advanced by British and Scottish governments between 2001 and 2007. The results suggest that the interactions between policy-makers and lobbyists are driven mainly by the expected policy costs for policy-makers, providing lobbyists with strong incentives to provide correct advice to policy-makers. Bernhagen found little support for the expectation that lobbyists can successfully persuade policy-makers to take a course of action that is beneficial to the lobbyist at the expense of wider constituencies.

There is little robust evidence in Britain that shows that direct lobbying actually works, in contrast to work overseas, such as in the US (Bergan 2009; Baumgartner et al. 2009). The main exception is Richardson and John (2012), which randomly assigned two different lobbying strategies in eight English local authorities, working with local lobby groups to deliver the letters to local councillors: one was a high-quality information strategy, the other a low-quality information strategy, with the finding being that strategy did not make a difference to the response except that the high-quality letter helped speed up reference of the problem mentioned by the lobbyist to a bureaucrat to help solve.

Binderkrantz and Pedersen's (2019) study of lobbying in Denmark and the UK, discussed in section 7.4.4, showed similarities between the two countries, with separate economic and citizens' groups seeming to favour insider and outsider methods, respectively. Interest groups choose the method that suits them, but insider approaches do seem to work better. Overall, '[c]itizen groups report a higher level of agenda-setting success and a lower level of decision-making influence than economic groups' (p. 92). This survey-based approach does not consider the preferences of state actors when accounting for the influence, returning to the classic problem of the attribution of power once again.

As shown in section 7.3, the classic producer or consumer group, whose activities are focused on formal political processes, needs to be compared with a wider array of advocacy and more informal groups that seek to organize and influence policy indirectly. Groups play an important role at the local level in helping volunteering and achieving social outcomes in partnership or in co-production with agencies where the influence is more subtle (Szreter 2002), often involving non-classic or excluded actors from the political process (Lowndes 2004). There has been a vast expansion of groups at the local level, often involved with the delivery of policy, such as voluntary associations, which is shown in a study of Birmingham, comparing 1970 with 1998 (Maloney, Smith, and Stoker 2016). However, it may be difficult for central policy-makers to navigate this complicated universe and find the groups that can act as alarm bells to overcome the information asymmetries in delivering public policies.

7.7 Conclusion

Interest, pressure, or advocacy groups play an important role in a democracy like Britain's. They help citizens represent their interests in ways that are less easily done by political parties and directly by voters, even though the best interest group campaigns usually involve parties and need supportive public opinion. Still, their role cannot be separated from the institutions of the state and the importance of party politics, such as the statecraft practised by political parties. The power of interest groups, a classic question in political science, is tied up with a consideration of the role of the state, as assessing a group's power involves understanding the preferences of the state or local state actors rather than simply assuming a one-way influence, a misunderstanding that has bedevilled studies of lobbying since the early days of political science in Britain and elsewhere.

Studies of interest groups show the importance of these groups to the delivery of public policy, which reveals a two-way relationship between groups and the state. There is a complex pattern of governance that makes policy-making complicated and a difficult terrain for governments or regional and local agencies. In today's turbulent politics, there is room for new advocacy groups to upset the equilibrium. It is not the case that some groups have inbuilt systemic advantages over public policy, such as the classic fears of business influence, so in some sense the fear that democracy might be undermined by private interests is probably overplayed. Nevertheless, the very unpredictability of the interest group world and the appearance of actors skilled in the use of social media may provide opportunities to influence the political agenda and to engage in more disruptive politics.

Further reading

It is a good idea to read at least one of the classic works, such as Richardson and Jordan (1979). The more recent accounts of interest group influence and lobbying are represented by the first Bernhagen (2012) study. The case study of the City and Brexit is also a very useful way to understand modern debates, in particular over the extent of the power of business groups (James and Quaglia 2018).

Essay and examination questions

Essay and examination questions could concern the question of the influence of groups, such as 'How powerful are interest groups in Britain?' or 'Is business a uniquely powerful pressure group in Britain?' Alternatively, the question could be about lobbying tactics, such as 'Does lobbying deliver the outcomes that interest groups desire?', which also concerns influence. A more descriptive question could be 'What kinds of pressure or interest groups are there in British politics today? What explains these differences?', which can draw on the typologies discussed in section 7.4, such as producer or consumer and insider or outsider. Another approach is to ask about a particular interest group chosen by the student as to how it illustrates the themes in this chapter, or to compare two interest groups with each other, especially if they contrast, such as a business group and a direct-action or protest movement.

Access the online resources for this chapter, including biannual updates, web links, and multiple-choice questions: www.oup.com/he/John1e

Chapter 8

Governing Through Bureaucracy

8.1 What is going to be in this chapter?

This chapter is about the central government departments, executive agencies, and other public bureaucracies in operation in the UK today, such as those in local and territorial governments. These bodies help make and implement public policies and run public services. The chapter reviews more general work on bureaucracy and public administration, and sets out the theory of politician–bureaucrat relationships (going back to the principal–agent model), before addressing the classic question of civil service influence over public policy. The later part of the chapter from section 8.6 onwards takes account of the diversity of bureaucratic organizations operating in Britain today. There is a discussion and review of the evidence of how politicians manage to satisfy their political objectives through delegating authority to these bodies.

8.2 Introduction

In this chapter, more direct forms of delegation than interest groups are discussed, which is the use of officials and bureaucratic structures (see Key term 8.1) to regulate society and the economy, implementing decisions and policies on behalf of politicians (Huber 2000). Returning to the foundations of British politics, the starting point is the unlimited legal power placed in the hands of Parliament out of which forms the government. Given this power, the government, when operating through Parliament, could rely on the courts to put laws and other changes into effect. Similarly, the powers of the executive, exercised through the Crown's prerogative powers, may give the impression that commands from the centre will be obeyed without any other structure being in place. In fact, organizational structures need to exist with public employees tasked with implementing public policy and running public services.

Bureaucracy involves a permanent or semi-permanent set of officials, who have expertise, and are located in a formal institutional structure with a hierarchy or its equivalent, which can take the instructions that politicians legitimately authorize. These people and institutional structures can ensure that a policy has a chance of working, as well as run the machinery of government so everyday problems are solved seamlessly. Bureaucracies exist at the centre in the form of departments of state; and they can be specialized within the centre as with communications divisions or technical advice committees; then operate at various spatial scales, such as in regional organizations, in the devolved territories, and in local government, either reporting to central government and its politicians, or to local and regional governments directly.

Key term 8.1 Bureaucracy

An organization, usually in the public sector, that is tasked with turning political decisions into implemented policies, and for running public services. As well as hierarchical structure, whereby commands come from the top and then are passed down the line, a variety of structures, such as team-based structures, still count as bureaucracy. In popular discourse, bureaucracy is associated with slowness, too much attention to procedures, and lack of initiative: but see section 8.5 for a different view.

8.2.1 The politics of bureaucracy

Much of what happens in a bureaucracy is technical, about getting things done in a practical way. Bureaucratic decisions seem to occur once political debate has taken place, manifestos agreed, and elections held. In the classic writing about bureaucracy, especially that written by the early twentieth-century sociologist Max Weber (1978, chapter XI), the power of the bureaucracy, which can get things done using the best scientific knowledge available, is inevitably political. Much of the advice ministers receive from bureaucrats they have neither the academic knowledge nor professional background to understand fully. Decisions about which course of action to take often involve political values about their assessment. As ministers turn over in office frequently, reshuffled by the prime minister to avoid them building up power bases, they may never acquire enough expertise to monitor civil servants effectively (Key term 8.2).

Many civil servants have political views of their own, even if they are submerged and not consciously articulated. These ideas inevitably affect, to varying degrees, how officials do their day-to-day work and the advice they give to politicians, even though most civil servants take great pride in offering neutral advice, and helping the politicians achieve their objectives.

Key term 8.2 Civil servant

Photo 8.1 Civil servants work for central government and state governments, and answer to the government, not a political party.

A civil servant is a permanent employee of central government, other national governments in the UK, and public agencies working under national governments. Other kinds of bureaucrat, such as officers, work in local government. Other specialist personnel, such as police and members of the armed services, retain their own status (see section 8.3.1).

Pure neutrality is hard to achieve in any case, and value preferences may affect how evidence is assessed, for example (see section 8.4). In practice, politicians and civil servants, especially those operating outside central government in local councils, often make policy choices together in a team.

The British tradition of law-making bestowed a lot of discretion on the bureaucracy and executive agencies to implement legislation in broad terms (Loughlin 1986), which gave civil servants and ministers the latitude to decide much of how policy takes place, without facing much challenge from the courts. The role of the courts has increased in recent years and policy-making has become more legally constrained (for example, in counter-terrorism, Walker and Cawley 2020). However, the UK is still different to some other countries in Western Europe, like Italy, such as where the legislature may tie the executive's hands (Huber 2000, 401). As officials are involved with political decisions, they are powerful key actors who can be compared with ministers and legislators. Like politicians, civil servants operate in a context of the agenda-setting process and under the influence of public opinion. The debate about representation comes into focus, just as it did in section 8.3.3, asking whether the bureaucracy should be representative of society as a whole.

8.2.2 Delegation to agencies

Politicians can delegate decisions to independent agencies to make them more independent and supposedly apolitical, such as the decision in 1997 to transfer decisions about the level of the interest rate from the Treasury to the Bank of England. Another example is the Office for Budget Responsibility, set up in 2010, which transfers the calculation of the state of public finances from the Treasury into a separate and independent body. But such transfers do not remove political considerations in that values and trade-offs are part of the decisions of these bodies just as much as before they were delegated: this is politics in the broad sense rather than of just party politics. Central government funds these agencies, appoints their heads, and the same staff move between the central civil service and these agencies. The attempt at depoliticization through delegation needs to be understood in broad political terms (Flinders and Buller 2006), whereby central political actors are seeking to guide preferred outcomes and political benefits through the way in which agencies are delegated.

8.3 Basic facts: UK bureaucracy

8.3.1 What is the civil service?

The civil service is called Her Majesty's Civil Service or the Home Civil Service, though such terms are not used anymore in government official information. It is the permanent bureaucracy that supports the Crown and by implication the government of the day, though there are some direct responsibilities to Parliament and to other bodies, such as the Scottish government. By permanent, this means that its members do not lose their jobs or need to re-apply for them when the party in government changes, as is the case in some countries, such as federal government in the US after a presidential election. Organizations that make up the civil service include central government departments and their agencies. There are also non-departmental government bodies (NDGBs), whose employees are not strictly part of the civil service, though many civil servants are seconded to them. Many NDGBs are advisory bodies, such as the Advisory Council on the Misuse of Drugs, and the Boundary Commission for England; others carry out particular functions, such as the Arts Council England, which distributes funding to arts organizations and groups (see here for a full list: www.gov.uk/government/organisations). There are twenty non-ministerial departments, which are at arm's length from government because of a need for independence, such as the Charity Commission, which regulates charities, or the UK Statistics Authority, which gives independent advice on the use of official statistics. Then there are 413 agencies and other public bodies, some of which deliver services on behalf of central government departments, such as the Environment Agency, which deals with flood protection, among other functions.

8.3.2 The grade structure and the Senior Civil Service (SCS)

The civil service includes a large number of people on a series of grades then set out into what is called the professions, which have particular expertise, such as research (see section 8.3.6), which is increasingly characterizing the civil service rather than the stereotype of a hierarchy. The Administrative Officer/Administrative Assistant (AO/AA) is the most junior post, carrying out administrative support and operational functions, and examples include prison officers and caterers. Then there is the Executive Officer (EO) who offers business and policy support, such as in finance, human resources, and Information Technology. The Senior Executive Officer/Higher Executive Officer (SEO/HEO) includes people who work on policy matters. Grades 6 and 7 are civil servants who are people with a lot of experience and have important policy job tasks.

In the UK, there is a lot of focus on the top grades. This part of the hierarchy used to be called the higher civil service, now the Senior Civil Service (SCS). This group form into the senior management team for each government department. The SCS is the elite, now numbering about 6,500 people, who guide policy and administration. They have been subject to a long debate about the political power of the civil service, particularly as they have been recruited, since the recommendation of the Northcote-Trevelyan report of 1854, separately to the rest of the civil service by competitive examination. The idea is that the civil service 'fast stream' attracts the brightest and best of university graduates, which inevitably makes them part of an elite, even if recruited competitively. In the SCS, directors are ultimately responsible for the policy work of their team and director generals oversee directors and work closely with the department's ministers. Each department also has a permanent secretary, who supports the minister at the head of the department, acts as the accounting officer (responsible for signing off public expenditure items), and is the person in charge of the day-to-day running of the department.

Photo 8.2 The 'glass ceiling' is a metaphor used to represent barriers in the careers of women and minority groups in the workplace.

8.3.3 Employment figures and representation

Figures from the Office for National Statistics (ONS) show that in March 2020 the number of people working in the civil service was 456,410, up from 445,480 in 2019 (Office for National Statistics 2020). On a full-time equivalent (FTE) basis, employment is 423,770, up from 413,910 in 2019. In the past, there was a lot of debate over whether the civil service reproduces or even enhances social inequalities through its lack of representativeness (see section 8.4.4). For the civil service as a whole today, there do appear to be reasonable levels of representation:

> 53.8 per cent are women, a decrease of 0.1 percentage point from the previous year; 13.2 per cent are ethnic minority background, up from 12.7 per cent in 2019; 12.8 per cent declare themselves as having a disability, up from 11.7 per cent in 2019; 5.0 per cent identify as being lesbian, gay, bisexual or recorded their sexual orientation as 'other' (LGBO), up from 4.9 per cent in 2019; 67.8 per cent are working at Executive Officer (EO) grade and above, up from 66.4 per cent in 2019 . . . and 36.1 per cent are aged under 40, up from 35.8 per cent in 2019. Of those with a known sexual orientation, 4.9 per cent of civil servants identify as being lesbian, gay, bisexual or recorded their sexual orientation as 'other' (LGBO). This has increased every year since data on sexual orientation has been captured in these statistics, and is up 1.2 percentage points since 2015. (Office for National Statistics 2020, 1)

Total levels of representation might disguise the concentration of male, white, older, and non-LGBTQ people in the higher grades, revealing what is called a 'glass ceiling' (Photo 8.2), a hidden barrier that prevents women and minority-group members progressing up to the top. So, it is important to look at the breakdown according to grade. Figure 8.1 shows the proportions across the five grades.

There are the expected gradients, with less equal representation at the higher grades. For example,

8

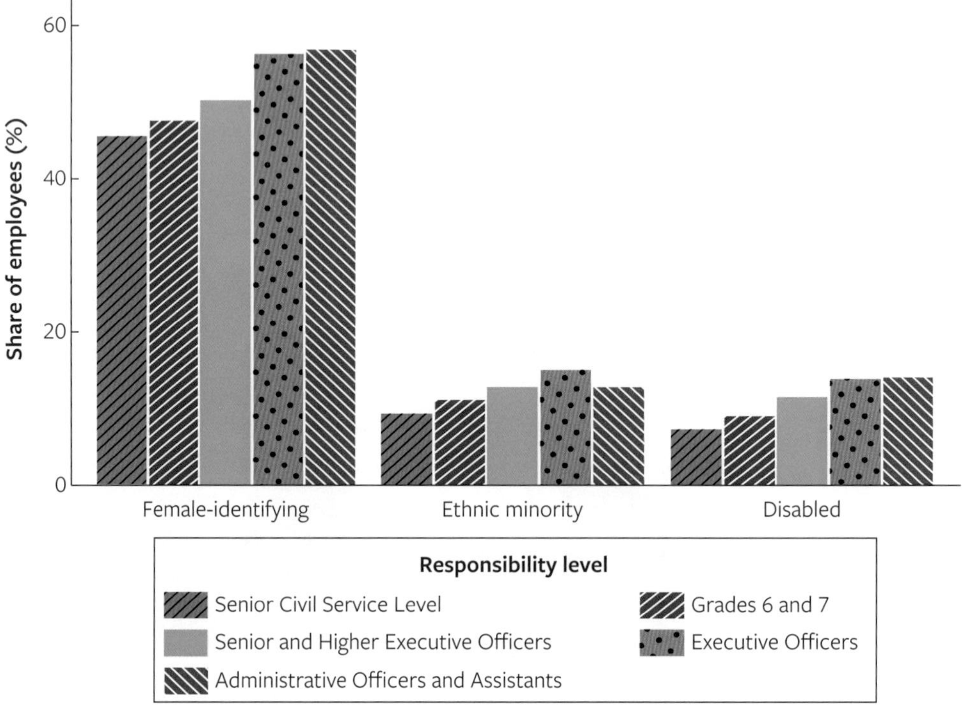

Figure 8.1 Representation in the civil service, March 2020.
Source: gov.uk: www.gov.uk/government/statistics/civil-service-statistics-2020

women comprise 45.0 per cent of the SCS, whereas they make up 56.2 per cent of administrative officers. This contrasts with 34.0 per cent in the senior grades in 2010. This progress may have come from the civil service's diversity and inclusion policies and how they are monitored as well as reflecting broader social changes.

Traditionally, senior civil servants were recruited from the major public (private) schools and from elite universities, Oxford and Cambridge in particular. There is less official information about social backgrounds. *Elitist Britain* (Sutton Trust 2019) collates evidence from *Who's Who*, LinkedIn, DODS People, internet searches, and direct contacts, which is a less conventional research method but still worth reporting with caveats. One indication of potential bias in favour of people from particular social backgrounds comes from data about applicants to the fast stream: in 2018, 55 per cent of applicants had parents in higher managerial, administrative, or professional occupations, whereas 13 per cent of applicants had parents working in routine or manual occupations; however, 68 per cent of those appointed to the fast stream in 2018 came from the first group (Sutton Trust 2019, 5): 'Civil service permanent secretaries (59 per cent), Foreign Office diplomats (52 per cent), and Public Body Chairs (45 per cent) have among the highest rates of independently educated in their ranks . . . with 56 per cent having graduated from Oxford or Cambridge, and 39 per cent having attended both a private school and Oxbridge.' The picture in this respect may still be quite restrictive for ethnic-minority groups (Institute for Government 2018) and women (Institute for Government 2017b).

8.3.4 **The organization of the civil service and ministers**

It is also important to know about the structure of government and where civil servants work, as well as the names of a few key personnel. At the centre is support for the prime minister and cabinet which is provided by the Cabinet Office, who have responsibilities for coordinating government, leading over intelligence, coordinating the government's response to crises, managing the UK's cyber security, promoting efficiency and reform across government, making the way government works more transparent, overseeing the civil service, and political and constitutional reform.

The key civil servant is the cabinet secretary, who is the UK's leading civil servant, responsible for coordinating the rest of the civil service, advising the prime minister, and supporting the cabinet. The role is usually combined with the head of the civil service post. In 2021 this position was occupied by Sir Simon Case. The Cabinet Office has its own ministerial structure to which civil servants report, like any government department (see the ministerial offices in Zoom-In 2.3). There is a management structure of senior civil servants who work within and alongside this hierarchical structure.

The other main central ministry at the centre of government is the Treasury, headed by the Chancellor of the Exchequer, and a team of ministers. This is the finance ministry which manages the economy, sets taxes and expenditure, and also monitors public expenditure throughout government, so has power over other government departments. There is a team of civil servants who work alongside ministers, which is slightly more top heavy than a government department with several permanent secretaries, rather like the Cabinet Office.

Then there are government departments that run things like transport, local government, and so on, which have a standard ministerial structure from secretary of state downwards (see Zoom-In 2.3), along with a senior management team running alongside that of ministers. There are currently twenty-three ministerial departments, which range from Department for Business, Energy and Industrial Strategy (BEIS) to the Office of the Leader of the House of Commons.

8.3.5 **The relationship between civil servants and ministers**

Either within the central state, such as the Cabinet Office and Treasury, or in departments, there is an expected relationship between civil servants and

Photo 8.3 The homepage of the Department for Business, Energy and Industrial Strategy on the UK government website.

ministers, which seeks to reinforce the conventional wisdom that civil servants advise, and ministers decide. Civil servants are not involved with party politics, even if we think their roles are political in a broader meaning of the term; that is, not party political but concerned with values and preferred outcomes. The most senior civil servants directly advise ministers by putting briefs to them and asking them to sign off decisions and appointments. These informal principles and working practices were drawn together in a ministerial and a civil service code (HM Government 2015). On political impartiality, the civil service code says that civil servants must 'serve the government, whatever its political persuasion, to the best of your ability in a way which maintains political impartiality and is in line with the requirements of this code, and no matter what your own political beliefs are, act in a way which deserves and retains the confidence of ministers, while at the same time ensuring that you will be able to establish the same relationship with those whom you may be required to serve in some future government' (gov.uk: www.gov.uk/government/publications/civil-service-code/the-civil-service-code). There are some provisions for when a civil servant believes the code has been breached, which involves protection for whistleblowing (reporting wrongdoing), procedures for a ministerial direction, and reporting upwards to the Civil Service Commission. In the end, it is up to the prime minister to hold ministers to account: to decide whether they have breached the code and whether they should leave office. For example, in November 2020, an independent inquiry found that the current home secretary, Priti Patel, had breached the code over bullying of civil servants, but she did not resign; nor did the prime minister, Boris Johnson, dismiss her.

8.3.6 The professions and scientific advice

Working to support the work of senior civil servants and ministers are specialized groups of public officials providing advice and services. This occurs through what is called the professions, such as commercial and procurement, communications (coms), finance, and digital data and technology. There is increasingly a functional model of government that cuts across departments and focuses on providing core functions. There is a vast diversity of functions that civil servants carry out. Even when personnel are working as private contractors, which are extensively used across government, they perform civil service or public roles, such as a prison officer working in a private as opposed to public prison.

One important role for civil servants is analysis, which involves using evidence to inform decision-making, employing about 1,700 people across the government machine, such as operational researchers, statisticians, economists, social researchers, actuaries, geographers, and data scientists/analysts. Many scientists and social scientists work for the civil service (indeed, perhaps readers of this book will have such a job in the future). These work to support the government's need for advice in making decisions. At the top of the civil service is the Government Chief Scientific Adviser and Head of Government Science and Engineering Profession, who in 2021 is Sir Patrick Vallance, who overall is charged with 'providing scientific advice to the prime minister and members of cabinet advising the government on aspects of policy on science and technology ensuring and improving the quality and use of scientific evidence and advice in government'. Within the NHS and Department of Health and Social Care, there are similar figures who have a degree of independence indicated by their job description and their professional standing, such as the Chief Medical Officer for England and the UK government's Chief Medical Adviser, currently Chris Whitty. These figures were very important during the Covid-19 crisis and became prominent public figures (in general, civil servants are not in the public glare), as it was increasingly important for the government to show the public that its policies were guided by science, and that is the purpose of these officials. Advisors fit within a political structure for making decisions, but need to show they are to a degree independent and drawing on scientific opinion and knowledge.

8.3.7 Beyond the central state

Beyond the civil service are the bureaucracies that serve other political authorities, such as the Scottish Civil Service, which works for the Scottish government (it is still part of the formal grade and employment structure of the civil service). There are similar bodies for the Welsh government and the Northern Ireland Executive. Outside the formal civil service are the cadres of officers that work for local authorities and whose members are answerable to the mayor or cabinets that run these bodies, as well as having professional obligations.

8.4 The power of the civil service debate

8.4.1 The civil service: the classic debate

One of the classic debates in British politics is about the power of the civil service to determine matters of public policy in place of or in addition to elected politicians. The introduction to this chapter highlighted that there is no clear dividing line between matters of administration, i.e. delivery matters, and making policy, which is about applying political values and preferences to the determination of the outputs and outcomes of government. Administrative decisions can often be another form of politics, which involves making collective choices based on values that might be contested by others. In any case, the classic relationship in the principal–agent model is between the political principal and the bureaucratic agent (Moe 1984) (see Zoom-In 1.4), where the politician needs to delegate activities based upon the need for expertise and capacity, but does not have the ability to monitor the agent fully. Even the classic bureaucratic behaviour of resistance, of slowing down or limiting implementation (see Key term 8.1), perhaps to preserve the integrity of the bureau and its working practices, can amount to an input in policy because outcomes are different from what the principal would want them to be and policy is not introduced as fast as could have been achieved.

8.4.2 The resilience of the traditional model

It is important to remember as a counterbalance to the civil service power argument that ministers have a large amount of power and ultimate sanction: they are the legitimate political actors who initiate policies and sign off decisions. Also, studies show that civil servants are very attached to the traditional model whereby the minister decides and civil servants administer or dispose, not just from interviews but from direct observation, as in Rod Rhodes' anthropological study of the civil service (Rhodes 2011, 306–7). There is even a view that the civil service can be *too* respectful of government views, not pointing out policy errors, which then cause governments more trouble down the line (Barker and Wilson 1997, 225) (see section 8.5 on policy disasters).

Also, principal–agent models do not say the agent always wins, as there are ways in which the principal can monitor the agent, such as by obtaining information from interest groups and developing alternative sources of expertise (McCubbins, Noll, and Weingast 1987). One example of how this can happen is the appointment of political advisors as temporary civil servants, what are called special advisors (SpAds), who can pick up on a lot of information and report it to the minister, and are trusted because of their political loyalty.

8.4.3 The public service ethos

The principal–agent model relies on personal self-interest as the driver, but it is widely recognized that those who work in the public sector are driven by values and a sense of public service, called the public service ethos (PSE) (Key term 8.3), observed in Britain, as with other countries, such as the US, using survey data (for example, John et al. 2008). The values come from a motivation to be a public servant, which might be stimulated at school and university; then fostered by working for a public organization. Whereas public service was once about traditional values of service, now civil servants might be motivated by dealing with pressing public problems, such as climate change. The civil service role has changed over time, with civil servants increasingly valuing empowerment and mission in their roles more than career development, as shown in a recent survey (Reeder 2020).

The PSE implies serving the minister who is elected to make decisions in the public interest, though it can also indicate civil servants following other values,

Key term 8.3 Public service ethos (PSE)

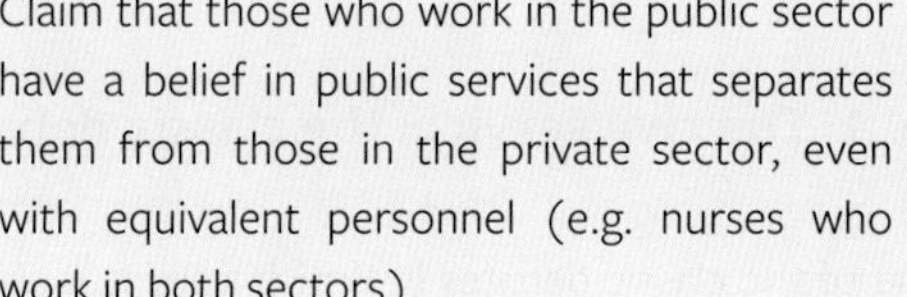

Claim that those who work in the public sector have a belief in public services that separates them from those in the private sector, even with equivalent personnel (e.g. nurses who work in both sectors).

such as in favour of human rights, which could conflict with government policies. Civil servants may think they need to intervene if a policy is damaging. When asked in a survey if civil servants regard it as legitimate if a minister proposes 'sharply damaging' policy or action, 50 per cent of senior civil servants mentioned they would comply, 41 per cent said they would 'write a minute or dissuade', 54 per cent said they would 'inform superiors within department', 32 per cent mentioned they would 'inform colleagues in other departments', 32 per cent said they would 'seek a different post, resign from service', only 4 per cent mentioned they would 'seek support outside government' (e.g. from MPs, interest groups), and none said they would sabotage (Barker and Wilson 1997, 235).

A self-interested civil servant might be easier to control. They may respond more to incentive than a principled person as incentives may be manipulated but principles are hard to compromise on (Grand 2010, 68). In addition, the personnel at the centre have loyalty to the state which might not amount to loyalty to a particular government, even though in constitutional theory the two are thought to be the same; as servants of the Crown they might think of themselves as having an interest in the survival and protection of the state.

8.4.4 Critique from the left

The belief about the power of civil servants comes from across the political spectrum, often from the experience of parties being in government. From the left-wing perspective, the civil service has been one of the causes of the lack of radicalism of Labour governments. Members of the left argued that the civil service was part of the ruling class, with its social class background in recruitment and in elite networks of which the civil service is part. With shared values with the governing elite, the civil service was portrayed as having an interest in subverting reforms and in preserving the existing state of affairs. At the time these critiques were made, the civil service had a very narrow recruitment from certain kinds of public (i.e. private) schools and Oxford and Cambridge University, top-tier universities, much more than they do today. For example, in 1958, fifty of the top seventy-three highest-level civil servants were educated at Oxford or Cambridge universities, three came from Eton, and eleven came from either Harrow, Winchester, Rugby, or Marlborough (Guttsman 1963, 336). This is a very small range, even of exclusive education establishments. Studies of elites stress that the people who have the same or similar background share common interests and values (Guttsman 1963). This view appeared in a book-length treatment of the right-wing bias of the service, entitled *The Civil Servants: An Inquiry into Britain's Ruling Class* (Kellner and Crowther-Hunt 1980). The book details many examples of civil service resistance to government policies, notably towards the programme of reform of the civil service. But it is not a systematic study by any means and is based on cases that illustrate rather than prove its argument. The main protagonist in the left-wing critique of the civil service was the Labour politician and former minister Tony Benn (Dave Richards and Smith 2014), but civil servants may have been working to the command of the prime minister against a controversial figure in cabinet.

8.4.5 Bureaucratic politics

Ministers and civil servants are caught up with rivalry between government departments, such as between the economics ministries and the spending departments, but this reflects more general divisions in politics between different objectives within a government, such as over spending levels, where ministers and civil servants are united in defending their respective departments. The lens of civil service power needs to be seen within what is called bureaucratic politics (Jenkins and Gray 1983). Nonetheless, it shows how both civil servants and politicians are part of the same

Key term 8.4 Bureaucratic politics

The rivalry for resources and favourable policies between agencies within the state, which can be used to explain policy choices.

culture, based on common assumptions and routines. The permanence of civil servants gives them an advantage in this framework in that they understand it much more than less experienced ministers. This culture of the civil service appears in some studies as very powerful and all-embracing, such as in the classic study of the Treasury, *The Private Government of Public Money* (Heclo and Wildavsky 1974). The two researchers detected a closed club of officials, who knew each other very well. They ran the finance ministry, consolidating their power from their links to allies right across the Whitehall machine.

8.4.6 The complaint from the right

The suspicion about civil service power has also come from the right, with a long pedigree (see Greenaway 1992). Right-of-centre thinkers and politicians, especially when radicalized in the 1970s, tend to think of the civil service as part of the centrist and collectivist establishment. Civil servants are believed to be keen to maintain the state's involvement and role in providing public services and believed to be resistant to more radical reforms based on the idea of returning parts of the state to the private sector. Civil servants might not want to champion quasi-markets whereby private sector models are applied to the management of public services, such as consumer choice of public service provider. The civil service might be representative of more progressive ideas out of step with parts of Britain living outside the metropolitan core. This argument is reviewed in Case Study 8.1.

8.4.7 Power over the machine: the bureau-shaping debate

One of the key arguments about bureaucratic influence is that civil servants care a lot about their own environment and organizational unit, as it affects them directly and influences their status within the official machine. In some public choice accounts, civil

Case Study 8.1 Brexit and the civil service

Another example of right-wing critique is that the civil service was biased *against* Brexit, and then conspired to have a stronger relationship with the EU in the period when Theresa May was prime minister (2016–19). The argument is that the civil service is made up of educated people who are largely opposed to Brexit (see basis of the Brexit vote in section 4.8.1). The policy that led to the Chequers agreement of 2018, which proposed keeping Britain in the regulatory orbit of the EU for many activities, appeared to look like compromise agreed by civil servants who brokered the agreement. But the cabinet was divided and May was trying to find a way through, with civil servants caught in the middle, or in ministries representing different interests. A report based on eighty-one interviews claimed there was no Brexit bias: 'No evidence emerges that civil servants undermine or thwart their minister or derail the Brexit negotiations' (Kakabadse et al. 2018, 3.1). This was based on interviews with both politicians and civil servants, so it is not quite an insider story, but again it is hard to prove the bias of civil servants one way or another.

servants seek to arrange things so that the total budgets under their command increase with their salaries and status increasing alongside it (Niskanen 1975). But does this happen? There have been a lot of tests of these bureaucratic strategies, such as whether some departments are better able to resist cutbacks during spending cuts, but this could be to do with the features of each organization rather than measuring the power of bureaucrats (Dunsire et al. 1989). The evidence in favour of the bureau-maximizing hypothesis is ambiguous (Blais and Dion 1991). In one approach, the power of bureaucrats was more directly assessed, which is Dunleavy's bureau-shaping argument (Dunleavy 1991). This is the idea that bureaucrats wish to maximize their core budget close to their operations and are less concerned with the size of other budgets they control, such as those that transfer to other organizations. The argument is that bureaucrats have an incentive to encourage reform, so they may reshape their organization to maximize the amount of core budget they administer in proportion to the total, as this allows them to work more on policy advice with close relationships to the minister that they prefer, which is characteristic of a high core budget authority. Dunleavy then argues that the move to breaking up departments by setting up agencies illustrated this argument as civil servants were very keen on pressing for this better alignment with their preferences. Plausible as this argument is, an interview-based study of civil servants designed to test this claim could not find any evidence in support (Marsh, Smith, and Richards 2000).

8.4.8 Experimental work

Stronger evidence can come from experimental studies done with civil servants, which can uncover hidden or unconscious bias that might not appear in a case study or an interview with a researcher. An experiment done with World Bank officials and those from the former Department for International Development (Banuri, Dercon, and Gauri 2017) found confirmation bias in this way. One group was told there was evidence of the impact of skin cream on a rash. Another group was told that there was evidence of income changes of the poorest 40 per cent when the minimum wage was increased in the local area. The results were more in favour of where the policy was introduced with the minimum wage. This example does not show that civil servants are biased against a minister, but it does show the ideas and values can be embedded and routinized so that a new minister probably gets socialized into a way of thinking by officials, especially when officials are given advice. This is more consistent with more general understandings of how bias operates in organizations, which is not usually through conscious discrimination but from the effect on working practices and decisions of often hidden assumptions (Bohnet 2016).

Another experiment was carried out by Wittels (2020, 53) with local bureaucrats in England to see if they would respond to local citizen preferences in place of instruction from their political principals using scenarios. She finds that, 'Results show that bureaucrats resist. When citizens and politicians agree, almost ninety per cent of bureaucrats shirk responding to demands and opt to provide their own advice. The rate of resistance decreases somewhat under conflict, in favour of the citizen group. Counter to what a risk-based model of bureaucrat behaviour would expect, on average, bureaucrats do not yield to politicians at a higher rate in the conflict scenario.'

8.4.9 Recent changes that may tilt the balance to ministers

Back in the 1970s, when allegations of the bias of the civil service were made, the civil service was more autonomous and self-confident. Given that governments have come into power with suspicions of the civil service, they have sought to take it under more precise control. The system of SpAds was introduced first in 1964, and part of this rise in prominence is the search for less reliance on officials. There are quite a large number of them—119 in 2019. In the end, although SpAds can become very powerful, they are there because of the minister and their role does not fundamentally affect that of the civil service, who learn to work with the advisors rather than against them (Yong and Hazell 2014). In fact, there are not very many SpAds when compared to civil servants. They cannot replace the work of officials—they usually do party business and liaison with No. 10, which civil servants cannot do (Rhodes 2011, 160).

Then there is the use of outsiders to do civil service roles, such as heads of agencies. Governments have been more assertive over civil service appointments to ensure that civil servants share their objectives. Outright dismissals are rare, but the prime minister in particular usually takes an interest in appointments, but this needs to be balanced with the role of the independent Civil Service Commission. In recent years, because of a lack of political fit and more assertiveness from ministers, forced or semi-forced resignations are more common, such as Sir Ivan Rogers, the government's chief diplomat to the EU, who left the civil service in 2017. His advice was not to the liking of Theresa May's Brexit-supporting government at the time. Then there are more frequent directions by ministers over civil servants, simply asserting their will against advice, breaking down the traditional model of behind the scenes and consensual decision-making (Institute for Government 2017a).

This phenomenon is called politicization of the civil service (Peters 2013). It means that parties in government are becoming increasingly assertive and more organized to resist the civil service view. But the result of greater politicization might be passivity and indifference to ministerial objectives (see here: www.instituteforgovernment.org.uk/blog/politicisation-civil-service-beware-straw-men). This reluctance to advise may have been a cause of policy blunders in recent years, as has been revealed in King and Crewe's study: 'even when officials had harboured serious reservations about ministers' bright ideas, they had failed openly to express their reservations . . . Several of the blunders we describe resulted, at least in part, from this formidable combination of ministerial activism and official reticence' (King and Crewe 2014, 335). To gratify ministers, civil servants may in the end rush to implement policies that turn out to be unworkable, undermining ministers in the long run.

Overall, there is a lot of strain on the civil service today, with over-assertive ministers and forced resignations of civil servants (Rutter 2020). These are signs that the traditional model has broken down, but there is no clear alternative to replace it.

8.4.10 **Summing up on civil service power**

Overall, it is hard to sustain the claim of systematic civil service bias and power, and to observe how much civil servants are focused on delivering the objectives of a new government, even when they might privately disagree. Occasions of the assertion of direct civil service power are rare and the more indirect influence over the routines of government and rules of the game has diminished over time as British governments have become more assertive and the old elite culture has lessened. Much depends on the chemistry of the relationship and the skill of the minister in working with the civil service team. Remember the distinction between power *to* and power *over* (Key term 2.5): civil servants are needed to create power *to*, which might even mean working independently of ministers. Letting civil servants be powerful to be able to give good advice that might challenge ministers, speaking truth to power, might be in the political interest of the government of the day. More power *over* might be at the price of less power *to*.

8.5 The capacity of the bureaucracy

A feature of British government is that the bureaucracy contributes to the quality of policy-making and governing efficiency, more generally supporting the work of political parties to get their objectives done. Given such demands of this role, there has been a lot of assessment of the capacity of the bureaucracy in achievement of this, which ranges from self-congratulation about being governed by the brightest and best (Campbell and Wilson 1995, 14–17), to dismay at the low quality of decision-making and tendency towards blunders or disasters in public policy (Dunleavy 1995b), or blame (if carefully made) for the UK's poor economic performance post-1945 (Hennessy 1989, 691–729). Then there is the argument that the civil service has fallen in performance through loss of morale, endless reform, and greater political control (Campbell and Wilson 1995). There is also a belief, but with no hard evidence to back it up, that the values underpinning effective bureaucracy and its overall competence have eroded, such as the decline in internal deliberation while policy is being made and the exclusion of civil servants from much decision-making (Foster 2005, 207). This has been linked to the decline of 'club government'—an informal set of close networks across government where the rules of the game are implicitly understood. This ensures some stability in the system and protects decision-makers from making rash choices based on short-term assessments (Moran 2007). In David Marquand's view, this loss of compass meant party elites were likely to launch a whole series of institutional reforms without much thought about how they knit together (Marquand 1981). However, as Moran (2007, 172) points out, there were probably just as many policy fiascos under club government as there are now. The greater politicization of decision-making is hard to assess as making policy based on evidence has always been political: in no jurisdiction in the world do policy-makers make policy purely on the evidence. Even Britain's highly developed procedures for feeding independent scientific advice into decisions needs information to be moderated and used within a political framework for making decisions. It is possible to see this tempering and balancing of advice, or even ignoring of it, during the Covid-19 crisis in Britain from 2020 (see section 11.3.4).

8.5.1 Civil service modernization

On top of this politicization is a long-running reform agenda designed to modernize the bureaucracy and to increase its efficiency, which includes criticisms of the government by amateurs, without technical and professional skills, recruited in the fast stream. Then there are efforts to introduce market principles into the evaluation of the civil service, such as reviews of efficiency in the 1980s. This was followed by the 'Next Steps' reforms that created agencies, with chief executives and some independence from government (see section 8.4.7), often called the agencification of government (see Key term 8.5).

In the David Cameron government there was a focus on opening up data. Later, the government set out a national digital strategy in November 2020 (Department for Digital, Culture, Media and Sport 2020).

There is a debate as to whether the civil service has been able to use effectively the opportunities given by digital resources and to harness the internet to improve the relations between the citizen and the state as part of more integrated and holistic forms of governance. Digital governance is usually thought to be poor in the UK compared to elsewhere, such as Australia, partly through the legacy of the New Public Management (NPM) reforms that had weakened

Photo 8.4 The Department for Digital, Culture, Media and Sport (DCMS) aims to protect and promote cultural and artistic heritage.

Key term 8.5 Agencification

The tendency to move away from long hierarchies of government departments to an array of semi-independent delivery agencies.

Key term 8.6 New Public Management (NPM)

Doctrine of injecting innovation and efficiency into the public sector by incentives and market mechanisms. Often involves the break-up of traditional bureaucracies. Examples include internal markets for services, contracting out, managing performance through indicators, and performance-related pay.

much central capacity in IT and handed over expertise to private companies contracting for services (Dunleavy et al. 2006).

8.5.2 Hood and Dixon's study

One study to assess the claims of efficiency and quality of policy-making was carried out by Hood and Dixon (2015) to assess the performance of NPM reforms (see Key term 8.6) introduced in British government, designed in part to reform the machine as a whole and the role of civil servants in it. They collected three decades of data on the efficiency, personnel, and outputs of government, only to discover that in this period of massive changes and reform there were no large discernible changes in outcomes as a result. Some outcomes even got worse with a growth in complaints and an increase in running costs. It may be the case that the bureaucracy is a classic example of path dependence, where essentially the same system of administration and government continues over time and any changes do not have a massive impact. These findings comport with another study showing the static productivity of government, if with some innovations and rises (Dunleavy and Carrera 2013). Overall, government does not appear to reap the advantages of IT changes, and is dogged by poor management and changes in policies. Nonetheless, even with these inconsequential reforms it is hard to substantiate whether the civil service has lost capacity in the last decades, contributing to policy failures, though this is King and Crewe's view from their case studies. On the other hand, the civil service performs well in comparative surveys of effectiveness, such as the high ranking in the International Civil Service Effectiveness (InCiSE) Index in 2019 (www.bsg.ox.ac.uk/about/partnerships/international-civil-service-effectiveness-index-2019).

8.5.3 Civil service as an innovator

By convention, the bureaucracy is a drag on innovation and reform. The stereotype has to do with the bureaucratic organization as conservative and wanting to avoid risks. In 2021 this view was associated with Dominic Cummings, Boris Johnson's chief advisor, appointed with a mission to shape up the civil service. He wrote in his blog (https://dominiccummings.com) on 2 January 2020:

> there are also some profound problems at the core of how the British state makes decisions. . . . Dealing with these deep problems is supported by many great officials, particularly younger ones, though there will naturally be many fears—some reasonable, most unreasonable . . . There is a huge amount of low hanging fruit—trillion-dollar bills lying on the street . . . We want to hire an unusual set of people with different skills and backgrounds to work in Downing Street.

But is it true? The stereotype is just that: just like the same images of over-zealous ministers who must be talked out of outlandish ideas. But there is a huge amount of innovation promoted by the UK central state. Cummings was hampered by his combative style, and resigned in November 2020. Other more politically adept entrepreneurs can get innovation off the ground, by persuading others to adopt an idea. One example was how the central state adopted ideas from behavioural economics to use new techniques to nudge people to carry out prosocial behaviours, like volunteering, giving, and recycling waste. The Cameron government (2010–16) set up the nudge unit, the Behavioural Insights Team in the Cabinet Office, a world pioneer introducing behavioural interventions, such as reminding people to pay their taxes on time. It had to battle with bureaucratic constraints but overcame them largely (John 2017a), acting as a trailblazer for innovations and a whole new field of government policy-making. These kinds of initiatives are hard to reconcile with the reputation of slow-moving of bureaucracies. In the end the team decided to wrest free of the civil service and the government agreed it could set up as an independent organization, a social purpose company, at arm's length from government, but jointly owned by the UK Cabinet Office, the charity Nesta, and employees. While there were bureaucratic constraints of running a nudge unit at the centre of government, the experience shows how innovation is possible in British central government.

8.6 Delegation and the continuation of politics by bureaucratic means

This chapter started with the focus on delegation (see section 8.2), which still needs to occur even with highly politicized ministers. Certain very technical tasks need to be organized even within the central service under the direct control of ministers, such as a system for allocating central government grants to local government based on the spending needs of each local authority, such as how many social workers to fund. Ministers could not decide this on their own without experts to advise them: to collect and manage the data and to carry out the statistical analysis. As a result, these activities are delegated within the bureaucracy, but the politicians may still have political objectives in mind when they oversee and sign off on these decisions. So, the question is whether such routines become a matter for administration, or whether political objectives are introduced, even if quite subtly. Some of these objectives could be policy objectives, which might be about ensuring that policy targets the needy, such as rewarding poorer local authorities, or about promoting competition between local authorities, such as letting authorities keep business rates if they manage their services well. Others may be about rewarding political followers or getting re-elected by targeting voters in politically important constituencies. But the politicians need civil servants to follow these political interests, even if in a submerged and non-conscious way. Political principals may have subtle ways to get compliance, which if true again points away from the civil service power hypothesis and shows how the executive can get its wishes carried out in a centralized system as exists in England.

8.6.1 **Agencies**

It also works with delegated agencies, which gets around the paradox that government delegates to these agencies to get a political benefit from making them independent of political interference, such as lower interest rates, but still wants them to follow partisan preferences. Delegation occurs because of a more general demand for de-politicization, whereby party politicians are taken out of public decisions (Flinders 2008). Delegation appears to make government less vulnerable to the charge of politicizing public policy. But at the same time government still wants these agencies to follow political objectives that they would have preferred to achieve when not delegated, which again requires government not only to overcome the classic principal–agent issues, but also to work with agencies who are formally independent. The answer to this problem is that independence is only relative, as there is central control of budgets and appointments to these bodies, which still need to be signed off by ministers. Also, there is the law of anticipated reactions (Friedrich 1937), whereby agents can follow the implied objectives of the principal without any direct communication: the objectives are effectively internalized. It might seem that these claims are hard to substantiate, but statistical work on public policy decisions can reveal the way this happens without supplying the smoking gun of a clear causal process that can be verified.

8.6.2 **Formula funding and political advantage**

There is a wealth of discourse on what is called distributive politics (Golden and Min 2013) (Key term 8.7), which suggests that the allocation of policy outcomes may be explained by the political advantage, such as targeting seats which ministers or committee members are representing, or to areas with many party supporters, or swing or marginal seats (Key term 5.10) where more resources can help a government party stay in power. This is helped by there being single constituencies where there is one representative to reward or whether there may be seats where only a few votes are needed to reverse or maintain a plurality of votes: the political advantage of the single-member FPTP electoral system. In the UK, it was often assumed that the impartiality of the civil service stopped governments doing this. But a number of studies of local government finance have shown that governments have adjusted the formula to reward marginal seats and local authorities where there is a government party in control (John and Ward 2001; Fouirnaies and Mutlu-Eren 2015). This relies on government and

Key term 8.7 Distributive politics

The way in which decisions in public policy reflect the political importance and power of certain locations and/or groups.

civil servants being able to tweak the formula so that an alternative politically advantageous specification can be implemented. This does not prove political interference in causal terms but sets up a plausible explanation, and also places Britain in a comparative context where such manipulation is routine, as in the US and Africa (Golden and Min 2013).

8.6.3 **Pork barrel politics**

Pork barrel is thought to be a feature of legislative dominant systems where committee chairs in the legislature give a power to skew resources to the home state (Stein and Bickers 1997), hence 'bringing home the bacon' in the US. This could feature in large public projects, such as the location of a military base. Although pork barrel sounds like malpractice, it is usually done perfectly legally. In fact, it can be seen as a feature of responsive constituency politics (see section 3.6.9), i.e. what an elected representative should be doing for their community, with the unfairness that some areas get resources because their representative is powerful, with others getting less than they should.

Just like Congressional committee chairs, ministers in the Westminster system can use their power to allocate resources to their constituencies. One study tests regeneration funds allocated to urban areas (John, Ward, and Dowding 2004). This study found that some of the areas received more funds because ministers had constituencies located there. In terms of delegation this means that civil servants based in government regional offices are able to reflect these political criteria in the communities that make successful bids. Another example is the allocation of grants to the Towns Fund, a scheme to benefit smaller urban centres set up in the summer of 2019. Hanretty (2021) analysed the data, comparing decisions for the Town Deals scheme with whether they met the criteria set by civil servants, finding that Conservative-held and marginal sets got the schemes more than other areas. The study does show the power of ministers over civil servants given how the decisions were different to the official criteria.

8.6.4 **Distributive politics and delegated agencies**

The same kinds of relationship can be found with agencies that are at arm's length, as these bodies still report to central government departments under the indirect control of the minister. Bertelli et al. (2014) looked at Arts Council grants designed to fund bodies such as theories or community arts, or opera. Looking at Grants for the Arts (GFA) in the UK between 2003 and 2006, and using statistical regression techniques, they find that local authorities with swing voters for the governing party in Westminster received more grants than did local authorities with their core supporters.

Politically, manipulation can affect other kinds of benefit that public authorities receive, such as officially measured performance scores. These scores are allocated by independent bodies at arm's length from government once again, suggesting impartiality and clean hands on the part of government. Bertelli and John (2010), however, find that local authorities got better performance scores from the former Audit Commission if they were in swing seats, and with authorities that shared the same partisan stripe as central governments. But some politics were also local as the political representatives on the commission were able to return resources back to their local authorities. As well as the central party getting advantages, this form of delegation allows more local representation to skew resources as in the traditional pork barrel.

8.6.5 Agency reorganization

The other way politics enters into the management of delegation is how these agencies are organized and run. Bertelli and Sinclair (2018) evaluate this argument in the context of a recent mass administrative reorganization by the British coalition government using statistical regression models. Their evidence suggests that termination is less likely for agencies salient in newspapers popular with the government's core supporters, but not those read by its minority coalition partner. Overall, media salience and the public information it creates matters in the government's decisions about agencies.

James et al. (2016) evaluate expectations of increased risk to agencies following transitions in government, prime minister, or departmental minister, and from the effect of a new political executive. Using evidence from executive agencies, they find that politics is more important than performance. Ministers seek to terminate agencies created by previous ministers, an effect that is reinforced by high media attention to the agency. Performance against agency targets is not associated with higher termination risk, and replacement agencies do not perform any better than those that were terminated. Overall, these studies show that executive politics is an important feature of administration of government policies, even over technical matters such as public finance decisions and the structure of agencies.

8.7 Conclusion

Politics is integral to bureaucracy, otherwise much that happens in the civil service could not be explained. Politicians drive the civil service and seek to realize their political objectives from it. Bureaucracy in Britain responds to this need by delivering policies the government and prime minister want. Civil service influence and power is exercised at the margin, concerned with managerial matters, and is expressed through the culture and operating assumptions the people and organizations have rather than in direct policy choices. While the will of the central executive is respected, there is much that goes on beyond the spectrum of the central gaze (which comes more into view in Chapter 9). When government is divided, these politicians and civil servant roles become more complicated. The civil service is also caught up in more general trends in politics which point to more divided governments and rebellious backbenchers, which means the system is harder to administer in such an impartial way as before. Add to that the complexity of government in the multi-country UK, with different policies being made at different levels of government. Capacity issues are part of the modern challenge to produce public policies that are fit for purpose that do not have fiascos and blunders inscribed into their design. These policy errors come from the fast-moving nature of politics, the impossible demands of politicians, and the in capacity of the government machine to produce well-crafted policies.

Further reading

One account of how the civil service works is Rod Rhodes' *Everyday Life in British Government* (2011), which has a lot of descriptive material. Offering a perspective of regrettable decline of the Whitehall machine is an incisive book by Christopher Foster (2005). For more specialist reading, there is the book by Hood and Dixon on the New Public Management reforms (2015). The more modern digital argument about civil service is contained in various publications by Dunleavy and Margetts (Dunleavy et al. 2006). For delegated governance, see Flinders (2008). The work on blame shifting is represented in the work of Christopher Hood (2010; see also Wood 2019).

Essay and examination questions

The classic civil service power question can be just 'How powerful is the civil service today?', or, with the principal–agent frame, 'To what extent does the principal–agent model explain the relationship between civil servants and ministers in Britain?' Other questions could be about the impact of the reform of the civil service to improve capacity, such as 'How effective is the reform of the civil service?' or the impact of New Public Management. More directly, it is possible to ask, 'Is the civil service to be blamed for policy blunders in Britain?', for which the reading by King and Crewe (2014) is the starting point, but could be followed up by their case studies, and the Covid-19 crisis as publications start to come out (e.g. Gaskell et al. 2020). A question about delegation could take the form, 'How can central government realize its political objectives and at the same time delegate responsibilities to agencies and local authorities?'.

Access the online resources for this chapter, including biannual updates, web links, and multiple-choice questions: www.oup.com/he/John1e

Chapter 9

Governing from Below

9.1 What is going to be in this chapter?

This chapter is the third of the four chapters covering the key aspects of delegation in British politics: the topic of decentralization and local/national self-government. After looking at some general principles, this chapter deals with local government in England, and government in the devolved territories/nations of Scotland, Wales, and Northern Ireland. The question of the rationale and general stability of the system is considered, with respect to the integrity of the UK as a whole.

9.2 Introduction

9.2.1 The complexity of decentralization

A lot about decentralization has already appeared in this book, such as in Chapter 8 on agencies and implementation, and also in how local representation features in parliamentary behaviour in Chapter 3. These examples illustrate how local issues and differences across a territory become important features of national politics. Then there are locally elected authorities, charged with running local services, arranged at various spatial scales, such as counties, cities, or even villages. These varied institutions of local/subnational governance and their allied agencies are closely intertwined with the central state and its organizations, as much of local government implements centrally authorized policies as well as making decisions of its own. Such interchanges mean that it is hard to separate out the two realms. National leaders have to struggle with achieving policy solutions that work for local people. In turn, some locally based politicians are also powerful, from which they seek to extract benefits, such as favourable distributions of resources and policies to deliver to their local constituencies and local areas they represent. In any case, the centre is fragmented into different parts, each of which is dealing with separate subcentral matters, such as the Treasury deciding the funding of infrastructure projects or the Department for Business, Energy and Industrial Strategy allocating energy efficiency projects based in local areas. At the same time, decentralized politics is split up into local authorities at different territorial levels, and even within local authorities as between service divisions. Moreover, there are higher-level subnational governments, such as at the regional/national level like the Scottish government; and then a range of non-elected agencies with a subnational remit, such as Local Enterprise Partnerships (LEPs) that interact with local government and Whitehall departments. Figure 9.1 is a simplified representation of this structure, just covering the elected authorities. UK Parliament is at the top, with powers delegated to the devolved territories of Scotland, Wales, and Northern Ireland, then each delegating power to local authorities, and also to a range of non-elected agencies. English local authorities sit

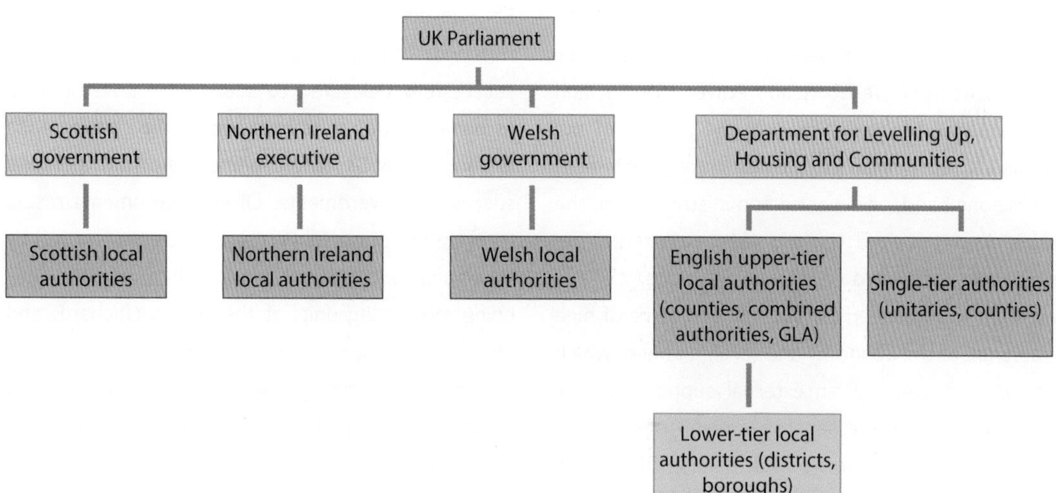

Figure 9.1 Elected governments in the UK.

9

under the government department responsible for local government (in practice also reporting to a range of other departments, such as Treasury, Transport, and so on). The lines in the figure should not be taken to mean that the higher level directs the lower as each are democratically elected and have autonomy. Powers are delegated, however, and could in theory be taken back by the UK Parliament.

9.2.2 Bulpitt's *Territory and Power*

Scholars have outlined frameworks of what is called intergovernmental or central–local relations (Rhodes 1988). These devices try to offer ways to get to grips with decentralization, usually based on understanding the levels of resources and powers of each level of governance, in particular between locally elected authorities and central government departments. Transactions between centre and locality are seen as exchanges of information and requests, with various elements of sanction—laws and finance at the central end, and experience and expertise on the subnational side. Scholars have come to believe it is better to examine the different tiers of governance together within the same framework, which can help explain subnational and national politics simultaneously.

One framework for examining this was set out by Jim Bulpitt in his *Territory and Power* (1983), and this is useful for understanding the politics of the whole UK rather than just English local government on the one hand, or devolved administrations on the other. He conceived the problem of decentralization as an expression of the central strategy of the UK state with its need to focus on problems of high statecraft of the economy and foreign affairs, which amounts to creating 'an external support system' that delivers concrete benefits in terms of economic opportunities and soft power, helping the central state realize its interests domestically, such as by getting an incumbent party re-elected. Other matters, such as running public services, were deemed less important. With such a detached strategy, central state actors aim to placate local and regional elites and satisfy their demands for degrees of autonomy. There was a decentralization of institutions in a series of separate and varied public bodies with different jurisdictions. This system was not organized in a systematic way, but was differentiated, reflecting local traditions. It was also modified continually out of expediency. As a result, the UK had a variegated pattern of decentralization, with much power exercised by a range of subnational authorities and their associated elites. It was done pragmatically, whereby the UK government used its legal power to transfer authority to other public authorities. And even though much has changed since Bulpitt wrote the book, not least the importance of public services for the central state, the argument is that the framework gives a lot of insight into the practice of decentralization. Zoom-In 9.1 gives a summary.

9.2.3 Stability or instability?

Bulpitt's framework, which stresses pragmatism and accommodation, would seem to point to stability. But, in fact, the seeds of instability are embedded within it. For one, governments started to worry about the performance of the very public services that have been successfully delegated to subnational governments, as dissatisfaction puts pressure on the centre (such as through PMQs) and can impinge on the electoral success of governments. Often governments resort to using the powerful weapons of central control by regulating more (Hood et al. 1999), and strengthening monitoring units at the centre (Richards and Smith 2006); but these initiatives can be done too quickly, without being based on local knowledge and experience of implementation, leading to policy failures and loss of reputation, such as policy disasters (see sections 1.4.7 and 11.3.4); then governments turn to decentralization once again to try to diffuse

Zoom-In 9.1 Bulpitt's framework for understanding British statecraft

This is about the political code and statecraft that helped govern the territories of the United Kingdom during the twentieth century, characterized by informal brokerage and the reluctance of the centre to deal with the detail of decentralized administration.

Key concepts:

- Territorial politics (the complex arena across the whole UK for the interplay of elites, interests, and values)
- Centre and periphery: the centre is the concentration of political interests, identity, and power occurring primarily in the capital, London, where the political and administrative elites had control over the levers of power; the periphery is the rest of the country
- High and low politics: high means matters of state, international policy, and the economy; low is about administration and public services. Assumed to be separated
- Dual polity: separation of high and low politics
- Official mind: the centre's sets of values and assumptions
- Statecraft: the practice of governing the dual polity, by careful and pragmatic balancing of the external support system and internal demands, including party advantage
- External support system: system of international relations and economic trading relations that satisfy demands of domestic politics

Further reading: *John (2008, introduction).*

the controversy. Overall, the strategy of offloading creates weaknesses in the resolve of the centre and limits its resources, encourages a lack of coherence in the system, and emboldens local elites to make further demands. In other words, Bulpitt's framework describes and offers understanding of the unstable pattern of governance that exists currently, whereby the UK's structure can fall apart from the very system of central–local tensions the central state has created and fostered. This framework, in which central elites set out their broad objectives, but in actual fact lack strong means of control when it comes to the detailed matters in the periphery, is a good way to understand how decentralized politics works, and shows how the inconsistencies of the political settlement of central–local relations feed back into the crisis of the nation state as a whole. Using the insights of Bulpitt's framework, it is possible to understand how the institutions work, such as local authorities and national government, and how the delivery of policies operates in this framework, some of which will be conveyed in section 9.3, but also by approaches to making policy in this highly complicated interdependent system, where policy errors and miscommunication are just as likely as policy successes and mutual accommodation.

9.2.4 Decentralization vs. centralization?

In some accounts, stretching back to J. S. Mill (1861, chapter XV), more decentralization and local autonomy are seen as beneficial in delivering better and more innovative public services and as a counter to the costs of ill-thought-out centralization. In other words, the tendency towards policy errors and blunders could be laid at the door of a central state that makes too hasty decisions and does not take advantage of local knowledge (Gaskell et al. 2020); but other accounts argue that more decentralization can create more confusion, the inefficient representation of regional interests, lack of planning and coordination, loss of efficiency, and even corruption (Prud'homme 1995). Unfortunately, the international evidence does not show whether more centralized or decentralized systems are better at making policy and deliver more effective outcomes as both can work in different places and contexts (Treisman 2007).

Alongside this debate about the advantages of decentralization runs the classic theme of representation and democratic responsiveness, which takes a different form because they are tied to different territorial spaces and their interests, whereas at the central level, there is an attempt to cohere these local interests into a central state strategy. Such variation justifies the normative ideal of local democratic autonomy: the desirability of local choices within the nation state even if they are not necessarily the right ones to make (Sharpe 1970). To this end, local government councillors and executives are elected by local people with their own interests and values. Local leaders and mayors try to forge strategies for their areas (which are composed of even smaller jurisdictions, such as local wards and villages), which in turn feeds into the pattern of representation as a whole. Then there is Scotland and Wales, where such autonomy has been forged more intently in recent years as power, finance, and functions have been transferred from the UK level very rapidly.

9.3 Basic facts: governing from below

9.3.1 Constitutional position of subcentral government

The starting point, as ever in British politics, is the question of a government's power to decide how other institutions operate and whether they are in existence or not. In countries with codified constitutions, such as Germany, territorial units of the state have constitutional protection. Moreover, states are usually represented in the second chamber of the legislature, a senate for added representation and legitimacy. State (and even local government) rights may be protected by a constitutional court, which does not exist in the same way in the UK. Local units, such as local government, or even the Scottish Parliament, owe their existence to statute as approved by the UK Parliament, which can be modified or taken away by a law of Parliament.

Subcentral government is a form of delegation of power, which corresponds to other kinds of delegation, such as to executive agencies, but does not give these bodies a permanent democratic mandate and sense of legitimacy, which might be expected from the election of politicians to run them as in Westminster. So, is local government no more than an agency set up by central government to deliver services? To avoid answering yes to that question, there was an attempt by academic lawyers to locate a protection of local government in a constitutional convention (Elliott 1981), which could even be recognized by the courts when interpreting statutory powers. As with other conventions not connected to the prerogative, it only exists as a loose commitment by political actors, which is easily overridden by political imperatives (Loughlin 1996). Scotland might be different. McLean (2010) argues that the Act of Union 1707 and its associated jurisprudence created a constitutional union of the two nations, qualifying whether Britain is a unitary state and in effect creating a union state. In the end, Parliament could amend the Act of Union, if it so pleased, but that is unlikely; nor will it repeal the legislation that sets up the Scottish Parlia-

Key term 9.1 Unitary state

A state where power is concentrated in one executive and not decentralized as in a federal constitution with extensive separation of power (see Key term 3.2). It is possible to refer to the *union* state to reflect the division of powers between Scotland and the rest of the UK.

ment. In that sense, devolution of powers in Scotland (and Wales) is entrenched in the political system, much like a constitutional convention. More specifically, the Sewel convention of 1998 says that when the UK Parliament wants to legislate on a matter within the devolved competence of the Scottish Parliament, Senedd Cymru/Welsh Parliament, or Northern Ireland Assembly, it will 'not normally' do so without the relevant devolved institution having passed a legislative consent motion. Even though the convention can be bypassed (as happened with the trade deal at the end of Brexit, and the government's single market legislative proposal in 2020), such breaches are rare.

9.3.2 **Basic features of English local government**

With English local government, an Act of Parliament sets up the kind of authority in operation in a particular area, which has a constitution, such as elections for local councillors, and a means for conducting business in the chamber of the council, and concentrated in the executive body. There are various types of local authority depending on where someone lives. In many areas there are county councils (twenty-six) which are large bodies that cover cities and rural areas (see Table 9.1), running the main subnational services, such as education, social care, transport, strategic planning, and economic development. The tier below counties is the non-metropolitan districts (192) that have a limited range of functions such as housing, waste collection, licensing, local planning, and local parks and amenities. In some of these areas outside the main metropolitan spaces, there are unitary authorities that have all the functions of the districts and counties (these emerged in the 1990s in a half-completed reform, which makes a complicated system even more so). The move to unitary councils is ongoing; for example, there is a consultation happening in Somerset to create a unitary council from the county and the districts. Then in urban areas, there are single-tier authorities: the metropolitan boroughs, much like the unitary authorities, with seven in Greater Manchester, five in Merseyside, four in South Yorkshire, five in Tyne and Wear, seven in the West Midlands, and five in West Yorkshire. There are thirty-two of these kinds of authorities in London, called the London boroughs, to which is added the City of London authority, which has an unusual set-up and arrangement for elections, though is still basically a local authority.

Some metropolitan areas are even more complicated as they have their own elected authorities. In London there is the Greater London Authority (GLA), which is an elected assembly with executive powers with a separate directly elected mayor, who reports to the assembly which has a scrutiny function and approves the budget. The mayor and GLA are responsible for policing, fire, transport, strategic planning matters, and various capacity building and promotion functions. Other areas have their own mayors, such as Cambridgeshire and Peterborough Combined Authority and the Greater Manchester Combined Authority. These new mayors have become prominent national figures, particularly as some already had a national stature before they stood for office, such as Andy Burnham, mayor of Greater Manchester in 2021, who was an MP and in Labour's shadow cabinet. For details of local governments' electoral systems, pattern of elections, and party competition, see section 5.3.3.

Photo 9.1 City Hall, the headquarters of the Greater London Authority (GLA), which comprises the Mayor of London and the London Assembly.

Table 9.1 The structure of English local government

Type of authority	Number
Two-tier	
County councils	26
District councils	192
Single-tier	
Unitary authorities	55
Metropolitan districts	36
London boroughs	32
City of London	1
Isles of Scilly	1
Total	343

Leadership in local government is either chosen locally to be a directly elected mayor by referendum, or by default a leader and cabinet (Gains, John, and Stoker 2005). Most are run by leader and cabinets. In 2021, there were only fifteen councils that had elected mayors, such as Liverpool City Council and Watford Borough Council. Finally, there is the lowest level of governance, the parish or town council, which is a form of direct democracy (see Key term 4.14) in operation outside the main metropolitan areas (though in practice having limited participation from residents: see Ryan et al. 2018). There are 10,472 parishes in England, mainly responsible for local amenities and minor planning matters. Successive governments have been encouraging community participation, such as through parishes, as implemented by the Localism Act 2011.

Local authorities can set a local tax, a property tax called the council tax, but this does not pay for all local services, only about a half at present, so there is a central grant allocated to local authorities based on a formula. Local government spending was about £98 billion in 2020/2021, about 10 per cent of total public expenditure. In 2021, the government looked to remove or reduce central government's share, and replace it with distributing non-domestic tax rates. This would be a change to the current system, to limit the central grant and rely on re-distributing non-domestic rates, but it is hard to implement.

9.3.3 Wales

Wales is a nation in the United Kingdom. With the English controlling some of its territory since Norman times, it was conquered in 1272, then put under common legal and administrative arrangements under a formal Act of Union in 1536. It has a population of 3.1 million and is about 20,800 square km in area. It has always had a distinct identity and culture, reinforced by the Welsh language (Cymraeg), spoken currently by about 20 per cent of the population, which is now an official language in official information and public dialogue, and a core part of much education provision. Since the nineteenth century, there has been a gradual development of modern Welsh-only institutions, such as the Church in Wales (the version of the Anglican church), many sports bodies, the Welsh National Opera, the Welsh national flag, and the University of Wales (a loose structure over and above some of the universities in Wales). In recent years, these kinds of institutions have been increasing in number and growing in importance, such as the Welsh-language channel, S4C, and many institutions created by the Welsh government.

Before devolution, most decisions about Wales were taken in Whitehall, with identical or very similar legislation to that in England. In 1965, a government office for Wales was set up headed by a Secretary of State for Wales, which showed the importance of administrative devolution at that time. Political devolution happened in 1999 after a narrowly won referendum in 1997, which led to the creation of the National Assembly for Wales (now Senedd Cymru), which over time gradually acquired responsibilities and law-making powers. The Parliament gained primary law-making powers following the second 2011 referendum, and some tax powers under the 2014 Wales Act. Under the Wales Act 2017 the Senedd can make laws on matters not reserved to the UK Parliament.

Photo 9.2 The Pierhead and the Senedd building in Cardiff Bay.

Sections 5.3.2 and 5.3.3 contain details about the parties and electoral systems in Wales. Out of the assembly emerges a government with a majority or the ability to get a majority in coalition. The assembly nominates the first minister of Wales; in 2021 this was Mark Drakeford. The first minister then appoints the other ministers, some of whom sit in the cabinet. There is a system of local government, twenty-two single-tier areas, with functions much like English local authorities, such as over waste collection and disposal, housing, planning, licensing, and local amenities.

9.3.4 Northern Ireland

Northern Ireland is a part of the United Kingdom located on the island of Ireland, with a population of 1.8 million. It is 14,130 square kilometres in size. Its history goes back to the 1921 partition of Ireland, after the Curragh army mutiny of 1914, where it was clear the army could not be used to keep Protestant communities in check, which led to the setting up of the separate territory with its own governance, the former Stormont Parliament, which was in existence from 1921–72. It had law-making powers as a devolved government, and a majoritarian electoral system that ensured power was held by the Protestant majority, which reinforced widespread discrimination against Catholics in the job market, and for public resources such as housing, as well as unfair treatment by the public services personnel, such as the police. After civil rights protests during the 1960s and then a violent campaign by the terrorist group the Irish Republican Army (IRA), direct rule was instituted in 1972. In spite of experiments in bringing the communities together, it lasted until the Good Friday agreement of 1998, which created the current power-sharing arrangements.

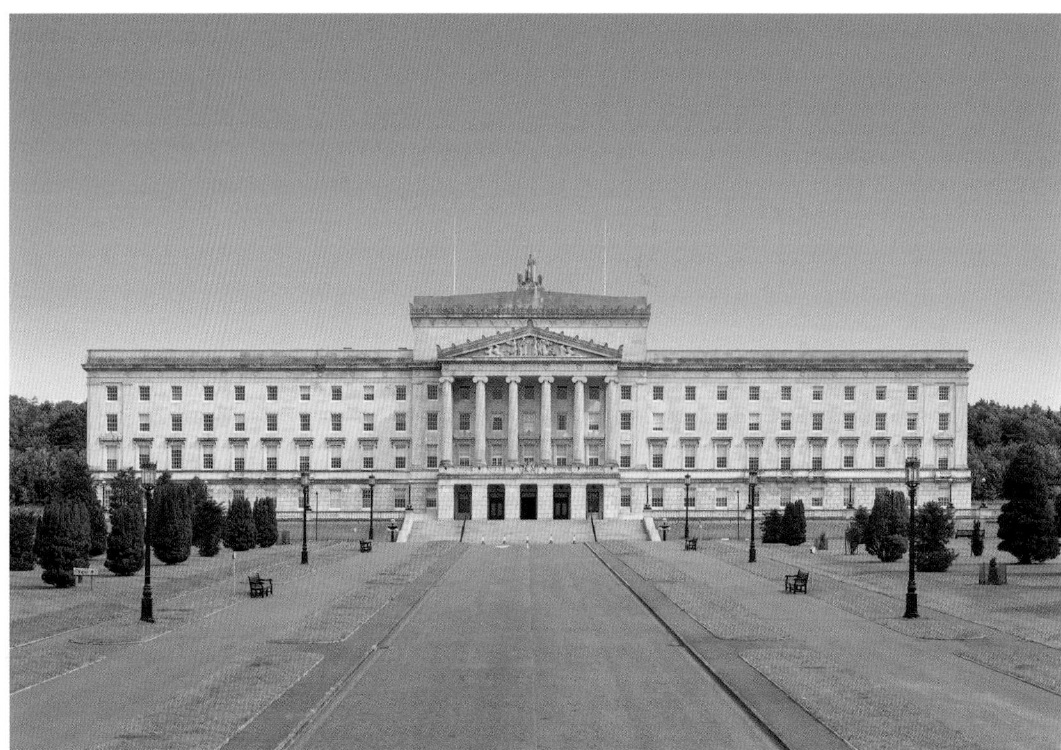

Photo 9.3 Northern Ireland Parliament and Government building in Stormont, Belfast.

The Northern Ireland Assembly is composed of ninety Members of the Legislative Assembly (MLAs). The Northern Irish Assembly nominates the Northern Ireland executive, which is responsible for most policy areas except reserved matters. Joint decision-making is inscribed into the constitutional arrangements, with the first minister and deputy first minister nominated as respectively the leaders of the largest and second largest groups or blocks in the assembly. Under the Belfast Agreement both blocs had to endorse the candidates for both posts, but under the 2006 St Andrews Agreement the largest party in the largest designation nominates the first minister even if the rest of that designation/bloc does not like the choice. The largest party in the second largest designation nominates the deputy first minister, with the same proviso. Ministers of the executive, except for the minister of justice, are nominated by the political parties in the assembly. The number of ministers a party can nominate is determined by its share of seats in the assembly. The executive takes decisions on policy in devolved responsibilities in Northern Ireland. Some functions are the subject of joint decision-making by members of the Northern Ireland executive in the North/South Ministerial Council (NSMC). The NSMC is a forum for Irish-Northern Irish consultation and co-operation, where they can come to agreed co-ordination on some issues across the island of Ireland if they wish to. Below the assembly, there is the system of local government, with eleven local councils, having a much more limited range of functions than in the rest of the UK.

9.3.5 Scotland

Scotland was an independent country up to the Act of Union in 1707, though it had shared a monarch with England since 1603. It has a population of just under 5.3 million and is 77,933 square kilometres in size. In the period since union, it retained its separate legal system, such as for criminal law, and many separate

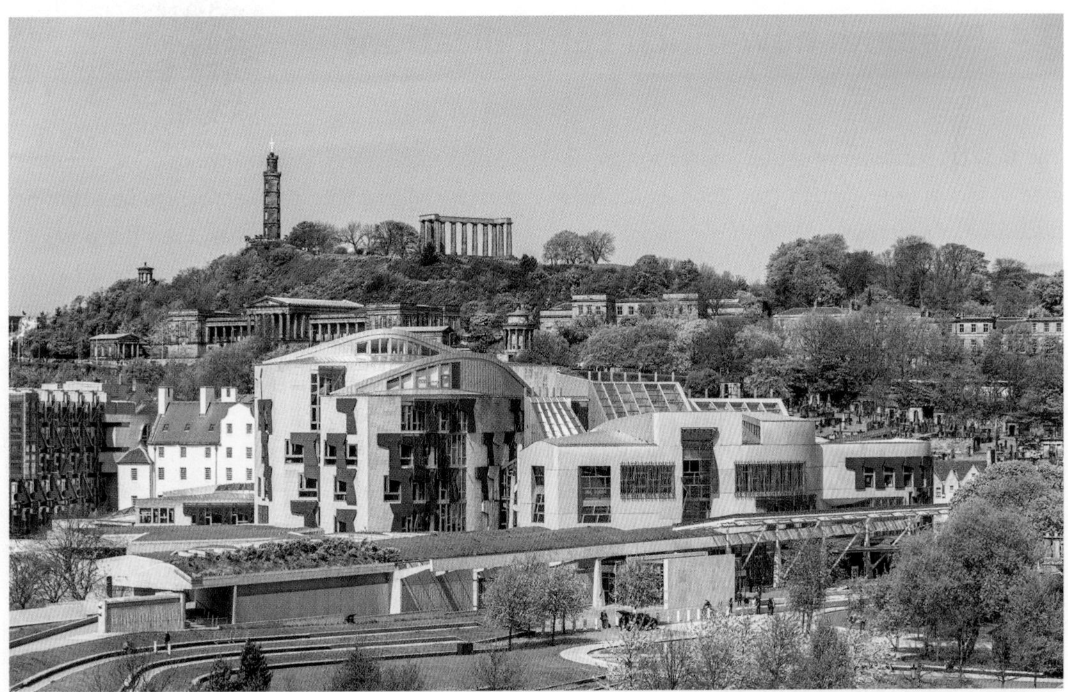

Photo 9.4 New Parliament House under Calton Hill, Edinburgh, Scotland. The site of the Scottish Parliament.

Scottish institutions carried on in existence as central to Scottish life, including religious bodies, the education system, and award of qualifications, making Scotland always more autonomous than Wales. A separate government department, the Scottish Office, was set up in 1885, with a Secretary of State, long before the Welsh equivalent. The Scottish Office had a Secretary of State of cabinet rank since the 1920s. The Scottish language of Gaelic is spoken by a small minority, about 1–2 per cent of the population, which might be seen to reduce Scottish separateness, but it means that nationalism is not associated so much with language as it is in Wales.

After a referendum was decisively won in 1997, a separate Scottish Parliament was set up in 1999 (see sections 5.3.2 and 5.3.3 for details about the party and electoral system). Over time the Scottish Parliament acquired more powers from Westminster. The Scotland Act 2012 provided a transfer of financial powers from Westminster, expanding the income tax-varying power to plus or minus 10p in the pound, and added a list of new legislative powers devolved from Westminster. Then the Scotland Act of 2016 devolved significant areas such as onshore oil and gas extraction, rail franchising, consumer advocacy and advice, and control over certain and removable taxes including Air Passenger Duty, and full control over Scottish income tax including income tax rates. In 2016, there was devolution of some social security connected to policy areas like housing/social care that were already non-reserved, leaving most of the welfare state/social security system at UK level, and unreserved eight specific social security benefits. Out of its £21.3 billion budget, about half is raised in Scotland.

The Parliament, made up of 129 members, nominates the first minister, who then appoints other ministers, including those in the cabinet, which runs the Scottish government, the executive body. The government supervises a structure of thirty-two councils.

9.4 England: how much centralization?

The British constitutional set-up implies a high degree of formal centralization (see Zoom-In 9.2 for a discussion of centralization). With law-making firmly placed in Westminster in England, with many delegated powers in the direct hands of ministers, and financial control subject to Treasury supervision in terms of the central grants and other kinds of expenditures, such as capital grants, there appears to be a tight degree of control from Whitehall. Even the power of general competence which local government has had since the Localism Act of 2011 does not get around the basic legal framework of central authorization.

Zoom-In 9.2 Centralization and decentralization

Centralization refers to the exercise of power and control by government at one territorial level over another, and more generally to the extent to which decisions and routines (even culture and media) are always routed through the UK nation state level rather than at subnational levels. Decentralization captures the opposite: the extent to which power is exercised outside the central state.

But centralization can co-exist with extensive delegation of powers to public authorities, as Parliament can choose to hand over powers to other bodies. This is consistent with the Bulpittian notions set out in section 9.2.2, reflecting a governing style that implies the offloading to other bodies of functions that the centre does not really want to administer. Given democratic control at the local level through parties and party organizations, and that in the past at least much of British law gave local authorities powers to do things rather than prescribe deeply, a high degree of practical decentralization emerged, where local authorities were trusted to get on with the job without very much central interference. Even though there have been many complaints about centralization going back to the 1930s (Robson 1933), this pragmatic form of decentralization over many spheres of policy-making and implementation was the norm (Griffith 1966), existing up to the 1980s, and continues in many sectors of activity away from the public glare.

The other perspective behind the decentralization argument is more practical: the sheer complexity of policy-making and implementation beyond the centre with the range of agencies and then interest groups and professional associations, each of which has some expertise and legitimacy to administer public services. Central departments could not control the whole system even if they would like to, as they do not have the capacity to do this in terms of central intelligence, personnel, and amount of time they have available, especially when spending so much time dealing with day-to-day crises. It is better to delegate and let the system to a certain extent govern itself, with central government steering from the top, and where local authorities have the experience and local knowledge to make most decisions. If things go wrong, government can seek to shift blame onto these organizations (Hood 2010). In practice, central government does sometimes want to exercise its levers over policy sectors, especially when a topic is politically contentious and highlighted in the media. Then commands will be issued and finance is made available. But the eye of the centre might then quickly move on to other crises and leave the local actors to get on with the job and to pick up the pieces.

Usually, these exercises in centralization go wrong and show the costs of intervention, even leading to 'policy messes' (Rhodes 1988) or disasters, and a lack of easy solutions rather than effective control. The centre can easily overreach itself. One example is local economic policies, where there have been successive attempts to take over policies run by local authorities, only for these powers to be returned again (see Pike and Tomaney 2009), such as with 'city deals' (Jones et al. 2017), then metro mayors (Deas 2014). The role of central government in the Covid-19 crisis is a neat example of the politics of centralization in England (see Case Study 9.1).

9.4.1 Academic studies of central–local politics

The theme of practical or pragmatic decentralization emerges in many academic accounts of central–local relations, such as Rhodes' work (1988), and of communities of decision-makers deciding matters away from the gaze of Whitehall (e.g. Jordan and Cairney 2013). This bottom-up perspective also appears in John's (2014) 'great survivor' metaphor of local government resilience and persistence of local government. Local government has retained much the same structure and functions and framework for political management over many decades of central initiative and reform, and is able to 'survive' the implantation of alternative forms of centrally directed administration in localities, such as local quangos or public bodies. Local government ends up as the trusted and go-to actor. Instead of rolling over, local authorities often find new things to focus on like they did for environment policy, economic policy, and police monitoring (Atkinson and Wilks-Heeg 2000). In the end, local government is regarded by central government as an effective way to decentralize functions. The essentially pragmatic culture within local government is reinforced in an equilibrium trap. The system stays in place, but does not prevent central interventions and its ability to constrain locally autonomous decision-making.

The counter to these arguments about decentralization is that there are pressures for central government to impose stricter controls over local government so the relatively permissive framework of delegation gets interrupted by the centre, which in the end can use its superior resources to enforce change over the long term, especially if the centre is unified over an issue. This happened under the governments led by Margaret Thatcher when local government became controlled by more radical Labour parties and the centre by a reforming right-wing government (Gyford 1985), but were largely defeated because of sustained use of the legal powers of central government (John 1994). Government can introduce performance management over all local authority services, while not subjecting central government departments to such controls (see Hood et al. 1999). In the austerity cuts of the 2010s, local government was expected to reduce capital and revenue expenditure by a far higher amount than other parts of the public sector, cuts of about 30 per cent (Lowndes and McCaughie 2013, 534), creating a huge challenge in managing the cuts (Eckersley and Tobin 2019).

The centralization–decentralization debate can be seen to omit key features of intergovernmental relationships in England, which is not so much about sharing policy-making, but more about the general stance of the central institutions and their personnel towards local government. This is highly embedded in elite culture in London, in that local government is seen as inferior, and that central ways of doing business are thought to be superior. This is the idea that there is an embedded 'cultural disdain' of local government (Greenwood 1981), with widespread distrust and lack of confidence in it (Jones and Travers 1994), as shown over Covid-19 (see Case Study 9.1).

9.5 Community power and local policy choices

A key question for local politics is the way in which a degree of local autonomy intersects with local power relationships. This is an important general question for any democratic organization as it is for British central government, in its relation to interest groups like business, for example, or the way certain groups are important within political parties and use them to get to power. But there are special reasons for wanting to consider the issue of who governs at the local level, which is partly to do with the fragmentation of local government in how local politics intersect with the powerful forces in society, changes in the focus of public opinion, and controversies in public policy. Local government is likely to be the middle site of intense local conflicts about resources and over culture, which makes it a cauldron for new ideas and where new groups can exercise power in Britain today. With these features, local government can become a centre for innovation, policies, and new management practices that can spread across a territory through the natural tendency of diffusion across jurisdictions (Gilardi 2010), especially at the subnational level (Brannan et al. 2008). It allows the observer to take the temperature of the body politic: to work out who has power and how power is used or not used for the common good. In this way, the study of local politics allows understanding of how British politics is evolving in response to changing social and

Case Study 9.1 Local government and the Covid-19 crisis

During the Covid-19 pandemic, the government often did not want to use local authorities as the means to implement its public health policies, often relying on private companies, such as the track and trace scheme (Gaskell and Stoker 2020). The government centralized power over public health through the agency, Public Health England, not using local authorities, which have established public health departments and could have been used to organize local test and trace, using their local knowledge (see case study of Leicester: Gill, Sridhar, and Godlee 2020). Then the government decided to involve local authorities later on, which seemed to get the 'worst of all worlds': inefficiency and ill-thought-out centralization, then the humiliation of having to change its mind afterwards (Calvert and Arbuthnott 2021, chapter 12). The relative failure of the early Covid-19 initiatives is put down to this lack of trust in local government.

Photo 9.5 The United Kingdom's NHS Covid-19 app and other contact tracing apps.

economic conditions, such as local representation of ethnic minorities. Policy-making is experienced on the front line in some respects and in different parts of the complex geography of the UK. With this intensity and variety of experiences from local areas, it is possible to see how local government and other local institutions can innovate to create better policies and institutional structures.

In spite of its experience of the front line, studies of local decision-making, particularly in cities such as

Birmingham (Newton 1976), show that decision-making in local areas remains closed within party groups in partnership with the professional cadres of officials and bureaucrats, with only certain interest groups allowed in—a version of the insider and outsider categories covered in section 7.4.4. This tends to limit the representative function of local government, and makes it vulnerable to capture by narrow policy-making coalitions, such as between planners and the private sector (Dunleavy 1981), such as shown over the causes of the Grenfell Tower fire (see Case Study 9.3). These studies uncovered the institutionalization of power within local government, which make community involvement and decentralization of power hard to achieve.

This theme of local closure comes out of the debates about leadership, with studies of local councillors replicating this closed form of decision-making (Copus 2004). Ironically, given the narrative of centralization and local innovation, it was central government who initiated reform of local government leadership, starting from the efforts of the flamboyant centrist-Conservative politician Michael Heseltine in the 1990s, then reforms to leadership promoted by New Labour, which introduced elected mayors into local government (see section 9.3.2). Then central government discovered that wider forms of territory than local government areas were a better centre for leadership: hence metro mayors. The introduction of metro mayors has created a cadre of leaders who can powerfully articulate local interests, linked to party, but also representing local areas (Gains 2015). As well as advantages in delivering leadership, there are only weak accountability mechanisms in place to hold these mayors to account (Terry 2017).

9.5.1 Some local autonomy after all?

The stereotype of local party and bureaucratic control can be overplayed. In most cities there has been a subtle interplay between interest groups, parties, bureaucrats, and communities with balancing actors between these elements, and where community representation comes through even if imperfectly. In a study of the impact of the London riots of 2011, Leon and John (2020) examine how voters punished the Conservative incumbents at the GLA election of 2012, in effect showing how white voters were able to express sympathy for the rioters in voter turnout and vote choice, showing accountability mechanisms at work.

There has been a revival of community initiatives and citizen participation in many cities, which have sometimes challenged local government leadership or provided alternatives (Durose and Richardson 2015). Local government has experimented with new forms of participation and its evaluation (John et al. 2019), such as citizen assemblies (Doherty et al. 2020) and budgeting exercises in cities such as Salford in Greater Manchester (Röcke 2014). There have been experiments in policy labs and community participation schemes, based on injecting innovation into local public policy (Marvin et al. 2018). There has also been an interest in behavioural public policy initiatives at the local level—nudges tested with randomized controlled trials (John and Blume 2017). In this way, local communities and areas are the places where these upswings in participatory politics can occur, with more traditional institutions like local government both challenged and brought into new debates. Local governments in England are part of a wave of innovations in democratic policy-making in evidence across Europe, such as in Scandinavia (Sørensen and Vabo 2020).

Local issues come to the fore with the concern about places that are 'left behind', seeming to contrast with the prosperity of metropolitan areas. The relative fortunes of small towns came up in the Brexit debate, and where many Brexit voters live. Jennings and Stoker's (2018) research on the 'two Britains' shows increasing polarization based on where people live. With central government financial support, these issues of inequality and deprivation can be addressed by local government, who often represent small towns. Hence, there is the 'levelling-up' agenda, which is being pursued by the Conservative government in 2021, while Labour's towns initiative (labourtowns.co.uk) aims to promote research and debate on this subject.

9.6 Conflict and contest

Acute conflicts and disputes about public policy happen at the local level because of the importance of service delivery and their access to competing social groups, and the presence of the groups and community organizations keen to highlight injustices. In urban areas such issues intersect with the sources of the key divisions in society today based on social class and race, reinforced by inequalities across space and in the consumption of state-funded housing services. In the view of an earlier generation of writers, cities were seen as sites of class conflict between rich and poor (Castells 1978). Given the importance of land in cities and its development, a lot of these conflicts centre on access to land and often the remodelling of public housing estates, as developers seek profits and middle classes want new places to live, or coalitions seek to preserve housing that sustains middle-class communities in urban centres, such as nineteenth-century terraces and squares (like in Islington, London). There were many conflicts in cities over these developments occurring over many decades (Raban 1974). They carry on today as land prices are high in urban areas, creating incentives to use financial instruments from the private sector to regenerate urban estates but inject private sector development with them to make them work financially; what some authors call a financialization of urban governance (Beswick and Penny 2018). But this has not always been seen as in the best interests of local residents (see Case Study 9.2).

Case Study 9.2 The Elephant and Castle redevelopment

The redevelopment of the large estate, Heygate, around the south London road interchanges at Elephant and Castle has seen community groups at loggerheads with the local council. Southwark London Borough Council is seeking to justify the large scheme in terms of social benefits, but has wrestled with the logistics of the financing options. The council claimed, 'From the outset, the council committed to build a series of early affordable housing developments, in and around Elephant and Castle, before any redevelopment of the estate began. This would give many Heygate tenants the opportunity to relocate elsewhere in the neighbourhood (if they wanted to) long before the estate became due for demolition' (see: www.southwark.gov.uk/regeneration/elephant-and-castle?chapter=4). But at the same time, the council gave the development of the scheme to a private company, entering into a financial partnership with it and sharing profits. Huge effort was made to consult over names and the design of the estate, but local communities still felt they had a lack of control over the development and were concerned about the extent of private housing. It remains a controversial scheme with arguments on both sides about the best way to develop the area.

Case Study 9.3 The Grenfell Tower fire

In 14 June 2017 a terrible fire occurred in a public housing tower block in central London, which rapidly got out of control and trapped residents inside, with the fire services struggling to cope and to rescue residents. Seventy-two people died and many others were traumatized, with their lives severely disrupted, facing loss of family, friends, and neighbours. In terms of public policy, there are a large number of issues to resolve, such as the procedures for evacuating high-rise buildings, which are being considered at a public inquiry (www.grenfelltowerinquiry.org.uk).

The dispute illustrates the role of central policy-making for the locality and highlights whether local government should be blamed for policies that led to the kind of cladding on the outside of the building that caused the fire to spread. Under pressure from austerity, the local authority appeared to choose a cheaper cladding which was more combustible than another expensive choice, hence contributing to the severity of the fire (Hodkinson 2019, 2). The attempt by central government to blame the local authority for the incident is only partially true given the complex policy environment, the extent of supervision by the public agencies that regulate cladding materials, and the role of the private sector in carrying out the work.

For some, the fire represents the salience of global capitalism, in how it is expressed at a local and global scale, and the prevalence of neo-liberal values in public policy, which negatively affect poor communities (Danewid 2020). What cannot be doubted is that poor, ethnic-minority citizens were not protected enough, and the incident reveals the inequalities in Britain today.

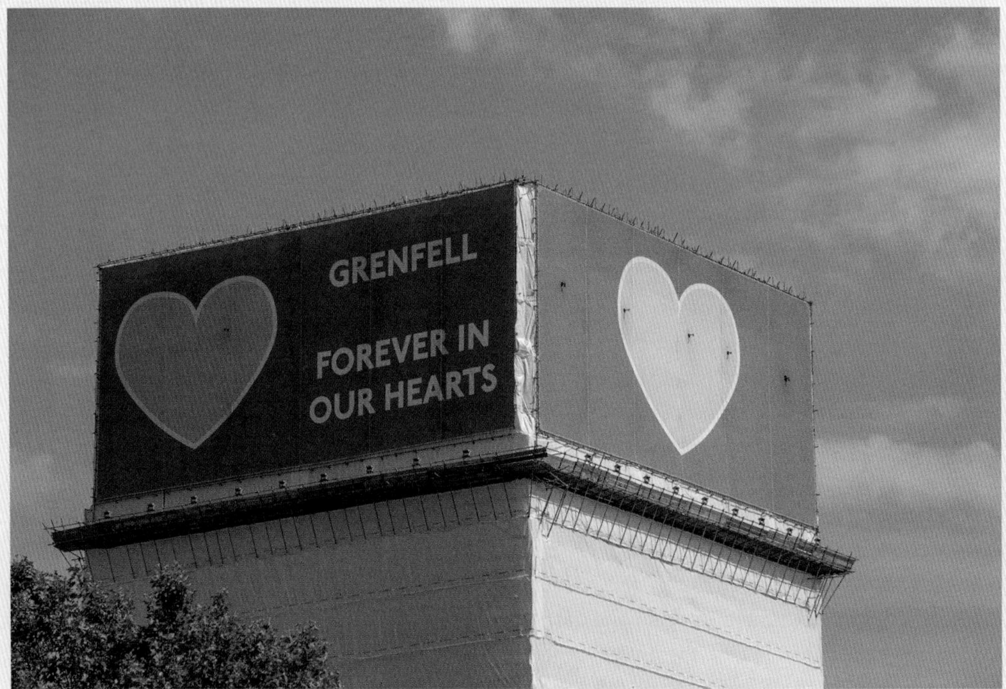

Photo 9.6 'Forever in our hearts' support banner on Grenfell Tower, London.

9

9.7 Territorial politics: towards the breakup of the UK?

English local government covers about 82 per cent of the population living in the UK, but what happens for the other 18 per cent is very different and also different between these territories. The system of devolution is also very important for understanding the whole system of decentralization and policy-making in the UK. Recall in section 9.2.2 that Bulpitt argued that the UK central state was keen to stay detached from territorial politics and wanted to find local elite collaborators to which to hand over decision-making, which is the reason for the complex structure of decentralization, which was the baseline from which devolution was overlaid at the start of the twenty-first century. From this historical continuity, this central strategy is replicated in the pattern of territorial politics happening today. The centre was largely pragmatic in handing over powers to devolved authorities and has sought to manage the system by devolving further powers downwards. As noted in section 1.3.13, the complexity of managing a set of semi-autonomous national governments has altered the national pattern of UK government, such as the executive through joint decision-making across the nations of the UK, and with Parliament having different voting rules depending on the jurisdiction. The changes in voting and party politics effectively create four political systems in the UK, each party competing in different ways, and giving different results for the UK political parties.

9.7.1 Northern Ireland

The Bulpittian framework certainly fits with the UK government's approach to Northern Ireland, where most functions were devolved for much of the twentieth century and the elites governed the province as they saw fit. In the end, the Northern Ireland issue showed the problems of relying on this kind of delegation in that it was not able to keep a lid on the problems of inequality and exclusion. The civil rights movement gained momentum in the 1960s when the strategy of detachment looked increasingly fragile. Yet even then, the UK government did not move to act decisively, until politics took a violent path in the early 1970s before it acted. Then direct rule from London and the period of 'the Troubles' ensued. The lack of any institutional solution at the time and the recurring violence and terrorist acts caused a leading political scientist to conclude 'the problem is that there is no solution' (Rose 1976, 139). The expert on resolving conflicts on divided societies reviewed all the options, declaring known institutional solutions of power-sharing or consociational democracy to be unworkable in Northern Ireland (Lijphart 1975).

In spite of a period of clampdown and even internment in the early 1980s, the modal act of the UK government was still usually accommodation, by finding a new set of elites to talk to. There were early links between the UK government to Sinn Féin and to the IRA, and that direction of travel towards including the Republicans and the Irish government in decision-making. In the medium term, the approach was about getting the Protestant communities and their elites to accept this loss of monopoly control. There were a few periods of reversion, such as in the early 1980s, with the hunger strikes by republican prisoners, such as Bobby Sands, and a crackdown; but over the decades a more normal practice of accommodation led to the Good Friday agreement of 1998 (which was a consociational solution many in the past thought unworkable). This also was paralleled by a change in political strategy from the Republican movement towards relying on electoral politics (Tonge 2006). Protestant communities often believe that the UK government is not

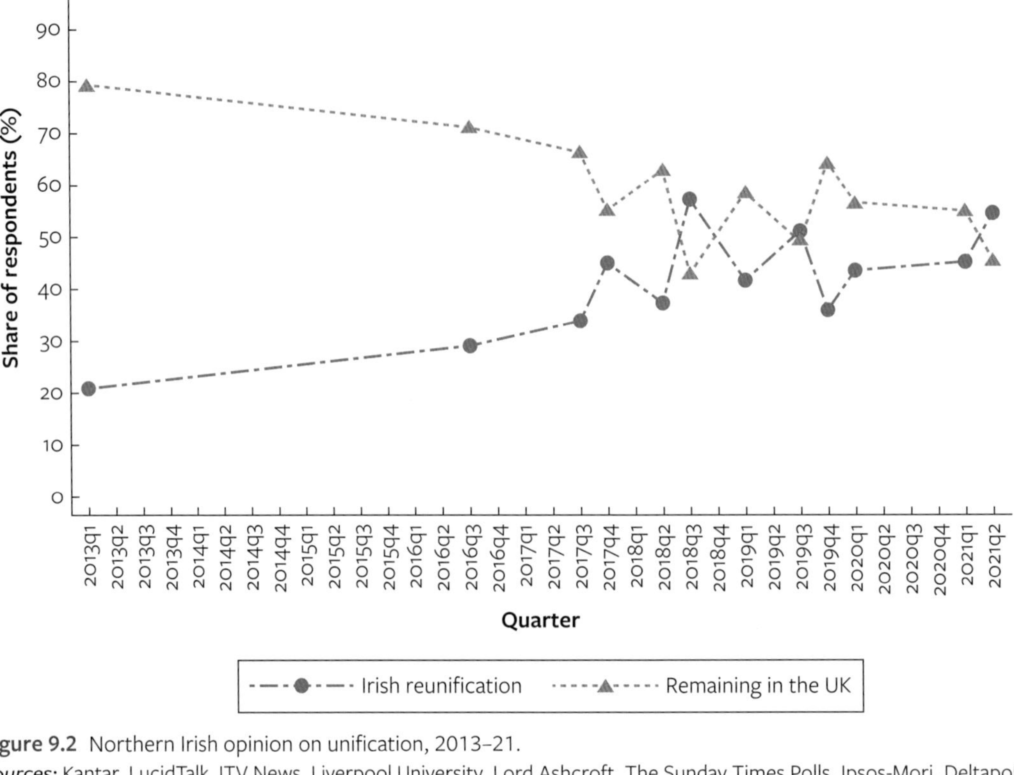

Figure 9.2 Northern Irish opinion on unification, 2013–21.
Sources: Kantar, LucidTalk, ITV News, Liverpool University, Lord Ashcroft, The Sunday Times Polls, Ipsos-Mori, Deltapoll, NILT, YouGov, ICM, ESRC

necessarily committed to keeping Northern Ireland in the union and believe that the territory will be 'sold out', which they think the Good Friday agreement seems to be a sign of, which again shows the cynical nature of the central approach to territorial management. The Withdrawal Agreement from the
9 European Union, signed in 2019, seems to confirm this idea that the UK government is not worried about Northern Ireland being treated differently from the rest of the UK, so there is in effect a customs border in the Irish sea. It is yet to be seen whether a UK government will anticipate a border poll that leads to the reunification of Ireland, which seems likely to happen in the long run (Tonge 2020). Although there has been growing support for unification, public opinion in Northern Ireland is split (see Figure 9.2).

9.7.2 **Wales**

The territorial management of Wales has drawn less attention than the other parts of the United Kingdom, partly because of the starting point of relative centralization, the smaller vote share of the nationalist party, the relative stability of the core Labour vote in supporting a Labour government in Wales, and less overt conflict between Wales and the British government. Figure 9.3 shows the seats received by the parties contesting the Welsh Assembly, which shows a stable picture, and contrasts with Scotland. There has been relative stability over time in preferences for independence and feelings of national identity more generally (Bradbury and Andrews 2010) (see Figure 9.4). But this should not distract attention from the scale of the change of the devolution settlement

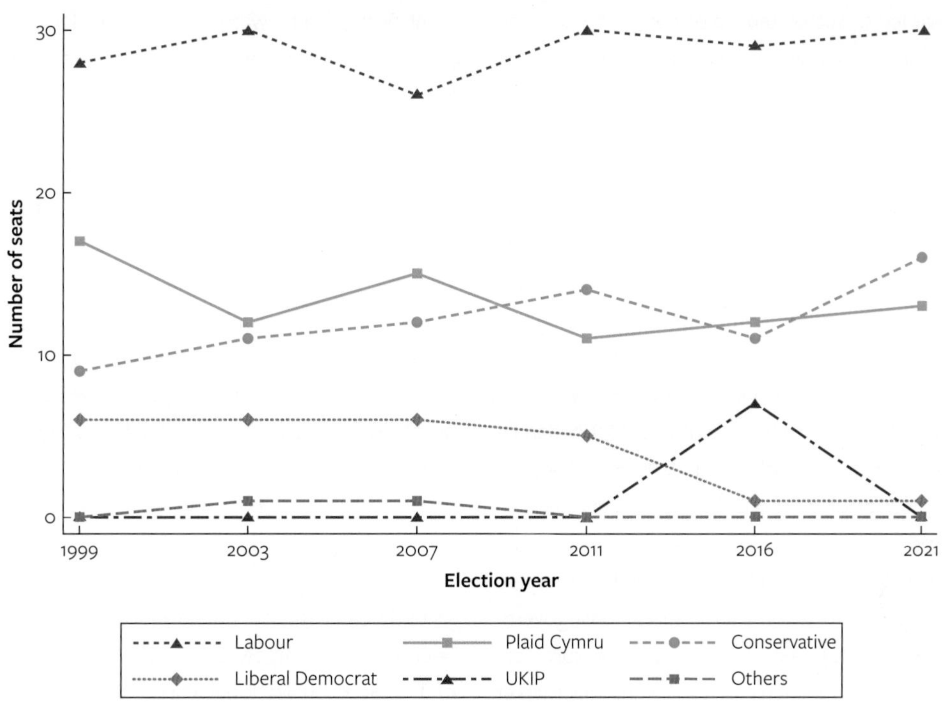

Figure 9.3 Seats held by parties in the Welsh Assembly/Senedd Cymru, 1999–2021.
Sources: Election Resources.org: http://electionresources.org/uk/sct-wls; BBC News: www.bbc.com/news/topics/cqwn14k92zwt/welsh-parliament-election-2021

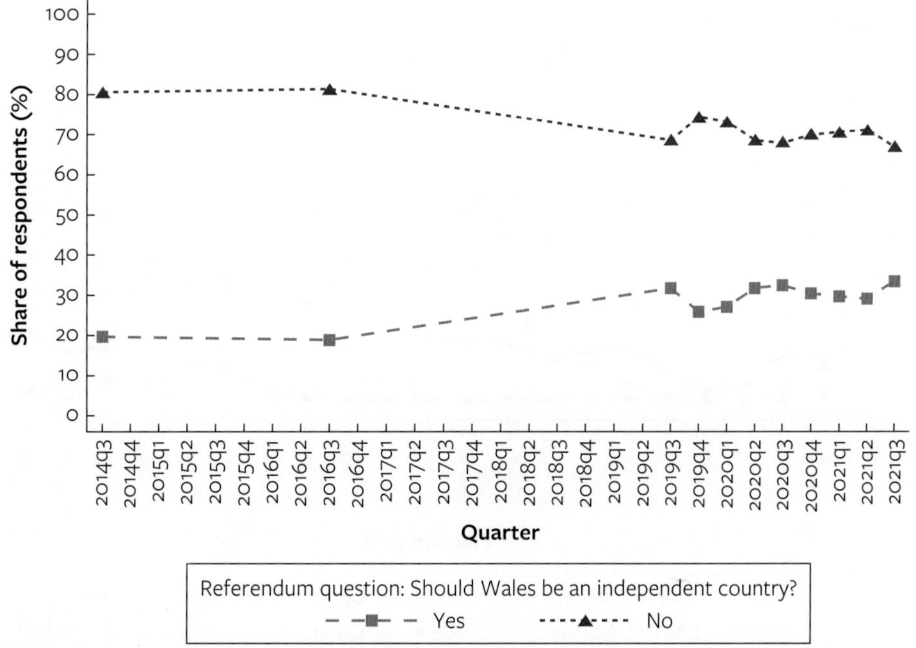

Figure 9.4 Views in Wales about independence, 2014–21.
Source: YouGov: https://yougov.co.uk/topics/politics/explore/topic/Welsh_Independence(popup:search/welsh%20 independence

9

which has led to such extensive powers being held and exercised in Wales, which has acquired a logic of its own in successive changes in the law and in acquiring new powers which the UK government is happy to do. This seemed to be an easy set of choices to make for the centre despite creating a set of conflicts over policy when previously there was central control, as was illustrated in the Covid-19 crisis with Wales' very different approach to public health control, with earlier decisions on lockdown and a different set of tools used, such as over shop and hospitality sector openings (see Case Study 1.2).

Brexit also creates tension (as it does for Scotland), not so much because of the underlying politics, as Wales voted for Brexit much like England, but because certain powers, such as over the single market and trading standards, revert from Europe to the UK. They can either be allocated to central or subnational government, with the UK government wanting to ensure economic regulation functions for the UK internal market are at the central level as in the classic Bulpittian argument of high and low politics. But this does leave the possibility of delegation to other areas that are deemed less important, such as agriculture. Tensions emerge because the Welsh economy is strongly reliant on EU trade and the Welsh government has expressed a desire to have a role in determining trade policy after Brexit. Agriculture and fisheries are key economic sectors, and West Wales and the Valleys was one of only two areas that received regional aid from the EU, causing difficulties of transition. Overall, the government has sought compromise rather than taking over new EU functions over the devolved territories (Bradbury 2021a), which is consistent with the Bulpittian approach.

9.7.3 Scotland

As outlined in section 9.3.5, the story in Scotland has been different, largely due to the electoral success of the Scottish National Party (SNP) since devolution, at general elections (see Figure 9.5), and

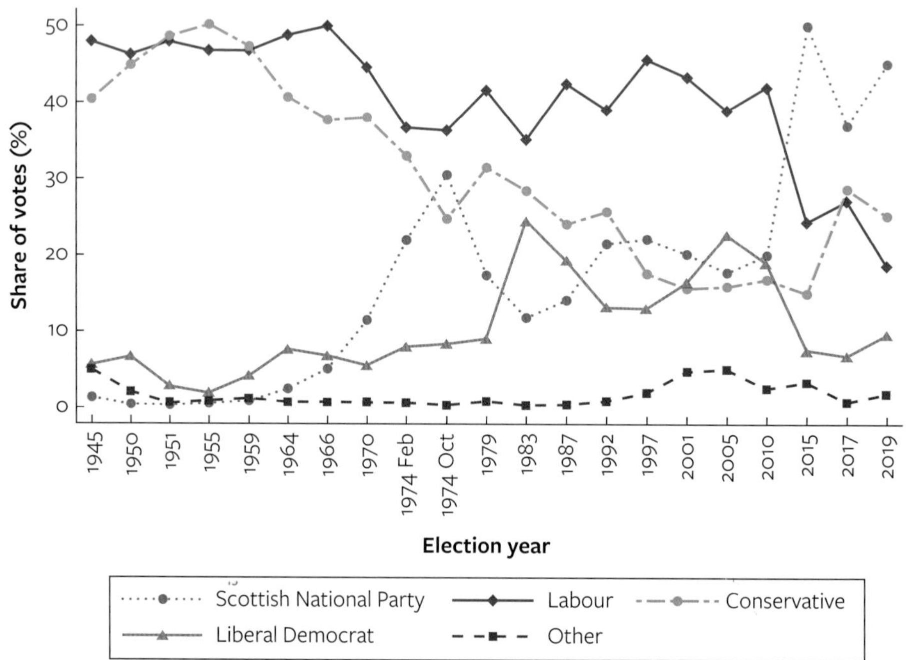

Figure 9.5 Share of votes in general elections in Scotland, 1945–2019, by political party.
Source: Audickas et al. (2020)

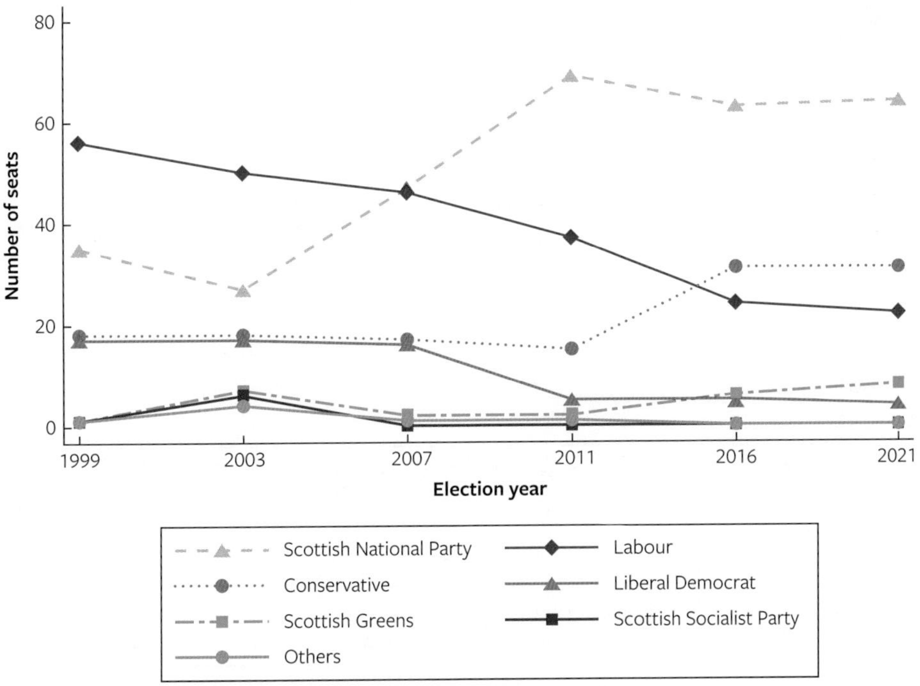

Figure 9.6 Seats in the Scottish Parliament, 1999–2021, by party.
Sources: ElectionResources.org: http://electionresources.org/uk/sct-wls; BBC News: www.bbc.com/news/topics/c37d28xdn99t/scottish-parliament-election-2021

in the Scottish Parliament (Figure 9.6), which has changed the political landscape dramatically. There is also the success of the Scottish government in using devolved powers and developing its policy capacity. This was helped by the prior existence of a Scottish political system with its different elements long before devolution (Kellas 1989). Even though the divergence in policy-making was not strong, even fairly slowly changing after devolution (Keating 2005), there was a prior system with the capacity to operate independently and legitimately so that in due course moving to a more autonomous and effective approach to policy-making. The Bulpittian strategy of the Westminster government created this baseline which in turn influenced the setting up of the Scottish Parliament as a project of containment, assuming that greater accommodation as a natural end point whereby the union would be sustained in a system where Scotland has a large amount of autonomy. But it was the electoral breakthrough of the Scottish National Party and the loss of support for Scottish Labour that created the impetus to use the powers in a different way, as the launchpad for independence.

Being in power has sustained the legitimacy of the SNP as a party of government in Scotland able to gain credit from wielding autonomy and using financial discretion for policies that are different and more generous than in England, such as no fees for students (except English ones), while successfully blaming Whitehall for policy failures, for example over the Covid-19 pandemic. The devolution experiment has demonstrated the case for independence and given the SNP the legitimacy to pursue it, though there is no counterfactual that would inform if devolution had proceeded more slowly or not at all or that there would be more national unity. As Scottish voters increasingly identify with the SNP, the party gains further legitimacy, which makes

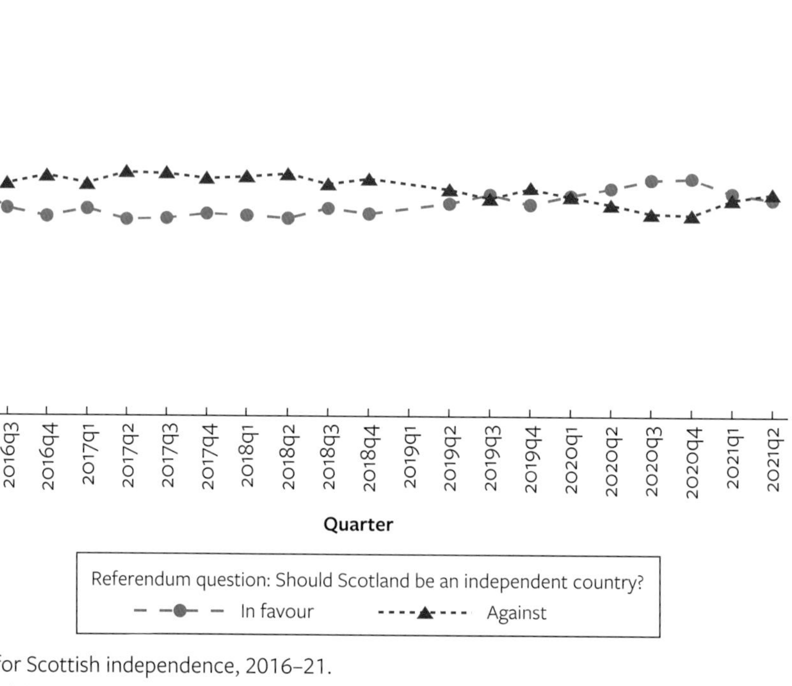

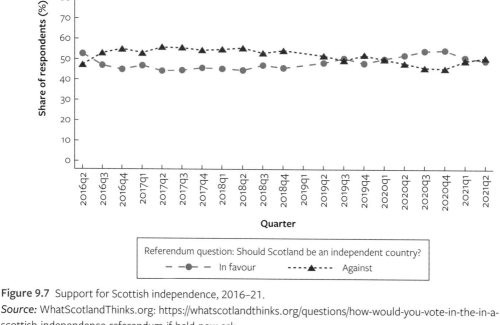

Figure 9.7 Support for Scottish independence, 2016–21.
Source: WhatScotlandThinks.org: https://whatscotlandthinks.org/questions/how-would-you-vote-in-the-in-a-scottish-independence-referendum-if-held-now-ask
Note: data are averages across all polls published each quarter of the share of respondents that favoured/opposed Scottish independence

the independence argument easier to make. This was shown by the change in support during the Scottish independence referendum campaign in 2014—how party support and anti-Westminster attitudes link together. The polling shows how split Scotland is over the issue of independence, with a rise in support for independence above 50 per cent during 2020, with a fall back in 2021 (see Figure 9.7, which has 'don't know' answers removed). A second referendum is inevitable at some point, which may result in independence.

9.8 Conclusion

Decentralization in British politics has formed into a complex pattern, where there are different dynamics in the various territories: relative centralization in England, power-sharing in Northern Ireland, pragmatic devolution in Wales, and then a strong push towards independence in Scotland, with Whitehall increasingly taking a hands-off approach. For a question about how centralized or decentralized British politics is, the answer would need to be based on where a person lives, with England rehearsing the conventional arguments about constitutional centralization and the rest of the country increasing decentralization, if not a form of federalism (leaving aside centralization over local government within Scotland, Wales, and Northern Ireland). Unifying these diverse arrangements is an approach to government from the British state which is both detached and at the same time interventionist, which helps create instability. Institutional reform is the norm, which is thought to address critiques of centralization and overload; but this strategy creates power bases for local elites, whether a mayor of Greater Manchester, first minister of Scotland or Wales, or first and deputy first ministers of Northern Ireland. While formal authority is in Westminster, in practice it is increasingly decentralized, but in a way that is destabilizing of the body politic, another factor contributing to political turbulence in British politics.

Further reading

In terms of the intellectual framework for this chapter, you can read Bulpitt's book, *Territory and Power* (1983); but it might be easier to read a summary or discussion, such as the author's introduction to the re-issued volume (Bulpitt and John 2008). For an overall summary of decentralization in the UK, see John and Copus (2010). The 'great survivor' piece is also a survey of the history and status of local government (John 2014), while Lowndes and Gardner (2016) offer a different perspective.

Northern Ireland has stimulated a plethora of publications, tracing the evolution of the conflict and the moves to its possible solution with the Good Friday agreement (e.g. Tonge 2006; O'Leary and McGarry 2016; O'Leary 2019). Wales has had less attention, but there are studies and reviews of devolution (Bradbury and Andrews 2010; Moon and Evans 2017). Scotland has generated literature mostly on parties and elections; less on policy-making. Very useful for understanding policy-making are the writings of Michael Keating (2005, 2010; Keating, Cairney, and Hepburn 2009) and James Mitchell (2013, 2019), who writes about Scotland in the context of devolution more generally. On devolution, see the Institute for Government report, *Has Devolution Worked*? (Paun and Macrory 2019), which contains an essay by Mitchell. The classic themes and constitutional discussion appear in Bogdanor (2001) and Jeffery (2007).

Essay and examination questions

Questions often revolve around the centralization–decentralization debate, such as 'How centralized is the United Kingdom/Britain/England?'. Another way to go is to ask about Bulpitt's framework, such as 'To what extent does the framework offered by Jim Bulpitt in *Territory and Power* explain how decentralization works in the United Kingdom?'. The other linked question is about local autonomy, especially in England, such as 'Is there much local autonomy in England?'.

Devolution questions can be about trying to explain the system as a whole, such as 'To what extent is the devolution settlement a stable form of decentralization?'. There are possible questions about conflict and its resolution in Northern Ireland, e.g. 'Was Richard Rose wrong to think there is no solution to the Northern Ireland problem?'. For Scotland, it could be 'Did devolution contribute to the strength for the support for Scottish independence?'.

Access the online resources for this chapter, including biannual updates, web links, and multiple-choice questions: www.oup.com/he/John1e

Chapter 10

Delegating Upwards

Challenges of International Politics

10.1 What is going to be in this chapter?

Much of what happens in British politics occurs because of its relationship to the international stage. Relationships to other states, international bodies, and the international economy need to be managed by the UK's political leaders and foreign and defence bureaucracies, to manage how to use Britain's voice in international matters. Then there is the delegation of powers to international organizations and the making of treaties. The chapter covers the UK's foreign policy and focuses on how functions are delegated to international organizations. The chapter tells the story of the EU as one of the most important international delegations culminating in the story of Brexit. This leads to a discussion of the UK's defence and security role. One key theme of the chapter is how success and failure in international politics feed back into domestic politics.

10.2 Introduction

10.2.1 International affairs as an agency problem

Just as governments delegate downwards to sub-national authorities, they also transfer authority and functions upwards to international bodies and organizations. This delegation occurs because some activities cannot be done very easily domestically so it makes sense to pool them across nation states. These acts of delegation often result from international diplomacy, say from an international agreement or treaty. Once an international agreement is made into law or agreed in an international treaty, then there is usually a body that administers this activity, with its own staff and political heads, which then creates the classic problem of delegation, that of ensuring that the wishes of the principal are realized in the actions of the agent (see Zoom-In 1.4). This is the problem of different preferences and asymmetric information but in the international arena (Hawkins et al. 2006). The additional issue is that instead of there being one principal and one or many agents, there are many principals in the form of other states that have also delegated the function. For a single state this creates the problem of realizing its preferences internationally when there are many other actors in play and a supranational agency as the co-ordinating organization.

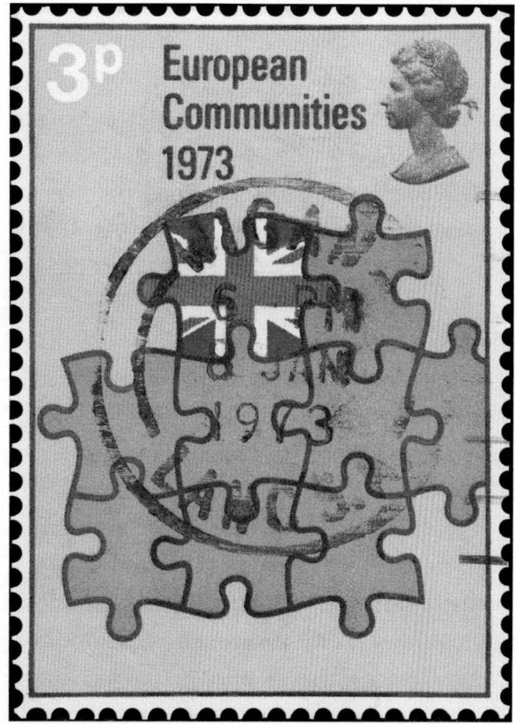

Photo 10.1 Postage stamp printed in the UK commemorating entry into the European Economic Community (EEC), 1973.

10.2.2 The historical context

In the past, the UK relied on its economic and military power to avoid or overcome these agency problems (linked to its status as a former centre of empire controlling, at one stage, large portions of the globe). It also used its economic size and political networks, for example its prestigious placement in international bodies such as the United Nations (UN) and the North Atlantic Treaty Organization (NATO), and fostered links with the leading world power, the USA. The UK sought to use its power and reputation in the world system of states to try to realize its objectives. While it is probably the case that the UK's actual status as a great power was over by the 1950s or earlier, it is certainly much more qualified in the present day. Where much international governance happens within international bodies, the UK is one of many influential players.

Showing the complexity of delegation was membership of the European Union (EU), and the decision in 1973 to join the then European Economic Community (EEC), which ended in 2020. Membership pooled some aspects of sovereignty into an international organization that has policy-making functions across many areas, with a tendency for scope, and the number of competences increases over time. There were many benefits from that relationship, and Britain was able to use its key place at the European decision-making table to extract many concessions and advantages (discussed in section 4.7.2). But there was a spill-over of European public policy into conflicts in domestic politics, and these tensions eventually led to Brexit.

Even after Brexit, the EU is a large political entity on Britain's doorstep and one of its main trading partners. The issue of linkage to EU regulation and de facto delegation to the EU remains. Even within a trade deal, certain matters, such as competition and other laws, are still decided by the EU, as part of the structure of the free trade agreement, with few or no UK laws being adopted by the EU in return. Even outside the free trade agreement, issues such as product standards and safety in effect require the UK to adhere to European regulations in order to trade with its largest partner. It makes sense to have domestic goods production carried out to the same standards as the main trading countries, as there would be too much cost in following too many standards at the same time, with the larger entity likely to set the preferred standards. This is European influence on domestic regulation just like pre-Brexit, even if done outside formal decision-making institutions. Powers are delegated upwards whether Britain has a say in them or not.

10.2.3 How international affairs affect domestic politics

The linkage of international to domestic politics is the key theme of this chapter, where there has been a potentially destabilizing relationship over time, possibly contributing to political turbulence more generally. In the Bulpittian universe, as outlined in section 9.2.2, the management of international relationships could be a source of stability in domestic politics, what he calls the 'external support system'. Elites seek international advantage to prioritize key state objectives, especially over the economy, which can then be used to placate local and other elites. Over time, however, it is possible to see the international sphere as one of relative failure to quell domestic politics because of the greater internationalization, even globalization, of the economy and its regulation, and the growing power of international bodies. Rather than supporting domestic politics, international policy-making became a source of tension that is linked to other pre-existing domestic issues, such as spatial economic inequality, and differences over culture, causing discontent focused on external actors as the perceived sources of these problems. This lack of containment of international issues reinforced differences within the integrated political organization of political parties, whereby international matters helped split these already diverse entities. Here the chapter gets heavily involved with Brexit and its aftermath, and how external relationships might work in a post-Brexit world.

10.2.4 Theoretical tools

Many of the theoretical tools needed to interpret the material have already been outlined, such as the principal–agent model (see Zoom-In 1.4), and the state theories of Jim Bulpitt (see section 9.2.2). Much of what has been learnt about the operation of the central state and its fragmentation applies to international relations and foreign policy, in particular the competition between bureaus, such as the Treasury and Home Office. Then the governance argument of different kinds of representation, from interest groups and sub-national authorities, makes it hard for a nation state to develop a consistent line in international negotiations. In this sense, concepts such as bureaucratic politics (see section 8.4.5) or the core executive (see section 2.6.8) become important in understanding the external international role. In fact, one classic book on international decision-making, *Essence of Decision*, which examines US and Soviet decision-making during the Cuban Missile Crisis of 1962, makes use of bureaucratic politics in one of its models (Allison 1971).

In addition to these insights, it is also useful to be aware of ideas from the study of international relations to understand how the British state operates internationally (see Sanders 1990, chapter 9). In fact, the analysis already presented in this book, such as with territorial politics, is not too far from realism, how scholars see states pursuing their interests (Waltz 1979) (see Key term 10.1). It is also possible to consider more ideational approaches which stress the role of ideas in shaping foreign policy and in explaining how states adopt an approach to international relations: idealism (Wilson 2011) (see Key term 10.2). Conceptions held by elites about the UK's role in the world matter, such as a view about closeness to America (Atlanticism), belief in European integration, or a desire to promote development and democratic accountability through humanitarian interventions and aid (Gamble 2017).

Key term 10.1 Realism

A theory used by international relations scholars to understand how states working in an international system realize their interests, in particular seeking security amid potential anarchy or conflict.

Key term 10.2 Idealism

A school of thought that claims that ideas, even morality, can help explain how actors conceive of their objectives, which shapes decision-making in the international arena. Origins in the late nineteenth century.

10.3 Basic facts: challenges of international politics

10.3.1 Domestic institutions concerned with external affairs

Certain parts of the central UK state seek to exercise monopoly over the management of external relations, assisted by the dominance of nation states in international institutions and international law. This makes the prime minister fundamental as a decision-maker, who is expected to have day-to-day relationships with other world political leaders. As the executive has the key role in making or changing international treaties and authorizing any military or humanitarian intervention, it follows that the prime minister and the cabinet are the core decision-makers. The Foreign, Commonwealth and Development Office (FCDO) is the lead department on international relations and diplomacy. It emerged in September 2020 as a merger of the Foreign and Commonwealth Office (FCO) and the Department for International Development (DFID). The FCO side is responsible for diplomacy, managing ambassadors located in other countries, and co-ordinating representation on international bodies; the development side handles the UK's large aid budget and other related policies. Also important is the Ministry of Defence (MOD), which runs the armed forces and is concerned with security, and any operations authorized by the UK government. Linked to these defence organizations is Britain's security and intelligence apparatus, the UK's Secret Intelligence Service, also known as MI6. Another important department, emerging post-Brexit, is the Department for International Trade (DIT). Trade deals and negotiation were once handled by the EU in tandem with national governments; now the DIT does this.

Other parts of the central state are also involved with foreign affairs, which was particularly the case when the UK was a member of the EU, when departments were involved with policies decided at the EU level, such as agriculture, energy, environment, and so on, which were handled by representation on ministerial groups in Brussels (the de facto centre for EU power and where key EU seats are hosted, including the European Commission, Council of the EU, and European Council). Researchers on the central state found this gradual Europeanization was an important development (see Key term 10.3), which changed power relationships within the state as well as its internal organization (Bulmer and Burch 2009). Post-Brexit, central departments will continue to have an international focus, such as on climate change policies, linked to international agreements, for example, involving the Department for Business, Energy and Industrial Strategy and Department for Environment, Food and Rural Affairs, as well as the FCDO. There are legislators with an interest in overseas matters, sitting on specialist select committees, such as the Foreign Affairs Select Committee. A range of specialist interest groups and experts advise on foreign policy matters. Subnational authorities are not formally part of external negotiations; but they have taken an interest in it, for example with Scotland setting up an office in Brussels: Scotland House Brussels. This is an example of para-diplomacy (see Key term 10.4), which operates under the radar, and even more so after Brexit.

Key term 10.3 Europeanization

Pre-Brexit claim that UK national and subnational policy-making are increasingly defined by relationships with the European Union.

Key term 10.4 Para-diplomacy

How non-central state actors can carry out diplomacy, leapfrogging over national governments.

10.3.2 International organizations

Britain has membership of key organizations by virtue of its economic size and past status as a world power, being one of the victors of the Second World War. Key is the United Nations (UN), where the UK has a permanent seat on the Security Council, which gives it a veto on substantive resolutions, and can be the means to conduct an international conflict. This also gives the UK a say over the many activities of the UN, not only peace and security, but also initiatives such as on climate change, sustainable development, human rights, disarmament, terrorism, humanitarian and health emergencies, gender equality, governance, and food production. The UK is also a key member of the North Atlantic Treaty Organization (NATO), the military alliance created in 1949 for the protection of Europe and North America, with an integrated command, where the UK also has membership of the North Atlantic Council (NAC), which is the principal political decision-making body. On leaving the EU the UK became a member of the World Trade Organization (WTO), so participates in part of its ministerial conferences which decide key policy. The UK is also part of the Group of Seven (G7) (Photo 10.2), which is an intergovernmental organization consisting of Canada, France, Germany, Italy, Japan, the United Kingdom, and the United States.

The heads of government of the member states, as well as the representatives of the EU, meet at the annual G7 summit. There are other organizations responsible for co-operation, such as the Organisation for Economic Co-operation and Development

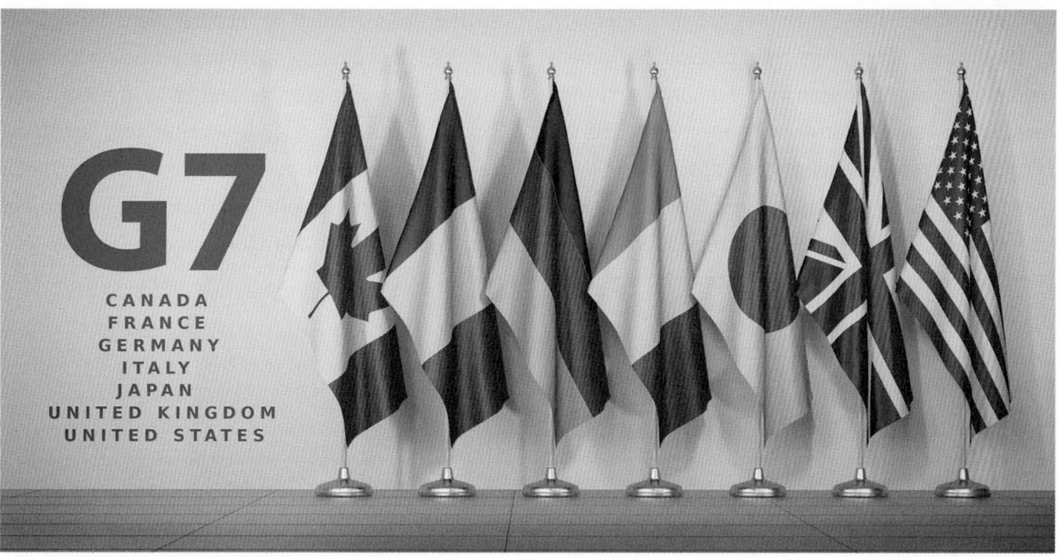

Photo 10.2 The UK is a member of the Group of Seven (G7).

(OECD), which is mainly about collating research and providing data from expert survey and research projects. Finally, the UK is a member of 'five eyes' (FVEY), a group of nations that share military intelligence with Australia, Canada, New Zealand, and the United States.

10.3.3 **Legal delegation**

In terms of legal delegation, the European Convention on Human Rights and its court, the European Court of Human Rights, are important. As a signatory, the UK needs to follow the convention in domestic law, which includes judgments made by UK courts (see section 3.7). This is much quicker now since the Human Rights Act 1998 incorporated the convention into UK law, with UK courts upholding it when hearing and deciding the verdict of cases. There are other courts that enforce international law, such as the United Nations International Court of Justice, the International Criminal Court, the International Labour Organization Administrative Tribunal, the International Tribunal for the Law of the Sea, the Permanent Court of Arbitration, and the World Bank International Centre for the Settlement of Investment Disputes, all of which have implications for what the UK may or may not do, both internationally and domestically, which is a consequence of the decision to delegate authority to these courts. Usually, there is no choice to be under the jurisdiction of these organizations and courts if the UK wants to trade and do business overseas. Moreover, there are advantages in ensuring that other states also behave according to these norms and laws, for the pursuit of trade, running a merchant navy, or finding justice for criminals outside the jurisdiction of domestic courts.

10.3.4 **Basic facts on the EU**

It is important to know some of the basics on EU decision-making. The EU is an international organization created by treaty, to which nation states delegate functions for decisions that have the status of EU law. Policy and laws, as well as a budget that funds the central activities of the EU and any programmes it authorizes, are proposed by the EU Commission and headed by commissioners who are nominated by nation states. These measures are then approved by the Council of Ministers and European Parliament before becoming European law. The European Parliament is the representative body, elected across the EU, which increasingly makes decisions and laws jointly with the Council of Ministers in a procedure called 'co-decision'. These directives and regulations are implemented by domestic law, the former by legislation or other laws decided by member state Parliaments and the latter directly applicable into domestic law. Laws and treaties are interpreted by the European Court of Justice (ECJ), which has final authority, seeking to resolve disputes when they occur. This is a simplified summary of EU decision-making, and further sources can provide a fuller picture (for example, Wallace et al. 2020).

10.4 Britain and the EU: the story

The most important delegation the UK engaged in was to the EU while it was a member state from 1973 to 31 January 2020, accepting its jurisdiction until the end of 2020. It is important to consider this example because UK politics and policy-making were intertwined with this institution, so much so that many authors thought that the UK was part of a system of multilevel governance, whereby subnational, national, and international (European) levels were working together in the same system (Bache and Flinders 2004), limiting the applicability of the Westminster model of nationally based and executive-led decision-making. Nation states remain the key actors in the EU, with subnational governments largely subordinate (states in federal systems such as Germany are exceptions), and national decision-making central to EU decision-making (Tsebelis and Garrett 2001; Moravcsik and Schimmelfennig 2009). Even when taking account of the influence of various institutions, such as the European Parliament, on EU policy-making (Wallace et al. 2020), the EU is still very much a nationally driven organization, but one with a powerful bureaucracy and developed legal order regulated by the ECJ (see section 10.3.4). Given the political controversy that started even before the UK's membership, it has had an explosive impact on UK politics, which led to Brexit. It is important to understand the EU and its intersection with national politics, especially with regard to the impact on political turbulence. So, this part of the chapter takes a historical turn to explain how the UK got to this point, and what the long-run impact of EU membership on UK politics is. Moreover, even after Brexit, the EU remains a powerful regulatory system on the UK's doorstep, with which it needs to interact over trade and international affairs. This means dealing with its regulatory and decision-making system, much like decision-makers in Canada have to pay close attention to the United States and what is happening in the US Congress and the Supreme Court.

At the core of the EU is a trading system, which created a large market that rivals the USA's, and which caused UK politicians and policy-makers from the 1950s to see it as in the country's interest to join economically, which led to a long campaign for membership (Wall 2012). As well as a perception of economic interest, the goal of membership was an ideas-based movement, based on a particular view about the UK's past, particularly an awareness of national decline as the empire gradually faded. There was also a belief in the UK about the need to modernize and go forward in a new international

10

project. In fact, in the 1950s there was participation in European projects, such as the Committee of European Economic Co-operation (CEEC), the Council of Europe, NATO, and the European Free Trade Association (EFTA), which showed how the political elites were coming to believe in more European co-operation.

Support for membership was considerable, reaching across the main parties, leading to an application when the Conservative Party was in government in 1963 and then with Labour in 1967 (both vetoed by France). But this project created a divide across left and right, sometimes splitting both into two, with an anti-market opposition to Europe on the left in the Labour Party and an anti-regulation faction within the Conservative Party. Before and just after the first referendum in 1975, the main split was on the left, but this switched to the right from the early 1980s while the left became more at ease and even supported the EU, especially over the more progressive social and employment policies that emerged from Europe, which the right increasingly despised. This had the effect of encouraging greater fragmentation of the party system, which was already weakening, causing more splits and more turbulence in UK politics. It also moved political argument from matters of economics and policy management to more fundamental issues about rights, freedom, equality, constitution, and political recognition either promoted within the EU or outside it, which could not be accommodated by compromise (for the background, see Evans and Menon 2017).

The mixture of economic and political reasons for action was also evident at the EU level, with economic advantages being pushed through the single market initiative, which came into law via the Single European Act of 1986. This measure, designed to improve free markets and competition across Europe, was championed by economic liberals, including the Conservative government at the time led by Margaret Thatcher, but also reflected federalist ideals, as were part of the project from the beginning.

10.4.1 Europeanization

In terms of policy-making, membership of the EU meant (in time) participation in a single but regulated market, where policy on trade transferred from nations to the EU, though each nation state continued to have a say in any trade policy the commission agreed on as they needed to approve it (having the right of veto). Member states participated in EU decision-making more generally as well as over those regulations. The signing of the Treaty of Rome and subsequent treaties meant transferring decision-making to the European level for specific functions, such as agriculture, fishing, energy, transport, and then other areas, such as the environment, which increased in number and scope over time. Nation states retained rights over decision-making in these areas, and control over other matters that were not delegated, such as over the welfare state. But there developed a system of regulation, a powerful legal order, with the ECJ also making policy as well as interpreting law as any constitutional court does (Dehousse 1998).

The result was a gradual Europeanization of policy-making in nation states (Featherstone and Radaelli 2003) (see Key term 10.3), as the effect of this legal regulation occurred over time, as the competences of the EU expanded and it became hard to contain regulation to certain areas. Some directives, such as over the contracting out of public services to private companies (The Transfer of Undertakings (Protection of Employment) Regulations 2006, otherwise known as TUPE), affected all aspects of government and administration irrespective of the competence of the EU, such as all cleaning contracts. This happened with central government departments and agencies (Jordan 2003), at the local level (John 1996), with private companies and associations encouraging many informal links to the EU (Bache and Jordan 2006).

It is difficult to ascertain the extent of Europeanization, with the claim in the late 1980s by the former president of the European Commission,

Jacques Delors, that 80 per cent of domestic law would in fact be European (speech to the European Parliament (EP), OJC 4 July 1988, p. 124). There have been a lot of calculations about how much is actually the case, with estimates ranging from 6 to 84 per cent (Miller 2014). It is a very hard figure to estimate as it makes assumptions about the amount of EU law in a piece of legislation, such as directly implementing a piece of legislation, or legislation crafted in compliance with a wide range of other European legislation. Yet the number may not itself be revealing (Exadaktylos and Radaelli 2012; Toeller 2012). It also does not acknowledge the qualitative dimension to Europeanization, which is about the alignment of policy-making across tiers of government. This includes the way public and private organizations seek to influence public policy, so they are part of a wider political system with influence going upwards and downwards. The Europeanization of public authorities may first be based on simple compliance with EU regulations and being prepared to win grants; but over time it involves thinking more ambitiously in European terms (John 1993). The impact of European policies on public administration and policy-making in the UK was profound, in law, finance, and within policy communities. Morphet (2013) claims that civil servants used to dress up many changes as domestic law when in fact they were European. Even today, European legislation is highly embedded into UK law and will not change much after leaving the EU, unless Parliament authorizes it. UK courts will likely be reading judgments from the ECJ to interpret these provisions for many years to come even if they are not required to do so. This is because they need to understand the meaning of the law and often the only way to do that is to look at prior ECJ decisions.

10.4.2 **Britain's influence in Europe**

To understand the nature of the UK–EU relationship and its stability, it is important to know about the ability of the UK state to exercise power in Europe. This is about political power and, much like other exercises of power in this book, for example over the UK Parliament (see section 3.2.5), it needs careful assessment (see section 2.6.7). Examining the extent of influence the UK had in Europe helps us understand the causal logic to the Brexit decision and informs whether delegation to EU was in fact destabilizing for domestic UK politics because of the lack of influence, or whether the Brexit argument was based on a narrative or construction of European politics that was helpful in fighting domestic political battles. Was the destabilizing aspect of Brexit to do with the power of narrative and framing (see section 6.7) or was there a more general separation of the UK from European politics, or even an element of both? In other words, finding out about the UK's role in Europe helps us determine the extent to which the Brexit decision was inevitable.

10.4.3 **The 'awkward partner' thesis**

Stephen George, in his book *Britain in Europe: An Awkward Partner* (1998), sought to account for the conflict between the UK and EU, with blocking tactics from Britain particularly in evidence. First, the UK came late to membership and had many problems adjusting to the method of governance in the community. Second, domestic political constraints held back British leaders from launching and/or selling pro-European initiatives to an apathetic domestic media and public. Third, there was an awkwardness on the part of UK elites, schooled in the 'winner takes all' Westminster system, in coming to terms with the horse-trading and coalition-building found elsewhere in Europe and as the standard way of reaching agreement in Brussels. The adversarial model of UK politics, commonly polarizing debates and political conflicts into two sides, epitomized by government and opposition, arrayed on opposite sides of the House of Commons, did not suit coalition and the more consensual style of politics found more commonly in Europe. Finally, there is an ideological preference for a special relationship with the US as the UK's main international partnership. Underpinning all of the above, George identified a fifth factor around the tone of British debates about Europe, which has served to underscore all of the previous factors in the minds of the UK's EU partners as a 'condescending, and at times almost contemptuous' (p. 39) approach to integration in the early years. George notes the resistance to joining in the 1950s as indicative that the UK still wanted to be a world power, and as a result it is less comfortable in the EU than other nation states. The UK may have been more reluctant than others in subsuming its external role into EU institutions, which themselves have international roles and presence. The British elite prefer a 'special relationship' with the US as the UK's main international partnership. George's thesis plays into the idea of UK separateness, and the uniqueness of UK institutions, discussed in Chapter 1.

There are some heavy critiques of George's research, such as by Buller (1995) who says that 'awkwardness' is not defined, and that other countries are awkward too (for example, Germany and France), and overall this is too much of a generalization. It is possible to find examples of the UK being co-operative, such as over food standards, and measures to promote the single European market. Other countries play domestic tactics too, such as German reluctance to pay out funds to less well-off European countries. George was sensitive to these issues, especially with the wording of the title of the book using 'an' rather than 'the' (though 'the awkward partner' does appear in the book, confusingly).

10.4.4 **Evidence for British influence in Europe**

How is it possible to resolve this influence claim? This links back to power again, but trying to assess the influence over (and from) a diverse unit with many entry points and over a lot of sectors is challenging. Robert Thomson's *Resolving Controversy in the European Union* (2011; for a summary, see Hix 2015) does have strong analysis of the question of national preferences and outcomes for 125 pieces of EU legislation between 1996 and 2008. He interviewed over 350 decision-makers to identify the positions of the member state governments, the EU Commission, and the European Parliament on each piece of law (on a 0–100 scale on each issue). Thomson shows the average distance between a government's policy position (on the 0–100 scale) and the final outcomes on over 300 issues involved. The UK was on average the fourth closest actor to final policy outcomes, and performed much better than France, Germany, and the EU Commission. As Simon Hix (2015) writes, 'We should be careful not to infer too much from these results, as what could be happening on some issues is that the UK wants only a minor policy change from a current policy while some other governments want more integrationist or regulatory policies. Then a compromise deal leads to an outcome which is more integrationist or regulatory than the UK would prefer, but is nonetheless closer to the UK's position than the positions of the other governments.'

10.4.5 **The elite bargain over EU membership**

Overall, it is important to be careful when assuming weak or strong influence of a country in the EU, which is likely to differ for each policy area and over time. The work of Thomson (2011) suggests a nuanced picture, and this can explain why UK elites were keen on EU integration because of the policy influence it gave them. This is at the heart of the elite strategy for Europe, using the EU platform for maintenance of power in a more complex world of many states and power blocs. It was a classic example of what Putnam (1988) calls a two-level game, whereby elites were playing the international arena to get a domestic payoff, but where the final international agreement ended up in a more co-operative outcome between international partners than would have been expected at first.

Understanding the UK's influence in the EU does not get around the idea that the French–German alliance is very powerful, for example over agenda-setting and governance changes. It may be the case that the UK had a lot of influence over more minor policy matters, such as trading standards, while the bigger decisions about governance were being made from the influence of France and Germany (and allied countries), which is often regarded as the 'motor' of EU integration (Webber 2005). The UK did not always get its way. For example, in 2011 Britain vetoed the Fiscal Compact, which required national budgets to be in balance or surplus; but the EU proceeded anyway by setting up a separate intergovernmental treaty that excluded the UK (Treaty on Stability, Coordination and Governance in the Economic and Monetary Union (TSCG), or the Fiscal Stability Treaty). There is also the impact of the UK conflictual tone and rough tactics in Europe. These open attacks were often done to please domestic audiences, but created considerable damage to the British international reputation that is hard to measure. For example, David Cameron's set-up of the European Conservatives and Reformists (ECR) Eurosceptic political group in the European Parliament in 2009, which the British Conservative MEPs joined, alienated the more moderate right parties in Europe.

10.4.6 **Disrupting the UK–EU equilibrium**

With the research of Thomson and argument of Hix, it could be argued that the UK had achieved a Bulpittian-style equilibrium (see section 9.2.2), playing for international influence to strengthen the UK economy via access to the single market, and favourable regulation. The UK also sought to minimize the negative effects in terms of exposure to free movement, blocked further European integration, and sought with public investment to try to limit greater inequality across the UK that might be thought to be caused by the EU. But this frame for international management did not last. Helen Thompson argues that the creation of the Eurozone, and its associated governance, destabilized this balance, by ensuring that Eurozone countries can push ahead with regulation and policy without any say from the UK (Thompson 2017). Blocking tactics could not be expected to work anymore. It is hard to prove this claim, and much of the changes in the Eurozone are highly technical so it is hard to see the spill-over into domestic politics, at least not in the way freedom of movement (or its perception) played a role in national debates and affected party competition. It is probably the case that the reasons for Brexit cannot be found in the logic of lack of power in Europe/marginalization or a failure of delegation. Rather, it is about how European politics and its narrative played into the climate of anti-politics; and how the EU was represented as a set of problems for voters, who were mobilized by skilful Eurosceptic advocates. By a simple cross on the referendum ballot paper, many marginalized or discontented groups could not only give voice to their concerns, but could also believe that change would happen as a result of the democratic process.

10.4.7 **Euroscepticism and the road to Brexit**

Euroscepticism is not unique to Britain, but it did become prevalent, which can be seen as a consequence of its imperial past and sense of national grandeur. It may have been more embedded in popular and elite culture in Britain than other European countries. It was fuelled by anti-politics and the growing cultural divide in the UK (see section 4.4.8). But public opinion data do not suggest overwhelming support for leaving the EU in the two decades before Brexit, and often less than a majority. Shown in Figure 10.1, there is only a gradual growth in the proportion of voters who wanted to leave the EU.

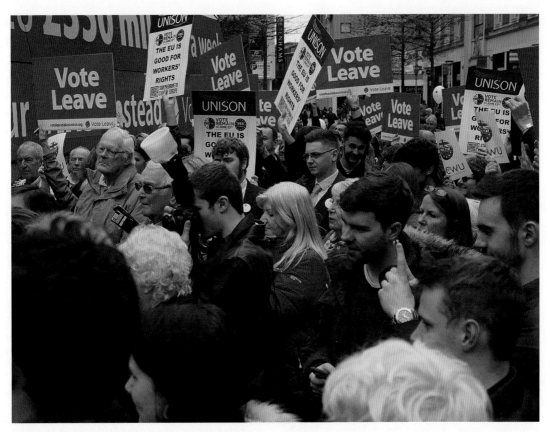

Photo 10.3 Vote Leave Brexit supporters demonstrate in Exeter, May 2016.

Key term 10.5 Euroscepticism

A feeling of hostility by some citizens and national politicians to the institutions and political project of the European Union, including criticism of the loss of autonomy of national governments to make independent decisions, such as over immigration. Can include belief in withdrawal from the EU, as in Brexit. Links to populism (Zoom-In 4.3).

Compared across Europe, Britain was more Eurosceptic than other countries, as shown through analysis of the regular Eurobarometer surveys (Carl, Dennison, and Evans 2019), and shown in Figure 10.2 from the Pew Research Centre surveys. This figure demonstrates that UK support for the EU is lower than in other European countries. This is a consistent finding even though support for the EU goes up and down in any country, such as in Germany during the migrant crisis of 2015 and 2016. So, the differences are not so great as might be thought, and often a majority of the UK public have a favourable view of the EU, at certain periods, even rising post-Brexit (see Figure 10.2).

Anti-EU attitudes were encouraged by the media (see section 6.4.3), factions within parties, and from the tactics of challenger parties, which sought to mobilize public opinion. The big shift was the change within the Conservative Party and its grassroots whereby Euroscepticism became overladen with libertarian

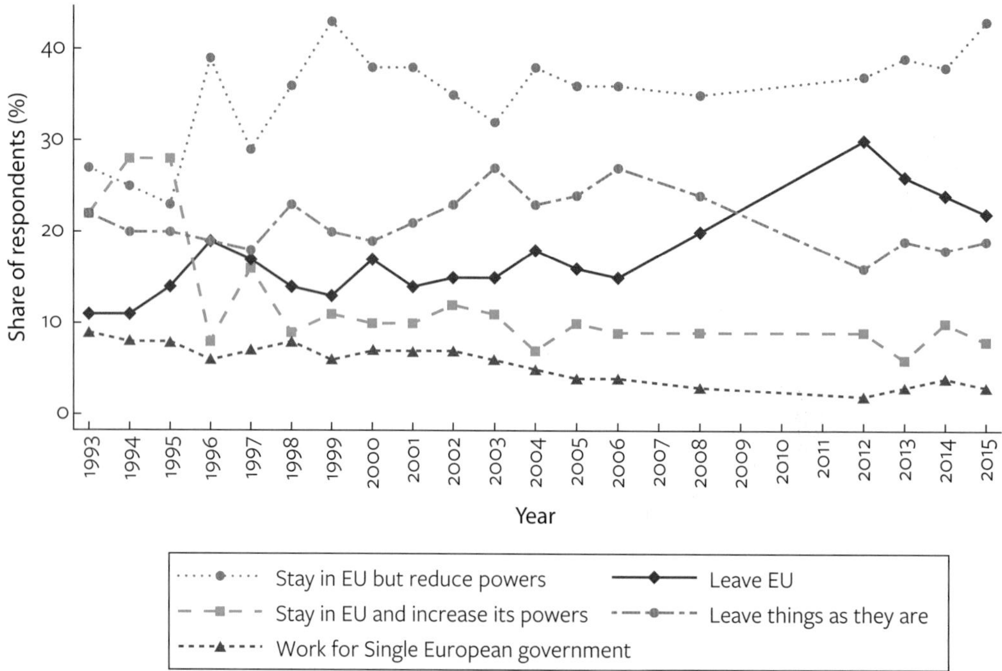

Figure 10.1 Attitudes towards Britain's relationship with the EU, 1993–2015.
Source: BSA: www.bsa.natcen.ac.uk/media/39024/euroscepticism.pdf

and British values. Important here is Margaret Thatcher's late conversion to Euroscepticism marked in the Bruges speech of 1988, which fuelled the right-wing elements within the Conservative Party, some of whom defected to the United Kingdom Independence Party (UKIP). Conservatives believed that their own government had capitulated to European integration, hence the rebellions against John Major's government during 1992–7, which included a campaign not to ratify the key Maastricht Treaty that created the Euro. It is significant in European terms that a major government party, partly in competition with UKIP, driven by its heartland membership, became largely Eurosceptic, with its originally strong pro-European wing becoming increasingly a minority voice. In the main, conservative parties in Western Europe, such as the CSU and CDU in Germany, have remained committed to the European project.

What gave the Eurosceptic movement force was the leakage of Eurosceptic ideas into the Labour heartlands, as these voters had become concerned about immigration, making the EU an easy target with its open borders (in spite of not being responsible for much immigration) and a range of cultural issues associated with inequality within England and Wales (Sobolewska and Ford 2020). This had been noted in support for the British National Party (BNP) in the 2000s where some core Labour voters became potential supporters of this far-right party, with one in five saying they might vote for it (John and Margetts 2009). Then came support for UKIP, which ranged outside the Conservative base (Ford and Goodwin 2014). Sobolewska and Ford (2020, 142–53) note that immigration levels resulted from a set of policy choices made by party elites, which was partly to do with bargains they had to make with other states and the EU, as well as a belief in the economic advantages of more immigration, especially from central Europe. The Labour government under Blair did not agree to transitional limits on immigration from central Europe in the mid-2000s when other EU countries did, which

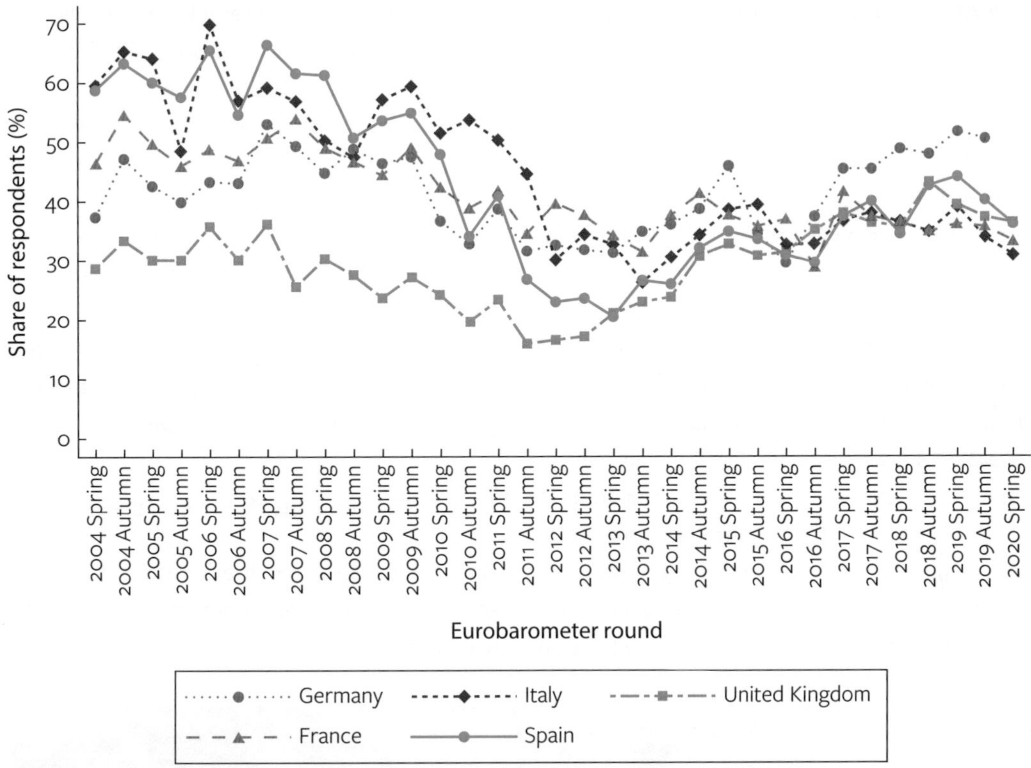

Figure 10.2 Extent of favourable views of the EU in selected European nations, 2004–20.
Source: Eurobarometer
Note 1: the figure shows for each country and Eurobarometer the addition of the share of respondents that answered 'very positive' and 'fairly positive' to the question 'In general, does the EU conjure up for you a very positive, fairly positive, neutral, fairly negative or very negative image?'
Note 2: for Germany and UK, population weights were used (Eurobarometer surveys East/West Germany and Great Britain/Northern Ireland separately and these are combined with population weights in the analysis). Post-stratification weights are used on those and all other countries

allowed significant numbers of EU citizens from countries, such as Poland, to move to and/or work in Britain (an example of the argument that much turbulence in British politics is due to the agency of elites in making ill-thought-out decisions).

The financial crisis and recession of 2008–9 hit traditional Labour-voting areas hard, making it challenging for enterprises located there to compete internationally when cheap manufactured goods, often from the rapidly industrializing countries in Asia, became more available in the international market in the 2000s. Research from Colantone and Stanig (2018) has explored the impact of competition in the UK, finding that the most severely affected areas voted Leave in 2016. Additional recent work examines the impact of housing prices on political outlooks and behaviour, finding that lower house prices outside London and the south-east conveyed feelings of insecurity and greater willingness to challenge the system (Ansell and Adler 2019).

The reasons why the referendum was called and lost by David Cameron, who campaigned for Remain, had much to do with statecraft, which is about how political leaders make judgements about how to get to their goals, having to balance conflicting objectives and resolve deep conundrums—one of the reasons high-level politics is so challenging (see section 2.6.2). Cameron made a particular choice to offer the referendum in the 2015 party manifesto, thus taking a huge risk. However, at the same time it is important to recognize the pressure on leaders to commit to policies, especially as there was a race between the parties to offer a referendum on EU membership, even the pro-EU Liberal Democrats. It also brings the analysis back to the problem of international delegation, and calculations by the elite to rebalance the loss of equilibrium by a popular vote. This strategy of rebalancing was evident in the relatively failed attempt to renegotiate the UK's relationship with the EU after the referendum had been called, aiming to limit migration or at least the welfare benefits of migrating from another EU country (a miscalculation as the EU was never going to agree). In this sense, the reasons for Brexit and its outcome have much to do with a balance between four elements which have been explored in this book: the style of executive government based on fast calculations, often mistakes, from the top (see section 2.6.2); waves of anti-politics and loss of support for traditional institutions (see section 4.4.8); fractures and loss of ebullience of the traditional political parties (see section 5.8.5); and then a loss of balance in international-focused statecraft, which caused difficulties that were hard to contain. Brexit needs to be understood in this multi-causal way. Feedback across the different elements of British politics—executive, citizen, party, and international—generated the 'perfect storm' of Brexit.

10.4.8 Britain and the EU post-Brexit

On 24 June 2016 the Brexit result (52:48) was announced in the early hours by the BBC (Shipman 2016, 449–65). The prime minister, David

Photo 10.4 The UK voted for Brexit by a narrow margin of just under 4 (3.78) per cent.

Cameron, resigned at 8.30am, agreeing to stay in office until a successor could be found. The pound dropped across all currencies. There was a sense that the country was rudderless, with the governor of the Bank of England, Mark Carney, as the main public figure offering reassurance and calm, seeking to stabilize the plummeting exchange rate. This was followed by an extraordinary leadership contest when Boris Johnson, one of the contenders, withdrew on 30 June 2016 after his main backer, Michael Gove, denounced and ran against him.

The political system was in turmoil. But gradually this ebbed, with the appointment of a new leader of the Conservative Party, Theresa May, who became prime minister on 11 July 2016. She used her powers to appoint a new cabinet and proceed with the Brexit process. But the political parties were divided, and Parliament deadlocked, unable to agree on Theresa May's deal with the EU. The key problems of managing delegation to the EU for policies associated with trade had not gone away, which disrupted the political parties that were more divided than ever over Brexit. The referendum had not solved the problem but had highlighted the lack of equilibrium and turbulence that caused Brexit, making the years 2016–19 highly unsteady and uncertain, exacerbated by May's decision to call the 2017 general election, and losing the small majority the Conservatives had won in 2015.

The institutions of government continued in place, despite being fractured by the split in the cabinet, between the more pro-EU Treasury (keen to have a deep partnership with the EU) and other departments closer to the preference of Brexiteer ministers. Public opinion also moderated, with immigration reducing in concern, as shown by evidence from surveys carried out across the referendum time period (Schwartz et al. 2020). The referendum to a certain extent had given sections of the UK people a voice. If a thermostatic view of public opinion is taken, whereby the responsiveness of governments to the public is noticed and appreciated by the public, alleviating their concerns (Wlezien 1995), then the Brexit decision could be seen as a response by the governing elite to concerns of certain sections of the public. In turn, it may be the case that the public noticed this response to their voice and this lessened their concerns on Brexit matters, such as immigration. The relationship between some sections of the public and the governing parties may have returned to a sort of equilibrium, so partly addressing the feedback and some of the turbulence of UK politics, caused by the negative feedback between publics, elites, and international politics that had built up over decades.

In the end, some voters had a chance to use the features of the UK political system to get a government that they wanted, as they could vote for the Conservative Party in marginal constituencies, giving Boris Johnson's government a way out of the deadlock, using Parliament and the eighty-seat majority to implement an executive-driven outcome. Yet, as soon as this was done, the UK was faced with the Covid-19 pandemic, revealing the weakness of the governing system almost at the point of this assertion of power (Calvert and Arbuthnott 2021). Meanwhile, the continuing trade negotiations over Brexit in 2020 showed that the problem of delegation had not gone away; rather, it has taken a different form. With all the same decisions generated by international co-operation, in terms of global rule-making, delegation problems still determine the policy process. In time, these regulatory changes may be less visible to voters than the EU, so less likely perhaps to cause political turbulence, because there is no one institution for voters and critics to focus on.

10.5 Non-EU international politics

10.5.1 Diplomatic leverage and military investment

The story of the UK and the EU is part of a wider issue about how the UK seeks to manage its relationships with the external world, where it does not have its perceived leverage to achieve international objectives singly or with a few other partners, with reduced power and presence, and a more complex world in which to achieve its objectives. British elites believed that its role as a global power was worth hanging on to because they believed in it on its own terms, as well as considering that it helped British security and economic interests (Sanders 1990). There may have been a domestic politics payoff in terms of prestige of the incumbent party. The UK has maintained a high degree of presence internationally. From its representation in key roles in organizations, the UK has developed diplomatic corps and networks, and a larger military expenditure which it has maintained relatively stable over time. Britain spends above average in terms of GDP, though other nations are close too, as Figure 10.3 shows.

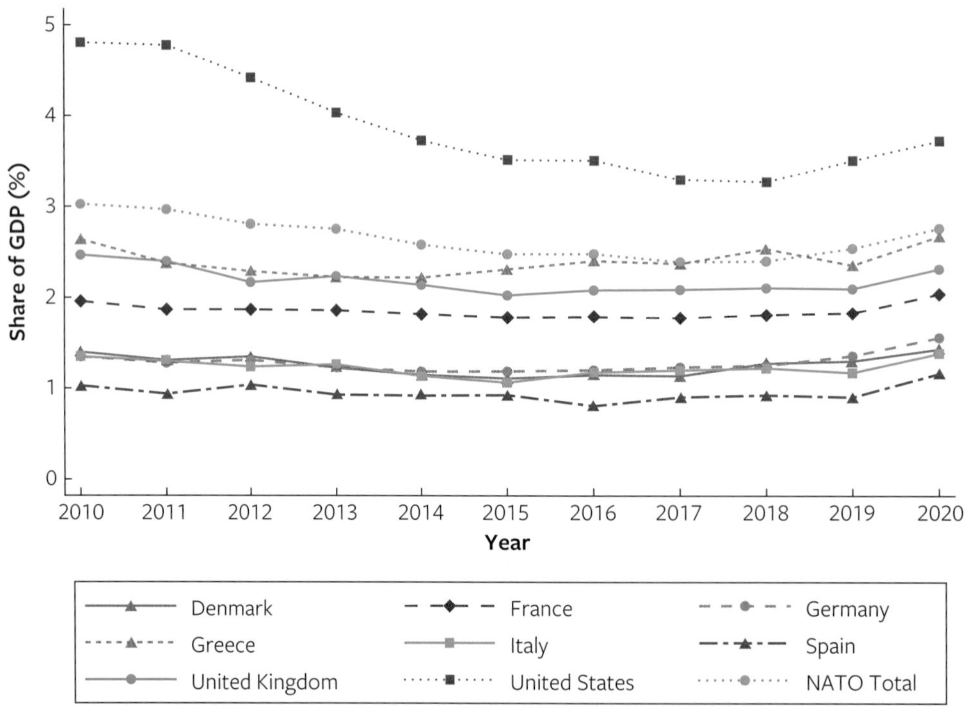

Figure 10.3 Defence expenditure as per cent of GDP for selected countries.

Sources: NATO: www.nato.int/cps/en/natohq/news_182242.htm and NATO: www.nato.int/cps/en/natohq/news_152830.htm.

Note 1: NATO Total refers to the total defence expenditure of all NATO countries added, divided by the total GDP of all NATO countries added

Note 2: 2020 values are NATO estimates

With this military presence, the UK might be thought to be a key player in world politics. But with the US's dominant world power status, this became difficult. The last hurrah of the old imperial strategy occurred in 1956 with the move to protect the Suez Canal, but when the US effectively shut down Britain and France's operation, the result was a national humiliation. This marked the end of an era, and that kind of action ceased for a long time, with even Britain not directly participating in US military efforts, such as the Vietnam War waged by the US from 1955 to 1975. Britain gradually retreated from empire, agreeing to the independence of most of its colonies (Sanders 1990, 101–3). This shift made it logical for British elites to pursue a European role.

There were examples of military intervention where superior military resources permitted successful conflicts, but where feedback into domestic politics was either positive or negative. In the case of the Falklands conflict of 1982, it was positive. On 2 April 1982, the Argentine army seized a little-known group of islands called the Falklands (which are a self-governing British Overseas Territory), some 8,000 miles from the UK, but only about 300 miles from the coast of Argentina. Argentina contested the islands' sovereignty, though with no sure claim in international law. With the invasion, UK politics was thrown into crisis, with the prime minister needing a solution quickly, but without a clear way of responding (Moore 2014, 664–66). Ultimately, the military managed to formulate a response, addressing the long supply chain of running a military operation so far from the UK with success lauded by the media and all supporters, bolstering the prime minister's reputation for decisiveness and helping secure the 1983 general election victory (Clarke and Stewart 1995). So, this conflict was a neat case study about how international affairs, if managed successfully, can support the incumbent in domestic politics, an example of the 'rally round the flag' effect which has been shown more generally for popularity in Britain (Lai and Reiter 2005). The more complex example is the invasion of Iraq in 2003 which is explored in Case Study 10.1. As with Brexit, it shows how choices in international statecraft negatively feed back into domestic politics.

10.5.2 Trade and international alliances

Since the late 2010s there has been less use of interventions and military power, perhaps the negative aftermath of Blair's adventures, with no intervention in the civil war in Syria after Cameron lost the House of Commons vote in 2013, and limited air operations authorized by Theresa May on 17 April 2018. The same approach was taken with the overthrow of General Gaddafi in August 2011, with Prime Minister Cameron permitting air strikes on Libya, but with no move to put 'boots on the ground'.

The focus of Cameron, May, and Johnson's premierships has been more on fostering international trade alliances. These have become more important post-Brexit, with the need to secure trade deals after leaving the European customs union. These have been largely low-key negotiations. The main high-profile relationship was managing the complicated relationship between the British government and President Trump, where the Conservatives claimed some linkage through the populist links to the Trump base and Brexit. But Britain found it hard to develop a relationship with Trump, focused as he was on domestic media, America first, and surviving endless crises. The attempt to develop a relationship with China also did not play well with Trump and his circle. The switch to President Biden in January 2021 also presented challenges as the UK may have been tainted by Trump and the president's interest in all-Ireland issues. The post-Brexit world is one of negotiation and balancing, as the UK's relative weak leverage can only be used marginally in a world of large trade blocs, in which it is a minor player. Case Study 10.2 on China illustrates these problems, as well as showing negative feedback into domestic politics.

Case Study 10.1 The 2003 Iraq war

This arose as part of the US's more assertive strategy against international terrorism, following the attacks of 11 September 2001, when terrorists highjacked planes across the United States, and flew them into prominent buildings, including the defence bureaucracy, the Pentagon, and then the twin towers of the World Trade Center in New York City, creating a massive loss of life from the rapid collapse of those two massive skyscrapers. Tony Blair, as UK prime minister and leading ally of the US, participated in the international response, focused on countering terrorism. The left-wing

Photo 10.5 An anti-Iraq war protest in London, February 2003. The Stop the War coalition marched through central London, seen here passing along The Embankment. Police estimated the number of protestors at 2,000,000.

(Continued)

Labour Blair overcame partisan differences to form a close working relationship with right-wing Republican President George Bush. This partnership suited the defence and security establishment of the UK, already highly linked into the US's defence and security institutions. The campaign to unseat Saddam Hussein, the former leader of Iraq, reflected a perceived link to international terrorism, which in fact was not strong, nor was it clear he was an international security threat, in spite of the Kuwait invasion (Chilcot 2016, 12–34). The stronger argument was based on Iraq's defiance of UN Security Council resolutions.

The war developed a logic of its own, as part of an approach to international policy of the United States, which was couched in an aspiration to spread democracy, but linked to the power of the right in US politics. Dangerous politically as it was for Blair, it played to his personality and vision and his wish to be seen as a world statesperson, having apparently solved Labour's internal problems. It probably reflected Blair's vanity and overweighting of his importance in the British–US relationship, which meant that the US could easily deploy Britain as a useful ally when many international partners were not so keen or opposed the 'war on terror', but without clear payoffs to the junior partner. His over-ambition reflects the fate of prime ministers in the British system noted in section 2.7. Even though it was relatively easy to remove Saddam Hussein and his regime, the aftermath to the Iraq war proved to be complicated. There were few clear objectives post-invasion. Creating a functioning democracy free of violence was a very difficult, if almost impossible task.

In terms of domestic politics, it was a miscalculation (or a calculated loss), as Blair became unpopular from the war, with protests against it. It cost Blair personal support from the electorate and in turn lost votes for Labour in the general election of 2005 over and above the normal incumbency loss (see Key term 5.9). Statistical analysis tracks the number of casualties with this loss of approval (Clarke et al. 2009, 137). The negative views about Blair helped give the Liberal Democrats an electoral boost. It also led to internal conflict within Labour and contributed to a decline in trust in politics (Strong 2017), especially with regard to any further military action (Gribble et al. 2015). As with Brexit, this shows how choices in international statecraft negatively feed back into domestic politics.

Case Study 10.2 The UK and China

China is becoming one of the world-leading economic powers, with significant military and diplomatic resources. In terms of international trade, it makes sense for the UK to develop stronger ties with China to sell goods and services into its market and to encourage inward investment into the UK. The City of London wishes to retain its status as a leading hub for renminbi currency trading. Such opportunities were seized by Prime Minister David Cameron and his Chancellor, George Osborne, through trade visits and successful planned investments in nuclear power. But such a strategy did not play well with the US under President Trump, 2017–21, who was in a trade dispute with China. China's military complex and intelligence capacity, and a perception of threat, did not play well domestically in the UK, with groups of Conservative MPs, such as former leader Sir Iain Duncan-Smith, opposed to stronger links to China. Theresa May hesitated to invest in the Chinese nuclear programme, while she entertained the idea of having Huawei, the communication company, provide a new generation of mobile internet. But the company ended up getting blocked from the 5G mobile network. There was controversy over the treatment of protestors in the former UK colony, Hong Kong. Then there was the international controversy over the treatment of the Uyghur Muslims in Xinjiang, a human rights crisis. UK MPs approved a motion declaring Uyghur Muslim genocide as a crime against humanity. Overall, the government faces two ways over China. On one hand, it is trying to keep its trade opportunities open with one of the world's largest economies, and on the other it aims to modify domestic concerns and uphold their moral obligation to condemn the inhumane actions of the Chinese government. In terms of the theme of the chapter, the China case study is an example of the UK state following a strategic policy, but with negative feedback into domestic politics, which leads to modification but not a fundamental change in foreign policy.

10.6 Humanitarian and ethical dimensions to British foreign policy

There are several strands to understanding foreign policy, and this chapter has emphasized the need to delegate functions, and the ways in which the management of external power can feed into domestic politics. The other dimension is that foreign policy can be justified and followed in its own terms by seeking to use power for moral ends. It can be argued that such concerns have always influenced UK foreign policy. But such concerns to reinvent UK external policies towards a different humanitarian and ethical dimension appeared as part of the rethink of the Cold War, where a lot of the investments, such as in troops based in Western Europe and the reliance on the nuclear deterrence, could be questioned. So, the armed forces have diversified to more flexible forms of delivery, towards more intelligence, combatting internal crime and dealing with 'rogue' states, and international action to protect communities. Such concerns appeared markedly under the Blair government from 1997 with an attempt towards ethical foreign policy (Williams 2002), whose concerns emerged strongly in the humanitarian intervention in Kosovo (Daddow 2009). Given the salience of economics and security, it is hard for these explicit ethical dimensions to be sustainable or plausible as a dominant strategy over time. Nor do agency problems go away as the typical form for these international organizations, such as the United Nations.

10.7 Aid

The main area for a more ethically driven foreign policy is overseas financial aid for support and other policy objectives in less developed countries. This is funded by the UK government and was part of a former ministry, the Department for International Development (DFID), which can either be bilateral, with one country or region, or multilateral, with jointly funded aid programmes such as the UN. Aid decisions follow the interests of the nation state, and links to security and trade, but reducing aid to these considerations is unfair. Partly because of the colonial history of the UK and continuing connections to countries in the Commonwealth, such as India and Kenya, this budget has been large, and enhanced in recent years. As with other aspects of international politics, the link to domestic politics is strong, if not dominant. As part of David Cameron's electoral strategy of making the Conservative Party electable, he committed to having aid at 0.7 per cent of Gross National Income (GNI) during the 2010 general election. This commitment was maintained up to 2020, which makes the UK a very generous aid giver. Comparing the Development Assistance Committee (DAC) countries (an international committee acting under the auspices of the OECD countries), the UK comes out very high, though not at the top, as shown in Figure 10.4. The UK was the first developed economy to carry out this commitment.

There are many factors which contributed to the Conservative Party coalition government in 2010, and their victory after the 2015 election. One of the key factors was the candidate differences in the 2010 election in which Gordon Brown's image was tarnished as an economic statesman after the financial crisis (Clarke et al. 2011, 240). It is likely that Cameron's commitment to 0.7 per cent in international aid alone did not contribute significantly to the outcome. Based on the costs of Labour incumbency, the prominence of economic issues, and the ability of the Liberal Democrats to seize the political agenda on TV, especially in TV debates, the Conservatives managed to capture the anti-politics mood in the 2010 campaign. Once the 0.7 per cent commitment had been made, the Conservatives had to do it, given that changing it would show lack of values, in spite of backbench opposition

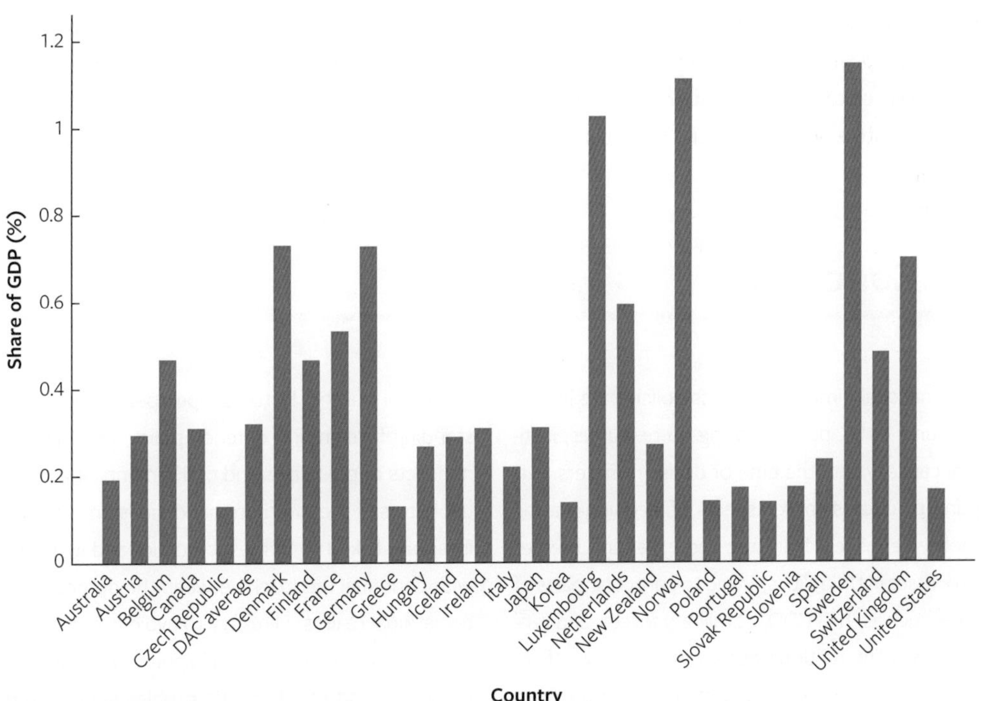

Figure 10.4 DAC members' net development assistance in 2020.
Source: OECD: https://data.oecd.org/oda/net-oda.htm

as austerity was being implemented in the rest of the public sector. Theresa May retained this pledge also. The 2019 general election found the Conservative Party carrying forward this idea in its manifesto: 'We will proudly maintain our commitment to spend 0.7 per cent of GNI on development' (Conservative and Unionist Party 2019, 53). However, by the spending review of 2020, the Conservatives decided to back down from the pledge to 0.5 per cent.

10.7.1 Agency issues and aid

Whether at 0.5 or 0.7 per cent, the commitment to aid is a large investment of resources, which are not just handed off, but need to follow policy objectives, and the government needs to show accountability for the spending of funds, as well as deal with the potential backlash against this spending and ensure the spending fits in with other objectives. Governments can also ensure their partisan preferences, such as for certain kinds of aid and country, affect aid allocation, with right-wing governments preferring 'trade for aid', where aid is linked to clear economic benefits of closer relationships with a country (Greene and Licht 2018).

The UK government cannot spend the aid money directly but needs to hand it to an international organization, such as the UN, or to donor countries, which administer it as part of their own programmes. But as the UK government does not have direct control and administration of these aid programmes, the principal–agent model becomes relevant once again (see Zoom-In 1.4), with local actors that have different objectives to those of the funder, such as rewarding clients or winning elections. Domestic administrations need to reward a local winning political coalition through which international policies may help them (Mesquita and Smith 2009). Programmes are not spent in ways that are planned (Canavire-Bacarreza, Neumayer, and Nunnenkamp 2015).

It is very hard for the UK government to overcome these agency problems. It spends a large amount of money on evaluating programmes to see if they work, but it is hard to get authoritative evidence, as the main evaluation tool is a randomized controlled trial, where places or people who get the programme are randomly allocated. Even though the UK government commissions many of these, the evidence tends to be incremental in progress as these trials are hard to carry out.

10.8 Conclusion

The international dimension and its policies are important features of UK politics, taking up resources, institutional capacity, and the time of decision-makers. It is tempting to discuss these aspects of decision-making and policy separately from the more general themes and processes in UK politics, linked to particular parts of UK state, such as the FCDO, its military forces, and representation on international bodies, which partly reflect the importance of international affairs that derived from the UK's former role as a great power, and its attempt to adapt to new power relations across the world.

Useful as the historical perspective is in understanding foreign and defence policy, especially in the mindsets of politicians and civil servants, it is more valuable to see the international dimension of politics as integrally linked to domestic politics and its problems, with continual feedback between the domestic and international realms. Elites try to avoid problems or gain advances in the international sphere partly in order to resolve or address domestic problems, but often lack the power in the international realm to do this successfully. In this chapter, the principal–agent model was highlighted to help understand these dilemmas and lack of agency. This has the advantage of comparing the UK state's dilemmas across a range of domains where delegation takes place, such as decentralization and management of executive agencies. International affairs are also a field where extensive forms of delegation take place, where the central state needs to get other actors to deliver its objectives, but may fail in this quest.

Brexit and its preceding politics illustrate these themes powerfully. Given the importance of this event in UK politics, it offers understanding of the whole British political system at a certain point in its development. The UK's relationship with the EU reveals the double-edged nature of the principal–agent relationship, with delegation having many advantages and policy wins, but also creating a lack of control and the potential for destabilizing feedback into UK politics. It also shows how the international realm, elite politics, political parties and their challengers, and mass opinion are connected together in a dynamic way, so is a fitting segue into the final part of the book, which summarizes the nature of UK politics.

Further reading

To get an overview of the historical context, see David Sanders' *Losing an Empire, Finding a Role* (1990). Another is Andrew Gamble's *Between Europe and America* (2017). There are more specialized treatments, such as of security (Walsh 2006). On the UK and the European Union, the general book by former civil servant Stephen Wall tells the story (2012). On Brexit, there is Evans and Menon's *Brexit and British Politics* (2017), Sobolewska and Ford's *Brexitland* (2020), and Thompson's essay on contingency and Brexit (2017).

Essay and examination questions

It is possible to start with some general and historical questions, such as 'What factors influence UK defence and security policy?' or 'How influential is Britain in international affairs?'. A more specialist question could focus on UK aid policy; for example, 'How do political factors shape Britain's aid policy?'. A more theoretical question could be 'Do ideas or interests guide UK foreign policy?'. Another question could be more closely related to the themes of this book, which is to take the principal–agent model as the guide, and link to the EU dimension, by asking, 'To what extent does the principal–agent model offer insight into Britain's external policies?'.

Questions about the role of the UK in Europe could focus on criticizing the awkward partner thesis, for example, 'Was the UK an awkward partner in Europe?'. Brexit could be addressed by 'What caused Brexit?' or 'Was Brexit inevitable?'.

Access the online resources for this chapter, including biannual updates, web links, and multiple-choice questions: www.oup.com/he/John1e

Chapter 11

Conclusion

The State of British Democracy

11.1 What is going to be in this chapter?

This chapter aims to pull together the information and evidence in this book to understand the nature of British politics, in particular to explain its more turbulent recent past. A table containing summaries of each chapter is offered, which relate to the themes of the book: party government and executive power, political turbulence, blunders/policy disasters, and the difficulties of achieving agency. Then there is a return to the debate about the quality of UK democracy, which began in Chapter 1.

11.2 Introduction

This chapter is a summary of the common themes and key points about British politics, which help make sense of current events, such as whether turbulence and instability now characterize British politics, and whether democracy can work well in these conditions. With these and other insights, it is possible to assess whether there is anything left for traditional understandings of British democracy or whether the country is in uncharted waters, without any clearly understood democratic mechanisms and not capable of producing effective policy outcomes. Overall, how does Britain fare as a democracy with its old and new features? Is it fated to produce policies that are bound to fail and not satisfy discontented publics, who cannot effectively punish politicians at the polls? Or does some form of accountability and responsiveness manage to seep through?

11.3 Recapitulation in five dimensions

Table 11.1 reviews the main arguments and findings in each chapter, with the first column (I) devoted to the basic or core findings, the main points; column II concerns the extent to which traditional concepts of party government and a powerful executive focused on re-election are still in evidence, especially with the insights of recent research; column III concerns the implications of the findings of each chapter about political turbulence—whether it is occurring and what drives it; column IV contains assessment on the extent to which the decision-making system contributes to policy disasters and what part of the political system is responsible; and finally, in column V, the extent of agency in the system is reviewed, especially in the context of extensive delegations of powers, which concerns how British politics is illuminated by the insights of the principal–agent model, elaborated at the start of the book in Chapter 1 (see Zoom-In 1.4).

With these basic summaries set out, it is now possible to review each of the five dimensions that have emerged across the findings from each chapter.

11.3.1 Dimension I: general points

With dimension I, the general findings, it is possible to observe the complexity and diversity of UK politics, as it has operated in a rapidly changing world. Chapters 7 to 10 outlined the extensive delegation to interest groups, agencies, subcentral authorities, and international organizations, showing the reality of making policy in a complex and asymmetric state. Institutional and constitutional arrangements have changed rapidly, such as over individual devolution settlements, which have increased the complexity of managing the system, and meant the centre has to seek compromise across the nations of the UK rather than run everything from Whitehall. Part B, on political behaviour and citizenship, showed how changeable citizen behaviour has been, which makes it harder for policy-makers to anticipate events and prepare for election contests.

Table 11.1 Key themes from Chapters 1–10

Short chapter titles	*I. General points*	*II. Extent of Party government*	*III. Increased turbulence*	*IV. Policy blunders*	*V. Agency problems*
The Starting Point	Persistence of the Westminster model; piecemeal reforms to the constitution	Survival of majoritarian government at the centre (e.g. 2019–); other periods of weakness	Decline of conventions leading to political risk-taking, e.g. high-stakes elections, referendums	Party alternation leading to rash decisions; high speed of executive decision-making	Imperfect single chain of command from voters to MPs to government
Leadership from the Top	Strong powers of the prime minister; vulnerability to challenge; costs of longevity in office; divided parties/cabinet	Control over the machine; some powers limited by Parliament; new rules on appointment	Source of rash political decisions from pressure on the prime minister	Ministerial initiatives; low capacity of centre to review policy	Limits of prime ministerial power to control Whitehall
Debating Politics and Making Laws	Gradual reform; increase in power; changes in representation	Less executive control over MPs, varies depending on majority/party unity	Growing intra-party conflicts; lurches by leaders to compensate	Growth of rebellions, leading to U-turns; still post-hoc review of decisions rather than pre-emptive	Limits of parliamentary control of executive because of asymmetry of information
What People Think and Do about Politics	Sustained participation and engagement with politics; growth of anti-politics; decline in political trust	Disaffection increases costs of ruling; loss of identification with main parties undermines their legitimacy	Latent support for populist parties, and for anti-establishment outcomes, in referendums	Rapid policy-making to deal with backlash; more U-turns; harder to legitimate policies	Stealth democracy and low knowledge about politics limits control of agents
Winning and Losing Elections	Decline of main parties; more complex party system; more perverse electoral outcomes	Majorities less likely; more partisan control over policy levers	Electoral shocks	Increased risk of losing office increases need for policy initiatives	End of cube law undermines electoral accountability from vote swings

Short chapter titles	*I. General points*	*II. Extent of Party government*	*III. Increased turbulence*	*IV. Policy blunders*	*V. Agency problems*
The Media and Agenda-Setting	Decline of traditional powerful media; expansion of social media	Partisan blaming of the media; lack of control over social media	Agenda-setting unpredictable; more surges in the agenda	24-hour news cycle and feedback surges make it hard to formulate policies	Lack of accurate information to review incumbents
Interest Groups	Diversification of interest groups; lack of power of traditional groups, such as business	State and partisanship still a factor behind interest group success	Links between groups and protest and use of social media	Link to agenda-setting and speed of politics	Interest groups not 'alarm bells' amid turbulent churn, which can help policy-makers
Governing Through Bureaucracy	Weakening of traditional civil service model; increasing delegation and complexity; more representative	Politicization increases control; achieves partisan objectives through anticipated reactions	Feedback through blunders	Link to blunders; costs of politicization and of NPM reforms	Government can overcome agency problems, but costly for capacity
Governing from Below	Sustained formal centralization in England, pragmatic decentralization continues; greater complexity and asymmetry; subnational politics have to deal with frontline issues and inequality	Partisan aims still achieved through funding and the pork barrel	Lack of policy learning because of attention span of the centre; capacity of localities not deployed systematically	Bulpittian offloading strategy destabilizing in the long term as it gives power to subcentral elite	Complexity of pragmatic reforms, hand-off policy leads to central weakness and loss of control
Delegating Upwards	Loss of control of the 'external support' system due to complexity of delegation	Harder to achieve partisan advantage from international strategy	Negative spill-overs into national politics	Complexity of international politics leads to more failures, e.g. Iraq 2003	Control of international policy hard in more complex international world, leads to loss of control of domestic political agenda

At the same time, there is much still to recognize in UK politics: the core elements of the constitutional arrangements remain in place, being reformed and adapting piecemeal, rather than being swept away or becoming completely anachronistic. If this were not the case, then some of the cases that have been decided in the Supreme Court in recent years, such as *Miller* and *Cherry*, would not be recognizable. Taking the arguments of the new institutionalists, this persistence of the parliamentary state is to be expected, as British politics contains fundamental standard operating procedures that have their own internal logic: rules of the constitution, informal norms, and the narratives that political actors adopt, maintaining the equilibrium of UK politics. For example, when a party gets a secure majority of MPs in Parliament, as Boris Johnson did in 2019, then some of the old routines of politics of executive dominance can return, with the opposition positioning for a future electoral contest, and other institutions behaving as expected, with civil service responsiveness, parliamentary quiescence (at least initially), and formally compliant local authorities (with the exception of the metro-mayors). Then there is the rhetoric of Brexit with concerns about national sovereignty and the role of Parliament in making laws, which means executive dominance of the cabinet and the central state, highlighted in the Covid-19 pandemic period from 2020 onwards when the executive was completely in charge (in England), and where it negotiated the final free trade deal with the EU for the UK without much reference to Parliament. This is very much traditional institutional politics. Yet, the foundation of this system in secure government majorities in Parliament may be insecure, with a majority for one party being as much able to vanish as to reappear. For the moment, Johnson's government looks secure, reaping a bounce in the polls in the 2021 local elections. But such boons can just be temporary in the fickle world of electoral politics. The rewards to the incumbent also benefited government in the other nations of the UK, especially in Scotland, with the SNP's desire for independence bolstered by its reputation for competence.

11.3.2 **Dimension II: executive dominance and party government**

In column II of Table 11.1, the issue of executive dominance and party government is revisited, which extends the theme of continuity. The tussle between Conservative and Labour remains, both seeking to be a party of government or remain as one, with electoral competition for majorities of House of Commons seats. With Sir Keir Starmer as Labour leader from 2020, a more traditional opposition-style politics has reappeared, as Labour seek to present themselves as responsible enough to form a government in their own right, while also holding the government to account for its failings; even Jeremy Corbyn (Labour leader 2015–20) was trying this tactic at PMQs and in the shadowing of government. It would seem that the experiment with parliamentary control over the executive in the 2017–19 government led by Theresa May was just that, and the lack of coordination of Parliament reveals the difficulty of finding an alternative to executive dominance in the UK system. Nonetheless, a lack of a majority for a new government could bring back these wrangles and experiments once again.

At the same time, it is possible to argue that the decline of constitutional conventions, and greater critique of the existing system of government coming from both main political parties, had led to more executive and partisan control of decision-making than forty years ago, which started up in earnest with Margaret Thatcher's control of the civil service and policy during the Conservative governments in office from 1979 to 1990, and has advanced since that time. This is the logic of party government. The greater politicization of public policy is the result of this newfound partisan assertiveness where governments are partisan in their management of the economy, through managing the political business cycle, and targeting public resources through the pork barrel (see section 8.6.3). The system of executive agencies and delegation shows the executive's interest can be realized in this framework of decentralization, maybe even at the cost of wider policy capacity. Party government is not at an end; it just operates in a more openly partisan manner, even if its foundations in support by the electorate have weakened.

11.3.3 **Dimension III: increased political turbulence**

From Chapter 1, this book has emphasized the ways in which different features of UK politics have heightened political turbulence, affecting political behaviour, public opinion, and the media agenda primarily, but also affecting executive, party, and policy choices, with changes in political behaviour and public policy linked together in a process of negative feedback. Part B of the book went through the first part of this claim, with Chapter 4 focusing on the decline of traditional allegiances and emergence of new parties and unpredictable referendum outcomes, Chapter 5 on electoral shocks, and Chapter 6 on agenda-setting. As was argued in Chapters 1 and 2, the central state had a hand in this turbulence, and it may have been the case that state managers had always taken electoral risks (think of Ted Heath's failed election gamble of February 1974, just like Theresa May's in 2017), but that risk-taking reached new heights as leaders had to manage events and contexts they had not faced before, such as a defecting electorate and divided parties. It is the thesis of this book that the friction created by the interaction of the features discussed in Parts A and B—traditional UK political institutions, on the one hand, and more volatile publics, on the other—has been the cause of the extent of turbulence in the UK. Moreover, this turbulence has not been helped by the delegation and fragmentation observed in Part C, in particular the negative feedback from delegated bodies, such as devolved parliaments, across the UK right back into the central state itself.

Turbulence is a key theme of this book, designed to help us understand UK politics and recent events, to bring together the literature in an up-to-date way, and to extend the ideas already there in classic studies of UK politics. Proving these changes is a challenge, however. Fieldhouse et al.'s (2019) study on electoral shocks shows increasing volatility of the electorate, but these changes have only been gradually unfolding, and to a lesser extent than the narrative about current UK politics might indicate. The most recent BES research suggests decreasing volatility in 2019 (The British Election Study Team 2021). Research comparing the volatility of the media agenda in the UK and Germany, taking as examples public opinion and the agenda of *The Times* and *Der Spiegel* over a fifty-year period, found little change in volatility over time, using various measures for these data series, and more change evident in Germany than in the UK (Camera et al. 2020). So, the research agenda for the phenomenon of political turbulence is wide open.

While more research takes place, the turbulence of British politics is likely to continue into future years. A second referendum on Scottish independence seems probable, sooner or later (Photo 11.1), which means the basic shape of the UK state could change, with the disruption produced by national separation and the need to forge a new set of relationships, much like Brexit. Then Ireland may be unified, especially as the unionist parties have received reduced levels of support in recent elections (Jon Tonge 2020). The UK state will be smaller, with implications for its other decentralized elements, which may also come to desire independence, such as Wales. Parts of the north of England, such as the northwest, show the same discontent and anti-Westminster stance pioneered by the SNP in Scotland.

Photo 11.1 A Scottish independence rally in Edinburgh, October 2019.

11.3.4 Dimension IV: policy disasters

The fourth theme of this book is the extent to which UK politics, especially recently, encourages blunders and policy disasters. In the traditional discourse, the institutions of politics, such as the monarchy and civil service, helped lead to responsible party government. But policy errors may be at the core of UK politics, to do with rapid decision-making caused by partisan competition and risk-taking by senior politicians, such as the prime minister. They are part and parcel of the Westminster model of decision-making. King and Crewe (2014) recount these kinds of failures over a long time period, such as the exchange rate mechanism (foolish entry and forced exit of a currency harmonization scheme), Millennium Dome (a large, expensive venue on the bank of the Thames), the NHS's programme for IT (and other IT programmes), and the London tube upgrade. Some of the same examples appear in Dunleavy's (1995b) review. What is significant in both accounts is that they lay the blame on institutions, with blunders happening irrespective of the party in power. In King and Crewe's study, rapid turnover of ministers in office, short time horizons, weak accountability to Parliament, centralization, executive isolation, and secrecy (leading to lack of deliberation) are key institutional factors. In Dunleavy's account, the role of cabinet committees, ministerial hyperactivism, and parliamentary weakness in scrutiny are factors, assisted by a fast-legislative schedule caused by executive dominance (see Zoom-In 11.1). Linked to the discussion in section 8.4.9, both sets of study authors blame the civil service for poor advice, either from arrogance or cultural disconnect from the real world as well as lack of expertise to monitor projects effectively. The treatment by Dunleavy implies that policy disasters have got more frequent, bolstered by faith in the New Public Management (NPM) techniques by

Zoom-In 11.1 Policy disasters according to Dunleavy (1995b)

Definition: 'significant and substantially costly failures of commission or omission by government' (Dunleavy 1995b, 52).

Examples: IT reforms, Trident nuclear programme.

Causes:

- Scale aggregation. Policy becomes aggregated into the core executive; government has a strong statist character; policy systems are not based on long-term partnerships with private and other public actors. Centralization means policy goes forward without checks.
- The 'fastest law in the west'. Ease at which the executive can get primary law through both chambers. Little scrutiny/cost benefit analysis by external bodies before legislation passed.
- Political hyper-activism. Obsessive political desire to re-organize administrative mechanisms and introduce radical policies. Politicians gain points with new initiatives (then move on).
- Arrogance of Whitehall. The cult of the amateur, without social science or statistical training, remains; and the basic idea of the civil servant is someone who can move from one brief to another, easily getting up to speed and confident they can have knowledge to outwit the specialists. The agencification of the central state intensifies this.
- Ineffective core executive checks and balances. Cabinet committees can be unstable; a radical proposal can emerge if one department and the Treasury backs it so it can sweep through.

Critique: no systematic comparison with other countries, or comparison with successes.

both ministers and civil servants (see Zoom-In 11.1). Another account by Mick Moran (2007) stresses the decline in club government, where everyone in the elite knew each other and kept each other in check, which led to hyperactive policy-making.

But it is hard to assess these claims robustly: has adherence to constitutional norms decayed? It is hard to know without getting into the minds of past and current decision-makers and very difficult to compare adherence to constitutional norms over time. There is also a critical literature, which focuses on the lack of clarity of definition of policy disasters, the contested character of these events, and the role of the media in shaping disasters (Hart and Gray 2005). Many disasters concern large capital investment projects in the public sector, where it is very hard to plan ahead and where the private sector also has massive problems delivering (for example, opening a new airport terminal). While some of the policy failures are truly massive, some can get sorted out over time. Many public projects that were thought of as disasters, such as those in Peter Hall's book *Great Planning Disasters* (1980), have become successes. For example, Sydney's opera house, which was bedevilled with design flaws and cost overruns, is now iconic and has probably earned the Australian government billions of dollars of tourist revenue alone. Some British disasters have turned around, with the Millennium Dome becoming a successful entertainment venue in recent years, in spite of still looking like an enormous circus tent. Error correction is one of the characteristics of democracy: realizing mistakes emerges from an open political culture where government, under public pressure, can find better solutions. Democracies are adaptable (Runciman 2015). And implementation is a long iterative process of organizations learning from each other, which can take many years, long after the bad headlines have been forgotten. The public policy scholar Paul Sabatier considered that about thirty years was an appropriate time period from which to measure policy successes (Sabatier 1986). Policies can be successful, including those in Britain, from greater collaboration and exchange between policy-makers (Dunlop, Radaelli, and Trein 2019).

It is difficult to find hard evidence that the UK makes poorer decisions than other countries, all of which have their own policy disasters and blunders, as shown in a review across Europe (Hart and Gray 2005). Disasters are not just a feature of centralized politics, as they happen in countries with divided government and checks and balances; for example, the regulation of financial crises across many countries, Berlin Brandenburg Airport in Germany, and criminal justice policy in Belgium. A systematic attempt to define disasters and measure them comparatively found that constitutional arrangements were not the cause of these policy failures (Jennings, Lodge, and Ryan 2018).

The policy errors around the UK government's response to the Covid-19 crisis have caused observers to revisit Dunleavy, Moran, and King's claims, as the UK's initial response appeared to be far worse than other countries (Gaskell et al. 2020). To what extent were central decision-makers at fault by not reading the warning signs that a reasonable policy-maker could have done? This is not judging policy-makers with the benefit of hindsight but working out what they could have done with the information at hand. Lack of full assessment of the evidence over Covid-19 is the conclusion of the eminent scholar of war and decision-making, Lawrie Freedman (2020). He observed the lateness of the UK response in March 2020, putting this down to the character of Boris Johnson rather than to the quality of the system of producing advice.

There is a long list of possible disasters following the Covid-19 pandemic, such as over digital technology. They reflect what the former head of the civil service, Gus O'Donnell (2020), called 'over-promise and under-deliver', the opposite of good public administration. There were numerous issues with the contact-tracing app, which the government claimed would be a 'world-beating' home-grown app for tracing cases of the virus. There were also mistakes over the procurement of Personal Protective Equipment (PPE). The report by the National Audit Office (NAO) stated that the 'government has budgeted an unprecedented £15 billion of taxpayers' money to buy PPE for England during 2020–21. It has paid very high prices given the very unusual market conditions, and hundreds of millions of pounds' worth of PPE will not be used for the original intended purpose'. Mass testing for the virus was slow to roll out, with promises not met. The UK had an initial advantage in having testing capacity, but struggled to deliver. Then there were high numbers of deaths in care homes caused by poor NHS planning, and lack of attention, though this was an international problem.

What about the successes? For example, the Nightingale hospitals, large backup hospital facilities successfully constructed with the help of the army, were organized in record time. But they were not used extensively. The ventilator scheme, whereby private companies were invited to compete to make these devices that were essential for the intensive care of Covid-19 patients, worked well: 'the ventilator challenge was undoubtedly a significant achievement, involving a huge effort from industry across the UK. In total it produced around 15,000 mechanical ventilators in just four months—around half the number now available to the NHS, and a volume that we understand would normally take years to produce' (House of Commons Public Accounts Committee 2020). Other solutions to tackle the impact of the virus on the UK were also successful, such as Treasury employment retention schemes, the use of official data from ONS, the commissioning of the vaccines, other planning in departments and agencies, and the initially successful public information campaign, 'Stay Home. Protect the NHS. Save Lives' (Photo 11.2). The vaccine roll-out was swift and well organized, with the UK proving faster than its European neighbours, such as France, Italy,

Photo 11.2 Government 'Stay Home' poster.

and Germany. The centralized top-down government approach to commissioning was successful this time. When investigations have been done on the period during the pandemic, it will be possible to know what lengths the government and civil servants went to in order to address all the challenges. Overall, given that the UK was in a crisis which was very fast-moving and with no prior experience of dealing with such a scale, perhaps some policy failures are understandable, but the ones that occurred that have to do with the nature of the UK state, such as the concentration of power in the cabinet and Whitehall, the partisan nature of party politics, the lack of trust of local government, and over-reliance on private contractors, may have made these problems worse than elsewhere (Gaskell and Stoker 2020). At the same time, there has been a lot of adaption and very rapid changes to all kinds of public and private organizations, as well as in citizen behaviour, which could be the foundation of other large and effective changes that societies need to make, showing some learning amid the chaos. This learning capacity could also be put to addressing large policy challenges like climate change (Runciman 2020).

11.3.5 Dimension V: agency loss

The fifth and final dimension explored in this book is the extent to which the political system reveals agency problems; that is, the difficulty of a principal controlling an agent, given information asymmetry and non-aligned interests. For this to work in the UK, there needs to be a single chain of command, from voters to MPs to government with signals going back to voters again, who pass judgment, and so ensure accountability (see section 1.4.5). This argument has been made by economists Persson and Tabellini (2005). They test whether some kinds of institutions can help achieve better policy outcomes, such as economic growth, and whether presidential and majoritarian systems do better than coalition and multi-party systems. Such ideas have also been used to assess clarity of responsibility for directly elected mayors, for example (Greasley and John 2011) and the ability of citizens to monitor corruption (Tavits 2007). This brings up a key problem of democracy of ensuring an element of popular control. Rather than a pluralist balance of power where all groups and voters negotiate a common interest that can be followed by those in political authority (Dahl 1961), democracies commonly have information gaps whereby some political actors may not easily control others or need to invest in additional strategies or institutional reforms to achieve their objectives (Strøm, Müller, and Bergman 2003).

Various features of UK politics now prevent the single chain of command working in a clear way, particularly from the emergence of more complex party politics at different levels. The decline of the cube law (see section 5.8.4), and the huge unpredictability of elections, means that election outcomes are determined by small groups of voters in some marginal seats who are different to other voters. Uniform swing relies on the idea that changes in the vote in marginal seats match those in safe seats, so that voters across the whole country change their vote preferences at the same time. In this case, it does not matter that a vote might not count in a safe seat because the changes in voters right across the country are moving in the same direction, which can be seen in a very decisive election when everyone is voting against the incumbent. Once that uniform swing breaks down, then a small number of voters in particular places get to decide the result, whereas other voters with different preferences remain powerless.

Clarity of responsibility in particular has been undermined by a series of reforms and institutional changes that mean the government of the day cannot be held fully responsible for the bulk of decisions made in public policy. This book has covered many of these factors, particularly from Chapters 7 to 10 (also see Flinders 2009). The first is the delegation of decisions to international agencies and institutions, which are subject to either collective decision-making across nation states and/or judicial rulings that are binding. It also applies to decisions about human rights with the European Court of Human Rights, decisions of the World Trade Organization, and the free trade and other agreements agreed between the UK and EU post-Brexit, as these are binding on the nation state and contain much regulation that must be implemented. When the electorate considers various policies and laws, whether on prisoner rights or food labelling, it cannot fairly blame the government directly, and if the government is blamed because voters do not know who is responsible, politicians cannot do anything directly about it, making the performance evaluation model inoperable. Many decisions have been delegated downwards to devolved national governments, such as the Scottish Parliament, so voters may not know which national government is responsible and politicians may seek to blame the other level of government for the problem through blame shifting. Even though it might be possible to decide matters of competence between the two, the two levels are intertwined together, especially politically. Most decision-making happens away from the central executive in Westminster, but in a complicated array of decentralized bodies, groups, and agencies, creating a form of governance that is hard to control and has considerable autonomy from central government, making the unified model of government only an official description of current practice (Jordan and Cairney 2013).

Governments also delegate decisions to independent bodies, such as the Bank of England, so they do not make the decisions, such as on interest rates, which insulates them from blame, a form of delegated governance, which might also be applied to the system of agencies and special-purpose bodies that have been given some degree of independence from the centre (Flinders 2008). It is argued that the courts have been strengthened, entrenching rights and using discretion to make policies independent of the executive (Ewing 2009) (see section 3.7). All these factors serve to undermine the single chain of accountability and the simplicity of the Westminster model.

The principal–agent story fits with more general critiques of UK democracy (see Zoom-In 1.4), which have to do with the concentration of power and lack of responsiveness, which is partly to do with the design of its institutions and poor incentives for elites to act responsively and in an accountable fashion. These critiques of UK democracy have sounded loud and clear for many decades in the demands for a codified constitution and electoral system reform (for example, Hirst 1989).

But there is a need to compare this critique with the findings in the comparative literature to gauge if British politics does in fact perform noticeably worse on various measures of responsiveness of governments to the electorate. In terms of policy programmes, the public spending of programmes does move in the direction of the median voter by looking at spending priorities over time (Hofferbert and Budge 1992). Public opinion data series over many decades show that by and large the public agenda of politicians largely follows changes in public preferences (Soroka and Wlezien 2005), such as for spending, or in terms of the most important problem that concerns the electorate at any one time (Jennings and John 2009). The UK fares reasonably well if not better on responsiveness and performance voting in comparative perspective, such as through the relationship between public opinion and public policy (Soroka and Wlezien 2010). Green and Jennings (2012) show that the electorate does indeed attribute responsibility for performance failures. Kam et al.'s (2020) comparative examination of the electorate's capacity to reward or sanction the incumbent government shows a degree of accountability across a range of electoral systems and constitutional setups, which depends on there being an extent of bipolarity, with party system fragmentation weakening accountability. This does not mean a British-style system always delivers accountability, but like any system, it has the potential to do so.

Finally, there are some signs that the institutions are responsive to a more diverse and even polarized electorate, with better representation of MPs, ministers, and in particular of the composition of senior civil servants (see section 8.3.3). Major crises such as the Grenfell Tower fire (see Case Study 9.3) have revealed the tension and inconsistencies in central and local policy-making and how the discrimination and poor receipt of services can be made part of a wider debate about inequality and representation. These issues have been further highlighted by the Covid-19 crisis. Democratic reform is on the agenda, with reformers considering how mechanisms, such as deliberative democracy with mini-publics and citizen assemblies (UCL 2017), can work alongside representative institutions.

Even if the mechanics of the single chain of command do not work clearly, it may be the case that democracy still operates in Britain *despite* the imperfection of its institutions rather than *because* of them—that some kind of responsiveness is in place if the conditions are right, as in the Kam et al. (2020) formulation, and exist in spite of the perversity of electoral signals and agency loss. Party control might still just be able to promote a version of clarity of responsibility as a benefit to decision-making and democratic accountability. It is still possible to 'kick out the rascals' or the incumbent, if the discontented voters are in the right constituencies, and this acts as some constraint on the behaviour of incumbents, much as they enjoy the fruits of office. The argument that democracy in Britain can at times work does not displace arguments for more reform, such as of the second chamber, electoral systems, rules of accountability, and the pattern of decentralization.

Access the online resources for this chapter, including biannual updates, web links, and multiple-choice questions: www.oup.com/he/John1e

References

Abreu, Maria, and Özge Öner. 2020. 'Disentangling the Brexit Vote: The Role of Economic, Social and Cultural Contexts in Explaining the UK's EU Referendum Vote'. *Environment and Planning A: Economy and Space* 52 (7): 1434–56.

Adams, James, Luca Bernardi, and Christopher Wlezien. 2019. 'Social Welfare Policy Outputs and Governing Parties' Left-Right Images: Do Voters Respond?' *The Journal of Politics* 82 (3): 1161–65.

Adams, James, Lawrence Ezrow, and Zeynep Somer-Topcu. 2011. 'Is Anybody Listening? Evidence That Voters Do Not Respond to European Parties' Policy Statements during Elections'. *American Journal of Political Science* 55 (2): 370–82.

Adonis, Andrew. 1990. *Parliament Today*. Manchester: Manchester University Press.

Alford, Robert R. 1967. 'Class Voting in the Anglo-American Political Systems'. In *Party Systems and Voter Alignments: Cross-National Perspectives*, edited by Seymour Martin Lipset and Stein Rokkan, 67–93. New York: Free Press.

Allen, Nicholas, and Nora Siklodi. 2016. 'Theresa May Asserts Control in a Revamped Cabinet-Committee System: British Politics and Policy at LSE'. http://blogs.lse.ac.uk/politicsandpolicy/theresa-may-asserts-control-in-a-revamped-cabinet-committee-system.

Allen, Nicholas, and Nora Siklodi. 'Objectivity and Falsehood: Assessing Measures of Positional Influence with Members of David Cameron's Cabinets'. *The British Journal of Politics and International Relations* 22 (2): 220–37.

Allen, Peter. 2018. *The Political Class: Why It Matters Who Our Politicians Are*. Illustrated edition. Oxford: Oxford University Press.

Allison, Graham T. 1971. *Essence of Decision: Explaining the Cuban Missile Crisis*. Boston, MA: Little, Brown.

Almond, Gabriel A., and Sidney Verba. 1963. *The Civic Culture: Political Attitudes and Democracy in Five Nations*. Princeton, NJ: Princeton University Press.

Anderson, Christopher J., and Yuliya V. Tverdova. 2001. 'Winners, Losers, and Attitudes about Government in Contemporary Democracies'. *International Political Science Review/Revue Internationale de Science Politique* 22 (4): 321–38.

Ansell, Ben. 2014. 'The Political Economy of Ownership: Housing Markets and the Welfare State'. *American Political Science Review* 108 (2): 383–402. https://doi.org/10.1017/S0003055414000045.

Ansell, Ben, and David Adler. 2019. 'Brexit and the Politics of Housing in Britain'. *The Political Quarterly* 90: 105–16.

Anstis, Shirley. 2020. *Black British Members of Parliament in the House of Commons: 22 Stories of Passion, Achievement and Success*. 1st edition. West Haven, CT: Envision Publishing.

Arter, David. 2004. *The Scottish Parliament: A Scandinavian-Style Assembly?* London: Routledge.

Ashe, Jeanette, Rosie Campbell, Sarah Childs, and Elizabeth Evans. 2010. ' "Stand by Your Man": Women's Political Recruitment at the 2010 UK General Election'. *British Politics* 5 (4): 455–80. https://doi.org/10.1057/bp.2010.17.

Atkinson, Hugh, and Stuart Wilks-Heeg. 2000. *Local Government from Thatcher to Blair: The Politics of Creative Autonomy*. 1st edition. Cambridge, UK; Malden, MA: Polity.

Audickas, Lukas, Noel Dempsey, and Philip Loft. 2019. 'Membership of UK Political Parties.' August. https://commonslibrary.parliament.uk/research-briefings/sn05125.

Audickas, Lukas, Philip Loft, and Richard Cracknell. 2020. 'UK Election Statistics: 1918–2019—A Century of Elections'. February. https://commonslibrary.parliament.uk/research-briefings/cbp-7529.

Austen-Smith, David, and John R. Wright. 1994. 'Counteractive Lobbying'. *American Journal of Political Science* 38 (1): 25–44. https://doi.org/10.2307/2111334.

Awan-Scully, Roger. 2018. *The End of British Party Politics?* London: Biteback Publishing.

Bache, Ian, and Matthew Flinders. 2004. 'Multi-Level Governance and the Study of the British State'. *Public Policy and Administration* 19 (1): 31–51. https://doi.org/10.1177/095207670401900103.

Bache, Ian, and Andrew Jordan. 2006. 'The Europeanization of British Politics'. In *The Europeanization of British Politics*, edited by Ian Bache and Andrew Jordan, 265–79. Palgrave Studies in European Union Politics. London: Palgrave Macmillan UK. https://doi.org/10.1057/9780230627321_17.

Bachrach, Peter, and Morton S. Baratz. 1962. 'Two Faces of Power'. *The American Political Science Review* 56 (4): 947–52.

Bagehot, Walter. 1873. *The English Constitution*. 1st edition. London: Chapman & Hall.

Bagehot, Walter, and R. H. S. Crossman. 1963. *The English Constitution. With an Introduction by R.H.S. Crossman*. London: Collins.

Bale, Tim. 2017. 'Tim Bale: Inside Labour's Massive Membership Base'. LabourList. https://labourlist.org/2017/10/tim-bale-inside-labours-massive-membership-base.

Bale, Tim. 2019. *Footsoldiers: Political Party Membership in the 21st Century*. 1st edition. London; New York: Routledge.

Banfield, Edward C. 1970. *The Unheavenly City: The Nature and Future of Our Urban Crisis*. Boston, MA: Little, Brown.

Banuri, Sheheryar, Stefan Dercon, and Varun Gauri. 2017. 'Biased Policy Professionals'. Policy Research Working Paper No. 8113. Washington, DC: World Bank.

Barber, Benjamin R. 1984. *Strong Democracy: Participatory Politics for a New Age*. Berkeley, CA: University of California Press.

Barker, Anthony, and Graham K. Wilson. 1997. 'Whitehall's Disobedient Servants? Senior Officials' Potential Resistance to Ministers in British Government Departments'. *British Journal of Political Science* 27 (2): 223–46. https://doi.org/10.1017/S0007123497000124.

Barnes, Samuel Henry, and Max Kaase. 1979. *Political Action: Mass Participation in Five Western Democracies*. London: Sage Publications.

Bartle, John, Sebastian Dellepiane-Avellaneda, and James Stimson. 2011. 'The Moving Centre: Preferences for Government Activity in Britain, 1950–2005'. *British Journal of Political Science* 41 (2): 259–85.

Bates, Stephen, Mark Goodwin, and Stephen McKay. 2017. 'Do UK MPs Engage More with Select Committees since the Wright Reforms? An Interrupted Time Series Analysis, 1979–2016'. *Parliamentary Affairs* 70 (4): 780–800. https://doi.org/10.1093/pa/gsx007.

Baumgartner, Frank R., and Bryan D. Jones. 1993. *Agendas and Instability in American Politics*. Chicago, IL: University of Chicago Press.

Baumgartner, Frank R., Jeffrey M. Berry, Marie Hojnacki, Beth L. Leech, and David C. Kimball. 2009. *Lobbying and Policy Change: Who Wins, Who Loses, and Why*. Chicago, IL: University of Chicago Press.

Beer, Samuel H. 1965. *Modern British Politics: A Study of Parties and Pressure Groups*. London: Faber.

Bell, John. 1985. *Policy Arguments in Judicial Decisions*. Oxford: Clarendon Press.

Benedetto, Giacomo, and Simon Hix. 2007. 'The Rejected, the Ejected, and the Dejected: Explaining Government Rebels in the 2001–2005 British House of Commons'. *Comparative Political Studies* 40 (7): 755–81.

Benn, Tony, and Chris Mullin. 1979. *Arguments for Socialism*. London: J. Cape.

Benton, Meghan, and Meg Russell. 2013. 'Assessing the Impact of Parliamentary Oversight Committees: The Select Committees in the British House of Commons'. *Parliamentary Affairs* 66 (4): 772–97.

Bergan, Daniel E. 2009. 'Does Grassroots Lobbying Work? A Field Experiment Measuring the Effects of an E-mail Lobbying Campaign on Legislative Behavior'. *American Politics Research* 37 (2): 327–52.

Bergman, Torbjörn, Wolfgang C. Müller, and Kaare Strøm. 2000. 'Introduction: Parliamentary Democracy and the Chain of Delegation'. *European Journal of Political Research* 37 (3): 255–60. https://doi.org/10.1111/1475-6765.00512.

Bernhagen, Patrick. 2012. 'Who Gets What in British Politics—and How? An Analysis of Media Reports on Lobbying around Government Policies, 2001–7'. *Political Studies* 60 (3): 557–77. https://doi.org/10.1111/j.1467-9248.2011.00916.x.

Bernhagen, Patrick. 2013. 'When Do Politicians Listen to Lobbyists (and Who Benefits When They Do)?' *European Journal of Political Research* 52 (1): 20–43. https://doi.org/10.1111/j.1475-6765.2012.02062.x.

Bernhagen, Patrick, and Thomas Bräuninger. 2005. 'Structural Power and Public Policy: A Signaling Model of Business Lobbying in Democratic Capitalism'. *Political Studies* 53 (1): 43–64. https://doi.org/10.1111/j.1467-9248.2005.00516.x.

Berry, Richard. 2015. 'Book Review: Making British Law: Committees in Action by Louise Thompson'. *British Politics and Policy at LSE* (blog). 13 December 2015. https://blogs.lse.ac.uk/politicsandpolicy/book-review-making-british-law-committees-in-action-by-louise-thompson.

Bertelli, Anthony M., and Peter John. 2010. 'Government Checking Government: How Performance Measures Expand Distributive Politics'. *The Journal of Politics* 72 (2): 545–58. https://doi.org/10.1017/s002238160999082x.

Bertelli, Anthony M., and Peter John. 2013. 'Public Policy Investment: Risk and Return in British Politics'. *British Journal of Political Science* 43 (4): 741–73.

Bertelli, A., and J. Sinclair. 2018. 'Democratic Accountability and the Politics of Mass Administrative Reorganization'. *British Journal of Political Science* 48 (3): 691–711.

Bertelli, Anthony M., Jennifer M. Connolly, Dyana P. Mason, and Lilian C. Conover. 2014. 'Politics, Management, and the Allocation of Arts Funding: Evidence from Public Support for the Arts in the UK'. *International Journal of Cultural Policy* 20 (3): 341–59. https://doi.org/10.1080/10286632.2013.786057.

Beswick, Joe, and Joe Penny. 2018. 'Demolishing the Present to Sell off the Future? The Emergence of "Financialized Municipal Entrepreneurialism" in London'. *International Journal of Urban and Regional Research* 42 (4): 612–32. https://doi.org/10.1111/1468-2427.12612.

Bevan, Shaun. 2015. 'Bureaucratic Responsiveness: Effects of Elected Government, Public Agendas and European Attention on the UK Bureaucracy'. *Public Administration* 93 (1): 139–58. https://doi.org/10.1111/padm.12113.

Bevan, Shaun, and Peter John. 2016. 'Policy Representation by Party Leaders and Followers: What Drives UK Prime Minister's Questions?' *Government and Opposition* 51 (1): 59–83.

Bevir, Mark, and R. A. W. Rhodes. 2006. 'Interpretive Approaches to British Government and Politics'. *British Politics* 1 (1): 84–112. https://doi.org/10.1057/palgrave.bp.4200001.

Binderkrantz, Anne Skorkjær, and Helene Helboe Pedersen. 2019. 'The Lobbying Success of Citizen and Economic Groups in Denmark and the UK'. *Acta Politica* 54 (1): 75–103. https://doi.org/10.1057/s41269-017-0076-7.

Birch, A. H. 1964. *Representative and Responsible Government: An Essay on the British Constitution*. London: Allen and Unwin.

Bischoff, Ivo. 2003. 'Determinants of the Increase in the Number of Interest Groups in Western Democracies: Theoretical Considerations and Evidence from 21 OECD Countries'. *Public Choice* 114 (1): 197–218. https://doi.org/10.1023/A:1020838017459.

Bite The Ballot, Toby S. James, ClearView Research, Oliver Sidorczuk, Kenny Imafidon, and Daniel McGrath. 2016. *Getting the 'Missing Millions' on to the Electoral Register: A Vision for Voter Registration Reform in the UK*. All Party Parliamentary Group on Democratic Participation. https://ueaeprints.uea.ac.uk/id/eprint/59301.

Blais, Andre, and Stephane Dion, eds. 1991. *The Budget-Maximizing Bureaucrat: Appraisals and Evidence*. Pittsburgh, PA: University of Pittsburgh Press.

Blau, Adrian. 2004. 'A Quadruple Whammy for First-Past-the-Post'. *Electoral Studies* 23 (3): 431–53. https://doi.org/10.1016/S0261-3794(03)00030-1.

Blick, Andrew. 2016. *The Codes of the Constitution*. London: Bloomsbury Publishing.

Blumenau, Jack. 2019. 'The Effects of Female Leadership on Women's Voice in Political Debate'. *British Journal of Political Science*, 1–22. https://doi.org/10.1017/S0007123419000334.

Bochel, John M., and David T. Denver. 1971. 'Canvassing, Turnout and Party Support: An Experiment'. *British Journal of Political Science* 1 (3): 257–69.

Bochel, Hugh, Andrew Defty, and Jane Kirkpatrick. 2015. ' "New Mechanisms of Independent Accountability": Select Committees and Parliamentary Scrutiny of the Intelligence Services'. *Parliamentary Affairs* 68 (2): 314–31. https://doi.org/10.1093/pa/gst032.

Bogdanor, Vernon. 2001. *Devolution in the United Kingdom*. Oxford: Oxford University Press.

Bohnet, Iris. 2016. *What Works*. Cambridge, MA: Harvard University Press.

Borge, Rosa, and Ana S. Cardenal. 2011. 'Surfing the Net: A Pathway to Participation for the Politically Uninterested?' *Policy & Internet* 3 (1): 1–29. https://doi.org/10.2202/1944-2866.1099.

Boudreau, Cheryl, and Arthur Lupia. 2011. 'Political Knowledge'. In *Cambridge Handbook of Experimental Political Science*, edited by Arthur Lupia, Donald P. Greene, James H. Kuklinski, and James N. Druckman, 171–84. Cambridge: Cambridge University Press. https://doi.org/10.1017/CBO9780511921452.012.

Bowler, Shaun. 2010. 'Private Members' Bills in the UK Parliament: Is There an "Electoral Connection"?' *The Journal of Legislative Studies* 16 (4): 476–94. https://doi.org/10.1080/13572334.2010.519457.

Bowler, Shaun, and Jeffrey A. Karp. 2004. 'Politicians, Scandals, and Trust in Government'. *Political Behavior* 26 (3): 271–87. https://doi.org/10.1023/B:POBE.0000043456.87303.3a.

Bradbury, Jonathan. 2021a. 'Welsh Devolution and the Union: Reform Debates after Brexit'. *The Political Quarterly*. https://doi.org/10.1111/1467-923X.12944.

Bradbury, Jonathan. 2021b. *Constitutional Policy and Territorial Politics in the UK. Volume 1: Union and Devolution 1997–2007*. 1st edition. Bristol: Bristol University Press.

Bradbury, Jonathan, and Rhys Andrews. 2010. 'State Devolution and National Identity: Continuity and Change in the Politics of Welshness and Britishness in Wales'. *Parliamentary Affairs* 63 (2): 229–49. https://doi.org/10.1093/pa/gsp029.

Bradbury, Jonathan, and James Mitchell. 2007. 'The Constituency Work of Members of the Scottish Parliament and National Assembly for Wales: Approaches, Relationships and Rules'. *Regional & Federal Studies* 17 (1): 117–45. https://doi.org/10.1080/13597560701189669.

Brady, C. 1999. 'Collective Responsibility of the Cabinet: An Ethical, Constitutional or Managerial Tool?' *Parliamentary Affairs* 52 (2): 214–29. https://doi.org/10.1093/pa/52.2.214.

Brannan, Tessa, Catherine Durose, Peter John, and Harold Wolman. 2008. 'Assessing Best Practice as a Means of Innovation'. *Local Government Studies* 34 (1): 23–38. https://doi.org/10.1080/03003930701770405.

Breitenbach, Esther. 2020. 'Scottish Women and Political Representation in the UK and Scottish Parliaments (1918–2020)'. *Open Library of Humanities* 6 (2): 14. https://doi.org/10.16995/olh.579.

Brians, Craig Leonard. 1997. 'Residential Mobility, Voter Registration, and Electoral Participation in Canada'. *Political Research Quarterly* 50 (1): 215–27. https://doi.org/10.2307/449036.

Brooks, Steve, and Owain Ap Gareth. 2016. *Women in the National Assembly*. Electoral Reform Society Cymru. www.electoral-reform.org.uk/wp-content/uploads/2017/06/Women-in-the-National-Assembly-of-Wales.pdf.

Budge, Ian, and Dennis J. Farlie. 1983. *Explaining and Predicting Elections: Issue Effects and Party Strategies in Twenty-Three Democracies*. London; Boston, MA: HarperCollins Publishers Ltd.

Budge, Ian, Hans-Dieter Klingemann, Andrea Volkens, Judith Bara, and Eric Tanenbaum, eds. 2001. *Mapping Policy Preferences: Estimates for Parties, Electors, and Governments 1945–1998*. Oxford; New York: Oxford University Press.

Buller, Jim. 1995. 'Britain as an Awkward Partner: Reassessing Britain's Relations with the EU'. *Politics* 15 (1): 33–42. https://doi.org/10.1111/j.1467-9256.1995.tb00018.x.

Bulmer, Simon J., and Martin Burch. 2009. *The Europeanisation of Whitehall: UK Central Government and the European Union*. Manchester: Manchester University Press. www.jstor.org/stable/j.ctt155jfnh.

Bulpitt, Jim. 1983. *Territory and Power in the United Kingdom: An Interpretation*. Manchester: Manchester University Press.

Bulpitt, Jim, and Peter John. 2008. *Territory and Power in the United Kingdom: An Interpretation*. Colchester: ECPR Press.

Burch, Martin. 1996. *The British Cabinet System*. Hoboken, NJ: Prentice Hall.

Burch, M., and I. Holliday. 1995. *The British Cabinet System*. Brighton: Harvester Wheatsheaf.

Burke, Edmund. 1790. *Reflections on the Revolution in France: And on the Proceedings in Certain Societies in London Relative to That Event. In a Letter Intended to Have Been Sent to a Gentleman in Paris*. J. Dodsley.

Butler, Daniel M. 2014. *Representing the Advantaged: How Politicians Reinforce Inequality*. Cambridge: Cambridge University Press.

Butler, David. 1978. *Coalitions in British Politics*. London: Macmillan.

Butler, David, and Uwe W. Kitzinger. 1976. *1975 Referendum*. 1st edition. London: Macmillan.

Butler, David E., and Donald E. Stokes. 1969. *Political Change in Britain: Forces Shaping Electoral Choice*. New York: St. Martin's Press.

Butler, David, Andrew Adonis, and Tony Travers. 1994. *Failure in British Government: Politics of the Poll Tax*. 1st edition. Oxford: Oxford Paperbacks.

Butt, Ronald. 1967. *The Power of Parliament*. London: Walker.

Butt, Sarah. 2006. 'How Voters Evaluate Economic Competence: A Comparison between Parties in and out of Power'. *Political Studies* 54 (4): 743–66. https://doi.org/10.1111/j.1467-9248.2006.00631.x.

Byrne, Bridget, Claire Alexander, Omar Khan, James Nazroo, and William Shankley. 2020. *Ethnicity, Race and Inequality in the UK: State of the Nation*. Bristol: Policy Press.

Cain, Bruce E., John A. Ferejohn, and Morris P. Fiorina. 1984. 'The Constituency Service Basis of the Personal Vote for U.S. Representatives and British Members of Parliament'. *American Political Science Review* 78 (1): 110–25.

Calvert, Jonathan, and George Arbuthnott. 2021. *Failures of State: The Inside Story of Britain's Battle with Coronavirus*. London: Mudlark.

Camera, Chico, Peter John, Helen Margetts, and Scott A. Hale. 2020. 'Measuring the Volatility of the Political Agenda in Public Opinion and News Media'. *Public Opinion Quarterly* (accepted).

Campbell, Colin, and Graham Wilson. 1995. *The End of Whitehall: Death of a Paradigm?* Wiley.

Campbell, Rosie. 2006. *Gender and the Vote in Britain: Beyond the Gender Gap?* Colchester: ECPR Press.

Campbell, Rosie, and Sarah Childs. 2015. 'Conservatism, Feminisation and the Representation of Women in UK Politics'. *British Politics* 10 (2): 148–68.

Campbell, Rosie, and Philip Cowley. 2014. 'What Voters Want: Reactions to Candidate Characteristics in a Survey Experiment'. *Political Studies* 62 (4): 745–65.

Campbell, Rosie, and Kristi Winters. 2008. 'Understanding Men's and Women's Political Interests: Evidence from a Study of Gendered Political Attitudes'. *Journal of Elections, Public Opinion and Parties* 18 (1): 53–74. https://doi.org/10.1080/17457280701858623.

Campbell, Rosie, Sarah Childs, and Elizabeth Hunt. 2018. 'Women in the House of Commons'. In *Exploring Parliament*, edited by Cristina Leston-Bandeira, and Louise Thompson. Oxford: Oxford University Press.

Campbell, Rosie, Philip Cowley, Nick Vivyan, and Markus Wagner. 2019. 'Legislator Dissent as a Valence Signal'. *British Journal of Political Science* 49 (1): 105–28. https://doi.org/10.1017/S0007123416000223.

Canavire-Bacarreza, Gustavo, Eric Neumayer, and Peter Nunnenkamp. 2015. 'Why Aid Is Unpredictable: An Empirical Analysis of the Gap Between Actual and Planned Aid Flows'. *Journal of International Development* 27 (May). https://doi.org/10.1002/jid.3073.

Carl, Noah, James Dennison, and Geoffrey Evans. 2019. 'European but Not European Enough: An Explanation for Brexit'. *European Union Politics* 20 (2): 282–304. https://doi.org/10.1177/1465116518802361.

Carpini, Delli. 1997. *What Americans Know about Politics and Why It Matters*. New edition. New Haven, CT: Yale University Press.

Castells, Manuel. 1978. *City Class and Power*. London: Macmillan International Higher Education.

Catalano, Ana. 2009. 'Women Acting for Women? An Analysis of Gender and Debate Participation in the British House of Commons 2005–2007'. *Politics & Gender* 5 (1): 45–68.

Chilcot, Lord. 2016. 'The Report of the Iraq Inquiry'. London: Report of a Committee of Privy Counsellors. www.gov.uk/government/publications/the-report-of-the-iraq-inquiry.

Childs, Sarah. 2004. 'A Feminised Style of Politics? Women MPs in the House of Commons'. *The British Journal of Politics and International Relations* 6 (1): 3–19.

Childs, Sarah. 2008. *Women and British Party Politics: Descriptive, Substantive and Symbolic Representation*. London: Routledge.

Childs, Sarah, and Philip Cowley. 2011. 'The Politics of Local Presence: Is There a Case for Descriptive Representation?' *Political Studies* 59 (1): 1–19. https://doi.org/10.1111/j.1467-9248.2010.00846.x.

Childs, Sarah, and Mona Lena Krook. 2008. 'Critical Mass Theory and Women's Political Representation'. *Political Studies* 56 (3): 725–36.

Childs, Sarah, and Mona Lena Krook. 2009. 'Analysing Women's Substantive Representation: From Critical Mass to Critical Actors'. *Government and Opposition* 44 (2): 125–45. https://doi.org/10.1111/j.1477-7053.2009.01279.x.

Christiansen, Lars, and Keith Dowding. 1994. 'Pluralism or State Autonomy? The Case of Amnesty International (British Section): The Insider/Outsider Group'. *Political Studies* 42 (1): 15–24.

Clarke, Harold D. 2004. *Political Choice in Britain*. Oxford: Oxford University Press.

Clarke, Harold D., and Marianne C. Stewart. 1995. 'Economic Evaluations, Prime Ministerial Approval and Governing Party Support: Rival Models Reconsidered'. *British Journal of Political Science* 25 (2): 145–70.

Clarke, Harold D., David Sanders, Marianne C. Stewart, and Paul F. Whiteley. 2003. 'Britain (Not) at the Polls, 2001'. *PS: Political Science and Politics* 36 (1): 59–64.

Clarke, Harold, David Sanders, Marianne Stewart, and Paul Whiteley. 2006. 'Taking the Bloom off New Labour's Rose: Party Choice and Voter Turnout in Britain, 2005'. *Journal of Elections, Public Opinion and Parties* 16 (1): 3–36.

Clarke, Harold D., David Sanders, Marianne C. Stewart, and Paul F. Whiteley. 2009. *Performance Politics and the British Voter*. Cambridge: Cambridge University Press.

Clarke, Harold, David Sanders, Marianne Stewart, and Paul Whiteley. 2011. 'Valence Politics and Electoral Choice in Britain, 2010'. *Journal of Elections, Public Opinion & Parties* 21 (2): 237–53. https://doi.org/10.1080/17457289.2011.562614.

Clarke, Nick, Will Jennings, Jonathan Moss, and Gerry Stoker. 2016. 'The Rise of Anti-Politics in Britain'. www.researchgate.net/publication/303496664_The_rise_of_anti-politics_in_Britain.

Clarke, Nick, Will Jennings, Jonathan Moss, and Gerry Stoker. 2018. *The Good Politician: Folk Theories, Political Interaction, and the Rise of Anti-Politics*. Cambridge: Cambridge University Press.

Clement, Matt. 2016. 'Medieval Riots'. In *A People's History of Riots, Protest and the Law: The Sound of the Crowd*, edited by Matt Clement, 49–76. London: Palgrave Macmillan UK. https://doi.org/10.1057/978-1-137-52751-6_3.

Coase, R. H. 1937. 'The Nature of the Firm'. *Economica* 6 (16): 386–405.

Coen, David, and Jeremy John Richardson. 2009. *Lobbying the European Union: Institutions, Actors, and Issues*. Oxford: Oxford University Press.

Colantone, Italo, and Piero Stanig. 2018. 'Global Competition and Brexit'. *American Political Science Review* 112 (2): 201–18. https://doi.org/10.1017/S0003055417000685.

Colebrook, Andrew, and Sarah Priddy. 2021. 'Ministers in the Conservative Governments: 2015, 2017 and 2019 Parliaments'. May. https://commonslibrary.parliament.uk/research-briefings/cbp-7335.

Coleman, James S. 1988. 'Social Capital in the Creation of Human Capital'. *American Journal of Sociology* 94 (January): S95–120. https://doi.org/10.1086/228943.

Conservative and Unionist Party. 2019. 'Conservative Manifesto 2019: Conservatives'. www.conservatives.com/our-plan.

Cook, Timothy E. 2005. *Governing with the News: The News Media as a Political Institution*. 2nd edition. Chicago, IL: University of Chicago Press.

Copus, Colin. 2004. *Party Politics and Local Government*. Manchester: Manchester University Press.

Cowley, Philip. 2004. 'Parliament: More Bleak House than Great Expectations'. *Parliamentary Affairs* 57 (2): 301–14. https://doi.org/10.1093/pa/gsh026.

Cowley, Philip. 2005. *The Rebels: How Blair Mislaid His Majority*. London: Politico's Publishing Ltd.

Cowley, Philip, and D. Kavanagh. 2016. *The British General Election of 2015*. New York: Springer.

Cowley, Philip, and Dennis Kavanagh. 2018. *The British General Election of 2017*. British General Election Series. London: Palgrave Macmillan. https://doi.org/10.1007/978-3-319-95936-8.

Cowley, Philip, and Philip Norton. 1999. 'Rebels and Rebellions: Conservative MPs in the 1992 Parliament'. *The British Journal of Politics & International Relations* 1 (1): 84–105.

Cowley, Philip, and Mark Stuart. 2014. 'In the Brown Stuff? Labour Backbench Dissent Under Gordon Brown, 2007–10'. *Contemporary British History* 28 (1): 1–23. https://doi.org/10.1080/13619462.2013.794694.

Crewe, Ivor. 1974. 'Do Butler and Stokes Really Explain Political Change in Britain?' *European Journal of Political Research* 2 (1): 47–92. https://doi.org/10.1111/j.1475-6765.1974.tb00748.x.

Crewe, Ivor. 1988. 'Has the Electorate Become Thatcherite?' In *Thatcherism*, edited by R. Skidelsky, 25–49. London: Chatto and Windus.

Crewe, Ivor, and Anthony King. 1995. *SDP: The Birth, Life, and Death of the Social Democratic Party*. Oxford: Oxford University Press.

Crick, Michael. 2018. *Sultan of Swing: The Life of David Butler*. London: Biteback Publishing.

Crossman, Richard Howard Stafford. 1979. *The Crossman Diaries: Selections from The Diaries of a Cabinet Minister, 1964–1970*. London: Hamilton.

Cunill, Marta Cantijoch, David Cutts, and Rachel Gibson. 2016. 'Moving Slowly up the Ladder of Political Engagement: A "Spill-over" Model of Internet Participation'. *The British Journal of Politics & International Relations* 18 (1): 26–48.

Curtice, John. 2010. 'So What Went Wrong with the Electoral System? The 2010 Election Result and the Debate About Electoral Reform'. *Parliamentary Affairs* 63 (4): 623–38.

Curtice, John. 2011. 'The Death of a Miserable Little Compromise: The Alternative Vote Referendum'. *Political Insight* 2 (2): 14–17. https://doi.org/10.1111/j.2041-9066.2011.00066.x.

Curtice, John. 2015a. *Scottish Independence Referendum 2014*. London: Biteback.

Curtice, John. 2015b. 'A Return to Normality? How the Electoral System Operated'. *Parliamentary Affairs* 68 (suppl. 1): 25–40. https://doi.org/10.1093/pa/gsv025.

Curtice, John. 2017. 'General Election 2017: A New Two-Party Politics?' *Political Insight* 8 (2): 4–8. https://doi.org/10.1177/2041905817726889.

Curtice, John. 2018. 'How the Electoral System Failed to Deliver—Again'. *Parliamentary Affairs* 71 (suppl_1): 29–45. https://doi.org/10.1093/pa/gsx060.

Curtice, John. 2020a. 'Brave New World: Understanding the 2019 General Election'. *Political Insight* 11 (1): 8–12.

Curtice, John. 2020b. 'A Return to "Normality" at Last? How the Electoral System Worked in 2019'. *Parliamentary Affairs* 73 (suppl. 1): 29–47. https://doi.org/10.1093/pa/gsaa021.

Curtice, John, and Holli Semetko. 1994. 'Does It Matter What the Papers Say?' In *Labour's Last Chance*, edited by Anthony Heath, Roger Jowell, and John Curtice with Bridget Taylor, 43–64. Brookfield, VT: Dartmouth.

Curtice, John, and Ben Seyd. 2003. 'Is There a Crisis of Political Participation?' In *British Social Attitudes: Continuity and Change Over Two Decades*, edited by Alison Park, John Curtice, Katarina Thomson, Lindsey Jarvis, and Catherine Bromley, 93–108. London: Sage Publications Ltd. https://doi.org/10.4135/9781849208628.n5.

Curtice, John, and Michael Steed. 1986. 'Proportionality and Exaggeration in the British Electoral System'. *Electoral Studies* 5 (3): 209–28. https://doi.org/10.1016/0261-3794(86)90012-0.

Custodi, Jacopo. 2020. 'Nationalism and Populism on the Left: The Case of Podemos'. *Nations and Nationalism*. https://doi.org/10.1111/nana.12663.

Cutts, David, Edward Fieldhouse, and Peter John. 2009. 'Is Voting Habit Forming? The Longitudinal Impact of a GOTV Campaign in the UK'. *Journal of Elections, Public Opinion & Parties* 19 (3): 251–63. https://doi.org/10.1080/17457280903073914.

Cutts, David, Matthew Goodwin, Oliver Heath, and Paula Surridge. 2020. 'Brexit, the 2019 General Election and the Realignment of British Politics'. *The Political Quarterly* 91 (1): 7–23.

Daddow, Oliver. 2009. ' "Tony's War"? Blair, Kosovo and the Interventionist Impulse in British Foreign Policy'. *International Affairs (Royal Institute of International Affairs 1944–)* 85 (3): 547–60.

Dahl, Robert A. 1956. *A Preface to Democratic Theory*. Chicago, IL: University of Chicago Press.

Dahl, Robert A. 1961. *Who Governs? Democracy and Power in an American City*. New Haven, CT: Yale University Press.

Dahlerup, Drude. 1988. 'From a Small to a Large Minority: Women in Scandinavian Politics'. *Scandinavian Political Studies* 11 (4): 275–98. https://doi.org/10.1111/j.1467-9477.1988.tb00372.x.

Dalton, Russell J. 2004. *Democratic Challenges, Democratic Choices: The Erosion of Political Support in Advanced Industrial Democracies. Democratic Challenges, Democratic Choices*. Oxford: Oxford University Press. www.oxfordscholarship.com/view/10.1093/acprof:oso/9780199268436.001.0001/acprof-9780199268436.

Dalton, Russell J. 2015. *The Good Citizen: How a Younger Generation Is Reshaping American Politics*. London: CQ Press.

Dalton, Russell J. 2017. *The Participation Gap: Social Status and Political Inequality*. Oxford; New York: Oxford University Press.

Dalton, Russell J., David M. Farrell, and Ian McAllister. 2011. *Political Parties and Democratic Linkage: How Parties Organize Democracy*. Comparative Study of Electoral Systems. Oxford; New York: Oxford University Press.

Danewid, Ida. 2020. 'The Fire This Time: Grenfell, Racial Capitalism and the Urbanisation of Empire'. *European Journal of International Relations* 26 (1): 289–313. https://doi.org/10.1177/1354066119858388.

Danigelis, Nicholas L., Melissa Hardy, and Stephen J. Cutler. 2007. 'Population Aging, Intracohort Aging, and Sociopolitical Attitudes'. *American Sociological Review* 72 (5): 812–30. https://doi.org/10.1177/000312240707200508.

Dearlove, John. 2011. *The Politics of Policy in Local Government: The Making and Maintenance of Public Policy in the Royal Borough of Kensington and Chelsea*. Cambridge: Cambridge University Press.

Deas, Iain. 2014. 'The Search for Territorial Fixes in Subnational Governance: City-Regions and the Disputed Emergence of Post-Political Consensus in Manchester, England'. *Urban Studies* 51 (11): 2285–2314. https://doi.org/10.1177/0042098013510956.

Dehousse, Renaud. 1998. 'The Juridification of the Policy Process'. In *The European Court of Justice: The Politics of Judicial Integration*, edited by Renaud Dehousse, 97–116. The European Union Series. London: Macmillan Education UK. https://doi.org/10.1007/978-1-349-26954-9_5.

Dekavalla, Marina. 2015. 'The Scottish Newspaper Industry in the Digital Era'. *Media, Culture & Society* 37 (1): 107–14. https://doi.org/10.1177/0163443714553565.

Dennison, James, and Bobby Duffy. 2021. 'Lockdown Scepticism and Brexit Support'. London: King's College London. www.kcl.ac.uk/policy-institute/assets/lockdown-scepticism-and-brexit-support.pdf.

Denny, Kevin, and Orla Doyle. 2008. 'Political Interest, Cognitive Ability and Personality: Determinants of Voter Turnout in Britain'. *British Journal of Political Science* 38 (2): 291–310. https://doi.org/10.1017/S000712340800015X.

Denver, David. 1998. *Elections and Voting Behaviour in Britain*. London: Macmillan International Higher Education.

Denver, David, Christopher Carman, and Robert Johns. 2012. *Elections and Voters in Britain*. London: Macmillan International Higher Education.

Department for Digital, Culture, Media and Sport. 2020. 'National Data Strategy'. www.gov.uk/government/publications/uk-national-data-strategy/national-data-strategy.

Dewan, Torun, and Keith Dowding. 2005. 'The Corrective Effect of Ministerial Resignations on Government Popularity'. *American Journal of Political Science* 49 (1): 46–56.

Dewan, Torun, and David P. Myatt. 2008. 'The Qualities of Leadership: Direction, Communication, and Obfuscation'. *American Political Science Review* 102 (3): 351–68.

Dewan, Torun, and David P. Myatt. 2010. 'The Declining Talent Pool of Government'. *American Journal of Political Science* 54 (2): 267–86.

Dicey, Albert Venn. 1889. *Introduction to the Study of the Law of the Constitution*. London: Macmillan and Company.

Dickson, Brice. 2015. 'Activism and Restraint within the UK Supreme Court'. *European Journal of Current Legal Issues* 21 (1). http://webjcli.org/article/view/399.

Dixon, Ruth M. 2021. 'Impact of the House of Lords: Analysis of Parliamentary Session 2016–17'. April. https://lordslibrary.parliament.uk/research-briefings/lln-2019-0100.

Dobreva, Diyana, Daniel Grinnell, and Martin Innes. 2020. 'Prophets and Loss: How "Soft Facts" on Social Media Influenced the Brexit Campaign and Social Reactions to the Murder of Jo Cox MP'. *Policy & Internet* 12 (2): 144–64.

Doherty, Bob, Yaadwinder Sidhu, Tony Heron, Chris West, Alice Seaton, Jane Gulec, Patricia Prado, and Paulina Flores Martinez. 2020. 'Citizen Participation in Food Systems Policy Making: A Case Study of a Citizens' Assembly'. *Emerald Open Research* 2 (May): 22. https://doi.org/10.35241/emeraldopenres.13609.1.

Donoughue, Bernard. 2006. *Downing Street Diary: With Harold Wilson in No. 10*. New edition. London: Pimlico.

Donoughue, Bernard. 2008. *Downing Street Diary*. New York: Random House.

Dorussen, Han, and Michael Taylor. 2003. *Economic Voting*. London: Routledge.

Dowding, Keith. 1996. *Power*. Maidenhead: Open University Press.

Dowding, Keith. 2013a. 'Prime Ministerial Power: Institutional and Personal Factors'. In *Understanding Prime-Ministerial Performance: Comparative Perspectives*, edited by Paul Strangio, Paul 't Hart, and James Walter. Oxford: Oxford University Press.

Dowding, Keith. 2013b. 'The Prime Ministerialisation of the British Prime Minister'. *Parliamentary Affairs* 66 (3): 617–35. https://doi.org/10.1093/pa/gss007.

Dowding, Keith, Peter John, and Daniel Rubenson. 2012. 'Geographic Mobility, Social Connections and Voter Turnout'. *Journal of Elections, Public Opinion and Parties* 22 (2): 109–22. https://doi.org/10.1080/17457289.2011.634589.

Downs, Anthony. 1957. *An Economic Theory of Democracy*. New York: Harper & Row.

Drewry, Gavin, and Study of Parliament Group. 1985. *The New Select Committees: A Study of the 1979 Reforms*. Oxford: Clarendon Press.

Driver, Stephen. 2011. *Understanding British Party Politics*. Cambridge, UK; Malden, MA: Polity Press.

Druckman, James N. 2001. 'The Implications of Framing Effects for Citizen Competence'. *Political Behavior* 23 (3): 225–56. https://doi.org/10.1023/A:1015006907312.

Druckman, James N., and Matthew S. Levendusky. 2019. 'What Do We Measure When We Measure Affective Polarization?' *Public Opinion Quarterly* 83 (1): 114–22. https://doi.org/10.1093/poq/nfz003.

Druckman, James N., Samara Klar, Yanna Krupnikov, Matthew Levendusky, and John Barry Ryan. 2020a. 'How Affective Polarization Shapes Americans' Political Beliefs: A Study of Response to the COVID-19 Pandemic'. *Journal of Experimental Political Science* August: 1–12. https://doi.org/10.1017/XPS.2020.28.

Druckman, James N., Samara Klar, Yanna Krupnikov, Matthew Levendusky, and John Barry Ryan. 2020b. 'Affective Polarization, Local Contexts and Public Opinion in America'. *Nature Human Behaviour* November: 1–11. https://doi.org/10.1038/s41562-020-01012-5.

Duffy, Bobby. 2020. 'Is Britain Really a Nation Divided?' *Political Insight* 11 (3): 22–25. https://doi.org/10.1177/2041905820958819.

Duffy, Bobby, Kirstie Anne Hewlett, Julian McCrae, and John Hall. 2019. 'Divided Britain? Polarisation and Fragmentation Trends in the UK'. September. https://kclpure.kcl.ac.uk/portal/en/publications/divided-britain-polarisation-and-fragmentation-trends-in-the-uk(6b45e664-f08d-4a09-822c-aa17c2c4a8ae).html.

Dunleavy, Patrick. 1981. *The Politics of Mass Housing in Britain, 1945–75: A Study of Corporate Power and Professional Influence in the Welfare State*. Oxford: Clarendon Press.

Dunleavy, Patrick. 1987. 'Class Dealignment in Britain Revisited'. *West European Politics* 10 (3): 400–19. https://doi.org/10.1080/01402388708424640.

Dunleavy, Patrick. 1991. *Democracy, Bureaucracy and Public Choice: Economic Explanations in Political Science*. London: Harvester Wheatsheaf.

Dunleavy, Patrick. 1995a. 'Estimating the Distribution of Positional Influence in Cabinet Committees under Major'. In *Prime Minister, Cabinet and Core Executive*, edited by R. A. W. Rhodes and Patrick Dunleavy, 298–321. London: Macmillan Education UK. https://doi.org/10.1007/978-1-349-24141-5_14.

Dunleavy, Patrick. 1995b. 'Policy Disasters: Explaining the UK's Record'. *Public Policy and Administration* 10 (June): 52–70. https://doi.org/10.1177/095207679501000205.

Dunleavy, Patrick. 2005. 'Facing Up to Multi-Party Politics: How Partisan Dealignment and PR Voting Have Fundamentally Changed Britain's Party Systems'. *Parliamentary Affairs* 58 (3): 503–32. https://doi.org/10.1093/pa/gsi049.

Dunleavy, Patrick. 2006. *The Westminster Model and the Distinctiveness of British Politics*. Basingstoke: Palgrave Macmillan.

Dunleavy, Patrick. 2012. 'Duverger's Law Is a Dead Parrot. European Political Scientists Need to Recognize That Plurality or Majority Voting Has No Tendency at All to Produce Two Party Politics'. *EUROPP* (blog). 20 June. https://blogs.lse.ac.uk/europpblog/2012/06/20/duvergers-law-is-dead.

Dunleavy, Patrick, and Leandro Carrera. 2013. *Growing the Productivity of Government Services*. Cheltenham: Edward Elgar Publishing. https://ideas.repec.org/b/elg/eebook/14497.html.

Dunleavy, Patrick, and Dominic Muir. 2013. 'Parliament Bounces Back: How Select Committees Have Become a Power in the Land'. *Democratic Audit Blog* (blog). www.democraticaudit.com/2013/07/18/parliament-bounces-back-how-select-committees-have-become-a-power-in-the-land.

Dunleavy, Patrick, and R. A. W. Rhodes. 1995. *Prime Minister, Cabinet and Core Executive*. London: Macmillan Education UK.

Dunleavy, Patrick, Alice Park, and Ros Taylor. 2018. *The UK's Changing Democracy*. London: LSE Press. https://doi.org/10.31389/book1.

Dunleavy, Patrick, Helen Margetts, Jane Tinkler, and Simon Bastow. 2006. *Digital Era Governance: IT Corporations, the State, and e-Government*. Oxford: Oxford University Press.

Dunlop, Claire A., Claudio M. Radaelli, and Philipp Trein, eds. 2019. *Learning in Public Policy: Analysis, Modes and Outcomes*. London: Palgrave Macmillan.

Dunsire, Andrew, Christopher Hood, and Meg Huby. 1989. *Cutback Management in Public Bureaucracies: Popular Theories and Observed Outcomes in Whitehall*. Cambridge: Cambridge University Press.

Durose, Catherine, and Liz Richardson. 2015. *Designing Public Policy for Co-Production: Theory, Practice and Change*. 1st edition. Bristol: Policy Press.

Durrant, Tim, Nicola Blacklaws, and Ketaki Zodgekar. 2020. 'Special Advisers and the Johnson Government'. October. www.instituteforgovernment.org.uk/publications/special-advisers.

Duverger, Maurice. 1963. *Political Parties: Their Organization and Activity in the Modern State*. New York: Wiley.

Eckersley, Peter, and Paul Tobin. 2019. 'The Impact of Austerity on Policy Capacity in Local Government'. *Policy & Politics* 47 (3): 455–72. https://doi.org/10.1332/030557319X15613701303511.

Eckstein, Harry. 1960. *Pressure Group Politics: The Case of the British Medical Association*. Stanford, CA: Stanford University Press.

Ekman, Joakim, and Erik Amnå. 2012. 'Political Participation and Civic Engagement: Towards a New Typology'. *Human Affairs* 22 (3): 283–300. https://doi.org/10.2478/s13374-012-0024-1.

Electoral Commission (Great Britain), ed. 2004. *Gender and Political Participation: Research Report, April 2004*. London: Electoral Commission.

Elliott, Michael. 1981. 'The Role of Law in Central-Local Relations'. https://blackwells.co.uk/bookshop/product/The-Role-of-Law-in-Central-Local-Relations-by-Michael-J-Elliott-Social-Science-Research-Council-Great-Britain/9780862260248.

Erikson, Robert S. 1988. 'The Puzzle of Midterm Loss'. *The Journal of Politics* 50 (4): 1011–29. https://doi.org/10.2307/2131389.

Evans, Elizabeth, and Lisa Harrison. 2012. 'Candidate Selection in British Second Order Elections: A Comparison of Electoral System and Party Strategy Effects'. *Journal of Legislative Studies* 18 (June). https://doi.org/10.1080/13572334.2012.673067.

Evans, Geoffrey, and Jonathan Mellon. 2020. 'The Re-Shaping of Class Voting: The British Election Study'. www.britishelectionstudy.com/bes-findings/the-re-shaping-of-class-voting-in-the-2019-election-by-geoffrey-evans-and-jonathan-mellon/#.XsKTt8bTV0s.

Evans, Geoffrey, and Anand Menon. 2017. *Brexit and British Politics*. New York: Wiley.

Evans, Geoffrey, and James Tilley. 2017. *The New Politics of Class: The Political Exclusion of the British Working Class*. Oxford; New York: Oxford University Press.

Evans, Geoffrey, Anthony Heath, and Mansur Lalljee. 1996. 'Measuring Left-Right and Libertarian-Authoritarian Values in the British Electorate'. *The British Journal of Sociology* 47 (1): 93–112. https://doi.org/10.2307/591118.

Evans, Jocelyn, and Jon Tonge. 2009. 'Social Class and Party Choice in Northern Ireland's Ethnic Blocs'. *West European Politics* 32 (5): 1012–30. https://doi.org/10.1080/01402380903065157.

Evans, Jocelyn, Kai Arzheimer, Rosie Campbell, and Philip Cowley. 2017. 'Candidate Localness and Voter Choice in the 2015 General Election in England'. *Political Geography* 59 (July): 61–71. https://doi.org/10.1016/j.polgeo.2017.02.009.

Ewing, Keith. 2009. 'Judiciary'. *The Oxford Handbook of British Politics*. July. https://doi.org/10.1093/oxfordhb/9780199230952.003.0015.

Exadaktylos, T., and C. Radaelli. 2012. *Research Design in European Studies: Establishing Causality in Europeanization*. New York: Springer.

Farrell, David M., and Rüdiger Schmitt-Beck. 2002. *Do Political Campaigns Matter? Campaign Effects in Elections and Referendums*. Hove: Psychology Press.

Featherstone, Kevin, and Claudio M. Radaelli. 2003. *The Politics of Europeanization*. Oxford: Oxford University Press.

Fenno, Richard F. 1978. *Home Style: House Members in Their Districts*. Boston, MA: Little, Brown.

Fieldhouse, Edward. 1995. 'Thatcherism and the Changing Geography of Political Attitudes, 1964–1987'. *Political Geography* 14 (1): 3–30. https://doi.org/10.1016/0962-6298(94)P4049-D.

Fieldhouse, Edward, and David Cutts. 2008. 'Diversity, Density and Turnout: The Effect of Neighbourhood Ethno-Religious Composition on Voter Turnout in Britain'. *Political Geography* 27 (5): 530–48. https://doi.org/10.1016/j.polgeo.2008.04.002.

Fieldhouse, Edward, Jane Green, Geoffrey Evans, Jonathan Mellon, Christopher Prosser, Hermann Schmitt, and Cees van der Eijk. 2019. *Electoral Shocks: The Volatile Voter in a Turbulent World*. Oxford; New York: Oxford University Press.

Finer, Samuel Edward. 1975. *Adversary Politics and Electoral Reform*. London: Anthony Wigram.

Fiorina, Morris P. 1981. *Retrospective Voting in American National Elections*. New Haven, CT: Yale University Press.

Flickinger, Richard S., and Donley T. Studlar. 1992. 'The Disappearing Voters? Exploring Declining Turnout in Western European Elections'. *West European Politics* 15 (2): 1–16. https://doi.org/10.1080/01402389208424903.

Flinders, Matthew. 2008. *Delegated Governance and the British State: Walking without Order*. Oxford: Oxford University Press.

Flinders, Matthew. 2009. *The Oxford Handbook of British Politics*. Oxford: Oxford University Press.

Flinders, Matthew, and Jim Buller. 2006. 'Depoliticisation: Principles, Tactics and Tools'. *British Politics* 1 (3): 293–318.

Foley, Michael. 2001. *The British Presidency*. 2nd edition. Manchester: Manchester University Press.

Foos, Florian, and Daniel Bischof. 2019. 'Can the Tabloid Media Create Eurosceptic Attitudes? A Quasi-Experiment on Media Influence in England', unpublished ms.

Foos, Florian, and Peter John. 2018. 'Parties Are No Civic Charities: Voter Contact and the Changing Partisan Composition of the Electorate'. *Political Science Research and Methods* 6 (2): 283–98. https://doi.org/10.1017/psrm.2016.48.

Foos, Florian, Peter Charles John, Christian Mueller, and Kevin Cunningham. 2020. 'Social Mobilisation in Partisan Spaces'. *The Journal of Politics* July. https://doi.org/10.1086/710970.

Ford, Robert. 2008. 'Is Racial Prejudice Declining in Britain? 1'. *The British Journal of Sociology* 59 (4): 609–36.

Ford, Robert, and Matthew J. Goodwin. 2014. *Revolt on the Right: Explaining Support for the Radical Right in Britain*. London: Routledge.

Foster, Christopher. 2005. *British Government in Crisis*. London: Bloomsbury Publishing.

Fouirnaies, Alexander, and Hande Mutlu-Eren. 2015. 'English Bacon: Copartisan Bias in Intergovernmental Grant Allocation in England'. *The Journal of Politics* 77 (3): 805–17. https://doi.org/10.1086/681563.

Franklin, Bob. 2006. *Local Journalism and Local Media: Making the Local News*. London: Routledge.

Franklin, Mark N. 1985. *The Decline of Class Voting in Britain: Changes in the Basis of Electoral Choice, 1964–1983*. Oxford: Clarendon Press.

Freedman, Lawrence. 2020. 'Scientific Advice at a Time of Emergency: SAGE and Covid-19'. *The Political Quarterly* 91 (3): 514–22. https://doi.org/10.1111/1467-923X.12885.

Friedrich, Carl J. 1937. *Constitutional Government and Politics: Nature and Development*. New York: Harper & Brothers Publishers.

Gains, Francesca. 2015. 'Metro Mayors: Devolution, Democracy and the Importance of Getting the "Devo Manc" Design Right'. *Representation* 51 (4): 425–37. https://doi.org/10.1080/00344893.2016.1165511.

Gains, Francesca, Peter C. John, and Gerry Stoker. 2005. 'Path Dependency and the Reform of English Local Government'. *Public Administration* 83 (1): 25–45.

Gamble, Andrew. 1974. *The Conservative Nation*. London: Routledge & Kegan Paul.

Gamble, Andrew. 1990. 'Theories of British Politics'. *Political Studies* 38 (3): 404–20.

Gamble, Andrew. 1994. *The Free Economy and the Strong State: The Politics of Thatcherism*. London: Macmillan Education UK.

Gamble, Andrew. 2017. *Between Europe and America: The Future of British Politics*. London: Macmillan International Higher Education.

Garnett, Mark. 2021. *The British Prime Minister in an Age of Upheaval*. 1st edition. Medford, OR: Polity.

Gaskell, Jen, and Gerry Stoker. 2020. 'Centralised or Multi-Level: Which Governance Systems Are Having a "Good" Pandemic?' *British Politics and Policy at LSE* (blog). 16 April. https://blogs.lse.ac.uk/politicsandpolicy/governance-systems-covid19.

Gaskell, Jen, Gerry Stoker, Will Jennings, and Daniel Devine. 2020. 'Covid-19 and the Blunders of Our Governments: Long-Run System Failings Aggravated by Political Choices'. *The Political Quarterly* 91 (3): 523–33. https://doi.org/10.1111/1467-923X.12894.

Gavazza, Alessandro, Mattia Nardotto, and Tommaso Valletti. 2019. 'Internet and Politics: Evidence from UK Local Elections and Local Government Policies'. *The Review of Economic Studies* 86 (5): 2092–2135.

Gavin, N. T. 2007. *Press and Television in British Politics: Media, Money and Mediated Democracy*. New York: Springer.

Gavin, Neil T. 2010. 'Pressure Group Direct Action on Climate Change: The Role of the Media and the Web in Britain—A Case Study'. *The British Journal of Politics & International Relations* 3 (12): 459–75.

Gavin, Neil T., and David Sanders. 2003. 'The Press and Its Influence on British Political Attitudes under New Labour'. *Political Studies* 51 (3): 573–91.

Geddes, Marc. 2019. *Dramas at Westminster: Select Committees and the Quest for Accountability*. Manchester: Manchester University Press.

George, Stephen. 1998. *An Awkward Partner: Britain in the European Community*. Oxford: Oxford University Press.

Gerber, Alan S., Donald P. Green, and Ron Shachar. 2003. 'Voting May Be Habit-Forming: Evidence from a Randomized Field Experiment'. *American Journal of Political Science* 47 (3): 540–50. https://doi.org/10.2307/3186114.

Ghonim, Wael. 2012. *Revolution 2.0: The Power of the People Is Greater Than the People in Power—A Memoir*. New York: Houghton Mifflin Harcourt.

Gibson, Rachel K., Wainer Lusoli, and Stephen Ward. 2016. 'Online Participation in the UK: Testing a "Contextualised" Model of Internet Effects'. *The British Journal of Politics and International Relations* June. https://journals.sagepub.com/doi/10.1111/j.1467-856x.2005.00209.x.

Gilardi, Fabrizio. 2010. 'Who Learns from What in Policy Diffusion Processes?' *American Journal of Political Science* 54 (3): 650–66.

Gill, Mike, Devi Sridhar, and Fiona Godlee. 2020. 'Lessons from Leicester: A Covid-19 Testing System That's Not Fit for Purpose'. *BMJ* 370 (July): m2690. https://doi.org/10.1136/bmj.m2690.

Gilroy, Paul. 2013. *There Ain't No Black in the Union Jack*. London: Routledge. https://doi.org/10.4324/9780203995075.

Glenn, Norval D., and Michael Grimes. 1968. 'Aging, Voting, and Political Interest'. *American Sociological Review* 33 (4): 563–75. https://doi.org/10.2307/2092441.

Goet, Niels D. 2019. 'Measuring Polarization with Text Analysis: Evidence from the UK House of Commons, 1811–2015'. *Political Analysis* 27 (4): 518–39. https://doi.org/10.1017/pan.2019.2.

Goet, Niels D., Thomas G. Fleming, and Radoslaw Zubek. 2020. 'Procedural Change in the UK House of Commons, 1811–2015'. *Legislative Studies Quarterly* 45 (1): 35–67. https://doi.org/10.1111/lsq.12249.

Golden, Miriam, and Brian Min. 2013. 'Distributive Politics Around the World'. *Annual Review of Political Science* 16 (1): 73–99. https://doi.org/10.1146/annurev-polisci-052209-121553.

Goldthorpe, John H., Catriona Llewellyn, and Clive Payne. 1987. *Social Mobility and Class Structure in Modern Britain*. Oxford: Clarendon Press.

Graham, Mark, and William H. Dutton, eds. 2019. *Society and the Internet: How Networks of Information and Communication Are Changing Our Lives*. 2nd edition. Oxford; New York: Oxford University Press.

Grand, Julian Le. 2010. 'Knights and Knaves Return: Public Service Motivation and the Delivery of Public Services'. *International Public Management Journal* March. https://doi.org/10.1080/10967490903547290.

Grant, Wyn. 1978. *Insider Groups, Outsider Groups and Interest Group Strategies in Britain*. Warwick: University of Warwick, Department of Politics.

Grant, Wyn. 1985. *Political Economy of Corporatism*. London: Macmillan International Higher Education.

Grant, Wyn. 2004. 'Pressure Politics: The Changing World of Pressure Groups'. *Parliamentary Affairs* 57 (2): 408–19. https://doi.org/10.1093/pa/gsh033.

Grasso, Maria Teresa, Stephen Farrall, Emily Gray, Colin Hay, and Will Jennings. 2019a. 'Thatcher's Children, Blair's Babies, Political Socialization and Trickle-Down Value Change: An Age, Period and Cohort Analysis'. *British Journal of Political Science* 49 (1): 17–36.

Grasso, Maria Teresa, Stephen Farrall, Emily Gray, Colin Hay, and Will Jennings. 2019b. 'Socialization and Generational Political Trajectories: An Age, Period and Cohort Analysis of Political Participation in Britain'. *Journal of Elections, Public Opinion and Parties* 29 (2): 199–221. https://doi.org/10.1080/17457289.2018.1476359.

Greasley, Stephen, and Peter John. 2011. 'Does Stronger Political Leadership Have a Performance Payoff? Citizen Satisfaction in the Reform of Subcentral Governments in England'. *Journal of Public Administration Research and Theory* 21 (2): 239–56. https://doi.org/10.1093/jopart/muq018.

Green, Donald P., and Alan S. Gerber. 2019. *Get Out the Vote*. 4th revised edition. Washington, DC: Brookings Institution Press.

Green, E. H. H. 1996. *The Crisis of Conservatism: The Politics, Economics and Ideology of the Conservative Party, 1880–1914: The Politics, Economics and Ideology of the British Conservative Party, 1880–1914*. 1st edition. London: Routledge.

Green, Jane, and Will Jennings. 2012. 'The Dynamics of Issue Competence and Vote for Parties in and out of Power: An Analysis of Valence in Britain, 1979–1997'. *European Journal of Political Research* 51 (4): 469–503. https://doi.org/10.1111/j.1475-6765.2011.02004.x.

Greenaway, John. 1992. 'British Conservatism and Bureaucracy'. *History of Political Thought* 13 (1): 129–60.

Greene, Zachary D. 2014. 'UK Voters See Divided Political Parties as Less Able to Make Sensible or Coherent Policies'. *British Politics and Policy at LSE* (blog). 22 November. https://blogs.lse.ac.uk/politicsandpolicy/uk-voters-see-divided-political-parties-as-less-able-to-make-sensible-or-coherent-policies.

Greene, Zachary David, and Matthias Haber. 2015. 'The Consequences of Appearing Divided: An Analysis of Party Evaluations and Vote Choice'. *Electoral Studies* 37 (March): 15–27. https://doi.org/10.1016/j.electstud.2014.11.002.

Greene, Zachary D., and Amanda A. Licht. 2018. 'Domestic Politics and Changes in Foreign Aid Allocation: The Role of Party Preferences'. *Political Research Quarterly* 71 (2): 284–301. https://doi.org/10.1177/1065912917735176.

Greenwood, R. 1981. 'Fiscal Pressure and Local Government in England and Wales'. In *Big Government in Hard Times*, edited by C. Hood, M. Wright, and M. Robertson. Oxford: Oxford University Press.

Gribble, Rachael, Simon Wessley, Susan Klein, David Alexander, Christopher Dandeker, and Nicola Fear. 2015. 'British Public Opinion after a Decade of War: Attitudes to Iraq and Afghanistan'. *Politics* 35 (June): 128–50. https://doi.org/10.1111/1467-9256.12073.

Griffith, John Aneurin Grey. 1966. *Central Departments and Local Authorities*. London: Allen & Unwin.

Griffith, John Aneurin Grey. 1974. *Parliamentary Scrutiny of Government Bills*. London: Allen and Unwin for PEP and the Study of Parliament Group.

Griffith, John Aneurin Grey. 1997. *The Politics of the Judiciary*. New York: Fontana.

Grimm, Pamela. 2010. 'Social Desirability Bias'. In *Wiley International Encyclopedia of Marketing*. American Cancer Society. https://doi.org/10.1002/9781444316568.wiem02057.

Grönlund, Kimmo, and Henry Milner. 2006. 'The Determinants of Political Knowledge in Comparative Perspective'. *Scandinavian Political Studies* 29 (4): 386–406. https://doi.org/10.1111/j.1467-9477.2006.00157.x.

Group, Glasgow University Media. 1976. *Bad News*. London: Routledge & K. Paul.

Guttsman, W. L. 1963. *The British Political Elite*. London: MacGibbon & Kee.

Gyford, J. 1985. *The Politics of Local Socialism*. London: George Allen & Unwin.

Habel, Philip, and Sarah Birch. 2019. 'A Field Experiment on the Effects of Ethnicity and Socioeconomic Status on the Quality of Representation'. *Legislative Studies Quarterly* 44 (3): 389–420.

Hall, Peter A. 1999. 'Social Capital in Britain'. *British Journal of Political Science* 29 (3): 417–61.

Hall, W., R. Tinati, and W. Jennings. 2018. 'From Brexit to Trump: Social Media's Role in Democracy'. *Computer* 51 (1): 18–27. https://doi.org/10.1109/MC.2018.1151005.

Hallsworth, Michael. 2018. 'Behavioural Government Using Behavioural Science to Improve How Governments Make Decision'. The Institute for Government. www.instituteforgovernment.org.uk/blog/government-must-tackle-bias-decision-making.

Hamilton, Alexander, and James Madison. 2015. *The Federalist Papers*. Scotts Valley, CA: CreateSpace Independent Publishing Platform.

Handsford, Thomas G., and Brad T. Gomez. 2010. 'Estimating the Electoral Effects of Voter Turnout'. *The American Political Science Review* 104 (2): 268–88.

Hanretty, Chris. 2013. 'The Decisions and Ideal Points of British Law Lords'. *British Journal of Political Science* 43 (3): 703–16.

Hanretty, Chris. 2014. 'Haves and Have-Nots before the Law Lords'. *Political Studies* 62 (3): 686–97. https://doi.org/10.1111/1467-9248.12041.

Hanretty, Chris. 2021. 'The Pork Barrel Politics of the Towns Fund'. *The Political Quarterly* 92 (1): 7–13. https://doi.org/10.1111/1467-923X.12970.

Hanretty, Chris, Benjamin E. Lauderdale, and Nick Vivyan. 2017. 'Dyadic Representation in a Westminster System'. *Legislative Studies Quarterly* 42 (2): 235–67.

Hansard Society. 2019. 'Audit of Political Engagement 16'. www.hansardsociety.org.uk/publications/reports/audit-of-political-engagement-16.

Hart, Paul 't, and Pat Gray. 2005. *Public Policy Disasters in Europe*. London: Routledge.

Hawkins, Darren G., David A. Lake, Daniel L. Nielson, and Michael J. Tierney. 2006. 'Delegation under Anarchy: States, International Organizations, and Principal-Agent Theory'. *Delegation and Agency in International Organizations* 3: 21.

Hay, Colin. 2002. *British Politics Today*. New York: Wiley.

Hay, Colin. 2013. *Why We Hate Politics*. New York: John Wiley & Sons.

Hay, Colin, and Ben Rosamond. 2002. 'Globalization, European Integration and the Discursive Construction of Economic Imperatives'. *Journal of European Public Policy* 9 (2): 147–67.

Heath, Anthony F. 2016. *Understanding Political Change: The British Voter 1964–1987*. New York: Elsevier.

Heath, Anthony F., Roger Jowell, and John Curtice. 1985. *How Britain Votes*. Oxford: Pergamon Press.

Heath, Anthony F., Roger M. Jowell, and John Curtice. 2001. *The Rise of New Labour: Party Policies and Voter Choices*. Oxford: Oxford University Press.

Heath, Anthony F., Stephen D. Fisher, David Sanders, and Maria Sobolewska. 2011. 'Ethnic Heterogeneity in the Social Bases of Voting at the 2010 British General Election'. *Journal of Elections, Public Opinion & Parties* 21 (2): 255–77. https://doi.org/10.1080/17457289.2011.562611.

Heath, Anthony F., Iain McLean, Bridget Taylor, and John Curtice. 1999. 'Between First and Second Order: A Comparison of Voting Behaviour in European and Local Elections in Britain'. *European Journal of Political Research* 35 (3): 389–414. https://doi.org/10.1023/A:1006924510899.

Heath, Anthony F., Stephen D. Fisher, Gemma Rosenblatt, David Sanders, and Maria Sobolewska. 2013. *The Political Integration of Ethnic Minorities in Britain*. Oxford: Oxford University Press.

Heath, Oliver. 2007. 'Explaining Turnout Decline in Britain, 1964–2005: Party Identification and the Political Context'. *Political Behavior* 29 (4): 493–516. https://doi.org/10.1007/s11109-007-9039-4.

Heath, Oliver. 2018. 'Policy Alienation, Social Alienation and Working-Class Abstention in Britain, 1964–2010'. *British Journal of Political Science* 48 (4): 1053–73.

Heclo, Hugh, and Aaron B. Wildavsky. 1974. *The Private Government of Public Money: Community and Policy Inside British Politics*. London: Macmillan.

Heffernan, Richard. 2003. 'Political Parties and the Party System'. In *Developments in British Politics*, edited by Patrick Dunleavy, Andrew Gamble, Richard Heffernan, and Gillian Peele. Vol. 7. London: Palgrave Macmillan. www.palgrave.com/products/title.aspx?PID=265379.

Heffernan, Richard. 2005. 'Exploring (and Explaining) the British Prime Minister'. *The British Journal of Politics and International Relations* 7 (4): 605–20. https://doi.org/10.1111/j.1467-856x.2005.00203.x.

Hennessy, Peter. 1989. *Whitehall*. London: Secker & Warburg.

Hibbing, John R, and Elizabeth Theiss-Morse. 2002. *Stealth Democracy: Americans' Beliefs about How Government Should Work*. Cambridge: Cambridge University Press. www.loc.gov/catdir/samples/cam031/2002073699.html.

Hindess, Barry. 1971. *The Decline of Working-Class Politics*. London: MacGibbon & Kee.

Hindmoor, Andrew. 2004. *New Labour at the Centre: Constructing Political Space*. Oxford: Oxford University Press.

Hindmoor, Andrew, Phil Larkin, and Andrew Kennon. 2009. 'Assessing the Influence of Select Committees in the UK: The Education and Skills Committee, 1997–2005'. *The Journal of Legislative Studies* 15 (1): 71–89. https://doi.org/10.1080/13572330802666844.

Hirst, Paul Q. 1989. *After Thatcher*. London: Collins.

Hix, Simon. 2015. 'Is the UK Marginalised in the EU?' *EUROPP* (blog). 20 October. https://blogs.lse.ac.uk/europpblog/2015/10/20/is-the-uk-marginalised-in-the-eu.

HM Government. 2015. 'The Civil Service Code'. gov.uk. www.gov.uk/government/publications/civil-service-code/the-civil-service-code.

Hobolt, Sara B., and Toni Rodon. 2020. 'Cross-Cutting Issues and Electoral Choice. EU Issue Voting in the Aftermath of the Brexit Referendum'. *Journal of European Public Policy* 27 (2): 227–45. https://doi.org/10.1080/13501763.2019.1701535.

Hobolt, Sara B., Thomas J. Leeper, and James Tilley. 2020. 'Divided by the Vote: Affective Polarization in the Wake of the Brexit Referendum'. *British Journal of Political Science*, February. www.cambridge.org/core/journals/british-journal-of-political-science.

Hodkinson, Stuart. 2019. *Safe as Houses: Private Greed, Political Negligence and Housing Policy After Grenfell*. Manchester: Manchester University Press.

Hofferbert, Richard I., and Ian Budge. 1992. 'The Party Mandate and the Westminster Model: Election Programmes and Government Spending in Britain, 1948–85'. *British Journal of Political Science* 22 (2): 151–82.

Höhmann, Daniel. 2020. 'When Do Men Represent Women's Interests in Parliament? How the Presence of Women in Parliament Affects the Legislative Behavior of Male Politicians'. *Swiss Political Science Review* 26 (1): 31–50. https://doi.org/10.1111/spsr.12392.

Hood, Christopher. 1983. *Tools of Government*. London: Macmillan International Higher Education.

Hood, Christopher. 2002. 'The Risk Game and the Blame Game'. *Government and Opposition* 37 (1): 15–37.

Hood, Christopher. 2010. *The Blame Game: Spin, Bureaucracy, and Self-Preservation in Government*. Princeton, NJ: Princeton University Press.

Hood, Christopher, and Ruth Dixon. 2015. *A Government That Worked Better and Cost Less? Evaluating Three Decades of Reform and Change in UK Central Government*. Oxford: Oxford University Press.

Hood, Christopher, Scott, Oliver James, George Jones, Colin Scott, and Tony Travers. 1999. *Regulation Inside Government: Waste Watchers, Quality Police, and Sleaze-Busters*. Oxford: Oxford University Press.

House of Commons. 2016. 'House of Commons: Women in the House of Commons after the 2020 Election—Women and Equalities Committee'. https://publications.parliament.uk/pa/cm201617/cmselect/cmwomeq/630/63002.htm.

House of Commons Public Accounts Committee. 2020. 'COVID-19: Supply of Ventilators'. https://committees.parliament.uk/work/621/covid19-supply-of-ventilators.

Huber, John D. 2000. 'Delegation to Civil Servants in Parliamentary Democracies'. *European Journal of Political Research* 37 (3): 397–413. https://doi.org/10.1023/A:1007033306962.

Hughes, Dr Melanie M., and Pamela M. Paxton. 2016. *Women, Politics, and Power: A Global Perspective*. 3rd edition. Los Angeles, CA: CQ Press.

Institute for Government. 2017a. 'Ministerial Directions'. The Institute for Government. 24 August. www.instituteforgovernment.org.uk/explainers/ministerial-directions.

Institute for Government. 2017b. 'Gender Balance in the Civil Service'. The Institute for Government. 20 October. www.instituteforgovernment.org.uk/explainers/gender-balance-civil-service.

Institute for Government. 2018. 'Ethnicity in the Civil Service'. The Institute for Government. 29 March. www.instituteforgovernment.org.uk/explainers/ethnicity-civil-service.

Inter-Parliamentary Union. 2021. 'Global and Regional Averages of Women in National Parliaments'. Parline: The IPU's Open Data Platform. 2021. https://data.ipu.org/women-averages.

James, Scott, and Lucia Quaglia. 2018. 'Brexit, the City and the Contingent Power of Finance'. *New Political Economy* 24 (2): 1–14. https://doi.org/10.1080/13563467.2018.1484717.

James, O., N. Petrovsky, A. Moseley, and G. Boyne. 2016. 'The Politics of Agency Death: Ministers and the Survival of Government Agencies in a Parliamentary System'. *British Journal of Political Science* 46 (4): 763–84.

Janis, Irving L. 1972. *Victims of Groupthink: A Psychological Study of Foreign-Policy Decisions and Fiascoes*. Oxford: Houghton Mifflin.

Jeffares, Stephen. 2014. *Interpreting Hashtag Politics: Policy Ideas in an Era of Social Media*. New York: Springer.

Jeffery, Charlie. 2007. 'The Unfinished Business of Devolution: Seven Open Questions'. *Public Policy and Administration* 22 (1): 92–108.

Jeffery, David. 2017. 'The Strange Death of Tory Liverpool: Conservative Electoral Decline in Liverpool, 1945–1996'. *British Politics* 12 (3): 386–407. https://doi.org/10.1057/s41293-016-0032-6.

Jenkins, Bill, and Andrew Gray. 1983. 'Bureaucratic Politics and Power: Developments in the Study of Bureaucracy'. *Political Studies* 31 (2): 177–93. https://doi.org/10.1111/j.1467-9248.1983.tb01340.x.

Jennings, Sir Ivor. 1948. *The Law and the Constitution*. London: University of London Press.

Jennings, Will, and Peter John. 2009. 'The Dynamics of Political Attention: Public Opinion and the Queen's Speech in the United Kingdom'. *American Journal of Political Science* 53 (4): 838–54. https://doi.org/10.1111/j.1540-5907.2009.00404.x.

Jennings, Will, and Peter John. 2010. 'Punctuations and Turning Points in British Politics: The Policy Agenda of the Queen's Speech, 1940–2005'. *British Journal of Political Science* 40 (July). https://doi.org/10.1017/S0007123409990068.

Jennings, Will, and Gerry Stoker. 2018. 'The Divergent Dynamics of Cities and Towns: Geographical Polarisation after Brexit'. *The Political Quarterly* 90 (S2): 155–66.

Jennings, Will, Martin Lodge, and Matt Ryan. 2018. 'Comparing Blunders in Government'. *European Journal of Political Research* 57 (1): 238–58. https://doi.org/10.1111/1475-6765.12230.

Jennings, Will, Nick Clarke, Jonathan Moss, and Gerry Stoker. 2017. 'The Decline in Diffuse Support for National Politics: The Long View on Political Discontent in Britain'. *Public Opinion Quarterly* 81 (3): 748–58. https://doi.org/10.1093/poq/nfx020.

Jogerst, Michael. 1993. *Reform in the House of Commons: The Select Committee System*. Lexington, KY: University Press of Kentucky.

John, Peter. 1993. *The Europeanisation of British Local Government: New Management Strategies*. Luton: Local Government Management Board.

John, Peter. 1994. 'Central-Local Government Relations in the 1980s and 1990s: Towards a Policy Learning Approach'. *Local Government Studies* 20 (3): 412–36. https://doi.org/10.1080/03003939408433737.

John, Peter. 1996. 'Europeanization in a Centralizing State: Multi-Level Governance in the UK'. *Regional & Federal Studies* 6 (2): 131–44. https://doi.org/10.1080/13597569608420972.

John, Peter. 2006. 'Explaining Policy Change: The Impact of the Media, Public Opinion and Political Violence on Urban Budgets in England'. *Journal of European Public Policy* 13 (7): 1053–68. https://doi.org/10.1080/13501760600924118.

John, Peter. 2009. 'Can Citizen Governance Redress the Representative Bias of Political Participation?' *Public Administration Review* 69 (3): 494–503.

John, Peter. 2014. 'The Great Survivor: The Persistence and Resilience of English Local Government'. *Local Government Studies* 40 (5): 687–704.

John, Peter. 2017a. 'Behavioural Science, Randomized Evaluations and the Transformation of Public Policy: The Case of the UK Government'. In *Psychological Governance and Public Policy*, edited by Jessica Pykett, Rhys Jones, and Mark Whitehead. Abingdon: Routledge.

John, Peter. 2017b. *Field Experiments in Political Science and Public Policy: Practical Lessons in Design and Delivery*. London: Taylor & Francis.

John, Peter, and Shaun Bevan. 2012. 'What Are Policy Punctuations? Large Changes in the Legislative Agenda of the UK Government, 1911–2008'. *Policy Studies Journal* 40 (1): 89–108. https://doi.org/10.1111/j.1541-0072.2011.00435.x.

John, Peter, and Toby Blume. 2017. 'Nudges That Promote Channel Shift: A Randomized Evaluation of Messages to Encourage Citizens to Renew Benefits Online'. *Policy & Internet* 9 (2): 168–83. https://doi.org/10.1002/poi3.148.

John, Peter, and Tessa Brannan. 2008. 'How Different Are Telephoning and Canvassing? Results from a "Get Out the Vote" Field Experiment in the British 2005 General Election'. *British Journal of Political Science* 38 (3): 565–74. https://doi.org/10.1017/S0007123408000288.

John, Peter, and Colin Copus. 2010. 'The United Kingdom: Is There Really an Anglo Model?' *The Oxford Handbook of Local and Regional Democracy in Europe*. 4 November. https://doi.org/10.1093/oxfordhb/9780199562978.003.0002.

John, Peter, and Helen Margetts. 2003. 'Policy Punctuations in the UK: Fluctuations and Equilibria in Central Government Expenditure since 1951'. *Public Administration* 81 (August): 411–32. https://doi.org/10.1111/1467-9299.00354.

John, Peter, and Helen Margetts. 2009. 'The Latent Support for the Extreme Right in British Politics'. *West European Politics* 32 (3): 496–513. https://doi.org/10.1080/01402380902779063.

John, Peter, and Hugh Ward. 2001. 'Political Manipulation in a Majoritarian Democracy: Central Government Targeting of Public Funds to English Subnational Government, in Space and across Time'. *The British Journal of Politics & International Relations* 3 (3): 308–39.

John, Peter, Ed Fieldhouse, and Hanhua Liu. 2005. 'The Civic Culture in Britain and America Fifty Years On'. www.academia.edu/2819084/The_Civic_Culture_in_Britain_and_America_Fifty_Years_On1.

John, Peter, Hugh Ward, and Keith Dowding. 2004. 'The Bidding Game: Competitive Funding Regimes and the Political Targeting of Urban Programme Schemes'. *British Journal of Political Science* 34 (3): 405–28.

John, Peter, A. Bertelli, W. Jennings, and S. Bevan. 2013. *Policy Agendas in British Politics*. New York: Springer.

John, Peter, Mark Johnson, Peter John, and Mark Johnson. 2008. 'Is There Still a Public Service Ethos?' In *British Social Attitudes: The 24th Report*, edited by Alison Park, John Curtice, Katarina Thomson, Miranda Phillips, Mark Johnson, and Elizabeth Clery, 105–26. London: Sage Publications Ltd. https://doi.org/10.4135/9781849208697.n5.

John, Peter, Sarah Cotterill, Alice Moseley, Liz Richardson, Graham Smith, Gerry Stoker, and Corinne Wales. 2019. *Nudge, Nudge, Think, Think: Experimenting with Ways to Change Citizen Behaviour*. Manchester: Manchester University Press.

Johns, Rob, and James Mitchell. 2016. *Takeover: Explaining the Extraordinary Rise of the SNP*. London: Biteback Publishing.

Johnston, Ron, and Charles Pattie. 2006. *Putting Voters in Their Place: Geography and Elections in Great Britain*. Oxford: Oxford University Press.

Johnston, Ron, Kelvyn Jones, and David Manley. 2018. 'Age, Sex, Qualifications and Voting at Recent English General Elections: An Alternative Exploratory Approach'. *Electoral Studies* 51 (February): 24–37. https://doi.org/10.1016/j.electstud.2017.11.006.

Jones, George W. 1964. 'The Prime Minister's Power'. *Parliamentary Affairs* 18 (2): 167–85.

Jones, George W. 1990. 'Mrs Thatcher and the Power of the PM'. *Contemporary Record* 3 (4): 2–6. https://doi.org/10.1080/13619469008581077.

Jones, George W., and Tony Travers. 1994. *Attitudes to Local Government in Westminster and Whitehall:*

A Report to the Commission for Local Democracy. London: CLD Ltd.

Jones, Harriet, and Michael D. Kandiah. 1996. *The Myth of Consensus: New Views on British History, 1945–64*. Houndmills: Palgrave Macmillan.

Jones, Owen. 2020. *This Land: The Struggle for the Left*. London: Penguin UK.

Jones, Peter, Martin Wynn, David Hillier, and Daphne Comfort. 2017. 'A Commentary on the City Deals in the UK'. *Journal of Public Affairs* 17 (3): e1661. https://doi.org/10.1002/pa.1661.

Jordan, Andrew. 2003. 'The Europeanization of National Government and Policy: A Departmental Perspective'. *British Journal of Political Science* 33 (2): 261–82.

Jordan, Grant, and Paul Cairney. 2013. 'What Is the "Dominant Model" of British Policymaking? Comparing Majoritarian and Policy Community Ideas'. *British Politics* 8 (3): 233–59.

Jordan, Grant, and W. Maloney. 2007. *Democracy and Interest Groups: Enhancing Participation?* London: Palgrave Macmillan. https://doi.org/10.1057/9780230223240.

Jordan, Grant, Frank R. Baumgartner, John D. McCarthy, Shaun Bevan, and Jamie Greenan. 2012. 'Tracking Interest Group Populations in the US and the UK'. In *The Scale of Interest Organization in Democratic Politics: Data and Research Methods*, edited by Darren Halpin and Grant Jordan, 141–60. Interest Groups, Advocacy and Democracy Series. London: Palgrave Macmillan. https://doi.org/10.1057/9780230359239_7.

Judge, David. 1993. *The Parliamentary State*. London: Sage Publications.

Judge, David. 2005. *Political Institutions in the United Kingdom*. Oxford: Oxford University Press.

Judge, David, and Cristina Leston-Bandeira. 2018. 'The Institutional Representation of Parliament'. *Political Studies* 66 (1): 154–72. https://doi.org/10.1177/0032321717706901.

Jungherr, Andreas, Gonzalo Rivero, and Daniel Gayo-Avello. 2020. *Retooling Politics: How Digital Media Are Shaping Democracy*. Cambridge; New York: Cambridge University Press.

Kakabadse, Andrew, Nada Kakabadse, Penny Moore, and Filipe Morais. 2018. 'Is Government Fit for Purpose? The Kakabadse Report'. Henley-on-Thames: Henley Business School. http://data.parliament.uk/writtenevidence/committeeevidence.svc/evidencedocument/public-administration-and-constitutional-affairs-committee/civil-service-effectiveness/written/79751.html#_ftn1.

Kalla, Joshua L., and David E. Broockman. 2018. 'The Minimal Persuasive Effects of Campaign Contact in General Elections: Evidence from 49 Field Experiments'. *American Political Science Review* 112 (1): 148–66.

Kam, Christopher, Anthony M. Bertelli, and Alexander Held. 2020. 'The Electoral System, the Party System and Accountability in Parliamentary Government'. *American Political Science Review* 114 (3): 744–60. https://doi.org/10.1017/S0003055420000143.

Kavanagh, Dennis, and Philip Cowley. 2010. *The British General Election of 2010*. London: Palgrave Macmillan.

Keane, John. 1991. *Media and Democracy*. Cambridge: Polity.

Keating, Michael. 2005. 'Policy Convergence and Divergence in Scotland under Devolution'. *Regional Studies* 39 (4): 453–63. https://doi.org/10.1080/00343400500128481.

Keating, Michael James. 2010. *The Government of Scotland: Public Policy Making after Devolution*. Edinburgh: Edinburgh University Press. https://abdn.pure.elsevier.com/en/publications/the-government-of-scotland-public-policy-making-after-devolution.

Keating, Michael, Paul Cairney, and Eve Hepburn. 2009. 'Territorial Policy Communities and Devolution in the UK'. *Cambridge Journal of Regions, Economy and Society* 2 (1): 51–66. https://doi.org/10.1093/cjres/rsn024.

Kellas, James G. 1989. *The Scottish Political System*. Cambridge: Cambridge University Press.

Kellermann, Michael. 2012. 'Estimating Ideal Points in the British House of Commons Using Early Day Motions'. *American Journal of Political Science* 56 (3): 757–71.

Kellermann, Michael. 2013. 'Sponsoring Early Day Motions in the British House of Commons as a Response to Electoral Vulnerability'. *Political Science Research and Methods* 1 (2): 263–80. https://doi.org/10.1017/psrm.2013.19.

Kellermann, Michael. 2016. 'Electoral Vulnerability, Constituency Focus, and Parliamentary Questions in the House of Commons'. *The British Journal of Politics and International Relations* 18 (1): 90–106. https://doi.org/10.1111/1467-856X.12075.

Kellner, Peter Ludwig, and Norman Crowther Crowther-Hunt Baron Crowther-Hunt. 1980. *The Civil Servants: An Inquiry into Britain's Ruling Class*. Boston, MA: Macdonald and Jane's.

Kelly, Scott. 2002. *The Myth of Mr. Butskell: The Politics of British Economic Policy, 1950–55*. Aldershot; Burlington, VT: Ashgate Publishing Limited.

Kelso, Alexandra. 2009. 'Parliament'. In *The Oxford Handbook of British Politics*. 16 July. https://doi.org/10.1093/oxfordhb/9780199230952.003.0013.

King, Anthony. 1975. 'Overload: Problems of Governing in the 1970s'. *Political Studies* 23 (2–3): 284–96.

King, Anthony. 1976. 'Modes of Executive-Legislative Relations: Great Britain, France, and West Germany'. *Legislative Studies Quarterly* 1 (1): 11–36. https://doi.org/10.2307/439626.

King, Anthony. 1981. 'The Rise of the Career Politician in Britain—And Its Consequences'. *British Journal of Political Science* 11 (3): 249–85.

King, Anthony. 1991. 'The British Prime Ministership in the Age of the Career Politician'. *West European Politics* 14 (2): 25–47. https://doi.org/10.1080/01402389108424843.

King, Anthony. 2007. *The British Constitution*. Oxford: Oxford University Press.

King, Anthony, and Nicholas Allen. 2010. '"Off with Their Heads": British Prime Ministers and the Power to

Dismiss'. *British Journal of Political Science* 40 (2): 249–78.

King, Anthony, and Ivor Crewe. 2014. *The Blunders of Our Governments*. London: Oneworld Publications.

King, Jeff. 2019. 'The Democratic Case for a Written Constitution'. *Current Legal Problems* 72 (1): 1–36. https://doi.org/10.1093/clp/cuz001.

Kingdon, John W. 1984. *Agendas, Alternatives, and Public Policies*. Boston, MA: Little, Brown.

Kirchheimer, O. 1966. 'The Transformation of the Western European Party Systems'. In *Political Parties and Political Development*, edited by Myron Weiner and Joseph LaPalombara. Studies in Political Development. Princeton, NJ: Princeton University Press.

Klapper, Joseph T. 1960. *Effects of Mass Communication*. Glencoe, IL: Free Press.

Krook, Mona Lena, and Diana Z. O'Brien. 2012. 'All the President's Men? The Appointment of Female Cabinet Ministers Worldwide'. *The Journal of Politics* 74 (3): 840–55.

Laakso, Markku. 1979. 'Should a Two-and-a-Half Law Replace the Cube Law in British Elections?' *British Journal of Political Science* 9 (3): 355–62. https://doi.org/10.1017/S0007123400001824.

Laakso, Markku, and Rein Taagepera. 1979. '"Effective" Number of Parties: A Measure with Application to West Europe'. *Comparative Political Studies*. https://doi.org/10.1177/001041407901200101.

Ladd, Jonathan McDonald, and Gabriel S. Lenz. 2009. 'Exploiting a Rare Communication Shift to Document the Persuasive Power of the News Media'. *American Journal of Political Science* 53 (2): 394–410.

Lai, B., and D. Reiter. 2005. 'Rally 'Round the Union Jack? Public Opinion and the Use of Force in the United Kingdom, 1948–2001'. *International Studies Quarterly* 49 (2): 255–72.

Lakin, Stuart. 2008. 'Debunking the Idea of Parliamentary Sovereignty: The Controlling Factor of Legality in the British Constitution'. *Oxford Journal of Legal Studies* 28 (4): 709–34.

Lamprinakou, Chrysa, Marco Morucci, Rosie Campbell, and Jennifer van Heerde-Hudson. 2017. 'All Change in the House? The Profile of Candidates and MPs in the 2015 British General Election'. *Parliamentary Affairs* 70 (2): 207–32. https://doi.org/10.1093/pa/gsw030.

Larcinese, Valentino. 2007. 'Does Political Knowledge Increase Turnout? Evidence from the 1997 British General Election'. *Public Choice* 131 (3): 387–411.

Lawless, Jennifer L. 2012. *Becoming a Candidate: Political Ambition and the Decision to Run for Office*. Illustrated edition. Cambridge; New York: Cambridge University Press.

Lazarsfeld, Paul F., and Robert King Merton. 1948. *Mass Communication, Popular Taste and Organized Social Action*. New York: Bobbs-Merrill, College Division.

Leduc, Lawrence. 2002. 'Opinion Change and Voting Behaviour in Referendums'. *European Journal of Political Research* 41 (6): 711–32.

Lee, Lucy, and Penny Young. 2013. 'A Disengaged Britain? Political Interest and Participation Over 30 Years'. In *British Social Attitudes: The 30th Report*, edited by A. Park, C. Bryson, E. Clery, J. Curtice, and M. Phillips, 62–86. London: NatCen.

Leon, Gabriel A., and Peter John. 2020. 'The Political Consequences of Urban Unrest: Vote Choices after the 2011 London Riots'. Unpublished.

Leslie, Patrick A., and Barış Arı. 2018. 'Could Rainfall Have Swung the Result of the Brexit Referendum?' *Political Geography* 65: 134–42.

Leston-Bandeira, Cristina, and Louise Thompson. 2018. *Exploring Parliament*. Oxford: Oxford University Press.

Lijphart, Arend. 1975. *The Politics of Accommodation: Pluralism and Democracy in the Netherlands*. Berkeley, CA: University of California Press.

Lijphart, Arend. 1999. *Patterns of Democracy: Government Forms and Performance in Thirty-Six Countries*. New Haven, CT: Yale University Press.

Lindblom, C. E. 1977. *Politics and Markets: The World's Political Economic Systems*. New York: Basic Books.

Linde, Jona, and Barbara Vis. 2017. 'Do Politicians Take Risks Like the Rest of Us? An Experimental Test of Prospect Theory Under MPs'. *Political Psychology* 38 (1): 101–17. https://doi.org/10.1111/pops.12335.

Linn, Suzanna, Jonathan Nagler, and Marco Morales. 2010. 'Economics, Elections, and Voting Behavior—Oxford Handbooks'. In *The Oxford Handbook of American Elections and Political Behavior*. Oxford: Oxford University Press. www.oxfordhandbooks.com/view/10.1093/oxfordhb/9780199235476.001.0001/oxfordhb-9780199235476-e-20.

Lipset, Seymour Martin, and Stein Rokkan. 1967. *Party Systems and Voter Alignments: Cross-National Perspectives*. Cambridge: Free Press.

Lizotte, Mary-Kate, and Andrew H. Sidman. 2009. 'Explaining the Gender Gap in Political Knowledge'. *Politics & Gender* 5 (02): 127. https://doi.org/10.1017/S1743923X09000130.

Loughlin, Martin. 1986. *Local Government in the Modern State*. Mytholmroyd: Sweet & Maxwell.

Loughlin, Martin. 1996. *Legality and Locality: The Role of Law in Central-Local Government Relations*. Oxford: Clarendon Press.

Loughlin, Martin. 2012. 'Prime Minister's Questions as Political Ritual'. *British Politics* 7 (4): 314–40.

Lovenduski, Joni. 1996. 'Sex, Gender and British Politics'. *Parliamentary Affairs* 49 (1): 1–16. https://doi.org/10.1093/oxfordjournals.pa.a028660.

Lovenduski, Joni. 2005. *Feminizing Politics*. New York: Wiley.

Lowndes, Vivien. 2004. 'Getting on or Getting By? Women, Social Capital and Political Participation'. *The British Journal of Politics & International Relations* 6 (1): 45–64. https://doi.org/10.1111/j.1467-856X.2004.00126.x.

Lowndes, Vivien, and Alison Gardner. 2016. 'Local Governance under the Conservatives: Super-Austerity, Devolution and the "Smarter State"'. *Local Government Studies* 42 (3): 357–75. https://doi.org/10.1080/03003930.2016.1150837.

Lowndes, Vivien, and Kerry McCaughie. 2013. 'Weathering the Perfect Storm? Austerity and Institutional Resilience in Local Government'. *Policy & Politics* 41 (4): 533–49. https://doi.org/10.1332/030557312X655747.

Lukes, Steven. 1977. *Power: A Radical View*. London: Macmillan.

Lundberg, Thomas Carl. 2014. 'Tensions Between Constituency and Regional Members of the Scottish Parliament Under Mixed-Member Proportional Representation: A Failure of the New Politics'. *Parliamentary Affairs* 67 (2): 351–70. https://doi.org/10.1093/pa/gss055.

Maggetti, Martino, and Philipp Trein. 2021. 'More Is Less: Partisan Ideology, Changes of Government, and Policy Integration Reforms in the UK'. *Policy and Society* April: 1–20. https://doi.org/10.1080/14494035.2021.1908673.

Mair, Peter, ed. 1990. *The West European Party System*. 1st Edition. Oxford; New York: Oxford University Press.

Maloney, William A. 1999. 'Contracting out the Participation Function: Social Capital and Chequebook Participation'. In *Social Capital and European Democracy*, 108–19. London: Routledge.

Maloney, William A., Graham Smith, and Gerry Stoker. 2016. 'Social Capital and Urban Governance: Adding a More Contextualized "Top-Down" Perspective'. *Political Studies* June. https://journals.sagepub.com/doi/10.1111/1467-9248.00284.

Margetts, Helen. 2017. 'Why Social Media May Have Won the 2017 General Election'. *The Political Quarterly* 88 (3): 386–90.

Margetts, Helen, Peter John, Tobias Escher, and Stéphane Reissfelder. 2011. 'Social Information and Political Participation on the Internet: An Experiment'. *European Political Science Review* 3 (3): 321–44. https://doi.org/10.1017/S1755773911000129.

Margetts, Helen, Peter John, Scott Hale, and Taha Yasseri. 2015. *Political Turbulence: How Social Media Shape Collective Action*. Princeton, NJ: Princeton University Press.

Marien, Sofie, Marc Hooghe, and Ellen Quintelier. 2010. 'Inequalities in Non-Institutionalised Forms of Political Participation: A Multi-Level Analysis of 25 Countries'. *Political Studies* 58 (1): 187–213.

Marmor, Theodore R., and David Thomas. 1972. 'Doctors, Politics and Pay Disputes: "Pressure Group Politics" Revisited'. *British Journal of Political Science* 2 (4): 421–42.

Marquand, David. 1981. 'Club Government: The Crisis of the Labour Party in the National Perspective'. *Government and Opposition* 16 (1): 19–36.

Marsh, David, T. O'Toole, and S. Jones. 2007. *Young People and Politics in the UK: Apathy or Alienation?* London: Palgrave Macmillan. https://doi.org/10.1057/9780230625631.

Marsh, David, and R. A. W. Rhodes. 1992. *Policy Networks in British Government*. Oxford: Clarendon Press.

Marsh, David, M. J. Smith, and D. Richards. 2000. 'Bureaucrats, Politicians and Reform in Whitehall: Analysing the Bureau-Shaping Model'. *British Journal of Political Science* 30 (3): 461–82.

Marshall, Geoffrey. 1971. *Constitutional Theory*. Oxford: Clarendon Press.

Marshall, Geoffrey. 1987. *Constitutional Conventions*. Oxford: Oxford University Press. https://doi.org/10.1093/acprof:oso/9780198762027.001.0001.

Marvin, Simon, Harriet Bulkeley, Lindsay Mai, Kes McCormick, and Yuliya Voytenko Palgan. 2018. *Urban Living Labs: Experimenting with City Futures*. London: Routledge.

Marylebone, Baron Quintin Hogg Hailsham of St. 1976. *Elective Dictatorship*. London: British Broadcasting Corporation.

McAllister, Laura, and Roger Awan-Scully. 2021. 'For Wales, Do Not See England? An Analysis of the 2017 General Election'. *Parliamentary Affairs* 74 (1): 138–57.

McCarty, Nolan, Keith T. Poole, and Howard Rosenthal. 2016. *Polarized America: The Dance of Ideology and Unequal Riches*. Cambridge, MA: MIT Press.

McCombs, Maxwell E., and Donald L. Shaw. 1972. 'The Agenda-Setting Function of Mass Media'. *The Public Opinion Quarterly* 36 (2): 176–87.

McCubbins, Mathew D., and Thomas Schwartz. 1984. 'Congressional Oversight Overlooked: Police Patrols versus Fire Alarms'. *American Journal of Political Science* 28 (1): 165. https://doi.org/10.2307/2110792.

McCubbins, Mathew D., Roger G. Noll, and Barry R. Weingast. 1987. 'Administrative Procedures as Instruments of Political Control'. *Journal of Law, Economics, & Organization* 3 (2): 243–77.

McDonald, Michael D., and Ian Budge. 2005. *Elections, Parties, Democracy: Conferring the Median Mandate*. Oxford: Oxford University Press. www.oxfordscholarship.com/view/10.1093/0199286728.001.0001/acprof-9780199286720.

McKay, Lawrence. 2020. 'Does Constituency Focus Improve Attitudes to MPs? A Test for the UK'. *The Journal of Legislative Studies* 26 (1): 1–26. https://doi.org/10.1080/13572334.2020.1726635.

McKenzie, Robert Trelford, and Allan Silver. 1968. *Angels in Marble: Working Class Conservatives in Urban England*. London: Heinemann Educational.

McLaren, Lauren, Anja Neundorf, and Ian Paterson. 2020. 'Diversity and Perceptions of Immigration: How the Past Influences the Present'. *Political Studies* June. https://doi.org/10.1177/0032321720922774.

McLean, Iain. 2001. *Rational Choice and British Politics: An Analysis of Rhetoric and Manipulation from Peel to Blair*. Oxford: Oxford University Press.

McLean, Iain. 2010. *What's Wrong with the British Constitution?* Oxford: Oxford University Press.

McMillan, Fraser. 2020. 'Devolution, "New Politics" and Election Pledge Fulfilment in Scotland, 1999–2011'. *British Politics* 15 (2): 251–69. https://doi.org/10.1057/s41293-019-00120-9.

Media Reform Coalition. 2021. 'Report: Who Owns the UK Media?' www.mediareform.org.uk/media-ownership/who-owns-the-uk-media.

Mellon, Jonathan, and Geoffrey Evans. 2016. 'The New Face of British Class Voting'. The British Election Study. www.britishelectionstudy.com/bes-resources/the-new-face-of-british-class-voting/#.XsNfTMbTV0s.

Mellon, Jonathan, and Christopher Prosser. 2017. 'Twitter and Facebook Are Not Representative of the General Population: Political Attitudes and Demographics of British Social Media Users'. *Research & Politics* July. https://doi.org/10.1177/2053168017720008.

Mellors, Colin. 1978. *The British MP: A Socio-Economic Study of the House of Commons*. Farnborough: Saxon House.

Mellows-Facer, Adam, Chloe Challender, and Paul Evans. 2019. 'Select Committees: Agents of Change'. *Parliamentary Affairs* 72 (4): 903–22. https://doi.org/10.1093/pa/gsz039.

Mendelsohn, M., and A. Parkin. 2001. *Referendum Democracy: Citizens, Elites and Deliberation in Referendum Campaigns*. New York: Springer.

Mesquita, Bruce Bueno de, and Alastair Smith. 2009. 'A Political Economy of Aid'. *International Organization* 63 (2): 309–40. https://doi.org/10.1017/S0020818309090109.

Mezey, Michael L. 1979. *Comparative Legislatures*. Publications of the Consortium for Comparative Legislative Studies. Durham, NC: Duke University Press.

Miliband, Ralph. 1961. *Parliament Socialism: A Study in the Politics of Labour*. London: G. Allen & Unwin.

Miliband, Ralph. 1972. *Parliamentary Socialism: A Study in the Politics of Labour*. London: Merlin Press.

Mill, John Stuart. 1861. *Considerations on Representative Government*. London: Parker, Son, and Bourn.

Miller, John. 2014. *The Glorious Revolution*. London: Routledge.

Miller, Vaughne. 2014. 'How Much Legislation Comes from Europe?' June. https://commonslibrary.parliament.uk/how-much-legislation-comes-from-europe.

Miller, Warren E., and Donald E. Stokes. 1963. 'Constituency Influence in Congress'. *The American Political Science Review* 57 (1): 45–56. https://doi.org/10.2307/1952717.

Miller, William L. 1991. *Media and Voters: The Audience, Content, and Influence of Press and Television at the 1987 General Election*. Oxford: Clarendon Press.

Milligan, Kevin, Enrico Moretti, and Philip Oreopoulos. 2004. 'Does Education Improve Citizenship? Evidence from the United States and the United Kingdom'. *Journal of Public Economics* 88 (9–10): 1667–95.

Milner, Henry. 2002. *Civic Literacy*. Hanover, NH: Tufts University Press.

Mitchell, James. 2000. 'New Parliament, New Politics in Scotland'. *Parliamentary Affairs* 53 (3): 605–21. https://doi.org/10.1093/pa/53.3.605.

Mitchell, James. 2013. *Devolution in the UK. Devolution in the UK*. Manchester: Manchester University Press. www.manchesterhive.com/view/9781847793270/9781847793270.xml.

Mitchell, James. 2019. '10. Has Devolution Strengthened the UK Constitution?' *Has Devolution Worked?*, 145. www.instituteforgovernment.org.uk/sites/default/files/publications/has-devolution-worked-essay-collection-FINAL.pdf.

Mitchell, James, and Ailsa Henderson. 2020. 'Tribes and Turbulence: The 2019 UK General Election in Scotland'. *Parliamentary Affairs* 73 (suppl. 1): 142–56. https://doi.org/10.1093/pa/gsaa027.

Moe, Terry M. 1984. 'The New Economics of Organization'. *American Journal of Political Science* 28 (4): 739–77. https://doi.org/10.2307/2110997.

Mondak, Jeffery J., and Mary R. Anderson. 2004. 'The Knowledge Gap: A Reexamination of Gender-Based Differences in Political Knowledge'. *The Journal of Politics* 66 (2): 492–512. https://doi.org/10.1111/j.1468-2508.2004.00161.x.

Moon, David S., and Tomos Evans. 2017. 'Welsh Devolution and the Problem of Legislative Competence'. *British Politics* 12 (3): 335–60. https://doi.org/10.1057/s41293-016-0043-3.

Moore, Charles. 2014. *Margaret Thatcher: The Authorized Biography, Volume One: Not for Turning*. London: Penguin.

Moore, Charles. 2015. *Margaret Thatcher: The Authorized Biography, Volume Two: Everything She Wants*. London; New York; Toronto; Dublin: Allen Lane.

Moore, Charles. 2019. *Margaret Thatcher: The Authorized Biography, Volume Three: Herself Alone*. London: Allen Lane.

Moran, Michael. 2007. *The British Regulatory State: High Modernism and Hyper-Innovation*. Oxford: Oxford University Press.

Moravcsik, Andrew, and Frank Schimmelfennig. 2009. 'Liberal Intergovernmentalism'. *European Integration Theory* 2: 67–87.

Morphet, Janice. 2013. *How Europe Shapes British Public Policy*. Bristol: Policy Press.

Morris, Richard. 2017. 'How the Lib Dems Learned to Love All-Women Shortlists'. 24 April. www.newstatesman.com/politics/staggers/2017/04/how-lib-dems-learned-love-all-women-shortlists.

Mortensen, P. B., C. Green-Pedersen, G. E. Breeman, L. Chaqués Bonafont, W. Jennings, P. John, A. Palau Roque, and A. Timmermans. 2009. 'Comparing Government Agendas: Executive Speeches in the Netherlands, United Kingdom, Denmark and Spain'. http://library.wur.nl/WebQuery/wurpubs/385602.

Mortimore, Roger, and Andrew Blick, eds. 2018. *Butler's British Political Facts*. London: Palgrave Macmillan. https://doi.org/10.1057/978-1-137-56709-3.

Moss, Jonathan, Nick Clarke, Will Jennings, and Gerry Stoker. 2016. 'Golden Age, Apathy or Stealth? Democratic Engagement in Britain, 1945–1950'. *Contemporary British History* 30 (4): 441–62. https://doi.org/10.1080/13619462.2016.1180982.

Mudde, Cas. 2004. 'The Populist Zeitgeist'. *Government and Opposition* 39 (4): 541–63.

Mudde, Cas, and Cristóbal Rovira Kaltwasser. 2012. *Populism in Europe and the Americas: Threat or Corrective for Democracy?* Cambridge: Cambridge University Press.

Mueller, Dennis C., and Peter Murrell. 1986. 'Interest Groups and the Size of Government'. *Public Choice* 48 (2): 125–45.

Mule, Rosa. 2001. *Political Parties, Games and Redistribution*. Cambridge: Cambridge University Press.

Mutz, Diana C. 2011. *Population-Based Survey Experiments*. Princeton, NJ: Princeton University Press.

Nadeau, Richard, Éric Bélanger, and Ece Özlem Atikcan. 2019. 'Emotions, Cognitions and Moderation: Understanding Losers' Consent in the 2016 Brexit Referendum'. *Journal of Elections, Public Opinion and Parties* 31 (1): 1–20. https://doi.org/10.1080/17457289.2019.1604528.

Neustadt, Richard E. 1960. *Presidential Power*. New York: New American Library.

Newman, Nic. 2020. 'Reuters Institute Digital News Report 2020', 112. https://reutersinstitute.politics.ox.ac.uk/sites/default/files/2020-06/DNR_2020_FINAL.pdf.

Newton, Kenneth. 1976. *Second City Politics: Democratic Processes and Decision-Making in Birmingham*. Oxford: Clarendon Press.

Newton, Kenneth, and Malcolm Brynin. 2001. 'The National Press and Party Voting in the UK'. *Political Studies* 49 (2): 265–85. https://doi.org/10.1111/1467-9248.00313.

Nickerson, David W. 2014. 'Do Voter Registration Drives Increase Participation? For Whom and When?' *The Journal of Politics* 77 (1): 88–101.

Niskanen, William A. 1975. 'Bureaucrats and Politicians'. *Journal of Law and Economics* 18 (3): 617–43.

Nixon, Jaqi. 1998. 'The Role of Black and Asian MPs at Westminster'. In *Race and British Electoral Politics*, edited by Shamit Saggar, 202–22. London: UCL Press.

Norpoth, Helmut. 2001. 'Divided Government and Economic Voting'. *The Journal of Politics* 63 (2): 414–35.

Norpoth, Helmut. 2006. 'Did the Media Matter? Agenda-Setting, Persuasion and Mobilization Effects in the British General Election Campaign'. *British Politics* 1 (2): 195–221.

Norris, Pippa, and Joni Lovenduski. 1995. *Political Recruitment: Gender, Race and Class in the British Parliament*. Cambridge: Cambridge University Press.

Norris, Pippa, John Curtice, David Sanders, Margaret Scammell, and Holli Semetko. 1999. *On Message: Communicating the Campaign*. London; Thousand Oaks, CA: Sage Publications Ltd.

Norton, Philip. 1975. *Dissension in the House of Commons: Intra-Party Dissent in the House of Commons' Division Lobbies 1945–1974*. London: Macmillan International Higher Education.

Norton, Philip. 1978. *Conservative Dissidents: Dissent within the Parliamentary Conservative Party, 1970–74*. London: Temple Smith.

Norton, Philip. 1980. *Dissension in the House of Commons: 1974–1979*. Oxford: Oxford University Press.

Norton, Philip. 1987. 'Dissent in the British House of Commons: Rejoinder to Franklin, Baxter, Jordan'. *Legislative Studies Quarterly* 12 (1): 143–52. https://doi.org/10.2307/440050.

Norton, Philip. 2003. 'Cohesion without Discipline: Party Voting in the House of Lords'. *The Journal of Legislative Studies* 9 (4): 57–72.

Norton, Philip. 2013. *Parliament in British Politics*. London: Macmillan International Higher Education.

O'Brien, Diana Z., and Jennifer M. Piscopo. 2019. 'The Impact of Women in Parliament'. In *The Palgrave Handbook of Women's Political Rights*, 53–72. New York: Springer.

O'Donnell, Gus. 2020. 'Handling Covid Crisis Required Stronger Leadership and a Better Use of a Wider Range of Evidence Says Gus O'Donnell'. The IFS. 24 September. www.ifs.org.uk/publications/15042.

Ofcom. 2019. 'Media Nations: UK 2019'. www.ofcom.org.uk/__data/assets/pdf_file/0019/160714/media-nations-2019-uk-report.pdf.

Office for National Statistics. 2018. 'Population of England and Wales'. 2018. www.ethnicity-facts-figures.service.gov.uk/uk-population-by-ethnicity/national-and-regional-populations/population-of-england-and-wales/latest.

Office for National Statistics. 2020. 'Civil Service Statistics: 2020'. gov.uk. www.gov.uk/government/statistics/civil-service-statistics-2020.

O'Grady, T. D. 2019. 'Careerists versus Coalminers: Welfare Reforms and the Substantive Representation of Social Groups in the British Labour Party'. *Comparative Political Studies* 52 (4): 544–78.

O'Leary, Brendan. 2019. *A Treatise on Northern Ireland, Volume III: Consociation and Confederation*. Oxford: Oxford University Press.

O'Leary, Brendan, and John McGarry. 2016. *The Politics of Antagonism: Understanding Northern Ireland*. London: Bloomsbury Publishing.

Page, Edward C. 1999. 'The Insider/Outsider Distinction: An Empirical Investigation'. *The British Journal of Politics and International Relations*. https://journals.sagepub.com/doi/10.1111/1467-856X.00011.

Paldam, Martin. 1986. 'The Distribution of Election Results and the Two Explanations of the Cost of Ruling'. *European Journal of Political Economy* 2 (1): 5–24. https://doi.org/10.1016/S0176-2680(86)80002-7.

Panitch, Leo. 1977. 'The Development of Corporatism in Liberal Democracies'. *Comparative Political Studies* 10 (1): 61–90. https://doi.org/10.1177/001041407701000104.

Park, Alice, Caroline Bryson, Elizabeth Clery, John Curtice, and Miranda Philips. 2012. 'British Social Attitudes: The 36th Report'. London: NatCen Social Research.

Parkinson, John. 2007. 'The House of Lords: A Deliberative Democratic Defence'. *The Political Quarterly* 78 (3): 374–81. https://doi.org/10.1111/j.1467-923X.2007.00866.x.

Pattie, Charles, and Ron Johnston. 1998. 'Voter Turnout at the British General Election of 1992: Rational Choice, Social Standing or Political Efficacy?' *European Journal of Political Research* 33 (2): 263–83. https://doi.org/10.1111/1475-6765.00383.

Pattie, Charles, Todd Hartman, and Ron Johnston. 2017. 'Incumbent Parties, Incumbent MPs and the Effectiveness of Constituency Campaigns: Evidence from the 2015 UK General Election'. *The British Journal of Politics and International Relations* 19 (4): 824–41. https://doi.org/10.1177/1369148117718710.

Pattie, Charles, Ron Johnston, and Edward A. Fieldhouse. 1995. 'Winning the Local Vote: The Effectiveness of Constituency Campaign Spending in Great Britain, 1983–1992'. *American Political Science Review* 89 (4): 969–83. https://doi.org/10.2307/2082521.

Pattie, Charles, Patrick Seyd, and Paul Whiteley. 2004. *Citizenship in Britain: Values, Participation and Democracy*. Cambridge: Cambridge University Press.

Paun, Akash, and Sam Macrory. 2019. 'Has Devolution Worked?' July. www.instituteforgovernment.org.uk/publications/has-devolution-worked.

Paxton, Pamela, Melanie M. Hughes and Tiffany D. Barnes. 2020. *Women, Politics, and Power: A Global Perspective*. 4th edition. Lanham, MD: Rowman & Littlefield Publishers.

Pedersen, Helene Helboe, and Jennifer vanHeerde-Hudson. 2019. 'Two Strategies for Building a Personal Vote: Personalized Representation in the UK and Denmark'. *Electoral Studies* 59 (June): 17–26. https://doi.org/10.1016/j.electstud.2019.02.010.

Pedersen, Mogens N. 1979. 'The Dynamics of European Party Systems: Changing Patterns of Electoral Volatility'. *European Journal of Political Research* 7 (1): 1–26. https://doi.org/10.1111/j.1475-6765.1979.tb01267.x.

Persson, Torsten, and Guido Enrico Tabellini. 2005. *The Economic Effects of Constitutions*. Cambridge, MA: MIT Press.

Peters, B. Guy. 2011. *Institutional Theory in Political Science: The New Institutionalism*. New York: Bloomsbury Publishing.

Peters, B. Guy. 2013. 'Politicisation: What Is It and Why Should We Care?' In *Civil Servants and Politics: A Delicate Balance*, edited by Christine Neuhold, Sophie Vanhoonacker, and Luc Verhey, 12–24. Public Sector Organizations. London: Palgrave Macmillan. https://doi.org/10.1057/9781137316813_2.

Pharr, Susan J, and Robert D Putnam. 2000. *Disaffected Democracies: What's Troubling the Trilateral Countries?* Princeton, NJ: Princeton University Press.

Phillips, D., John Curtice, M. Philips, and J. Perry. 2017. 'British Social Attitudes: The 35th Report, Voting'. London: The National Centre for Social Research.

Pike, Andy, and John Tomaney. 2009. 'The State and Uneven Development: The Governance of Economic Development in England in the Post-Devolution UK'. *Cambridge Journal of Regions, Economy and Society* 2 (1): 13–34. https://doi.org/10.1093/cjres/rsn025.

Pitkin, Hanna F. 1967. *The Concept of Representation*. Berkeley, CA: University of California Press.

Pogrund, Gabriel, and Patrick Maguire. 2020. *Left Out: The Inside Story of Labour Under Corbyn*. New York: Random House.

Polsby, Nelson W. 1975. 'Legislatures'. In *Handbook of Political Science*, vol. 5, edited by Fred I. Greenstein and Nelson W. Polsby. Reading, MA: Addison-Wesley.

Powell, G. Bingham. 2000. *Elections as Instruments of Democracy: Majoritarian and Proportional Visions*. New Haven, CT: Yale University Press. http://books.google.com/books?hl=en&lr=&id=GIMZmYdvfREC&oi=fnd&pg=PR9&dq=info:FYne4rGqSAUJ:scholar.google.com&ots=HhAHjZISl5&sig=-zZ_m9qJy76yPpNp3DoYNrJXfCc.

Powell, G. Bingham Jr, and Guy Whitten. 1993. 'A Cross-National Analysis of Economic Voting: Taking Account of the Political Context'. *American Journal of Political Science* 37 (2): 391–414.

Pressman, Jeffrey L., and Aaron Wildavsky. 1984. *Implementation: How Great Expectations in Washington Are Dashed in Oakland; Or, Why It's Amazing That Federal Programs Work at All, This Being a Saga of the Economic Development Administration as Told by Two Sympathetic Observers Who Seek to Build Morals on a Foundation*. Berkeley, CA: University of California Press.

Prosser, Christopher. 2018. 'The Strange Death of Multi-Party Britain: The UK General Election of 2017'. *West European Politics* 41 (5): 1226–36. https://doi.org/10.1080/01402382.2018.1424838.

Prosser, Christopher, Edward Fieldhouse, Jane Green, Jonathan Mellon, and Geoffrey Evans. 2020. 'Tremors but No Youthquake: Measuring Changes in the Age and Turnout Gradients at the 2015 and 2017 British General Elections'. *Electoral Studies* 64 (April): 102–129. https://doi.org/10.1016/j.electstud.2020.102129.

Prud'homme, Rémy. 1995. 'The Dangers of Decentralization'. *The World Bank Research Observer* 10 (2): 201–20. https://doi.org/10.1093/wbro/10.2.201.

Pulzer, Peter. 1967. *Political Representation and Elections in Britain*. London: Allen & Unwin.

Putnam, Robert D. 1988. 'Diplomacy and Domestic Politics: The Logic of Two-Level Games'. *International Organization* 42 (3): 427–60.

Putnam, Robert D. 2000. *Bowling Alone: The Collapse and Revival of American Community*. London: Simon and Schuster.

Putnam, Robert D., Robert Leonardi, and Raffaella Y. Nanetti. 1994. *Making Democracy Work: Civic Traditions in Modern Italy*. Princeton, NJ: Princeton University Press.

Puwar, Nirmal. 2004. *Space Invaders: Race, Gender and Bodies Out of Place*. Illustrated edition. Oxford; New York: Berg Publishers.

Quinn, Thomas. 2013. 'From Two-Partism to Alternating Predominance: The Changing UK Party System, 1950–2010'. *Political Studies* 61 (2): 378–400. https://doi.org/10.1111/j.1467-9248.2012.00966.x.

Quinn, Thomas. 2016. 'The British Labour Party's Leadership Election of 2015'. *British Journal of Politics and International Relations* 18 (4): 759–78.

Quintelier, Ellen, and Jan W. van Deth. 2014. 'Supporting Democracy: Political Participation and Political Attitudes. Exploring Causality Using Panel Data'. *Political Studies* 62 (S1): 153–71. https://doi.org/10.1111/1467-9248.12097.

Qvortrup, Matt. 2017. 'The Rise of Referendums: Demystifying Direct Democracy'. *Journal of Democracy* 28 (3): 141–52. https://doi.org/10.1353/jod.2017.0052.

Raban, Jonathan. 1974. *Soft City*. New York: E. P. Dutton.

Rallings, Colin, and Michael Thrasher. 2013. *Local Elections in Britain*. London: Routledge.

Ramsay, Gordon, and Martin Moore. 2016. 'Monopolising Local News: Is There an Emerging Local Democratic Deficit in the UK Due to the Decline of Local Newspapers?' May. https://doi.org/10.18742/pub01-026.

Ranney, Austin. 1954. *The Doctrine of Responsible Party Government, Its Origin and Present State*. Champaign, IL: University of Illinois Press.

Rawnsley, Andrew. 2001. *Servants of the People: The Inside Story of New Labour*. London: Penguin.

Rawnsley, Andrew. 2010. *The End of the Party*. London: Penguin.

Raymond, Chris. 2016. 'Why British Politics Is Not a Two-Party System'. *Political Insight* 7 (3): 28–31. https://doi.org/10.1177/2041905816680418.

Reeder, Neil. 2020. 'Organizational Culture and Career Development in the British Civil Service'. *Public Money & Management* 40 (8): 559–68. https://doi.org/10.1080/09540962.2020.1754576.

Reeves, Aaron, Martin Mckee, and David Stuckler. 2015. '"It's The Sun Wot Won It": Evidence of Media Influence on Political Attitudes and Voting from a UK Quasi-Natural Experiment'. *Social Science Research* 56 (December). https://doi.org/10.1016/j.ssresearch.2015.11.002.

Renwick, Alan. 2010. *The Politics of Electoral Reform: Changing the Rules of Democracy*. Cambridge: Cambridge University Press. https://doi.org/10.1017/CBO9780511676390.

Renwick, Alan, and Jean-Benoit Pilet. 2016. *Faces on the Ballot: The Personalization of Electoral Systems in Europe. Faces on the Ballot*. Oxford: Oxford University Press. https://oxford.universitypressscholarship.com/view/10.1093/acprof:oso/9780199685042.001.0001/acprof-9780199685042.

Rheault, Ludovic, Kaspar Beelen, Christopher Cochrane, and Graeme Hirst. 2016. 'Measuring Emotion in Parliamentary Debates with Automated Textual Analysis'. *PLoS ONE* 11 (12): e0168843.

Rhodes, R. A. W. 1988. *Beyond Westminster and Whitehall: The Sub-Central Governments of Britain*. London: Unwin Hyman.

Rhodes, R. A. W. 2005. 'Is Westminster Dead in Westminster (and Why Should We Care)?' January. https://citeseerx.ist.psu.edu/viewdoc/download?doi=10.1.1.545.8552&rep=rep1&type=pdf.

Rhodes, R. A. W. 2011. *Everyday Life in British Government*. Oxford: Oxford University Press.

Rich, Paul B. 1990. *Race and Empire in British Politics*. Cambridge: CUP Archive.

Richards, David, and Martin J. Smith. 2006. 'Central Control and Policy Implementation in the UK: A Case Study of the Prime Minister's Delivery Unit'. *Journal of Comparative Policy Analysis: Research and Practice* 8 (4): 325–45. https://doi.org/10.1080/13876980600971151.

Richards, Dave, and Martin Smith. 2014. 'The Lessons of Tony Benn as a Cabinet Minister: Breaking the Rules and Paying the Price'. *British Politics and Policy at LSE* (blog). 19 March. https://blogs.lse.ac.uk/politicsandpolicy/the-lessons-of-tony-benn-as-a-cabinet-minister-breaking-the-rules-and-paying-the-price.

Richards, David, and Martin Smith. 2016. 'The Westminster Model and the "Indivisibility of the Political and Administrative Elite": A Convenient Myth Whose Time Is Up?' *Governance* 29 (4): 499–516.

Richardson, Jeremy John, and A. Grant Jordan. 1979. *Governing under Pressure: The Policy Process in a Post-Parliamentary Democracy*. New York; Oxford: Basil Blackwell.

Richardson, Liz, and Peter John. 2012. 'Who Listens to the Grass Roots? A Field Experiment on Informational Lobbying in the UK'. *The British Journal of Politics and International Relations* 14 (4): 595–612.

Riker, William H. 1986. *The Art of Political Manipulation*. New Haven, CT: Yale University Press.

Robson, William A. 1933. 'The Central Domination of Local Government'. *The Political Quarterly* 4 (1): 85–104. https://doi.org/10.1111/j.1467-923X.1933.tb02271.x.

Röcke, Anja. 2014. *Framing Citizen Participation: Participatory Budgeting in France, Germany and the United Kingdom*. New York: Springer.

Rooij, Eline A. de. 2012. 'Patterns of Immigrant Political Participation: Explaining Differences in Types of Political Participation between Immigrants and the Majority Population in Western Europe'. *European Sociological Review* 28 (4): 455–81.

Rose, Richard. 1968. 'Class and Party Divisions: Britain as a Test Case'. *Sociology* 2 (2): 129–62. https://doi.org/10.1177/003803856800200201.

Rose, Richard. 1974. *The Problem of Party Government*. New York: Springer.

Rose, Richard. 1976. *Northern Ireland: Time of Choice*. Washington, DC: American Enterprise Institute for Public Policy Research.

Rose, Richard. 1980. *Do Parties Make a Difference?* London: Macmillan.

Rose, Richard. 1990. 'Inheritance Before Choice in Public Policy'. *Journal of Theoretical Politics* 2 (3): 263–91. https://doi.org/10.1177/0951692890002003002.

Rose, Richard, and Phillip L. Davies. 1994. *Inheritance in Public Policy: Change without Choice in Britain*. New Haven, CT: Yale University Press.

Rosenberg, Joshua. 2020. *Enemies of the People? How Judges Shape Society*. Bristol: Policy Press.

Runciman, David. 2015. *The Confidence Trap: A History of Democracy in Crisis from World War I to the Present*. Updated edition with a new afterword by the author. Princeton, NJ; Oxford: Princeton University Press.

Runciman, David. 2018. *How Democracy Ends*. Main edition. London: Profile Books.

Runciman, David. 2020. 'Talking Politics— 296: Did Covid Kill the Climate?' www.talkingpoliticspodcast.com/blog/2020/296-did-covid-kill-the-climate.

Russell, Andrew T., and Edward Fieldhouse. 2005. *Neither Left nor Right: The Liberal Democrats and the Electorate*. Manchester: Manchester University Press.

Russell, Meg. 2013. *The Contemporary House of Lords: Westminster Bicameralism Revived*. Oxford: Oxford University Press.

Russell, Meg. 2020. 'Brexit and Parliament: The Anatomy of a Perfect Storm'. *Parliamentary Affairs* June. https://doi.org/10.1093/pa/gsaa011.

Russell, Meg, and Jonathan Bradbury. 2007. 'The Constituency Work of Scottish and Welsh MPs: Adjusting to Devolution'. *Regional & Federal Studies* 17 (1): 97–116. https://doi.org/10.1080/13597560701189644.

Russell, Meg, and Philip Cowley. 2016. 'The Policy Power of the Westminster Parliament: The "Parliamentary State" and the Empirical Evidence'. *Governance* 29 (1): 121–37. https://doi.org/10.1111/gove.12149.

Russell, Meg, and Daniel Gover. 2017. *Legislation at Westminster: Parliamentary Actors and Influence in the Making of British Law. Legislation at Westminster*. Oxford: Oxford University Press. www.oxfordscholarship.com/view/10.1093/oso/9780198753827.001.0001/oso-9780198753827.

Russell, Meg, and Daniel Gover. 2021. 'Taking Back Control: Why the House of Commons Should Govern Its Own Time'. www.ucl.ac.uk/constitution-unit/taking-back-control-why-house-commons-should-govern-its-own-time.

Russell, Meg, Daniel Gover, and Kristina Wollter. 2016. 'Does the Executive Dominate the Westminster Legislative Process? Six Reasons for Doubt'. *Parliamentary Affairs* 69 (2): 286–308. https://doi.org/10.1093/pa/gsv016.

Russell, Meg, and Ruxandra Serban. 2020a. 'The Muddle of the "Westminster Model": A Concept Stretched Beyond Repair'. *Government and Opposition*, 1–21. https://doi.org/10.1017/gov.2020.12.

Russell, Meg, and Ruxandra Serban. 2020b. 'An Ageing and Distinctly Cloudy Term: Why It Is Time for the "Westminster Model" to Be Retired'. British Politics and Policy at LSE. 11 August. https://blogs.lse.ac.uk/politicsandpolicy.

Rutter, Jill. 2020. 'The New Doctrine of Ministerial Irresponsibility'. UK in a Changing Europe. 27 August. https://ukandeu.ac.uk/the-new-doctrine-of-ministerial-irresponsibility.

Ryan, Matt, Gerry Stoker, Peter John, Alice Moseley, Oliver James, Liz Richardson, and Matia Vannoni. 2018. 'How Best to Open up Local Democracy? A Randomised Experiment to Encourage Contested Elections and Greater Representativeness in English Parish Councils'. *Local Government Studies* 44 (6): 1–22.

Saalfeld, Thomas. 2003. *The United Kingdom: Still a Single 'Chain of Command'? The Hollowing Out of the 'Westminster Model'*. Delegation and Accountability in Parliamentary Democracies. Oxford: Oxford University Press. https://oxford.universitypressscholarship.com/view/10.1093/019829784X.001.0001/acprof-9780198297840-chapter-21.

Saalfeld, Thomas. 2011. 'Parliamentary Questions as Instruments of Substantive Representation: Visible Minorities in the UK House of Commons, 2005–10'. *The Journal of Legislative Studies* 17 (3): 271–89.

Saalfeld, Thomas, and Kalliopi Kyriakopoulou. 2010. *Presence and Behaviour: Black and Minority Ethnic MPs in the British House of Commons*. The Political Representation of Immigrants and Minorities. London: Routledge. 6 October. https://doi.org/10.4324/9780203843604-22.

Sabatier, Paul A. 1986. 'Top-Down and Bottom-Up Approaches to Implementation Research: A Critical Analysis and Suggested Synthesis'. *Journal of Public Policy* 6 (1): 21–48. https://doi.org/10.1017/S0143814X00003846.

Sanders, David. 1990. *Losing an Empire, Finding a Role: An Introduction to British Foreign Policy Since 1945*. London: Macmillan International Higher Education.

Sanders, David. 1991. 'Government Popularity and the Next General Election'. *The Political Quarterly* 62 (2): 235–61. https://doi.org/10.1111/j.1467-923X.1991.tb00856.x.

Sanders, David, Anthony Heath, Stephen Fisher, and Maria Sobolewska. 2014. 'The Calculus of Ethnic Minority Voting in Britain'. *Political Studies* 62 (2): 230–51. https://doi.org/10.1111/1467-9248.12040.

Särlvik, Bo, and Ivor Crewe. 1983. *Decade of Dealignment: The Conservative Victory of 1979 and Electoral Trends in the 1970's*. Cambridge: Cambridge University Press.

Sasse, Tom, Tim Durrant, Emma Norris, and Ketaki Zodgekar. 2020. 'Government Reshuffles: The Case for Keeping Ministers in Post Longer'. www.instituteforgovernment.org.uk/publications/government-reshuffles-keeping-ministers-post-longer.

Savage, Mike. 2015. *Social Class in the 21st Century*. London: Pelican.

Schattschneider, E. E. 1960. *The Semi-Sovereign People*. New York: Holt, Rinehart and Winston.

Schmitter, Philippe C. 1974. 'Still the Century of Corporatism?' *The Review of Politics* 36 (1): 85–131.

Schmitter, Philippe C., and Gerhard Lehmbruch. 1979. *Trends Toward Corporatist Intermediation*. London: Sage Publications.

Schofield, Norman. 2004. 'Equilibrium in the Spatial "Valence" Model of Politics'. *Journal of Theoretical Politics* 16 (4): 447–81. https://doi.org/10.1177/0951629804046150.

Schudson, Michael. 1989. 'The Sociology of News Production'. *Media, Culture & Society* 11 (3): 263–82. https://doi.org/10.1177/016344389011003002.

Schwartz, Cassilde, Miranda Simon, David Hudson, and Jennifer van-Heerde-Hudson. 2020. 'A Populist Paradox? How Brexit Softened Anti-Immigrant Attitudes'. *British Journal of Political Science*, 1–21. https://doi.org/10.1017/S0007123419000656.

Scully, Roger, and Richard Wyn Jones. 2012. 'Still Three Wales? Social Location and Electoral Behaviour in Contemporary Wales'. *Electoral Studies* 31 (4): 656–67. https://doi.org/10.1016/j.electstud.2012.07.007.

Searing, Donald. 1994. *Westminster's World: Understanding Political Roles*. Cambridge, MA: Harvard University Press.

Searing, D., and C. Game. 1977. 'Horses for Courses: The Recruitment of Whips in the British House of Commons'. *British Journal of Political Science* 7 (3): 361–85.

Searing, Donald D., William G. Jacoby, and Andrew H. Tyner. 2019. 'The Endurance of Politicians' Values Over Four Decades: A Panel Study'. *American Political Science Review* 113 (1): 226–41. https://doi.org/10.1017/S0003055418000692.

Seawright, David, and John Curtice. 2008. 'The Decline of the Scottish Conservative and Unionist Party 1950–92: Religion, Ideology or Economics?' *Contemporary British History* June. https://doi.org/10.1080/13619469508581341.

Seldon, Anthony. 2008. *Blair Unbound*. New York: Simon and Schuster.

Seldon, Anthony, and Raymond Newell. 2019. *May at 10*. London: Biteback Publishing.

Sharpe, L. J. 1970. 'Theories and Values of Local Government'. *Political Studies*. https://journals.sagepub.com/doi/10.1111/j.1467-9248.1970.tb00867.x.

Sheffer, Lior, Peter John Loewen, Stuart Soroka, Stefaan Walgrave, and Tamir Sheafer. 2018. 'Nonrepresentative Representatives: An Experimental Study of the Decision Making of Elected Politicians'. *American Political Science Review* 112 (02): 302–21.

Shell, Donald. 1992. *The House of Lords*. London: Harvester.

Shephard, Mark, and Paul Cairney. 2005. 'The Impact of the Scottish Parliament in Amending Executive Legislation'. *Political Studies* 53 (2): 303–19. https://doi.org/10.1111/j.1467-9248.2005.00530.x.

Shephard, Mark, and C. J. Carman. 2007. 'Electoral Poachers? An Assessment of Shadowing Behaviour in the Scottish Parliament'. *Journal of Legislative Studies* 13 (4): 483–96.

Shipman, Tim. 2016. *All Out War: The Full Story of How Brexit Sank Britain's Political Class*. London: William Collins.

Shipman, Tim. 2017. *Fall Out: A Year of Political Mayhem*. London: HarperCollins UK.

Siaroff, Alan. 2003. 'Two-and-a-Half-Party Systems and the Comparative Role of the "Half"'. *Party Politics* 9 (3): 267–90. https://doi.org/10.1177/13540688030090003001.

Skinner, Gideon, Roger Mortimore, and Daniel Spielman. 2019. 'How Britain Voted in the 2019 Election'. Ipsos MORI. www.ipsos.com/ipsos-mori/en-uk/how-britain-voted-2019-election.

Slapin, Jonathan B., and Justin H. Kirkland. 2019. 'The Sound of Rebellion: Voting Dissent and Legislative Speech in the UK House of Commons'. *Legislative Studies Quarterly*. https://doi.org/10.1111/lsq.12251.

Slapin, Jonathan B., Justin H. Kirkland, Joseph A. Lazzaro, Patrick A. Leslie, and Tom O'Grady. 2018. 'Ideology, Grandstanding, and Strategic Party Disloyalty in the British Parliament'. *American Political Science Review* 112 (1): 15–30.

Smets, Kaat. 2012. 'A Widening Generational Divide? The Age Gap in Voter Turnout through Time and Space'. *Journal of Elections, Public Opinion & Parties* 22 (4): 407–30.

Smith, Alastair. 2003. 'Election Timing in Majoritarian Parliaments'. *British Journal of Political Science* 33 (3): 397–418.

Smith, Alastair. 2004. *Election Timing*. Cambridge: Cambridge University Press.

Smith, Martin J. 1999. *The Core Executive in Britain*. London: Macmillan.

Smith, Timothy Hallam. 2013. 'Are You Sitting Comfortably? Estimating Incumbency Advantage in the UK: 1983–2010—A Research Note'. *Electoral Studies* 32 (1): 167–73. https://doi.org/10.1016/j.electstud.2012.12.002.

Sobolewska, Maria. 2005. 'Ethnic Agenda: Relevance of Political Attitudes to Party Choice'. *Journal of Elections, Public Opinion and Parties* 15 (2): 197–214. https://doi.org/10.1080/13689880500178781.

Sobolewska, Maria, and Robert Ford. 2020. *Brexitland: Identity, Diversity and the Reshaping of British Politics*. Cambridge: Cambridge University Press.

Sobolewska, Maria, E. Fieldhouse, and D. Cutts. 2013. 'Taking Minorities for Granted? Ethnic Density, Party Campaigning and Targeting Minority Voters in 2010 British General Elections'. *Parliamentary Affairs* 66 (2): 329–44. https://doi.org/10.1093/pa/gss088.

Sørensen, Eva, and Signy Irene Vabo. 2020. 'Introduction: A Public Innovation Perspective on Change in Local Democracy'. *Innovation Journal* 25 (1): 1–19.

Soroka, Stuart N., and Christopher Wlezien. 2005. 'Opinion–Policy Dynamics: Public Preferences and Public Expenditure in the United Kingdom'. *British Journal of Political Science* 35 (4): 665–89.

Soroka, Stuart N., and Christopher Wlezien. 2010. *Degrees of Democracy: Politics, Public Opinion, and Policy*. Cambridge: Cambridge University Press.

Spirling, Arthur, and Iain McLean. 2006. 'UK OC OK? Interpreting Optimal Classification Scores for the UK House of Commons'. *Political Analysis* 15 (1): 85–96.

Spirling, Arthur, and Kevin Quinn. 2010. 'Identifying Intraparty Voting Blocs in the U.K. House of Commons'. *Journal of the American Statistical Association* 105 (490): 447–57.

Spoon, Jae-Jae, and Heike Klüver. 2019. 'Party Convergence and Vote Switching: Explaining Mainstream Party Decline across Europe'. *European Journal of Political Research* 58 (4): 1021–42. https://doi.org/10.1111/1475-6765.12331.

Stein, Robert M., and Kenneth N. Bickers. 1997. *Perpetuating the Pork Barrel: Policy Subsystems and American Democracy*. Cambridge: Cambridge University Press.

Stimson, James A., Michael B. MacKuen, and Robert S. Erikson. 1995. 'Dynamic Representation'. *American Political Science Review* 89 (3): 543–65.

Stoker, Gerry. 2006. *Why Politics Matters: Making Democracy Work*. London: Palgrave Macmillan. https://eprints.soton.ac.uk/47278.

Stoker, Gerry. 2016. *Why Politics Matters: Making Democracy Work*. 2nd edition. London: Palgrave Macmillan.

Stoker, Gerry, and Colin Hay. 2017. 'Understanding and Challenging Populist Negativity towards Politics: The Perspectives of British Citizens'. *Political Studies* 65 (1): 4–23. https://doi.org/10.1177/0032321715607511.

Stokes, Donald E. 1963. 'Spatial Models of Party Competition'. *American Political Science Review* 57 (2): 368–77. https://doi.org/10.2307/1952828.

Strøm, Kaare, Wolfgang C. Müller, and Torbjörn Bergman. 2003. *Delegation and Accountability in Parliamentary Democracies. Abstract and Keywords*. https://doi.org/10.1093/019829784X.001.0001.

Strong, James. 2017. *Public Opinion, Legitimacy and Tony Blair's War in Iraq*. London: Taylor & Francis.

Studlar, Donley T., and Ian McAllister. 2002. 'Does a Critical Mass Exist? A Comparative Analysis of Women's Legislative Representation since 1950'. *European Journal of Political Research* 41 (2): 233–53. https://doi.org/10.1111/1475-6765.00011.

Sturgis, Patrick, and Will Jennings. 2020. 'Was There a "Youthquake" in the 2017 General Election?' *Electoral Studies* 64 (April): 102065. https://doi.org/10.1016/j.electstud.2019.102065.

Sturgis, Patrick, Jonathan Jackson, and Jouni Kuha. 2020. 'Lockdown Scepticism Is Part of the Brexit Divide'. *LSE BREXIT* (blog). 8 June. https://blogs.lse.ac.uk/brexit/2020/06/08/20111.

Sunstein, Cass R. 2017. *#Republic: Divided Democracy in the Age of Social Media*. Princeton, NJ: Princeton University Press.

Sutton Trust. 2019. 'Elitist Britain?' gov.uk. www.gov.uk/government/publications/elitist-britain.

Sweet, Alec Stone. 2000. *Governing with Judges: Constitutional Politics in Europe. Governing with Judges*. Oxford: Oxford University Press. www.oxfordscholarship.com/view/10.1093/0198297718.001.0001/acprof-9780198297710.

Szreter, Simon. 2002. 'The State of Social Capital: Bringing Back in Power, Politics, and History'. *Theory and Society* 31 (5): 573–621.

Taagepera, Rein. 1986. 'Reformulating the Cube Law for Proportional Representation Elections'. *American Political Science Review* 80 (2): 489–504. https://doi.org/10.2307/1958270.

Tate, Katherine. 2003. *Black Faces in the Mirror: African Americans and Their Representatives in the US Congress*. Princeton, NJ: Princeton University Press. https://books.google.co.uk/books?hl=en&lr=&id=jO8k3i_vti8C&oi=fnd&pg=PR7&ots=nFOlwCVH8x&sig=owWZ-M7Fih07aVE1YqWOtjxwx-A0.

Tavits, Margit. 2007. 'Clarity of Responsibility and Corruption'. *American Journal of Political Science* 51 (1): 218–29. https://doi.org/10.1111/j.1540-5907.2007.00246.x.

Terry, Chris. 2017. 'Who's Going to Hold the New Metro Mayors to Account?' *Democratic Audit UK*. www.democraticaudit.com/2017/05/03/whos-going-to-hold-the-new-metro-mayors-to-account.

The British Election Study Team. 2021. 'Volatility, Realignment and Electoral Shocks: Brexit and the UK General Election of 2019—The British Election Study'. www.britishelectionstudy.com/bes-findings/volatility-realignment-electoral-shocks/#.YBOtWOCnwkh.

Thomas, Alex. 2021. 'The Heart of the Problem: A Weak Centre Is Undermining the UK Government'. January. www.instituteforgovernment.org.uk/publications/weak-centre-government.

Thompson, E. P. 1971. 'The Moral Economy of the English Crowd in the Eighteenth Century'. *Past & Present* 50: 76–136.

Thompson, Helen. 1996. *The British Conservative Government and the European Exchange Rate Mechanism, 1979–1994*. Hove: Psychology Press.

Thompson, Helen. 2017. 'Inevitability and Contingency: The Political Economy of Brexit'. *The British Journal of Politics and International Relations* 19 (3): 434–49. https://doi.org/10.1177/1369148117710431.

Thompson, Louise. 2015. *Making British Law: Committees in Action*. 1st edition. Houndmills; New York: AIAA.

Thomson, Robert. 2011. *Resolving Controversy in the European Union: Legislative Decision-Making before and after Enlargement*. Cambridge: Cambridge University Press.

Tickell, Adam, Peter John, and Steven Musson. 2005. 'The North East Region Referendum Campaign of 2004: Issues and Turning Points'. *The Political Quarterly* 76 (4): 488–96.

Tilley, James, and Geoffrey Evans. 2014. 'Ageing and Generational Effects on Vote Choice: Combining Cross-Sectional and Panel Data to Estimate APC Effects'. *Electoral Studies* 33 (March): 19–27. https://doi.org/10.1016/j.electstud.2013.06.007.

Toeller, Annette Elisabeth. 2012. 'Claims That 80 Per Cent of Laws Adopted in the EU Member States Originate in

Brussels Actually Tell Us Very Little about the Impact of EU Policy-Making'. *EUROPP* (blog). 13 June. https://blogs.lse.ac.uk/europpblog/2012/06/13/europeanization-of-public-policy.

Tonge, Jon. 2006. *Northern Ireland*. Cambridge: Polity.

Tonge, Jon. 2020. 'General Election 2019: Northern Ireland'. *Political Insight* 11 (1): 13–15. https://doi.org/10.1177/2041905820911740.

Tonge, Jonathan, Maire Braniff, Thomas Hennessey, James W. McAuley, and Sophie Whiting. 2014. *The Democratic Unionist Party: From Protest to Power*. Oxford: Oxford University Press.

Tonge, Jonathan, Stuart Wilks-Heeg, and Louise Thompson, eds. 2020. *Britain Votes: The 2019 General Election*. Oxford: Oxford University Press.

Topaloff, Topaloff. 2017. 'The Rise of Referendums: Elite Strategy or Populist Weapon?' *Journal of Democracy* 28 (3): 127–40.

Toynbee, Polly, and David Walker. 2015. *Cameron's Coup: How the Tories Took Britain to the Brink*. London: Guardian Faber Publishing.

Treisman, Daniel. 2007. *The Architecture of Government: Rethinking Political Decentralization*. Cambridge: Cambridge University Press.

Trenaman, Joseph Mazzini, and Denis McQuail. 1961. *Television and the Political Image: A Study of the Impact of Television on the 1959 General Election, by Joseph Trenaman and Denis McQuail*. London: Methuen.

Trumm, Siim. 2018. 'Representation in Wales: An Empirical Analysis of Policy Divisions between Voters and Candidates'. *The British Journal of Politics and International Relations* 20 (2): 425–40. https://doi.org/10.1177/1369148117740284.

Tsebelis, George. 2011. *Veto Players: How Political Institutions Work*. Princeton, NJ: Princeton University Press.

Tsebelis, George, and Geoffrey Garrett. 2001. 'The Institutional Foundations of Intergovernmentalism and Supranationalism in the European Union'. *International Organization* 55 (2): 357–90.

Tufte, Edward R. 1973. 'The Relationship between Seats and Votes in Two-Party Systems'. *The American Political Science Review* 67 (2): 540–54. https://doi.org/10.2307/1958782.

Turnbull-Dugarte, Stuart J. 2020. 'The European Lavender Vote: Sexuality, Ideology and Vote Choice in Western Europe'. *European Journal of Political Research* 59 (3): 517–37. https://doi.org/10.1111/1475-6765.12366.

Uberoi, Elise. 2017. 'Turnout at Elections'. July. https://commonslibrary.parliament.uk/research-briefings/cbp-8060.

UCL. 2017. 'New Report: Blueprint for a UK Constitutional Convention'. The Constitution Unit. 2 June. www.ucl.ac.uk/constitution-unit/news/2017/jun/new-report-blueprint-uk-constitutional-convention.

UKICE. 2021. 'UK Trade Post-Brexit: Challenge or Opportunity?' UK in a Changing Europe. 3 March. https://ukandeu.ac.uk/uk-trade-post-brexit.

UK Parliament. 2018. 'UK Gender-Sensitive Parliament Audit 2018. Report of the Gender-Sensitive Parliament Audit Panel to the House of Commons Commission and the House of Lords Commission'. London. www.parliament.uk/globalassets/documents/lords-information-office/UK-Parliament_-Gender-Sensitive-Parliament-Audit_Report_DIGITAL.pdf.

University College, London, Constitution Unit, Independent Commission on Referendums. 2018. *Report of the Independent Commission on Referendums*. London: London University College and Constitution Unit.

Vannoni, Matia. 2015. 'The (Un)Heavenly Chorus in British Politics: Bringing the What, the When and the How Questions into the Analysis of Interest Group Influence'. *British Politics* 10 (3): 378–88. https://doi.org/10.1057/bp.2015.6.

Vannoni, Matia, and Peter John. 2018. 'Using Sequence Analysis to Understand Career Progression: An Application to the UK House of Commons'. *The Political Methodologist*, August. https://kclpure.kcl.ac.uk/portal/en/publications/using-sequence-analysis-to-understand-career-progression(2fca1817-2161-4a9e-beff-ef194264c2e6).html.

Verba, Sidney, Norman H. Nie, and Jae-on Kim. 1987. *Participation and Political Equality: A Seven-Nation Comparison*. Chicago, IL: University of Chicago Press.

Verba, Sidney, Kay Lehman Schlozman, and Henry E. Brady. 1995. *Voice and Equality: Civic Voluntarism in American Politics*. Cambridge, MA: Harvard University Press.

Vile, M. J. C. 1967. *Constitutionalism and the Separation of Powers*. Oxford: Oxford University Press.

Vivyan, Nick, and Markus Wagner. 2012. 'Do Voters Reward Rebellion? The Electoral Accountability of MPs in Britain'. *European Journal of Political Research* 51 (2): 235–64. https://doi.org/10.1111/j.1475-6765.2011.01998.x.

Vivyan, Nick, Markus Wagner, Konstantin Glinitzer, and Jakob-Moritz Eberl. 2020. 'Do Humble Beginnings Help? How Politician Class Roots Shape Voter Evaluations'. *Electoral Studies* 63 (February): 102093. https://doi.org/10.1016/j.electstud.2019.102093.

Vowles, Jack, Gabriel Katz, and Daniel Stevens. 2017. 'Electoral Competitiveness and Turnout in British Elections, 1964–2010'. *Political Science Research and Methods* 5 (4): 775–94.

Vries, Catherine E. De, and Sara B. Hobolt. 2020. *Political Entrepreneurs: The Rise of Challenger Parties in Europe*. Princeton, NJ: Princeton University Press.

Wäckerle, Jens. 2021. 'How the Parliamentary Labour Party Achieved Gender Parity and Why the Conservatives Still Lag Behind'. *British Politics and Policy at LSE* (blog). 11 January. https://blogs.lse.ac.uk/politicsandpolicy/women-mps-labour-conservatives.

Walker, Clive, and Oona Cawley. 2020. 'The Juridification of the UK's Counter Terrorism Prevent Policy'. *Studies in Conflict & Terrorism* February: 1–26. https://doi.org/10.1080/1057610X.2020.1727098.

Walker, Stephen G., and George L. Watson. 1989. 'Groupthink and Integrative Complexity in British Foreign Policy-Making: The Munich Case'. *Cooperation and Conflict* 24 (3): 199–212. https://doi.org/10.1177/001083678902400306.

Wall, Stephen. 2012. *The Official History of Britain and the European Community, Vol. II: From Rejection to Referendum, 1963–1975*. London: Routledge.

Wallace, Helen, Mark A. Pollack, Christilla Roederer-Rynning, and Alasdair R. Young. 2020. *Policy-Making in the European Union*. New York: Oxford University Press USA.

Walsh, James I. 2006. 'Policy Failure and Policy Change: British Security Policy After the Cold War'. *Comparative Political Studies* 39 (4): 490–518. https://doi.org/10.1177/0010414005275562.

Walter, Stefanie. 2019. 'Better off without You? How the British Media Portrayed EU Citizens in Brexit News'. *The International Journal of Press/Politics* 24 (2): 210–32. https://doi.org/10.1177/1940161218821509.

Waltz, Kenneth Neal. 1979. *Theory of International Politics*. Reading, MA: Addison-Wesley.

Ward, Hugh, and Peter John. 1999. 'Targeting Benefits for Electoral Gain: Constituency Marginality and the Distribution of Grants to English Local Authorities'. *Political Studies* 47 (1): 32–52.

Ward, Stephen, Rachel Gibson, and Wainer Lusoli. 2003. 'Online Participation and Mobilisation in Britain: Hype, Hope and Reality'. *Parliamentary Affairs* 56 (4): 652–68.

Wardle, Huon, and Laura Obermuller. 2019. '"Windrush Generation" and "Hostile Environment": Symbols and Lived Experiences in Caribbean Migration to the UK'. *Migration and Society* 2 (1): 81–89. https://doi.org/10.3167/arms.2019.020108.

Watts, Jake, and Tim Bale. 2019. 'Populism as an Intra-Party Phenomenon: The British Labour Party under Jeremy Corbyn'. *The British Journal of Politics and International Relations* 21 (1): 99–115. https://doi.org/10.1177/1369148118806115.

Weale, Albert. 2018. *The Will of the People: A Modern Myth*. 1st edition. Cambridge: Polity Press.

Webber, Douglas. 2005. *The Franco-German Relationship in the EU*. London: Routledge.

Weber, Max. 1978. *Economy and Society: An Outline of Interpretive Sociology*. Berkeley, CA: University of California Press.

Wenzelburger, Georg, Carsten Jensen, Seonghui Lee, and Christoph Arndt. 2020. 'How Governments Strategically Time Welfare State Reform Legislation: Empirical Evidence from Five European Countries'. *West European Politics* 43 (6): 1285–1314. https://doi.org/10.1080/01402382.2019.1668245.

Wheatley, Jonathan. 2015. 'Restructuring the Policy Space in England: The End of the Left–Right Paradigm?' *British Politics* 10 (3): 268–85. https://doi.org/10.1057/bp.2015.35.

White, Hannah. 2015. 'Select Committees under Scrutiny'. London: Institute for Government. www.instituteforgovernment.org.uk/sites/default/files/publications/Under%20scrutiny%20case%20studies%20final_0.pdf.

Whiteley, Paul F. 2011. 'Is the Party Over? The Decline of Party Activism and Membership across the Democratic World'. *Party Politics* 17 (1): 21–44. https://doi.org/10.1177/1354068810365505.

Whiteley, Paul F., and Patrick Seyd. 2002. *High-Intensity Participation: The Dynamics of Party Activism in Britain*. Ann Arbor, MI: University of Michigan Press.

Williams, Paul. 2002. 'The Rise and Fall of the "Ethical Dimension": Presentation and Practice in New Labour's Foreign Policy'. *Cambridge Review of International Affairs* 15 (April): 53–63. https://doi.org/10.1080/09557570220126243.

Wilson, Peter. 2011. 'Idealism in International Relations'. LSE Research Online. http://eprints.lse.ac.uk/41929/1/Idealism%20in%20international%20relations%20(LSERO).pdf.

Wittels, Annabelle Sophie. 2020. 'The Effect of Politician-Constituent Conflict on Bureaucratic Responsiveness under Varying Information Frames'. 4x8q2. *SocArXiv*. Center for Open Science. https://ideas.repec.org/p/osf/socarx/4x8q2.html.

Wlezien, Christopher. 1995. 'The Public as Thermostat: Dynamics of Preferences for Spending'. *American Journal of Political Science* 39 (4): 981–1000. https://doi.org/10.2307/2111666.

Wolak, Jennifer, and Michael McDevitt. 2011. 'The Roots of the Gender Gap in Political Knowledge in Adolescence'. *Political Behavior* 33 (3): 505–33.

Wolbrecht, Christina, and David E. Campbell. 2007. 'Leading by Example: Female Members of Parliament as Political Role Models'. *American Journal of Political Science* 51 (4): 921–39. https://doi.org/10.1111/j.1540-5907.2007.00289.x.

Wolinetz, Steven B. 1991. 'Party System Change: The Catch-All Thesis Revisited'. *West European Politics* 14 (1): 113–28. https://doi.org/10.1080/01402389108424835.

Wood, David M., and Philip Norton. 1992. 'Do Candidates Matter? Constituency-Specific Vote Changes for Incumbent MPs, 1983–1987'. *Political Studies* 40 (2): 227–38. https://doi.org/10.1111/j.1467-9248.1992.tb01381.x.

Wood, Matthew. 2019. *Hyper-Active Governance: How Governments Manage the Politics of Expertise*. Cambridge: Cambridge University Press.

Xenos, Michael, Ariadne Vromen, and Brian D. Loader. 2014. 'The Great Equalizer? Patterns of Social Media Use and Youth Political Engagement in Three Advanced Democracies'. *Information, Communication & Society* 17 (2): 151–67. https://doi.org/10.1080/1369118X.2013.871318.

Yong, Ben, and Robert Hazell. 2014. *Special Advisers: Who They Are, What They Do and Why They Matter*. London: Bloomsbury Publishing.

Zaller, John R. 1992. *The Nature and Origins of Mass Opinion*. Cambridge; New York: Cambridge University Press.

INDEX

Note:

Tables, figures, and photos are indicated by an italic *t, f,* and *p* following the page number. Key politicians, public figures and political thinkers are identifiable by their full forename, whereas academic researchers are identifiable by their first initials.

N